The
DICTIONARY
of
HISTORIC
NICKNAMES

The
DICTIONARY
of
HISTORIC NICKNAMES

A Treasury of More than 7,500 Famous and Infamous Nicknames from World History

CARL SIFAKIS

Facts On File Publications
460 Park Avenue South
New York, N.Y. 10016

THE DICTIONARY OF
HISTORIC NICKNAMES

Library of Congress Cataloging in Publication Data

Sifakis, Carl.
   Dictionary of historic nicknames.

   Bibliography: p.
   Includes index.
   1. Nicknames. 2. Biography. I. Title.
CT108.S53   1983   920'.02   82-15430
ISBN 0-87196-561-5

Printed in the United States of America

10 9 8 7 6 5 4 3 2 1

For Meisi

ACKNOWLEDGMENTS

Among the Facts On Filers I must specifically thank for their supervision or assistance are Ed Knappman, for his cogent comments, Joe Reilly, Ophelia Batalion and Kate Kelly.

INTRODUCTION

*"The first Rotarian was the first man
to call John the Baptist 'Jack'"*

—**H. L. Mencken**

The meaning of a nickname born in the smoke and cacaphony of battle has been debated by scholars since the American Civil War. On July 21, 1861 *Old Jack's* Virginians stood unmarked by the horrors of the Battle of First Manassas. It was 9:15 A.M., an hour when what was to be a great Confederate victory looked like anything but that. The remnants of a battered force of 3,600 Confederate troops were facing a continuous, withering attack by some 14,000 Union soldiers. The most beleaguered unit was Brigadier General Barnard Elliott Bee's Third Brigade.

A correspondent for the *Charleston Mercury* reported:

Bee rode up and down his lines encouraging his troops by everything that was dear to them to stand up and repel the tide which threatened them with destruction. . . .At last his own brigade dwindled to a mere handful, with every officer killed or disabled. He rode up to General [Thomas J.] Jackson and said, "General, they are beating us back."

The reply was "Sir, we'll give them the bayonet." General Bee immediately rallied the remnants of his brigade and his last words to them were: "There is Jackson, standing like a stone wall. Let us determine to die here, and we will conquer. Follow me." His men obeyed his call. . . .

What did Bee mean by describing Jackson "standing like a stone wall"? Was he admiring him for coolly holding his ranks? Or was he contemptuously referring to Jackson as a "stone wall" for his failure to come to the aid of the Third Brigade? History provides no answer, since a moment after Bee's rallying cry he fell mortally wounded.

Had Bee survived, what would have happened if he had brought charges against Jackson for an alleged failure to act? Jackson to this day would still be known as *Stonewall Jackson,* but the sobriquet would be one of infamy and disgrace. His career would probably have ended at Bull Run and the military course of the great rebellion could possibly have been far different. Bee, however, did not live to tell a tale of cowardice (if again that interpretation of his remark is valid) and the heroic legend of *Stonewall Jackson* grew, fostered by Southern propagandists who understood the value of heroes and how nicknames could be used to promote them.

However, such sobriquets often produce complications for other, less heroic, personalities. Almost every heroic nickname invites ridicule in the form of variations on it. Thus the German Kaiser, Frederick William II (better known to American soldiers in World War I as *Kaiser Bill*), was lampooned by the British as early as the turn of the century as *Frederick the Greatest,* an unfavorable comparison to *Frederick the Great*. Similar misfortune befell Confederate general William Lowther Jackson. Considered by his own men to be somewhat less than the compleat military leader that *Stonewall Jackson* was regarded as, he was disparagingly called *Mudwall Jackson.*

A nickname is no less than an attempt at instant biography. Although a nickname such as *Shortie* may not tell it all, it certainly imparts helpful information about its referent. Most likely it refers to someone of short stature, but it could also be applied facetiously to someone who is very tall. Nicknames are often prime examples of perversity. Some are merely descriptive and others are honorific, affectionate, neutral, vulgar, mean, biting or pejorative. Certain nicknames may be worn as badges of honor by their owners as they celebrate some laudatory real or imaginary accomplishment. Others only seem to bestow honor but have the opposite effect. Philip III of France, for example, was contemptuously nicknamed *The Daring* because he was perceived as cowardly.

Subtlety is not always involved, however, in the application of an unwanted sobriquet. When the French called Charles III *The Simple,* they really meant it—and they had good reason, since in his simplicity he trusted Count Herbert of Vermandis, who promptly

flung him into prison. When the braggart Napoleonic general Jean Baptiste Jules Bernadotte maneuvered himself into position as crown prince of Sweden, he did his best to enhance his public standing all around. Assuming the name of Charles Jean, he finally offered his services as mediator between the vanquished French and the victorious allies. His old comrades in arms dubbed him *Charles Jean Charlatan.*

Nicknames have a consuming way about them that few can escape. They overwhelm a person, caressing and embracing him, and only seldom do they loosen their hold and then only for good cause. When John F. Kennedy entered the White House, he felt his nickname of *Jack* unbefitting his new office and requested newsmen not to use it. It was one of the few times that the media obliged in such matters, but Kennedy had something better to offer as a replacement. He pointed out that *JFK* was shorter and provided an unmistakable message in a headline. It took almost two decades for Dwight D. Eisenhower's original nickname to be shortened to just plain *Ike* from *Ugly Ike,* a typical childish cruelty to describe his toothy, mouselike look. Similarly, James Butler Hickok was originally known as *Duck Bill* because of his long nose and protruding lip. However, as his stature as a deadly gunfighter grew, it became an exercise in prudence to address him as *Wild Bill* instead.

Sometimes it becomes necessary to "sanitize" a nickname, as was the case with *Black Jack Pershing,* the commanding general of U.S. troops in Europe during World War I. It seemed in rather poor taste to let a military leader fighting for democracy and freedom be identified by his original sobriquet—*Nigger Jack Pershing.* The reference was to Pershing's previous command of black troops and reflected not only racial bias against such troops but also a feeling of resentment within the Army officer corps that any officer who took such a command did so because it offered the chance for quicker promotion. Thus a campaign was launched to call Pershing *Black Jack,* certainly less offensive, with the implication the sobriquet reflected merely his stern character and dour disposition.

Nicknames no doubt date back to the caveman, and they appear with the first written histories. John A. Wilson, the noted Egyptologist of the University of Chicago, found nicknames about as common—and often as uncomplimentary—in ancient Egypt as they are around the world today. Some of the old-time favorites translate into our equivalents of *Red, Tiny, Baldy, Ape, Frog, Lazy, Donkey* and *Big Head.* Such sobriquets were not restricted to commoners but extended to the families of the god-kings. One king's son was called *The Cat,* and another king's daughter, Uyhet-ibu, was dubbed *Nosy.*

Not surprisingly some of history's most famous personages have come down to us mainly by their nicknames. The Greek philosopher Aristocles became better known to Athenians—and to posterity—by his nickname, *Plato,* meaning "broad-shouldered." Roman orator and statesman Marcus Tullius gained his surname of *Cicero* from the Latin word *cicer* meaning wart. Plutarch notes that he had "a flat excrescence on the tip of his nose."

It has been observed that nicknames tend to be more derogatory when applied by those in a higher social position to describe persons of lower stature. However, as the sobriquet *Princess Nosy* bears witness, history is replete with nastiness going up the ladder as well. For every *Good Queen Bess* (Queen Elizabeth I of England) we can find a *Brandy Nan* (Queen Anne of England), a tribute to Anne's devotion to the bottle.

The word "nickname" was originally "ekename," or extra name, and its use has changed over the centuries. At first each man had but one name, but eventually it was necessary to make identifications more precise. So John became John (the) Smith or John (the) Baker or John (the) Butcher. These second names were called in Middle English "ekenames." Ekename evolved into "nekename" and finally "nickname." In a sense all surnames were originally nicknames, but in many cases their meanings have been lost through centuries of disuse of certain words or the alterations of names as families moved from one country and culture to another.

For a time nicknames were often more erudite than they are now. Characters of mythology and works of literature inspired many nicknames. In some cases the sobriquet of a living person was passed on to another who ended up achieving more lasting fame, and as a result the original meaning of the nickname was lost.

A 19th century observer, Edmond About, suggested in the *Revue de Deux Mondes* that the political history of many nations could be written in the form of a compendium of national epigrams and *vaudevilles*—facetious ditties at which the French excelled. Another observer, F. L. Oswald, concurred but added, "A collection of historical nicknames would, however, serve the same purpose in a still more compendious form. There are sobriquets that sum up all the physical and moral characteristics of an individual and sometimes of a party or even a whole nation."

Thus it is somewhat surprising that no book on the subject appears to have been written in the English language until 1887, when Albert Romer Frey's *Sobriquets and Nicknames* was published. Frey bemoaned the fact that the origins of so many nicknames remained veiled in mystery. The search for many of these origins required industrious literary detective work. Fortunately, numerous others have since taken up the hunt. Certainly, the works of grass-roots American historian Waldo Koop are both delightful and informative in his tedious tracing of nicknames of the West, especially the transformation of miner Matt Konarsky into *Telephones Tchaikovsky*.

This volume, attempting to trace some 7,500 nicknames, does not pretend to be the complete compendium Oswald sought. The emphasis here as often as possible is on those instant biographies that illuminate a person's time and place in some way, from ancient Egypt's royal courts to the 20th century mansions and back lots of Hollywood. No effort has been made to list every *The Great* in history, or every *The Fat*, *The Short* or *The Tall*. Still, as a matter of record, Napoleon is listed as *The Little Corporal*. In addition the sobriquet justified that of *The Little Signor* for Victor Emmanuel III of Italy, expressing the yearning, sometimes anguish, of a people wishing for greatness from their less than exemplary monarch. Similarly, the dubbing of Thomas Jefferson as *Long Tom*, among his many more honorific sobriquets, deserves special attention since at 6 feet 2½ inches he was extremely tall for his era. Today *Long Tom* would never have to stoop to pass through a doorway.

Other sources with more complete listings of nicknames are available to the researcher, but because of space limitations they are no more than an enumeration of·names, without explanations of them. Two of the best of such recent offerings are *Pseudonyms and Nicknames Dictionary*, edited by Jennifer Mossman and containing some 17,000 original names and 22,000 assumed ones, and the four-volume (including supplements) *Handbook of Pseudonyms and Personal Nicknames*, compiled by Harold S. Sharp. A good source, although limited to the United States, is George Earlie Shankle's *American Nicknames*, fairly complete through 1937, with some additions in a second edition through 1955.

The Dictionary of Historic Nicknames attempts a worldwide survey of nicknames of all ages, with special emphasis on the current in realization of the fact that some personages in a later period may well otherwise fade into obscurity. Nicknames today appear in every walk of life. Some are bestowed in the same way and for the same reasons as in the days of the caveman, but many reflect history and culture and are based as often an a person's deeds as on mere description. Military men have them, as do rulers, politicians, religious leaders, harlots, athletes, criminals and show business personalities.

Sobriquets in the last-named category are, of course, largely public relations creations, but some celebrity nicknames have had genuine origins. Before he ever became a famous comedian, *Groucho Marx* was a dedicated poker player who carried his money in a "grouch bag," or stripteaser's G-string, and the name *Groucho* eventually carried over into the Marx Brothers act. Brother *Chico* also sported a genuine nickname, having gained his from the admiration of his brothers for his constant success with the "chickies." Because he was so sickly as a child, *Gummo Marx* was often sent forth by Mama Marx wearing rubbers, rain or shine; thus the name *Gummo*. *Harpo*'s sobriquet can perhaps be dismissed as more of a show business title, although it should be noted that many of his acquaintances preferred calling him *Harpo*. Somehow his real name, Adolph, just didn't seem to fit. Research has failed to uncover any convincing origin for *Zeppo*'s nickname, including explanations tracing it to a cigarette lighter or a zeppelin (see entry).

Lupe Velez bore a nickname that was a classic Hollywood inside joke which few among the general public understood. She was *The Mexican Spitfire* or *Firecracker*. She was also a lady with a penchant for finding her way into gentlemen's beds, and while this was hardly a breach of movieland etiquette, she did have a disconcerting habit of "popping off"—like a firecracker—about her affairs. Nor, indeed, was Marie McDonald's sobriquet *The Body* considered a "hype." In addition to paying tribute to her figure, it reflected the sum of her acting talents and was therefore a nickname well earned.

Hollywood nicknames have often been employed for savage effect, born of rivalry, jealousy or the venom of gossip columnists, and sometimes even out of actual artistic disputes. Thus F. Scott Fitzgerald referred to Joe Mankiewicz as *Monkeybitch*. Perhaps a bit more bitchy were those who found Loretta Young's off-screen personality less than pleasing and referred to her as *Gretch the Wretch* (her real name is Gretchen). Her ex-husband Grant Withers popularized *The Steel Butterfly* as another of her sobriquets, coming close to *The Iron Butterfly* for Jeanette MacDonald, who had the ability to terrorize most of her colleagues, particularly, her acting and singing partner, Nelson Eddy. Kay Francis, always noted for her tightfistedness, was called *Hetty Green*, and French import Claudette Colbert was always so demanding of her cameramen that they called her *The Frantic* or *Fretting Frog*.

Few categories can boast as many colorful nicknames as the crime world. *Golf Bag Sam Hunt* was a Capone gunman who packed an automatic shotgun with his golf clubs, and *Duck Walk* was a Chicago gun moll of the same era whose strut was greatly affected by the two .38s she wore holstered to her knees, at the ready when her man needed them. *Billy the Clock* is an arsonist widely acclaimed in the underworld for his very accurate celluloid

timing devices. *Kissing Sam* is a pickpocket who can perform the most difficult act of the light-fingered profession, that of lifting a victim's billfold from an inside coat pocket while standing face to face, close enough to kiss him.

Many underworld names are bestowed with high honors. Frank Costello was *The Prime Minister* because of his extraordinary success at bribing politicians. Johnny Torrio was *The Brain* because he had great organizing ability and because so many of his tenets became the principles on which the national crime syndicate was built. *Hot Stove Jimmy Quinn* was a politician with the reputation of being "so crooked he'd steal a hot stove." *Umbrella Mike Boyle,* business agent of the Electrical Workers' Union No. 134 in Chicago during the 1920s, derived his nickname by standing at a bar on certain days of the week with an unfurled umbrella into which building contractors seeking to avoid labor troubles would deposit their cash levies.

Other criminals could not abide their nicknames. *Bugsy Siegel* was called Ben by his friends and *Bugsy,* the underworld was fond of saying, only by his dead enemies—that "bugs" he got when so addressed. One who actually killed over the use of his nickname was public enemy Charles Arthur Floyd, better knows as *Pretty Boy Floyd*. He murdered the two Ash brothers of the Kansas City underworld as much because they insisted on calling him *Pretty Boy* as for any other reason. Even when Floyd was shot down in an Ohio corn field in 1934 by FBI agents and one, standing over him, announced, "You are *Pretty Boy Floyd,*" the fatally wounded gangster snarled out what were virtually his last angry words: "I'm Charles Arthur Floyd!"

Scarface Al Capone was another gangster who did not appreciate his nickname. Capone, who had gotten the scar in a whorehouse altercation in Brooklyn during his youth, resented the repeated appearance of his nickname in the Chicago papers. In 1929 Capone called on Merrill C. Meigs, publisher of Hearst's *Evening American,* to protest. Although Meigs was impressed with Capone's presentation of his case, he pointed out that the mobster was a most newsworthy character. Capone retorted, "Does your newspaper consider it fair play to refer to a physical disfigurement every time it mentions my name?"

Meigs admitted he had never considered the matter. He told Capone he would think about it and discuss it with his editors. The next day Capone called to get Meigs' answer and was told that *Scarface* would no longer be used in the newspaper except in a direct quote from someone like a police official. Meigs told friends he had reached the decision with no feeling of compulsion. "The man was right," he said. "I just had not thought of it before." It was, to say the least, a prudent decision, especially considering Capone's muscle and ability to disrupt newspaper distribution if he desired.

Journalists have generally been reluctant to give up nicknames. Harry Guzik, a long-time procurer and payoff man for the Capone mob, became known as *Greasy Thumb Guzik* because, he said, he peeled off so many bills from the huge roll he carried that he could never get the grease off his thumb. When Harry died, newspapermen transferred the nickname to his younger brother Jake, who was the top payoff man for the syndicate. The nickname was too good to die.

In the sports world nicknames have always abounded, many of them bordering on the show biz approach. Star Yankee centerfielder Joe DiMaggio was *The Yankee Clipper* and Henry Aaron, baseball's top home run hitter, was *Hammerin' Hank.* But many other names were truly descriptive of personal traits. *Dizzy*

Dean earned his nickname not merely for being dizzy, which he most certainly was, but because he could drive others dizzy with his inane actions and chatter. *The Diz* even offered scholarly comments on the matter of nicknames, once saying: "Most all ballplayers got nicknames, and Birdie Tebbetts's is Birdie because he's always ahollerin' like a little ole kinairy bird."

Perhaps two of the most descriptive and logical nicknames in the game were those given brothers Paul and Lloyd Waner of the Brooklyn Dodgers, who were known as *Big Poison* and *Little Poison* respectively. Both were "poison" to enemy pitchers. On many occasions Lloyd, often hailed as the greatest singles hitter of all time, would get on base, and brother Paul, a slugger, would drive him home with an extra-base hit. The origin of the *Poison* sobriquet, however, had nothing to do with hitting ability . Lloyd was extremely thin (for this reason he had earler gained the moniker *Muscles*) and once when he was playing in New York, a fan in the stands made a loud comment in typical Brooklynese about Lloyd being a "little poison," meaning little person. The nickname stuck and later acquired its other meaning.

Baseball nicknames are not bestowed lightly, however, and the ones that fans read in the sports pages are not always those used in the dugout. While the great Lou Gehrig was called *The Iron Horse* for his ability to play in so many successive games, he was addressed differently by his teammates, who, referring to his more tangible attributes, called him *Biscuit Pants.* Athletes seldom have the right to confer their own nicknames upon themselves. When in 1980 Yankee catcher Rick Cerone advised the media that he thought he could be called *The Italian Stallion,* there was no sudden outburst of agreement. Two New York television sportcasters allowed he might earn the moniker after several years of "proving himself," one presumes with the bat and otherwise as well.

When a sports nickname takes, it can become inseparable from the athlete. Thus *Babe Ruth* was always the *Babe*. A woman contestant on a TV quiz show once proved a very poor loser when she failed to give *Babe Ruth*'s real name. She said it was *Babe Ruth*. Informed the correct answer was George Herman Ruth, she replied: "That's insane. Everybody knows his name was *Babe Ruth*." The lady made it clear that she thought she was being robbed, and for a time she refused to leave the set.

Of course nicknames are a part of all sports. Byron White, who became a Supreme Court justice, was a star at the University of Colorado and later with Pittsburgh in the professional ranks. In his gridiron days he was called *Whizzer White*. By the time he joined the High Court he was known as Justice Byron White—except to some capital wag who observed that the group formerly known as The Nine Old Men had become Eight Old Men and a *Whizzer*.

In boxing Jack Dempsey, a former hobo from Manassa, Colo., battled his way to the heavyweight campionship in 1919 as *The Manassa Mauler*. When he was tried on draft evasion charges the following year, which he beat, he was caustically referred to as *The Manassa Slacker*. Heavyweight champion Joe Louis was famed as *The Brown Bomber,* but earlier in his career he had been dubbed *The Detroit Destroyer,* an identification that failed to convey fully his destructive punching power. After his rematch one-round victory over Max Schmeling in 1938, *The Detroit Destroyer* was forgotten, forever replaced by *The Brown Bomber*.

Perhaps the fight game's best sobriquet went not to a boxer but to matchmaker and manager *Greasy Vest Weill*. Regarded by many sportswriters as a rather unsavory character in an unsavory racket, Weill's personal appearance reflected this perception. His title may well have been originated by columnist Dan Parker, who in any event could always turn a deft phrase about it. He once wrote:

In the boxing business he is variously and with some affection (although his personal popularity is open to grave question) known as *The Vest, The Weskit King* and *Greasy Vest*. These sobriquets date back to his salad days when he took his meals on the fly and the fly retaliated by taking his meals on Al. One could always tell then what Weill had been eating over a two-week period. But the fault wasn't entirely his as he was too busy riding day coaches all over the country with his fighters to pay much attention to his sartorial getup.

Nicknames were just as numerous in the Old West as they have been in the sports world. Among the most colorful was that of *Liver Eating Johnston,* who sported that very accurate sobriquet because of his habit, born of a personal vendetta, of killing Indians and feasting on their livers. Johnston's uncommon and unsightly eating habits may have accounted for a total of 300 victims.

Similarly, Alfred (of Alferd) Packer won a permanent spot in Colorado folklore as *The Man Who Ate Democrats* when he consumed five companions during a dangerous trek through mountain snows. Upon his conviction in 1873, the presiding judged leaned down from the bench and roared with considerable distaste, "Packer, you depraved Republican son of a bitch, there were only five Democrats in Hinsdale County, and you ate them all!"

Historian Duncan Emrich has stated that it was an old Wild West custom for miners and cowboys and the like to name each other. They bestowed such names as *Crooked-Nose Pete* and *Cock-Eyed Frank* and *Sleepy Otto* and *Baldy Golden* and *Blind Dick*. *Dirty-Face Jack* was probably a miner who handled explosives and showed his line of work in his appearance. *Strawberry Yank* had a whiskey-induced red nose, but *Fat Jack,* up Montana way, was as lean as a fence rail. *Christmas-Tree Murphy* once killed a man with a Christmas tree, and anyone expecting a fair gunfight with *Dark Alley Jim* was not only stupid but dead. *Peg-Leg Annie* lost her foot after she nearly froze to death in a snowstorm on Bald Mountain. *Slot-Machine Ida* was uncontrollable near those one-armed bandits in Nevada and *Shoestring Annie* was famed for her sales pitch: "Buy a pair of shoelaces, you God-damned cheapskate!"

As Bret Harte noted in his short story "Tennessee's Partner":

At Sandy Bar in 1854 most men were christened anew. Sometimes these appellatives were derived from some distinctiveness of dress, as in the case of "Dungaree Jack"; or from some peculiarity of habit, as shown in "Saleratus Bill," so called from an undue proportion of that chemical in his daily bread; or from some unlucky slip, as exhibited in "The Iron Pirate," a mild, inoffensive man who earned that baleful title by his unfortunate mispronunciation of the term "iron pyrites." Perhaps this was the beginning of a rude heraldry.

Legends of how many characters of the Old West got their nicknames are filled with inaccuracies. *Bat Masterson* did not get his from any habit of thumping his foes over the head with his walking stick. His given name was Bartholomew, which he could not abide. He insisted on being addressed as *Bat* and even changed his official name to William Barclay Masterson.

Historian Waldo Koop has researched many frontier nicknames that help explain why the West was so wild. Take the case of *Catacorners Ketchum*, a miner victimized by his Bible-spouting partner who took off with the fruits of all their diggings. Ketchum became part of the folklore of the West with these angry words: "If I ever ketch that sneak he'll get a Bible crammed down his throat, catacorners."

In Butte, Mont., there was a Polish miner named Matt Konarsky who became celebrated as *Telephones Tchaikovsky*. Konarsky often pecked out two-fingered tunes on pianos in the local saloon or the parlor of his boarding house. Being so talented and Polish, he was immediately nicknamed *Tchaikovsky*. The *Telephones* appendage came one day when he was donning his street clothes in the mine change room after his tour in the shaft. A fellow miner, an Irishman, spotted him wearing a double truss that, with its black rubber pads, much resembled a telephone operator's headset. "Lord God," the Irish miner exclaimed, "will ye have a look at the tiliphones on old Tchaikovsky!" Hence *Telephones Tchaikovsky*.

Political nicknames are often more savage than most, and no American president has been spared them. In addition to being *The Great Emancipator* and *Honest Abe*, Lincoln was to his enemies *The Buffoon, The Baboon, Caesar, The Jester, Massa Linkum* and *The Tyrant*, among others.

Certainly the most fitting sobriquet of all for any president was *Silent Cal*, applied to *Calvin Coolidge*. At a White House dinner Coolidge was sitting next to a lovely young thing who said to him "Mr. President, I have made a bet which I hope you will help me win."

Coolidge looked at her.

She went on, "It is that I will engage you in conversation for at least five minutes."

There followed a gap of silence. Then Coolidge said, "You lose."

Of course, Democrats always said Coolidge's nickname was most appropriate, that he was silent because he really had nothing to say.

Perhaps even more subject to wicked nickname barbs than U.S. presidents have been their first ladies. Recently former president Richard Nixon appeared on television to bemoan the custom of nicknaming president's wives, especially calling his wife *Plastic Pat* and Nancy Reagan *First Mannequin.* Rosalyn Carter was called *The Iron Magnolia,* an allusion to the perception by many that she was made of far sterner stuff than Jimmy Carter. Bess Truman's strong desire to remain almost totally in the background caused her to be dubbed *The Last Lady of the Land.* However, easily the most "sinning" first lady in the view of hardened politicians was *Lemonade Lucy,* Mrs. Rutherford Hayes, who really shook the existing order when she refused to serve anything stronger than lemonade in the White House.

As mentioned earlier, royalty has never been exempt from nicknames of the most unflattering variety. Before there was a monarchy in France, the strongest leader in the early 5th century was Clodion, nicknamed *The Hairy* because of his luxuriant beard. His growth was said to have excited the contempt of several of his less favored courtiers, who, one historian recounts, "probably could not grow beards." In 8th century France, Childeric III, nicknamed *The Stupid,* was deposed by *Pepin the Short,* thus ending the Merovingian dynasty. And, as was their fashion, when the French called John (Jean) II *The Good,* they were deliberately lying through their teeth about one of the worst sovereigns in the nation's history.

Naturally, sexual propensities among royalty are seldom ignored. Czar Alexander III was nicknamed *The Young Steer* in his crown prince days. He did not seem to have slowed down with the passing years; all that was ever dropped from the appellation was *Young.* Although much of the British press is most circumspect about it, the fact remains that the Fleet Street nickname for England's Prince Andrew is *Randy Andy.*

Today many parents recognize care must be exercised in naming a child if they wish to control his or her nickname, and even so the cause may well be lost. Writing in the *New York Times,* Josef Berger told of a mother who settled on Eric for her son because she was satisfied she could cope with *Rick* or *Rickie* as a nickname. So much for a mother's best-laid plans. The neighborhood kids called him *Ear-ache.*

Certain surnames bear their own special forenames. For instance, many a Drummond has been called *Bulldog* and Streets have been dubbed *One Way* or *Dead End.* If Cecil Rhodes of South African fame had been born a century later, he probably would have been called Dusty, the fate of most Rhodes of Rhoades, in his childhood.

The care and feeding of nicknames require their changing use in different circumstances. According to H. Van Buren of the East-West Culture Learning Institute, a name generally comes in three distinct varieties. First there is a person's official name, for instance, Stewart. Then there is the nickname of Stew. And there's the affectionate nickname of Stewie. Almost always these nicknames are formed from the first syllable of the first name and the affectionate version come by adding an "ee" sound.

Affection fades from a nickname as anger (and thus formality) grows. Thus, according to the Van Buren theory, a parent's tone and name calling would progress as follows:

Debbie, no.
Deb, don't.
Deborah Ann, you've been told twenty times not to do that.
Deborah Ann Smith, stop that instantly!

Van Buren notes it is the nature of nicknames that many male versions have no affectionate nicknames, such as in the case of Phillip, Roger, Lester and Carleton, but most female versions do—such as Ann, Edith, Grace and Ruth. Van Buren argues that in the United States nicknames have a masculine connotation and affectionate nicknames a feminine one. It is far more common for males to be addressed by their nicknames and females by their affectionate nicknames, not for reasons of affection as much as indications of "childishness."

For most men, affectionate nicknames offer a childish ring to be shed in the transition from boyhood to manhood. Often, Van Buren notes, it is a battle for a boy to get his mother to start using his nickname instead of its diminutive variation . . . and he will probably never get his grandmother to do so. It is a form of sibling rivalry for a sister to embarrass "big brother" by using his "baby name."

This objection to the male diminutive does not apply to sports or show business, where such personalities as Sammy Davis, Willie Mays, Reggie Jackson, Woody Hayes and the like can thrive since they are in an activity exempted from society's normal rules.

Politicians are sometimes permitted such an exception, with the use of the diminutive often taking on a macho character, such as in the case of *Teddy Roosevelt*. Robert Kennedy's supporters used *Bobby* in the same masculine sense, while his foes used the name disparagingly, trying to stress what they considered his "childishness."

For whatever reasons all people in all cultures make use of nicknames. Certainly this was true of the American Indians. Many of their nicknames were bestowed by whites and the Indians returned the favor. Indian nicknames tended to go to the heart of matters. There has long been a historical controversy about whether or not Andrew Jackson engaged in large-scale extermination of Indians, as his political foes always charged. *Old Hickory* (he was supposedly as tough as hickory) denied the charge, but the Indians may well have provided the answer with their nickname for him—*Sharp Knife*. Sam Houston may well have been *The Father of Texas* to the whites, but to the Indians he was *Big Drunk*.

A different dichotomy of views existed in the case of John Churchill, the first duke of Marlborough. He was referred to as *The Silly Duke* because he would cut off conversation that bored him or of which he disapproved by remarking, "Oh, silly! Silly!" His enemies at court used the name behind his back. Although it might seem that Marlborough would have been more ill-treated by his military rivals than by fellow Englishmen, the more tolerant French, in typical Gallic manner, called him *The Handsome Englishman*.

It should be noted that there are variations between spoken and written nicknames. The former is more often descriptive, physically, mentally or morally, and the latter tends to be more of a capsulated characterization of a career. The written version is as much a nickname as the verbal, although hardly any neighbors of George Bernard Shaw would have said, "Hi there, *Wag of Whitehall Court*." What they would say—out of hearing range— was: "Here comes *Old Hair-and-Teeth*."

The more controversial a person the more nicknames he may gain. It is not always possible to list them all. Daniel Defoe, counting both nicknames and pseudonyms, sported well over 200, but his lifestyle was probably best summed up by that of *The Sunday Gentleman*. Considerably and constantly in debt, he was often dodging bailiffs, emerging only on Sundays dressed in his finest raiment, since he was safe from their clutches on the Sabbath.

Far more persons in this volume reveled in their nicknames than resented them, and many made a consistent effort to live up to them. English poet and verse satirist Alexander Pope, the literary dictator of his age, was called by admirers *The Bard of Twickenham*. Those who felt the sting of his scathing invective nicknamed him *The Wasp of Twickenham*. Pope most certainly enjoyed being *The Wasp* far more, once writing:

Yes, I am proud; and must be proud, to see Men not afraid of God afraid of me.

There is considerable self-serving in attempts to explain away nicknames. Many individuals alter the real reason for their own or other's nicknames. The Chicago police could hardly be expected to appreciate the meaning of *Greasy Thumb Guzik's* moniker, thus officials have with a straight face told feature writers that he was originally so identified because he had been a waiter with the obnoxious habit of getting his thumb in the soup, hence he became *Greasy Thumb*. Now, was that Harry or Jake? To maintain credibility, this theory requires that the errant thumb characteristic be a family trait.

Nicknames are often applied anonymously, and for good reason. Retribution for an unwanted or hated nickname can be awesome if the sobriquet is directed against the mighty. When William Collingborne wrote his famous rhyme—

The Cat, the Rat and Lovel our Dogge Rulen all England under an Hogge.

—he was referring to King Richard III of England and his three associates, Sir Richard Ratcliffe, William Catesby and Lord Lovel. For this offense against the crown, Collingborne was hanged and, while still alive, had his heart ripped from his body.

Happily, not all nicknames elicit such murderous responses. Indeed, *Dasher Abbandando*, the second entry in the book, doubtlessly relished in telling and retelling the hilarious or, perhaps more accurately, violent origin of his nickname.

The entries in this book are for the most part listed by the subject's name; however, a fair number are placed under the nickname when it is better known that the individual's real name, or the true identity is unknown or uncertain or the nickname is a collective one. Nicknames in the text of each entry are italicized. However, nicknames that are merely variations or diminutives of proper names—Bob or Bobby—initials—FDR—or physical description—Fatty—are generally not in italics.

Some disputes will inevitably arise over the origin or meaning of certain sobriquets. Probably some observers will feel the identification of the first entry, Hank Aaron, as *Bad Henry* can be explained as black argot, present-day usage of *Bad* to indicate greatness, exceptional skill or accomplishment. However, many sportwriters have noted that *Bad Henry* has been used and was most likely originated by certain "purists" of the game who were unhappy that Aaron had shattered the home run record of *The Mighty Bambino, Babe Ruth*. Thus it may be noted that nicknames can be pithy word portraits of man, his era and indeed ourselves, depending on how we use them.

A

AARON, HENRY LOUIS "Hank" (1934–)

As baseball's leading home run hitter with a career total of 755, Henry "Hank" Aaron exceeded even Babe Ruth's output. His batting skill earned him the appellation *Hammerin' Hank*. In addition to most home runs Aaron holds the record for runs batted in (2,297) and total bases (6,856). Some baseball "purists" refer to him as *Bad Henry* for deposing Ruth, leading observers to wonder if the nickname would have been coined if Aaron had been white.

ABBANDANDO, FRANK "the Dasher" (1910–1942)

One of Murder Inc.'s most productive "hit men," Frank Abbandando took part in an estimated 50 contract killings, but he earned his sobriquet on a nearly bungled assignment. Contracted to "rub out" a longshoreman, he aimed his gun at point-blank range, only to have the weapon misfire. Thoroughly embarrassed, Abbandando dashed around the block so fast that he actually came up behind his target again, this time pumping three fatal bullets into him. Abbandando was thereafter known by his fellow killers as *The Dasher*. He was executed in 1942.

ABBAS (721?–754)

The methods of Abbas (Abdul-Abbas) for achieving and maintaining power as the first caliph of the Abbasside dynasty of Bagdad are aptly described by his nickname *The Bloodshedder*.

ABBE, CLEVELAND "Old Prob" (1838–1916)

American meteorologist and astronomer Cleveland Abbe was one of the first to make daily weather forecasts based on reports telegraphed from other parts of the country. Beginning in 1869, his predictions about the "probable" weather appeared in a column called "Probabilities," printed locally in Cincinnati and subsequently carried in newspapers around the country. He bylined the column "Old Prob" when he was barely 30. His pioneering forecast methods led to the establishment of the U.S. Weather Bureau, an achievement for which he was dubbed *The Father of the Weather Bureau.*

Abdul the Damned—See ABDUL-HAMID II.

ABDUL-HAMID II (1842–1918)

Abdul-Hamid II, sultan of Turkey, was called *The Great Assassin* in recognition of the enormous number of persons he had killed to maintain power. He was also known as *Abdul the Damned*, since it was believed he was certain to be overthrown and probably assassinated. To protect himself the sultan had his Yildiz Palace in Constantinople heavily guarded and his private rooms fitted with alarm systems, trap doors and mirrors set at angles to reveal hidden intruders. Life-sized wax dummies of the sultan, reclining on lounges or sitting in chairs, were set in windows in hopes of drawing an assassin's fire. Faced throughout his regime with such dissident movements as the Young Turks, he was finally deposed and sent into exile in 1909.

ABDUL-JABBAR, KAREEM (1947–)

Beginning in the mid-1970s, star basketball center Kareem Abdul-Jabbar (born Lew Alcindor) was referred to by the press and public in Los Angeles as *The Franchise* in recognition of his vital role in leading the Los Angeles Lakers to the NBA championship.

ABDULLAH, MOHAMMAD
(c. 1902–1982)

Sheik Mohammad Abdullah, an important figure in India's struggle for independence, was also a dominant force in securing limited autonomy for Moslem Kashmir within the predominantly Hindu country. This achievement earned him the respect of his countrymen as *The Lion of Kashmir*.

ABEEL—See Cornplanter.

ABERNATHY, JOHN *(1764–1831)*

The eminent English surgeon Dr. John Abernathy was called *Doctor My-Book* because he never lost an opportunity to promote his writings. When asked a question by a patient, he often replied, "Read my book," which was titled *Surgical Observations*.

Abolitionist of the Abolitionists, The— See SEWARD, WILLIAM H.

Abominable No-Man, The—See ADAMS, SHERMAN.

ABPLANALP, ROBERT H.
(1922–   )

American inventor and business tycoon Robert H. Abplanalp became a millionaire with his invention of an aerosol dispenser, bringing him acclaim as *The Aerosol King*. He won greater public recognition during the administration of Richard M. Nixon as *The President's Other Friend*, an allusion to the fact that he and fellow millionaire Bebe Rebozo were Nixon's only close friends.

Abraham Lincoln of the Sea—See FURUSETH, ANDREW.

Absolute Wisdom, The—See WOOD, MATTHEW.

ABU BAKR "The Upright"
(c. 573–634)

The father-in-law of Mohammed and his only companion during the Hegira, Abu Bakr was the first Moslem caliph and Mohammed's successor. Honored as *The Upright,* he began the great expansion of Islam as a world religion.

ABU NASR MOHAMMED AL FARABI *(?–950)*

Celebrated physician and composer Abu Nasr Mohammed al Farabi was nicknamed *The Orpheus of Arabia* for his musical works. Once, we are told, while he accompanied musicians at court with his lute, the prince asked him to play some of his own works. He produced a three-part composition which he distributed to the band. The first threw the ruler and his courtiers into fits of laughter, the second turned them all to tears and the third lulled everyone, including the musicians, to sleep.

ABU YUSUF ALKENDI *(?–880)*

Arabian physician and philosopher Abu Yusuf Alkendi authored well over 200 philosophical works, earning the praise of his friends as *The Great Astrologer* and *The Philosopher of the Arabs*. One of the earliest translators and commentators of Aristotle, he also has been called *The*

Phoenix of His Age, since he represents his culture's first philosophical revolt against Islamism.

Abyssinian Prince, The—See BRIDGETOWER, GEORGE AUGUSTUS POLGREEN.

ABZUG, BELLA (1920–   )

A former representative from New York and an ardent advocate of civil liberties and women's rights, Bella Abzug is often referred to affectionately by supporters as *Battling Bella, Bellicose Bella* or *Hurricane Bella,* nicknames used less kindly by her political foes. Some Abzug supporters prefer not to describe her outspoken political style and dub her instead *Mother Courage.*

ACCARDO, ANTHONY "Tough Tony" (1906–   )

Usually called *Tough Tony,* Chicago syndicate boss Anthony Accardo is also known rather affectionately in the underworld as *Joe Batters.* This "handle" derives from his early years with Al Capone, when he was famous for his proficiency with a baseball bat as a slugger for the mob.

Accidental President, The—See FILLMORE, MILLARD; JOHNSON, LYNDON BAINES.

Accused, The—See BORDEN, LIZZIE.

Achilles of England, The—See WELLINGTON, ARTHUR WELLESLEY, FIRST DUKE OF.

ACHILLINI, ALESSANDRO (1463–1512)

An Italian physician and philosopher, Alessandro Achillini was celebrated by his contemporaries as *The Second Aristotle.*

Acid Doctor, The—See DE KAPLANY, GEZA.

Acid Drop—See AVORY, HORACE EDMUND.

ACTON, JOHN EMERICH EDWARD DALBERG-ACTON, LORD (1834–1902)

Although he has been nicknamed *The Historian Who Never Wrote a Book,* Lord Acton is one of the most important historians of all time. A professor of modern history at Cambridge University, he planned the great *Cambridge Modern History,* and is most often remembered for the observation, "All power tends to corrupt; absolute power corrupts absolutely." Acton held that a historian must be a moralist and that he is bound to condemn every historical figure who fails to maintain high virtue. This lofty standard led to his being dubbed *Acton the Severe.*

Acton the Severe—See ACTON, JOHN EMERICH EDWARD DALBERG-ACTON, LORD.

ADAMS, ABIGAIL (1744–1818)

Because John Adams, second president of the United States, relied heavily on the political advice of his wife, Abigail Smith Adams, his political foes referred to her as *Mrs. President.*

ADAMS, ALBERT J.—See Meanest Gambler in New York, The.

ADAMS, EVA B. *(1908–   )*

Eva B. Adams, the administrative assistant to Sen. Pat McCarran of Nevada from 1939 until his death in 1954, was often described as Nevada's *Third Senator* because of the political influence she exerted in Washington. She served as director of the U.S. Mint from 1961 to 1969.

ADAMS, HENRY BROOKS *(1838–1918)*

Henry Adams, one of America's greatest historians and the grandson of President John Quincy Adams, spent his life in a frustrated pursuit of power and thought of himself as a failure. He called himself *The Boston Amateur,* an opinion seconded by biographers who consider him an Adams born too late. As democratic America boomed in the industrialized 19th century, it was no longer possible to control affairs from the study, as others in his family had done, and Adams never took his ideas to the marketplace of public opinion.

ADAMS, JOHN *(1735–1826)*

The second president of the United States, John Adams was nicknamed *The Colossus of Independence* by Thomas Jefferson to honor his skillful orator before the Continental Congress on behalf of independence. Adams was also called *Old Sink or Swim,* a nickname that derived from his response to a royalist who urged him to give up the colonial cause: "Sink or swim, live or die, survive or perish, I am with my country from this day on." A stocky 5 feet 7 inches tall, Adams became quite plump in middle age and while serving as Vice President under Washington, he was called *His*

Rotundity—behind his substantial back—by members of the Senate. Adams resented the unflattering sobriquet and once offered a statement in his defense: "I have one head, four limbs, and five senses, like any other man, and *nothing peculiar in any of them.* . . . I have no miniature and have been too much abused by painters ever to sit to anyone again."

ADAMS, JOHN QUINCY *(1767–1848)*

John Quincy Adams, sixth president of the United States, was nicknamed *Second John* because he was the son of former president John Adams. But his opponents called him *The Massachusetts Madman,* for reasons described in an anonymous tract of the time: "Well has he been called 'The Massachusetts Madman.' He boasts that he places all his glory in independence. If independence is synonymous with obstinacy, he is the most independent statesman living." In his later years, Adams returned to the House of Representatives, where he was referred to as *Old Man Eloquent* in recognition of his talent for oratory.

ADAMS, MAUDE *(1872–1953)*

Probably the most popular actress of the American stage in the early 1900s, Maude Adams scored her greatest triumphs in the plays of James M. Barrie and was known as *The Barrie Actress.* Described as almost nunlike in her private life, she often went to live in convents, resulting in the sobriquet *The Original I-Want-To-Be-Alone Woman.*

ADAMS, SAMUEL *(1722–1803)*

American patriot Samuel Adams is known as *The Father of the American Revolution* for his constant agitation against the British and his refusal to compromise with them. He and John Hancock were the only two men excluded from an offer of general pardon by the British in 1775. Loyalists disdainfully called Adams *The Would-be Cromwell of America,* perhaps somewhat of a blunder in the Protestant colonies.

ADAMS, SHERMAN *(1899–   )*

Often described as the most powerful unelected official in U.S. history, Sherman Adams was the chief assistant to President Dwight Eisenhower, and he totally dominated the Eisenhower White House. His "O.K.—S.A." or "NO—S.A." carried almost the same weight as the president's signature. The latter response, extremely common, led to his being nicknamed *The Abominable No-Man.* Because of his abrasive, distant and self-righteous manner, Adams was also called *The Iceberg.* He was eventually driven from power after the "Vicuna coat" scandal which revealed that he was "on the take" from a New England textile manufacturer.

ADAY, MARVIN LEE—See Meat Loaf.

ADDERLEY, JULIAN "Cannonball" *(1928–1975)*

Leading jazz saxophonist Julian Adderley acquired the nickname of *Cannibal* as a youth for his reputation at school for devouring all manner of food. Adults later misunderstood the word to be *Cannonball,* and that name stuck to him thereafter.

ADDISON, JOSEPH *(1672–1719)*

English essayist and poet Joseph Addison is called *The English Atticus* as a form of tribute, but the nickname was originally applied to him derisively by Alexander Pope to avenge a number of real or imagined slights. Pope portrayed Addison satiri-

cally as Atticus in his poem *Epistle to Arbuthnot,* the final couplet reading:

> Who would not smile if such a man
>   there be?
> Who would not laugh if Addison
>   were he?

In its present version the couplet reads:

> Who but must laugh, if such a man
>   there be?
> Who would not weep, if Atticus
>   were he?

Some of Addison's contemporaries also dubbed him *The Literary Machiavel,* because after bestowing great praise on Pope's translation of the *Iliad,* he proceeded to publish a rival translation of his own.

Addisonian, The—See IRVING, WASHINGTON.

ADELIS, PETE—See Leather Lung Pete.

ADENAUER, KONRAD *(1876–1967)*

Known affectionately to the German people as *Der Alte* or *The Old Man,* Konrad Adenauer was the first chancellor of the postwar Federal Republic of Germany, or West Germany. Some have noted that in periods following military defeat the German people seem to gravitate toward grandfatherly leaders, as was the case with Paul von Hindenburg after World War I.

Adlai Stevenson of Songwriters, The— See PORTER, COLE.

ADLER, MORTIMER *(1902–   )*

American philosopher Mortimer Adler has been called the *Poobah of Popularizers* for what one critic calls his "highly successful career mingling the goods of scholarship with the tinsel of merchandising." Many observers find his attempts at conveying ideas from the academy to the populace quite successful, and they can live with the sobriquet, as indeed Adler himself probably can.

Admirable, The—See EZRA, ABRAHAM BEN MEIN IBN.

Admirable Doctor, The—See BACON, ROGER.

Admiral on Horseback, The—See HORTHY, MIKLOS VON NAGYBANYA.

Admiral of the Mosquitoes, The—See COLUMBUS, CHRISTOPHER.

Adonais—See KEATS, JOHN A.

Adonis, Joe: JOSEPH DOTO *(1902–1972)*

A member of the controlling board of the national crime syndicate at its inception in the early 1930s, racket boss Joseph Doto adopted the name *Adonis* because he considered himself the spitting image of Aphrodite's handsome lover.

Adonis of the French Revolution, The— See CHENIER, ANDRE.

Adulterer, The—See HAMILTON, ALEXANDER.

Advance Agent of Emancipation, The—See MOTT, LUCRETIA.

Adversity Hume—See HUME, JOSEPH.

Adviser of Presidents, The—See BARUCH, BERNARD M.

Aerosol King, The—See ABPLANALP, ROBERT H.

AESCHYLUS *(525–456 B.C.)*

Called *The Father of Greek Tragedy,* Aeschylus was the first dramatist to introduce a second actor into drama. Although he is believed to have written about 90 plays, only seven survived in their entirety.

Aeschylus of France, The— See CREBILLON, PROSPER JOLYOT DE.

Aesop of Arabia, The—See NASSAR BEN HARETH.

Aesop of France, The—See LA FONTAINE, JEAN DE.

Affidavit Boies—See BOIES, HORACE.

African Astronomer, The—See BANNEKER, BENJAMIN.

African Roscius, The—See ALDRIDGE, IRA.

Africa's Angry Young Man—See MBOYA, THOMAS JOSEPH.

AGNES, COUNTESS OF DUNBAR AND MARCH—See Black Agnes.

AGNEW, SPIRO T. (1918–   )

The discredited vice president of the United States under Richard Nixon, Spiro T. Agnew was referred to by his political enemies at *The White Knight* and *Spiro T. Eggplant,* given him by the "eggheads" he attacked. The most insulting of all his nicknames is probably *Nixon's Nixon.*

Agreeable Sea Wolf, The—See JONES, JOHN PAUL.

AIKEN, MARGARET—See Great Witch of Balwery, The.

AIUPPA, (JOSEPH JOHN) JOE "Ha Ha" (1907–   )

Joe *"Ha Ha"* Aiuppa, an old-time Capone muscleman, had by 1980 become Mafia boss of Cicero, Ill., and reputedly head of the entire Chicago mob. Aiuppa got the name *Ha Ha* because he never cracked a smile.

AKBAR THE GREAT (1542–1605)

Akbar the Great, the third Mongol ruler of Hindustan and the descendant of Genghis Khan and Tamerlane, unified most of Indian subcontinent, a task he began on coming to the throne at the age of 14. Regarded as the 16th century's greatest Asian Renaissance prince, he possessed a huge library of 24,000 volumes. Although illiterate, he delighted in having the books read to him, thus accumulating a vast store of information and memorizing endless verses of poetry. Called *The Guardian of Mankind,* he was acclaimed for his justice, which was such "that everyone wronged feels he has the emperor on his side." Throughout his life Akbar attempted to wipe out religious differences in his immense empire through his own religion, the Din-i-Ilahi, or "Divine Faith." While Akbar's unification of his subjects did not last, his descendants nevertheless held the throne until 1858 when India was absorbed by the British Crown.

Alaric-Cotin—See FREDERICK THE GREAT.

ALBANI, FRANCESCO (1578–1660)

Italian painter Francesco Albani was known as *The Anacreon of Painters* because of the softness and sensuousness of his style. His canvasses were said to have captured the pagan sensuousness ascribed to the Greek lyric poet Anacreon.

ALBERT II, DUKE OF AUSTRIA (1289–1358)

Disparaged early in his reign as *The Lame* because of a physical deformity, Albert II, duke of Austria, proved to be a shrewd and thoughtful ruler. By the end of his reign he was universally known as *The Wise.*

ALBERT III, DUKE OF AUSTRIA (1347–1395)

Albert III, duke of Austria, was frequently called *Albert with the Tress* because of his custom of entwining in his hair a lock of his wife's or that of other comely ladies.

ALBERT IV, DUKE OF AUSTRIA (1377–1404)

After a pilgrimage to the Holy Land, Albert IV, duke of Austria, turned from court life to one of religious devotion and for a time lived in a Carthusian monastery. Called *The Pious* for his devout practices, he left the duties of state to his cousin William, whose popularity in that role may be judged by his sobriquet The Delightful.

ALBERT, PRINCE OF MONACO (1958–   )

According to the gossip press, Prince Albert, the eldest child of Princess Grace and Prince Rainier of Monaco, has been dubbed *The Sun King,* after the despotic Louis XIV of France, by his sisters Caroline and Stephanie. This sibling disparagement is said to arise from the young women's complaint that Albert interferes too often in their personal lives.

Albert the Good: ALBERT OF ENGLAND (1819–1861)

Prince Albert of Saxe-Coburg-Gotha, the German husband and prince consort of Queen Victoria of England, was nicknamed *Albert the Good* for his devotion to his wife and adopted country. When he died of typhus at the age of 42, Victoria insisted on being referred to as Victoria the Good in his honor. Because of her long periods of absence from the public eye while she mourned her loss, however, her more common sobriquet was The Widow at Windsor.

Albert the Workingman or Albert: ALEXANDRE MARTIN (1815–1895)

Alexandre Martin, better known in French politics as *Albert the Workingman* or *Albert,* was a mechanic who played important roles in the revolu-

tions of 1830 and 1848. A follower of socialist Louis Blanc, he was the first laborer to participate in a French government. Sentenced to life imprisonment after the 1848 revolution, he was pardoned in 1859 by Louis Napoleon.

Albert with the Tress—See ALBERT III, DUKE OF AUSTRIA.

ALBERTUS MAGNUS (1193?–1280)

German theologian, philosopher, scientist and writer, Albertus Magnus, among the great thinkers of the Dominican order, gained the sobriquet *Doctor Universalis,* or *Universal Doctor.* One of his pupils was Thomas Aquinas. Albertus Magnus spent much of his later years seeking ways to unite Christian theology and Aristotelianism. He was canonized by Pius XI in 1932.

Albino King, The—See EDWARD THE CONFESSOR.

Alcidas—See TROUSSE, MARQUIS DE LA.

ALCUIN (735–804)

Brought to France from England to superintend the studies of Charlemagne, Alcuin was known as *The School-Mistress of France.* He instructed the young king in rhetoric, logic and astronomy while regulating the lectures and disciplines of medieval universities.

Aldiborontiphoscophornio—See BALLANTYNE, JOHN.

ALDRIDGE, IRA (1810?–1867)

Accounts of the early life of Ira Aldridge, the great black Shakespearean tragedian, vary, but it is doubtful that he ever was a slave in his native Maryland. He was apparently the son of a freeman, and he may well have traveled to England as the manservant of actor Edmund Kean. In any event, we know that Aldridge studied acting and appeared as Othello at London's Covent Garden to enthusiastic audiences. He was hailed in both Europe and America as *The African Roscius,* after the Roman slave who became an actor in the first century B.C. and made both his master and himself extremely wealthy, eventually buying his freedom.

ALEICHEM, SHALOM (1859–1916)

Jewish short story writer and journalist Shalom Aleichem has been nicknamed *The Yiddish Mark Twain* for his poetic folk tales about Jewish life in late 19th century Russia. One of his stories was adopted for the stage musical and film *Fiddler on the Roof.*

ALEMBERT, JEAN LE ROND D' (1717?–1783)

Eighteenth century French philosopher and mathematician Jean le Rond d'Alembert edited the *French Encyclopedia* with Diderot and wrote its extended introduction, gaining the designation *The Father of French Philosophy*. He was also dubbed *The Mazarin of Letters* since his influence on the literature of his day was as profound as Cardinal Mazarin's had been on politics during the previous century.

ALEXANDER II OF RUSSIA (1818–1881)

Although hailed as *The Emancipator* for freeing the serfs, Czar Alexander II of Russia was not a popular ruler. His inadequate distribution of land left of peasants virtual serfs of the state as they struggled to reimburse the crown for excessive prices paid to aristocratic landowners. Several attempts were made on Alexander's life, and he was finally assassinated in 1881.

ALEXANDER III OF RUSSIA (1845–1894)

In his crown prince days Alexander III, czar of Russia, was nicknamed *The Young Steer*. He retained the appellation in later years, although *Young* was dropped from it.

Alexander of the North—See CHARLES XII OF SWEDEN.

Alexander the Coppersmith—See HAMILTON, ALEXANDER.

ALEXANDER THE GREAT (356–323 B.C.)

Alexander the Great, the *Conquerer of the World,* preferred or at least exploited the nickname *Madman of Macedonia,* which often caused foes to lay down their arms in fear.

ALFONSO I OF ARAGON AND NAVARRE (ALFONSO VII OF LEON AND CASTILE) (?–1157)

Alfonso I of Aragon and Navarre, who later became Alfonso VII of Leon and Castile, was nicknamed *The Fighter* because he engaged in 29 battles to win and hold his thrones.

ALFONSO I OF ASTURIAS (693–757)

Alfonso I, king of Asturias, is apparently the first monarch to have been nicknamed *The Catholic*. He was particularly zealous in building and making endowments for great churches and monasteries.

ALFONSO V, KING OF NAPLES, ARAGON AND SICILY (1385–1458)

Alfonso V, king of Naples, Aragon and Sicily, was dubbed *The Magnanimous* because, after coming to the throne, he destroyed a list of names of nobles who had been hostile to him. This generous act gained him an important measure of support.

Alfonso the Good: ALFONSO IX OF CASTILE (1155–1214)

King Alfonso IX of Castile, the first monarch in Europe to institute severe laws against prostitution, won for his efforts the sobriquet *Alfonso the Good.* White slavers were banished from the country, and landlords renting rooms to prostitutes were fined and their houses confiscated by the crown, moreover, brothel keepers had to free all prostitutes, most of whom were little more than slaves, and find them husbands within a short period of time or be beheaded.

Alfonso the Wise: KING ALFONSO OF CASTILE AND LEON (1221–1284)

Alfonso X, ruler of the Spanish kingdoms of Castile and Leon, made his court a center of learning and a melting pot of Eastern and Western cultures. He was to become known as *Alfonso el sabio* or *Alfonso the Wise,* for such works as the *Siete Partidas,* a compilation of Roman and canon law, and the Alfonsine Tables in astronomy. His last years were spent fighting a civil war against elements determined to stamp out all non-Christian influences. When he died in 1284, only Seville was still loyal to him. Chroniclers of the era belittled him as a "wise" king who "studied the heavens and watched the stars, while losing the earth and his kingdom."

ALGER, HORATIO, JR. (1834–1899)

Horatio Alger, Jr., the American author of some 125 books which taught two generations of boys that success and riches could come to even the humblest newsboy through virtuous effort, was nicknamed *Holy Horatio* in his youth because of his unflinching religious manner. Ironically, although he preached the virtues of morality in achieving reward, Alger died penniless.

ALI, MUHAMMAD (1942–   )

Before the world's heavyweight boxing champion changed his name from Cassius Clay to Muhammad Ali, his "magnificient lip" won him the nicknames *Cassius the Brashest* and *Gaseous Cassius.* Despite his obvious bent toward showmanship, many boxing experts agree that he is *The Greatest,* his self-proclaimed sobriquet.

ALINSKY, SAUL D. (1909–1972)

American poverty fighter and social activist Saul D. Alinsky dedicated his life to counseling poor and powerless groups throughout the country in the use of picket lines, strikes, boycotts and sit-downs to pressure landlords, local political machines and the business establishment into meeting their demands. He dubbed himself *The Professional Radical.*

All Dwight—See MACDONALD, DWIGHT.

All Round About Cleveland—See CLEVELAND, BENJAMIN.

All-Around Wonder, The —See WILLIAMS, RICHARD PERRY.

ALLEN, ETHAN (1737–1789)

American Revolutionary War hero Ethan Allen led his Green Mountain Boys, considered to be among the best of the era's frontier fighting men, with such verve that he was called *The Robin Hood of the Forest*.

ALLEN, FRED (1894–1956)

American radio comedian Fred Allen was hailed as *The King of the Quick Quip* for his acerbic adlibs, but he was unable to achieve the same success on television. Although he enjoyed some renown as a TV quiz show participant, he stood as proof that a quick quip comic is only as fast as his writers.

ALLEN, JOHN—See Wickedest Man in New York, The.

ALLEN, JOHN M. (1846–1917)

A representative from Mississippi from 1885 to 1901, John M. Allen was affectionately known as *Private John*. He often declared he had been "the only private in the Confederate army," reflecting the humorous, widely held belief that everyone who served in the southern army had been an officer.

ALLEN, THOMAS (1743–1811)

During the American Revolution Rev. Thomas Allen gained the sobriquets *The Fighting Parson* and *The Fighting Parson of Bennington Fields* for leading a force of Massachusetts patriots in Vermont's Battle of Bennington.

ALLEN, WILLIAM "Fog Horn" (1806–1879)

A senator from Ohio from 1837 to 1849, William Allen was called *The Ohio Gong* because of his stentorian voice. He gained the sobriquet *Fog Horn* when he made himself heard at a Democratic rally even though his political opponents kept a steam whistle blowing nearby.

ALLEYN, SIMON (fl. mid-16th century)

Throughout the religious troubles of 16th century England, Simon Alleyn, the parish priest in Bray in Berkshire, never lost his head. Twice a Papist and twice a Protestant during the various reigns of Henry VIII, Edward VI, Bloody Mary and Elizabeth, he was celebrated in song as *Always Vicar of Bray*.

Almighty Mac—See MACARTHUR, DOUGLAS.

ALTERIE, LOUIS "Two Gun" (1892–1935)

A throwback to Wild West cowboys, *Two Gun Alterie* was one of Chicago's most colorful and deadly killers during the 1920s. A leading, though dim-witted, member of the Dion O'Banion gang, he strutted around with a gun on each hip and demonstrated his marksmanship by shooting out lights in saloons. He frequently challenged rival gangsters to shootouts in Chicago's downtown area at high noon. An exasperated Mayor William E. Dever once moaned, "Are we still abiding by the code of the Dark Ages?"

ALTGELD, JOHN "Pardon" (1847–1902)

John Altgeld, governor of Illinois, wrote the final chapter to the unsavory Haymarket Affair—the 1886 labor bombing in Chicago—when in 1893 he pardoned eight anarchists convicted of the crime. Five had died in the meantime, four on the gallows and one a prison-cell suicide. This act of courage prompted his enemies to label him John *Pardon* Altgeld and ruined his political career.

ALVES, CASTRO (1847–1871)

Brazilian romantic poet Castro Alves was an apostle of social justice who often recited his verses at political rallies, earning the nickname *The Poet of the Slaves*.

Always Ready—See RUBIROSA, PORFIRIO.

***Always Vicar of Bray, The*—See ALLEYN, SIMON.**

AMADEUS VIII, FIRST DUKE OF SAVOY (1383–1451)

Considered one of the most brilliant political thinkers of his day, Amadeus VIII, first duke of Savoy, was almost always consulted in negotiations among the powers of Europe. He gained the sobriquet *The Pacific* because he frequently offered ways to avert direct confrontations. At being the victim of an assassination attempt, Amadeus VIII relinquished the throne to his son Louis and retired to a more tranquil life on the shores of Lake Geneva at La Ripaille with some of his most trusted lords. His court there was considered a place of religious austerity, and he was called *The Hermit*

of La Ripaille. His estate was actually a seat of high living and luxury, however, so much so that "La chère de la Ripaille" entered the language as a synonym for delicious cuisine and elegance of all kinds.

AMBERG, LOUIS "Pretty" (1898–1935)

Famed in journalistic circles as the ugliest gangster in America, Louis Amberg was jokingly nicknamed *Pretty* by reporters. Damon Runyon immortalized him in his fiction and newspaper columns as the Brooklyn gangster who stuffed corpses into laundry bags and he revealed that when New York's playboy mayor, Jimmy Walker, first laid eyes on *Pretty* in a night club, he took a vow to stay off booze. Amberg himself often bragged that Ringling Brothers Circus once offered him a job as the missing link. He was the victim of an underworld assassination in 1935.

***Ambidextrous Chief Executive, The*—See GARFIELD, JAMES A.**

***Ambling Alp, The*—See CARNERA, PRIMO.**

AMBREE, MARY (c. 1584)

Mary Ambree, a heroine mentioned in many old ballads, was nicknamed *The English Joan of Arc* for taking part in the siege of Ghent in 1584 to avenge the death of her lover.

AMECHE, DON (1908–   )

Movie actor Don Ameche became so identified with his portrayal of Alexander Graham Bell in a film of the same title that he was humorously dubbed *The Inventor of the Telephone*. For years in children's lore it was one of the most popular adult nicknames of any American with the possible exception of Honest Abe and The Father of His Country.

American Bewick, The—See ANDERSON, ALEXANDER.

American Blackstone, The—See KENT, JAMES.

American Caesar, The—See GRANT, ULYSSES S.

American Carlyle, The—See EMERSON, RALPH WALDO.

American Devil, The—See MCDOUGAL, DAVID STOCKTON.

American Dreyfus, The—See BALLINGER, RICHARD ACHILLES.

American Eagle, The—See CLARK, MARK WAYNE.

American Fabius, The—See WASHINGTON, GEORGE.

American Gauguin, The—See LEETEG, EDGAR.

American Goldsmith, The—See IRVING, WASHINGTON.

American Hogarth, The—See SHAHN, BEN.

American Jack Sheppard, The: JACK MAHANEY (1844–?)

One of the most celebrated American criminals of the 19th century, Jack Mahaney was called *The American Jack Sheppard* because, like his British counterpart, he continually made daring escapes from prison. He twice escaped from Sing Sing, twice from New York City's Tombs Prison and several times from other eastern prisons. He also escaped from speeding trains, miraculously avoiding serious injury. A popular figure in the sensational press of the time, Mahaney, in keeping with his nickname, avoided capture to the end, and his ultimate fate is unknown.

American Kipling, The—See LONDON, JACK.

American Leonardo, The—See MORSE, SAMUEL F.B.

American Louis Philippe, The—See FILLMORE, MILLARD.

American Mouth of the Year—See MITCHELL, MARTHA.

American Pitt, The—See STEVENS, THADDEUS.

American Scott, The—See COOPER, JAMES FENIMORE.

American Socrates, The—See HOOK, SIDNEY.

American Wordsworth, The—See
BRYANT, WILLIAM CULLEN.

America's First Libber—See
ANTHONY, SUSAN B.

America's Greatest Showman—See
TODD, MIKE.

America's Homer—See **RICE,
GRANTLAND.**

America's Leading Juvenile Forever—
See **FAIRBANKS, DOUGLAS.**

America's One-Eyed Jewish Negro—
See **DAVIS, SAMMY, JR.**

America's One-Man Newspaper—See
WINCHELL, WALTER.

America's Self-Made Man—See
WALKER, MARY EDWARDS.

America's Sweetheart—See **OAKLEY,
ANNIE; PICKFORD, MARY.**

America's Tuning Fork—See
SEEGER, PETE.

AMIN DADA, IDI "Big Daddy"
(1924–   )

Probably the most prolific practitioner of political
mass murder in 20th century Africa, Idi Amin,
while president of Uganda, caused the deaths of an
estimated 90,000 Lango and Acholi tribesmen
from 1971 to 1974. Suspicious of everyone, he
accused Asians in Uganda of painting themselves
black with shoe polish, and he threatened severe
reprisals. Still, he liked to pose as a savior of his
people, and he gave himself the nickname of *Big
Daddy*. He was ousted from power and forced to
flee the country in 1979.

AMMONIUS (c. 175–242)

A former porter, the famed Alexandrian philosopher Ammonius was nicknamed *Saccus,* or *Sack-
bearer.*

Amorous, The—See **PHILLIPE THE
AMOROUS.**

Amorous Amazon, The—See
SAMPSON, DEBORAH.

Anacreon Moore—See **MOORE,
THOMAS.**

Anacreon of Germany, The—See
FLEMING, PAUL.

Anacreon of Painters, The—See
ALBANI, FRANCESCO.

Anacreon of Painting, The—See
BOUCHER, FRANCOIS.

Anacreon of the Guillotine, The:
BERTRAND BARERE DE VIEUZAC
(1753–1841)

Bertrand Barere de Vieuzac, a member of the
Committee of Public Safety during the Reign of
Terror in France, was called *The Anacreon of the
Guillotine*. Some saw in his flowery language and
conviviality with hapless victims a sensuousness
associated with the verses of the Greek lyric poet
Anacreon.

*Anacreon of the Twelfth Century,
The*— See MAPES, WALTER.

ANASTASIA, ALBERT (1903–1957)

Dubbed by the press and law enforcement officials *The Lord High Executioner of Murder Inc.*, Albert Anastasia established leadership of that underworld organization in the 1930s with Louis ''Lepke'' Buchalter. Anastasia was murdered in a New York barbershop in 1957 in a rub-out as efficient as any he planned or carried out.

Anatomist of Humanity, The—See **MOLIERE.**

Ancient Mariner, The—See **PERRY, GAYLORD.**

ANDERSEN, HANS CHRISTIAN (1805–1875)

''The Ugly Duckling,'' one of Hans Christian Andersen's most popular fairy tales, might have served as the author's autobiography, if not for its happy ending. Described as having a sharp nose, extremely small eyes, legs disproportionately long for his body and very large feet, Andersen was cruelly called *The Stork,* often by passing strangers unaware of who he was.

ANDERSON, ALEXANDER (1775–1870)

America's first wood engraver, Alexander Anderson was nicknamed *The American Bewick,* after Thomas Bewick, his more famous English predecessor. Anderson illustrated a large number of books and was still practicing his craft when he died at the age of 95.

ANDERSON, CHARLIE (fl. c. 1896–1900)

One of the most successful prospectors of the Klondike gold rush, Charlie Anderson was known as *The Lucky Swede*. While drunk he bought a claim for $800, which he tried to sell later when desperate for cash. Finding no takers and forced to work the mine, Anderson struck ore and in four years took out $1.2 million worth of gold. His lucky strike lured thousands of fortune hunters to Alaska.

ANDERSON, DOROTHY MAE STEVENS—See Deep Freeze Woman, The.

ANDERSON, JOSEPH REID (1813–1892)

The director of the famed Tredegar Iron Works of Richmond, Va., during the Civil War, Joseph R. Anderson, a West Point graduate, served briefly as a brigadier general in the Confederate Army before being returned to his factory by the war department. During the war he was dubbed *The Krupp of the Confederacy*, after the German family of armament makers, for playing a key role in keeping the rebel army supplied with ordnance.

ANDERSON, MARIAN (1902–   )

The first black artist to sing a major role at New York's Metropolitan Opera, Marian Anderson was nicknamed *The Philadelphia Lady* after the Daughters of the American Revolution in 1939 denied her permission to sing in that city's Constitution Hall because of her race. As an unofficial apology, first lady Eleanor Roosevelt welcomed her to the Lincoln Memorial in Washington, D.C., where the contralto sang to an integrated audience of 75,000.

ANDERSON, ROBERT (1805–1871)

The commander of the Union garrison at Fort Sumter, S.C. at the outbreak of the Civil War, Robert Anderson was dubbed *The Hero of Fort Sumter* upon his evacuation to New York. It was a strange title for a pro-slavery Kentuckian. At the end of the war he returned to the scene of his fame to re-raise the U.S. flag.

ANDERSON, WILLIAM—See Bloody Bill Anderson.

ANDREW, PRINCE OF ENGLAND (1960–   )

The more outspoken elements of the British press have in recent years dubbed Prince Andrew of England *Randy Andy* because of his amorous liaisons. Some say that such behavior has almost become a matter of tradition among the princes of the royal house.

Angel of Death, The—See MENGELE, JOSEF.

Angel of Mercy of Prison Reform—See DIX, DOROTHEA LYNDE.

Angel of Sing Sing, The—See LAWES, KATHRYN.

Angel of the Assassination, The—See CORDAY, CHARLOTTE.

Angel of the Battlefields, The—See BARTON, CLARA.

Angel of the Death Cells, The—See SCOFFEL, KATHERINE.

Angel of the Prisons, The—See TUTWILER, JULIA STRUDWICK.

Angelic Doctor, The—See THOMAS AQUINAS.

ANGENSOLA, BARTOLOMEO LEONARDO DE (1562–1631) and LUPERCIO LEONARDO DE (1559–1613)

Brothers, the Spanish poets Lupercio and Bartolomeo Leonardo de Angensola shared the same sobriquet, *The Spanish Horace,* applied to them individually by various critics.

ANGHIERA, PIETRO MARTIRE (1457–1526)

Italian historian and royal chronicler Pietro Martire Anghiera, the diplomatic representative of the court of Ferdinand and Isabella of Spain and later dean of the Cathedral of Granada, wrote the initial account of the discovery of America, for which he was designated *The First Historian of America.* Remarkably, the work did not appear until 1516.

ANGILBERT (?–814)

Charlemagne dubbed the French writer Angilbert *The Homer of the Franks.*

Angry Man of the Press, The—See PEGLER, WESTBROOK.

Angry Young Man, The—See OSBORNE, JOHN.

Animal Lover, The—See RIPON, MARQUESS OF.

Animated Adenoid, An—See FORD, FORD MADOX.

Ann the Word—See LEE, ANN.

ANNE, DUCHESSE DE MONTPENSIER—See Mademoiselle, La Grande.

ANNE, PRINCESS OF ENGLAND (1950–)

Because she was the only female competitor at the 1976 Olympics not required to submit to a sex test, Princess Anne of England was dubbed by the press *The Perfect Female.*

ANNE, QUEEN OF ENGLAND (1665–1714)

Queen Anne of England was called, behind her back, as *Brandy Nan* because of her renown as a tippler. A graffiti verse that first appeared on her statue in St. Paul's churchyard goes:

Brandy Nan, Brandy Nan, left in the
   lurch,
Her face to the gin-shop, her back to the
   church.

ANNE OF CLEVES (1515–1557)

England's King Henry VIII labeled Anne of Cleves, his fourth wife, *The Mare of Flanders* upon seeing her for the first time. "I like her not," he said. Unable to consummate the politically arranged union, he bought her off and had the marriage annulled and his minister Thomas Cromwell executed for advising the match.

Anne of the Thousand Days—See BOLEYN, ANNE.

Another Machiavel—See BRUTE, LORD.

ANSELMI AND SCALISE: ALBERT ANSELMI (?–1929) and JOHN SCALISE (?–1929)

Having grown up together as children in Sicily, American gangsters Albert Anselmi and John Scalise were inseparable in the 1920s during Chicago's Capone era. Called simply Anselmi and Scalise and nicknamed *The Mutt and Jeff of Murder,* they always worked together and specialized in the "handshake kill." While one shook hands with the hapless victim, holding his gun hand, the other stepped up and shot him in the head. Fittingly, the inseparable pair died together, their heads bashed in by Al Capone with an Indian club at a party given in their "honor."

ANSGAR OF DENMARK (801–864)

Ansgar of Denmark is remembered as *The Apostle of the North* for having brought Christianity to Scandinavia in the 9th century.

ANTHEIL, GEORGE (1900–1959)

An avant garde American composer of ballets and film scores, George Antheil was hailed by fans as *The Exponent of Futurism* and derided by those who could not abide his work as *The Bad Boy of Music.*

ANTHONY, JOHN J. (1898–1970)

John J. Anthony, whose radio counseling show "The Goodwill Hour" was must listening for millions of Americans for more than 20 years, was plain Mr. Anthony to his fans and *Mr. Agony* to his detractors.

ANTHONY (or ANTONY), ST. (251–356)

An Egyptian Christian who gave away his considerable possessions at age 20 to become a hermit, St. Anthony later formed colonies of hermits that came to be called monasteries—the first religious communities. He is known as *The Father of Monachism* and *The Father of Monks*.

ANTHONY, SUSAN B. (1820–1906)

The leader of the woman-suffrage movement, Susan B. Anthony has been called *The Champion of Women's Rights* and, in contemporary times, *America's First Libber*.

Anti-Chain-Store Patman—See PATMAN, WRIGHT.

Antichrist of Wit, The—See QUERNO, CAMILLO.

Anti-McFarlane—See MCFARLANE, WILLIAM D.

Anti-Machiavel—See BENTHAM, JEREMY.

Anti-Scot—See RITSON, JOSEPH.

Anti-War Knutson—See KNUTSON, HAROLD.

ANTOINE DE BOURGOGNE (1421–1504)

The son of Philip the Good, Antoine de Bourgogne was celebrated for his bravery in combat as *Le Grande Batard,* or *The Great Bastard*.

ANTONINUS (86–161)

The Roman emperor Antoninus was nicknamed *The Pious* because he insisted that his predecessor and adoptive father, Hadrian, be classed as a god.

Ape Deeming—See DEEMING, FREDERICK BAILEY.

APELLES (c. 330 B.C.)

The ancient Greek painter Apelles has been called *The Greatest Painter of Antiquity* and *The Prince of Painters*. Some two generations earlier another Greek painter, Parrhasius, had bestowed the latter compliment upon himself to ensure his place in history. History has found the sobriquet more appropriate to Apelles. (See Parrhasius.)

Apollo of Portugal, The—See CAMOENS, LUIS.

APOLLONIUS OF ALEXANDRIA (?–240 B.C.)

Apollonius of Alexandria was dubbed *Grammaticorum Princeps,* or *The Prince of Grammarians,* by the Romans because he was the first to organize Latin grammar into a system.

Apollo's Messenger—See MESSINGER, PHILIP.

Apostate, The—See JULIAN (FLAVIUS CLAUDIUS JULIANUS); MACKINTOSH, JAMES.

Apostate Politician, The—See SWIFT, JONATHAN.

Apostle of Aestheticism, The—See
WILDE, OSCAR.

Apostle of Cold Water, The—See
GOUGH, JOHN BATHOLOMEW.

Apostle of Communist Causes—See
CARLSON, EVANS F.

Apostle of Culture, The—See
ARNOLD, MATTHEW.

Apostle of Disunion, The—See
JULIAN, GEORGE WASHINGTON.

Apostle of Free Trade, The—See
BRIGHT JOHN; COBDEN,
RICHARD.

Apostle of Gaul, The—See MARTIN,
ST., BISHOP OF TOURS.

Apostle of Infidelity, The—See
VOLTAIRE.

Apostle of Liberty, The—See
JEFFERSON, THOMAS.

Apostle of Peace, The—See LADD,
WILLIAM.

Apostle of Temperance—See
MURPHY, FRANCIS.

Apostle of the Alps—See BERNARD
OF MENTHON, ST.

Apostle of the North, The—See
ANSGAR OF DENMARK; GILPIN,
BERNARD.

*Apostle of the Scottish Reformation,
The*—See KNOX, JOHN.

Apostle of the Sword, The— See
MOHAMMED.

Apostle of Unitarianism, The—See
CHANNING, WILLIAM ELLERY.

Apostle to the Indians, The—See
ELIOT, JOHN.

*Apostle to the Sioux Indians,
The*—See HARE, WILLIAM
HOBART.

APPIANI, ANDREA (1754–1817)

Andrea Appiani, an Italian fresco artist, was dubbed *The Painter of the Graces* while court painter to Napoleon Bonaparte. Francois Boucher, the favorite of Louis XV in the previous century, had been so nicknamed, and Napoleon felt his artist was entitled to the same honor. Experts tend to agree that Appiani was more deserving of the nickname then Boucher.

*ARBUCKLE, ROSCOE "Fatty"
(1887–1933)*

Ill-fated movie comic great *Fatty* Arbuckle saw his career end in a national scandal after the death of starlet Virginia Rappe in his San Francisco hotel suite during a wild party in 1921. After three sensational trials, the actor was acquitted of killing the young women while raping her, but his movie contracts were dropped and several of his completed films were scrapped. The 300-pound Arbuckle had been known humorously to the public as the *Prince of Whales,* a sobriquet thereafter used with derogatory intent.

ARCARO, EDDIE *(1916–)*

Considered by many turf experts the greatest jockey of all time, Eddie Arcaro was called *The King of the Stakes Riders* because his percentage of winners in high-purse events was much higher than in average races. Racing fans affectionately (or perhaps otherwise if they lost a bet) dubbed him *Banana Nose* because of his large nose. According to a track joke, this was how Arcaro won so many photo finishes ''by a nose.''

Arch Appeaser, The—See CHAMBERLAIN, NEVILLE.

Arch Priest of Anti-Masonry, The—See STEVENS, THADDEUS.

Arch-Bugger of Bloomsbury, The—See STRACHEY, LYTTON.

ARCHIBALD, MARQUIS OF ARGYLE *(1598–1661)*

Archibald, Marquis of Argyle, was nicknamed *The Presbyterian Ulysses* by Scottish compatriots. Although full of cunning and constantly plotting to aid Charles II of England, he was said to be motivated always by what was good for his native Scotland.

Architect of Nature, An—See BURBANK, LUTHER.

Architect of the Welfare State, The—See NASH, WALTER.

ARETINO, PIETRO *(1492–1556)*

Pietro Aretino, an Italian writer of comedies and barbed sonnets, was dubbed *The Scourge of Princes* for his satirical poems directed against leading personalities of the day. Actually, these were often scurrilous attacks for the purpose of blackmail, a safe enough vocation for Aretino, who always operated with royal or papal protection.

ARIOSTO, LUDOVICO *(1474–1533)*

The noted Italian Renaissance poet Ludovico Ariosto, author of the epic poem, *Orlando Furioso,* was called *The Homer of Ferrara.* Three centuries later Lord Byron dubbed him *The Southern Scott,* after Sir Walter Scott.

ARISTIDES *(530?–468? B.C.)*

The Athenian statesman and general Aristides was nicknamed *The Just,* notably for organizing a system of equitable assessments in financing the Delian League, a defensive alliance of Greek states.

Aristocrat of the Bank Robbers, The— See SHINBURN, MARK.

ARISTOPHANES *(c. 448–385 B.C.)*

Although only 11 of his plays survive, the Greek poet Aristophanes is known as *The Father of Comedy* and *The Creator of the New Comedy,* the latter for developing a new style of comedy dealing with vices instead of personalities. Aristophanes' works exhibit a lustiness of humor, much of which is played down in modern versions, as in his antiwar comedy *Lysistrata.*

ARISTOTLE *(384–322 B.C.)*

Dubbed by Plato *The Talent of the Academy,* the Greek philosopher Aristotle is more commonly known as *The Pope of Philosophy.* That identification is used both by his admirers, who hold him in unbridled reverence, and by his detractors, who insist he exercised for centuries an almost despotic influence on Western thought.

ARLINGTON, JOSIE *(1864–1914)*

New Orleans' most famous brothel keeper, Josie Arlington was designated *The Snootiest Madam in America.* Putting on airs in her lavish *Chateau Lobran D'Arlington,* a name she legally adopted, Josie attempted to pass herself off as an aristocrat, as in this account carried in the gutter press of the day: "Society is graced by the presence of a bona-fide baroness, direct from the Court of St. Petersburgh. The baroness is at present residing incog. at the Chateau d'Arlington, and is known as La Belle Stewart." The baroness was soon exposed by the knowledgeable sporting crowd as a former hoochy-koochy dancer at the Chicago World's Fair. Many of Josie's other imports proved to be impostors as well, but her establishment and its successor, The Arlington, continued to be accepted as the most discriminating of its kind in the city.

Arm & Hammer—See HAMMER, ARMAND.

Armorer of Gangland, The—See FRANTIZIUS, PETER VON.

ARMOUR, PHILIP D. *(1832–1901)*

Philip D. Armour, the American meat-packing executive, was nicknamed *The Pork Baron* because of his many innovations in the field, including on-premise slaughtering and the utilization of waste parts, or, as he put it, "all the pig but the squeal."

ARMSTRONG, GERALD RALPH *(1942–   )*

Jerry Armstrong, a professional shareholder and stockholder rights advocate, is the bane of American corporation executives. Journalists have labeled him *The Corporate Gadfly.*

ARMSTRONG, HENRY *(1912–   )*

Henry Armstrong, dubbed by sports writers *Homicide Hank,* was the only boxer to hold three world's titles—featherweight, lightweight and welterweight—simultaneously. He was also described as *The Human Buzzsaw* because of his style of constantly boring in on an opponent until he simply overwhelmed him.

ARMSTRONG, LOUIS *(1900–1971)*

The great jazz trumpeter and entertainer Louis Armstrong, who helped moved the black folk music of New Orleans into the mainstream of American music, was called *Satchmo,* a contraction of satchelmouth. An interviewer once asked Armstrong if he felt hurt by the name. His answer was a widemouthed grin.

ARMSTRONG, LUCILLE *(191?–   )*

Lucille Armstrong, wife of the late jazz great Louis Armstrong, was dubbed by her husband *Brown Sugar,* which has now entered the American language as a variation on the "black is beautiful" theme.

Army's One-Man Hit Parade, The— See LOESSER, FRANK.

Army's Topmost Sarge, The—See
WOOLDRIDGE, WILLIAM O.

ARNOLD, BENEDICT (1741–1801)

Having previously been a hero in the Revolution, Benedict Arnold was called *The Traitorous Hero* when he switched sides and joined the British. Thereafter he was referred to simply as *The Traitor*. In time the nickname was dropped, and Benedict Arnold became an American synonym for traitor.

ARNOLD, MATTHEW (1822–1888)

The English poet, essayist and critic Matthew Arnold was known as *The Apostle of Culture* and *The Sainte-Beuve of English Criticism,* after the distinguished French critic. Arnold's main thesis was that the middle class had to give up its "Philistine," money-grubbing contempt for intellectuality and instead embrace the clarity of Hellenism and the moral seriousness of the Hebrews. Critics of Arnold found his pessimism rather trying and often referred to him as *Poor Matt.* As Robert Louis Stevenson said after his death: "Poor Matt. He's gone to heaven, no doubt—but he won't like God."

Aroostook Potato, The—See
BREWSTER, RALPH OWEN.

Arsonist, The—See **CAESAR, JULIUS.**

ARTHGAL, EARL OF WARWICK (c. 4th century)

Arthgal, the first earl of Warwick, said to have lived around the time of King Arthur, was called *The Bear* for once having strangled such a beast with his arms. The Warwick crest carries the emblem of a bear.

ARTHUR, CHESTER A. (1830–1886)

Chester A. Arthur, the 21st president of the United States, was one of several called *His Accidency,* for having succeeded to the office on the assassination of President Garfield. Possessed of considerable grace and polish, he garnered such sobriquets as *First Gentleman of the Land, Prince Arthur,* and *The Dude President.* As for his political abilities, he was called *A Nonentity with Side Whiskers.* After completing his partial term, Arthur sought the Republican nomination and a full term but gained neither.

Artichoke King, The—See
TERRANOVA, CIRO.

Artist of Damnation, The—See
EDWARDS, JONATHAN.

Artist of the Poor, The—See **DE SICA, VITTORIO.**

Artist of the Revolution, The—See
DAVID, JACQUES LOUIS.

Artist with Brush and Lute, The—See
GIORGIONE DA CASTELFRANCO.

ASCH, SHOLEM (1880–1957)

Among the accolades given author Sholem Asch was the sobriquet *The Jewish Dickens.*

ASHLEY, CHESTER (1790–1848)

In the 1840s Arkansas politician Chester Ashley refused to accept the pronunciation of his state's name as "Ark-en-saw" and insisted that its proper pronunciation was "Ar-Kansas." Elected to the

U.S. Senate in 1844, he obstinately refused to answer roll calls unless addressed as *The Senator from Ar-Kansas*, which became his official nickname. Long after Ashley had left the scene, the state officially adopted the pronunciation "Ark-en-saw."

ASHTON, RALPH *(c. late 15th century)*

English landowner Sir Ralph Ashton (or Assheton) was disparagingly referred to by his tenants as *The Black Knight of Ashton*, an allusion to the huge levies he placed on them. After he was killed, the borough of Ashton-under-Lyne held an annual celebration called the "Riding of the Black Lad."

ASIMOV, ISAAC *(1920–   )*

Isaac Asimov, one of the most highly regarded science and science fiction writers in the United States, has been described as *The Writer of the Universe*, an allusion both to his subject matter and awesome output. In 1979 he published his 201st book and is still going strong.

Aspasia of Lyons—See LABE, LOUISA.

Assassination Witness, The—See LINCOLN, ROBERT TODD.

Assassin's Assassin, The—See RUBY, JACK.

Assistant President, The—See ROOSEVELT, ELEANOR.

ASTOR, MARY *(1906–   )*

Many Hollywood directors considered Mary Astor the consummate movie actress because of her ability to get a scene right the first time, dubbing her *One-Take Astor*.

ATATURK, MUSTAPHA KEMAL *(1881–1938)*

The Father of the Turks, Mustapha Kemal Ataturk took his country into the modern world by abolishing the caliphate, closing religious courts and schools and instituting a modern legal system. Historians weigh his courage, honesty and patriotism against his intellectual narrowness, brutality and taste for debauchery. Yet Ataturk was indeed *The Schoolmaster of Turkey*, teaching his people a new script in Latin letters to replace the Arabic, educating, emancipating and enfranchising women, and reforming the nation's banking and farming systems.

ATHANASIUS *(c. 297–373)*

One of the four great Greek Doctors of the Church and bishop of Alexandria for 40 years, Athanasius was known as *The Father of Orthodoxy* for his persistent struggle against various heresies, especially that of the Adrians. He was unswerving in this task even though he was exiled five times from his see as a result.

Atheist, The—See HOBBES, THOMAS.

ATHERTON, CHARLES GORDON "Gag" *(1804–1853)*

An antebellum Democratic representative from New Hampshire, Charles Gordon Atherton was known as *Gag Atherton* for attempting to solve the problem of slavery by containing it with the Gag Resolution, which required that any bill concerning slavery in either house of Congress be tabled. The resolution was adopted in 1838 and lasted for six years before being repealed.

Atlas of America, The—See
WASHINGTON, GEORGE.

Atomic Traitors, The—See
**ROSENBERG, JULIUS AND
ETHEL.**

ATTENDOLO, MUZIO (1369–1424)

Famed for his military prowess, Italian soldier of fortune Muzio Attendolo was called *Sforza* or *Stormer of Cities*. He founded the house of Sforza.

Attila of Authors, The—See
SCIOPPIUS, GASPAR.

Attila the Nun: PFEIFFER, JANE CAHILL (1932–   )

A former executive of IBM who in 1978 rose to be the $225,000-a-year chairman of NBC, Jane Cahill Pfeiffer has been called *Attila the Nun* because she spent six months in a convent in her youth and because of her skills as a corporate infighter. Before she was deposed after a two-year reign, she was known to have brought a strong sense of morality to the NBC post, some saying it was more of the ''avenging angel'' quality.

ATTLEE, CLEMENT RICHARD (1883–1967)

The Labor prime minister of Great Britain during the closing months of World War II, Clement Attlee was often savaged by the Tories as *The Modest Little Man*. After a short pause the phrase ''with much to be modest about'' was added. Not surprisingly, the sobriquet was the work of his predecessor Winston Churchill.

Attorney General for Runaway Slaves, The—See **CHASE, SALMON P.**

Attorney-General of the Lantern, The—See **DESMOULINS, CAMILLE.**

ATTUCKS, CRISPUS (1723?–1770)

Crispus Attucks, killed by the British in the Boston Massacre, has been dubbed *The First American Negro Martyr*.

AUBREY, JAMES T., JR. (1918–   )

Movie executive James T. Aubrey obtained his nickname *The Smiling Cobra* in the rough-and-tumble world of network television when he was the programming chief of CBS during the 1960s.

Auction Block—See **BLOCK, JOHN R.**

AUGUSTINE, ST. (354–430)

Known as one of the greatest defenders of the Christian faith, St. Augustine of Hippo was so brilliant in his written refutations of heresies and opposition to schisms that he was accorded the sobriquet *The Hammer of the Heretics*.

Augustus of Arabic Literature, The—
See **MAMOUN.**

AURELIAN (LUCIUS DOMITIUS AURELIANUS) (c. 212–275)

Installed as Roman emperor in 270, Aurelian forced the Goths back across the Danube, defeated Palmyra, reconquered Egypt and once again restored Roman rule to Gaul and Britain. For these accomplishments he was hailed as *The Restorer of the Roman Empire*.

Australia's Martin Luther King—See **PERKINS, CHARLES NELSON.**

Austrian Wench, The—See **MARIE ANTOINETTE.**

Autocrat of the Quacks, The—See **HEADLEY, JOEL TYLER.**

Available Man, The—See **GARFIELD, JAMES A.**

AVERILL, JAMES (?–1889)

An example of the big lie as a nickname is Jim Averill's *The King of the Cattle Thieves*. A small Wyoming rancher, he and Cattle Kate (Ella Watson) were lynched in 1889 by henchmen of the great cattle barons after they were accused, almost certainly falsely, of being major cattle thieves. The lynchings were but the opening move in the notorious Johnson County War to destroy homesteaders.

AVILA, JOHN B. (1865–1937)

Coming to California from the Portuguese Azores, John B. Avila planted the first sweet potato fields there in 1888 and turned the vegetable into a major commercial crop. He is known as *The Father of the Sweet Potato Industry*.

Avonian Willy—See **SHAKESPEARE, WILLIAM.**

AVORY, HORACE EDMUND (1851–1935)

A celebrated English judge noted for his cold manner but incisive interpretations of the law, Mr. Justice Avory was nicknamed by lawyers *Acid Drop* because of his caustic wit when setting aside their contentions.

Awful Gardner—See **GARDNER, ORVILLE.**

Awfully Weirdly—See **BEARDSLEY, AUBREY.**

Axis Sally: MILDRED ELIZABETH SISK (1900–   ) and RITA LOUISE ZUCCA (1912–   )

More than one female radio propagandist for the Nazis during World War II was known to GIs as *Axis Sally*. The two most infamous Americans were Mildred Elizabeth Sisk and Rita Louise Zucca.

AYESHA (c. 611–c. 678)

The favorite wife of Mohammed was accorded the sobriquet *Um-mu-l-Mu' minim*, or *The Mother of Believers*.

B

Babe Ruth of Hockey, The—See **MORENZ, HOWARD WILLIAM "Howie"; RICHARD, MAURICE.**

Babe Ruth of Japan, The—See **OH, SADAHARU.**

Babe Ruth of Polo, The—See **HITCHCOCK, THOMAS, JR.**

BABEUF, FRANCOIS NOEL (1764–1797)

Fanatical French revolutionist Francois Noel Babeuf proclaimed himself *The Tribune of the People* in a journal of the same name he launched in 1794. He fought the Directory in the most violent language, and was called *A Second Robespierre.* Convicted of conspiring to reestablish the Convention of 1793, Babeuf heaped scorn on his judges before going to the guillotine in 1797.

Baboon, The—See LINCOLN, ABRAHAM.

Baby—See HARLOW, JEAN.

Baby Doc—See DUVALIER, JEAN-CLAUDE.

Baby Elephant—See O'HARA, MAUREEN.

Baby Face Nelson—See NELSON, GEORGE "Baby Face."

Baby Flo: FLORA MAE KING JACKSON (1930–1965)

Flora Mae King Jackson, one of the great ladies of the American circus, tipped the scales at 840 pounds. She was known to her colleagues as *Baby Flo.*

Baby Murphy—See MURPHY, AUDIE.

Baby Savior, The—See STRAUS, NATHAN.

Baby Star—See WATERS, ETHEL.

Babykins—See HALL, REV. EDWARD WHEELER.

BACALL, LAUREN (1924–   )

In Lauren Bacall's pre-Hollywood modeling days in her native New York City, she was known as *The Windmill* because of her long arms and legs and swinging walk.

BACH, JOHANN CHRISTIAN (1735–1782)

Composer Johann Christian Bach, the 11th son of Johann Sebastian Bach, was much sought after by various localities, being hailed in Italy as *The Milan Bach* while serving as an organist in that city. When he was lured to England in 1759, he was proudly hailed there as *London Bach,* much to the distress of the Milanese. He lived in London for the last 23 years of his life, producing a number of operas and religious choral works.

BACH, JOHANN SEBASTIAN (1685–1750)

Until the time of his death, Johann Sebastian Bach was called *The Old Wig* by his contemporaries and even by his talented sons, who considered him merely the composer of "dead music." As a result many of his scores were lost, and it was not until a century after his death that the public slowly came to appreciate his works.

BACHARACH, BURT (1929–   )

U.S. composer and pianist Burt Bacharach was acknowledged by the press as being *The Music Man of the 1970s.*

Bachelor President, The—See BUCHANAN, JAMES.

Backbone—See CLEVELAND, GROVER.

Backstairs Intriguer, The—See HOPKINS, HARRY L.

BACON, FRANCIS (1561–1626)

Sir Francis Bacon, the English statesman, philosopher and essayist, rose to high positions of power under Elizabeth I and especially her successor, James I. Convicted of taking bribes and dismissed from his post as lord chancellor, he was nicknamed *The British Socrates* because, like the ancient Greek sage, he ended his life in official disfavor.

BACON, JOHN (?–1346)

John Bacon (or Bacho or Baconthrope), an English Carmelite monk and schoolman, was hailed in Rome as *The Resolute Doctor* because, according to Pansa, he had "furnished the Christian religion with armor against the Jews stronger than any of Vulcan's."

BACON, MARY (1949?–   )

A successful female jockey, Mary Bacon became known at racetracks as *The Bunny Jockey* after posing for a pictorial feature in *Playboy* magazine. One newspaper suggested she could always be bet on to "Show."

BACON, ROGER (c. 1214–1294)

English Franciscan philosopher and scientist Roger Bacon considered natural science a complement to faith, not a contradiction of it, and he fought to place sciences in the curriculum of medieval universities. His popularity with students and scientists led to such sobriquets as *The Father of Philosophy, The Admirable Doctor* and *Doctor Mirabilis,* or *Wonderful Doctor.*

Bad Boy of American Publishing, The—See STUART, LYLE.

Bad Boy of Music, The—See ANTHEIL, GEORGE.

Bad Boy of Opera, The—See CORELLI, FRANCO.

Bad Eartha, The—See KITT, EARTHA MAE.

Bad Henry—See AARON, HENRY LOUIS "Hank."

Bad News—See GALLOWAY, JAMES.

BADEN-POWELL, ROBERT STEPHENSON SMYTHE (1857–1941)

The founder of the Boy Scouts and the Girl Guides, Robert Stephenson Smythe Baden-Powell earned the nickname *The Butterfly Spy* while a British military intelligence officer during the Boer War. Often disguising himself as a butterfly enthusiast, he drew pictures of the insects, which contained detailed information about military forts and other data.

Badinguet—See NAPOLEON III.

BAER, MAX (1909–1959)

World heavyweight champion Max Baer was often called *Madcap Maxie* for his antics outside, and occasionally inside, the ring.

BAEZ, JOAN (1941–   )

Joan Baez is known as *The Non-Violent Singer* because of her commitment to numerous protest and peace movements.

BAGENAL, BEAUCHAMP (1741–1801)

Having taken part in more than 20 duels, Irish eccentric Beauchamp Bagenal won considerable fame in 18th century Ireland as *The Duellist*. Crippled from an accident, he preferred to duel in the churchyard of Killinane, County Carlow, where he faced his adversary's fire propped upright against a tombstone.

BAILEY, ANNE HENNIS TROTTER— See Mad Anne.

BAILEY, F. LEE (1933–   )

Celebrated defense lawyer Francis Lee Bailey is a confident, compelling, and flamboyant courtroom figure who has successfully defended such clients as Dr. Sam Sheppard and Captain Ernest L. Medina, accused of killing civilians at Vietnam's My Lai. Bailey also convinced the state of Massachusetts to go for less than a capital case against the Boston Strangler. Bailey's track record and his habit of flying a private jet to various trials around the country has caused courtroom rivals and more staid members of the bar to call him *The Flying Mouth*.

BAILEY, NATHAN (?–1742)

The compiler of the most complete English dictionary of his day, Nathan Bailey was called *Philologos*, meaning "a lover of words." Johnson relied on the work to a considerable extent for his famous dictionary.

BAILLIE, JOANNA (1762–1851)

Scottish dramatist and poet Joanna Baillie gained such accolades as *Shakespeare in Petticoats* and *The Sister of Shakespeare*.

BAILLIE, ROBERT (?–1684)

Scottish republican patriot Robert Baillie was styled *The Scottish Sidney* after Englishman Algernon Sidney. Baillie was executed in 1684. John Milton derisively dubbed him *Scotch What d'ye call*.

BAKER, ANDERSON YANCEY (1876–1930)

Although a multimillionaire, Anderson Yancey Baker insisted on serving as sheriff of Hidalgo County, Tex., from 1912 to 1930. He was dubbed *The Millionaire Sheriff*.

BAKER, HOWARD, JR. (1925–   )

Republican Senator Howard Baker of Tennessee gained the nickname *Old Two-to-Ten* during his days as an attorney because of his talent for winning light sentences for convicted clients.

BAKER, JOHN "Home Run" (1886–1955)

Major league baseball slugger John Baker became *Home Run Baker* in 1911 when he led the league with nine home runs, and followed up with two home runs in the World Series. If those statistics seem less than impressive compared with present day records, it must be remembered that Baker competed in the "dead ball" era. It can only be speculated how well he might have hit with today's lively ball.

Baker, The—See LOUIS XVI.

Baker's Wife, The—See MARIE ANTOINETTE.

BALL, JOE (1892–1938)

Joe Ball, described as Texas' most ghoulish murderer, was known as *The Gator Lover* even before his homicidal peculiarities were exposed. This was because in the 1930s Ball ran a tavern in Elmendorf, Tex., called the Sociable Inn, where he kept alligators in a pond out back. Crowds were always on hand at mealtime to see him feed live stray dogs and cats to the awesome reptiles. Ball's place was also famed for its beautiful waitresses, who never seemed to remain on the job for long. It turned out that the tavern owner had become the lover of many of the women, and had murdered them when they became pregnant or otherwise troublesome. To the everlasting delight of the nation's sensational crime publications, it was disclosed that *The Gator Lover* had fed more than dogs and cats to his "pets." Ball shot himself to death when authorities closed in on him.

BALL, JOHN (?–1381)

A leader of England's Wat Tyler peasant revolt of 1381, clergyman John Ball was labeled by Richard II *The Mad Priest* for preaching the worth of common man. ("When Adam delved and Eve span, Who was then the gentleman?") The rebels marched toward London, burning prisons, destroying buildings and taking Canterbury on the way.

Richard II promised reforms but instead had some of the leaders murdered and imprisoned others. With the king in attendance, *The Mad Priest* was hanged, drawn and quartered.

BALLANTYNE, JOHN (1776–1821)

Exercising a writer's prerogative, Sir Walter Scott gave John Ballantyne, his Scottish publisher, a number of nicknames. Because Ballantyne had a dignified, almost pompous, air, Scott called him *Aldiborontiphoscophornio.* Grateful to the publisher for the unceasing corrections and revisions of his manuscripts, Scott also referred to him as *Fidus Achates,* harkening back to the mythological Achates, the friend of Aeneas. When Ballantyne wanted Scott to reveal his authorship of *Waverly,* Soctt playfully dubbed him *Picaroon,* or rogue.

BALLINGER, RICHARD ACHILLES (1858–1922)

Secretary of the interior under President William Howard Taft, Richard A. Ballinger was accused of favoritism in the allotment of coal-land claims in Alaska. Taft exonerated Ballinger, who nevertheless resigned from office, being labeled by supporters *The American Dreyfus.* Long after Ballinger's death in 1922, Harold Ickes, secretary of the interior under Franklin D. Roosevelt, ordered an official investigation into the case, and, as a result, Ballinger's name was cleared.

Balloon Buster, The—See LUKE, FRANK, JR.

Balloon Tytler—See TYTLER, JAMES.

BALOGH, HARRY (1891–1961)

Boxing announcer Harry Balogh, whose flowery introductions of fighters for many years at New

York's Madison Square Garden set the pattern for the technique, was labeled by the press *The Czar of Circumlocution*.

Banana Nose—See ARCARO, EDDIE.

Bananas, Joe: JOSEPH BONANNO (1905–   )

Top mafioso Joseph Bonanno has never shown the aversion to his nickname exhibited by other criminals to theirs. He accepts the press-endowed *Joe Bananas* as, if nothing else, a useful Americanization of his name, in contrast to the old "dons," who sought to maintain Sicilian traditions.

BANDARRA, GONALO ANNES (c. 1505–1556)

An obscure Portuguese cobbler, Gonalo Annes Bandarra was called *The Portuguese Nostradamus*, after the French-Jewish astrologer who was his contemporary. Bandarra was condemned by the Inquisition in 1541, but he managed to escape capture.

Bandit Queen, The—See STARR, BELLE.

Bandit Queen of India, The—See DEVI, PHOOLAN.

BANIER, JOHAN (1595–1641)

Put in charge of the Swedish army after the death of King Gustavus Adolphus, Gen. Johan Banier overran virtually all of Germany with such harshness that he was feared as *The Lion of Sweden*. It was said that he exhibited the same fierce behav-

ior when he took a princess of Baden as a wife. It has never been established whether Banier died of poisoning in 1641 or from the intemperance and indulgences of his lifestyle.

Banjo Eyes—See CANTOR, EDDIE.

BANKHEAD, TALLULAH (1903–1968)

The distinguished U.S. stage and screen actress Tallulah Bankhead, called *Tallu* by her friends, was accorded the tribute *The Darling of the Gods*.

BANKHEAD, WILLIAM B. (1874–1940)

One of a long line of Alabama Democratic statesmen, William B. Bankhead was the speaker of the House of Representatives from 1917 until his death in 1940. Although he had a distinguished political career, he was most appreciative of being called *Tallulah's Papa*, after his famous actress daughter, Tallulah Bankhead.

Bankrupt, The—See EDWARD III, KING OF ENGLAND.

BANKS, NATHANIEL PRENTISS (1816–1894)

Capitalizing on his working class background, Nathaniel Prentiss Banks made political hay out of the sobriquet *Bobbin Boy*, earned for working as a child in a Massachusetts cotton mill. He won several high offices, including the governorship of Massachusetts. Although he had no military experience, he became one of the Civil War's many "political generals," a career that proved to be a dismal failure. Routed twice by Stonewall Jackson in 1862, he was forced to flee the field, leaving behind vast quantities of supplies. Jackson's ill-provisioned men were duly grateful for the windfall and dubbed their hapless benefactor *Old Jack's Commissary General* or more simply *Commissary Banks.*

BANNEKER, BENJAMIN (1731–1806)

Self-taught black scientist Benjamin Banneker, one of the foremost U.S. astronomers of his day, for several years published an almanac and astronomical ephemeris for the mid-Atlantic states. Dubbed *The African Astronomer,* he assisted in the 1789 survey of the District of Columbia, and was an early black pamphleteer against slavery.

BARBARA, JOSEPH, SR. (1905–1959)

Infamous for the underworld conference held at his Apalachin, N.Y., mansion in 1957, Joseph Barbara, Sr., gained the unwanted sobriquet *The Underworld's Host.* After his cover identity was destroyed with the arrest of some 60 Mafia figures in a police raid on the conference, Barbara moved elsewhere. He died two years later, and the 58-acre estate was later sold for use as a tourist attraction.

Barbara Wa-wa—See WALTERS, BARBARA.

Barbed Tongue, The—See LONGWORTH, ALICE LEE ROOSEVELT.

Barber, The—See COMO, PERRY; MAGLIE, SAL.

BARBERI, MARIA—See Tombs Angel, The.

BARBIE, KLAUS (1913–   )

The Gestapo chief of Lyons, France, during World War II, Klaus Barbie gained the awesome sobriquet *The Hangman of Lyons* for his torture of prisoners and deportation of Jews to concentration camps. The war criminal successfully hid out in South America for decades, but finally was extradited to France for trial in 1983.

Bard of Arthurian Romance, The—See TENNYSON, ALFRED LORD.

Bard of Avon, The—See SHAKESPEARE, WILLIAM.

Bard of Erin, The—See MOORE, THOMAS.

Bard of Prose, The—See BOCCACCIO, GIOVANNI.

Bard of the British Navy, The—See DIBDIN, CHARLES.

Bard of Twickenham, The—See POPE, ALEXANDER.

BARDOT, BRIGITTE (1934–   )

French film actress Brigitte Bardot is known as *The Sex Kitten,* a sobriquet transferred to her private life because of her storied romantic liaisons. In an interview at the age of 40 she boasted she "must have a man every night," which sent the publicity makers to their calculators and, after arbitrarily subtracting 76 nights a year for various distractions, they determined that the formidable *Sex Kitten* had had 4,980 nights of sexual activity.

Barefoot Boy from Wall Street, The— See WILLKIE, WENDELL L.

Barker, Dock or Doc: ARTHUR BARKER (1898–1939)

Whether *Dock* or *Doc* was the nickname of Arthur Barker, one of the most brutal public enemies of the 1930s, has long been a matter of dispute among his biographers. Evidence supports *Dock,* which may have been later shortened by the press and public to *Doc,* but no satisfactory explanation of the origin of either has been forthcoming.

BARKLEY, ALBEN W. (1877–1956)

Alben W. Barkley got the nickname *Dear Alben* from a letter so addressed to him by President Franklin C. Roosevelt in 1937, asking to use his influence as a senator to pass a bill that would enable Roosevelt to "pack" the Supreme Court with justices sympathetic to his policies. When Barkley was elected vice president in 1948, the term *Veep* was popularized in affection for him, the first time it was used for a vice president.

BARKLEY, ELIZABETH JANE RUCKER HADLEY (1912–1964)

Elizabeth Jane Barkley married The Veep, Vice President Alben W. Barkley, while he was in office and by extension was nicknamed *The Veepess* by the press. She was not comfortable with the sobriquet and complained it sounded like the name of a snake.

BARNARD, JOHN (1685–1764)

Few English politicians enjoyed the popularity of John Barnard, a merchant, sheriff, alderman and the mayor of London. His universally applauded efforts to clean up 18th century London included clearing the city of vagrants and beggars and lowering the penalties on youthful offenders, a great many of whom he is credited with reforming. He also strove to ensure that no arrested person would spend a night behind bars without the accusation against him being heard first. Although he was devoted to the English countryside and had a suburban residence, he resolutely lived in London while in office to avoid being accused of fearing city life. Dubbed by citizens *The Father of London,* he was called *The Great Commoner* by William Pitt, whose own admirers later applied the nickname to Pitt himself.

BARNATO, BARNETT ISAACS "Barney" (1852–1897)

Noted Jewish speculator and capitalist Barnett Isaacs "Barney" Barnato made a fortune developing the Kimberly diamond mines, which were thought to have been exhausted. Because the mines were located in the Kaffir tribe country of South Africa, Barnato was known as *The Kaffir King.* He committed suicide by jumping into the sea.

BARNES, LEROY "Nicky" (1932 or 1933–   )

Harlem narcotics king Leroy "Nicky" Barnes was described by blacks and the press as *Mr. Untouchable* because he seemed to be immune to legal interference—until sentenced to life imprisonment in 1978.

BARNUM, PHINEAS T. (1810–1891)

The entrepreneur extraordinaire of entertainment, Phineas T. Barnum was called *The Prince of Showmen* and, perhaps more accurately, *The Prince of Humbugs,* the latter because he used so many fakes in his circus in the belief that the public loved to be fooled. He is credited with saying, although he did not originate the observation, "There's a sucker born every minute." It is a measure of his stature that legendary circus impresario John Ringling North is called The Greatest Showman Since Barnum.

Barnum of Basketball, The—See SAPERSTEIN, ABE.

Barnum of Broadway, The—See MERRICK, DAVID.

BARNWELL, JOHN (1671–1724)

Irish-American pioneer John Barnwell became celebrated in the colonies as *Tuscarora John* for protecting the Roanoke settlement against the Tuscarora Indians. He led the campaign that defeated the tribe so thoroughly that it was forced to flee Virginia and the Carolinas for New York.

Barrel-Mirabeau—See MIRABEAU, VICOMTE DE.

Barrie Actress, The—See ADAMS, MAUDE.

BARROW, CLYDE—See Bonnie and Clyde.

BARROW, ISAAC (1630–1677)

Charles II of England dubbed his chaplain, Isaac Barrow, *The Unfair Preacher*. Barrow, an accomplished classical scholar, mathematician and theologian, was noted for the exhaustiveness of his sermons, which the king said were "unfair" to those that followed them.

BARRY, JOHN (1745–1803)

Commodore John Barry was more deserving than John Paul Jones of the accolade *The Father of the American Navy*. The first commander commissioned by the Continental Congress, he trained many of the cadres who later achieved fame in U.S. naval history.

BARRYMORE, JOHN (1882–1942)

One of the great actors of the American stage, John Barrymore was known as *The Great Profile* because of his matinee-idol looks and his brilliant performances in many roles, ranging from *Peter Ibbetson, Richard III* and *Hamlet* on the stage to *Rasputin, Don Juan* and *Doctor Jekyll and Mr. Hyde* on the screen. Acting, drinking and romance occupied about equal portions of Barrymore's time. *The Great Profile's* later years, plagued by alcoholism, were spent playing movie roles parodying his former greatness.

Barrymore of the Brain Trust, The— See TUGWELL, REXFORD G.

BART, JEAN (c. 1650–1702)

A noted and highly successful French naval commander and privateer under Louis XIV, Jean Bart was nicknamed by his English and Dutch foes *The French Devil*.

BARTER, RICHARD—See Rattlesnake Dick.

BARTLEY, JAMES (1870–1909)

In 1891 English sailor James Bartley was in one of two long boats from the whaling ship *Star of the East* pursuing a harpooned whale. The thrashing beast capsized Bartley's boat, and he and another crewman vanished in the sea. Brought alongside the ship and killed, the whale was cut open. The next day Bartley was found in its stomach, barely alive. He had lost his hair, and his face, hands and neck were bleached unnaturally white by the whale's gastric juices. Bartley lived another 18 years and was nicknamed *A Modern Jonah,* a sobriquet engraved on his tombstone in his native Gloucester, England.

BARTON, BRUCE (1886–1967)

A founder of the major advertising agency Batten, Barton, Durstin & Osborn, Bruce Barton was a two-term Republican representative from New York from 1937 to 1941. He was called *The Great Repealer* for continually introducing bills to repeal various New Deal legislations.

BARTON, CLARA (1821–1912)

Because of her self-sacrificing work as a nurse during the Civil War, Clara Barton was nicknamed *The Angel of the Battlefield* by grateful soldiers. She founded the American Red Cross in 1881 and served as its president for the next 23 years.

BARTON, ELIZABETH (1506?–1534)

A domestic servant turned prophetess, Elizabeth Barton gained considerable fame for her trances and visions. She entered a priory where she acquired the nickname *The Nun of Kent* and began making political utterances, denouncing enemies of the Catholic Church and prophesizing a terrible fate for Henry VIII if he divorced Catherine to marry Anne Boleyn. When Henry had quite enough, she was made to confess she was an impostor and then executed, along with the monk who was her confessor and a number of other priests.

BARTRAM, JOHN (1699–1777)

Designated *The Father of American Botany* for his work in the field, John Bartram founded the first botanical gardens in the United States, at Kingssessing, Pa. He was also called *Botanist to the King,* a measure of the esteem in which his work was held in England as well.

BARUCH, BERNARD M. (1870–1965)

American public servant and financier Bernard M. Baruch accumulated a huge fortune between 1889 and 1913 and actually enlarged it during the Depression through shrewd stock market moves. A respected unpaid adviser to every U.S. president from Woodrow Wilson to John F. Kennedy, he was known as *The Adviser of Presidents.*

Baseball's Kissing Bandit: MORGANA (?–   )

Morgana, an exotic dancer, is known as *Baseball's Kissing Bandit* for her habit of jumping from her seat and running onto the field to kiss ballplayers. Her uniform consists of sneakers, shorts and a very tight sweater. She first struck in 1969, swarming over Pete Rose, and during the next decade struck a total of a dozen times, with players only twice being able to avoid her clutches. ''A pretty good batting average,'' she has observed.

Basement Barnum, The—See ROSE, BILLY.

Bashful Billionaire, The—See HUGHES, HOWARD.

BASIL II (958?–1025)

Byzantine emperor Basil II, one of the greatest military commanders of his time, engaged in virtually continuous warfare with the Germans, Saracens and especially the Bulgarians. He was hailed as *Bulgaroktonos,* or *Slayer of Bulgarians.*

BASS, SAM (1851–1878)

Described in "The Ballad of Sam Bass" as "a kinder-hearted fellow you seldom ever see," train robber Bass has entered western folklore as *The Robin Hood of Texas* and *The Good Badman*. In point of fact one would be hard put to find any act that made him a genuine Robin Hood, but he was loose with the money he stole, and if there was a way for a gunman to become popular in Texas, it was as a free spender.

Bass John—See SPREULL, JOHN.

Bastard of Orleans, The—See DUNOIS, JEAN.

Batavian Buffoon, The—See ERASMUS, DESIDERIUS.

Batman and Robin: DAVID GREENBERG (1943–) and ROBERT HANTZ (1943–)

New York City policemen David Greenberg and Robert Hantz made so many arrests as a team, especially in narcotics cases, they were nicknamed *Batman and Robin*.

BATTAGLIA, SAM "Teets" (1908–1973)

Chicago syndicate mobster Sam Battaglia was called *Teets* for either or both of the following reasons: He had an extremely well-developed chest as a youth; later, as a member of the notorious 42 Gang he extorted money from businessmen under the threat ". . .or I'll bust ya in da teets." *Teets* himself preferred the latter explanation.

Batters, Joe—See ACCARDO, ANTHONY "Tough Tony."

Battery Dan—See FINN, DANIEL E.

Battle Annie—See Queen of Hell's Kitchen, The.

Battle Axe Gleason—See GLEASON, PATRICK JEROME.

Battling Barkeep—See GALENTO, ANTHONY "Two-Ton Tony."

Battling Bella—See ABZUG, BELLA.

Baugh, Slinging Sammy: SAMUEL ADRIAN BAUGH (1914–)

Football star Sammy Baugh was nicknamed *Slinging Sammy* because he was one of the best and hardest-throwing passers in the game. The story is often told of how Baugh was being flattened consistently by an opposing tackler after he had released the ball. Finally, Baugh called another passing play, faded back and, as the lineman came barrelling in on him, cut loose with the football, taking dead aim at the would-be tackler's helmet. Its force knocked the lineman out, and thereafter *Slinging Sammy* was subjected to no more cheap shots from opponents.

BAYARD, PIERRE DU TERRAIL, CHEVALIER DE (1473?–1524)

Pierre du Terrail, Chevalier de Bayard, a great French military hero famed for his impetuous bravery, was nicknamed *The Knight Without Fear and Blame*. It was a measure of the esteem in which he was held that many great fighting men thereafter gained his name as a sobriquet, including John Paul Jones, The Bayard of the Sea, American Revolutionary War general Francis Marion, The Bayard of the South, and John Laurens, The Bayard of the Revolution.

Bayard of the Revolution, The—See LAURENS, JOHN.

Bayard of the Sea, The—See JONES, JOHN PAUL.

Bayard of the South, The—See MARION, FRANCIS.

BAYLE, PIERRE (1647–1706)

Pierre Bayle, author of the French *Historical and Critical Dictionary,* was honored as *The Father of Modern Skepticism* for his immense influence on European philosophy and literature. He is regarded as the parent of the great French Encyclopedists who blossomed in the 18th century.

BEAL, ABRAHAM (c. 1803–1872)

Anglo-American philanthropist Abraham Beal began reforming drunkards and helping prisoners return to honest lives in his native England, where he won the appellation *The Prisoner's Friend.* Relocating in the U.S. in his mid-forties, he continued his altruistic activities until his death in 1872.

BEAME, ABE (1906–   )

The first Jewish mayor of New York City, Abe Beame was nicknamed *Spunky* in his youth because his boundless energy and enthusiasm belied his diminutive size.

BEAN, ROY (c. 1825–1903)

A legendary Texas frontier judge in whose saloon legal sessions were held, Roy Bean proclaimed himself *The Law West of the Pecos,* an appellation accepted by citizens. He dispensed his own brand of justice whether or not he held an official judgeship at the moment.

Bear, The—See ARTHGAL; BRADY, JAMES; HOBBES, THOMAS.

Bear Tracks—See MURPHY, JOHN "Bear-Tracks."

Bearded Iceberg, The—See HUGHES, CHARLES EVANS.

Beard That Made Poughkeepsie Famous, The—See SMITH BROTHERS.

BEARDSLEY, AUBREY (1872–1898)

English author and illustrator Aubrey Beardsley, known for his unique illustrations for *The Rape of the Lock, The Savoy, Lysistrata, The Yellow Book, Volpone* and others, had a style that was exceedingly precious and at the same time often ribald or grotesque. He was nicknamed *Awfully Weirdly* and *Daubaway Weirdsley,* the latter an invention of the British humor magazine *Punch.*

Bearer of Bad News, The—See RIVLIN, ALICE MITCHELL.

BEARES, JAMES D. (?–1870)

A member of Louisiana's notorious "black-and-tan" legislature after the Civil War, James D.

Beares was described after his death by a newspaper as "one of the most profligate and corrupt senators under the radical regime, and whose vote for a measure was only to be obtained by substantial pecuniary reward. His corruption was so notorious that he earned the sobriquet *'Where does Beares come in?'* " Beares was shot dead in 1870 by his prostitute mistress, who was not prosecuted, allegedly because she knew so many secrets about the political scandals of the day.

Bear-Leader, The—See BOSWELL, JAMES.

Beast, The—See CROWLEY, ALEISTER.

Beast Butler—See BUTLER, BENJAMIN.

Beast of Buffalo, The—See CLEVELAND, GROVER.

Beau Brummel of Broadway, The—See FAY, LARRY.

Beau Brummel of the Army—See MACARTHUR, DOUGLAS.

Beau Brummel of the Coast, The—See Harrington, Happy Jack.

Beau Brummel of the Senate, The—See LEWIS, JAMES H.

Beau James—See WALKER, JAMES J.

Beau Jess of Washington Court House—See SMITH, JESSE.

Beau Nasty—See FOOTE, SAMUEL.

BEAUCHAMP, RICHARD DE (1382–1439)

Often cited as the pinnacle of medieval chivalry, Richard de Beauchamp, 12th earl of Warwick and regent of France, was called *The Father of Curtesie*. According to Emerson, the French emperor informed Henry V of England "that no Christian king had such another knight for wisdom, nurture and manhood, and caused him to be named The Father of Curtesie."

Beauclerc—See HENRY I, KING OF ENGLAND.

BEAUMARCHAIS, PIERRE AUGUSTIN CARON DE (1732–1799)

Pierre Augustin Caron de Beaumarchais is said to have modeled the leading character of his play *Mariage de Figaro* after himself, thus giving rise to his nickname *The Figaro of His Age*. De Beaumarchais (an elegant amendment to his surname Caron) wrote operas and satires as well as plays and was an accomplished musician, a talented painter, a more than satisfactory actor and a mechanic. For a time he was also a magistrate and a political figure, and he was almost always involved in arguments in court and in his private life. Fortunately, he was an accomplished duelist, earning and surviving the sobriquet *The Prince of Quarrellers*.

BEAUREGARD, PIERRE GUSTAVE TOUTANT (1818–1893)

As the first Confederate general to fight and win a battle in the Civil War, P.G.T. Beauregard gained the sobriquet *The Hero of Sumter*. A great admirer of Napoleon, Beauregard was known for his Napoleonic reports and speeches, which earned him the nickname *Little Napoleon*. As second in command of the Confederate forces at Shiloh, he drafted the orders for the attack with a copy of Napoleon's order for the Battle of Waterloo at his side. Some have observed that the battle might have turned out differently if he had used a plan for one of Napoleon's victories instead.

Beautiful Bob—See TAYLOR, ROBERT.

Beautiful Half of a Poet, A—See TENNYSON, ALFRED LORD.

Beautiful Little Knitter, A—See WOOLF, VIRGINIA.

Beautiful Rope-Maker, The—See LABE, LOUISA.

Beautifyer, The—See HOGARTH, WILLIAM.

Beauty—See STUART, JAMES EWELL BROWN "Jeb."

Beaver, The—See BEAVERBROOK, LORD.

BEAVERBROOK, LORD WILLIAM MAXWELL AITKEN (1879–1964)

Canadian-born press magnate Lord Beaverbrook was referred to by the staff of his British newspaper the *Daily Express* as *The Beaver,* not simply as a play on his name but because of his constant attention to the publication's affairs.

BECCARIA, MARCHESE DE (1738–1794)

An early and brilliant foe of capital punishment and judicial torture, Marchese de Beccaria penned his famous *Of Crimes and Punishment* in 1764 while only in his twenties, winning for himself the sobriquet *The Protector and Defender of Humanity*. A member of a wealthy Milan family of soldiers, judges and clergy, he explained in his writings he was denuded of feelings of humanity after eight fanatical years of education under the Jesuits, until he broke free through the influence of Montesquieu and the French Encyclopedists. Through a cooperative prison governor, Beccaria was able to witness and gather evidence on secret accusations, tortures, the religious Inquisition, and the punishment of death for the most trivial of offenses. The abolition of capital punishment in many countries in the past 200 years has been attributed to Beccaria's influence.

BECKER, CHARLES (1846–1906)

Charles Becker, considered by many experts to be the greatest bank note forger in American counterfeiting history, was colorfully dubbed *The Master Maker of the Queer*.

BECKET, THOMAS "à" (1118–1170)

Thomas Becket had possibly the shortest and perhaps the most malicious nickname in history. It was an "*à*" stuck between his proper names. The inference was that there was something sinister about the Archbishop of Canterbury and that he was somehow not quite English. Becket was born in England, and, although his parents were of French origin, there seemed to have been no contemporary use of the "*à*." But after his death his detractors made subtle use of it to suggest all was not proper about the murdered archbishop.

BECKX, PETER (1794–1887)

With a certain amount of awe for his political power, the Italians nicknamed Peter Beckx, superior-general of the Society of Jesus, or Jesuits, *The Black Pope*.

BEDA, NOEL (?–1537)

French theologian and doctor of the Sorbonne Noel Beda was as famous for his gross eating habits as for his learning, and he was called *gros soupier,* or *The Great Sopper* for the way he avidly sopped up his food with bread. According to his contemporary Rabelais, Beda's main contribution to the world was a book on the excellence of tripe, with the implication that his most noteworthy feature was his tremendous stomach.

Bedeviled Viking, The—See STRINDBERG, AUGUST.

Bee, The—See SOPHOCLES

BEEBE, LUCIUS (1902–1966)

Lucius Beebe, the newspaper columnist, poet, author and bon vivant noted for his luxurious lifestyle, was designated *The Social Historian of Cafe Society.* Some of his subjects objected to his gossipy reports and countered by calling him *Luscious Lucius,* an allusion to his elegant, often effeminate dress.

BEECHER, LYMAN (1755–1863)

American clergyman Lyman Beecher was nicknamed *The Father of Brains* or *The Father of More Brains Than Any Other Man in America* because of the accomplishments of so many of his children. A professor of theology who preached at a number of churches in the East and in Cincinnati, he numbered among his children Catherine Esther, a leading educationist; Edward, a clergyman and college president; Charles, a pastor, an accomplished musician and later Florida's superintendent of public instruction; Henry Ward, a leading preacher, reformer and for a time mentioned for the U.S. presidency; and Harriet Beecher Stowe, the abolitionist and author of *Uncle Tom's Cabin.*

Beelzebub M. Goldwater—See GOLDWATER, BARRY M.

Beethoven of the Flute, The—See KUHLAU, FRIEDRICH DANIEL RUDOLPH.

Begging Bishop, The: JOHN HACKET (1592–1670)

Bishop John Hacket raised all the funds for the rebuilding of the Cathedral of Lichfield, England by personally soliciting donations from passersby. After eight years of standing in the same location, he raised the equivalent of about $75,000 and became known as *The Begging Bishop.*

BEHAM, HANS SEBALD (c. 1500–1550)

A noted painter and engraver who produced exceedingly small prints, Hans Sebald Beham was called *The Little Master.*

BEJAZET I, SULTAN OF THE TURKS (1347–1403)

Bejazet I, sultan of the Turks, was nicknamed *The Thunderbolt* for the speed with which he moved his troops. He was defeated by the Mongol invader Timur in 1402 and died the following year.

Believe-It-or-Not Man, The—See RIPLEY, ROBERT.

Believer, The—See FORD, CLARA.

BELINSKY, VISARION GRIGORYEVICH (1810–1848)

The fearless and passionate Russian critic Visarion Grigoryevich Belinsky, an outspoken foe of Russian absolutism, was perhaps the country's most influential writer of his day as the literary critic of the widely read monthly *Home Annals*. Belinsky, or *Furious Visarion* as friends like Turgenev called him, considered it the critic's duty to be "the tutor of society." He wrote, "Ever since I was a child I have considered it to be a most agreeable offering to the God of Truth and Reason to spit in the face of public opinion whenever it was stupid or mean or both." He is particularly famous for a letter to Gogol, written shortly before his death from consumption, in which he attacked Gogol's reactionary views.

BELL, ALEXANDER GRAHAM (1847–1922)

Scottish-born teacher of the deaf and the first inventor to patent the telephone and exploit it commercially, Alexander Graham Bell was dubbed *The Father of the Telephone.*

Bell, Tom: THOMAS J. HODGES (1825–1856)

Thomas J. Hodges, alias Tom Bell, was the only physician known to have taken to the western bandit trail. Called *The Outlaw Doc,* he designed a sheet-iron protector to shield his vital areas from bullets. The device didn't protect him, however, from a California posse, which caught him in 1856 with the help of an informer and put a rope around his unprotected neck.

BELL, WILLIAM (c. 1761)

During the month of March in 1761, William Bell, a soldier in England's Life Guards, was celebrated as *Doomsday Bell*. London had been hit by a minor earthquake on Feb. 8 and by another on March 8. Noting the tremors had struck exactly four weeks apart, Bell warned that a third would strike in 28 days and that it would mean the total destruction of the world. He made scores of speeches around the city and convinced a large number of people that his prediction was accurate; even some disbelievers decided it might be prudent to leave town as the dread day approached. Numerous Londoners sought shelter in outlying villages, where they were charged exorbitant rates, and many others sought refuge aboard boats on the Thames. On doomsday, April 5, nothing much happened, and on the following day Bell was seized and cast into Bedlam, London's madhouse. Thereafter *Doomsday Bell* was called *Mad Bell*.

Belle of Amherst, The—See DICKINSON, EMILY.

Belle of New York, The—See PRADO, KATIE.

BELLI, MELVIN (1907–   )

Flamboyant San Francisco lawyer Melvin Belli has been dubbed *The King of Torts* for his ability to win huge settlements for his clients in damage suits.

Bellicose Bella—See ABZUG, BELLA.

Bellona—See EATON, MARGARET O'NEILL.

BELMONTE, JUAN (1892–1962)

In one season a lone Spanish bullfighter Juan Belmonte killed 200 bulls in 109 bullfights, having previously gained great popularity with aficionados for his unorthodox style and the nickname *The Crazy Suicide*. Scorning the technique of sidestepping a charging bull, Belmonte, once he had picked his ground, would dig in his feet and maneuver the beast around with his cape. He often climaxed this feat by kneeling inches from the bull's nose and daring the animal to gore him. Indeed, many did. Ironically, the man who so often nonchalantly faced the moment of truth in the bull-ring was a nervous stutterer in private life.

Beloved Man of the Four Nations, The—See HAWKINS, BENJAMIN.

BELSUNCE, HENRI FRANCOIS (1671–1755)

According to a contemporary account, during the great plague that struck Marseilles in the 18th century, Bishop Henry Francois Belsunce "exerted himself by night and day to succor the dying, cheer the despairing, comfort the afflicted." His Christian·devotion won him the appellation *The Good Bishop,* as he is still remembered today.

BEMIS, MRS. CHARLES—See China Polly.

Bench-Leg—See HANSON, ROGER WEIGHTMAN.

BENDER, CHARLES ALBERT "Chief" (1883–1954)

Since Philadelphia Athletics pitcher Charles Albert Bender was a Chippewa Indian, it never occurred to baseball fans to call him anything other than *Chief* or *Chief Bender.*

Bendigo: WILLIAM THOMPSON (1811–1880)

British professional boxer and heavyweight champion Bendigo, whose real name was William Thompson, was known as *The Reformed Pugilist* after retiring from the ring in 1851 to become an evangelist. His reformation proved to be a long process that included 28 jail terms for violations of the anti-fight law. He had been lectured on the evils of sin during each prison stay.

Benefactor—See POTOLEMY III.

Benefactor, The—See PTOLEMY VII.

BENGA, OTO—See Man in the Zoo, The.

BENJAMIN, JUDAH PHILIP (1811–1884)

The attorney general and secretary of war under Confederate President Jefferson Davis during the Civil War, Judah Philip Benjamin was called *The Brains of the Confederacy,* an accolade sometimes used as a disparagement of Davis. Upon the defeat of the South, Benjamin fled to England, where he became a highly esteemed lawyer.

BENTHAM, JEREMY (1748–1832)

British philosopher and reformer Jeremy Bentham, the leader of the so-called Philosophic Radicals, was known as *The Father of Utilitarianism.* He believed that the only good was pleasure and the only evil, pain, and that the duty of government and social institutions was to promote the greatest happiness for the greatest number of people. His judgment that parliamentary reform was an essential prerequisite to all other reforms brought him the sobriquet *Anti-Machiavel.*

The great utilitarian to the end, Bentham left his large fortune to University College in London, with the provision that his preserved body be displayed annually at the meeting of the board of directors. Dr. Southward Smith performed a complete dissection and an anatomical lecture for both medical students and the public, which Bentham had stipulated, and the bones were then reassembled into a skeleton capped with a wax mask of his face. The body was then clad in Bentham's clothing and displayed sitting upright in an armchair in a glass-covered mahogany case. For the next 92 years Bentham was listed as "present" at the meetings but "not voting." In 1924 Bentham's corpse was put on display in an exhibit area at the college.

BENTON, THOMAS HART (1782–1858)

As a U.S. senator from Missouri for 30 years, Thomas Hart Benton was a hard-money advocate who called for the issuance of only gold coins. Labeled by foes *The Gold Humbug,* he became so identified with gold coins that they were often referred to as Benton's Mint Drops.

BERCHLINGEN, GOETZ VON—See Goetz of the Iron Hand.

BERGER, HENRY (?–1929)

Honoring an odd request from Hawaiian King Kamehameha V in 1872, Emperor Wilhelm of Prussia dispatched Capt. Henry Berger, a military officer, to organize and direct a Royal Hawaiian Band. Over the next 43 years Berger became famous as *The Hawaiian Musikmeister,* writing some of Hawaii's most popular songs, such as "Aloha Oe" and "Hawaii Ponoi." Berger insisted he faithfully picked up native tunes, but many experts perceive a strong resemblance to the folk tunes of Germany in his Hawaiian melodies.

BERGH, HENRY (1811–1888)

Sent to St. Petersburg by President Lincoln, diplomat Henry Bergh became so sickened by the common practice of flogging animals in Russia that he physically intervened with a peasant brutally flailing an overloaded donkey. Resigning his post, he returned to the United States where, in 1866, he founded the American Society for the Prevention of Cruelty to Animals, and became famous as *The Father of the ASPCA.*

BERIA, LAVRENTI P. (1899–1953)

The hated and feared Soviet secret police chief Lavrenti P. Beria was known as *The Himmler of Russia,* an apt description Nikita Khrushchev used to justify having him killed in 1953.

BERKELEY, BUSBY (1895–1976)

Known for his lavish motion picture musical productions featuring hundreds of dancers, choreographer Busby Berkeley was dubbed *The Wizard of the Chorus Line.* His movies are now regarded as a lost art.

BERKELEY, GEORGE (1684–1753)

The distinguished Irish philosopher and writer George Berkeley, bishop of Cloyne, was designated *The Irish Plato.*

BERKOWITZ, DAVID—See Son of Sam.

BERKOWITZ, ITZHAK DOV (1885–1967)

Israeli author Itzhak Dov Berkowitz, who often told the story of his people, was dubbed *The Voice of the Uprooted.*

BERMAN, OTTO "Abbadabba" (1889–1935)

Dubbed *Abbadabba Berman,* mathematical genius Otto Berman was the underworld's "adding machine" in the 1920s and 1930s. As an aide to racket king Dutch Schultz, he used his own formula to juggle race track betting handle totals so that the numbers game could be fixed to pay off on lesser-played numbers; he was credited with bilking players of an extra million dollars a week. When Schultz was assassinated in 1935, Berman was inadvertently killed with him, depriving the Lucky Luciano-Vito Genovese mob—which took over the operation—of millions of dollars annually because no one was able duplicate his technique.

BERNADOTTE, JEAN BAPTISTE JULES (1763–1844)

Long a supporter and leading general of Napoleon, Jean Baptiste Jules Bernadotte maneuvered his way into the succession to the Swedish throne as Charles Jean. He enjoyed the French dictator's approval in this, but he turned against Napoleon when his mentor's fortunes waned, and for this act of disloyalty his old comrade-in-arms disparaged him as *Charles Jean Charlatan*.

BERNARD, SAMUEL (1651–1739)

English capitalist Samuel Bernard was nicknamed *Lucullus* by detractors who saw similarities between him and the "rich fool" of ancient Rome who spent his great wealth in ostentatious display.

BERNARD OF MENTHON, ST. (923–1008)

French churchman St. Bernard of Menthon, who founded the hospices in the Alps, was dubbed *Apostle of the Alps*.

BERNHARDT, SARAH (1844–1923)

The magnetic French tragedienne Sarah Bernhardt was known as *The Divine Sarah*, a tribute first paid her by Oscar Wilde. She is credited with having had more than 1,000 lovers.

BERNSTEIN, THEODORE (1904–1979)

The much-storied head of the copy desk at the *New York Times*, Ted Bernstein was the author of several books on journalism and correct usage of the English language. As the newspaper's long-time enforcer of editorial standards, he was regarded by many journalists as *The Governess* of the *Times*.

BERTHOLLET, CLAUDE LOUIS, COUNT (1748–1822)

While experimenting with the effects of carbonic acid on human beings, medical researcher Count Claude Louis Berthollet subjected himself to the experiment and died as a result, gaining the sobriquet *The Martyr to Science*.

BERTILLON, ALPHONSE (1853–1914)

The inventor of the Bertillon system of identification, the predecessor of the fingerprint system, French lawman Alphonse Bertillon was labeled *France's Greatest Detective*, this despite some lamentable errors such as the bungled Dreyfus case.

Best Abused Man in England, The— See DENNIS, JOHN.

*Best Congressman West of the Mississippi, The—*See VOORHIS, JERRY.

*Best Inspector General, The—*See PEARSON, DREW.

Best of Cut-Throats, The—See WELLINGTON, ARTHUR WELLESLEY, FIRST DUKE OF.

Best Undressed Woman in America, The—See LEE, GYPSY ROSE.

Bet-a-Billion Curtice—See CURTICE, HARLOW HERBERT.

Bet-a-Million—See GATES, JOHN W. "Bet-a-Million."

BETHUNE, THOMAS GREENE (1849–1908)

Black American musical prodigy Thomas Greene Bethune was sadly exploited in exhibitions around the world as *Blind Tom*. Although blind and virtually an idiot, he had the uncanny ability of being able to play on the piano any popular of classical composition after hearing it once. Born of slave parents, he bore the name of his former master.

Betrayer of Norway, The—See QUISLING, VIDKUN.

BETTERTON, THOMAS (1635–1710)

The great English actor Thomas Betterton was nicknamed *The British Roscius* after the famed Roman slave turned actor. As one critic said, "He alone was born to speak what only Shakespeare knew to write." In later years David Garrick received a similar sobriquet.

BETTY, WILLIAM HENRY WEST (1791–1874)

A brilliant child English actor, William Henry West Betty was hailed as *The Infant* or *Young Roscius,* an honorific after ancient Rome's famous comic actor Roscius. After making his debut in Belfast in 1803, Betty appeared in London's Covent Garden and drew crowds so large that troops had to be called out to control them. On one occasion William Pitt adjourned the House of Commons so that members could see him perform. By the time he retired in 1806, he had become enormously wealthy.

BEVIN, ERNEST (1881–1951)

Powerful British union leader Ernest Bevin served as the Labor government's foreign minister from 1945 to 1951, during which time he helped lay the basics of NATO and was savaged by his foes as *The Foreign Office's Charlie McCarthy.*

BICKERDYKE, MARY A. "Mother" (1817–1901)

Mary Bickerdyke, better known to the Union wounded during the Civil War as *Mother Bickerdyke,* was perhaps the second most famous nurse of that conflict, after Clara Barton. Because of the way she took command of every situation, she was called *The Brigadier Commanding Hospitals* by doctors and officers under whom she technically served.

BICKMORE, ALBERT SMITH (1839–1914)

American educator and naturalist Albert Smith Bickmore is credited with being *The Father of the Museum,* for having conceived the idea and implementing the founding of New York's American Museum of Natural History. Much of the museum's original, extensive collection of marine animal specimens was gathered personally by Bickmore from around the world.

Biddenden Maids, The: MARY AND ELIZABETH CHULKHURST (1100–1134)

The Biddenden Maids was a nickname given to the sisters Mary and Elizabeth Chulkhurst of Biddenden, England, who were born joined together.

BIDDLE, CLEMENT (1740–1814)

Clement Biddle was called *The Quaker Soldier* by Philadelphians because, despite his religious beliefs, he organized a group of Quaker volunteers to battle the Paxton Boys, a band of frontier ruffians who had planned to attack the city in 1764, because it offered protection to friendly Indians. Later, during the Revolutionary War, Biddle was a prime mover in organizing a Quaker volunteer unit for the Continental Army.

BIDDLE, JOHN (1615–1662)

Religious reformer John Biddle, who penned a number of anti-Trinitarian tracts in 17th century England, is designated *The Father of English Unitarianism.*

BIDDLE, NICHOLAS (1786–1844)

As president of the Second Bank of the United States, Nicholas Biddle exercised enormous political power, much to the distress of those opposing the concept of a National Bank. Since there was little doubt that Biddle extended his influence by paying money to certain newspapers, he was called *Emperor Nick of the Bribery Bank.*

BIERCE, AMBROSE (1842–1914?)

Journalist and short story writer Ambrose Bierce was called *Bitter Bierce* because of the grotesque, cynical and sardonic nature of his fiction. Bierce disappeared in Mexico in 1914 and was never heard from again.

Big Band's Black Man, The—See HENDERSON, FLETCHER.

Big Bankroll, The—See ROTHSTEIN, ARNOLD.

Big Casino—See GARRETT, PAT(RICK FLOYD).

Big Chief—See CURTIS, CHARLES.

Big Chief, The—See TAFT, WILLIAM HOWARD.

Big Clown, The—See GRAY, L. PATRICK.

Big Daddy—See AMIN DADA, IDI "Big Daddy."

Big Drunk—See HOUSTON, SAMUEL.

Big Eyes Schurz—See SCHURZ, CARL.

Big Feller, The—See SULLIVAN, TIMOTHY "Big Tim."

Big Foot Wallace—See WALLACE, WILLIAM "Big Foot."

Big Navy Claude—See SWANSON, CLAUDE A.

Big Nose Parrot: GEORGE CURRY (1841–1882)

Colorful western outlaw George Curry was called *George Parrot* by other cattle rustlers because of his large nose. Some lawmen missing the meaning of his nickname, compounded the insult by identifying him as *Big Nose Parrot.*

Big Poison—See WANER, PAUL AND LLOYD.

Big Six—See MATHEWSON, CHRISTY.

Big St. Bernard, A—See FORD, GERALD RUDOLPH.

Big Stiff, The—See GATES, JOHN W. "Bet-a-Million."

Big Train—See JOHNSON, WALTER.

Bigamy Young—See YOUNG, BRIGHAM.

Biggest Liar in the World, The—See RIPLEY, ROBERT.

BILBO, THEODORE GILMORE (1877–1947)

One of the most imposing unreconstructed southern politicians of the 20th century, Mississippi Sen. Theodore Gilmore Bilbo was referred to by friend and foe in the Capitol as simply *The Man.* Blacks also called him that since he typified the white power structure. He often used the term himself as a form of self-esteem only slightly below the royal "we." In addition, he was called *The Two-Edged Knife* because of his cutting ability in debate.

Bill the Builder—See THOMPSON, WILLIAM HALE "Big Bill."

Bill the Butcher—See POOLE, WILLIAM.

Billie the Kid—See RUSSELL, WILLIAM E.

BILLINGS, G. K. G. "Horseback" (1861–1937)

As the long-time chairman of the board of Union Carbide, G. K. G. Billings was noted for spending lavishly on his pleasures, which included an estimated half million dollars a year for his hobby of yachting. He gained the sobriquet *Horseback Billings* for a party he threw at Manhattan's Louis Sherry restaurant for an estimated cost of $250 a plate. Society writers were unimpressed by an event where guests dined while seated on their mounts. Besides its being an uncomfortable affair, the steeds soiled the banquet room floor, which hardly added to the elegance of the event.

BILLINGTON, JOHN (?–1630)

Even before the *Mayflower* arrived in Massachusetts, John Billington proved to be the rowdiest of its 102 pilgrims. Reprimanded and punished by Captain Miles Standish aboard ship for numerous blasphemous harangues by having his feet and neck tied together, he did not improve his behavior in succeeding years. Billington became known as *The Black Sheep of the Plymouth Colony,* a sobriquet he more than lived up to in 1630 when he killed another settler to become the first murderer in America (in terms of a white man killing a white man). He was hanged.

Billionaire Bachelor, The—See RICHARDSON, SID.

Billionaire Recluse, The—See HUGHES, HOWARD.

Billy Goat Devol—See DEVOL, GEORGE.

Billy Sunday of Japan—See KIMURA, HENRY SEIMATSU.

Billy the Kid (1859–1881)

Why William Bonney or Henry McCarthy, whichever was his real name, was nicknamed *Billy the Kid* is unknown, since he started killing about the age of 15, par for western badmen. Possibly he may have acquired the nickname *The Kid* because he tended to hang out with older lawbreakers. For a time he was big on the gambling circuit with an older man named Pat Garrett. Adept at cards, Garrett and Billy were referred to respectively as Big Casino and Little Casino, the latter perhaps subsequently shortened to *The Kid.* Garrett even-

tually became a lawman and killed his former partner in a celebrated ambush.

Billy the Kid: BILLY CLAIBORNE (1860–1882)

One of the survivors of the famed western gunfight at the O.K. Corral, Billy Claiborne was a young gunslinger who went around demanding to be referred to as *Billy the Kid.* It was not a sobriquet easily earned, since he had to kill three men who laughed in his face for attempting to appropriate the famous nickname. In November 1882 *Billy the Kid II* demanded that a noted shootist named Buckskin Frank Leslie honor him with the title. Leslie, working behind the bar of the Oriental Saloon in Tombstone, Ariz., removed his apron, stepped outside with Claiborne and promptly gunned him down. They marked his grave just plain Billy Claiborne, not *Billy the Kid.*

Biographer of the Dispensable Man, The— See SMITH, H. ALLEN.

Birdman of Alcatraz, The—See STROUD, ROBERT F.

BIRDSEYE, CLARENCE (1886–1956)

Justifiably called *The Father of Frozen Foods,* Clarence Birdseye developed his freezing process after observing the food-preserving methods of Eskimos. He is also known to some as *The Father of Invention,* since he went on to hold more than 250 patents for varied inventions, ranging from a process for converting sugar cane into paper pulp to a recoilless harpoon gun for whalers.

BISHOP, CORBETT (1906–1961)

It would be difficult to find a more committed American pacifist than Corbett Bishop, often described as *The Pacifist Absolutist*. A violator of the World War II draft law, he declined to cooperate in any way with his prosecutors and refused to eat, observe normal sanitary habits or even move while under arrest. Declining food and water during 426 days of three prison confinements, he had to be force-fed and carried in and out of court by FBI agents, before finally winning an unconditional release. His guards agreed Bishop never exhibited any personal hostility toward them. Bishop once summed up his attitude: "The authorities have the power to seize my body; that is all they can do. My spirit will be free."

Bishop, The—See DE SAPIO, CARMINE.

Bishop of Hell, The: GAINHAM, JOHN *(fl. 1700–1740)*

While incarcerated for bad debts in London's Fleet Street Prison for some 40 years, clergyman John Gainham married approximately 36,000 couples. Because most of the parents of those married did not approve of their marital choices, Gainham was called *The Bishop of Hell*.

BISMARCK, OTTO VON *(1815–1898)*

Prince Otto von Bismarck, who called his policies "blood and iron," was nicknamed *The Iron Chancellor* and *The Man of Blood and Iron* for unifying Germany under Prussian leadership by bluster, shrewd diplomacy and war.

Bismarck of Asia, The—See LI-HUNG CHANG.

Biscuit Pants—See GEHRIG, LOU.

Bitch of Buchenwald, The—See KOCH, ILSE.

Bite 'em—See MORELLET, ANDRE.

Bitter Bierce—See BIERCE, AMBROSE.

BIXBY, HORACE—See Lightning Pilot, The.

Black Agnes: AGNES, COUNTESS OF DUNBAR AND MARCH *(?–1369)*

Called by the English *Black Agnes* not only for her swarthy complexion but for her fighting spirit, Agnes, countess of Dunbar and March, was famed for her defense of Dunbar Castle during the absence of her husband. She forced the earl of Salisbury to retire in ignominy after 19 weeks of failing to breach the walls.

Black Babe Ruth, The—See GIBSON, JOSH.

Black Dahlia, The: ELIZABETH SHORT *(1925–1947)*

Elizabeth Short, a starstruck young girl who sought fame and fortune in Hollywood, constantly appeared at studio casting offices dressed entirely in black as a gimmick to gain attention. She became known as *The Black Dahlia*, and in 1947, when she was murdered in a particularly brutal fashion, newspapers picked up the nickname. The case remains unsolved, and, after a fashion, *The Black Dahlia* achieved the fame she had always sought.

Black Dan— See WEBSTER, DANIEL.

Black Death, The—See BLACKBURNE, JOSEPH HENRY.

Black Douglas: JAMES, LORD OF DOUGLAS (1286–1330)

James, lord of Douglas, was nicknamed *Black Douglas* by the fearful English because of his cunning raids on the Scottish border. Most likely the nickname came about because of the ruse he used to capture Roxburgh castle in 1314, when he dressed his men to look like black oxen.

Black Giant, The—See KOHL, HELMUT.

Black Giant of White Spirituals, The—See JACKSON, GEORGE PULLEN.

Black Hand, The—See MURPHY, CHARLES F.

Black Horowitz, The—See WALLER, FATS.

Black Jack—See PERSHING, JOHN JOSEPH.

Black John Brown, The—See VESEY, DENMARK.

Black King of the Gamblers, The—See HARRIS, MAC.

Black Knight of Ashton, The—See ASHTON, RALPH.

Black Maria: MARIA LEE (c. 1840s)

Maria Lee was a black woman who ran a particularly notorious Boston lodging house for seamen that was constantly being raided by police. Whenever a police wagon was seen leaving the waterfront packed with boisterous characters, it was generally assumed to be coming from *Black Maria's*. In time her nickname was given to the police wagon as well, as any such vehicle has since been called a Black Maria.

Black Monk, The—See REINHARDT, AD.

Black Nigger—See RUSSELL, BILL.

Black Pearl, The—See PELE.

Black Pope, The—See BECKX, PETER.

Black Prince, The: EDWARD, PRINCE OF WALES (1330–1376)

Edward, Prince of Wales, the eldest son of Edward III, was an accomplished warrior hailed as *The Black Prince* because of his distinctive black armor.

Black Ralph Nader, The—See SIMS, PHILIP.

Black Republican Blair—See BLAIR, FRANCIS PRESTON, JR.

Black Rifle: CAPTAIN JACK
(fl. mid-18th century)

Captain Jack, the only known name for this American frontier settler, took up a vendetta against the Ohio Indians after his wife and children were trapped in their burning cabin and slaughtered during his absence. For safety he painted his face and body dark while tracking the Indians, who called him *Black Rifle*.

Black Russell—See RUSSELL, JOHN.

Black Sheep of the Plymouth Colony, The—See BILLINGTON, JOHN.

Black Sheep Sarah—See CHURCHILL, SARAH.

Black Swallow of Death, The—See BULLARD, EUGENE.

Black Swan, The—See GREENFIELD, ELIZABETH TAYLOR.

Black Terror, The—See RICHMOND, BILL.

BLACKBURNE, JOSEPH HENRY
(1841–1924)

One of the foremost players in the history of chess, English great Joseph Henry Blackburne was dubbed *The Black Death*.

BLACKMUN, HARRY A. *(1908–   )*

Supreme Court Justice Harry Blackmun authored the Court's 1973 landmark decision legalizing abortion, and he has been a target of the antiabortion movement ever since. Among the nicknames and epithets hurled at him are *Butcher of Dachau, Pontius Pilate* and *King Herod*.

BLACKSTONE, WILLIAM
(1723–1780)

Sir William Blackstone, the famed English jurist and author of the classic *Commentaries on the Laws of England*, a basic text for generations of lawyers, was accorded the ultimate accolade of his profession—*The Lawyer*.

BLACKWOOD, WILLIAM
(1777–1834)

English publisher William Blackwood, who started *Blackwood's Magazine*, was known to his writers as *Ebony*.

BLAINE, JAMES G. *(1830–1893)*

A leading Republican politician who was the party's unsuccessful candidate for president in 1884, James G. Blaine became known as *The Uncrowned King* while serving as secretary of state under President Benjamin Harrison from 1889 to 1892 because he was generally regarded as the real power behind the office. His supporters also called him *The Plumed Knight*, while foes referred to him as *The Tattooed Man*, an allusion to the Ancient Greek Phryne, who had the names of political scandals with which he was connected tattooed on his skin.

Blaine's Irishman—See EGAN, PATRICK.

BLAIR, FRANCIS PRESTON, JR.
(1821–1875)

An antebellum Democratic representative, Francis Preston Blair, Jr., advocated a gradual and voluntary emancipation of the slaves rather than civil war, but to Democrats from slaveholding states this idea made him little better than a Republican. They denounced him as *Black Republican Blair,* and other Democrats favoring the same course of action all became known as Black Republicans.

BLAKE, WILLIAM *(1757–1827)*

English poet, artist, engraver and mystic William Blake was also a crusader against social injustice, especially against children, and a supporter of both the French and American Revolutions. Because of his stand in favor of independence for the American colonies, he won the sobriquet *The Prophet Against Empire.*

BLAND, JAMES A. *(1854–1911)*

Known as *The Prince of Negro Songwriters,* James A. Bland was born free in New York in 1854. He wrote ''Carry Me Back to Ol' Virginny'' in 1878, and it became the official state song of Virginia in 1940. Although he received little attention in America during his lifetime, he was a leading light of England's music halls for more than 20 years.

BLANKENBURG, RUDOLPH *(1843–1918)*

Rudolph Blankenburg, one of the Philadelphia's most potent political reformers and the city's mayor from 1911 to 1915, was nicknamed *Old Dutch Cleanser* in recognition of his reforms and German origins.

BLANTON, THOMAS LINDSAY *(1872–1957)*

Rep. Thomas Lindsay Blanton, who served consecutively for all but two years from 1917 to 1936, was known in the congressional cloakroom as *Hold*

That Line because it was considered virtually impossible to get him to change his political positions.

Blazing Star, A—See WARBURTON, WILLIAM.

BLIGH, WILLIAM *(1754–1817)*

Capt. William Bligh, remembered for his sadistic treatment of the crew of the *H.M.S. Bounty,* whose 1789 mutiny is the most notorious in history, was also involved in two other rebellions, earning him the nickname *The Man of Mutinies.* In 1797 Bligh was removed from the command of the *H.M.S. Director* after a mutiny calling for higher pay and stronger grog, which had been watered down to reduce drunkenness. In 1808 Bligh had to be removed from office as governor of New South Wales, Australia when his curtailing of alcohol sales resulted in the Rum Rebellion. Through it all Bligh was supported by the Admiralty but not by the British public, which referred to him as *That Bounty Bastard.*

Blind, The—See DIDYMUS.

Blind Emperor, The—See LOUIS III OF THE HOLY ROMAN EMPIRE.

Blind Magistrate, The—See FIELDING, JOHN.

Blind Mechanician, The: JOHN STRONG *(1732–1798)*

Although sightless from birth, Englishman John Strong proved to be a mechanical genius and was dubbed *The Blind Mechanician.*

Blind Naturalist, The—See HUBER, FRANCOIS.

Blind Poet, The—See GROTO, LUIGI; MILTON, JOHN.

Blind Poetess, The—See HAMILTON, JANET.

Blind Preacher, The—See MILBURN, WILLIAM HENRY; WADDEL, JAMES.

Blind Savant, The—See GORE, THOMAS PRYOR.

Blind Tom—See BETHUNE, THOMAS GREENE.

Blind Traveler, The—See HOLMAN, JAMES.

Blind White Devil, The—See BUCKLEY, CHRISTOPHER, A. "Blind Boss."

BLOCK, JOHN R. *(1919–   )*

As the U.S. secretary of agriculture under President Ronald Reagan, John R. Block was commonly called *Auction Block,* after farm foreclosures increased greatly due to depressed economic conditions.

Blockhead, The—See WORDSWORTH, WILLIAM.

Blonde Alibi, The—See ROLFE, LOUISE.

Blonde Bombshell, The—See HARLOW, JEAN.

BLOOD, THOMAS *(1618–1680)*

Col. Thomas Blood became famous in England as *The Crown Stealer* after a nearly successful attempt to remove the British crown jewels from the Tower of London in 1671. Caught with two confererates at the outer tower gate, Blood had with him the orb and ceremonial crown, but surprisingly, the culprits were not executed. King Charles II was so taken by the sheer gall of the plot that he granted all three a royal pardon and gave Blood a position at court. Later historical study has led to speculation that The Merry Monarch had been in on the plot to finance his playboy lifestyle and thus dared not let Blood go to trial.

Bloodiest Man in American History, The— See QUANTRILL, WILLIAM CLARKE.

Bloodshedder, The—See ABBAS.

Bloodthirsty, The—See MOULAY ISMAIL.

Bloody Bill Anderson: WILLIAM ANDERSON *(1840–1864)*

The most vicious guerrilla in Quantrill's Raiders during the Civil War was column leader William Anderson, who earned the sobriquet *Bloody Bill* for delighting in shooting down unarmed men and boys he figured were loyal to the Union. After he split from Quantrill, who was too peaceful for his liking, *Bloody Bill* led the raid on Centralia, Mo., numbering in his band 17-year-old Dingus James, better known as Jesse James. Anderson was shot from his saddle a month later in an engagement with Union troops.

Bloody Bridles Waite—See WAITE, DAVIS HANSON.

Bloody Butcher, The—See CUMBERLAND, WILLIAM AUGUSTUS, DUKE OF.

Bloody Mary: MARY I (1516–1558)

England's Mary Tudor, or Mary I, the daughter of Henry VIII, was dubbed *Bloody Mary* for her persecution of Protestants. The Bloody Mary, that "queen among drinks," was not, some saloon historians tell us, named after Mary I but rather after Mary Queen of Scots.

Bloody One-Handed, The—See LOISON, LOUIS HENRI, COMTE.

Bloody Shirt Foraker—See FORAKER, JOSEPH B.

BLOOMER, AMELIA JENKS (1818–1894)

A 19th century woman suffrage advocate, abolitionist and Unionist, Amelia Jenks Bloomer enjoyed her greatest fame for introducing an article of female apparel called the bloomer. The liberating garment was adopted by feminists in general, and Amelia Bloomer became known as *The Bloomer Girl,* a sobriquet she retained even when recruiting men in Iowa to fight for the northern cause in the Civil War.

Bloomer Girl, The—See BLOOMER, AMELIA JENKS.

BLOW, SUSAN ELIZABETH (1843–1916)

Traveling to Germany in 1870, young schoolteacher Elizabeth Blow learned of the concept of kindergarten originated there by Friedrich Froebel, and upon her return to the United States she convinced officials in St. Louis, Mo., to try the system. Called *The Mother of the Kindergarten,* she later founded a school to train kindergarten teachers and lived to see the system spread to every part of the country.

BLUCHER, GEBHARD LEBERECHT VON (1742–1819)

Gebhard Leberecht von Blucher, prince of Wahlstadt, was the Prussian field marshal who played key roles in the defeats of Napoleon at Leipsig in 1813 and at Waterloo in 1815. To his adulating countrymen he was *Marshal Forwards,* but Napoleon, not surprisingly, was less gracious and referred to him as *The Drunken Old Hussar.* Von Blucher took special pains to see to it that the latter sobriquet was correctly translated into German—*Der Versoffene Husar* (the "Old" being understood in this reference).

BLUDHORN, CHARLES (1930–1983)

Charles Bludhorn, an Austrian-American financier and business executive who built Gulf and Western into a giant conglomerate, was dubbed by Wall Streeters, more in awe than in disparagement, as *The Mad Austrian.*

Blue Jeans Governor, The—See WILLIAMS, JAMES DOUGLAS.

Blue Jeans Williams—See WILLIAMS, JAMES DOUGLAS.

Bluebeard: HENRI DESIRE LANDRU (1869–1922)

The nickname *Bluebeard* has been applied to many mass killers of women ever since the wife murderer first appeared in Charles Perrault's *Conte du Temps* in 1679. Today *Bluebeard* is most associated with the notorious Henri Desire Landru, who lured 10 women to their deaths over a period of five years with proposals of marriage. Early accounts in the French press after his arrest in 1919 described his beard as black or even blue-black, clearly an attempt to fit him better to the *Bluebeard* legend. Alas, Landru's beard was actually reddish brown, but no matter, he would forever be *Bluebeard*.

Bluebeard Hoch—See HOCH, JOHANN.

Bluff King Hal—See HENRY VIII.

BLUM, LEON (1872–1950)

Three-time prime minister of France, socialist Leon Blum was called *The Revolutionary in Pearl-gray Gloves,* a reference to his ability to communicate effectively with both factory workers and intellectuals. Because of his economic programs in the 1930s, he was also referred to as *The Father of France's New Deal.*

Blundering Brougham—See BROUGHAM, HENRY PETER, LORD.

Boar, The—See RICHARD III.

Bobbin Boy—See BANKS, NATHANIEL PRENTISS.

Bobby Fischer of Checkers, The—See HELLMAN, WALTER.

Bobby Fischer of His Day, The—See NIMZOWITSCH, ARNOLD.

Bobby Milk—See DE NIRO, ROBERT.

BOCCACCIO, GIOVANNI (1313–1375)

Poet and storyteller Giovanni Boccaccio, the author of the *Decameron,* probably Western Europe's most celebrated collection of stories, was celebrated as *The Prince of Story-Tellers.* He was also referred to as *The Bard of Prose.*

Boccaccio of the Nineteenth Century, The—See MONTIFAUD, MARC DE.

BOCCHERINI, LUIGI (1743–1805)

Famed Italian composer Luigi Boccherini was known for music that was marked by natural melody and fluent instrumentals, but his style was distinctly less than original. A profound admirer of Haydn, Boccherini imitated the former's style to such an extent that he was dubbed in music circles *Haydn's Wife.*

Body Love MacFadden—See MACFADDEN, BERNARR.

Body, The—See MCDONALD, MARIE.

Body Sellers, The: WILLIAM BURKE (c. 1792–1829) and WILLIAM HARE (c. 1792–1870?)

A pair of notorious graverobbers who supplied certain medical schools in Edinburgh, Scotland with bodies for experimentation, William Burke and William Hare eventually found such labors too difficult and decided it was easier to supply corpses by getting hapless victims drunk and strangling them. *The Body Sellers,* as they became known when apprehended in 1829, were charged with several murders. Burke was hanged, while Hare went free for testifying against his partner. An unpopular decision that had Hare on the run from angry mobs for weeks thereafter. The verb ''to burke'' derives from William Burke and means to kill by suffocation with few or no signs of violence.

BOGART, HUMPHREY (1899–1957)

Durable film ''tough guy'' Humphrey Bogart is known throughout the world as simply Bogie. His movie image is said to be an accurate reflection of his personality, and his nickname in the movie colony was *Whiskey Straight*.

BOIES, HORACE (1827–1923)

A leading Iowa politician who was elected governor in 1884 after switching from the Republican to the Democratic Party, Horace Boies was known as *Affidavit Boies* because he had such an honest face. He was a prime candidate for the Democratic presidential nomination in 1892.

BOILEAU-DESPREAUX, NICHOLAS (1636–1711)

French poet and critic Nicholas Boileau-Despreaux was nicknamed *The Law-Giver of Parnassus* for having methodically laid down the rules for almost every form of poetry in his *L'Art Poetique*. He was also called *The Flatterer* because he dedicated a number of his works to King Louis XIV, leaving his foes perplexed about how to attack him.

Boiling Water—See LEE, CHARLES.

BOISJOLIN, JACQUES FRANCOIS (1761–1841)

Having versified his thoughts on botany, Jacques Francois Boisjolin was known in later years as *The French Erasmus Darwin*.

BOLBER, MORRIS (c. 1890–1938)

Dr. Morris Bolber was infamous during the 1930s as *Philadelphia's Murdering Faith Healer*. When a female client wished to be rid of her spouse, Bolber and his aides would ''cast a spell'' on the man—for a fee—and, seemingly miraculously, he would soon be dead, generally from a sudden ''sickness'' or ''accident.'' It was estimated that between 30 to 50 Philadelphians in the Italian community died under Bolber's touch before he was sent to prison.

Boleslav the Mighty: BOLESLAV I OF POLAND (c. 966–1025)

Boleslav I, or *Boleslav the Mighty,* was honored as the *Charlemagne of Poland* because he enlarged the Polish domain by taking over lands left to his two brothers and seizing territories from the Bohemians, Pomeranians and Hungarians. He held these lands against the opposition of the Holy Roman emperors Otto III and Henry II, and forced or prevailed upon the latter to bestow on him the title King of Poland.

BOLEYN, ANNE (1507–1536)

Anne Boleyn, the second wife of King Henry VIII of England, lasted about three years before going to the block after Henry charged her with adultery with five men, including her own brother. Henry and his supporters called her *The Great Whore* and insisted she had actually had 100 lovers. Because of the length of her reign, she was also known as *Anne of the Thousand Days*. Just before her execution Anne predicted to her ladies-in-waiting that the people would have a new nickname for her: ''I shall be Queen Anne Lack-Head.'' However, it never caught on.

BOLIVAR, SIMON (1783–1830)

Called *The Liberator* and *The Washington of Colombia,* South American revolutionist Simon Bolivar led the liberation movement that freed northern South America from Spanish imperial rule. Uniting what are now several countries into one state, the Republic of Colombia, he tried to rule as a virtual dictator but faced separatist revolts in several areas, which broke away and formed independent states. *The Liberator* died in relative obscurity.

BOLTON, "Ice Box" BERNIE (c.1870–?)

Bernie Bolton, a gambler and con man who worked with the notorious Soapy Smith in the Klondike, had previously been a safe-blower of rather poor repute. He was saddled with the nickname *Ice Box Bernie* following one particularly embarrassing job in which he dynamited open an ice box in a meat market, mistaking it for a safe.

Bombast Russell—See RUSSELL, WILLIAM HOWARD.

Bomber Harris—See HARRIS, ARTHUR "Bomber."

BONANNO, JOSEPH—See Joe Bananas.

BONAPARTE, CHARLES JOSEPH (1851–1921)

Charles Joseph Bonaparte was a Baltimorian whose political interest in reform were questioned by foes, who referred to him as *The Imperial Peacock of Park Avenue,* an allusion to the exclusive area of the city where he lived and to the fact that he was the grandson of Napoleon Bonaparte. He was also labeled *Souphouse Charlie* because of his financial support of such charitable institutions as soup kitchens.

Boneless Wonder, The—See MACDONALD, RAMSAY.

Boney—See NAPOLEON BONAPARTE.

Boney Mahoney—See SOMERS, SUZANNE.

Bonehead—See MERKLE, FRED "Bonehead."

BONIFACE VIII, POPE (1228–1303)

Pope Boniface VIII was a most denounced pontiff, having been accused by foes of heresy, simony, licentiousness, haughtiness, despotism and other vices, which earned him the nicknames *The Prince of the New Pharisees* and *The Misleader of the Papacy.*

BONIN, WILLIAM (1947–   )

In 1981 34-year-old truck driver William Bonin was charged with being California's notorious *Freeway Killer,* who murdered 12 young men, ages 12 to 19, and dumped their bodies along freeways in 1979 and 1980.

Bonne Reine, La—See FRANCE, CLAUDE DE.

BONNET, STEDE—See Gentleman Pirate, The.

BONNEY, WILLIAM—See Billy the Kid.

Bonnie and Clyde: BONNIE PARKER (1910–1934) and CLYDE BARROW (1909–1934)

Bonnie Parker and Clyde Barrow were a famous Depression-era outlaw duo who robbed and murdered their way through Texas, New Mexico and Missouri, until they were killed in an ambush by Texas Rangers and sheriff's deputies. Together they were nicknamed *Bonnie and Clyde;* Barrow was also known as *Public Enemy No. 1 of the Southwest.* They were the subjects of a highly stylized 1967 movie titled with their nicknames.

Bonnie Prince Charlie—See STUART, CHARLES EDWARD.

BONNIVARD, FRANCOIS DE (1496–c. 1570)

Francois de Bonnivard, a Geneva politician and prelate, was nicknamed *The Prisoner of Chillon* after being confined in the dungeon of the Castle of Chillon for six years. He became the hero of Lord Byron's poem ''The Prisoner of Chillon.''

Book Doctor, The—See HALDLEMAN-JULIUS, EMANUEL.

BOOLE, ELLA A. (1858–1952)

The long-time president of the Women's Christian Temperance Union, Dr. Ella A. Boole was known as the unbending *Iron Chancellor of Prohibition.* Gray, motherly and plump, she spent 50 years fighting the evils of drink as well as vices of dancing, card-playing and theatergoing.

BOONE, DANIEL (1734–1820)

Daniel Boone, the pioneer, hunter and Indian fighter, was celebrated by the European Roman-tics as one of the most notable Americans of his era. He was called *The Noble Savage* and, by Lord Byron, *The Happiest Among Mortals.* The Indians too acknowledged his celebrity with the nickname *Wide Mouth,* perhaps based on one of his physical characteristics, because the Indians had come to know him as a man who could speak most glowingly but not always credibly.

Boone of the Rockies, The—See BRIDGER, JIM.

BOOTH, JOHN WILKES (1838–1865)

After his assassination of Abraham Lincoln in 1865, actor John Wilkes Booth was celebrated in much of Dixie as *The South's Avenging Angel.*

BOOTH, WILLIAM (1829–1912) and CATHERINE (1829–1890)

William Booth, the English preacher who founded the Salvation Army in 1865, organized it along military lines and assumed the title of *General Booth.* His wife Catherine, beloved within the organization, was called *The Mother of the Salvation Army.*

BORAH, WILLIAM E. (1865–1940)

A long-time senator from Idaho, William E. Borah was called *The Lone Lion,* for adopting positions that often placed him in lonely opposition to the entrenched establishment. During his unsuccessful attempt to prosecute labor leader Big Bill Haywood for murder, for instance, he enraged many fellow Republicans by simultaneously supporting the cause of organized labor and opposing business monopolies. During World War I he supported civil liberties at a time when the issue of free speech was less than popular. He subsequently opposed the League of Nations as being imperialist and later backed some aspects of the New Deal while attacking others. As always, *The Lone Lion* was prepared to stand alone.

BORDE, ANDREW—See Merry Andrew.

BORDEN, LIZZIE (1860–1927)

Lizabeth Andrew Borden was accused of killing her parents in 1892, but in a famous New England murder trial she was found innocent. She nevertheless was generally considered guilty, and for years thereafter the press often referred to her as *The Accused*. She was also subjected to one of the most famous bits of doggerel in American history:

> Lizzie Borden took an axe
> And gave her mother forty whacks.
> When she saw what she had done
> She gave her father forty-one.

BORMANN, MARTIN (1900–1945?)

Top Nazi official Martin Bormann was known as *The Brown Eminence* after he rose to the position of Hitler's deputy because his brutal execution of orders made him the quintessential Brown Shirt. Despite reports that he died trying to escape the Russians during the fall of Berlin, Bormann is said to be still alive and is the most wanted war criminal.

Born-Again Pornographer, The—See FLYNT, LARRY.

Boss—See FORD, JOHN.

Boss, The—See SPRINGSTEIN, BRUCE; TRUMAN, BESS.

Boss of the Bunny Empire—See HEFNER, HUGH.

Boss Thief—See HAYES, RUTHERFORD B.

Boss with the White Forehead, The—See CLUM, JOHN P.

Boston Amateur, The—See ADAMS, HENRY.

Boston Strangler, The: ALBERT H. DESALVO (1933–1973)

A mass murderer who killed 13 women in Boston over a 20-month period beginning in June 1962 was dubbed by the press *The Boston Strangler*. He was finally caught and identified as Albert H. DeSalvo, a man with a long list of sex offenses. Even after his incarceration for life, the public's morbid fascination with him continued. His letters drew high prices at auction. A sample quotation from one: "Boston people are sexpots, they all love sex. . . . Most broads are just waiting to get so-called raped." DeSalvo was proud of a paperback book about him and constantly tried to slip copies of it to female visitors at the institution where he was kept for a period. He had inscribed on the books: "Can't wait to get my hands around your throat." Another inmate or several inmates stabbed DeSalvo to death in his cell at the Walpole State Prison in 1973.

Boston Strong Boy, The—See SULLIVAN, JOHN L.

BOSWELL, JAMES (1740–1795)

Although he wrote what is considered the greatest English biography, *The Life of Samuel Johnson*, James Boswell was subjected to many barbs by those who sought to deflate Johnson's reputation. Horace Walpole called Boswell *Johnson's Zany* and Macaulay chimed in with *A Talebearer*. Others tried to dismiss him as *A Feather in the Scale* and *The Curious Scrapmonger*. More affectionately,

Boswell was called *The Bear-Leader,* because he was Johnson's constant companion. Johnson called him *Bozzy* but at times was exasperated by him and once declared, "Sir, you have but two topics, yourself and me. I am sick of both."

Botanist to the King—See BARTRAM, JOHN.

Bottomless Pit, The—See PITT, WILLIAM (the Younger).

BOUCHER, FRANCOIS (1704–1770)

The French painter Francois Boucher was dubbed *The Anacreon of Painting* and *The Painter of the Graces,* excessive tributes given solely because he was the favorite painter of Louis XV. For the same reason he was also hailed as *The French Raphael,* which many experts consider nothing short of blasphemy. They suggest, if anything, he be called *The Raphael of the Parc-aux-Cerfs,* which was a house in Versailles notorious as a harem of the king.

BOULANGER, GEORGES ERNEST JEAN MARIE (1837–1891)

The original *Man on Horseback,* Gen. Georges Boulanger shook the Third French Republic to its foundations during the 1880s by rallying numerous military officers to his side with appeals to their monarchical and clerical sentiments and the promise of a war of revenge against Germany. A skillful rabble-rouser, he rode down the boulevards of Paris on a prancing black war horse and, gesturing toward the Chamber of Deputies, gave cry to throwing the rascals out. He had powerful men behind him, but when the time came in 1889 for him to stage a coup, *The Man on Horseback* lost his courage and fled to Belgium. Two years later, when his nickname was being used to lampoon him, he committed suicide.

Bounty Bastard, That—See BLIGH, WILLIAM.

BOURDEILLE, PIERRE DE (1527–1614)

The French diarist Pierre de Bourdeille, lord of Brantome, has come down to us as *The Pepys of His Age.* But while the great British diarist supplied us with a wealth of important historical facts, de Bourdeille had a more limited viewpoint. As one critic stated, "If he could have kept his eyes upon [his age's] best rather than upon its worst features, [he] might possibly have been its Plutarch."

BOW, CLARA (1905–1965)

After starring as a passionate flapper in the movie *It* in 1927, actress Clara Bow was heralded as *The It Girl,* the pronoun signifying unlimited sexuality. When Gary Cooper, who had a small part in the movie, began keeping company with her, he was labeled The It Boy, an embarrassing sobriquet that allegedly caused him to break off the relationship.

BOWDLER, THOMAS (1754–1825)

The editor of the 10-volume *Family Shakespeare,* published in 1818, Englishman Thomas Bowdler chopped from the bard's works all phrases and scenes he felt to be indelicate. His prudish act of censorship resulted in the term *bowdlerize* and earned his the sobriquet *The Father of Bowdlerizing.*

Boy-Baccaleur, The—See WOLSEY, THOMAS.

Boy Explorer, The—See SIPLE, PAUL ALLMAN.

Boy General, The—See CUSTER, GEORGE ARMSTRONG.

Boy Genius, The—See WELLES, ORSON.

Boy Governor, The—See MASON, STEVENS THOMSON.

Boy-Hero of the Confederacy, The: SAM DAVIS (1842–1863)

A 21-year-old spy for the South during the Civil War, Sam Davis was honored as *The Boy-hero of the Confederacy* after choosing to be hanged rather than accept clemency in exchange for revealing the identity of his spy superior. Ironically, that man, Capt. Henry Shaw, a captive in the same Union prison, watched from his cell window as Davis went silently to the scaffold.

Boy Major, The—See PELHAM, JOHN.

Boy Mayor, The—See RUSSELL, WILLIAM E.

Boy Orator of the Platte, The—See BRYAN, WILLIAM JENNINGS.

Boy Preacher, The—See FURMAN, RICHARD; KENNEDY, CRAMMOND.

Boy Robot, The—See FISCHER, ROBERT JAMES.

Boy Scout, The—See DEWEY, THOMAS E.

Boy Socialist, The—See LONDON, JACK.

Boy Wonder of Wall Street, The—See RUBINSTEIN, SERGE.

BOYD, BELLE (1843–1900)

When her mother was being molested by a Union soldier, 18-year-old Belle Boyd killed him, thus beginning her long career as a thorn in the side of the federal army. Becoming a Confederate espionage agent, she reported directly to Brig. Gen. Jeb Stuart and Gen. Stonewall Jackson, providing valuable information that contributed to several of the South's early victories. Arrested and imprisoned twice, she was feared and hated in the North, where the press dubbed her *The Secesh Cleopatra,* the adjective being a slang term for Secession.

BOYLE, MICHAEL J. "Umbrella Mike" (fl. 1920s)

The business agent of a mob-dominated electrical workers union local in Chicago, Michael J. Boyle was dubbed *Umbrella Mike* because of his practice of standing at the bar of a nearby saloon twice weekly with an unfurled umbrella. Building contractors were assured labor peace by dropping donations into the umbrella.

BOZZARIS, MARKOS (c. 1788–1823)

Greek patriot and soldier Markos Bozzaris has been dubbed *The Leonidas of Modern Greece,* after the hero-warrior of ancient Sparta. Bozzaris' heroism at the Battle of Kerpenisi in 1823 closely paralleled the events at Thermopylae, and he is celebrated in Fitz-Green Halleck's poem ''Marco Bozzaris.''

Bozzy—See BOSWELL, JAMES.

BRADDOCK, JAMES J. *(1905–1974)*

Boxer James J. Braddock was nicknamed *The Forgotten Man* and *The Cinderella Man* because he had gone from a prominent and lucrative boxing career to obscurity and public welfare during the Great Depression, then came back to win heavyweight championship and a new fortune.

BRADFORD, WILLIAM *(1590–1657)*

Englishman William Bradford, a framer of the Mayflower Compact and a long-term governor of the Plymouth Colony, wrote the famous chronicle *History of Plimmoth Plantation* and other works that provide the first thorough account of life in the New World. He is credited with being *The Father of American History.*

BRADLEY, OMAR N. *(1893–1981)*

One of the top U.S. military leaders of World War II, Gen. Omar N. Bradley was known as *The GI's General.* He was highly popular with the troops, whose perception of him was that of a commander who always sought to mimimize losses to his men. Especially on the Sicilian front, this was in sharp contrast to the troops' view of Gen. George Patton, whose Old Blood and Guts sobriquet was explained by GI's as meaning "our blood and his guts."

BRADSHAW, JOHN *(1602–1659)*

John Bradshaw, the English lawyer who was president of the court that sentenced Charles I to death, was known as *The King's Murderer.*

Brady, Diamond Jim: JAMES BUCHANAN BRADY *(1857–1917)*

The noted millionaire and gourmand James Buchanan Brady was known as *Diamond Jim Brady* because of the valuable jewelry he wore. Valued at $2 million, his collection of jewelry included a set of shirt studs, vest studs and cuff links that cost $87,315. Never embarrassed by his gilt and glitter, *Diamond Jim* once said, "Them as has 'em wears 'em."

BRADY, JAMES *(1940–   )*

Presidential press secretary James Brady, who was critically wounded during the assassination attempt on Ronald Reagan in 1981, is nicknamed *The Bear.* As a child he was called *Pooh-Bear.*

BRAHE, TYCHO *(1546–1601)*

The noted Danish astronomer Tycho Brahe was nicknamed *Golden Nose* because he lost his nose in a duel and wore a replacement made of gold.

BRAHMS, JOHANNES *(1833–1897)*

The foremost exponent of the Romantic school of music, Johannes Brahms composed symphonies, piano works, concerti, chamber music, etc. His versatility inspired invective from a number of other composers, including Peter Ilich Tchaikovsky, who called him *Scoundrel Brahms* because he was "a giftless bastard."

Brain, The—See ROTHSTEIN, ARNOLD.

Brains of the Confederacy, The—See BENJAMIN, JUDAH PHILIP.

Brains of the Justice Department, The—See REHNQUIST, WILLIAM.

BRAITHWAITE, RICHARD
(1588–1693)

A minor pastoral poet of 16th century England, Richard Braithwaite anonymously wrote a book titled *Drunken Barnaby's Four Journeys to the North of England*, an account of the life of a wastrel. When Braithwaite died at the very ripe old age of 105, he was regarded as a "well bred gentleman and a good neighbor." More than a century later, in 1820, researchers determined he was the author of the book, and he has since borne the posthumous nickname *Drunken Barnaby*.

BRAND, MAX (1892–1944)

The author of 530 full-length books—notably the Dr. Kildare stories and countless westerns—Max Brand was called *The King of the Pulp Writers*. He died in Italy in 1944 while on a reporting assignment at the front. He was 51 years old at the time, which meant he had written a book on an average of every two weeks during his career as an author.

BRANDEIS, LOUIS D. (1856–1941)

Supreme Court Justice Louis D. Brandeis was called *The People's Attorney* for his long fight against financial monopolies, especially those of railroads and life insurance companies. He was also in the forefront of liberal causes, such as the campaign to establish minimum wage and hours laws. As a justice he was famous for many powerful dissenting opinions, usually in support of popular causes.

Brandy Nan—See ANNE, QUEEN OF ENGLAND.

BRAUN, WERNHER VON
(1912–1977)

German rocket expert Wernher von Braun avoided capture by the Russians during World War II and was taken prisoner by the Americans, who shipped him to the United States as a "ward of the Army" with 112 of his fellow scientists. He became a foremost figure in the U.S. space program, and was labeled by some *Our Nazi* to distinguish him from German scientists who had gone to work for the Russians, becoming *Their Nazis*.

Brave Jersey Muse, The—See PRYNNE, WILLIAM.

Bravest of the Brave, The—See NEY, MICHEL.

Brazilian Bombshell, The—See MIRANDA, CARMEN.

Brazilian Bonanza, The—See MIRANDA, CARMEN.

Bread-father, The—See SOWER, CHRISTOPHER.

Breadline Charlie (fl. 1920s)

One of America's legendary beggars, *Breadline Charlie* (his real name is unknown) carried in his pocket small chunks of stale bread that he would drop surreptitiously on a crowded street. Diving at the pavement with shrieks of joy, he would devour the crumbs as though he had not eaten in days, a routine that won him pity and cash from passersby.

Breeches Maker, The: DANIELE DA VOLTERRA *(1509–1566)*

When in 1555 Pope Paul IV ordered the removal of Michelangelo's paintings from the Sistine Chapel on the grounds they were obscene, he relented in the face of outraged protests, provided that all naked figures, including the angels and the Virgin Mary in *The Last Judgment,* had clothes painted on them. The task fell to Michelangelo's pupil Daniele da Volterra, who thereafter was referred to as *The Breeches Maker.*

BRENNAN, PETER J. *(1919–)*

Union leader Peter J. Brennan, the secretary of labor under President Richard Nixon, was known as *The Loyal Hard Hat* because of his firm support of the latter's Vietnam War policies, as were many real-life hardhats.

BREWSTER, RALPH OWEN *(1888–1961)*

When Maine Sen. Ralph Owen Brewster was a representative, his district included potato-growing Aroostook County. He was dubbed *The Aroostook Potato* by other representatives because he kept potatoes on display in his Washington office and gave away sacks of them to voters.

BREZHNEV, LEONID *(1906–1982)*

Soviet citizens gave Communist leader Leonid Brezhnev the whispered nickname *The Honest Dictator* in recognition of the fact that he granted much more personal freedom than had Stalin. In the last several years before his death Brezhnev threw lavish birthday parties for himself and encouraged being toasted as *The Most Celebrated Author on the Planet.*

BRICKNER, GUSTAVE A. *(1912–)*

Renowned as *The Human Polar Bear,* ice swimmer Gustave Brickner is most famous for his dip in Pennsylvania's Monongahela River on January 24, 1963, when the water temperature was 32 degrees F and the wind-chill factor was minus 85 degrees.

Bride of the Mafia, The—See HILL, VIRGINIA.

Brides in the Bath Murderer, The—See SMITH, GEORGE JOSEPH.

BRIDGER, JIM *(1804–1881)*

Western pioneer and scout Jim Bridger was nicknamed *The Boone of the Rockies,* a comparison few could quarrel with since, like Daniel Boone, he was an accomplished spinners of tall tales about his alleged accomplishments.

BRIDGETOWER, GEORGE AUGUSTUS POLGREEN *(1780?–1845)*

During his debut at London's Drury Lane Theater in 1790, George Augustus Polgreen Bridgetower, a young mulatto, drew tumultuous applause for a violin solo played between parts of the Messiah. Hailed thereafter as *The Abyssinian Prince,* he played the *Kreutzer Sonata* in concert with Beethoven in 1803.

Brigadier Commanding Hospitals—See BICKERDYKE, MARY A. "Mother."

BRIGHT, JOHN (1811–1889)

Like his partner-in-politics Richard Cobden, John Bright was a well-to-do English manufacturer who was the emotional oratorical genius behind the Anti-Corn-Law League. Abolition of the Corn Laws, which put a tariff on imports of that vital foodstuff as well as other foods, led to lower food prices for the masses and, consequently, lower production costs for manufacturers. Bright was particularly outspoken following the failure of the potato crop in Ireland in 1845 and the resultant famine that caused the death by starvation of over a million people. His brilliant and impassioned pleas for repeal could not long be resisted, and the change was effected the following year. Both he and Cobden shared the sobriquet *The Apostle of Free Trade*. (See also Cobden, Richard.)

BRILLAT-SAVARIN, ANTHELME (1755–1826)

The famed French gastronome Anthelme Brillat-Savarin was celebrated as *The Muse of the Stomach* after he published his book, or rather his bible, of good eating, *Physiologie du gout*. Among his observations were: ''Animals feed, man eats''; ''The fate of nations depends on how they are fed''; ''Tell me what you eat and I'll tell you what you are.'' A lawyer and judge, he was forced to flee his homeland for a time during the Revolution and spent that period in the quest of the enjoyment of good food and wine. Of Adam and Eve, he wrote: ''You, first parents of the human race, who ruined yourselves for an apple, what would you have done for a turkey cooked with truffles? But in Eden there were neither cooks nor confectioners.—How I pity you!''

BRINKLEY, JOHN RICHARD ''Goat Gland'' (1885–1942)

One of the most successful medical quacks in American history, John R. Brinkley made millions by convincing rich aging men that transplants of goat gonads would reawaken them sexually. His fame spread as *Goat Gland Brinkley,* despite frequent harassment by authorities who eventually stripped him of his radio stations, which he used to peddle various quackeries.

Britain's Mr. America—See COOKE, ALISTAIR.

British Aristides, The—See MARVELL, ANDREW.

British Homer, The—See MILTON, JOHN.

British Orson Welles, The—See RUSSELL, KEN.

British Roscius, The—See BETTERTON, THOMAS.

British Socrates, The—See BACON, FRANCIS.

Broad-Shouldered—See HAAKON II, KING OF NORWAY.

Broadway Butterfly, The—See GORDON, VIVIAN; KING, DOT.

Broadway Joe—See NAMATH, JOSEPH WILLIAM.

Broadway Rose: ROSE DYM (1912–)

A famous professional beggar who flourished in New York in the 1930s and 1940s, *Broadway Rose* was generally identified as Rose Dym, born Anna Dym. Starting out in 1929 as an eager teenage autograph hunter on Broadway, she made such a pest of herself that celebrities gave her money just to get rid of her. Soon she was asking for cash, refining her technique until she accepted only folding money. Jack Dempsey once fled his own restaurant when *Broadway Rose* showed up to put the bite on his famous customers. She would not take money from non-celebrities, sending them on their way with a scathing rejection: "Go get yourself a reputation, jerk, before I'll take your scratch." *Broadway Rose* disappeared from the Broadway scene when celebrities deserted the area.

BRODIE, WILLIAM (1759–1788)

A respected 18th century businessman and town councilman of Edinburgh, Scotland, William Brodie led a second life by night as the head of a band of cutthroats and thieves. When finally apprehended and hanged in 1788, he was labeled *The Man with Two Lives.* A century later Robert Louis Stevenson based a famous novel on his career, and Brodie has since been remembered as *The Real Dr. Jekyll and Mr. Hyde.*

Bronco Charlie—See MILLER, CHARLES "Bronco Charlie."

BRONFMAN, SAMUEL (1891–1971)

Canadian-American distillery tycoon Samuel Bronfman became one of the most respected men in Canada as the owner of Seagram & Sons, Ltd. He earned much of his fortune of $400 million—which won him recognition as *The Richest Man in Canada*—by supplying liquor to the great American bootleg gangs during Prohibition.

BROOKS, PRESTON S. "Bully" (1819–1857)

Angered by a harsh abolitionist speech made by Sen. Charles Sumner of Massachusetts in May 1856 in which he attacked a number of southern senators—Rep. Preston S. Brooks of South Carolina charged into the Senate chamber and proceeded to batter Sumner over the head with his heavy cane. The assault left Sumner nearly blind in one eye and disabled him for many years, but Brooks received scores of canes and whips from southern admirers. Dubbed *Bully Brooks,* he later apologized for his attack, which led many antebellum representatives to arm themselves with pistols or bowie knives, or both, while in the Capitol.

Brother Devil—See PEZZA, MICHELE.

Brother George—See LIBERACE, GEORGE J.

Brotherly, The—See PTOLEMY II.

BROUGHAM, HENRY PETER, LORD (1778–1868)

English orator, jurist, statesman and scientist Lord Henry Brougham was nicknamed *Harry Twitcher* because of a muscular affliction in his face. Politically, he collected a number of unflattering sobriquets, including *Blundering Brougham* from Lord Byron, *The God of Wiggish Idolatry* from Sir Walter Scott and *Foaming Fudge* from Disraeli.

BROWN, (Edmund G., Jr.) JERRY (1938–)

When he was the young Democratic governor of California, Jerry Brown was labeled *Governor Moonbeam* by those who found his opinions and stands a bit too mystical or "farout."

BROWN, LAUNCELOT "Capability" (1715–1783)

Famous English gardener Launcelot Brown laid out the great gardens of Kew and Blenheim and those of many other 18th century estates. He was called *Capability Brown* because, after viewing grounds to be worked on, he usually observed the land had "capability."

BROWN, MOLLY—See Unsinkable Molly Brown, The

BROWN, MORDECAI "Three-Fingered" (1876–1948)

Mordecai Brown, a premier baseball pitcher in the early 1900s, was called *Three-Fingered Brown* because he had lost half the index finger of his pitching hand in a farming accident. The stub was credited with allowing him to develop one of the best curve balls of all time, since it let him put an extra spin on the ball.

Brown, Three-Finger—See LUCCHESE, THOMAS.

BROWN, WILLIAM JOHN—See Done Brown.

Brown Bomber, The—See LOUIS, JOE.

Brown Eminence, The—See BORMANN, MARTIN.

Brown Sugar—See ARMSTRONG, LUCILLE.

Brown-Nose of the Year, The—See MAGRUDER, JEB STUART.

BROWNING, ROBERT (1812–1889)

Critics labeled poet Robert Browning *The Danton of Modern Poetry* for his literary style, which offered a realism and rugged abruptness that many found alive with emotion. The sobriquet was not universally accepted, however. Tennyson saw his style as reflecting a poet who "has plenty of music in him, but he cannot get it out."

BRUMM, GEORGE FRANKLIN (1878–   )

One of the more short-winded members of Congress during the 1920s and 1930s, George Franklin Brumm was nicknamed *Three-Minute Brumm* by colleagues because he never exceeded that amount of time when addressing the House of Representatives.

BRUMMEL, GEORGE BRYAN "Beau" (1778–1840)

George Bryan Brummel, a leader of fashionable London society, brought moderation and simplicity to men's apparel by, among other innovations, replacing breeches with trousers. Known as *Beau Brummel,* he lived an extravagent life and ultimately went insane and died in an asylum.

BRUNDAGE, AVERY (1887–1975)

As president of the International Olympic Committee from 1952 to 1972 and, previously, the U.S. Olympic Association, Avery Brundage was known as *Slavery Brundage* because of his insistence that participating athletes remain free of professionalism and any remuneration.

BRUNO, ANGELO (1910–1980)

Angelo Bruno, the leader of the Philadelphia Mafia, was called *The Gentle Don* because of his ability to keep peace within his organization. However, he was shot-gunned to death in 1980, an event that marked the beginning of a stuggle for control of organized crime in Philadelphia and the enticing new area of Atlantic City, where gambling had recently been legalized.

BRUNO, GIORDANO (1548–1600)

Influenced by Copernicus and other early scientists, Giordano Bruno, a 16th century Dominican friar, deserted his monastery and broke from scholasticism to become a hunted wanderer for the rest of his life. The more he contemplated the Copernican universe, the more he rejected all religious dogmas. Denounced by Rome as *The Heretic,* Bruno did not have time to systemize his thought before being captured and burned at the stake in Rome in 1600.

Brutus—See FELTON, JOHN.

BRUTUS, LUCIUS JUNIUS (fl. 500 B.C.)

One of the first to hold the supreme office of consul in the republic of ancient Rome, Lucius Junius Brutus played a leading part in the expulsion of Tarquin, the last of the city-state's kings. He earned the sobriquet *Stupid* for having two of his sons put to death for conspiring to restore the Tarquin dynasty.

BRYAN, WILLIAM JENNINGS (1860–1925)

William Jennings Bryan, a three-time Democratic candidate for president, was called *The Boy Orator of the Platte* by the press during his first try for the office in 1896. He was 36 years old at the time, only one year older than the minimum age for a presidential candidate.

BRYANT, PAUL WILLIAM "Bear" (1913–1983)

Legendary football coach *Bear Bryant* was known as *The Great Rehabilitator* for his success in re-building football teams at four U.S. colleges: Maryland, Kentucky, Texas A&M and, for the last 25 years, his alma mater, Alabama. He ended his career with 323 wins, 85 losses and 17 ties, probably the most successful record in the sport. Fellow coach Bum Phillips dubbed him *The John Wayne of the Football World,* but his most common sobriquet was *Bear,* often described as a reflection of his gruff, demanding style with players. The tag actually went back to his youth, however, when he wrestled a bear in an Arkansas theater. "There was a poster out front with a picture of a bear, and a guy was offering a dollar minute to anyone who would wrestle the bear," he explained. "The guy who was supposed to wrestle the bear didn't show up, so they egged me on. They let me and my friends into the picture show free, and I wrestled this scrawny bear to the floor. I went around later to get my money, but the guy with the bear had flown the coop. All I got out of the whole thing was a nickname."

BRYANT, WILLIAM CULLEN (1794–1878)

One of the country's first formal versifiers, William Cullen Bryant was designated *The Father of American Poets*. The title *The American Wordsworth* was also bestowed on him because his nature poetry was often compared with that of the English bard. Bryant's poems include "Thanatopsis" and "To a Waterfowl."

Bubbles—See SILLS, BEVERLY.

BUCHALTER, LOUIS (1897–1944)

Labeled by J. Edgar Hoover "the most dangerous criminal in the United States" during the 1930s, Louis Buchalter was the head of Murder Inc., and more commonly known as *Louis Lepke.* The name derived from "Lepkeleh," an affectionate Yiddish diminutive meaning Little Louis, which he was called by his mother. In mob circles *Lepke*— who went to the electric chair in 1944—

was anything but affectionate. As one mob associate noted with considerable awe, "Lep loves to hurt people."

BUCHANAN, JAMES (1791–1868)

As the 15th president of the United States, James Buchanan was called *The Bachelor President* because he never married. He was also called *Ten-cent Jimmy* because of his advocacy of low tariffs and low wages. His pro-southern bias in the bitter dispute over slavery made him unpopular, and Buchanan did not seek reelection. He retired to his home in Wheatland, near Lancaster, Pa., and lived out his days as *The Sage of Wheatland*.

BUCHHOLZ, HORST (1933–   )

German movie actor Horst Buchholz's nickname, *The Teutonic James Dean,* has proved to be more wish than reality. While he has won acclaim as an actor, he has failed to attract the cult following of the deceased but still popular American star.

Buckey—See O'NEILL, WILLIAM O. "Buckey."

BUCKINGHAM, WILLIAM ALFRED (1804–1875)

As governor of Connecticut from 1858 to 1865, William Alfred Buckingham was said to have been one of the Union's staunchest supporters among chief executives of the states. He was dubbed by all, including Lincoln, *Staunch Buckingham*.

BUCKLEY, CHRISTOPHER A. "Blind Boss" (1845–1922)

Christopher A. Buckley, Democratic boss of San Francisco from the early 1870s to 1890—probably the most politically corrupt era in the city's history—was known as *Blind Boss Buckley* after losing his vision in 1882. He nonetheless kept firm control of graft in the city and was able to recognize visitors by the way they shook hands (and, it was said, judge new acquaintances on their susceptibility to graft). The city's Chinese, who had to pay tribute for the right to practice gambling and prostitution and to sell opium, referred to the rapacious Buckley as *The Blind White Devil*.

BUCKNER, SIMON BOLIVAR (1823–1914)

While on sick leave from the Civil War, Confederate general Simon B. Buckner recuperated in Richmond, where he spent so much time writing poetry—an unlikely activity in the wartime Confederate capital—that he became known as *Simon the Poet*.

BUCKNILL, THOMAS TOWNSEND— See Sentimental Tommy.

Buffalo Bill: WILLIAM FREDERICK CODY (1846–1917)

Plainsman, pony express rider, Army scout and above all, showman, William Frederick Cody first achieved fame as a hunter for the Kansas Pacific Railroad by killing more buffalo (69) in one day than had the previous record-holder, *Buffalo Bill Comstock* (a mere 46). Cody thereafter appropriated the nickname *Buffalo Bill* and went on to greater fame as the star of his own Wild West show. (See also Matthewson, William *"Buffalo Bill."*)

Buffalo Hangman, The—See CLEVELAND, GROVER.

Buffoon, The—See HITLER, ADOLF; LINCOLN, ABRAHAM.

Bugs—See MORAN, GEORGE "Bugs."

Builder and the Beast, The—See WHITE, STANFORD.

BULETTE, JULIA C. (?–1868)

A frontier prostitute who rose to the level of madam and was hailed for her civic virtues, Julia C. Bulette was called *The Queen of the Comstock,* much to the dismay of the higher-minded society women of Virginia City, Nev. When she was murdered in 1868, it was said that every man in town marched in the funeral procession with the wives remaining out of sight so as not to see their husbands. The scene left little doubt as to Julia's right to her title.

Bull Head—See SUMNER, EDWIN VOSE.

Bull Moose, The—See ROOSEVELT, THEODORE.

Bull of Bavaria, The—See STRAUSS, FRANZ JOSEF.

Bull Run Russell—See RUSSELL, WILLIAM HOWARD.

BULLARD, EUGENE (1894–1961)

The world's first black combat aviator was an American named Eugene Bullard, who won his recognition from France rather than the United States during World War I. In 1914 he joined the French Foreign Legion and subsequently transferred to the French Flying Corps, where he earned the nickname *The Black Swallow of Death.* When the United States entered the war it was announced that all American pilots serving with the French would be commissioned as officers in the U.S. Army Air Corps, but because he was black, Bullard's application was ignored. He remained with the French and won the Croix de Guerre for heroism, only to be shifted later to the French infantry, allegedly because of bigotry. After the war Bullard became a bandleader in Paris, married a countess and owned several nightclubs. During World War II he served with the French underground. Receiving no further recognition, he later returned to the United States, where he lived out his last years in Harlem working at menial jobs. When he died in 1961 he was buried in the French War Veterans cemetery at Flushing, N.Y.

Bull-Dog of la Valliere, The—See RIVE, JEAN JOSEPH.

BULLER, REDVERS HENRY (1839–1908)

Although he had earned a considerable reputation in earlier military campaigns, English general Sir Redvers Henry Buller proved most ineffective in fighting the Boers in South Africa. After suffering several major defeats, he was labeled *Sir Reverse* by the public and even by his own men.

Bully Brooks—See BROOKS, PRESTON S.

Bum, The—See ELLSBERG, DANIEL.

BUNBURY, HENRY WILLIAM (?–1811)

Superior English caricaturist Henry William Bunbury was called *The Second Hogarth,* a nickname that may have been bestowed on him by painter Sir Joshua Reynolds.

Bunco—See KELLY, JOSEPH "Bunco."

Bungalow Mind—See HARDING, WARREN G.

BUNKE, HAYDEE TAMARA (?–1967)

The German Communist comrade of revolutionary Che Guevera, Haydee Tamara Bunke was called *The Unforgettable Guerrilla*. She died in Bolivia in 1967, as did her mentor Guevera.

Bunny—See WILSON, EDMUND.

Bunny Jockey, The—See BACON, MARY.

BURBANK, LUTHER (1849–1926)

American botanist Luther Burbank pioneered the improvement of many food plants through grafting, hybridization and other methods, and he developed such flowers as the Shasta daisy and the Burbank rose. Celebrated as *The Plant Inventor*, he preferred to think of himself as *An Architect of Nature*, the title of his autobiography. In recent years some have rather unkindly dubbed him *The Lysenko of the New World*, since he held to the Russian agronomist's largely discredited theory that environmental characteristics of plants can be inherited. Coming earlier to the study of botany, Burbank had more excuse for his theory for which he employed none of the Russian's strong-armed methods of acceptance.

BURFORD, ANNE M. (Gorsuch) (1942–   )

Anne M. Burford, during her tenure as embattled director of the scandal-ridden Environmental Protection Agency under Ronald Reagan, was known to agency employees as *The Ice Queen* for her seeming aloofness.

Burglar's Lobby in Washington, The—See WILLIAMS, EDWARD BENNETT.

BURGOYNE, JOHN (1722–1792)

Somewhat of a dandy, British general and dramatist John Burgoyne was nicknamed *Gentleman Johnny* by American colonists. He returned to England in defeat following his surrender at Saratoga in 1777 and was widely derided as *General Swagger* and, in various poems and ballads, as *Sir Jack Brag* and *That Martial Macaroni*. His honor was eventually restored and he resumed a successful career as a writer of witty comedies.

BURKE, ARLEIGH "31-Knot" (1901–   )

Adm. Arleigh Burke of the U.S. Navy gained recognition during World War II in the Pacific as *31-knot Burke* for maneuvering his destroyer fleet against the enemy with astonishing speed and skill.

BURKE, EDMUND (1729–1797)

Edmund Burke, the British statesman generally regarded as the founder of the modern Conservative Party, was called *The Dinner-Bell* due to his habit of making such long speeches in Parliament that members missed their dinners.

BURKE, ELMER "Trigger" (1917–1958)

Regarded by the 1950s' underworld as one of the most dependable of "hitmen," Elmer *"Trigger"* Burke earned his monicker not simply for his ability as a tommy-gunner but because of the uninhibited and mindless way he used the weapon. Assigned to eliminate Joseph "Specs" O'Keefe, a member of the gang that pulled the great Brinks robbery, who was suspected of informing, he pursued his quarry through the streets of Boston firing burst after burst from a machine gun. He managed only to wound O'Keefe, however, who then started talking to the police. Burke died in the electric chair in 1958 for one of his many murders.

BURKE, JAMES (1809–1845)

James Burke, an English deaf mute who was the world's heavyweight boxing champion from 1833 to 1839, was known affectionately by the British public as *The Deaf'un*. The first English champion to venture to the United States in search of competition, he found a dearth of worthy challengers. His foremost opponent was a bruiser named Tom O'Connell, who lasted 10 minutes in a bout with him near Harts Island, N.Y.

BURKE, WILLIAM (1870–?)

Reformed criminal William Burke became known as *Philadelphia's Jean Valjean* in 1912, after the ill-fated hero of Victor Hugo's novel *Les Miserables*. An accomplished burglar who had served seven years in a Massachusetts prison, he settled in Philadelphia after his release and became an honest cigar store proprietor. He married and in 1911 was elected to the city council on a reform ticket. Unfortunately, he was recognized by a former convict who began to blackmail him, prompting Burke to resign his position and admit his past. He then faded into an embittered obscurity.

BURKE, WILLIAM—See Body Sellers, The.

BURNS, ARTHUR F. (1904–)

Arthur F. Burns, former chairman of the Federal Reserve Board, was often called by detractors *The Sugar Daddy of Big Bankers*.

BURNS, ROBERT (1759–1796)

Scottish poet Robert Burns was known as *The Peasant Bard* for using dialect in his verses. On a more personal level he was called *The Fornicator* by his fellow churchgoers following publication of his poem "The Fornicator," which detailed his affair with "Betsy," a servant girl in his mother's household. Burns was permitted to remain in the church after receiving a rebuke before the congregation.

BURNS, ROBERT ELLIOTT (1890–1965)

America's most famous chain gang escapee, Robert Elliott Burns was responsible for ending the inhuman Georgia chain gang system by creating a public uproar with a book and movie about his experiences. Burns, after numerous efforts by Georgia authorities to have him returned were rebuffed by northern officials, spent the rest of his life fighting for penal reform. He was called *The Man Who Broke a Thousand Chains*.

BURNS, WILLIAM J. (1858–1932)

The founder of the American detective agency that bears his name, William J. Burns was often described both in government and private service as *Never Fail Burns* and *The Incredible Detective*. The former sobriquet was considered rather excessive by the controversial Burns, but not even his most vehement detractors could deny that some of his detective work truly incredible. Despite being involved in labor union scandals and the Teapot Dome case, Burns undoubtedly deserved the evaluation once made of him by the *New York Times*: "the greatest detective certainly, and perhaps the only really great detective, the only detective of genius whom the country has produced."

Burns of the Green Mountains, The— See EASTMAN, CHARLES G.

BURR, AARON (1756–1836)

Aaron Burr, vice president of the United States under Thomas Jefferson, lost the race for governor of New York and, holding Alexander Hamilton responsible, killed him in a duel in 1804. He later conspired with Gen. James Wilkerson to invade Mexico and form an independent nation, for which he was tried for treason but acquitted in 1807. He nonetheless was saddled thereafter with such negative sobriquets as *The Napoleon of the West, The Great American Rascal* and *The Mephistopheles of Politics.*

BURRITT, ELIHU (1811–1879)

Elihu Burritt of Connecticut, a noted 19th century Biblical scholar and linguist, was known as *The Learned Blacksmith,* after having left the forge for his new calling.

BURROWES, PETER (1752–1841)

Irish Judge Peter Burrowes was often called *The Goldsmith of the Bar* because his squeaky voice was similar to that of poet and dramatist Oliver Goldsmith, whose wretched way of talking had earned him the sobriquet *Goldy.*

BUSSY, GEORGE (1735–1805)

Englishman George Bussy, who held many posts in the court of George III, was called *The Prince of Macaronis.* A Macaroni at the time was a fop who affected elegant manners and was given to such fashionable tastes as Italian food. When Yankee Doodle Dandy stuck a feather in his cap and called it macaroni, he was twitting the British.

Buster—See DEWEY, THOMAS E.

Buster—See KEATON, JOSEPH FRANCIS "Buster."

Butch—See LA GUARDIA, FIORELLO H.

Butcher Boy, The—See WANDERER, CARL.

Butcher Grant—See GRANT, ULYSSES S.

Butcher Hood—See HOOD, JOHN BELL "Butcher."

Butcher of Budapest, The—See KHRUSHCHEV, NIKITA.

Butcher of Cesena, The—See CLEMENT VII, POPE.

Butcher of Culloden, The—See CUMBERLAND, WILLIAM AUGUSTUS, DUKE OF.

Butcher of Dachau—See BLACKMUN, HARRY A.

Butcher of England, The—See TIPTOFT, JOHN.

Butcher's Dog, The—See WOLSEY, THOMAS.

BUTE, LORD (1713–1792)

Lord Bute of England was often called *Another Machiavel* because of his influence over King George III and a number of the nation's statesmen. His most popular nickname was *The Wire-Master,* and he was often so caricatured in published drawings that showed him standing behind a box and manipulating wires to make several of the king's ministers dance.

BUTKUS, DICK "the Animal" (1942–)

The great middle linebacker of the Chicago Bears football team, Dick Butkus was nicknamed *The Animal* because of the way he punished opponents daring to pass through his area of defense. Equally colorful is the accolade of *The Guru of Gore*.

BUTLER, BENJAMIN (1818–1893)

One of the most hated Union generals in the South during the Civil War, Ben Butler occupied New Orleans, where his command was marked by such incidents as the hanging of William Mumford for tearing down the American flag and his infamous "Woman Order," in which he declared that "when any female, shall, by word, gesture, or movement, insult or show contempt for any officer or soldier of the United States, she shall be regarded and held liable to be treated as a woman of the town plying her avocation." Known throughout the Confederacy as *Beast Butler,* he was declared an outlaw by Jefferson Davis. Later, falsely accused of stealing silver from a church, he was dubbed *Spoons Butler*. Residents of New Orleans showed their low opinion of him with the nickname *Picayune Butler,* the appellative of the black barber in the basement of the St. Charles Hotel. His own troops referred to him as *Cock-eye* because one of his eyes was afflicted with strabismus.

BUTLER, SAMUEL (1835–1902)

British novelist Samuel Butler, the son of a clergyman, refused to take up the cloth and instead wrote satires of contemporary religion, winning the sobriquet *The Earnest Atheist*. He was also called *The Mid-Victorian Modern* because his writing opened the way for the frank expression of unorthodox attitudes, long repressed in the Victorian era.

BUTLER, SMEDLEY DARLINGTON (1891–1940)

Gen. Smedley Darlington Butler of the U.S. Marine Corps was nicknamed *Old Gimlet Eye* by his men because of his fierce, glaring eyes. It was said that even in the dark he could spot whether or not uniform buttons had been polished.

BUTLER, THOMAS (1748–18??)

Col. Thomas Butler, an Irish-American, was nicknamed *The Navarre of the American Revolution* because his leadership and bravery on the battlefield resembled that of France's Henry of Navarre, or Henry IV.

Butter—See SPRING, TOM.

Butterfingers—See MORAN, THOMAS B. "Butterfingers."

Butterfly Spy, The—See BADEN-POWELL, ROBERT STEPHENSON SMYTHE.

BUTTERWORTH, MARY (1686–1775)

Mary Butterworth, a 30-year-old housewife with seven children, was the leader of one of the first successful counterfeiting rings in America. Probably the first woman of her calling, she was dubbed *The Kitchen Counterfeiter* because she did all the work in her kitchen with a hot iron and some starched muslin.

BYRD, HARRY F. (1887–1966)

Harry F. Byrd, the Virginia governor who subsequently served as a U.S. senator from 1933 until 1965, was nicknamed *Mr. Economy* because of his reputation as a fiscal conservative.

BYRON, AUGUSTA ADA (1815–1852)

Lord Byron nicknamed his daughter Augusta Ada *The Little Electra* because, he said, he expected that when she came of age she would remain loyal to him against her mother, as in the manner of the mythological Greek princess Electra, who helped avenge the murder of her father by her mother.

C

Cabinet Judas, The—See FORRESTAL, JAMES V.

CADE, JOHN "Jack" (?–1450)

Promising to end royal abuses, English rebel Jack Cade gathered a large army of men from Kent and Sussex and marched on London, winning the nickname *Jack-Amend-All*. His force of 30,000 defeated a royal army but later accepted a pardon and dispersed. Cade was then seized and executed.

CADMUS OF MILETUS (fl. mid-6th century B.C.)

The ancient Greek Cadmus of Miletus is the earliest scribe about whom there is definite information. Dubbed *The World's First Historian,* he wrote a history of Ionia and speculated on the cause of the periodic flooding of the Nile.

CADOUDAL, GEORGES (1771–1804)

French conspirator Georges Cadoudal was nicknamed *The Great Bullet-Head* for being an unswerving and unrepentant royalist. He fled to England in 1800 and subsequently refused an offer of a rich pension from Napoleon to serve him as a lieutenant-general. He returned to France in 1802 and formed an ill-fated conspiracy to overthrow Napoleon. He was executed in 1804. Napoleon said of him, "His mind was cast in the true mould; in my hands he would have done great things."

Caesar—See LINCOLN, ABRAHAM.

CAESAR, JULIUS (102 or 100–44 B.C.)

During his Egyptian campaign Julius Caesar besieged the palace at Alexandria and had his forces fire the Egyptian fleet. Flames quickly spread to the docks and set buildings on fire including the fabulous 250-year-old Alexandrine library. Although he could readily have had the conflagration extinguished, Caesar allowed the building and all its great manuscripts and ancient scrolls to be destroyed, earning the disparaging sobriquet *The Arsonist.*

CAFARELLI (1703–1795)

Cafarelli (or Caffareli), a famous castrated Italian opera singer of the 18th century, was nicknamed *The Insolent,* a mood not at all uncommon among the castrati of that day, especially in their middle and later years.

CAILLET, GUILLAUME (?–1359)

French revolutionary Guillaume Caillet, who led an uprising of 20,000 peasants against the government, has come down to us as *The Jack Cade of France,* after the ill-fated 15th century English rebel. (See Cade, John "Jack.")

CAIN, JAMES M. (1892–1977)

U.S. novelist James M. Cain, the author of such "hard-boiled" fiction as *The Postman Always Rings Twice* and *Double Indemnity,* as well as 16 other books, was dubbed *The Poet of the Potboiler.*

CAIN, PATRICK J. (1878–1949)

U.S. theatrical scenery warehouser Patrick Cain was known among Broadway theater folk as *The Custodian of Flops*.

Cain of Literature, The—See HENLEY, JOHN; HILL, JOHN.

Calamity Jane: MARTHA JANE CANNARY (1852–1903)

An exceptionally plain, hard-driving frontier drunk and prostitute, Martha Jane Cannary was romantically linked in a number of dime novels with Wild Bill Hickok, who in reality regarded her as no more than one of the boys. She dressed as a man and was nicknamed *Calamity Jane* because, according to some, a calamity or wild event was sure to take place whenever she was around, especially when she was drunk. An even less flattering theory is that the name referred to her looks.

CALDER, ALEXANDER (1898–1976)

Internationally acclaimed U.S. artist Alexander Calder was called *The Magical Maker of Mobiles* for his moving sculptures and *The Magical Maker of Stabiles* for his huge stationary outdoor pieces.

CALHOUN, JOHN C. (1782–1850)

John C. Calhoun carried two sets of nicknames: One referred to his almost constant agitation for war against England, the other to his unending support of slavery. Thus, he was called *The Warhawk* for encouraging the War of 1812 and, later, as secretary of war under President James Monroe, for preparing for what he believed would be certain further conflict with the British. As a pro-slaver he was called *The Napoleon of Slavery* and *The Great Nullifier*, the latter for his support of the doctrine of nullification.

California Hercules, The—See JEFFRIES, JAMES J.

CALIGULA (12–41)

The Roman emperor Caligula, who became more brutal and irrational as illness affected his mind, was called *The Horse Emperor* after he bestowed the rank of consul upon his favorite horse, Incitatus. The beast enjoyed all the honors of the office and was stabled in an ivory manger, where it was provided with a gold goblet from which to drink wine.

CALLEY, WILLIAM (1943–   )

Although convicted by court-martial of the mass murder of civilians at My Lai during the Vietnam War, Lt. William Calley of the U.S. Army retained a hard core of supporters who referred to him as *Hero Calley*.

CALLIMACHUS (fl. 5th century B.C.)

The early Greek sculptor Callimachus has been designated *The Father of the Corinthian Column*.

Callous Ox, The—See KALTENBRUNNER, ERNST.

CALVIN, JOHN (1509–1564)

Hounded from his native France and the Rhineland because of his religious convictions, Protestant reformer John Calvin settled in Geneva in 1536 but was expelled two years later because of the strictness of his system. In 1541, however, the Geneva council prevailed upon him to return because the town had become disorganized spiritually and morally in his absence. He remained there the rest of his life, a powerful voice of Protestantism who was referred to as *The Pope of Geneva.*

CAMBIO, ARNOLFA DEL
(1232–1300)

Because some authorities see similarities between the works of 13th century architect and sculptor Arnolfo del Cambio, a predecessor of Michelangelo, and those of Michelangelo, he has been called *The Michelangelo of the Middle Ages.*

CAMDEN, WILLIAM *(1551–1623)*

For his history of England, a work described as "the common sun where-at our modern writers have all lighted their little torches," William Camden was dubbed *The Nurse of Antiquity, SchoolMaster Camden* and *The English Strabo,* after the illustrious Greek geographer-historian.

Camel-Driver of Mecca, The—See MOHAMMED.

CAMERON, EVAN *(1629–1719)*

Sir Evan (or Ewen) Cameron, the great fighting Scot of Lochiel, was called *The Ulysses of the Highlands* after having been held hostage for six years by the marquis of Argyll. He later engaged in famous feuds with the Macdonalds and the Macintoshes and, at various times, fought the English.

CAMOENS, LUIS *.(1524–1579)*

Called *The Homer of Portugal* and *The Apollo of Portugal* for the beauty of his poetry, Luis Camoens, author of the *Lusiad,* stands as an example of a personage who reaped no benefit from his laudatory sobriquets. He was allowed to die in the streets in abject poverty.

CAMP, WALTER CHAUNCEY
(1859–1925)

Although he did not invent football, Walter Camp is credited with being *The Father of American Football* for having totally altered the rules of the game. Football was little more than a parody of English rugby until Camp introduced the line of scrimmage, reduced the number of players from 15 to 11, conceived the idea of four downs and created the position of quarterback. The result was a game that turns millions of American wives into "widows" every Sunday afternoon during the football season.

CAMPAGNA, LOUIS "Little New York" *(1900–1955)*

Louis Campagna was a mindless, brutal gangster whom Al Capone imported to Chicago as a trusted bodyguard. He once planned an assault on the Chicago Detective Bureau lockup to get at a rival gangster being held there and was foiled only when he and his men were recognized. Capone personally nicknamed him *Little New York Campagna* to demonstrate to his enemies that he had the ability to import all the muscle he needed to triumph over them.

CAMPBELL, MARY—See Highland Mary.

Canadian Kipling, The—See SERVICE, ROBERT WILLIAM.

Canadien Comet, The—See MORENZ, HOWARD WILLIAM "Howie."

Canary Who Couldn't Fly, The—See
RELES, ABE.

Candid Spoilsman, That—See
FARLEY, JAMES A.

CANHAM, ERWIN D. "Spike" (1904–1982)

The long-time editor of the *Christian Science Monitor*, Erwin D. Canham was credited by media critics with helping to make the new paper one of the most respected and influential in the United States. His nickname *Spike*, unusual for a man of his dignified bearing, bestowed on him by columnist Roscoe Drummond. "Erwin was such a scholarly type that I thought he needed a nickname," Drummond explained. "So I gave him the most incongruous one I could think of."

CANIFF, MILTON (1907–   )

American cartoonist Milton Caniff who created the comic strips "Terry and the Pirates," "Steve Canyon" and "Male Call," has been dubbed *The Rembrandt of the Comic Strip*.

CANNARY, MARTHA JANE—See
Calamity Jane.

Cannibal—See **ADDERLEY, JULIAN "Cannonball."**

CANNING, CHARLES JOHN "Clemency" (1812–1862)

While serving as governor-general of India, Charles John Canning, son of the British statesman George Canning, crushed the great Sepoy Rebellion of 1857 and was made the country's first viceroy the following year. Surprisingly lenient in his policy toward natives after the uprising, he was attacked by political opponents, who nicknamed him *Clemency Canning*. The sobriquet has often been erroneously attributed to his father.

CANNING, GEORGE (1770–1827)

Called *The Cicero of the British Senate* by his friends and *The Zany of Debate* by his opponents, English statesman George Canning was a master orator few could best with a cutting remark. Even non-politicians felt his verbal lash, as when a clergyman once asked him:
    "How did you like my sermon, Mr. Canning?"
    "You were brief," Canning responded.
    "Yes, you know I avoid being tedious."
    "But you *were* tedious."

CANNON, ISABELLA W. (1902–   )

In 1976, at the age of 74, Isabella W. Cannon ran—in sneakers—as the Democratic candidate for mayor of Raleigh, N.C. Nicknamed *The Little Old Lady in Tennis Shoes*, for wearing sneakers throughout the campaign, she won the race handily and continued to wear her sneakers to work at city hall.

CANNON, JAMES, JR. (1864–1944)

One of the most colorful and controversial foes of liquor, American Methodist bishop James Cannon, Jr., was dubbed *The Dry Messiah* for his considerable effort in helping pass the Eighteenth Amendment, which imposed prohibition on the land. In 1928 he was deeply involved in a political controversy with Sen. Carter Glass of Virginia, who denounced him as *The Methodist Pope* for opposing Al Smith's run for the presidency, allegedly on the grounds Smith was a Catholic. During a subsequent scandal, evidence presented to Senate committees and church governing bodies indicated that Cannon had hoarded flour and other scarce foods during World War I and that, more recently, he had made a killing in a gambling operation in stocks. Cannon was also charged with violation of the Corrupt Practices Act, for having accounted for only $17,000 of $65,000 given him by a leading businessman "to elect Hoover." Cannon was acquitted of the charges and his church exonerated him, or at least forgave his errant ways. Still, the bishop's influence as a moral leader dropped quite a bit, and he went into semiretirement a few years later as *The Lost Leader*.

CANNON, JOSEPH GURNEY (1836–1926)

A noted leader of reactionary Republicans, Joseph Gurney Cannon of Illinois ruled the House of Representatives despotically as chairman of the Rules Committee and, from 1903 to 1911, as speaker of the House. Official biographies claim his nickname was *Uncle Joe,* but in the House cloakroom he was called *Czar Cannon.* He was finally stripped of the power to appoint committees by a coalition of Democrats and Progressive Republicans.

Cannon King, The—See KRUPP, ALFRED.

CANO, ALONZO (1600–1676)

Seventeenth century Spanish painter, architect and sculptor Alonzo Cano has been designated *The Spanish Michelangelo.*

CANTINFLAS (1917–   )

The mustached Mexican actor-comedian Cantinflas, who often played a befuddled Everyman, has been dubbed *Mexico's Charlie Chaplin.*

CANTOR, EDDIE (1892–1964)

American comedian and song-and-dance man Eddie Cantor was nicknamed *Banjo Eyes,* a physical description he was said not to have appreciated until he heard it used with affection by fans.

Cap the Knife—See WEINBERGER, CASPAR.

Cap the Suitcase—See WEINBERGER, CASPAR.

CAPERN, EDWARD (1819–1894)

Assuredly the only British rural letter carrier to merit an entry in the *Dictionary of National Biography,* Edward Capern won attention as *The Postman Poet* because of his verses, published from 1856 on. They won critical acclaim for their imaginative simplicity in depicting rural scenes and situations.

CAPONE, ALPHONSE "Scarface Al" (1899–1947)

Legendary gang leader Alphonse Capone was known as *Scarface Al* due to a huge scar on his left cheek, received, he said, while fighting in the famed "Lost Battalion" in France. Alas, Capone never served in World War I. While employed as a bouncer in a Brooklyn saloon-bordello, he was scarred by a knife wielded by a hoodlum named Frank Galluccio in a fight over a young lady's charms. (See also Introduction.)

CAPONE, JAMES (1887–1952)

James Capone, the eldest brother of Chicago gang leader, Al Capone, left the fold long before the other Capone brothers became mobsters. Taking the name Richard James Hart, he became a lawman in Nebraska, earning the nickname *Two Gun Hart*. His surprising true identity was not revealed until 1940. He was not entirely the "white sheep" of the Capone family, however, having lost his police job in Homer, Neb. because of dishonesty.

CAPONE, RALPH "Bottles" (1893–1974)

An older brother of Chicago gang leader Al Capone, Ralph Capone was in charge of the mob's efforts during Prohibition to control the soda water used in mixed drinks. He set up a number of soda-water plants and was referred to thereafter by the underworld as *Bottles*.

CAPOTE, TRUMAN (1924–   )

U.S. novelist and short story writer Truman Capote has been called *The Glitterati Tiny Terror* for revealing the intimate secrets of his rich and famous friends. When cries of outrage met the publication of excerpts of his gossipy book *Answered Prayers,* in the mid-1970s, Capote was puckishly, some say sadistically, delighted. "They knew I was a writer, that this is my job. Were they really so stupid that they thought I wouldn't write about them?" Among other tidbits Capone has left for posterity is his claim that he has slept with all of his psychiatrists.

Capsize Kid, The—See TURNER, TED.

Captain Jack—See Black Rifle.

Captain Louisa—See LABE, LOUISA.

Captain Outrageous—See TURNER, TED.

Captain Rag—See SMITH, EDMUND.

Captain Shrimp—See STANDISH, MILES.

CARAVAGGIO, MICHAELANGELO MERISI DA (1565–1609)

Michaelangelo Merisi da Caravaggio has been called the first "popular" artist, for seeking to duplicate reality exactly. His paintings were filled with realistic depictions of corpses, holy executions and flagellations, and the artistic merit of his works was the subject of hot disputes. Called *The Master of Light and Violence* for both his canvases and his private life, he prowled the streets of Rome after dark, always armed and seeking quarrels. In 1606 he was forced to go into hiding after committing a murder over a gambling dispute. Subjected to many wounds, prison mistreatment and illnesses, Caravaggio died at the age of 44.

CARAWAY, HATTIE (1878–1950)

Hattie Wyatt Caraway, Democratic senator from Arkansas and the first woman elected to that body, was nicknamed *Knitting Hattie* because she frequently brought her knitting to the Senate chamber.

CARDIAC, JEAN LOUIS (1719–1726)

A French child prodigy known as *The Wonder Child,* Jean Louis Cardiac could recite the alphabet at three months and translate Latin into French and English at the age of four. He also mastered Greek and Hebrew and had accumulated advanced knowledge in history, geography and arithmetic by the time he was six. He died at the age of seven.

Cardinal's Hangman, The—See LAFFEMAS, ISAAC DE.

Carl Sagan of Union Dumping, The—See DEMARIA, ALFRED T.

CARLETON, MARY (c. 1642–1673)

An English criminal, bigamist, thief and actress, Mary Carleton was called *The German Princess* and *The Counterfeit Lady* after having swindled large sums of money from leading figures in London society by pretending to be of German royal blood and the heiress to a considerable fortune. She even acted in a play she had written about her alleged life. Finally exposed as a fraud, she was charged as a swindler, but was acquitted due to her considerable guile and masterful performance in the dock. The scandal brought her even more celebrity as *The German Princess,* but her luck failed, and in 1672 she was charged with a number of thefts, found guilty and hanged at Tyburn on Jan. 22, 1673. Before her execution she admitted she was not even German but merely the daughter of a Canterbury Cathedral chorister.

CARLETON, WILLIAM (1798–1869)

For his farming origins, his tributes to love and his portraits of rustic life, Irish writer William Carleton earned the sobriquet *The Prose Burns of Ireland.*

Carlo Khan—See FOX, CHARLES JAMES.

Carlos—See Carlos the Jackal.

Carlos the Jackal: ILICH RAMIREZ SANCHEZ (1949–   )

Considered by law enforcement agencies to be the most dangerous terrorist in the world during the 1970s and 1980s, Venezuelan Ilich Ramirez Sanchez is better known by the sobriquet *Carlos the Jackal* or *Carlos.* His deadly trail has been littered with innocent victims: travelers caught in the Tel Aviv airport massacre in 1972; four murdered in Paris, including two French intelligence officers, in 1975; the kidnapping of OPEC ministers in Vienna in 1975, during which three people were killed; and Israeli athletes at the 1972 Munich Olympics.

CARLSON, EVANS F. (1896–1947)

One of the most heroic if controversial military figures of World War II, Lt. Col. Evans F. Carlson of the U.S. Marine Corps became famous as the leader of Carlson's Raiders, whose battle cry was "Gung Ho." However, he was accused of being a leftist and an *Apostle of Communist Causes* by *Time* magazine because of his controversial comments. Of the armed forces he said: "Our greatest weakness is the caliber of our officers." Of capitalism: "I burn up . . . when I think of all the good guys who went out and got killed to protect the rights of a handful of sons of bitches to make more money for themselves." Despite later attacks on him for his political naivete, Carlson finished the war as one of the nation's most decorated fighting men, and they still sing songs in the Marine Corps about a man who fought World War II his own way.

CARLYLE, THOMAS (1795–1881)

Scottish historian and essayist Thomas Carlyle was called *The Censor* and *The Censor of the Age* because of his fault-finding and critical spirit. He is sometimes called *The Chelsea Philosopher,* having taken up residence at Cheyne Row, Chelsea in 1834 and remaining there for the rest of his life.

CARNEGIE, ANDREW (1835–1919)

U.S. industrialist Andrew Carnegie was called *The Steel King.* Later, when he sold his interests to U.S. Steel and turned to philanthropic Carnegie Endowments, including his Endowment for International Peace, he was called *The Prince of Peace.* It remained for the writer John Dos Passos to append to the latter sobriquet the phrase ''except in time of war.''

CARNERA, PRIMO (1906–1967)

The world heavyweight boxing champion of 1933–34, Primo Carnera was viciously exploited by his backers and referred to as *The Ambling Alp,* a description not only of his physical size but of his mental abilities. It was said tht 105 percent of him was sold to investors and that Primo was allowed to keep the rest. He ended up broke and finished his days parodying himself on the wrestling circuit.

CARNOT, LAZARE NICOLAS MARGUERITE (1753–1823)

French general Lazare Nicolas Marguerite Carnot reorganized the French revolutionary armies in 1793 to score great victories over the interventionists. Republican in outlook, he retired rather than serve under Napoleon but returned in 1814 when the nation was threatened by the Allies. Napoleon's minister of the interior during the Hundred Days, he was sent into exile after Waterloo. His remains were finally returned to Paris in 1889 and he was given the honorary designation *Org-*

anizer of Victory for his contribution to the French Revolution.

CARPENTIER, GEORGES (1894–1975)

The French heavyweight boxer who fought Jack Dempsey in the ring's first million-dollar gate, Georges Carpentier was called *The Orchid Man* for his classic good looks and elegant lifestyle, qualities rather at odds with the image of the average pugilist.

CARR, JOHN (1772–1832)

Sir John Carr, an illustrious English lawyer turned travel writer, was nicknamed *Jaunting Carr,* an allusion to his many journeys. Oddly, he resented the name to his dying day as an indication his works were not being taken seriously. Later practitioners of his craft would greatly welcome such a ready identification.

CARR, WILBUR JOHN (1870–1942)

U.S. assistant secretary of state from 1924 to 1937 and, later, U.S. minister to Czechoslovakia, Wilbur John Carr was called *The Father of the U.S. Foreign Service* for playing a key role in basing careers in the Service on merit rather than on political patronage.

CARRE, MATHILDE (1910–   )

An undercover French spy known as *The Cat,* Mathilde Carre was unmasked early in World War II by the Germans and induced to become a double spy to save her life. She betrayed well over 100 Allied agents before her double-dealing was revealed. Imprisoned, she was sentenced to death after the liberation of France, a punishment later reduced to life imprisonment.

Carrots—See GISH, LILLIAN.

CARSON, JOHNNY (1925–   )

Johnny Carson, the most-watched U.S. late night television personality for more than two decades, has been appropriately nicknamed *The Prince of Darkness.*

CARTER, (JAMES EARL) JIMMY (1924–   )

Jimmy Carter, the 39th president of the United States, was nicknamed *Hot,* short for *Hot Shot,* by his father. Because of the family peanut business, it was inevitable that he would later be dubbed *The Peanut Politician.* Sen. Robert Dole, Republican of Kansas, labeled him *A Chicken-fried McGovern* and then twisted the knife further by saying, "I take that back because I've come to respect McGovern."

CARTER, ROSALYNN (1927–   )

Within the Washington establishment First Lady Rosalynn Carter was nicknamed *The Iron Magnolia* to indicate that she had a degree of tough-willed backbone some felt lacking in President Jimmy Carter.

Cartesius—See DESCARTES, RENE.

CARTWRIGHT, ALEXANDER JOY— See Father of Baseball, The.

CARUSO, ENRICO (1873–1921)

Opera great Enrico Caruso has been called *The Man with the Orchid-lined Voice, Italy's Greatest Tenor* and *The World's Greatest Tenor.* In Italy the last sobriquet is considered a redundancy.

CARVER, GEORGE WASHINGTON (1864–1943)

Born a slave, black U.S. botanist and chemist George Washington Carver was a teacher who made important discoveries in the commercial application of various farm products. He was dubbed *The Peanut Man* for developing scores of methods for the use of the peanut, which led to the development of a huge and varied industry. He was also known as *The Sweet Potato Man* for similar reasons.

CASS, LEWIS (1782–1866)

Unlike many other officials who have overseen American Indian affairs, Lewis Cass was noted for treating Indians with respect and genuine affection. While he was in charge of the Michigan Territory from 1813 to 1831, the Indians called him *The Great Father at Detroit.*

Cassandra of the Columnists—See THOMPSON, DOROTHY.

CASSIDY, BUTCH (1866–1909 or 1937)

Western outlaw Robert LeRoy Parker, better known as Butch Cassidy, appropriated the name Cassidy from an older badman he admired, and he picked up *Butch* while hiding out from the law working as a butcher's assistant. It was said that everyone, including his employer, felt he gave housewives a very good measure with their meat.

CASSINI, OLEG (1913–   )

Irrepressible Italian-American designer Oleg Cassini is often called *The Rebel of Seventh Avenue* by the fashion press for marching to the beat of a different drummer in his styles.

Cassius the Brashest—See ALI, MUHAMMAD.

CASTEL, GUIDO DI *(fl. 14th century)*

In spite of his great wealth and power, Guido di Castel of Reggio was known as *The Simple Lombard* because he treated all people equally and offered his castle as a sanctuary for those exiled from other courts.

CASTLEREAGH, ROBERT STEWART *(1769–1822)*

Viscount Castlereagh, the reactionary leader of the Tories and Britain's foreign minister from 1812 to 1822, took part in the cynical Congress of Vienna to restore the balance of power in Europe after the Napoleonic Wars. He was often referred to by foes as *The Swell-foot Tyrant,* an unkind phrase coined by Shelley in reference to his gout. Byron called him *The Intellectual Eunuch.* Highly unpopular at home, he eventually killed himself.

Cat, The—See CARRE, MATHILDE.

Cat Lady of San Francisco, The—See MEIER, SALLY.

Catacorners—See KETCHUM, CATACORNERS.

CATALANI, ANGELICA *(1780–1849)*

A great Italian soprano who made her debut in Venice at the age of 15, Angelica Catalani was considered unsurpassed in bravura singing, for which she was designated *The Italian Nightingale.*

CATESBY, WILLIAM—See Rat, Cat and Lovel our Dogge.

CATHERINE THE GREAT OF RUSSIA *(1729–1796)*

Catherine the Great of Russia much preferred to be called *The Little Mother of All the Russians,* but she was fittingly referred to as *The Modern Messalina,* after the lascivious empress of ancient Rome. Catherine's young lovers were selected by her former paramour Grigori Potemkin, screened by her personal physician and checked for virility by a lady-in-waiting. She was also called the *Semiramis of the North,* after Semiramis, the 20th century B.C. queen of Assyria, who was said to have chosen the strongest men for her lovers and to later have had them put to death to guarantee their silence. By contrast the grateful Catherine sent her former lovers from court to huge estates she had created for them.

Catholic, The—See ALFONSO I OF ASTURIAS; ISABELLA I OF CASTILE and ARAGON.

CATINAT, NICHOLAS *(?–1712)*

Nicholas Catinat, marshal of France, was known to his soldiers with considerable affection as *Father Thoughtful* because of the caution and judgment he exhibited before committing them to action.

CATLIN, GEORGE *(1796–1872)*

U.S. traveler, writer and painter George Catlin has been dubbed *The Pictorial Historian of Aboriginal America* for his hundreds of depictions of Indians and Indian scenes in North and South America.

Cato of the Age, The—See PRYNNE, WILLIAM.

Cattle Kate (1862–1889)

Notorious prostitute Ella Watson ran a bawdyhouse in Sweetwater, Wyo., where cowboys frequently paid in cattle for services rendered. She was lynched by hirelings of large cattle interests seeking to cut losses suffered by ''rustlers.'' Cattle Kate's lynching was a prelude to the Johnson County War between established cattle ranchers and new settlers.

CAVALCANTI, GUIDO (c. 1250–1300)

Italian philosopher and poet Guido Cavalcanti, a friend of Dante, was called *The Other Eye of Florence*. Like Dante, he was forced into exile for his political views.

CAVETT, RICHARD "DICK" (1936–   )

Dick Cavett, the American television personality and interviewer, is known in the trade as *The Happy Talker*.

CECIL, WILLIAM LORD BURLEIGH (1563–1612)

The crafty William Cecil (Lord Burleigh) was accorded several disparaging sobriquets, including *The Weasel* and *Machiavel*. King James I of England (James VI of Scotland) likened his minister to a hunting dog set among his courtiers in a kennel and called him *The Little Beagle*.

CELLIER, ELIZABETH (fl. 1680s)

Elizabeth Cellier, an English Protestant who converted to Catholicism when she married a Frenchman, was a noted London midwife implicated in the anti-Roman agitations of Titus Oates. Known as *The Popish Midwife,* she was accused of various Vatican-inspired plots against the crown, most of which had been fabricated by Thomas Dangerfield, the so-called Restoration Rogue. Acquitted, she was later convicted of libel for her writings concerning the treatment of prisoners at Newgate.

Celtic Homer, The—See OSSIAN.

Censor of the Age, The—See CARLYLE, THOMAS.

Century White—See WHITE, JOHN.

Cerberus of the Treasury, The—See ELLSWORTH, OLIVER.

CERMAK, ANTON J. (1873–1933)

During the 1930s some knowledgeable crime authorities in Chicago insisted that when Mayor Anton J. Cermak was shot and killed in Miami, Fla., in a 1933 assassination attempt on President-elect Franklin D. Roosevelt, gunman Joseph Zangara really got the man he was after. According to this theory, Zangara said he was out to murder Roosevelt simply as a cover for a gangland ''hit.'' Cermak, elected on a reform ticket, was at odds with the Capone mob, but reform in Chicago then being a relative matter, he allegedly was interested only in replacing one set of gangsters with another. Cermak had been known since early in his political career as *Ten Percent Tony,* the figure reportedly being his standard cut in kickbacks and other deals.

CERQUOZZI, MICHAEL ANGELO (1600–1660)

Italian painter Michael Angelo Cerquozzi, renowned for his vivid portraits of great battles and shipwrecks, was accorded the sobriquet *The Michaelangelo of Battle Scenes.*

Cerro Gordo Williams—See
WILLIAMS, JOHN STUART.

CEZANNE, PAUL (1839–1906)

Dubbed *The Father of Modernism* near the end of his life, French painter Paul Cezanne enjoyed no acceptance from the art world until 1895, when the famous dealer Vollard embraced his works. His influence on painting has been enormous, especially among the Impressionists, whose compositions emphasize masses of color rather than lines.

CHADWICK, CASSIE (1857–1907)

Cassie Chadwick, a Canadian female crook who married into a Cleveland society family in the 1890s, swindled various banks around the country of perhaps $20 million by claiming to be the illegitimate daughter of Andrew Carnegie. Using forged documents and fake bonds to indicate that Carnegie had settled a fortune on her but would not acknowledge his parentage until after his death, she was able to obtain huge bank loans. After she was exposed and sent to prison—where she died in 1907—she was widely celebrated as *Goldbrick Cassie.*

CHADWICK, HENRY—See Father of Baseball, The.

Chairman of the Board, The—See **FORD, WHITEY; SINATRA, FRANK.**

CHAMBERLAIN, NEVILLE (1869–1940)

Returning from Berlin after signing the 1938 Munich Agreement between England, France, and Germany, British Prime Minister Neville Chamberlain was hailed by enthusiastic crowds in Lon-

don as *The Savior of European Peace* for heading off World War II. When Hitler invaded Poland, Chamberlain was ridiculed as *The Arch Appeaser.*

CHAMBERLAIN, WILT "the Stilt" (1936–)

Basketball center Wilt Chamberlain, who holds records in the National Basketball League for highest points per game and most rebounds, scored a record 100 points in one game. At 7 feet 1 inches tall, he was given the appropriate nickname *Wilt the Stilt.*

Chamberlain-Umbrella Policy Man, A—See **KENNEDY, JOSEPH P.**

CHAMBERS, MARILYN (1952–)

Marilyn Chambers, an American actress-model, was dubbed *Mrs. Clean of Pornographic Movies* after embarrassing Procter & Gamble by taking up a career in soft-core films while her image as a mother holding a baby graced boxes of Ivory Snow detergent and appeared in an expensive advertising campaign.

CHAMBORD, COMTE DE: HENRI CHARLES FERDINAND MARIE DIEUDONNÉ D'ARTOIS (1820–1883)

Because he was born after his father, the Duc de Berri, was assassinated, the Comte de Chambord (Henri Charles Ferdinand Marie Dieudonné d' Artois) was dubbed *Dieu-Donné,* or *The God-Given,* and *l'Enfant du Miracle,* or *The Miraculous Child.*

CHAMPDIVERS, ODETTE DE (fl. late 14th century)

When King Charles VI of France succumbed to long periods of madness, Queen Isabeau abandoned him to a horse-dealer's daughter named Odette de Champdivers, who greatly resembled her. The public referred to Odette as *The Little Queen,* and it was said that Charles VI never knew the difference between the two. During brief periods of saneness Charles VI's bed apparently was graced by his true wife, and between 1395 and 1401 the queen gave birth to four children, although it is doubtful that some or any of them were legitimate.

CHAMPEAUX, WILLIAM DE *(c. 1070–1121)*

The 12th century French philosopher William de Champeaux, a founder of scholastic realism, was honored as *The Venerable* and *The Pillar of Doctors.*

Champagne Tony—See LEMA, ANTHONY "Champagne Tony."

CHAMPION, EDME *(1764–1853)*

A Parisian jeweler who sold his stock and became an anonymous benefactor of the poor, Edme Champion was known as *Le Petit Manteau-Bleu,* or *The Little Blue-Cloak,* because of the coat he habitually wore. Keeping his identity secret for 13 years, Champion could be seen on the streets of Paris dispensing soup and giving out clothes to the needy. Champion, a beacon of hope to the indigent, in the harsh winter of 1829–30 alone, gave out some 40,000 bowls of soup and an inestimable amount of coats, shoes, and other garments. Finally identified in 1830, he was by popular demand nominated chevalier of the *Legion d'Honneur.*

Champion of the Virgin, The—See CYRIL OF ALEXANDRIA, ST.

Champion of Women's Rights—See ANTHONY, SUSAN B.

CHANDLER, RAYMOND *(1888–1959)*

Because he was considered to have raised the detective story to a certain level of eloquence, Raymond Chandler, creator of private eye Philip Marlowe, was called *The Poet of Violence.*

CHANDLER, WALTER *(1897–1967)*

A former Memphis mayor and Tennessee Democratic representative, Walter Chandler was dubbed *One-Man-One-Vote Chandler* after his suit to reapportion the Tennessee legislature resulted in the Supreme Court's 1962 landmark one-man, one-vote ruling.

CHANEY, LON *(1883–1930)*

Fully deserving of being called *The Man of a Thousand Faces,* actor Lon Chaney was the leading authority on movie makeup and wrote the entry on the subject for the *Encyclopedia Britannica.* A very private person, he used his makeup to avoid being recognized in public.

CHANG CHUNG-CH'ANG *(c. 1880–c.1935)*

The notorious Chinese warlord Gen. Chang Chung-Ch'ang was celebrated for his sexual abilities as *The General with Three Long Legs.* He was also called *The Dog-Meat General* because he ate the meat of a black chow dog daily, regarding it to be an aphrodisiac. He fostered the sobriquet *72-Cannon Chang* because his "manhood" was said to equal a stack of 72 silver dollars in diameter and length.

CHANNING, WILLIAM ELLERY
(1780–1842)

Known as *The Apostle of Unitarianism*, American clergyman William Ellery Channing was also nicknamed *Little King Pepin* by supporters, who regarded his gentle nature and religious fervor as unequaled since Pepin the Short, the 8th century king of the Franks.

CHAPIN, CHARLES (1858–1930)

Charles Chapin, the famous city editor of the *New York Evening World*, was an unfeeling boss who thought nothing of firing reporters on Christmas Eve. In 1918 he murdered his sleeping wife because he was in poor health and desperate financial straits and feared she would have to exist in poverty. Sentenced to serve from 20 years to life, Chapin mellowed in prison and, under Warden Lewis E. Lawes, became the famed *Rose Man of Sing Sing*, filling the prison grounds with impressive arrays of flowers. Horticulturists trekked to the prison to see his work, and it was said that many prisoners entering the death house paused outside to inhale the fragrance of his roses. In 1930 repair work necessitated ripping up his gardens, and Chapin died in grief shortly thereafter.

CHAPLIN, CHARLES "Charlie"
(1889–1977)

The great motion picture comedian, director, and producer Charlie Chaplin was nicknamed *The Little Tramp*, after his famous silent-screen character. Shortly before World War II, he also became known as *A Twentieth Century Moses* for making large cash contributions to organizations that helped many German Jews escape Nazi persecution and eventual extermination.

CHAPMAN, ~~~

Notorious robber, jewel thief and murderer Gerald Chapman was nicknamed *The Count of Gramercy Park* because between crimes he lived the life of a leisured gentleman in that exclusive section of Manhattan.

CHAPMAN, JOHN—See Johnny Appleseed.

Chappaquiddick Chicken, The—See KENNEDY, EDWARD M.

CHARLEMAGNE OF POLAND, THE— See Boleslav the Mighty.

CHARLES I OF ENGLAND
(1600–1649)

The ill-fated Charles I of England was known as *The Man of Blood* by Puritans and *The Last Man* by Parliamentarians determined that he would be the last king of England. After his execution he was known as *The Royal Martyr*. His son, later Charles II, was called The Son of the Last Man by Parliament when it offered a reward for his capture.

CHARLES II OF ENGLAND
(1630–1685)

The unconventional morality of Charles II won for the Restoration English king the sobriquet *The Merry Monarch*. He had at least 13 mistresses, the most famous being actress Nell Gwyn—called *The Protestant Whore*—and acknowledged 14 illegitimate children. Less flatteringly, he was also known as *Old Rowley* after a stallion in the royal stud. Earlier, when he was being hunted by

Parliament, he was called *The Son of the Last Man,* The Last Man being his father, Charles I, whom the Parliamentarians had executed in an attempt to abolish the English throne.

CHARLES II OF SPAIN (1661–1700)

King Charles II of Spain was disparagingly nicknamed by the English *Lord Strutt,* which probably said it all.

CHARLES IV OF THE HOLY ROMAN EMPIRE (1316–1378)

Charles IV, emperor of the Holy Roman Empire, was mockingly referred to as *Pfaffen-Kaiser,* or *Parson's Emperor,* since he was elevated to the throne by the Pope.

CHARLES V OF THE HOLY ROMAN EMPIRE (1500–1558)

Holy Roman emperor Charles V thoroughly relished the sobriquet of *The Second Charlemagne,* even though his reign was beset by internal uprisings, emerging Protestantism and colonial problems. *The Second Charlemagne* finally walked away from it all, turning over the empire to his brother Ferdinand in 1556, and retiring to a monastery.

CHARLES XII OF SWEDEN (1682–1718)

Called the *Alexander of the North* by his supporters and *The Madman of the North* by his foes during the Great Northern War of 1700 to 1720, Charles XII of Sweden defeated the Danes, Russians, Saxons, and Poles in a number of battles. He was beaten at Poltava in 1709 while attempting an overly ambitious invasion of Russia. Forced to take refuge in Turkey, he soon returned to the wars and invaded Norway in 1714. He was killed in an attack on a fortress in 1718.

CHARLES ALBERT, KING OF PIEDMONT (1798–1849)

As a youth in his twenties, Charles Albert made no secret of his hatred for the domineering Austrians. When he came to power, however, he was effectively squelched by Austrian foreign minister Metternich. As the revolutionary spirit spread throughout the Italian kingdoms, he gingerly returned to the anti-Austrian policies of his youth, but his subjects were hardly impressed, nicknaming him *Re Tentenna,* or *Vacillating King.* Finally, in 1848, Charles Albert declared war on Austria, only to be badly beaten and routed early the next year. Forced to sue for peace and sign a personal pledge of good behavior, the king shortly thereafter abdicated in favor of his son, Victor Emmanuel II—who would later drive out the Austrians. Charles Albert died in exile a few months later, and it was said of him by a historian "that nothing in his public life became him like the leaving of it."

Charles Jean Charlatan—See BERNADOTTE, JEAN BAPTISTE JULES.

CHARLES JOSEPH, PRINCE DE LIGNE (1735–1814)

Regarded by many as a pretentious fop, Field Marshal Charles Joseph of Austria, Prince de Ligne, was caricatured as *The Prince of Coxcombs.*

CHARLES MARTEL (688–741?)

Charles Martel, the mayor of the palace of Austrasia—a Frankish kingdom straddling part of

realm and was called *The Hammer* for smashing a numerically superior Moslem army at the Battle of Tours and Poiters in 732 and bringing an end to Arab invasions from Spain.

Charles the Affable: CHARLES VIII OF FRANCE (1470–1498)

King Charles VIII of France was known as *Charles the Affable,* a sobriquet that may have had a special meaning. In 1495 his troops, made up of men of many nations, invaded Italy. They entered Naples, where the disease of syphilis is said to have originated. Upon dispersing they were believed to have spread the ''whore's disease'' throughout Europe.

Charles the Bad: CHARLES II, KING OF NAVARRE (1332–1387)

Charles II, king of Navarre, won the appellation *The Bad* because of his treachery and constant plotting to gain the French throne. During the Hundred Years War, he forced John II of France to yield lands to him in Normandy to further his ambitions for the crown.

Charles the Fair: CHARLES IV, KING OF FRANCE (1294–1328)

Like his father, Philip IV, Charles IV, king of France, was said to have been one of the handsomest men in the world, and he was thus called *Charles the Fair.* In Philip's case, however, the sobriquet was intended disparagingly as a comment on his tyrannical and unjust reign. Charles's rule was brief and unimportant, and with his death the monarchy passed to the House of Valois.

Charles the Mad: CHARLES VI OF FRANCE (1368–1422)

Charles VI of France came to the throne at the age of 12 amidst such adulation that he was called *Charles the Well-Beloved.* As his mental health deteriorated, however, during what would finally total 44 bouts of madness, his nickname changed to *The Silly* to *The Foolish,* and, finally, to *Charles the Mad.*

Charles the Simple: CHARLES III OF FRANCE (879–929)

Attacked by French barons for what they considered his simple-minded policy of making constant concessions to the Norse invaders under Rollo, Charles III of France was called *Charles the Simple.* When he gave away Normandy and his daughter in marriage to Rollo, the nobles deposed him in 922 and clapped him into prison.

Charles the Well-Served: CHARLES VII OF FRANCE (1403–1461)

King Charles VII of France was honored as *The Well-Served* and *The Victorious* after the deeds of Joan of Arc stirred him from earlier inaction. He ended the Hundred Years War by driving the English out of France except for Calais.

Charles the Wise: CHARLES V OF FRANCE (1337–1380)

King Charles V of France was hailed as *Charles the Wise* because of what were considered his many brilliant accomplishments. These included driving the English out of most of France, putting down serious uprisings, strengthening the army and the tax system and building the Bastille.

***Charlie Chaplin of the Pulpit*—See
SUNDAY, BILLY.**

CHARTIER, ALAIN (1386–1458)

Noted French poet and litterateur Alain Chartier, praised for writing prose as picturesque as poetry, was viewed as *The Father of French Eloquence.* On one occasion the dauphin's wife, Margaret of Scotland, found him asleep in a chair and kissed his lips in tribute to the ''sweet words which flowed from them.''

CHASE, SALMON P. (1808–1873)

Ohio abolitionist politician Salmon P. Chase, secretary of the treasury under Abraham Lincoln, was sneered at by opponents for his antislavery views and referred to as *The Attorney General for Runaway Slaves* because he gave many of them legal aid. He was also called *The Father of Greenbacks* for being instrumental in the passage of the Legal Tender Act, which made paper money legal currency.

CHATTERTON, THOMAS (1752–1770)

English juvenile prodigy, poet and author Thomas Chatterton was nicknamed *The Marvelous Boy* by his admirers. While a young boy Chatterton unearthed parchments in a Bristol church where his father was sexton and composed and added poems to them, which he pretended were the work of the medieval monk Thomas Rowley. He sent the parchments to many prominent persons, including Horace Walpole, who for a time accepted them as genuine. Chatterton later moved to London, where he did some hack writing before committing suicide in poverty at the age of 17. He is the subject of Alfred de Vigny's tragedy *Chatterton.*

CHAUCER, GEOFFREY (1340–1400)

The greatest of the English poets of the Middle Ages and the bridge to the dawning Renaissance, Chaucer, author of the the *Canterbury Tales,* gained many accolades. Among these were *The Father of English Poetry, The Flower of Poets, Tityrus,* from Spenser, and *The Morning Star of Song,* from Tennyson.

***Chaucer of Artists, The*—See
DUERER, ALBRECHT.**

***Chauffeured Communist, The*—See
HALL, GUS.**

CHAVEZ, CESAR (1927–   )

Labor leader Cesar Chavez, the Mexican-American founder of the United Farm Workers, employs marches as a major weapon in his nonviolent arsenal and has been dubbed *The Marcher.*

CHECKER, CHUBBY (1941?–   )

Chubby Checker, the black American singer and dancer who introduced a new dance craze during the early 1960s, was logically dubbed *The Twist King.*

***Chemical Messiah, The*—See LEARY,
TIMOTHY.**

CHENEY, FRANCES NEEL (1906–   )

American librarian Frances Neel ''Fanny'' Cheney has been dubbed *The Library Profession's No. 1 Reference Reviewer.*

CHENIER, ANDRE (1762–1794)

Brilliant young French poet Andre Chenier, who attempted to Hellenize French verse, changed during the French Revolution from a fervid partisan of the Jacobins to their bitter foe. Imprisoned, he wrote some of his most stirring and most defiant works there, including *Iambes* and *La jeune captive*, before going to the guillotine in 1794. When the first collected edition of his works appeared a quarter of a century later, he was celebrated as *The Adonis of the French Revolution*.

CHEOTSIN *(fl. 12th century)*

Cheotsin, a Chinese ruler of the 12th century, has been dubbed *The Sardanapalus of China* for having committed suicide after his defeat by Woowong, his successor. According to legend, the great Assyrian ruler Sardanapalus burned himself and his palace after being besieged by his enemies.

Cherubic Master of Suspense, The— See HITCHCOCK, ALFRED.

CHESTERFIELD, PHILIP DORMER STANHOPE, LORD *(1694–1773)*

British statesman, orator and man of letters Lord Chesterfield, famed for his *bon-mots* and repartee, was known to his admirers as *The Prince of Wits*. Less than enamoured of him was King George II, who called him *A Tea-Table Scoundrel* who "tells little womanish lies to make quarrels in families; and tries to make women lose their reputations, and make their husbands beat them, without any object but to give himself airs."

CHESTERTON, GILBERT KEITH *(1874–1936)*

English author G. K. Chesterton was often called *The Master of Paradox,* but not by his critics. Among these was Ezra Pound, who called him *A Vile Scum on a Pond.* In recent years an effort has been made to resurrect his reputation as *A Tremendous Trifle,* a nickname based on his 1909 collection of essays, *Tremendous Trifles,* on the theory that he had much to say.

CHEVALIER, MAURICE *(1888–1972)*

French entertainer Maurice Chevalier was called *The Man in the Straw Hat.* His popularity in the United States during the early 1930s was such that it was estimated he accounted for perhaps five to ten percent of the sales of straw hats annually.

CHIABRERA, GABRIELLO *(1552–1637)*

Italian lyric poet Gabriello Chiabrera was nicknamed *The Italian Pindar* or *The Pindar of Italy,* after the Greek poet. The Italian word *Chiabreresco* derives from his surname and has come to mean Pindaric.

CHIANG KAI-SHEK *(1887–1975)*

Chinese nationalist leader Generalissimo Chiang Kai-shek was referred to disdainfully by the Allied military, especially by the American mission headed by Gen. "Vinegar" Joe Stilwell, as *Peanut*. There has been some effort to claim that *Peanut* was simply the code name for Chiang, but a reading of Stilwell's diaries clearly indicates that the general meant what he said.

Chicago's Arch Criminal—See O'BANION, DION.

Chicago's Grand Old Lady—See HUDLUN, ANNA ELIZABETH.

Chicken Plucker, The—See RIGGS, BOBBY.

Chicken-Fried McGovern, A—See CARTER, JIMMY.

Chief, The—See HOOVER, HERBERT.

Child Commissioner, The—See ROZELLE, PETE.

Child of Hell, A—See EZZELINO DI ROMANO.

Child of Light, The—See WOOLMAN, JOHN.

Childeric the Stupid: CHILDERIC III OF THE MEROVINGIANS (fl. 8th century)

In 8th century France, Childeric III of the Merovingians, was called *Childeric the Stupid* because his ineptness ended the dynasty when he was overthrown by Pepin the Short. Pepin's son Charlemagne unified the Franks and became the Holy Roman emperor.

Children's Poet, The—See LONGFELLOW, HENRY WADSWORTH.

CHILDS, WILLIAM (1865?–1938)

U.S. restaurateur William Childs can hardly be credited with inventing the hotcake, but he made it standard American breakfast fare in a chain of restaurants in big-city America, where he was hailed as *The Hotcake Baron*.

CHIN SHI HUANG-TI—See Tigerheart.

Chin, The—See GIGANTE, VINCENT.

China Polly: MRS. CHARLES BEMIS (1852–1933)

China Polly, a beautiful 20-year-old Chinese slave girl, became the bride of Idaho gambler Charley Bemis in one of the Old West's most storied couplings. She was also called *The Poker Bride* for having been won by Bemis as part of a poker pot. She nursed him back to health when he was badly wounded in a gunfight, after which they became a thoroughly devoted married couple.

Chinese Gordon—See GORDON, CHARLES GEORGE.

Chinese Harrison—See HARRISON, BENJAMIN.

Chinese Pompadour, The—See YANG KUEI-FEI.

Chinless Wonder, The—See KILGALLEN, DOROTHY.

Chivalrous Saracen, The—See SALADIN.

CHIVINGTON, JOHN M.
(1821–1894)

Minister-soldier John M. Chivington preached the word of God for 17 years until he joined the Union Army in 1861 and became known as *The Fighting Parson*. He had rejected a chaplain post and requested a "fighting" commission rather than a "praying" one. His victories over the Confederates in New Mexico made him a military hero, but his wanton slaughter of some 450 Indian men, women, and children in the Sand Creek Massacre in 1864 stigmatized him and forced his resignation from the army.

Chocolate Eclair, A—See
MCKINLEY, WILLIAM.

Chocolate King, The—See
HERSHEY, MILTON S.

CHOU EN-LAI (1898–1976)

Premier Chou en-Lai was called *Peking's Man for All Seasons* for his ability to survive the twists and eddies that have typified politics in the People's Republic of China since its founding in 1949.

Christian Atticus, The—See **HEBER, REGINALD.**

Christian Caligula, The—See **JOHN XII, POPE.**

Christian General, The—See **HOWARD, OLIVER OTIS "Bible-Quoting."**

Christian the Cruel: CHRISTIAN II OF DENMARK (1481–1550)

Christian II of Denmark was known as *The Cruel* and, more vividly, *The Nero of the North*. His massacre of Swedes in 1520 led to rebellion and dissolution of the union with Sweden. He was deposed in 1523 and ended his days in prison.

CHRISTINA OF SWEDEN
(1626–1689)

Coming to the Swedish throne at the age of 18, Queen Christina became a patroness of men of the arts and sciences, lavishing titles, land and money on them and, not surprisingly, winning their tribute as *The Miracle of Nature*. Among those attracted to her court was Descartes. In 1654 she abdicated and, dressed as a man, fled Stockholm for Rome, where she converted to Roman Catholicism. She twice attempted to regain her throne and failed, but continued her pursuit of learning and accumulated a vast library, which on her death was acquired by Pope Alexander VIII.

CHRISTOPHER III OF SWEDEN—
See **King Bark.**

CHULKHURST, ELIZABETH AND MARY—See **Biddenden Maids, The.**

CHURCHILL, JOHN (1650–1722)

John Churchill, duke of Marlborough, won the sobriquet *Silly Duke* because of his penchant for putting down conversations of which he disapproved by remarking, "Oh, silly! Silly!" His opponents at court delighted in using the name behind his back. His military enemies, the French, were far more tolerant and respectful, calling him *The Handsome Englishman*.

CHURCHILL, SARAH (1915–1982)

Sarah Churchill, the controversial actress daughter of Winston Churchill, was noted for her flamboyant lifestyle, which won her the nickname *Black Sheep Sarah* for the aggravation she caused her father. She said she preferred being called *The Lamb Who Strayed from the Fold,* and summed up her life as having ''burned my scandals at both ends.''

CHURCHILL, WINSTON (1874–1965)

Winnie, the nickname of Winston Churchill, was used at different times as a term of endearment and derision. While he was at Harrow, it was used mockingly after his father, Randolph Churchill, succumbed to a syphilitic mental breakdown in the House of Commons. His fellow students chanted: ''Randolph Churchill lost his head, Winnie Churchill pissed in bed.'' The youthful nickname, Churchill later said, haunted him the rest of his life.

CIANO, COUNT GALEAZZO (1903–1944)

The son-in-law of Benito Mussolini and Italy's fascist foreign minister Count Galeazzo Ciano earned the enmity of the Nazis for seeking to break up the Axis and keep Italy out of World War II. Goebbels referred to Ciano as *That Poisoned Mushroom,* and the Nazis finally forced Musssolini to have him arrested and shot in the back, tied to a chair, as a traitor.

CIBBER, COLLEY (1671–1757)

English poet Colley Cibber was one of many who felt the wrath of Alexander Pope, known as The Wasp of Twickenham. Labeled *The King of Dulness* by Pope, Cibber earned the great man's enmity by criticizing a play written by Pope and John Gay, *Three Hours After Marriage.* Pope had previously savaged Lewis Theobald by satirizing him in his poem *The Dunciad* as *The King of Dunces.* In 1743 Pope issued a new version of *The Dunciad* and substituted the name Cibber for Theobald, ensuring that the two thereafter shared that derogatory nickname.

Cicero (107–43 B.C.)

The great Roman orator and statesman Marcus Tullius is better known as Cicero, a sobriquet that became his surname. Cicero derives from the Latin *cicer* for wart. As Plutarch noted, he had ''a flat excrescence on the tip of his nose.'' The nickname Cicero has been passed down through history to honor other great orators.

Cicero of America, The—See LIVINGSTON, ROBERT R.

Cicero of France, The—See MASSILLON, JEAN BAPTISTE.

Cicero of Germany, The—See JOHANN, ELECTOR OF BRANDENBURG.

Cicero of the British Senate, The—See CANNING, GEORGE.

Cicero of the Revolution, The—See LEE, RICHARD HENRY.

Cicero's Mouth—See POT, PHILIPPE.

Cid, El (c. 1043–1099)

El Cid, or *The Master,* was the name given to the great national hero of Spain for his exploits against

he was also called El Cid Campeador, or The Lord Champion.

Cigar, The—See
GALANTE, CARMINE.

Cincinnatus of the West, The—See
WASHINGTON, GEORGE.

Cinderella Man, The—See
BRADDOCK, JAMES J.

Cinque, General Field Marshal—See
DEFREEZE, DONALD D.

Circe of the Revolution, The—See
ROLAND, JEANNE MANON PHILIPON.

Citizen Equality—See **PHILIPPE, DUC D'ORLEANS.**

Citizen King, The—See **LOUIS PHILIPPE I OF FRANCE.**

Citizen of Heaven—See **GRAHAM, BILLY.**

City Builder, The—See **SANCHO I, KING OF PORTUGAL.**

CLAIBORNE, BILLY—See **Billy the Kid.**

CLARE, JOHN (1793–1864)

Nineteenth century English poet John Clare, the self-educated son of a farm laborer, gained celeb-

1820. Known as *The Peasant Poet of Northamptonshire,* he was also called *The Poet Married to Nature* and wrote that after his death nature would be his widow. Delicate of body and mind, Clare spent the years after his 43rd birthday in asylums, save for a brief escape in 1841. Many students of poetry insist he wrote his deepest and most beautiful poems during his more lucid moments in confinement.

CLARK, ABRAHAM (1726–1794)

One of the first attorneys in the American Colonies to provide free or low-cost services to clients who could not afford to pay, Abraham Clark, a signer of the Declaration of Independence, was nicknamed *The Poor Man's Counsellor.*

CLARK, CHARLES DISMAS (1901–1963)

Known as *The Hoodlum Priest,* Charles Dismas Clark was a Catholic clergyman who helped some 3,500 former convicts toward rehabilitation at his St. Louis, Mo., "halfway house." A movie was made of his career in 1961.

CLARK, MARK WAYNE (1896–)

A forceful U.S. Army general during World War II, Mark Clark was known as a brilliant but vain commander. But Winston Churchill, who appreciated ego in military men, thought highly enough of Clark to dub him *The American Eagle,* noting that he had the special American knack for commanding troops of mixed nationalities.

CLARK (or CLARKE), RICHARD—
See **Deadwood Dick.**

CLARKE, MARCELLUS JEROME—
See **Sue Mundy.**

CLARKE, MCDONALD (1798–1842)

American poet McDonald Clarke bore the nickname *The Mad Poet* for having a writing style that went far beyond his era's allowances for poetic license. He died in an asylum. His career has often been compared with that of the English poet and dramatist Nathaniel Lee, who bore the same nickname and suffered a rather similar fate.

CLARKE, SAMUEL (1599–1682)

A noted English compiler of books, Samuel Clarke was anagramed and nicknamed *Suck All Cream,* an allusion to the fact that he sucked all the cream from all authors while having none himself.

CLARKSON, JAMES SULLIVAN "Headsman" (1842–1918)

The first assistant postmaster general under Republican president Benjamin Harrison, James Sullivan Clarkson accomplished something of a political miracle in his first 20 months in office by axing 32,335 Democratic appointees from their Post Office jobs. Democratic newspapers dubbed him *Headsman Clarkson.*

CLARKSON, THOMAS (1760–1846)

English humanitarian Thomas Clarkson, an early guiding force in the movement to abolish slavery, devoted his life and sacrificed his health to the cause, winning praise from the poet Coleridge as *The Moral Steam Engine.* Clarkson began by battling to eliminate the slave trade, with the realization that by subtracting its great profit he would inevitably doom the institution itself. When the Act of 1807 ended English traffic in slaves, Wordsworth noted in a sonnet: "Clarkson, it was an obstinate hill to climb." He lived to see the Emancipation Bill of 1833 free all slaves in British possessions, but not long enough to see the eradication of slavery in all civilized countries.

CLAY, CASSIUS MARCELLUS, SR. (1810–1903)

Cassius Marcellus Clay, Sr., a cousin of U.S. statesman Henry Clay, was a Kentuckian who fought numerous challenges for remaining loyal to the Union in the Civil War and thereby earned the nickname *The Kentucky Duel Fighter.* Although he never lost a duel, he was singularly ineffective in his first confrontation. Like his opponent, Clay missed his three allowed shots and had to agree the dispute was resolved—this despite the fact that he was a fine marksman who could normally hit a suspended string at 10 paces three times out of five. Asked how he could fail to hit his man, he responded, "That damned string never had no pistol in his hand."

CLAY, HENRY (1777–1852)

Among the congressional zealots from western states eager for a war with the British in 1812, Kentuckian Henry Clay, nicknamed *The Western Star,* stood in the front ranks. In later years, he became known as *The Great Compromiser* for his roles in the Missouri Compromise of 1820, the tariff compromise of 1833 and the Compromise of 1850. Among his less flattering sobriquets was *Judas of the West,* given him by supporters of Andrew Jackson after he threw his backing to John Quincy Adams in the 1824 presidential race, ignoring the instructions of his state's legislature. Adams named Clay secretary of state, which brought the cry of "deal" from Jacksonians.

Clean Gene—See MCCARTHY, EUGENE.

CLEBURNE, PATRICK RONAYNE (1828–1864)

One of the few Confederate heroes in the Civil War's western campaigns, fighting Irishman Patrick R. Cleburne became a favorite of President

label him *Stonewall of the West,* after Gen. Stonewall Jackson. In any event, having a hero within
the bickering command structure of the Army of
Tennessee was in itself a propaganda coup for the
South. Like the man with whom he shared the sobriquet *Stonewall,* Cleburne died in battle.

CLEM, JOHN LINCOLN (1851–1937)

After being turned down by one regiment, John
Lincoln Clem entered the Civil War at the age of
nine by unofficially attaching himself to the 22nd
Michigan Infantry as a drummer. His monthly pay
of $13 was donated by officers. At the battle of
Shiloh in 1862, his drum was destroyed by an artillery shell as he was beating the advance. His
fame spread immediately as *Johnny Shiloh,* and it
is believed he was the inspiration for the song and
play *The Drummer Boy of Shiloh.* Johnny went
on to greater glory at the battle of Chickamauga.
Carrying a musket that had been shortened for him,
he was confronted by a mounted rebel colonel and
wounded and captured him, thus becoming *The
Drummer Boy of Chickamauga.* Later that year he
was captured by Confederates, who showed off
their famous prize. Exchanged for another prisoner,
he finished out his service as an army courier.

CLEMENCEAU, GEORGES
(1841–1929)

A two-time premier of France, Georges Clemenceau was called *The Tiger* because of his political
ruthlessness.

Clemens Non Papa—See CLEMENT, JACQUES.

CLEMENT, JACQUES (?–c. 1558)

A celebrated Franco-Flemish musician-composer
of the 16th century, Jacques Clement was so renowned that he was accorded the sobriquet *Clemens

Clement VI.

CLEMENT VII, POPE (1341–1394)

Robert of Geneva, who became the infamous 14th
century antipope Clement VII, was known as *The
Butcher of Cesena.* During the Papal States War
of the 1370s, he induced that town's citizens to
lay down their arms on the promise of church
forgiveness. He then ordered his mercenaries to
commit wholesale rape and slaughter as an example to other cities not to resist papal authority.

CLEMENT XIV, POPE (1705–1774)

Pope Clement XIV was referred to as *The Protestant Pope* because he ordered the suppression of
the Jesuits in his 1773 brief "Dominus ac Re-
demptor noster."

CLEOPATRA (69–30 B.C.)

As part of his dream of greater empire, as well as
for romantic reasons, Mark Anthony dubbed
Cleopatra, the last queen of Egypt, *The Queen of
Queens.*

CLEVELAND, BENJAMIN
(1738–1806)

Revolutionary War hero Benjamin Cleveland, who
led Cleveland's Bulldogs (called Cleveland's Devils by the English) in battle in North Carolina, was
referred to as *All Round About Cleveland.* He
weighed more than 400 pounds.

CLEVELAND, GROVER (1837–1908)

Grover Cleveland, the 22nd and 24th president of
the United States, had the distinction of having
many nicknames hurled derisively at him not only
by opposition Republicans but by members of his
own Democratic Party. The reform Tilden wing

of the Democratic Party called him *The Pretender* and accused him of being insincere about his high ideals. Samuel Tilden himself dubbed him *Backbone,* alluding to his corpulence, and once said, "Backbone! He has so much of it, it makes him stick out in front." The kindest sobriquet about his physical dimensions was *Uncle Jumbo.* Democratic Tammany Hall, to whom he would not bow, referred to him as *The Stuffed Prophet.* The Republicans had their favorite disparagements as well, calling him *The Buffalo Hangman* because in his previous role as sheriff of Erie County, N.Y., he had been required to hang a convicted murderer. They also called him *The Dumb Prophet,* alleging that he often would not express himself on important questions. While his supporters hailed him as *The People's President, The Man of Destiny* and, simply, *Our Grover,* certainly his most common nickname was the disparaging *The Beast of Buffalo.* This arose from the acknowledged fact that he had fathered an illegitimate child and unsubstantiated reports that he beat the lovely young wife he had married during his second year in the White House.

Clicquot—See FREDERICK WILLIAM IV OF PRUSSIA

CLIFFORD, ROSAMUND—See Fair Rosamund.

CLIFTON, DAN—See Dynamite Dick.

CLIVE, ROBERT, LORD *(1725–1774)*

Robert Clive, the English general and statesman who helped found the British empire in India, is generally celebrated as *Clive of India.* The East Indians nicknamed him *Sabut Jung,* or *The Daring in War.*

Clodion the Hairy (fl. c. 428)

Before a monarchy developed in France, one of the most powerful leaders of the 5th century was *Clodion the Hairy,* so called for his luxuriant beard, which was said to have excited the contempt of some of his less favored courtiers. According to one historian, this was because they "probably could not grow beards."

CLOOTZ (or CLOOTS), JEAN BAPTISTE *(1755–1794)*

Fiery French revolutionary Jean Baptiste Clootz (or Cloots) was never in doubt as to his mission in life. He nicknamed himself *The Orator of the Human Race.*

Clothes Horse, The—See CRAWFORD, JOAN.

CLOVIS II OF FRANCE *(?–656)*

The first of 10 early French monarchs to be called *The Do-Nothing King,* Clovis II of the Merovingians was a figurehead under control of the major domus, or head of the palace. The Do-Nothing Kings remained in place until 741, when Pepin the Short seized the crown.

Clown Prince of Baseball, The—See VEECK, WILLIAM LOUIS.

Clown Prince of Racing, The—See SACHS, EDWARD.

Clownish Sycophant, The—See WORDSWORTH, WILLIAM.

Clubber—See WILLIAMS, ALEXANDER S. "Clubber."

CLUM, JOHN P. (1851–1932)

American pioneer, actor, Indian agent and editor John P. Clum is generally credited with developing the concept of the Indian Police in the American West. Having organized a force on the San Carlos Reservation, he earned the tribe's fierce loyalty as *The Boss with the White Forehead.*

Clutching Hand, The: PIETRO MORELLO (1880–1930)

Few New York mafiosi in the 1920s inspired more fear in the Italian community than Pietro Morello, who was nicknamed *The Clutching Hand.* When Lucky Luciano prepared to move against the top Mafia leaders, he realized he would first have to have *The Clutching Hand* eliminated. Gunmen caught Morello in a moment of weakness— while he was counting money.

Clyde—See FRAZIER, WALT "Clyde."

Coach—See FORD, JOHN.

COATES, ROBERT (1771–1848)

Having accumulated great wealth in the West Indies, Robert Coates became a celebrated leader of London fashion in the early 19th century and was nicknamed *Diamond Coates.* He was also referred to as *Romeo Coates* because of his love for amateur theatricals and his willingness to expend some of his fortune on them.

COBBETT, WILLIAM (1763–1835)

Known for his biting invective, British journalist and reformer William Cobbett fled to Philadelphia from England to escape reprisals for his writings. eralist newspaper filled with his barbed comments, which won him the sobriquet *Peter Porcupine.* Returning to England, he moved to the left and used his *Political Register* to support labor and agrarianism. For a time censorship problems drove him back to the United States, but Cobbett returned to England once more and continued his dual career as a militant reformer in Parliament and a political writer until his death.

Cobbler, The—See WILSON, HENRY.

COBDEN, RICHARD (1804–1865)

Richard Cobden and John Bright, another wealthy English manufacturer, launched the Anti-Corn Law League, which was pledged to wipe out tariffs on imported grain. Because of their energetic and successful campaign Cobden and Bright were both dubbed *The Apostle of Free Trade.* The laws were repealed in 1846, partly in response to the League's emotional appeals for cheaper food for the masses, and partly because free trade was to the advantage of the country's manufacturers. Since England had a massive head start in the production of machinery and abundant supplies of coal and iron, it needed free markets in other countries for its goods. The stripping away of the country's protectionist tariffs was a powerful argument for reciprocity. (See also Bright, John.)

Cock-eye—See BUTLER, BENJAMIN.

CODY, WILLIAM FREDERICK—See Buffalo Bill.

COELLO, ALONZO (1515–1590)

Portuguese portrait painter Alonzo Coello was called *The Titian of Portugal* because his work closely resembled that of the contemporary Italian Renaissance painter.

COHAN, GEORGE M. *(1878–1942)*

Patriotic actor, director, and songwriter George M. Cohan dominated the Broadway scene for so long that he was called, among other sobriquets, *Mr. Broadway, The Prince of the American Theater* and, of course, *The Yankee Doodle Dandy,* the title of a motion picture about his life as well as a very popular song.

COHEN, MICKEY *(1913–1976)*

Notorious California gangster Mickey Cohen was dubbed *Snow White* by the press for one of his "good guy" capers. Reading a news account about a 63-year-old widow who had been forced out of her home, Cohen became incensed. A crooked radio repairman had gotten the city marshal to put up for auction the widow's $4,000 home, when she refused to pay his inflated repair bill, then bought the house for a mere $26.50. The gambler dispatched seven of his boys to teach the repairman a lesson, which they proceeded to do by thumping him to within an inch of his life, breaking his skull and right arm in the process. Unfortunately, two rookie policemen happened along and arrested all seven. Cohen was also charged, and the press, learning the motivation for the slamming, dubbed him *Snow White* and his hoodlums the Seven Dwarfs. Cohen followed with a typically grand gesture by lifting the attachment and returning the house to the widow, with an extra cash gift.

COHN, HARRY *(1891–1958)*

Harry Cohn, the tyrannical, much-hated founder and president of Columbia Pictures, was dubbed *King Cohn,* reflecting his idea that studio moguls had a divine right, which allowed them to make imperious sexual demands on numerous actresses.

Coiner of Weasel Words—See WILSON, WOODROW.

COLBERT, CLAUDETTE *(1905–   )*

French-born Hollywood actress Claudette Colbert was referred to as *The Fretting Frog* by most of the cameramen who worked with her because of the demands she made on them. It was said she never allowed her right profile to be photographed, which cameramen dubbed "the dark side of the moon," because it was never seen.

Cold War Witch, The—See THATCHER, MARGARET.

COLERIDGE, SAMUEL TAYLOR *(1772–1834)*

British poet, critic and philosopher Samuel Coleridge was known to his admirers as *A Second Johnson* and *Old Man Eloquent.* The sentiment was not universal, however. Lord Byron dubbed him *Coleridge Muddling,* and Carlyle called him "a weak, diffusive, weltering, ineffectual man."

Coleridge Muddling—See COLERIDGE, SAMUEL TAYLOR.

COLL, VINCENT *"Mad Dog"* *(1909–1932)*

A baby-faced Irish-American gangster of the bootleg era, Vincent Coll awed police and rival gangsters alike with his utter disregard for human life, as when he shot down several children in an effort to hit a criminal foe. When *Mad Dog* or *Mad*

death in a phone booth, newspapers correctly predicted that police would show little interest in finding his killers.

COLLINS, CHURTON (1848–1908)

Famed English critic Churton Collins found that his was a field ripe for tit-for-tat. Disagreeing with his opinions, Alfred Lord Tennyson dubbed him *A Louse in the Locks of Literature,* a sobriquet that lasted the rest of Collins' life.

COLLINS, JOHN (1624–1683)

While still in his early twenties, English mathematician John Collins won the nickname *The English Mersenne* from the master himself, the French natural philosopher Marin Mersenne.

COLLINS, JOHN NORMAN (1947–   )

John Norman Collins was infamous as *Michigan's Co-ed Murderer,* following his 1970 arrest for the sexually motivated murders of seven female college students in the Ypsilanti area. He was convicted and sentenced to life imprisonment.

COLLINS, JOSEPH LAWTON "Lightning Joe" (1896–   )

Gen. Joseph Lawton Collins achieved fame during World War II as *Lightning Joe Collins* for being an aggressive and exuberant commander who believed in fast-moving military strokes. The sobriquet was further attested to by his well-documented practice of quickly removing subordinates whom he judged to be not up to their jobs.

Colonel Blimp—See LOW, DAVID.

Colonel Yes-Yes—See SADAT, ANWAR.

Colorado Charley—See UTTER, CHARLES H.

Colossus of Graft, The—See MURPHY, CHARLES F.

Colossus of Independence, The—See ADAMS, JOHN.

Colossus of Roads, The—See MCADAM, JOHN L.

COLSON, CHARLES W. "Chuck" (1919–   )

Chuck Colson, a White House aide to President Richard Nixon during the Watergate era, was known as a man who would walk over his own grandmother to serve Nixon. Tabbed *The White House Hatchet Man* and *The Master of Dirty Tricks,* he served a prison term for Watergate crimes and emerged from jail "born again." He was then referred to, not always with forgiving grace, as *Colson the Christian.*

Columbia's Gem of the Ozone—See KALTENBORN, H. V.

COLUMBUS, CHRISTOPHER (1451–1506)

The discoverer of America, Christopher Columbus was nicknamed *The Admiral of the Mosquitoes* by his men because in his great "enterprise of the Indies" he instead reached the Caribbean islands, where the insects vastly outnumbered the gold and other riches he found there.

Columbus of the Atomic Age, The—See **FERMI, ENRICO.**

COMBE, WILLIAM (1741–1823)

When he had money, English adventurer and writer William Combe, the creator of *Doctor Syntax,* was known as *Count Combe* because of his extravagant mode of dress. He was at various times a private soldier, waiter, cook, law student, hack writer and heir to a considerable family fortune. He quickly squandered the last, as well as his income from such literary endeavors as *The Diaboliad* and the three *Tours of Doctor Syntax,* and spent much of his life in debtors prison.

Combination Machiavelli, Svengali and Rasputin, A—See **HOPKINS, HARRY L.**

COMESTOR, PETER (?–1185?)

French theologian and ecclesiastical writer Peter Comestor was called *The Great Eater* because of his amazing appetite for food—much of which he could not digest—as well as his omnivorous reading habits.

COMFORT, ALEX (1920–)

Alex Comfort, the best-selling author of *The Joy of Sex: A Gourmet's Guide to Love Making* and *More Joy of Sex* is a PhD in biochemistry who has been dubbed by *Time* magazine *The Expansive Apostle of Coitus.* Of sex, Comfort says, "There is nothing to be afraid of, and never was."

Commander of the Faithful, The—See **OMAR I.**

Commisary Banks—See **BANKS, NATHANIEL PRENTISS.**

Commodore, The—See **VANDERBILT, CORNELIUS.**

COMMODUS, LUCIUS AELIUS AURELIUS (161–192)

Roman emperor Commodus dubbed himself *Hercules Secundus,* or the *Second Hercules,* for his exploits in the amphitheater. A vain exhibitionist, he took part in many gladitorial combats, reportedly killing at least 100 lions and never needing more than a single blow to dispose of each of them. In 192 *Hercules Secundus* was strangled by a wrestler.

COMMONER, BARRY (1917–)

Biologist Barry Commoner, a leading spokesman for environmental protection and the development of solar energy, is called *The Paul Revere of Ecology.*

Communist Capitalist, The—See **ENGELS, FRIEDRICH.**

COMO, PERRY (1912–)

At the height of his popularity, during the 1940s and 1950s, popular singer Perry Como was nicknamed *The King of the Jukes,* for his many hit recordings. Como was long referred to as *The Barber* because he had previously worked at that trade, at such a young age he had to stand on a milk-bottle case to cut patrons' hair. He is also called *Mr. Relaxation* because of his casual style of singing.

Compulsive Spy, The—See HUNT, E. HOWARD.

COMSTOCK, ANTHONY (1844–1915)

Devoting his life to ridding art and literature of all he considered "lewd and lascivious," moral crusader Anthony Comstock was known to some as *The Roundsman of the Lord* and to others as *The Great American Bluenose*. In 1913 he said, "In 41 years I have convicted persons enough to fill a passenger train of 61 coaches—60 coaches containing 60 passengers and the 61st almost full. I have destroyed 160 tons of obscene literature." He proudly claimed he had hounded 16 persons to death, either through fear or suicide, to satisfy his puritanism. Among his successes were the firing of Walt Whitman from his government job for the publication of *Leaves of Grass,* the arrest of Victoria Woodhull, a female candidate for president, and the banning of Margaret Sanger's books on birth control in New York. George Bernard Shaw said of him, "Comstockery is the world's standing joke at the expense of the U.S."

COMTE, AUGUSTE (1798–1857)

French philosopher Auguste Comte won the sobriquet *The Father of Positivism* for devising a system of thought that held that which is good here is good everywhere and if there is a future life, the best preparation for it is to live fully in the here and now. On a personal level Comte was hardly up to his philosophy, which he regarded as a new religion that would save humanity. He twice suffered mental collapses and attempted suicide at least once.

Concord Rebel, The—See THOREAU, HENRY DAVID.

CONDORCANQUI, JOSE GABRIEL (1742–1781)

Eighteenth century South American revolutionist Jose Gabriel Condorcanqui, who sought to free his native Peru from Spanish suppression, was called by his supporters *The Last of the Incas*.

Coney Island Killer, The—See Cyclone Louie.

CONFORTE, JOSEPH (?–)

Known as *Nevada's Master Pimp,* Joe Conforte owned the state's most famous legal bordello, the Mustang Ranch, for more than a quarter of a century. In 1980 it was announced that Conforte sold the brothel to Madam Gina Wilson for a sum reported to be $19.8 million.

CONFUCIUS (551–479 B.C.)

While Confucius is often designated *The Philosopher of China* and *The Moral Censor of China,* to his mother he was *Little Hillock,* because of a protuberance on the top of his head.

Congressional Playboy, The—See ZIONCHECK, MARION A.

Connecticut Tax Lady, The—See KELLEMS, VIVIEN.

CONNERY, SEAN (1930–)

British actor Sean Connery has been called *Mr. Kisskiss Bangbang,* an apt critique of his James Bond movie roles.

CONNORS, CHARLES "Ice Wagon" (?–1933)

One of the most rapacious and daring gangsters of the 1920s and 1930s, Charles Connors was nicknamed *Ice Wagon Connors* by the underworld for the most unfortunate of reasons. Years before his underworld assassination, he crashed a robbery getaway car into an ice wagon and was saddled with the moniker thereafter.

Conquered Hero, The—See NASSER, GAMAL ABDEL.

Conquering Lion, The—See HAILE SELASSIE.

Conqueror of the Matterhorn, The— See WHYMPER, EDWARD.

CONRAD, JOHN (1957–)

A young Boulder, Colo., waiter who has been subjected to various psychological studies for his amazing memory, John Conrad has demonstrated the ability to memorize as many as 19 complete dinner orders at a time and fill them without a single omission, whether entree, vegetable, condiment, dressing, etc. He has been labeled by journalists *A Memory for All Seasonings*.

CONRAD, JOSEPH (1857–1924)

Ukrainian-born British novelist and short story writer Joseph Conrad was called *The Sea Dreamer*, since many of his tales were set on the great waters of the world, especially on the Indian Ocean. Many critics take exception to the sobriquet, however, and insist he should be classified with the great Continental (especially French) writers for his finely crafted studies of character. The image of a "sea dreamer," they say, fails to convey this ability.

CONRAD II, KING OF GERMANY AND HOLY ROMAN EMPEROR (c. 984–1039)

One of the most resourceful of medieval German monarchs, Conrad II was called *The Salic* for his Salic Code, which held that freeholds could not have their lands taken from them except by a finding of their peers. Conrad II's purpose was to protect vassals from the arbitrary power of their lords and also to strengthen the power of the monarchy and limit that of the nobles. He gained for the crown the allegiance of both the burghers and vassals.

Conscience of Congress, The—See FENWICK, MILLICENT.

Contemporary Cassandra, The—See THOMPSON, DOROTHY.

CONVERSE, HARRIET (1836–1903)

American Indian folklore writer Harriet Converse was nicknamed *The Watcher* by Indians for the way she studied their ways. Because of the great good she did for the Six Nations tribe, she was made a chief in 1891.

Converted Jacobin, The— See WORDSWORTH, WILLIAM.

COOGAN, JACKIE (1914–)

During the 1920s child actor Jackie Coogan was called *The Youngest Millionaire*. After starring

he became the youngest person ever to accumulate a million dollars.

COOK, DEWITT CLINTON—See Moon Maniac, The.

COOK, FREDERICK A. *(1865–1940)*

Dr. Frederick A. Cook was generally regarded as the loser in the dispute with Robert Peary over which explorer actually reached the North Pole in 1908. The overwhelming opinion was that Cook fabricated his claims, for which he was labeled *The False Explorer*. In the 1920s Cook was convicted in a Texas oil-land sales fraud and sentenced to 14 years imprisonment, winning the additional nickname *Prince of Losers*. He was released in 1931 and granted a pardon shortly before his death in 1940 by President Franklin D. Roosevelt. By that time, ironically, the lands sold in the scheme were selling at prices considerably higher than the so-called fraud figure.

COOKE, ALISTAIR *(1908–   )*

British-born journalist and television personality Alistair Cooke, popular on both sides of the Atlantic, has been nicknamed *Britain's Mr. America*.

COOLIDGE, CALVIN *(1872–1933)*

Calvin Coolidge, the 30th president of the United States, was a man of few words who had no nicknames other than *Silent Cal*—save for the childhood *Red*. His political opponents claimed he made a national institution out of holding his tongue only because he had nothing to say. Coolidge differed a bit in emphasis and once commented, "If you don't say anything, you won't be called on to repeat it." (See also Introduction.)

Coolidge of the West, The—See LANDON, ALFRED M.

COOPER, ALICE *(1948–   )*

U.S. rock-and-roll singer Alice Cooper has been called *Mr. America, Schlock Rock's Godzilla,* and *The Queen of Rock 'n' Rouge,* the last for his outrageous makeup and onstage antics.

COOPER, GARY *(1901–1961)*

Film actor Gary Cooper may have been the shy-but-sturdy Coop in later years, but during the 1920s he was known as *The It Boy* as the result of his romantic involvement with Clara Bow, Hollywood's celebrated It Girl. Cooper had played a small role in the 1927 film *It*, which starred Miss Bow and sparked a torrid love affair that kept columnists supplied with endless saucy gossip about their escapades. However, the actor blanched at being saddled with the nickname, and the affair came to an end.

COOPER, JAMES FENIMORE *(1789–1851)*

Author James Fenimore Cooper won the accolade *The American Scott* because he was inspired by the writings of Sir Walter Scott and shared the same fondness for outdoor themes.

COOPER, SAMUEL *(1609–1672)*

Noted English miniaturist Samuel Cooper was accorded the sobriquet, by Walpole, of *Van Dyck in Little*.

COPERNICUS, NICHOLAS (1473–1543)

Called *The Father of Modern Astronomy*, Polish churchman and mathematician Nicholas Copernicus proved that the Earth was not the center of the solar system and that our planet revolves around the sun, rather than vice versa. The theory was not new, Pythagoras having suggested it long before, so perhaps Copernicus' older sobriquet *The Reformer of Astronomy* is more valid.

COPPOLA, MICHAEL "Trigger Mike" (1904–1966)

Syndicate gangster *Trigger Mike Coppola* earned his nickname not only because he killed to order for the Lucky Luciano-Vito Genovese family but because he murdered one of his wives and drove another to suicide on the suspicion they might betray him to the law. Shortly after the murder of Joseph Scottoriggio, a Republican candidate for Congress in 1946, Coppola's wife died suddenly after giving birth. The police suspected *Trigger Mike* of the crime and also believed he murdered his wife in her hospital bed for fear she would talk. In fact, *Trigger Mike's* second wife later said he bragged that he had killed his first wife. Fearing *Trigger Mike's* vengeance, his second wife subsequently took an overdose of sleeping pills.

CORALLO, ANTONIO "Tony Ducks" (c. 1925–   )

East Coast mobster Antonio Corallo long ago became known as *Tony Ducks* by admiring mafioso because he has been rather successful overall in "ducking" conviction.

CORBETT, JAMES J. "Gentleman Jim" (1866–1933)

Heavyweight boxing champion James J. Corbett was dubbed *Gentleman Jim* for his behavior both inside and outside the ring. A former bank teller, he dressed conservatively and like to wear evening clothes. He was also conversant with the English classics. Inside the ring, his gentlemanliness was demonstrated by a scientific boxing style that contrasted with the standard wade-in-and-slug approach of his day. He won the championship from John L. Sullivan in 1892, the first gloved championship match fought under Marquis of Queensbury Rules. Corbett ignored the boos and catcalls of "tap dancer" from the crowd as he danced away from the champion in the early rounds. He knocked out a weary Sullivan in the 21st round. For years thereafter some Sullivan partisans continued to disparage Corbett as *The Tap Dancer*.

CORDAY, CHARLOTTE (1767–1793)

Charlotte Corday, the 24-year-old daughter of an impoverished family of minor nobility, was shaken by the execution of royalists during the French Revolution, and she determined the extremist Jean Paul Marat had to die. Under the ruse of wishing to inform on royalist traitors, she was admitted to Marat's chambers on July 13, 1793, and, while he was bathing, she stabbed him to death in his tub. In short order Corday became known as *The Angel of the Assassination* and went to the guillotine.

Corduroy Killer, The—See FISCHER, ROBERT JAMES.

CORELLI, FRANCO (1921–   )

Temperamental Italian opera tenor Franco Corelli has long been called *The Bad Boy of Opera* for

soprano Birgit Nilsson on the neck during a performance because she outlasted him on a high note.

Cormorant, The—See MARRIOTT, JOHN.

Corn and Callous Pyle—See PYLE, CHARLES C. "Cash and Carry."

CORNEILLE, PIERRE (1606–1684)

French dramatist Pierre Corneille was called *The Father of French Tragedy* and *The Shakespeare of France*. The latter is perhaps an excessive accolade, although he certainly painted powerful portraits of classical tyrants and conquerors. The sobriquet was probably used far more in other countries and after Corneille's lifetime, since most Frenchmen of his period were rather puzzled by Shakespeare and called him The Lord of British Pandemonium.

Corner Memory Thompson—See THOMPSON, JOHN.

CORNFELD, BERNARD (1927–   )

Bernie Cornfeld, the flamboyant U.S.-born mutual fund executive who built a gigantic financial investment empire in Europe, was hailed as *The Midas of the Mutual Funds* until his bubble burst in the early 1970s and thousands of investors lost millions.

Cornfield Sherlock, The— See PARKER, ELLIS.

Corn-Law Rhymer, The— See ELLIOTT, EBENEZER.

Cornplanter: ABEEL (c. 1732–1836)

Seneca Indian chief Abeel was nicknamed *Cornplanter* by the whites of New York and Pennsylvania because he encouraged his faction of the tribe to adopt the white man's agricultural techniques. After serving the French against the Colonies, he later aided the newly formed republic and undertook missions to hostile tribes on behalf of the U.S. government, always demanding payment for his aid. He accumulated some 1,300 acres of land in Pennsylvania, much of it in payment "for his valuable services to the whites." He chose land in isolated areas, where for a time at least the Cornplanter Senecas were safe from encroachment.

Coroner of the Stars, The—See NOGUCHI, THOMAS.

Corporal Violet—See NAPOLEON.

Corporate Gadfly, The— See ARMSTRONG, GERALD RALPH.

Corrector, The—See CRUDEN, ALEXANDER.

CORRIGAN, DOUGLAS "Wrong-Way" (1907–   )

Douglas Corrigan won fame in July 1938 for taking off from Floyd Bennett Field in New York for Los Angeles and flying through fog to Dublin,

Ireland, allegedly by mistake. Corrigan's "wrong-way" non-stop ocean hop captured the imagination of a Depression-weary nation and world, and he became the most celebrated flyer since Charles Lindbergh. He was known thereafter as *Wrong-Way Corrigan*.

CORTELLINI, CAMILLO *(c. 17th century)*

Regarded highly for his virtuosity with the violin, Camillo Cortellini, an Italian composer of church music, was given as a sobriquet the name of the instrument itself. He was called simply *The Violin*.

CORVINUS, MATTHIAS, KING OF HUNGARY *(1442–1490)*

Matthias Corvinus, 15th century king of Hungary, employed well over 30 amanuenses, including four librarians in Florence, to transcribe books for his lavish library at Buda, thus gaining the sobriquet *The Lorenzo de Medici of Hungary,* after his Italian contemporary. At his death the library contained 30,000 volumes, of which only about 300 survive, the remainder having been destroyed by invading Turks, who ripped them apart for the gold ornaments in their bindings.

COSELL, HOWARD *(1920–   )*

Originally an attorney and now a leading television personality, controversial sports commentator Howard Cosell is called *The Mouth*. Many sports fans complain he never stops talking, but they never fail to dial him in, if only to hate him.

COSTELLO, FRANK *(1891–1973)*

As the acknowledged *Prime Minister of the Underworld,* Frank Costello handled the crime syndicate's dealings with dignitaries of the "legit world"—the police, judges, and politicos—to obtain protection for the mob.

COUE, EMILE *(1857–1926)*

French mental healer Emile Coue was hailed as a genius when he arrived in the United States in 1923 to promote his sure-fire program for happiness and peace of mind. It was quite a simple idea, even if Americans considered the name of his therapy, autosuggestion, rather clumsy. Coue's secret was summed up in 12 words: "Day by day in every way I am getting better and better." All one had to do was keep repeating that sentence, and happiness was assured, said *The Pied Piper of Contentment,* as he was dubbed. Evidently to make sure they had the words exactly right, thousands jammed the little Frenchman's lectures or took courses at newly established Coue Institutes. But after a time Coueism lost its appeal, and the public even told jokes about it, including the following:

Woman: "My husband thinks he's sick. He's always complaining."

Coue: "Well, just tell him that day by day in every way he is getting better and better."

Woman (some days later): "I have even worse trouble now."

Coue: "What is it, my dear lady?"

Woman: "Now my husband thinks he's dead."

COUGHLIN, FATHER CHARLES E. *(1891–1979)*

The notorious *Radio Priest* of the 1930s, Father Charles E. Coughlin, achieved an enormous following during the Depression with his strident, rasping brogue and virulent anti-semitism. Some 30 million listeners tuned in to his Sunday afternoon broadcasts to hear him denounce Franklin Delano Roosevelt and Jews and communists, the latter two being, he insisted, one and the same. A poll in 1934 showed that Father Coughlin was sec-

outspoken harangues—including the approval of Hitler's treatment of the Jews—caused *The Radio Priest* to lose some of its outlets, and in 1940 Church superiors forced him off the airwaves, although he was allowed to retain his pulpit. His magazine *Social Justice* was ordered discontinued by the government at the outbreak of World War II and it eventually folded.

Count Combe—
See COMBE, WILLIAM.

Count of Gramercy Park, The—See CHAPMAN, GERALD.

Counterfeit Lady, The—
See CARLETON, MARY.

Countess Who Cures the Blues, The—See PIAZZA, "Countess" WILLIE V.

COUZENS, JAMES (1872–1935)

Sen. James Couzens of Michigan, one of the richest men ever to serve in Congress, was nicknamed *The Croesus of the Senate*. Noted for his donations to philanthropic organizations, he was also referred to as *The Poor Man's Friend*.

Coward of Chappaquiddick, The—See KENNEDY, EDWARD M.

Cowboy Jess—See WILLARD, JESS.

Cowboy Philosopher, The—See ROGERS, WILL.

COWLEY, ABRAHAM (1618–1667)

A 17th century English poet whose works were highly esteemed in their time, although far less today, Abraham Cowley was hailed as *Our Pindar,* after the illustrious Greek lyric poet. The duke of Buckingham, perhaps the most ecstatic admirer of Cowley's verses, declared he deserved a combined accolade as the "Pindar, Horace, and Virgil of England."

COX, JACK (1921–   )

Texas politician Jack Cox was disparagingly called *The Turncoat Opportunist* in 1962 when he changed loyalties and switched from the Democratic to the Republican Party. The nickname was originated by Gov. John R. Connally, who was a Democrat at the time but did the same thing himself a few years later.

COYSEVOX, ANTOINE (1640–1720)

Noted Spanish-born French painter Antoine Coysevox was called *The Van Dyck of Sculpture,* after Sir Anthony Van Dyck

CRABB, CHRISTOPHER COLUMBUS (1852–1935)

Christopher Columbus Crabb was known as *Mr. Solid Man,* a solid man being a term for the lover of a prostitute. Rising from a $14-a-week clerk in Chicago's Marshall Field department store, he became the adviser and financial manager of Lizzie Allen, one of the city's fabled madams of the 19th century. Remarkably, he was at the same time the financial manager of a number of other madams. Trusted implicitly by all and said never to have stolen a cent, he was so highly regarded that Allen willed him $300,000, and another madam left him $150,000. Thereafter a sort of elder statesman of vice, he died extremely wealthy, leaving the bulk of his fortune to the Illinois Masonic Orphans' Home.

CRABB, LIONEL (1910–1956)

Britian's greatest frogman during World War II, Lionel Crabb, almost single-handedly cleared the depths around Gibraltar of mines and armed Italian frogmen while removing bombs attached to the hulls of British warships. After the war he worked in underwater intelligence against the Russians and became known as *The Frogman Spy*. He died in Portsmouth harbor while apparently on a spy mission against three Soviet warships.

Cradle Duke, The—See **Godfrey the Courageous.**

CRANE, STEPHEN (1871–1900)

Brilliant young writer Stephen Crane was hated by many members of the New York Police Department, who called him *The French Whore Lover*. Crane had testified in the case of a police officer accused of brutality against a streetwalker who had failed to give him a cut of her revenues. The police vendetta continued against Crane during the last four years of his life, and he was subjected to such continuous harassments as frequent police raids on his room in search of opium. Crane twice left the city because of the police but returned and died of tuberculosis.

CRASSUS, MARCUS LICINIUS (c. 115–53 B.C.)

Known as *Dives*, or *The Rich*, Roman politician and financial speculator Marcus Licinius Crassus accumulated great wealth through what Plutarch called "fire and rapine." Since Rome had no fire department, Crassus formed his own 500-man brigade, which rushed to each fire but did nothing until Crassus negotiated payment with the property owner. Most of Crassus' enormous wealth came from the civil war of 88–83 B.C. when, as a lieutenant to Lucius Cornelius Sulla, he bought up captured enemy property at rock-bottom prices. Showing a murderous inability to stick to the prescribed list of victims, Crassus killed many innocent landholders in his insatiable greed for property. According to a legend which may be deliciously apocryphal, *Dives* was captured by Syrians during a military campaign and put to death by having molten gold poured down his throat and being decapitated.

CRAWFORD, JOAN (1903–1977)

Hollywood actress Joan Crawford was dubbed *The Clothes Horse* by Depression-era critics because she wore a lavish wardrobe when so many Americans were ill-fed and ill-clothed. She defended her actions to the press by proclaiming: "I, Joan Crawford, I believe in the dollar. Everything I earn, I spend."

Crazy Bet—See **VAN LEW, ELIZABETH.**

Crazy Jane—See **JOANNA LA LOCA.**

Crazy Marsh—See **MARSH, SYLVESTER "Crazy."**

Crazy Suicide, The— See **BELMONTE, JUAN.**

Creator of the "Eclectic Readers," The—See **MCGUFFEY, WILLIAM HOLMES.**

Creator of the New Comedy, The—See **ARISTOPHANES.**

CREBILLON, PROSPER JOLYOT DE *(1674–1762)*

Regarded as a master of portraying terror and rage, French classical dramatist Prosper Jolyot de Crebillon gained the accolade *The Aeschylus of France.*

***Creeping Jesus*—See ZUKOR, ADOLPH.**

***Creepy*—See KARPIS, ALVIN "Creepy."**

CRICHTON, JAMES "The Admirable" *(1560?–1582)*

Scottish prodigy James Crichton was nicknamed *The Admirable Crichton* since he had perfectly mastered 10 foreign languages by the age of 15. After fighting with great distinction with the French Army and winning fame as a superb swordsman, he went to Italy at the age of 19 to serve as tutor and dueling instructor to the duke of Mantua's son, Prince Vincenzo, a ruffianly youth. Set upon in the street one night by three masked robbers, Crichton killed one, routed another, and spared the third when he unmasked himself. Recognizing Prince Vincenzo, Crichton immediately kneeled and held his sword by the point, offering it with devotion to his master. The mean Vincenzo seized the weapon and ran his tutor through. The prince was sent into exile for the killing, and the entire court wore mourning for *The Admirable Crichton* for three quarters of a year.

***Crime Fighter, The*—See NAST, THOMAS.**

CRIPPS, STAFFORD *(1889–1952)*

Winston Churchill often referred to British statesman Sir Stafford Cripps as *God.* What he pre-

for the grace of God, goes God."

***Critic of Progress, The*—See WELLS, H. G.**

CROCKETT, DAVY *(1786–1836)*

Davy Crockett, a frontiersman and teller of tall tales, was called *The Munchhausen of the West* because of his amazing claims. The original Baron von Munchhausen, a fictitious character created by Rudolf Erich Raspe in 1785, has become the symbol of impossible and highly mendacious, though amusing, adventures. Now remembered as the *King of the Wild Frontier,* a modern-day coinage, Davy said he "kilt 47 b'ars" in one month and single-handedly chopped to pieces a cougar with his "good old shiv." An oft in-and-out Tennessee congressman, he headed for Texas and died in 1836 at the Alamo, his greatest moment of glory.

***Croesus of the Senate, The*—See COUZENS, JAMES.**

CROISET, GERARD *(1909–   )*

Celebrated for using his psychic abilities to help police in Europe and America solve crimes and missing persons cases, Gerard Croiset is called *The Radar Brain* and *The Dutchman with the X-ray Mind.*

CROKER, THOMAS CROFTON *(1798–1854)*

Besides being the author of *Fairy Legends of the South of Ireland,* Thomas Crofton Croker was a man of extremely short stature. Sir Walter Scott nicknamed him *The King of the Fairies.*

CROMWELL, OLIVER (1599–1658)

Oliver Cromwell, the English revolutionary who became lord protector of England after the overthrow of the monarchy, was called many things by friend and foe. To some he was *God's Englishman,* but to others he was *The Man of Sin* and *The Usurper.* He was also called *Ironsides,* a name taken from the famous regiment he led in England's civil war.

CROMWELL, RICHARD (1626–1712)

The son of Oliver Cromwell, Richard Cromwell succeeded his father as lord protector of England. His short rule, lasting from September 1658 to May 1659, was marked by such ineptness and timidity that he was forced to resign. He was referred to with disdain as *Queen Dick.*

CROMWELL, THOMAS (c. 1485–1540)

Thomas Cromwell, the son of a blacksmith, rose to high position as the earl of Essex. Appointed vicar-general by Henry VIII of England to suppress the monasteries, he completed the task to his own enrichment, winning the nickname *The Hammer* (or *The Maul) of the Monks.* Cromwell was later executed for treason by Henry for arranging a royal marriage with Anne of Cleves, whom the King found to look like a "Flanders mare."

CRONKITE, WALTER LELAND, JR. (1916–   )

U.S. radio and television news commentator Walter Cronkite enjoyed tremendous public respect and often turned up on polls as the most trusted man in the country. Fans often called him *Uncle Walter,* a nickname given him by colleagues.

Crookback—See RICHARD III.

CROSBY, HARRY LILLIS "Bing" (1903–1977)

Crooner Harry Lillis Crosby was given the nickname *Bing* at the age of seven by his parents because of his fondness for a Sunday comic strip called *Bingville Bugle.*

Crowbar Man, The: PHINEAS P. GAGE (1823–1861)

An amazing medical oddity, railroad worker Phineas P. Gage was tamping down an explosive charge at Cavendish, Vt., on Sept. 13, 1848, when he inadvertently sparked the powder. The blast propelled a 13-1/4-pound tamping iron through his brain and out the top of his head. Remarkably, Gage never lost consciousness while being taken by oxcart to a hotel a mile away, where doctors cleaned his wound. Although he suffered periods of severe vomiting and hemorrhaging, he recovered. Blinded in his left eye and left with a 3½-inch-wide hole in his skull, he eventually resumed work, becoming celebrated as *The Crowbar Man* and living for nearly three more years. His skull, together with the tamping iron, is on display in the Harvard Medical School's museum.

CROWLEY, ALEISTER (1875–1947)

Aleister Crowley, perhaps the greatest master of the occult in the 20th century, was an irreligionist who founded his own "faith" based on black magic, sexual orgies and blood sacrifice—practices that caused his expulsion from a number of countries. While the press reviled him as *The Beast,* he took pride in his self-proclaimed sobriquet, *Wickedest Man in the World.*

CROWLEY, FRANCIS "Two Gun" (1911–1931)

Somewhat of a 20th century counterpart of Billy the Kid, Francis Crowley was dubbed by the press *Two Gun Crowley,* although there is no evidence he ever went on one of his robberies or murder sprees with more than one gun. Famous as the target of a dramatic siege by 300 New York police officers in 1931, which resulted in his capture, he later attempted to escape from the Sing Sing death house. In the end he died without the braggadocio of the newspaper-bred *Two Gun Crowley,* telling Warden Lewis E. Lawes, who regarded him as having totally reformed, to ''give my love to mother'' just before the switch was thrown.

Crown Prince, The—See MCADOO, WILLIAM GIBBS; SULZBERGER, ARTHUR OCHS.

Crown Prince of the New Deal, The—See ROOSEVELT, JAMES.

Crown Stealer, The—See BLOOD, THOMAS.

CROWNE, JOHN (?–1703)

Seventeenth century English dramatist John Crowne was labeled *Starch Johnny* by his contemporaries ''because of the unalterable stiffness and propriety of his collar and cravat.''

CRUDEN, ALEXANDER (1701–1770)

Alexander Cruden, a London bookseller who compiled *The Concordance of the Holy Scriptures,* appropriated for himself the sobriquet *The Corrector,* which aptly described his view of his mis-

between the two editions of his *Concordance,* in 1737 and 1761, Cruden thought it his duty to expunge all graffiti that struck him at odds with good morals, and he carried with him a sponge at all times for that purpose.

Cruel, The—See HENRY VI OF GERMANY.

Crybaby Leo—See TOLSTOY, LEO.

Crying Howe— See HOWE, WILLIAM F.

Cuddly Dudley—See MOORE, DUDLEY.

Cufflinks Carl—See SANDERS, CARL.

Cultured Perelman—See SHULMAN, MAX.

CUMBERLAND, RICHARD (1732–1811)

English playwright Richard Cumberland called *The Man Without a Skin* because he was incapable of tolerating even the smallest measure of adverse criticism.

CUMBERLAND, WILLIAM AUGUSTUS, DUKE OF (1721–1765)

The third son of George II, William Augustus, duke of Cumberland, had a dismal record against the French in military battle. But he scored an outstanding victory over the Highlanders under Prince

Charles Edward on Culloden Moor in 1746, ending all hopes for the British Stuart dynasty. His cruelty in dealing with foes both during and after battle earned Cumberland the sobriquets *The Butcher of Culloden* and *The Bloody Butcher*.

CUMMINGS, E. E. *(1894–1962)*

e. e. cummings (Edward Estlin Cummings) gained fame as an *enfant terrible* of American letters because of his highly individualistic and eccentric non-use of punctuation and capitalization in his poetry. Other writers wreaked their revenge on him with the nickname *LOWER CASE CUMMINGS*—in capital letters.

Cuncator—See VERRUCOSUS, QUINTUS FABIUS MAXIMUS.

CUNNINGHAM, MARY *(1952–)*

Mary Cunningham rose from secretary to corporate vice president of the Bendix company within a span of 12 months, but she later quit amid a burst of publicity about her relationship with Bendix chairman William Agee, who insisted she had earned every promotion along the way. In June 1982 Agee married Cunningham, who was then holding an executive position with Seagram & Son, and the press promptly dubbed her *First Lady of Bendix*. Some more outspoken reporters insisted the term had been first used behind her back during her Bendix days.

Curator of the Secrets of 62 Nations, The—See HAMMARSKJOLD, DAG.

Curious Scrapmonger, The—See BOSWELL, JAMES.

Curly Lashes—See MOUNTBATTEN, LORD LOUIS.

CURRY, GEORGE—See Big Nose Parrott.

Curthose: ROBERT II, DUKE OF NORMANDY *(c. 1056–1134)*

Robert II, duke of Normandy and the eldest son of William the Conqueror, was nicknamed *Curthose* because he was short and stout. A fearsome warrior despite his appearance, he nevertheless is remembered for his nickname, which became a description of short socks or boots.

CURTICE, HARLOW HERBERT *(1893–1962)*

General Motors president Harlow Herbert Curtice became known in business circles as *Bet-a-Billion Curtice* in 1954. When most businessmen were fearfully predicting a major economic slump, he announced in a speech to 500 of the nation's top executives, "No depression is in my vision." After he declared GM would spend a billion dollars on expansion during the next two years in anticipation of a boom in car sales, *Bet-a-Billion's* optimism proved contagious, and the nation went on a giant buying spree. Some observers said he had literally talked the country out of an ecomomic slump.

CURTIS, CHARLES *(1860–1936)*

Charles Curtis, vice president of the United States under Herbert Hoover, was nicknamed *Big Chief* because of his Indian blood.

CUSHMAN, PAULINE (1833–1893)

A New Orleans-born belle who was an intelligence agent for the Union during the Civil War, Pauline Cushman won fame as *The Spy of the Cumberland*. She crossed the lines on numerous occasions, until she was finally captured and sentenced to hang. Rescued by Union troops attacking Shelbyville, Tenn., she was lionized thereafter in the North and by Abraham Lincoln personally as a frequent White House guest. After the war she had a successful stage career, then an unhappy marriage. A later stage comeback after leaving her husband proved unsuccessful, and, after working as a cleaning woman in San Francisco, she committed suicide in 1893. At the time of her death, she was remembered once more and given a big funeral and a tombstone engraved with her nickname.

CUSTER, GEORGE ARMSTRONG (1839–1876)

Colorful military man George Armstrong Custer gained the sobriquet *The Boy General* only two years after graduating from West Point, when he was made a brigadier general of volunteers during the Civil War. Later, as he sought new fame and rank with the U.S. Army in the West, he was known as *The Scourge of the Indians*. His troops called him *Ringlets* and the Indians *Yellow Hair* because of his long, curly blond hair. When he died at the Battle of Little Big Horn, the Indians did not scalp him, out of respect for *Yellow Hair,* it was said. But most likely the explanation was that he had killed himself and Indians did not take the hair of a suicide.

Custodian of Flops, The—See CAIN, PATRICK J.

Cut-rate Showman, The—See TODD, MIKE.

Cyclone Louie: VACH LEWIS (1882–1908)

Vach Lewis, an early 20th century amusement park strong man known professionally as *Cyclone Louie,* was also a professional assassin known as *The Coney Island Killer*. Whenever murder victims turned up in New York's Coney Island with their necks virtually wrung like chickens, everyone in the area, including the police, knew it was the work of *Cyclone Louie,* but proving it was another matter. He was murdered in 1908 by an ambush party of 20 rival gangsters, almost all of whom pumped bullets into him.

Cyclops Cinderella—See LAKE, VERONICA.

Cynic Parasite, The— See THACKERAY, WILLIAM MAKEPEACE.

CYRIL OF ALEXANDRIA, ST. (376–444)

Christian theologian St. Cyril of Alexandria was called *The Champion of the Virgin* and *The Doctor of the Incarnation*. A supporter of the scriptural interpretation of the Alexandrian School, which opposed Chrysostom of the Antioch School, he championed orthodoxy against Nestorius, who objected to calling the Virgin Mary the mother of God.

Czar Cannon—See CANNON, JOSEPH GURNEY.

Czar of Circumlocution, The—See **BALOGH, HARRY.**

Czech Forerunner of Protestantism, The—See **HUS, JOHN.**

D

Dad—See **PRICE, STERLING.**

Dame de Beaute, La—See **SOREL, AGNES.**

DAMIENS, ROBERT FRANCOIS (1715–1757)

By attempting to assassinate Louis XV of France in 1757, Robert Francois Damiens secured his own demise and the nickname *The Devil*.

Damned Cowboy, That—See **ROOSEVELT, THEODORE.**

Damned Little Flycop, That—See **WOOLDRIDGE, CLIFTON.**

Dancing Chancellor, The—See **HATTON, CHRISTOPHER.**

Dandy King, The—See **MURAT, JOACHIM.**

Dandy of Country Music, The—See **DEAN, JIMMY RAY.**

DANGERFIELD, THOMAS (1650?–1685)

One of the great false witnesses in English history, Thomas Dangerfield was a key figure in the so-called Meal Tub plot, in which he alleged that the Catholics planned the assassinations of the king, the earl of Shaftesbury and others. He was discredited in court and died in custody, tarred with the sobriquet *The Restoration Rogue*.

Danish Luther, The—See **TAUSEN, HANS.**

Danish Moliere, The—See **HOLBERG, LOUIS, BARON DE.**

Danish Plautus, The—See **HOLBERG, LOUIS, BARON DE.**

DANTE ALIGHIERI (1265–1321)

The author of *The Divine Comedy* celebrated Italian poet, Dante Alighieri was dubbed by Byron *The Great Poet-Sire of Italy*. Nicknaming himself *The White Flower,* Dante likened himself to a flower bent and closed by the night frost and then blanched by the sun—the symbol of reason—thus opening its leaves. Dante describes the effect of the sun on him through a speech by Virgil as the latter persuades him to follow his guidance.

DANTON, GEORGES JACQUES (1759–1794)

French revolutionist Georges Jacques Danton led the Tuileries riot of 1792 and headed the Jacobins known as *The Mirabeau of the Mob.* In 1794, himself doomed to the guillotine, he told his executioner, "Afterward, show my head to the people. It is a head worth looking at."

Danton of Modern Poetry, The—
BROWNING, ROBERT.

*D'AQUINO, IVA—***See Tokyo Rose.**

*Daring in War, The—***See CLIVE, ROBERT, LORD.**

*Dark Cloud, The—***See ROBESON, PAUL.**

*Dark Menace, The—***See WILLS, HENRY.**

*Darling of the Gods, The—***See BANKHEAD, TALLULAH.**

DARROW, CLARENCE SEWARD (1857–1938)

Regarded as probably America's greatest lawyer, Clarence Seward Darrow was famed as *The Defender of the Damned,* a sobriquet he earned for saving defendants almost certain to be convicted from guilty verdicts and others from even more certain death penalties. Perhaps the oustanding example of the latter was Darrow's triumph in saving thrill-slayers Nathan Leopold and Richard Loeb from execution for the 1924 murder of young Bobby Franks, their experiment in the perfect crime.

*D'Artagnan of the A.E.F., The—***See MACARTHUR, DOUGLAS.**

Charles Darwin, who developed the theory of organic evolution through natural selection, was accorded such accolades as *The Great Naturalist* and *The Sage of Down House,* a reference to his home. As a youth he was called *Gas* by his father because his chemical experiments often ended in explosions. He was also called *Ratcatcher* because of his research with insects and animals. On his epic scientific voyage aboard the H.M.S. *Beagle,* Darwin was referred to by Capt. Fitz-Roy and other officers as *Philos,* short for philosopher.

*Darwin of Sex, The—***See ELLIS, HAVELOCK.**

*Darwin's Bulldog—***See HUXLEY, THOMAS HENRY.**

*Daubaway Weirdsley—***See BEARDSLEY, AUBREY.**

DAUGHERTY, HARRY M. (1860–1941)

President Warren G. Harding put more trust in Attorney General Harry M. Daugherty than any other of his associates, which goes far to explain the disgrace into which his administration fell. Daugherty, instrumental in bringing Harding to the presidency, was nicknamed *The President-maker.* Also called *Foxy Harry,* he was involved in much of Ohio Gang's dubious activities. He later had to stand trial in a bizarre multimillion-dollar alien property swindle. He beat the charge but was by then already totally discredited.

*Daughter of the Gods, The—***See NILSSON, BIRGIT.**

DAVID, JACQUES LOUIS (1748–1825)

Founder of the modern French school of painting, Jacques Louis David was the artistic superintendent of the grand national fetes of the French Revolution. A complete Jacobin, he cast his vote for the death of Louis XVI. His most famous painting of the revolutionary period is probably *Murder of Marat*. His nickname *The Artist of the Revolution* did not work in his favor in 1816, when he was banished from France.

DAVIDSON, JO (1883–1952)

American sculptor Jo Davidson, known for his forcefully realistic busts of his contemporaries—Roosevelt, Mussolini, Will Rogers, Gen. Pershing and Marshals Foch and Joffre—was given the sobriquet *The Plastic Historian*.

DAVIS, GARRY (1921–   )

American World War II bomber pilot Garry Davis, who renounced his U.S. citizenship, is the self-proclaimed *World Citizen No. 1*.

DAVIS, JEFF (1862–1913)

Jeff Davis, a colorful Arkansas politician who served as state attorney general and later governor during the early 20th century, was affectionately nicknamed *Pint-a-Day Davis* by voters. When his Baptist church withdrew fellowship from him on charges of drinking, he responded that he was just a "pint-a-day" Baptist kicked out by "quart-a-day" deacons. He asked voters who had ever imbibed to vote for him, and it appears most of them did.

DAVIS, JEFF (1883–1968)

Dubbed *King of the Hobos,* Jeff Davis founded the Hobos of America and long sought to differentiate hobos from tramps and bums in the public's mind.

DAVIS, NATHAN SMITH (1817–1904)

Dr. Nathan Smith Davis, a noted physician and editor of medical journals, was acknowledged as *The Father of the American Medical Association*. He was the driving force in bringing together medical delegates from throughout the country in Philadelphia in 1847 to establish the organization.

DAVIS, SAM—See Boy-Hero of the Confederacy

DAVIS, SAMMY, JR. (1925–   )

Known as *Mr. Wonderful* for his many talents, black entertainer, television personality and actor Sammy Davis, Jr., who lost his eye in an automobile accident, gained the nickname *America's One-eyed Jewish Negro* following his conversion to Judaism.

DAWSON, CHARLES (1864–1916)

English lawyer, fossil hunter and antiquarian Charles Dawson became known as *The Wizard of Sussex* after his discovery in 1908 of an allegedly ancient human skull with an ape-like jaw. The remains became known as "Piltdown Man" and were verified as belonging to "the missing link" between ape and man. Dawson died in 1916, his sobriquet intact, but he lost it in 1953 when scientists determined he had been a colossal hoaxer who

by staining it the color of mahogany with iron salt and bichromate.

DAY, DORIS (1924–)

Blonde Doris Day, the Hollywood singer and actress, has been called *The Golden Tonsil, The Tomboy with a Voice* and alluding to her great earning power, *The Three-Million-Dollar Freckled Corporation.* She took some offense at being known in the movie colony as *The Virgin,* a reference to the type of role she insisted upon playing, which gave rise to the joke variously attributed to Groucho Marx and Oscar Levant: "I knew Doris Day before she was a virgin."

DE CLARE, RICHARD (?–1176)

Richard de Clare, second earl of Pembroke, became famous for his bravery in many military campaigns in Ireland, and his soldiers nicknamed him *Strongbow.*

DE KAPLANY, GEZA (1926–)

Convicted of one of California's most heinous crimes, the torture-murder of his beautiful 25-year-old model-wife in 1962, Dr. Geza de Kaplany was dubbed *The Acid Doctor* by the press and sentenced to life imprisonment. Although his jury was assured by a spokesman for the state that he would be classified as a "special-interest prisoner" almost certain never to be paroled, de Kaplany became a cause celebre in 1976 when it was learned he had been quietly released and put on a plane for Taiwan, where there was urgent need, it was said, for a cardiac specialist.

De Lawd—See KING, MARTIN LUTHER, JR.

DE NIRO, ROBERT (1945–)

New York-born movie actor Robert De Niro was nicknamed *Bobby Milk* while growing up in the city's Little Italy section because he was such a pale and thin child.

DE QUINCEY, THOMAS (1785–1859)

English essayist Thomas De Quincey became known as *The English Opium-Eater* after the publication of his classic *Confessions of an English Opium-Eater.* The habit was generally credited with reducing his literary output.

DE RUYTER, MICHAEL (1607–1676)

The great Dutch admiral Michael De Ruyter, who savaged the English fleet and sailed his flotilla up the Medway and Thames in 1667 and towed off the flagship *Royal Charles,* was called *The Trembling Admiral.* The nickname was not a reflection on his courage, which was almost boundless, but rather the description of a slight tremor suffered in all his limbs, the result of bad fish eaten in his youth.

DE SAPIO, CARMINE (1908–)

New York Tammany Hall leader Carmine De Sapio, who went to prison for conspiracy, had long been known as *The Bishop* for the soft-spoken, if ironhanded, way he ran Tammany politics. Following his fall from grace, De Sapio was given the sobriquet *The Last of the Great New York Bosses,* a "last-of" appellation with more truth to it than most.

DE SICA, VITTORIO (1901–1974)

Italian neo-realist movie director Vittorio De Sica dubbed himself *The Artist of the Poor* because he preferred to use common laborers rather than professional actors and to film in the streets rather than in studios.

DE VALERA, EAMON (1882–1975)

Irish statesman Eamon de Valera fought for Irish independence from England in the Easter Rebellion of 1916 and served as prime minister and president of Ireland for many years. The tall leader was affectionately nicknamed *The Long Fellow* by supporters.

Deacon Jim—See MILLER, JAMES P. "Deacon Jim."

Deadly Asp, The—See PARKER, DOROTHY.

Deadwood Dick: RICHARD CLARK (or Clarke) (1845–1910)

A Deadwood, S.D., settler who drove a stage out of town for many years, Richard Clark (or Clarke) claimed to be the real *Deadwood Dick,* the tough-fighting, fast-shooting hero of scores of dime novels bearing the publisher's line, "Truth is stranger than fiction." Several other *Deadwood Dicks* claimed the honor, but Clark turned his claim into a personal industry by offering for sale to tourists rusty guns with bogus histories, pinup pictures of himself and homemade Indian scalps.

Deaf and Dumb Demagogue, The—See UMAI.

Deaf Charley—See HANKS, O. C. "Deaf Charley."

Deaf 'Un, The—See BURKE, JAMES.

DEAN, JAY HANNA "Dizzy" (1911–1974)

Perhaps the most colorful of all American baseball players, Jay Hanna Dean, born Jerome, was called *Dizzy* not simply because he was but because of his ability to drive others totally dizzy as well. A typical *Dizzy* tale concerns a female English journalist who became so exasperated with his bizarre use of language in an interview that she said, "Mr. Dean, don't you know the King's English?" *The Diz* blinked, reflected and responded, "Sure I do, and so's the Queen." (See also Introduction.)

DEAN, JIMMY RAY (1928–   )

American country and western singer Jimmy Dean is called *The Dandy of Country Music.*

DEAN, JOHN W., III (1938–   )

John W. Dean III, counsel to President Richard Nixon, was the key prosecution witness in the Watergate hearings that tumbled Nixon from power. Dean was one of the three men involved in the affair or its aftermath who were labeled *Mr. Clean.* Some Nixon supporters used the term disparagingly to cast a reflection on his neat appearance as an indication of effeminacy while Nixon opponents hailed him for coming completely clean in his testimony. (See also Ford, Gerald R., and Richardson, Elliot Lee.)

Dean of American Criminologists, The—See SUTHERLAND, EDWIN H.

Dean of American Letters, The—See WILSON, EDMUND.

Dean of Black Classical Composers, The—See STILL, WILLIAM GRANT.

Dean of Chicago Gunmen, The—See STEVENS, WALTER.

Dean of Commentators, The—See KALTENBORN, H. V.

Dean of the House, The—See SABATH, ADOLPH JOACHIM.

Dear Alben—See BARKLEY, ALBEN W.

Death on a Pale Horse—See WIRZ, HENRY.

Death Valley Scotty: WALTER SCOTT (1875–1954)

A showman ''desert rat'' who claimed to have found a great gold strike in Death Valley, Walter Scott won the nickname *Death Valley Scotty* when he was a youth driving 20-mule-team borax wagons across the desert. Around 1900 Scotty was promoting Death Valley as a gold-mine bonanza and extracting a fair amount of money from backers. By 1904 Scotty was flush with money, which he claimed to have made from a huge gold strike. But the money more likely came from a millionaire promoter named Albert M. Johnson. By the time *Death Valley Scotty* died in 1954, Scotty's Castle, and exotic Moorish structure he and Johnson had built, was a main tourist attraction in Death Valley.

Debonair Bandit, The—See HEDGEPETH, MARION C.

DEBS, EUGENE V. (1855–1926)

U.S. socialist leader Eugene V. Debs was known to his devoted supporters as *The Lover of Mankind* and *No. 9653,* his prison number. In 1920, while imprisoned for violating the Espionage Act, he ran for the presidency and polled almost a million votes.

DEE, JOHN (1527–1608)

An adviser and astrologer to Queen Elizabeth I of England, John Dee did much to foster learning in England. The author of 79 books, he convinced Elizabeth to form a royal library, which was the precursor to the British museum. While greatly interested in the sciences, Dee was also a devotee to witchcraft and demonology, gaining the sobriquet *Queen Elizabeth's Merlin.*

DEEMING, FREDERICK BAILEY (c. 1853–1892)

Australian and English mass murderer Frederick Deeming, executed in Australia in 1892 despite a strong plea of insanity, was held by many to be fully worthy of his nickname *Mad Fred.* He gained the additional sobriquet *Ape Deeming* after his death because part of his skeleton was used to illustrate the theory that he was closer to the anthropoid ape than to modern man.

Deep Freeze Woman, The: ANDERSON, DOROTHY MAE STEVENS (1929?–1974)

A derelict, Dorothy Mae Stevens became famous in 1951 as *The Deep Freeze Woman.* Having passed out from drinking she lay all night in a Chicago alley as the temperature plunged to 11 below zero. Her body temperature fell to 64.4; the blood in her legs was said to have frozen solid; her respiration slowed to three breaths a minute; her pulse rate dropped to 12; and her eyeballs had all but turned to ice. Remarkably, *The Deep Freeze Woman* believed to have been 22 years old at the time, was saved by doctors who had predicted she could not survive. Although she had to remain in the hospital for six months and lost both her legs and nine fingers, she lived another 23 years.

Defender of the Damned, The—See **DARROW, CLARENCE SEWARD; ROOT, GLADYS TOWLES.**

Defender of the Union, The—See **WEBSTER, DANIEL.**

DEFOE, DANIEL (1660?–1731)

British journalist and novelist Daniel Defoe probably had at least 200 sobriquets and pseudonyms, the latter of which may have been useful in his persistent troubles with the law. This problem was probably best illustrated by his nickname *The Sunday Gentleman,* acquired because he stayed in hiding from bailiffs during the week and then appeared in elegant attire on Sundays, when he was safe from their grasp.

DEFORGE, EVARISTE DESIRE (1753–1814)

Evariste Desire Deforge, Chevalier de Parny, was designated *The French Tibullus* by Voltaire for his elegaic and erotic poetry.

DEFREEZE, DONALD D. (1944–1974)

Black American revolutionary Donald D. DeFreeze was the self-proclaimed *General Field Marshal*

Cinque of the Symbionese Liberation Army, six of whose members, including Cinque, died in a blazing gun battle with police in Los Angeles in 1974. The original Cinque was an African slave who led a mutiny and took control of a slave ship. He was eventually freed by an American court after his case was pleaded by former President John Quincy Adams.

DEKKER, ALBERT (1905–1968)

Film actor Albert Dekker was for many years known secretly among the Hollywood set as *Mr. Kink* for his private peccadilloes. Committing suicide in his bathroom, he lived up to his nickname by hanging himself while wearing handcuffs and women's silk lingerie. His "Final Notices," all of them less than raves, were lipsticked on his body.

DELANEY, JOHN "Crooked Nick" (fl. late 19th century)

A vicious murderer and member of New Orleans' notorious Yellow Henry Gang, John Delaney got the underworld monicker *Crooked Neck* not because of a physical affliction but in tribute to his supreme talent as a garroter. It is a measure of the competence of police of that era that *Crooked Neck Delaney* was not imprisoned until 1892, after about a decade and a half of undisturbed murderous activity.

Delayer, The—See **VERRUCOSUS, QUINTUS FABIUS MAXIMUS.**

Delight of Mankind, The—See **TITUS.**

Delightful, The—See **WILLIAM, DUKE OF AUSTRIA.**

Deliverer, The—See WILLIAM OF ORANGE.

Deliverer of America, The—See WASHINGTON, GEORGE.

DELMAS, DELPHIN MICHAEL (1844–1928)

One of the great defense lawyers of his day, Delphin Michael Delmas was known as *The Silver-tongued Spellbinder*. In his heralded defense of Harry Thaw during the sensational Stanford White murder trial in 1906, he espoused the theory of "dementia Americana," a uniquely American neurosis suffered by U.S. males who believe every man's wife is sacred. Somehow the jury bought Delmas' thesis, even though Thaw killed White because he had been sexually involved with Mrs. Thaw before Thaw even knew her. Saved from the electric chair, Thaw was incarcerated in a mental institution, a remarkable achievement that one newspaper said no one but *The Silver-tongued Spellbinder* could have accomplished.

DELOREAN, JOHN ZACHARY (1925–)

Considered a maverick during his Detroit days, U.S. automobile executive John DeLorean was labeled *The Non-Organization Man*. Following his arrest in 1982 on drug charges, including allegedly plotting to distribute huge amounts of cocaine, he was humorously dubbed *The Inventor of the Snowmobile*.

DEMARA, FERDINAND WALDO, JR. (1921–1982)

Celebrated as *The Great Imposter*, Ferdinand Waldo Demara, Jr., was for many years America's

ous times this high school dropout was, among other impersonations, a naval surgeon, a Trappist monk in a Kentucky monastery, a cancer-research biologist, a hospital orderly, a doctor of philosophy, a schoolteacher, a recreational officer at a maximum security prison and a deputy sheriff. The subject of a book and movie about his career and careers, he was once asked to explain the motivation for his impersonations. "Rascality, pure rascality," he replied.

DEMARIA, ALFRED T. (1937–)

Alfred T. Demaria, a New York lawyer and strategist for the decertification of unions, is known to the press and the corporate world as *The Carl Sagan of Union Dumping*. Not surprisingly, union officials have a different sobriquet for him the most common being *A Pernicious Germ*.

DEMOCRITUS (c. 460 B.C.–c. 357 B.C.)

The ancient Greek thinker Democritus was called *The Laughing Philosopher* for the way he cheerfully laughed at the follies of man. He was said to have blinded himself so that he would be less distracted by the doings of man while engaged in his philosophical speculations.

Demon in the Belfry, The—See DURRANT, WILLIAM "Theo."

DEMPSEY, JACK (1895–1983)

Considered by many the greatest heavyweight fighter of all time, Jack Dempsey, a former hobo from Manassa, Colo., stormed to the championship in 1919 and was hailed as *The Manassa Mauler*. The following year, while being unsuccessfully prosecuted for draft evasion, he was often called *The Manassa Slacker*. The nickname no longer applied during World War II when Coast Guard commander Dempsey went into Tarawa under fire, an "old man" among the boys.

DENHAM, JOHN (1615–1669)

When Puritan poet George Withers was taken prisoner by the Royalists and sentenced to death for treason, Sir John Denham successfully interceded with Charles I, saying, "If your Majesty kills Withers, I will then be the worst poet in England." Thereafter Denham was called *The Second-worst Poet.*

DENNIS, JOHN (1657–1734)

English critic-turned-writer John Dennis brought down on himself a torrent of criticism when he turned to poetry and drama. Pope and Gay dubbed him *Sir Tremendous,* and others called him *The Royal Midas* since, they averred, everything he wrote turned to disaster. So complete was the rejection of his work that he became known as *The Best Abused Man in England.* At little loss to answer his detractors, Dennis lashed out so fiercely with his own critical comments that he was also called *Python.*

Deplorable Verlaine—See VERLAINE, PAUL.

Der Alte—See ADENAUER, KONRAD.

DERBY, CHARLOTTE, COUNTESS OF (1601–1664)

Charlotte, countess of Derby, won the nickname *The Warrior Lady of Latham* during the English Civil War for defending her castle at Latham for eight months in the absence of her husband, until she was finally relieved by Prince Rupert.

DESALVO, ALBERT H.—See The Boston Strangler.

DESCARTES, RENE (1586–1650)

French philosopher and mathematician Rene Descartes, known as *The Father of Modern Philosophy,* held that there is no principle whose truth could not be doubted, save the belief in one's own existence ("I doubt, therefore I am"). Dubbed *Cartesius* for formulating the principles of Cartesian coordinates and C curves, he is also designated *The Founder of Analytic Geometry.*

Desert Fox, The—See ROMMEL. ERWIN.

Desiccated Calculating Machine, The—See GAITSKELL, HUGH.

DESMOULINS, CAMILLE (1762–1794)

One of the earliest rabble-rousers of the French Revolution, Camille Desmoulins was a leader of the mob who presided over summary executions on the streets and hanged "enemies of the people" from street lamps. He thus became known and feared as *The Attorney General of the Lantern.*

Destroyer of the League of Nations, The— See LODGE, HENRY CABOT.

Detroit Destroyer, The—See LOUIS, JOE.

DEVEREUX, ROBERT (1567–1601)

Robert Devereux, second earl of Essex, the favorite of Queen Elizabeth I of England, was noted

diers of France called him *The English Achilles*. Historians note that had his spirit and courage been matched by other talents and achievements Essex could have achieved greatness.

DEVI, PHOOLAN *(1955–   )*

Phoolan Devi, a young Indian woman turned dacoit (the country's criminal class), terrorized even the lawless Chambal Valley of central India from 1979 to 1983, when she became known as *The Bandit Queen of India*. In one particularly brutal crime, which endeared her to many villagers and peasants, she and her gang slaughtered some 20 local landlords. All told, she and her decoits committed at least 70 acts of banditry and probably some 50 murders before she surrendered to authorities in 1983. Having lost 17 of her men in recent shoot-outs with police, she gave up, while thousands of her admirers cheered, after apparently being promised ''humane treatment'' and given assurances she would not suffer the death penalty.

Devil, The—See DAMIENS, ROBERT FRANCOIS; LEDAIN, OLIVER; PAGANINI, NICCOLO.

Devil David—See FORMAN, DAVID.

Devil on Two Sticks, The—See MORTON, OLIVER.

Devil's Adjutant, The—See WALLER, JOHN.

DEVOL, GEORGE *(1829–1902)*

Known along the Mississippi as *The Steamboat Sharper,* George Devol was probably the most talented, if not the most honest, riverboat gambler of the 19th century. In all, by his own estimate,

degenerative casino gambler, who lost most of it at faro, keno and roulette. He was also a top-flight head-butter and often settled gambling disputes by butting even pistol-armed opponents unconscious. He won numerous butting contests, for which he was dubbed *Billy Goat Devol*.

Devourer of Books, The—See MAGLIABECCHI, ANTHONY.

DEWEY, JEDEDIAH *(1714–1778)*

Jedediah Dewey, a colonial clergyman in Bennington, Vt., was nicknamed *The Fighting Parson*—a sobriquet accorded other fighting men later in U.S. history—because he not only preached but fought actively against the British during the Revolutionary War until his death in 1778.

DEWEY, THOMAS E. *(1902–1971)*

Thomas E. Dewey, the unsuccessful Republican candidate for U.S. president in 1944 and 1948, made his reputation as a fearless prosecutor of underworld figures in New York, where he won the nickname *Gangbuster*. Democrats shorted that to just plain *Buster* and also referred to him as *The Boy Scout*. The most disparaging sobriquet bestowed on him was *Little Man on the Wedding Cake,* which, considering his height and mustachioed formality, was as inspired as it was cruel. Among those credited with, or claiming credit for, inventing the nickname was Alice Roosevelt Longworth, the daughter of Theodore Roosevelt and the presiding grande dame and wit of Washington society; Harold Ickes; Walter Winchell; and Ethel Barrymore. Ickes was not its originator, although he probably savaged Dewey more than anyone. One of his most famous comments alluded to Dewey's youthful age when he first declared his candidacy: ''Dewey has thrown his diaper in the ring.''

Diamond Coates—See COATES, ROBERT.

Diamond-Tooth Lil—See PRADO, KATIE.

DIBDIN, CHARLES (1748–1814)

The author of some 900 sea songs, Charles Dibdin was styled *The Bard of the British Navy* and, by some, *The True Laureate of England*.

Dick Turpin of Journalism, This—See PULITZER, JOSEPH.

DICKINSON, EMILY (1830–1886)

American poet Emily Dickinson wrote some 1,800 poems, but only a handful were published before her death. The daughter of a leading Amherst attorney, she withdrew totally from society while in her late twenties, and her nickname went from *The Belle of Amherst* to *The Nun of Amherst*. After her death in 1886, her poetry, rich in imagery and unique in style, became much acclaimed.

DICKINSON, JOHN (1732–1808)

A leader of moderate forces in the Continental Congress, John Dickinson opposed outright separation from England and voted against the Declaration of Independence. He was nicknamed *The Penman of the American Revolution* for the many pamphlets and political papers he wrote. Under the pseudonym Fabius he later offered a famous series of open letters backing adoption of the Constitution.

Dictator Goebel—See GOEBEL, WILLIAM.

Dictator of Beale Street, The—See HARRIS, MAC.

Dictator of Letters—See VOLTAIRE.

DIDYMUS (c. 313–398)

Having lost his sight in childhood, Didymus, the Alexandrian churchman and scholar, was called *The Blind*. Despite this affliction, he became one of the most learned men of his era.

DIES, MARTIN (1901–1972)

Martin Dies, a member of the House of Representatives for most of the years from 1931 to 1959, was the first chairman of the House Committee on Un-American Activities. He originally gained national fame in the 1930s when he charged that the New Deal and the CIO were infiltrated by communists. Both he and his committee were at times described by opponents as *Loaded Dies*.

DILGER, HUBERT CASIMIR ANTON (1836–1911)

In 1861 Hubert Dilger took a leave of absence from the Baden Mounted Artillery to take part in the American Civil War, adding a distinctly German touch to the conflict. The countryside in which his new Ohio battery served was rugged, so he discarded the regulation trousers in favor of more rugged breeches made from doeskin, which he was accustomed to wearing in Germany. As the accomplishments of his battery grew, Dilger became

Army.

DILLINGER, JOHN "Kill Crazy" (1902–1934)

The most infamous and celebrated public enemy of the 1930s, John Dillinger was called *Kill Crazy Dillinger,* although there is the strong possibility he killed only one man, a police officer, in a gunfight. His gang killed many more, often against his specific orders.

Dillinger of the 1960s, The—See WILCOXSON, BOBBY RANDELL "One-Eye."

DILLON, JACK (1891–1942)

American boxer Jack Dillon (Ernest Cutler Price), generally recognized as light-heavyweight boxing champion from 1913 to 1916, was called *Jack the Giant Killer* for his ability to give away weight to opponents.

DINEMANDY, JEAN (c. 1510–1588)

Sixteenth century poet Jean Dinemandy (or Dorat) was hailed as *The French Pindar,* after the Greek lyric poet, whose style enjoyed an exuberant rebirth during the Renaissance. King Charles IX created for Dinemandy the office of Poete Royal.

DINGELL, JOHN D. (1926–   )

The powerful head of the House Energy and Commerce Committee, Rep. John D. Dingell, Democrat of Michigan, is considered by colleagues to be a liberal on all matters save those involving the vironmentalists have called him *Tailpipe Johnny* because of his bids to weaken pollution limits on cars. His sponsorship of what opponents dubbed the "Dirty Air Act" earned him the sobriquet *Dirty Dingell.*

Dinner-Bell, The—See BURKE, EDMUND.

DIRKSEN, EVERETT MCKINLEY (1896–1969)

Sen. Everett McKinley Dirksen, Republican of Illinois, famed for his melodious oratory, was often referred to as *The Wizard of Ooze.*

Dirty Dingell—See DINGELL, JOHN D.

Dirty Hun, The—See STROHEIM, ERIC VON.

Dirty Rotten Coward Who Shot Mr. Howard, The—See FORD, ROBERT NEWTON.

Disco Sally: SALLY LIPPMAN (1900–1982)

Sally Lippman, who achieved fame in her seventies as the fast-talking queen mother of Manhattan night life, was nicknamed *Disco Sally.* A former lawyer, she created a happening in 1980 when she married her 30-year-old dancing partner at a wild disco party.

Disease-Demonized Soul, A—See PULITZER, JOSEPH.

DISRAELI, BENJAMIN (1804–1881)

The British statesman, novelist and founder of the modern Conservative party, Benjamin Disraeli was called *Dizzy* by his supporters as a play on his name. Actually, the sobriquet was used to counter foes, who dubbed him *Dizzy* when he first entered Parliament for his bizarre mode of dress and for what they regarded as his even more bizarre political stands.

Disturber of the Peace, The—See MENCKEN, HENRY LOUIS.

Divine Madman, The—See MICHELANGELO.

Divine One, The—See RAPHAEL.

Divine Sarah, The—See BERNHARDT, SARAH.

Divorce Judge, The—See SABATH, JOSEPH.

DIX, DOROTHEA LYNDE (1802–1889)

Called *The Angel of Mercy of Prison Reform*, Dorothea Lynde Dix was a consumptive 39-year-old teacher when she took up the cause of improving the treatment of prisoners, the insane and mentally ill. Her work was credited not only with improving conditions in the United States and Canada but in England and Europe as well.

Dizzy—See DEAN, JAY HANNA "Dizzy"; DISRAELI, BENJAMIN.

Dizzy Dean—See DEAN, JAY HANNA "Dizzy."

DOBIE, GILMOUR *"Gloomy Gil"*

One of the foremost college football coaches in history, Gilmour Dobie was nicknamed *Gloomy Gil* because he was always pessimistic about his team's chances. Yet he produced 14 unbeaten teams over 31 years and in 1924, was given college football's first 10-year coaching contract at Cornell.

Doc—See SIMON, NEIL.

Doctor, The—See HEAD, EDITH.

Dr. Doom—See KAUFMAN, HENRY.

Doctor Mirabilis—See BACON, ROGER.

Doctor My-Book—See ABERNATHY, JOHN.

Dr. No—See TREURNICHT, ANDRIES PETRUS.

Doctor of the Incarnation, The—See CYRIL OF ALEXANDRIA, ST.

Dr. Rock—See SCHMITT, HARRISON R.

Doctor Slop—See STODDART, JOHN.

Dr. Strangelove—See TELLER, EDWARD.

Doctor Universalis—See ALBERTUS MAGNUS.

DODSLEY, ROBERT (1703–1764)

Robert Dodsley, later an important London publisher, editor and author, was nicknamed *The Livery Muse* after writing a volume of poetry called *The Muse in Livery* while in service to a Miss Lowther.

Doer, The—See SCHMIDT, HELMUT.

Dog Detective, The—See MILLER, DAISY ORR.

Dog-Meat General, The—See CHANG CHUNG-CH'ANG.

DOLAN, DANDY JOHNNY (c. 1850–1876)

One of the most brutal New York gangsters of the 19th century, *Dandy Johnny Dolan* was so called because he was a fashion plate of the underworld. He enhanced his wardrobe in a particularly dangerous manner, by making it a habit to appropriate items of clothing and jewelry from his victims. He was eventually caught in possession of a cane with a metal handle carved in the likeness of a monkey, as well as the watch and claim of a slain businessman, and he was convicted of murder and hanged.

DOLCI, DANILO (1925–   )

Italian social worker Danilo Dolci has become known as *The Gandhi of Sicily*. Giving up his career as an architect to fight poverty on the island after witnessing an infant die from malnutrition, he taught the unemployed how to organize. He has also led "upside-down strikes"—as when the unemployed repaired a road, unpaid and without permission—which resulted in his imprisonment. Incurring further governmental wrath by publishing the pathetic stories of small boys who sold themselves for vice in order to buy food, he was jailed for obscenity. He has faced stern opposition from the three most powerful forces on the island: the government, the Church and the Mafia. Although conceded to be neither a communist nor a fellow traveler, he was awarded Russia's Lenin Peace Prize in 1956.

DOLE, JAMES DRUMMOND (1877–1958)

A Bostonian who moved to Hawaii in 1899, James Drummond Dole became a major pineapple grower who improved the quality of the fruit so that it could be canned and shipped all over the world. For his achievement he became known as *The Hawaiian Pineapple King*.

DOLET, ETIENNE (1509–1546)

A lifelong student of Cicero and humanism in the 16th century, Frenchman Etienne Dolet came under suspicion of heresy several times and was saved on one occasion by friends who intervened with the king of France. Setting up a printing press in Lyons, he was arrested several more times for publishing heretical books. In 1546, having been found guilty of an alleged mistranslation of Plato and accused of thus denying the immortality of the soul, he was burned at the stake in Paris. He has since been remembered as *The Martyr of the Renaissance*.

DOLLFUSS, ENGELBERT
(1892–1934)

Right-wing Austrian dictator Englebert Dollfuss, who sought to rally his country against the Nazis, was referred to as *The Pocket Dictator* because of his small stature. Hitler ridiculed Dollfuss with the nickname for thinking he could stand up against the might of Germany. The Nazis assassinated Dollfuss in 1934, but the attempt at a *putsch* failed, and Austria remained outside Hitler's orbit for another four years.

Dollheart—See JOHN LACKLAND.

Don Juan of Literature, The—See SAINTE-BEUVE, CHARLES AUGUSTIN.

Dona Juana—See MARIA LOUISA, QUEEN OF SPAIN.

Done Brown: WILLIAM JOHN BROWN (1805–1857)

William John Brown, a member of the House of Representatives in the 1840s, sought to be named speaker but failed in that ambition. He complained bitterly to friends that he had been "done," and his political foes thereafter nicknamed him *Done Brown*.

Donehogawa—See PARKER, ELY SAMUEL.

DONNELLY, IGNATIUS—See Prince of Cranks, The.

Do-Nothing King, The—See CLOVIS II OF FRANCE.

Don't Keir Hardie—See HARDIE, KEIR.

Doomsday Bell—See BELL, WILLIAM.

DORE, JOHN FRANCIS (1881–1938)

Winning reelection as mayor of Seattle, Wash., in 1936, after forming an alliance with both Dave Beck of the Teamsters Union of the AFL and Harry Bridges of the CIO, John Francis Dore was nicknamed *The Labor Mayor*. After the election he repudiated the "radical" CIO and announced the AFL would prevail as the labor union in Seattle.

DORIA, ANDREA (1468–1560)

The celebrated Genovese admiral and statesman Andrea Doria was styled *The Father of Peace* and *The Liberator of Genoa,* having freed the city from the French in 1528.

DORSEY, TOM (1899–   )

Tom Dorsey, the author of more than 1,000 songs, including "Precious Lord, Take My Hand," has been accorded the sobriquet *The Father of Gospel Music*.

DOSTOEVSKI, FEODOR (1821–1881)

Russian novelist Feodor Dostoevski led perhaps as dissolute and desperate a life as many of his characters. Although he did not engage in love affairs until he was 34, he led a frenzied sex life

quis de Sade, a sobriquet coined by his contemporary Ivan Turgenev.

DOTO, JOSEPH—See Adonis, Joe.

DOTY, SILE (1800–1876)

The complete burglar of the 19th century, Sile Doty was nicknamed *The King of the Hotel Thieves* because he raised that activity to a fine art. He bought scores of locks, disassembled and studied them and designed skeleton keys to fit various types of locks. He developed a tool that could be inserted in a door and turn a key on the other side. He boasted, and the police agreed, that he could break into any hotel room in the United States.

Double No-Hit—See VANDER MEER, JOHNNY.

DOUBLEDAY, ABNER (1819–1893)

Nicknamed *The Father of Baseball* because he supposedly designed the first baseball diamond and made the first rules of the modern game, Abner Doubleday actually did none of these things. Although a prolific writer of magazine articles on various subjects after the Civil War, he never wrote a word about the game he allegedly invented. Baseball had been created earlier in England under the name of "Rounders," and the rules of the game, almost identical to baseball as played today, can be found in *The Boy's Own Book,* published in London in 1828. Additionally, Jane Austen refers to baseball in a novel written about 1798. A more accurate sobriquet for Doubleday, and a novel play on his name, was *Old Forty-eight Hours,* acquired when he was a Civil War general noted for the deliberate and slow-moving direction of his command. It was said that he thought there were 48 hours in a day.

DOUBLEDAY, FRANK NELSON (1862–1934)

The founder of what was to become the publishing firm of Doubleday & Company, Inc., Frank Nelson Doubleday was nicknamed *Effendi*, the Arabic word for chief. Rudyard Kipling first coined the name, which derives from Doubleday's initials, F.N.D.

Doubting Thomas—See THOMAS THE APOSTLE.

Dough Moose—See PERKINS, GEORGE W.

DOUGHTON, ROBERT L. "Muley" (1863–1954)

A colorful long-time representative to Congress from North Carolina, Robert L. Doughton was nicknamed *Muley* Doughton because he had electioneered riding a mule in several of his early campaigns for office. He later served as chairman of the powerful House Ways and Means Committee for 19 years.

DOUGLAS, ARCHIBALD, FOURTH EARL OF (?–1424)

Archibald, the fourth earl of Douglas, was nicknamed *Tine-Man,* or a man who loses. After losing an eye at Homildon, he was taken prisoner by Percy in 1402. Joining forces with Percy that same year against Henry VI of England, he was taken prisoner and sent back to Scotland. He later made his way to France, where he was killed at the Battle of Verneuil in Normandy. As one historian noted: "No man was lesse fortunate, and it is no lesse true that no man was more valorous."

DOUGLAS, HELEN GAHAGAN (1900–1980)

U.S. politician and actress Helen Gahagan Douglas, wife of actor Melvyn Douglas, ran for U.S. senator in California in 1950 against and up-and-coming right-wing congressman named Richard M. Nixon. She was defeated by a particularly vicious red-baiting campaign in which Nixon dubbed her *The Pink Lady*. For his tactics in that campaign, Nixon won the sobriquet Tricky Dick.

DOUGLAS, JAMES (1371?–1443)

Scottish nobleman James, the seventh earl of Douglas, was nicknamed *The Gross*. He was fat, indolent and peace-loving, the three grossest characteristics of the time.

DOUGLAS, STEPHEN (1813–1861)

Because he was barely 5 feet tall, Stephen A. Douglas, Abraham Lincoln's long-time political foe, was called *The Little Giant*. The two men also had been rivals during the early 1840s for the affections of Mary Todd, who chose ''my tall Kentuckian'' over the ''very little Little Giant.''

DOUGLAS, WILLIAM (1724–1810)

The lecherous fourth duke of Queensberry, William Douglas was the consummate ''dirty old man.'' Leering at women from the window of his Piccadilly house he sent his groom out to bid for their favors and became known as *The Rake of Piccadilly*. Famous for orgies held on his estates, Douglas carried on affairs with women ranging from duchesses to prostitutes. *Old Q,* as he was called, even hired the former physician of Louis XV of France to keep him alive and supervise his orgies. When Douglas died at the age of 86, more than 70 unopened love letters were found in his bed.

DOW, NEAL (1804–1897)

Neal Dow earned the nickname *The Father of Prohibition* because he was Maine's driving force in the 1848 statewide ban on the manufacture and sale of intoxicating beverages, the nation's first.

DOWNER, ELIPHALET (?–1806)

American patriot Dr. Eliphalet Downer, who fought the British at Lexington and elsewhere, was nicknamed *The Fighting Surgeon of the Revolution*. He remained popular with both sides, however, and he not only treated British wounded but collected donations of money, food and supplies for them among the rebel colonists.

DOYLE, ARTHUR CONAN (1859–1930)

English physician and author Sir Arthur Conan Doyle, the creator of Sherlock Holmes, was later nicknamed *The Man Who Hated Sherlock Holmes* because he desired for many years to kill off the fictional detective. He once wrote to his mother: ''I think of flaying Holmes. . .and winding him up for good. He takes my mind from better things.'' His mother replied, ''You won't! You can't! *You mustn't!*'' Finally overcome by an ''overwhelming overdose of him,'' Doyle finished Holmes off at Reichenbach Falls in Switzerland. ''You brute!'' a reader wrote him. So severe was the public's reaction that Doyle was forced to resurrect Holmes. Even his plot to kill off Holmes by asking for more money for his stories failed: His hungry publisher paid.

Doyle took an interest in real-life criminal cases and solved a number of them himself, including clearing wrongfully accused men. For this he was called *The Man Who Was Sherlock Homes*.

Dragon, The—See DRAKE, FRANCIS.

DRAKE, FRANCIS (c. 1540–1596)

English navigator and privateer Sir Francis Drake was such a successful freebooter that he was celebrated in England as *The Terror of the Spanish Main*. The Spaniards nicknamed him *The Dragon*.

Dreck—See ECK, JOHANN.

DREISER, THEODORE (1871–1945)

Novelist Theodore Dreiser, whose brooding, detailed style made him his era's prime exponent of naturalism, was nicknamed *Our Bitter Patriot*. An enthusiastic supporter of the Soviet Union, Dreiser took a strong interest in principles espoused by the Quaker religion near the end of his life.

DRESSLER, MARIE (1871–1934)

U.S. comedienne and actress Marie Dressler was nicknamed *The Grand Old Lady of the Movies*. The Hollywood set called her *Queen Marie*.

DREYFUS, ALFRED (1859–1935)

Alfred Dreyfus, Jewish French Army officer and member of the general staff, was the subject of a notorious military frame-up when he was convicted of being a spy for the Germans and sent to Devil's Island for life in 1894. Becoming known as *The Semitic Sacrifice*, Dreyfus was finally cleared through the aid of many prominent persons, especially Emile Zola. The Dreyfus conviction provided the strong initial impulse for modern Zionism and convinced Theodor Herzl, the founder of the movement, of the need for a Jewish homeland.

Dribblepuss—See LEHR, LEW.

DRINAN, ROBERT (1920–   )

American Jesuit priest Rev. Robert Drinan, a former liberal Democratic representative, was labeled by his more conservative critics *The Mad Monk of Massachusetts*.

DRUCCI, VINCENT "Schemer" (1895–1927)

One of the most colorful if deadly Chicago gangsters of the 1920s, Vincent Drucci was called *The Schemer* because of his off-the-wall ideas for committing various robberies and kidnappings. A member of the O'Banion gang—the enemies of Al Capone—*The Schemer* was said to have once planned to murder Capone in a Turkish bath. The story, which even if apocryphal still characterizes the quality of Drucci's schemes, went that he almost strangled Capone before his bodyguards appeared in the steam room. *The Schemer* was said to have fled stark naked, jumping into his car and driving off.

Drummer Boy of Chickamauga, The—See CLEM, JOHN LINCOLN.

Drunkard, The—See MICHAEL III, EMPEROR OF THE EAST; WENCESLAS VI OF BOHEMIA.

Drunken Barnaby—See BRAITHWAITE, RICHARD.

Drunken Old Hussar, The—See BLUCHER, GEBHARD LEBERECHT VON.

Dry Hole Stebbins—See STEBBINS, GRANT C.

Dry Messiah, The—See CANNON, BISHOP JAMES, JR.

Dry Wind, The—See GUYER, ULYSSES SAMUEL.

DRYDEN, JOHN (1631–1700)

Regarded by many as the greatest English writer of the Restoration period, English poet and dramatist John Dryden was referred to in later life as *The Squab Poet,* a reference to his corpulence. He was particularly so disparaged by those who found his conversion to Catholicism offensive because such conversions had become politically expedient.

Dryden of Germany, The—See OPITZ, MARTIN.

DU BARTAS, SALUSTIUS (1544–1591)

A one-time officer in Gascon and thus called *A Gascon Moses,* 16th century writer Salustius Du Bartas wrote the seven-book epic poem *The Week of Creation,* gaining the sobriquet *The French Angel.* Milton borrowed heavily from it for his *Paradise Lost.*

DU SABLE, JEAN BAPTISTE POINT (c. 1745–1818)

A native of Haiti and a "free Negro," Jean Baptiste Point Du Sable started the first trading post at the "place of the wild onions" in the 1770s, thus gaining the sobriquet *The Father of Chicago.*

DUCHESNE, ROSE PHILIPPINE (1769–1852)

The founder of several Catholic convents and a teacher in mission schools for Indians of the American West, Rose Philippine Duchesne was nicknamed by the Potawotomi tribe *The Woman Who Always Prays.*

Duchess, The—See HARDING, FLORENCE DEWOLFE.

Duchess of Death, The—See SPINELLI, JUANITA "Duchess."

Duchess of Park Avenue, The—See HAMPTON, HOPE.

DUCHIN, EDWIN FRANK "Eddie" (1909–1951)

American jazz pianist and bandleader Eddie Duchin was known in his prime as *The Magic Fingers of Radio.*

Duck Bill—See HICKOK, JAMES BUTLER "Wild Bill."

Duckie Wuckie—See MEDWICK, JOE "Duckie Wuckie."

Dude President, The—See ARTHUR, CHESTER A.

Duel Fighter, The—See JACKSON, ANDREW.

Duellist, The—See BAGENAL, BEAUCHAMP.

DUERER, ALBRECHT (1471–1528)

Albrecht Duerer, the great German religious painter and graphic artist, was a dedicated lover of mirth and thus was nicknamed *The Chaucer of Artists*. Despite his love for the joy of laughter, Duerer never employed his art for ribald or obscene representations, then very much in fashion. In that sense the association of him with Chaucer becomes somewhat inappropriate.

DUFF, MRS. MARY (1794–1857)

Without dispute actress Mrs. Mary Ann Duff was recognized in the 19th century as *The Queen of the American Stage.* She was also celebrated as *The Siddons of America*, an allusion to the famed British tragedienne Sarah Siddons.

Dugout Doug—See MACARTHUR, DOUGLAS.

Duke—See WAYNE, JOHN.

Duke of Birmingham—See POWELL, JAMES ROBERT.

Dullest Briton of Them All, The—See TROLLOPE, ANTHONY.

DUMAS, ALEXANDER, PERE (1802–1870)

The prolific French author of hundreds of novels (it is suspected with a considerable number of collaborators), Alexander Dumas pere was celebrated as *The Fourth Musketeer*. There is considerable dispute over the reason for the nickname, taken of course from his highly successful *The Three Musketeers*. Some said it referred to his in Garibaldi's expedition of 1860, while others considered it a tribute to his long string of sexual escapades.

Dumas of the Indians, The—See GLOUX, OLIVIER.

Dumb Bell Murderer, The—See GRAY, JUDD.

Dumb Ox—See THOMAS AQUINAS.

Dumb Prophet, The—See CLEVELAND, GROVER.

Dumb-Dumb—See FORD, GERALD RUDOLPH.

Dumbest Man in Congress, The—See SCOTT, WILLIAM LLOYD.

Dummy Hoy—See HOY, WILLIAM E. "Dummy."

DUMONT, ELEANOR—See Madame Mustache.

DUNBAR, PAUL LAURENCE (1872–1906)

The chief black voice in U.S. literature of his day, Paul Laurence Dunbar became known as *The Poet Laureate of His People* for his novels and poems.

Dungeon Man of San Quentin, The—See MORRELL, ED.

DUNLAP, WILLIAM (1766–1839)

American painter, historian, theater manager and playwright William Dunlap was called *The Father of American Drama* for being the country's first professional dramatist.

DUNN, ROSA—See Rose of Cimarron.

DUNNE, IRENE—See First Lady of Hollywood.

DUNOIS, JEAN (1403–1468)

Jean Dunois, a natural son of Louis, duke of Orleans, was nicknamed *The Bastard of Orleans*. He was one of the greatest of French generals.

DUNS SCOTUS, JOHN (1265?–1308?)

Scottish theologian and philosopher John Duns Scotus was nicknamed *Doctor Subtilis,* or *Subtle Doctor,* because of his often hair-splitting doctrines, which distinguished him from other theologians, especially Thomas Aquinas. He also won fame as *The Marian Doctor* for being the first to defend the idea of the Virgin Mary's Immaculate Conception. The controversy he started raged for some five centuries before the idea was made a doctrine of the Catholic Church. Supporters of Duns, or "Dunses," remained an important voice in Christian theology until they were attacked by theologians of the Renaissance. Such "Dunses," later "Dunces," were called foolish hair-splitters who made objections for the sake of objecting. In time the word dunce came to mean a person who has no ability to absorb real learning.

DUNSTAN, JEFFREY (1759–1797)

A British mayor of Dunstan in the 18th century, Sir Jeffrey Dunstan was nicknamed *Old Wigs* because of the lavish hairpieces he wore. He often resold them later at a profit.

DURANT, WILLIAM CRAPO (1861–1947)

Pioneer automobile manufacturer William Crapo Durant, the founder of General Motors, was known during his long reign as *The General of General Motors*. It is a part of advertising lore that no more than his middle initial appeared in print in references to the corporation's products.

DURANTE, JIMMY (1893–1980)

Famous U.S. comedian Jimmy Durante was called *Schnozzola* because of his large nose. According to some accounts, he acquired the nickname well before it became his show business moniker. One theory has it that as an inveterate horse player he always bet horses "on the schnozzola" or nose—to win.

DURIEUX, TILLA (1880–1971)

German stage actress Tilla Durieux pioneered the Eliza Doolittle role in the 1913 production of George Bernard Shaw's *Pygmalion* and 20 years later was forced into exile. Returning to Berlin at the age of 71 to resume her stage career, she was hailed as *The Grand Old Lady of the German Theater*.

DURKIN, MARTIN P. (1894–1955)

The long-time president of the United Association of Plumbers & Steamfitters, Martin P. Durkin was nicknamed *The Plumber,* a sobriquet that orig-

President Dwight D. Eisenhower. It arose from a description of Eisenhower's nine-man cabinet as being composed of "eight millionaires and a plumber."

DUROCHER, LEO "Lippy" (1906–)

Baseball player and manager Leo Durocher was called *The Lip* or *Lippy Durocher* because of his technique of heckling opponents and umpires. His cry to his pitcher to "stick it in his ear" proved somewhat disconcerting to many rival batters.

DURRANT, WILLIAM "Theo" (1872–1898)

William "Theo" Durrant became known around the world as *The Demon in the Belfry* for the murder of two girls in San Francisco in 1895. An American version of Dr. Jekyll and Mr. Hyde, Durrant was a college senior and dedicated church-goer who took on several church duties. After having raped a number of girls in church, he killed two who either resisted or threatened to go to the police. Hiding the bodies in the belfry, he was eventually apprehended and, after a sensational trial and drawn-out appeals, hanged.

DUSE, ELEONORA (1859–1924)

Described by many students of the theater as the greatest actress of her time and perhaps of all time, Italian luminary Eleonora Duse was often called, as Victor Hugo dubbed her, *Duse the God*. Critic James Huneker once wrote of her: "Duse's art borders on the clairvoyant. . .her silences are terrifying." Tuberculosis forced her to retire from the stage in 1909, but after her wealth was wiped out by inflation, she resumed acting in 1921, even though only one of her lungs functioned. She disdained an offer of a pension from Italian dictator Benito Mussolini. In 1924, while on a triumphant

in Pittsburgh, Pa., and died.

Duse the God—See DUSE, ELEONORA.

Dutch Billy—See WILLIAM OF ORANGE.

Dutch Hogarth, The—See HOUBRAKEN, JAKOB.

Dutchman with the X-ray Mind, The—See CROISET, GERARD.

DUVALIER, FRANCOIS (1907–1971)

Like many bloody dictators, Francois Duvalier had a penchant for an innocuous nickname, and he encouraged the use of *Papa Doc* for himself. His regime was nonetheless a reign of terror, and under his rule Haiti's economy deteriorated.

DUVALIER, JEAN-CLAUDE (1951–)

Inheriting dictatorial control of Haiti on the death of his father, Francois Duvalier (Papa Doc), Jean Claude Duvalier launched a reign that he claimed would open a new era of enlightened rule for the bloodstained country. Instead, *Baby Doc*, as he was immediately nicknamed, proved the equal of Papa Doc in operating a police state where torture and murder remained the norm.

DWYER, WILLIAM V. "Big Bill" (1883–1946)

Big Bill Dwyer was known in the 1920s as *The King of the Bootleggers*, before he was charged with evading $2 million in taxes for only two years—not income but actual taxes. When he emerged from prison, Dwyer announced he was going straight, and surprisingly, he did. Becoming a leading sportsman, he brought ice hockey to New York and opened several race tracks around the country. A major New York horse race, the Dwyer Stakes, is named in his honor.

DYER, MARY (?–1660)

Mary Dyer, a devoted Quaker who became known as *The Quaker Martyr* following her execution, was expelled twice from Boston because of her religion, a capital offense in the Massachusetts Bay Colony. When she returned for the second time in 1660, she was hanged on the Boston Common.

DYLAN, BOB (1941–   ): ROBERT ZIMMERMAN

U.S. singer and songwriter Bob Dylan, whose songs were anthems of the 1960s civil rights movement, has been dubbed *The Radical Prophet of American Youth.*

DYM, ROSE—See Broadway Rose.

Dynamite Dick: DAN CLIFTON (1865?–1896?)

Dan Clifton, a member of Oklahoma's Doolin Gang, was nicknamed *Dynamite Dick* because of his penchant for using the explosive on robberies and in fights with the law. He became the most ''killed'' outlaw in America, as reward-hungry posses and bounty hunters tried to pass off any shot-up corpse for the real thing. Clifton had lost three fingers in a caper and some claimants, alas, cut off the wrong three fingers. The real *Dynamite Dick* was said to have been killed in a shoot-out in 1896, but that may have been another outlaw named Buck McGregg. In which case *Dynamite Dick* apparently rode off into the sunset.

E

Eagle of Divines, The—See THOMAS AQUINAS.

Eaglet, The—See NAPOLEON II.

EARHART, AMELIA (1898–1937?)

Amelia Earhart, who in 1932 became the first woman to fly solo across the Atlantic, was of course instantly nicknamed *Lady Lindy,* after Charles Lindbergh. She disappeared in 1937 while attempting to fly around the world.

EARLE, GEORGE H., III (1890–1974)

The governor of Pennsylvania from 1935 to 1939, and the first Democrat to hold that post in 44 years, George H. Earle was nicknamed *The Little New Dealer* because he closely patterned his administration after the federal policies of Franklin Roosevelt.

EARLY, JUBAL ANDERSON (1816–1894)

Confederate general Jubal A. Early was not a particularly old commander, but rheumatism contracted during the Mexican War ruined his posture and made him appear much older than he was. When Early was assigned to his first command at the beginning of the Civil War, his troops started referring to their ancient-looking commander as *Old Jubilee* or *Old Jube.* The name stuck with him throughout the war.

Earnest Atheist, The—See BUTLER, SAMUEL.

EARP, WYATT (1848–1929)

A legendary gunfighter of the Old West who has come down to us as a sterling upholder of law and order, Wyatt Earp never had that reputation with his contemporaries. He and Bat Masterson made up the duo known in Dodge City, Kan., as *The Fighting Pimps*. Instead of devoting themselves to keeping the peace, they spent much of their time as cardsharps, procurers and hired guns until new elections sent them elsewhere in the West.

EASTMAN, CHARLES G. (1816–1861)

Since many of his verses dealt with the ordinary man in everyday surroundings and circumstances, Vermont poet Charles Gamage Eastman was dubbed *The Burns of the Green Mountains*.

Easy Ed—See MEESE, EDWIN, III.

EATON, MARGARET O'NEILL (1796–1879)

Because Margaret O'Neill Eaton, wife of John H. Eaton, Andrew Jackson's secretary of war, was only a Washington innkeeper's daughter, many other cabinet members and their wives snubbed her, despite pleas from the president. They often called her *Pothouse Peggy* and *The Gorgeous Hussy*. Since a number of cabinet members threatened to resign if forced to receive her, the newspapers nicknamed her *Bellona*, the goddess of war.

Ebony—See BLACKWOOD, WILLIAM.

Eccentric Explorer, The—See WATERTON, CHARLES.

ECK, JOHANN (1486–1543)

A German religionist critic of Martin Luther, Dr. Johann Eck coined for him the term Doctor Luder, meaning a worthless fellow. Luther returned the compliment by thereafter referring to Dr. Eck as *Dreck,* meaning dirt in German.

Economic Pessimist, The—See MALTHUS, THOMAS ROBERT.

EDDY, NELSON (1901–1967)

Motion picture and stage baritone Nelson Eddy, who teamed with soprano Jeanette MacDonald in numerous films, was known disparagingly in the trade as *The Singing Capon*. The inside joke went that his eye makeup and lipstick made him look lovelier than his female partner and that she greatly resented it.

EDEN, ANTHONY (1897–1977)

Britain's foreign secretary under Winston Churchill and, later, prime minister, Anthony Eden was subjected to barbed sobriquets from the opposition Labor Party concerning his secondary role to Churchill. The most savage nickname was one coined by Aneurin Bevan—*The Juvenile Lead*.

Edgar the Peaceful: EDGAR OF ENGLAND (944–975)

King Edgar of England was put on the throne at the age of 15 by nobles dissatisfied with the rule of his brother Edwy. Unlike Edwy's reign, Edgar's was marked by peace, gained to some extent by his ceding some territories, and he was nicknamed *Edgar the Peaceful*.

Edison of American Parachute Design, The—See IRVIN, LESLIE L.

Edison of Crime Detection, The—See HEINRICH, EDWARD OSCAR.

EDWARD, PRINCE OF ENGLAND (1964–)

It has been said that the further an immediate member of the British royal family is from the throne, the more harsh the nicknames concocted by the nation's press for him becomes. Thus Prince Edward has appeared in headlines as *His Royal Rudeness*.

EDWARD, PRINCE OF WALES—See Black Prince, The.

EDWARD III OF ENGLAND (1312–1377)

Edward III of England gained the sobriquet *The Bankrupt* when his ambition led to the onset of the costly Hundred Years War and his own financial ruin. Faced with a $7 million loan he could not repay in 1339, he was the first ruler in the world to go bankrupt, under a petition of bankruptcy, brought by his creditors.

EDWARD VI OF ENGLAND (1538–1553)

Unlike his father, Henry VIII, King Edward VI of England was a most religiously inclined monarch. Nicknamed *The Saint*, he often took notes during sermons and applied the lessons learned to his kingly doings, an attitude that not surprisingly inspired the preachments of his divines. As a result of one sermon, Edward VI founded the St. Thomas and Bridewell hospitals. He was also referred to as *The Josiah of England*, after the young king of Judah during whose tenure religion was reformed.

Edward Longshanks: EDWARD I OF ENGLAND (1239–1307)

Edward I of England, called *Edward Longshanks* for the obvious reason, was also nicknamed *The Hammer of the Scots* because of his long campaigns against the Scots under Baloil and, later, William Wallace (who in turn was nicknamed in Scotland The Hammer and Scourge of England).

Edward the Confessor (c. 1004–1066)

The pre-Norman English king *Edward the Confessor*, so called because of his reputed sanctity, was also known as *The Albino King*. He had red eyes, skin like milk and a snow white beard and hair.

Edward the Fat Man (fl. late 19th century)

In the late 1800s one of the great sights of New York City was *Edward the Fat Man*, who sat on Broadway in an enormous armchair. The famed French gastronome Anthelme Brillat-Savarin visited America and included a word picture of *Edward the Fat Man* in his famous book on good eating, *Physiologie du gout*. He described him as having three chins, each more than a foot long, and fingers "like those of the Roman emperor who used his wife's bracelets for rings."

Edward the Martyr (963?–978)

As a young man the pre-Norman English king Edward, the son of Edgar, was nicknamed *Edward the Martyr*. During his short rule from 975 to 978, he was unable to control his kingdom and was murdered at Corfe, probably at the instigation of his stepmother, Aelfthryt, who was ambitious for her own son, Aethelred. Viewed as a martyred saint, Edward was consecrated at Shaftesbury.

Edward the Robber: EDWARD IV OF ENGLAND (1442–1483)

Edward IV of England was disparagingly referred to as *Edward the Robber* because he ruled autocratically and accumulated great wealth without regard to the will of Parliament.

EDWARDS, JONATHAN (1703–1758)

Colonial clergyman and theologian Jonathan Edwards was nicknamed *The Artist of Damnation* because of his particularly frightening sermons that described sinners meeting an angry God. He was made president of what is now Princeton University some five weeks before his death in 1758.

Effendi—See DOUBLEDAY, FRANK NELSON.

Egalite—See PHILIPPE, DUC D'ORLEANS.

EGAN, PATRICK (1841–1919)

Irish-American politician Patrick Egan was subjected to the political barbs of the foes of President James G. Blaine and denounced as *Blaine's Irishman* and *The Escaped Jailbird*. Egan, who was appointed to the post of minister plenipotentiary to Chile, had come to the United States from Ireland, where he had once been tried for and acquitted of treason.

Egghead—See STEVENSON, ADLAI.

EHRLICHMAN, JOHN (1925–   )

Before he was caught up in the Watergate scandal and sentenced to prison, John Ehrlichman, President Richard Nixon's chief domestic assistant, was known as *Wisdom*. The sobriquet was not used much after Watergate. During Nixon's first term, Ehrlichman far preferred being called *The White House Fireman*, as he anticipated bureaucratic blazes and dampened political fires. He and two other top presidential assistants, H. R. Haldeman and Henry Kissinger, all of Germanic background, were often accused of being a "Berlin Wall" around Nixon. Ehrlichman was also nicknamed *Von Ehrlichman* by grumbling politicians. Kissinger attempted to separate himself from his two compatriots by referring to them as *The Praetorian Guard*.

Eighth Wonder of the World, The—See TEMPLE, SHIRLEY.

Eight-Ulcer on a Four-Ulcer Job, An—See HUME, PAUL.

EISENBERG, LOUIS (1928–   )

A $225-a-week office building maintenance worker, Louis Eisenberg was known on the job as *Louie the Lightbulb,* because his main chore was replacing burned-out light bulbs. In 1981 *Louie the*

Lightbulb won $5 million in New York state's LOTTO game and became the biggest known lottery winner in history. Unlike many others who have gained sudden wealth, Eisenberg announced he had no intention of continuing to work.

EISENHOWER, DWIGHT DAVID
(1890–1969)

Dwight David Eisenhower was known in his toothy youth in Abilene, Kan., as *Ugly Ike* and *Little Ike* (brother Edgar was Big Ike), and he was often an object of derision. "It made us scrappers," Edgar Eisenhower once explained. By the time he entered West Point, biographer Peter Lyon stated, *Ugly Ike* was able to stand up to the harshness of military life because "he had had the unnecessary vanities kicked out of him." By the time he became Allied commander in Europe during World War II his nickname was simply *Ike*. A shortened uniform jacket worn by American GIs became known as an Ike or Eisenhower jacket.

EISENSTEIN, SERGEI (1898–1948)

Upon his arrival in America, the great Russian filmmaker Sergei Eisenstein was referred to as *The Russian Cecil B. De Mille*. It was a misnomer, since the brilliant director proved unable, or perhaps unwilling, to churn out popular commercial films. Dispirited, he returned to the USSR in the 1930s and had to make a public confession for "forgetting Socialism."

Elegant Hoosier Tunesmith, The—See PORTER, COLE.

Elegant Oakley—See HALL, ABRAHAM OAKLEY.

Elegant One, The—See HALL, ABRAHAM OAKLEY

Elephant Man, The: JOHN MERRICK (1863–1890)

Englishman John Merrick was called *The Elephant Man* because he was a nightmarish creature who looked more or less like a man but had many of the characteristics of an elephant. In his early life he could earn an income only in freak shows, whose impresarios seldom provided him with much to eat. Finally, through public donations, he got enough funds to be housed in a bed-sitting room and bathroom in a London hospital, the first home he had ever known.

Merrick was extremely intelligent and a voracious reader, especially of romantic novels, and he was visited by many women volunteers, who decorated his room. Even Queen Victoria visited him on several occasions. He died at the age of 27 because he wanted to sleep "like other people." As his head was so big and heavy, he slept in a bed in a sitting position, his back propped by pillows, with his knees drawn up and his arms wrapped around his legs. Then he rested his head on his knees. One night he simply lay back on a pillow, and his head apparently fell backward, dislocating his neck.

ELGAR, EDWARD WILLIAM (1857–1934)

English organist and composer Sir Edward Elgar became known as *Queen Victoria's Favorite Composer,* but the honor did not prevent the wrath of others from descending on him. George Bernard Shaw called him *One of the Seven Humbugs of Christendom* and *The Figurehead of Music in England.*

Elijah of the Reformation, The—See FAREL, GUILLAUME.

ELIOT, JOHN (1604–1690)

The first Indian mission in New England was established by Pastor John Eliot of the Massachusetts Bay Colony, who translated the Bible into the Algonquin dialect, producing the first Bible in any language printed in America. Called *The Apostle to the Indians,* he converted some 4,000, who were then warred on as traitors by other Indians. During King Philip's war the vengeance-seeking colonists, finding it difficult to catch the raiding Indians, instead attacked and slaughtered the unresisting convert Indians living in Eliot's specially built mission villages, despite the minister's desperate efforts to save them.

ELIZABETH, ELECTRESS PALATINE (1596–1662)

The wife of Frederick V, Elector Palatine, Elizabeth—of England's Stuart line— was disparaged as a *Snow Queen* who would rule with her husband when he became king of Bohemia but only through the winter. According to the Jesuits, both she and her husband (The Snow King) would vanish with the first rays of the spring sun. The Catholic forces carried the day in battle, and *The Snow Queen* and her royal husband had to flee, fulfilling the prediction. Elizabeth's admirers called her *The Queen of Hearts* because of her amiable disposition even in adversity.

ELIZABETH, PRINCESS OF THE PALATINE (1618–1680)

The beautiful daughter of Frederick V, Elector Palatine, Princess Elizabeth was noted for her dazzling beauty, marred only by a sharp aquiline nose that would at times turn cherry red. When that happened, *The Red-Nosed Princess,* as she was dubbed, would hide away in her apartment. Once summoned to a royal affair by her sister, Princess

me go with this nose?'' To which her sister replied, ''Will you wait till you get another?''

ELIZABETH I OF ENGLAND (1533–1603)

Elizabeth I of England was called *Good Queen Bess* by her subjects. Because she never married, she was also referred to as *The Virgin Queen.* Another nickname was *The World's Wonder,* sometimes used facetiously by opponents in connection with the previous sobriquet. John Penry called her *The Untamed Heifer.* He was executed in 1593 for uttering seditious words against the monarch.

ELIZABETH PETROVNA, EMPRESS OF RUSSIA (1709–1762)

Elizabeth Petrovna, empress of Russia and an avowed sensualist, was known throughout the courts of Europe as *L' Infâme Catin du Nord,* or *The Infamous Harlot of the North.*

ELLIOTT, EBENEZER (1781–1841)

As the author of *Corn-Law Rhymes,* a collection of poems that rallied public opinion in England against the notorious corn laws and by causing their repeal, advanced English capitalism, Ebenezer Elliott was dubbed *The Corn-Law Rhymer.* As Carlyle noted: ''Is not the corn-law rhymer already a king?''

ELLIOTT, ROBERT G. (1874–1939)

Robert G. Elliott, the official executioner for New York and five other states, dispatched in the electric chair a total of 387 people—believed to be a world record. He was nicknamed *The Legal Killer.*

ELLIS, HAVELOCK (1859–1939)

Because of his seven-volume *Studies in the Psychology of Sex,* a pioneering work on the subject based on a scientific, sociological approach rather than moral judgment, Havelock Ellis was given the sobriquet *The Darwin of Sex.*

ELLSBERG, DANIEL (1930–   )

The research associate who made public the Pentagon Papers, Daniel Ellsberg became known, at least to those who approved of his act, as *The Last Great American Hero.* Within the Nixon White House he was referred to as *The Bum.*

ELLSWORTH, OLIVER (1745–1807)

The first U.S. senator to be regarded as a watchdog over federal expenditures, Oliver Ellsworth of Connecticut was nicknamed *The Cerberus of the Treasury.* His watchfulness over disbursements was not always appreciated within the Treasury, where it was noted that in Greek mythology Cerberus was the three-headed dog which guarded the gates of Hades.

Elvis the Pelvis—See PRESLEY, ELVIS.

ELWES, JOHN (1714–1789)

One of the most colorful and eccentric English misers, John Elwes has been called *The Penurious Parliamentarian.* Although extremely rich, he was described as having "become proverbial in the annals of avarice." Worth a half million pounds, he never spent more than £50 a year on his upkeep and wore ragged clothes and, for many years, a wig he had found in the gutter. In Parliament his col-

leagues noted that since he had only one suit he could never become a turncoat. At his home Elwes often sat in the kitchen with his servants to save on fuel in other rooms; when his stable boy put out hay for a visitor's horses, Elwes would slip out and retrieve it. He quit Parliament after 12 years because he did not wish to expend the money necessary to be returned to office.

Emancipator, The—See ALEXANDER II OF RUSSIA.

Emancipator of the Plater, The—See JACOBS, HIRSCH.

Emanuel the Fortunate or *the Happy:* EMANUEL I OF PORTUGAL (1469–1521)

Emanuel I, king of Portugal, was called *Emanuel the Fortunate* or *Emanuel the Happy,* not so much as a description of him as of his reign, which has been described by historians as the Golden Age of Portugal. He raised the country to the foremost naval power of Europe. Because of his great efforts on behalf of education and the arts and sciences, he was also dubbed *The Portuguese Maecenas,* after the great Roman patron of the arts and letters.

EMERSON, RALPH WALDO (1803–1882)

The poet and philosopher Ralph Waldo Emerson was often called *The American Carlyle* because, like the British historian Thomas Carlyle, he was greatly influenced by German thought and literature. Living in Concord, Mass., he was quite naturally also designated *The Sage of Concord.*

Emperor Nick of the Bribery Bank— See BIDDLE, NICHOLAS.

Emperor of Believers, The—See
OMAR I.

Emperor of Pugilism, The—See
JACKSON, JOHN "Gentleman
Jack."

Emperor of the Caribbean, The—See
KEITH, MINOR COOPER.

Emperor of the Mountains, The—See
PETER.

Empress of the Blues, The—See
SMITH, BESSIE.

Enchanting Rebel, The—See
MENKEN, ADAH ISAACS.

Enduring Fascist, The—See
FRANCO, FRANCISCO.

ENG and CHANG—See Siamese
Twins, The.

ENGELS, FRIEDRICH (1820–1895)

The cofounder of modern communism with Karl
Marx, Friedrich Engels authored with Marx *The
Communist Manifesto* and carried to completion
Capital after Marx's death. Extremely well off,
he supported Marx financially and became known
as *The Communist Capitalist.*

Engineer of Success, The—See
WILSON, THORNTON ARNOLD.

English Achilles, The—See
DEVEREUX, ROBERT.

English Alexander, The—See
HENRY V OF ENGLAND.

English Aristophanes, The—See
FOOTE, SAMUEL.

English Atticus, The—See ADDISON,
JOSEPH.

English Brutus, The—See WILKES,
JOHN.

English Hog, The—See
MACREADY, WILLIAM
CHARLES.

English Horace, The—See JONSON,
BEN.

English Joan of Arc, The—See
AMBREE, MARY.

English Juvenal, The—See OLDHAM,
JOHN.

English Marcellus, Our—See
HENRY, PRINCE.

English Merlin, The—See LILLY,
WILLIAM.

English Mersenne, The—See
COLLINS, JOHN.

English Opium-Eater, The—See DE QUINCEY, THOMAS.

English Palladio, The—See JONES, INIGO.

English Rabelais, Our—See NASH, THOMAS.

English Rabelais, The—See SWIFT, JONATHAN.

English Roscius, The—See GARRICK, DAVID.

English Socrates, The—See JOHNSON, SAMUEL.

English Solomon, The—See HENRY VII.

English Strabo, The—See CAMDEN, WILLIAM.

ENNIUS, QUINTUS (239–169 B.C.)

As the first among the Romans to write heroic verses and poetry in highly polished Latin, Quintus Ennius has been accorded the title *The Father of the Latin Poets*. Later students of literature have also dubbed him *The Roman Chaucer*.

ENO, WILLIAM PHELPS (1858–1945)

Internationally acclaimed for the introduction of modern traffic regulations, New York-born William Phelps Eno originated one-way streets, stop signs, pedestrian safety islands and taxi stands and issued the first manual of police traffic regulations. He designed the circular traffic pattern around the Arc de Triomphe in Paris and induced that city to ban car horns in the 1930s. Although he was called *The Father of Traffic Safety*, Eno himself never drove a car, having been certain in 1900 that the fad would never last. When he had to bow to the inevitable, he bought a car but relied on a chauffeur to guide him through traffic.

Era-of-Good-Feeling President, The—See MONROE, JAMES.

ERASMUS, DESIDERIUS (1466–1536)

Dutch humanist Desiderius Erasmus, the great representative of the northern Renaissance, has gained such laudatory sobriquets as *The Glory of Netherland, The Glory of the Priesthood, The Viking of Literature* and *The Voltaire of the Sixteenth Century*. He managed to bring down on himself the wrath of both Catholics and Lutherans, however. The latter often called him *Errans Mus,* while the Jesuit Raynaud coined for him the nickname *The Batavian Buffoon*.

Eric Bloodaxe or Bloody Axe: ERIC, KING OF NORWAY (?–954?)

Eric, king of Norway from 930 to 934, gained the surname *Bloodaxe* or *Bloody Axe* because he usurped the throne by killing several of his brothers and exhibited great cruelty towards his people. Deposed by his half-brother, Haakon, he fled to England and ruled Northumbria. He was killed in battle around 954.

Eric Evergood: ERIC I OF DENMARK (1056–1103)

The first European king to go on a pilgrimage to Palestine, Eric I of Denmark was called *Eric*

died in Cyprus.

Eric the Lamb: ERIC III OF DENMARK (?–1147)

Regarded by many of the barons and the general populace of Denmark as an ineffectual ruler, Eric III was derided as *Eric the Lamb*. He finally abdicated in 1147.

Eric the Memorable: ERIC II OF DENMARK (?–1137)

Eric II of Denmark was referred to as *Eric the Memorable* by his subjects since his reign from 1134 to 1137 was marked by a fierce civil war.

Eric the Romantic: ERIC XIV OF SWEDEN (1533–1577)

Having written love letters to Queen Elizabeth I of England for seven years, Eric IV of Sweden became known as *Eric the Romantic*. Besides seeking to marry the English monarch, he at various times proposed marriage to Mary Queen of Scots and a number of royal princesses. He finally married Catherine Karin, the daughter of a corporal. He became mentally unbalanced and his brother John was proclaimed king. It is presumed he was poisoned in 1577 while in prison.

Eric the Saint: ERIC IX OF SWEDEN (?–1160)

A most zealous Christian, Eric IX of Sweden led a crusade to Finland in 1157, and for his many acts of piety, such as forcing the defeated Finns to be baptized, he was called *Eric the Saint*.

ERIGENA, JOHN SCOTUS (?–875)

Ninth century philosopher John Scotus Erigena has been designated *The Last of the Platonists* for his attempts to unite Christianity with the finer points of ancient philosophies.

Errans Mus—See ERASMUS, DESIDERIUS.

ERVIN, SAMUEL JAMES, JR. (1896–)

The senator from North Carolina who drew national attention during the televised Senate Watergate hearings, Sam Ervin was nicknamed *The Po' Ol' Country Lawyer,* a phrase that roled musically off his tongue.

Escaped Jailbird, The—See EGAN, PATRICK.

Escaping Professor, The: ROY GARDNER (1888–1940)

One of the most colorful criminals of the 1920s, Roy Gardner was a multifaceted character who taught English literature in college, published works on 17th century literature and suddenly turned to big-time robbery. Because he escaped custody several times with cunning tricks, the press soon nicknamed him *The Escaping Professor*.

ESCOFFIER, GEORGES AUGUSTE (1846–1935)

Probably the most famous French chef in history, Georges Auguste Escoffier helmed the kitchens at the Reine Blanche in Paris, the Grand Hotel in

Monte Carlo and the Savoy, Ritz and Carlton in London. He was famed as *The King of Chefs and The Chef of Kings*.

Eternal Flapper, The—See HOPPER, EDNA WALLACE.

Ethelred the Unready: ETHELRED II OF ENGLAND (968–1016)

King Ethelred II of England ruled at the height of the Danish invasions and was labeled *The Unready* for his inability to stop raids. He was forced to flee across the English Channel to Rouen in 1013. More generous critics of his reign referred to him as *Ethelred the Ill-Advised*.

Europe's Liberator—See WELLINGTON, ARTHUR WELLESLEY, FIRST DUKE OF.

EVERT LLOYD, CHRIS (1954–   )

American tennis star Chris Evert Lloyd has been dubbed *Miss Frigidaire* by much of the British public. For some reason British tennis fans find her cool, deliberate and glacial-faced playing style somewhat disconcerting in a game of such fired-up competitiveness.

Everybody's Second Choice—See HARDING, WARREN G.

Evil Krogh—See KROGH, EGIL.

Evita of the Orient, The—See MARCOS, IMELDA.

Executive Ass, The—See TYLER, JOHN.

Expansive Apostle of Coitus, The—See COMFORT, ALEX.

Explorer of the Spirit, The—See SWEDENBORG, EMANUEL.

Exponent of Futurism, The—See ANTHEIL, GEORGE.

Expounder of the Constitution, The—See WEBSTER, DANIEL.

Exterminator, The—See MONTBARS.

Extra Billy—See SMITH, WILLIAM "Extra Billy."

Eye, The—See PINKERTON, ALLAN.

EYTAN, RAFAEL (1932–   )

Because he was a firm believer in military solutions to Israel's problems and scoffed at peaceful negotiations, Israeli chief of staff Gen. Rafael Eytan gained the nickname *Israel's Patton*. He was credited with planning the 1981 raid that destroyed Iraq's atomic reactor as well as the 1982 invasion of Lebanon.

EZRA, ABRAHAM BEN MEIR IBN (1092–1167)

The celebrated Spanish Jew Abraham ben Meir ibn Ezra was called *The Admirable* for his noted accomplishments as a philologist, mathematician, poet, astronomer and commentator on the Bible. He is the Rabbi Ben Ezra of Robert Browning's poem of the same name.

Perhaps the most feared Italian of his day, Ezzelino di Romano, the tyrant of Padua, became known as *The Son of the Devil* and *A Child of Hell*. It was said that with a single look he could make even the boldest of men quake in fear. His cruelty to prisoners, men and women, was almost unparalleled. When he was finally overthrown, he remained unreconstructed. Ripping the bandages from his wounds, he was defiant and fierce to the last.

Called *The Palace Prowler,* 31-year-old Michael Fagan broke into Buckingham Palace on several occasions. One night in July 1982 he sat on Queen Elizabeth's bed and talked to her until she was finally able to summon help and have him taken into custody. After young Fagan's arrest, his father described him as a "royal fanatic." Fagan's exploits were reminiscent of those of Edward Jones, or "In-I-Go Jones," who broke into the palace four times during the reign of Queen Victoria. (See also Jones, Edward.)

F

FAIR, JAMES "Slippery Jim" (1831–1894)

One of the great bonanza kings of Nevada's Comstock Lode, James Fair may have been the most hated of the silver millionaires. He was called *Slippery Jim Fair,* and newspapers referred to him as "gross, greedy, grasping, mean and malignant." After once lending money to a needy acquaintance, he then foreclosed and took away the man's business and home. When it was suggested he was being a bit unkind, Fair replied, "A man who can't afford to lose shouldn't sit in a poker game." His obituaries read almost like celebrations. One editor wrote, "I have yet to hear a good word spoken of him. Never did I meet a man of good intelligence who had dealings with him of any sort who did not detest him."

FABER, JOHANN (c. 1470–1541)

Johann Faber, a leading German opponent of the Reformation, was called *Malleus Hereticorum*—after one of his works—or *The Hammer of the Heretics.*

FABRE, JEAN HENRI (1823–1915)

Because his 10-volume *Souvenirs entomologiques* was considered to be a masterpiece of patient and minute observation of insects, French entomologist Jean Henri Fabre was dubbed *The Insects' Homer.*

Fair Maid of Kent, The—See JOAN OF KENT.

Fair Perdita: ROBINSON, MRS. MARY DARBY (1758–1800)

An actress of some ability and a novelist and poet of somewhat less, Mrs. Mary Darby Robinson attracted considerable attention as Perdita in a pro-

Factory King, The—See OASTLER, RICHARD.

duction of Shakespeare's play *The Winter's Tale,* especially from the Prince of Wales, later to become George IV. When she became his mistress, they exchanged nicknames: She was his *Fair Perdita,* and he was her Florizel, the prince of Bohemia in the play. After the affair cooled, she became the mistress of Charles James Fox, the Whig statesman, and later died in extreme poverty.

Fair Rosamund: CLIFFORD, ROSAMUND *(?–1176)*

Because of her rare beauty Rosamund Clifford, the mistress of Henry II of England, was called *Fair Rosamund* even by the Saxons, who hated the king. Henry was said to have built a subterranean labyrinth in Blenheim Park as a retreat for visits with the lady.

FAIRBANKS, CHARLES W. *(1852–1918)*

Vice president of the United States during the second term of Theodore Roosevelt, Charles W. Fairbanks was so reserved and formal that he was often called *Icebanks.* The fact that he represented the wing within the Republican Party that opposed Roosevelt added to the chilliness of the relationship between the two men.

FAIRBANKS, DOUGLAS *(1883–1939)*

Swashbuckling film star Douglas Fairbanks, famed for his athletic prowess, was nicknamed *The Fourth Musketeer.* He was also called *America's Leading Juvenile Forever.*

FALLON, WILLIAM J. *(1886–1927)*

Known as *The Great Mouthpiece,* William J. Fallon was New York's greatest criminal lawyer of the 1920s, numbering among his clients thieves, stock swindlers, second-story men, pimps, mad-

ams, prostitutes, gangsters and murderers, most of whom were guilty and most of whom he got off. He was so successful at his craft that he was also called *The Jail Robber.* Not above bribing a juror to get a hung jury, Fallon was once brought to trial on such a charge but was acquitted. He immediately approached the press table and whispered to Nat Ferber of the *New York American,* the reporter who had dug up the case against him, "Nat, I promise you I'll never bribe another juror."

False Explorer, The—See COOK, FREDERICK A.

False Hair on the Chest—See HEMINGWAY, ERNEST.

False Monty, The—See JAMES, CLIFTON.

False Prophet, The—See MOHAMMED AHMED.

Fanatic of Vice, The—See SADE, MARQUIS DE: DONATIEN ALPHONSE FRANCOIS.

FAREL, GUILLAUME *(1489–1565)*

Exiled from France, French Protestant reformer Guillaume Farel traveled throughout Europe preaching vehement Reformation sermons and becoming known as *The Scourge of the Priests* and *The Elijah of the Reformation.* He persuaded Calvin to lead the Reformation in Geneva.

FARINELLI, CARLO BROSCHI *(1705–1782)*

Regarded as the greatest of Italy's castrati singers, Carlo Broschi Farinelli was called throughout his

the *Il Ragazzo,* or *The Lad.* "One God and one Farinelli!" a woman in London cried after hearing him sing opera. Farinelli was particularly lionized in Spain, where he was made a prince. He lived out his last years in splendor in Bologna in what has been called "a fairy castle." However, he long suffered a severe melancholia as the result of his castration, a barbarous custom inflicted on him to preserve his youthful soprano.

FARLEY, JAMES A. *(1888–1976)*

The Democratic politician who handled Franklin D. Roosevelt's presidential campaigns in 1932 and 1936, James A. Farley was known as *Smiling Jim.* He was also called *A Political Thor* and *That Candid Spoilsman,* the last an allusion to his firm belief in the principles of patronage.

FARMER, FANNIE MERRITT *(1857–1915)*

A stroke victim crippled for long periods of time, Fannie Farmer established her own school of cookery in Boston and became known as *The Mother of Level Measurement.* She stressed the importance of using standard, level measurements and following recipes to the 1/8 of a teaspoonful. Eschewing instructions for a "dash," "pinch" or "spoonful," she gave precise quantities. She made her "spoonful" an exact size, since spoons in that era had no standard dimensions. She is credited with considerably raising the cooking skills of the average housewife—or man.

Farmer George—See GEORGE III.

Farmer President, The—See HARRISON, WILLIAM HENRY.

FAROUK I *(1920–1965)*

Even after he was overthrown as king of Egypt by a coup in 1952, mammoth playboy Farouk I continued to be called *Prince Charming.* He earned the sobriquet because the numerous women who struck his fancy could always count on being lavished with gifts for their favors.

Farthing Jamie—See LOWSHER, JAMES.

FARWELL, CHARLES B. *(1823–1903)*

A U.S. senator from Illinois in the late 19th century, Charles B. Farwell, much to his dismay, was nicknamed *Poker Charley.* It may well have been a political "dirty trick," since he earnestly informed constituents that he didn't even know how to play the game.

Fat Adonis of Forty (or Fifty)—See GEORGE IV.

Fat Boy, That—See MAHARAJ JI.

Fat One, The—See GOERING, HERMANN.

Fat Paunch—See PTOLEMY VII.

Father Goose—See SENNETT, MACK.

Father of Abolition, The—See HOPKINS, SAMUEL.

Father of Abolitionism, The—See GARRISON, WILLIAM LLOYD.

Father of American Anthropology, The—See MORGAN, LEWIS HENRY.

Father of American Botany, The—See BARTRAM, JOHN.

Father of American Drama, The—See DUNLAP, WILLIAM.

Father of American Football, The—See CAMP, WALTER CHAUNCEY.

Father of American History, The—See BRADFORD, WILLIAM.

Father of American Literature, The—See IRVING, WASHINGTON.

Father of American Newspapers, The—See HARRIS, BENJAMIN.

Father of American Orchestral Music, The—See GRAUPNER, JOHANN CHRISTIAN GOTTLIEB.

Father of American Pediatrics, The—See JACOBI, ABRAHAM.

Father of American Poets, The—See BRYANT, WILLIAM CULLEN.

Father of American Political Cartoonists, The—See NAST, THOMAS.

Father of American Surgery, The—See PHYSICK, PHILIP SYNG.

Father of Analytic Psychology, The—See JUNG, CARL GUSTAV.

Father of Anarchy, The—See WARREN, JOSIAH.

Father of Anesthesia, The—See MORTON, WILLIAM THOMAS GREEN.

Father of Animal Magnetism, The—See MESMER, FRANZ ANTON.

Father of Arabic Literature, The—See MAMOUN.

Father of Automation, The—See WIENER, NORBERT.

Father of Baseball, The: ALEXANDER JOY CARTWRIGHT (1800–1892); HENRY CHADWICK (1824–1908)

Alexander Cartwright designed the baseball diamond, formed the first team (New York Knickerbockers) and authored the first set of rules in the 1840s. Traveling west by wagon train to hunt for gold, he taught other pioneers how to play the game. Henry Chadwick wrote the first official rule book and developed the scoring system as it is basically followed today. (See also Doubleday, Abner.)

Father of Basketball, The—See NAISMITH, JAMES.

Father of Bowdlerizing, The—See BOWDLER, THOMAS.

Father of Brains, The—See BEECHER, LYMAN.

Father of British Socialism, The—See OWEN, ROBERT.

Father of Chemistry, The—See VILLENEUVA, ARNAUD DE.

Father of Chicago, The—See DU SABLE, JEAN BAPTISTE POINT.

Father of Chop Suey, The—See LI-HUNG CHANG.

Father of Clockmaking, The—See TOMPION, THOMAS.

Father of Comedy, The—See ARISTOPHANES.

Father of Country Music, The—See RODGERS, JAMES CHARLES "Jimmy."

Father of Curtesie, The—See BEAUCHAMP, RICHARD DE.

Father of English Poetry, The—See CHAUCER, GEOFFREY.

Father of English Prose, The—See WYCLIFFE, JOHN.

Father of English Unitarianism, The—See BIDDLE, JOHN.

Father of English Water Color, The—See SANDBY, PAUL.

Father of Errors, The—See LILLY, WILLIAM.

Father of Etherization, The—See MORTON, WILLIAM THOMAS GREEN.

Father of Experimental Physiology, The—See GALEN, CLAUDIUS.

Father of Fingerprinting in America, The—See FAUROT, JOSEPH A.

Father of France's New Deal, The—See BLUM, LEON.

Father of Frankish History, The—See GREGORY OF TOURS.

Father of French Eloquence, The—See CHARTIER, ALAIN.

Father of French History, The—See VILLEHARDOUIN, GEOFFROI DE.

Father of French Philosophy, The—See ALEMBERT, JEAN LE ROND D'.

Father of French Poetry, The—See THIBAUT IV.

Father of French Prose, The—See VILLEHARDOUIN, GEOFFROI DE.

Father of French Tragedy, The—See CORNEILLE, PIERRE; GARNIER, ROBERT.

Father of Frozen Foods, The—See BIRDSEYE, CLARENCE.

Father of German Literature, The—See LESSING, GOTTHOLD EPHRAIM.

Father of German Poetry, The—See OPITZ, MARTIN.

Father of Gospel Music, The—See DORSEY, TOM.

Father or Greek Tragedy, The—See AESCHYLUS; THESPIS.

Father of Greenbacks, The—See CHASE, SALMON P.

Father of His Country, The—See WASHINGTON, GEORGE.

Father of His People, The—See LOUIS XII OF FRANCE.

Father of History, The—See HERODOTUS.

Father of Homeopathy in America, The—See HERING, CONSTANTINE.

Father of Humanism, The—See PETRARCH, FRANCESCO.

Father of India, The—See GANDHI, MOHANDA "Mahatma."

Father of International Law, The—See GROTIUS, HUGO.

Father of Invention, The—See BIRDSEYE, CLARENCE.

Father of Jests, The—See MILLER, JOE.

Father of Letters, The—See FRANCIS I OF FRANCE; MEDICI, LORENZO DE'.

Father of Lies, The—See HERODOTUS; RANDOLPH (OF ROANOKE), JOHN.

Father of London, The—See BARNARD, JOHN.

Father of Medicine, The—See HIPPOCRATES.

Father of Modern American Journalism, The—See PULITZER, JOSEPH.

Father of Modern Astronomy, The—See COPERNICUS, NICHOLAS.

Father of Modern Ballet, The—See FOKINE, MICHEL.

Father of Modern French Poetry, The—See MALHERBE, FRANCOIS DE.

Father of Modern Geography, The—See MERCATOR, GERARDUS.

Father of Modern Philosophy, The—See DESCARTES, RENE.

Father of Modern Skepticism, The—See BAYLE, PIERRE.

Father of Modern Surgery, The—See PARE, AMBROISE.

Father of Modernism, The—See CEZANNE, PAUL.

Father of Monachism, The—See ANTHONY (or ANTONY), ST.

Father of Monks, The—See ANTHONY (or ANTONY), ST.

Father of Moral Philosophy, The—See THOMAS AQUINAS.

Father of More Brains Than Any Other Man in America, The—See BEECHER, LYMAN.

Father of Negro Songs, The—See GRAUPNER, JOHANN CHRISTIAN GOTTLIEB.

Father of Orthodoxy, The—See ATHANASIUS, ST.

Father of Parody, The—See HIPPONAX.

Father of Peace, The—See DORIA, ANDREA.

Father of Pennsylvania, The—See PENN, WILLIAM.

Father of Philosophy, The—See BACON, ROGER.

Father of Phrenology, The—See GALL, FRANZ JOSEPH.

Father of Poetry, The—See ORPHEUS.

Father of Positivism, The—See COMTE, AUGUSTE.

Father of Printing, The—See GUTENBERG, JOHANN.

Father of Prison Reform, The—See OSBORNE, GEORGE O.

Father of Progressive Relaxation, The—See JACOBSON, EDMUND.

Father of Prohibition, The—See DOW, NEAL.

Father of Realism, The—See HOWELLS, WILLIAM DEAN.

Father of Reclamation, The—See WISNER, EDWARD.

Father of Ridicule, The—See
RABELAIS, FRANCOIS.

Father of Rock n' Roll, The—See
PRESLEY, ELVIS.

Father of Roman Satire, The—See
LUCILIUS, CAIUS.

Father of Russian History, The—See
NESTOR.

Father of Russian Marxism, The—See
PLEKHANOV, GEORGI.

Father of Santa Claus, The—See
MOORE, CLEMENT CLARKE.

Father of Scavenger's Daughter, The:
SKEFFINGTON, WILLIAM (*fl. early to mid-16th century*)

William Skeffington, a lieutenant at the Tower of London, was Henry VIII's prize torturer. He was called *The Father of Scavenger's Daughter,* that being an instrument of torture consisting of a piked iron frame which compressed the victim's body and caused bleeding especially from the nostrils.

Father of Science Fiction, The—See
VERNE, JULES.

Father of Secession, The—See
RHETT, ROBERT B.

Father of Sentiment, The—See
ROUSSEAU, JEAN JACQUES.

Father of Slum Clearance, The—See
RIIS, JACOB AUGUST.

Father of Smoke Control, The—See
WOLK, ABRAHAM L.

Father of Soda Pop, The—See
PHYSICK, PHILIP SYNG.

Father of Space Medicine, The—See
STRUGHOLD, HUBERTUS.

Father of Spoonerisms, The—See
SPOONER, WILLIAM ARCHIBALD.

Father of Swedish Music, The—See
ROMAN, JOHAN.

Father of Sweet Jazz, The—See
GOLDKETTE, JEAN.

Father of Television, The—See
ZWORYKIN, VLADIMIR KOSMA.

Father of Texas, The—See
HOUSTON, SAMUEL.

Father of the American Medical Association—See **DAVIS, NATHAN SMITH.**

Father of the American Navy, The—See **BARRY, JOHN.**

Father of the American Revolution, The—See **ADAMS, SAMUEL.**

Father of the ASPCA, The—See
BERGH, HENRY.

Father of the Atom Bomb, The—See
OPPENHEIMER, J. ROBERT.

*Father of the Atomic Submarine,
The*—See RICKOVER, HYMAN G.

Father of the Blues, The—See
HANDY, W. C.

Father of the Constitution, The—See
MADISON, JAMES.

*Father of the Continental Congress,
The*—See FRANKLIN, BENJAMIN.

*Father of the Corinthian Column,
The*—See CALLIMACHUS.

*Father of the Eighteenth Amendment,
The*—See SHEPPARD, MORRIS.

Father of the H-Bomb, The—See
TELLER, EDWARD.

Father of the Hershey Bar, The—See
HERSHEY, MILTON S.

Father of the Historical Novel, The—
SCOTT, WALTER.

*Father of the Homestead Act,
The*—See JOHNSON, ANDREW.

Father of the House, The—See
KELLEY, WILLIAM DARRAGH;
MACON, NATHANIEL.

*Father of the Juvenile Court,
The*—See LINDSEY, BEN B.

*Father of the Kindergarten,
The*—See FROEBEL, FRIEDRICH.

Father of the Latin Poets, The—See
ENNIUS, QUINTUS.

*Father of the Mail Order Catalog,
The*—See FRANKLIN, BENJAMIN.

Father of the Marseillaise, The—
See ROUGET DE LISLE, CLAUDE
JOSEPH.

*Father of the Modern Innkeeping
Industry, The*—See WILSON,
CHARLES KEMMONS.

Father of the Museum, The—See
BICKMORE, ALBERT SMITH.

Father of the Music Hall, The—See
PASTOR, TONY.

Father of the New Economics—See
KEYNES, JOHN MAYNARD.

Father of the Newsreel, The—See
PATHE, CHARLES.

Father of the Official Communique—
See STANTON, EDWIN M.

*Father of the One-Way Ride, The—*See
WEISS, HYMIE "the Polack."

*Father of the Patent Office, The—*See
RUGGLES, JOHN.

*Father of the Poets, The—*See
SPENSER, EDMUND.

*Father of the Pony Express, The—*See
RUSSELL, WILLIAM HEPBURN.

*Father of the Poor, The—*See GILPIN,
BERNARD.

*Father of the Potteries, The—*See
WEDGWOOD, JOSIAH.

*Father of the Quartering Act,
The—*See GAGE, THOMAS.

*Father of the Skyscraper, The—*See
GILBERT, CASS.

*Father of the Soviet Hydrogen Bomb,
The—*See SAKHAROV, ANDREI
DMITRIEVICH.

*Father of the Steamboat, The—*See
FULTON, ROBERT.

*Father of the Stove, The—*See
FRANKLIN, BENJAMIN.

*Father of the Sweet Potato Industry,
The—*See AVILA, JOHN B.

*Father of the Tabloid, The—*See
PATTERSON, JOSEPH MEDILL.

*Father of the Tariff, The—*See
HAMILTON, ALEXANDER.

*Father of the Telegraph, The—*See
MORSE, SAMUEL F. B.

*Father of the Telephone, The—*See
BELL, ALEXANDER GRAHAM.

*Father of the Tommy Gun, The—*See
THOMPSON, JOHN T.

*Father of the Turks, The—*See
ATATURK, MUSTAPHA KEMAL.

*Father of the Typewriter, The—*See
SHOLES, CHRISTOPHER
LATHAM.

*Father of the U.S. Air Force,
The—*See LOWE, THADDEUS, S. C.

*Father of the U.S. Foreign Service,
The—*See CARR, WILBUR JOHN.

*Father of the Volstead Act, The—*See
VOLSTEAD, ANDREW J.

*Father of the Watch, The—*See
HENLEIN, PETER.

Father of the Weather Bureau,
The—See ABBE, CLEVELAND
"Old Prob."

Father of Traffic Safety, The—See
ENO, WILLIAM PHELPS.

Father of Utilitarianism, The—See
BENTHAM, JEREMY.

Father of Vorticism, The—See
LEWIS, WYNDHAM.

Father of West Point, The—See
THAYER, SYLVANUS.

Father of Whist, The—See HOYLE,
EDMOND.

Father of Wonder Drugs, The—See
WAKSMAN, SELMAN ABRAHAM.

Father Thoughtful—See CATINAT,
NICHOLAS.

Fatty—See TAYLOR, ELIZABETH.

FAULKNER, RALPH—See King of
the Swashbucklers, The.

FAUROT, JOSEPH A. (1872–1942)

Although he was only a lowly detective sergeant
on the New York City police force in the early
1900s, Joseph A. Faurot is regarded as *The Father
of Fingerprinting in America.* He constantly bad-
gered the high brass to accept the new English sys-

tem of identification was finally adopted
to solve several cases
minals, and the method
rot used fingerprints
ous officials.

Favored Child of Vic..., The—See
MASSENA, ANDRE.

FAY, LARRY (1889–1933)

A notorious American gangster of the 19..s and
early 1930s and boss of the New York City milk
racket, Larry Fay was nicknamed *The Beau
Brummel of Broadway.* It was a facetious description for someone described by one newspaperman
as "a sadistic, over-dressed, little man, horse-faced
and stricken with a touch of megalomania." Fay
was shot to death by a doorman of a nightclub he
owned, when he denied him a small raise.

Fearless, The—See JOHN, DUKE OF
BURGUNDY.

Fearless Frances—See PERKINS,
FRANCES.

Feather in the Scale, A—See
BOSWELL, JAMES.

Federal Bull-Dog, The—See
MARTIN, LUTHER.

Federal Farmer, The—See LEE,
RICHARD HENRY.

FELTON, JOHN (?–1628)

Few assassins in history were as lionized as
Englishman John Felton, executed in 1628 for
killing the unpopular duke of Buckingham. He was

labeled *Honest Ja...* *Brutus* because, like that
Roman, it was ...had killed a tyrant. He
was also calle...*David*. As Disraeli later
wrote: "The p...f Felton to London, after the
assassination,...ed a triumph. Now pitied, and
now blessed,...hers held up their children to be-
hold the sav...f the country; and an old woman
exclaimed,...bless thee, little David.' Felton
was near...ainted before he reached the me-
tropolis...

Female Bill Hart, The—See GUINAN,
TEXAS.

---

*Female Brain of the SLA,
The*—See SOLTYSIK, PATRICIA.

Female Evel Knievel, The—See
LAWLER, DEBBIE.

Female Howard, The—See FRY,
ELIZABETH.

Female Marine, The—See SNELL,
HANNAH.

Female Plutarch, The—See LEWIS,
ESTELLE ANNA BLANCHE
ROBINSON.

Female Robin Hood, The—See
STARR, BELLE.

FENWICK, MILLICENT (1910–   )

A U.S. representative from New Jersey from 1975
to 1983 and an unsuccessful Republican candidate for the Senate in 1982, Millicent Fenwick, a
former fashion model, was a grandmother when
first elected to Congress. Because of her habit of
smoking a pipe, she was dubbed *The Pipe*. Perhaps a more substantive sobriquet, first applied to
her by television newscaster Walter Cronkite,
was *The Conscience of Congress*.

FERDINAND II OF THE TWO SICILIES (1810–1859)

Because of the wholesale bombardment of several
cities, especially Messina, Ferdinand II of the Two
Sicilies was fearfully referred to by the civilian
population during the revolutionary battles of 1849
as *King Bomba* or *Bomb*.

Ferdinand the Inconstant: FERDINAND I OF PORTUGAL (1345–1383)

Ferdinand I, king of Portugal, earned his nickname *The Inconstant* both in affairs of the heart
and affairs of state. He shocked royal society by
jilting the daughter of the king of Castile in favor
of a beautiful Portuguese noblewoman, Leonora
Telles. His policies were equally inconsistent in
his relations with Castile and England.

FERGUSON, RICHARD—See Galloping Dick.

FERGUSON, ROBERT (1638–1714)

One of the great political intriguers in English
history, Independent preacher Robert Ferguson,
a Scot, was labeled *Judas* by Dryden but was
more simply called *The Plotter*. He was at various
times a supporter of Monmouth's ascension to
the throne, a participant in the Rye House Plot
to assassinate James II, a member of Monmouth's
army and a preacher for the cause of James on
some occasions and for the Prince of Orange
on others.

FERMI, ENRICO (1901–1954)

Enrico Fermi, the Italian-born physicist, led the group that achieved the first man-made nuclear chain reaction, and he directed the building of the first atomic pile, resulting in the development of the atomic bomb. He was dubbed *The Columbus of the Atomic Age*.

FERNANDEL (1903–1971)

Long-faced, toothy-grinned French screen comedian Fernandel was often referred to by his affectionate and dedicated fans as *Horse Face*.

FETCHIT, STEPIN (1902–   )

Black American actor Stepin Fetchit achieved Hollywood fame as a slow-moving, dim-witted comic, leading many blacks in recent years to disparagingly refer to him as *The White Man's Negro*. Born Lincoln Theodore Monroe Andrew Perry, he took his professional name from a race-horse on which he won a considerable sum of money.

Fiddle and the Bow, The: OLIVER HARDY (1892–1957) and STAN LAUREL (1890–1965)

The Screen comedy team of Oliver Hardy and Stan Laurel was designated *The Fiddle and the Bow*. It was apparently a genuine nickname given them by the public rather than by a motion picture publicity department.

Fiddle-Dee-Dee—See LEIGH, VIVIEN.

Fidus Achates—See BALLANTYNE, JOHN.

FIEDLER, ARTHUR (1894–1979)

Symphony conductor Arthur Fiedler was, according to many, Boston's finest tourist and cultural attraction and he was celebrated as both *Mr. Boston* and *Mr. Pops*.

FIELDING, JOHN (1722–1780)

Noted Bow Street magistrate Sir John Fielding, who had been blinded in his youth, was called *The Blind Magistrate*. He was credited with knowing countless thieves and other criminal offenders by the sound of their voices.

FIELDING, TEMPLE (1913–1983)

One of the foremost American writers of travel books, Temple Fielding was dubbed *The King of European Guides*.

Fielding Among Painters, A—See HOGARTH, WILLIAM.

FIERRO, RODOLFO (?–1920)

The most devoted and bloodiest follower of Mexican bandit-revolutionary Pancho Villa, Gen. Rodolfo Fierro was nicknamed *Pancho Villa's Butcher*. He eagerly carried out all executions ordered, sometimes making it clear that Villa was too lenient in dealing with traitors. In his most awesome escapade, he captured 300 of Gen. Victoriano Huerta's soldiers and offered to let them escape rather than be executed if they could make it over a wall one at a time. He picked off every one with his rifle. *The Butcher* was feared even by his own men and when he fell from his mount while fording a river and was drowning under the weight of a money belt loaded with gold, none came to his aid.

Fiery Face—See JAMES II OF SCOTLAND.

Fifth Beatle, The—See KAUFMAN, MURRAY.

Figaro of His Age, The—See BEAUMARCHAIS, PIERRE AUGUSTIN CARON DE.

Fighter, The—See ALFONSO I OF ARAGON AND NAVARRE (ALFONSO VII OF LEON AND CASTILLE).

Fighting Atheist, The—See INGERSOLL, ROBERT G.

Fighting Commissary, The—See GINTER, LEWIS.

Fighting Con, The—See HUNTER, BOBBY LEE.

Fighting Parson, The—See ALLEN, THOMAS; CHIVINGTON, JOHN M.; DEWEY, JEDEDIAH.

Fighting Parson of Bennington Fields, The—See ALLEN, THOMAS.

Fighting Pimps, The—See EARP, WYATT; MASTERSON, WILLIAM BARCLAY "Bat."

Fighting Prelate, The: HENRY SPENSER (fl. late 14th century)

A warlike bishop of Norwich during the reign of England's Richard II, Henry Spenser was called *The Fighting Prelate.*

Fighting Quaker, The—See GREENE, NATHANAEL.

Fighting Surgeon of the Revolution, The—See DOWNER, ELIPHALET.

Figure of Fun, The—See ROOSEVELT, ELEANOR.

Figurehead of Music in England, The—See ELGAR, EDWARD WILLIAM.

FILLMORE, MILLARD (1800–1874)

Like John Tyler before him, President Millard Fillmore was called *His Accidency* and *The Accidental President,* since he stepped up from the vice presidency on the death of the president. He was often called *The American Louis Philippe* because of his close resemblance in physical appearance and aristocratic inclinations to the French monarch. Others refered to him as *The Handsome Mediocrity.*

Film Maker Who Always Goes Just Too Far, The—See RUSSELL, KEN.

Filthy Story-Teller, Despot, Liar, Thief, Braggart, Buffoon, Usurper, Monster, Ignoramus, Old Scoundrel, Perjurer, Robber, Swindler, Tyrant, Field-Butcher, Land-Pirate—See **LINCOLN, ABRAHAM.**

Financier of the American Revolution, The—See **MORRIS, ROBERT "Bobby the Treasurer."**

FINDLEY, PAUL (1921–)

Until his defeat for reelection in 1982, Illinois Republican representative Paul Findley was an outspoken supporter of the Palestinian and Arab causes in the Middle East, a position that prompted foes to nickname him *Yasser Arafat's Best Friend in Congress.*

FINK, MIKE (1770–1823)

Mike Fink was called *The King of the Keelboatmen* and *Snapping Turtle* because of his reckless, fighting behavior. The legend of his battles and killings have become part of Mississippi River mythology.

FINN, DANIEL E. (1849–1910)

A New York state assemblyman in the late 1800s, Daniel E. Finn won the sobriquet *Battery Dan* because he successfully defeated one of the worst land grabs in the city's history. The scheme would have allowed private companies to divide Battery Park into pier sites.

Fire Angel, The—See **HUDLUN, ANNA ELIZABETH.**

Firebrand—See **MARCANTONIO, VITO.**

FIRPO, LUIS ANGEL (c. 1895–1960)

The Wild Bull of the Pampas is a boxing sobriquet worthy of Argentine heavyweight Luis Angel Firpo. In 1923 Firpo and world heavyweight champion Jack Dempsey engaged in one of the bloodiest battles in ring history. During the first round the challenger actually knocked Dempsey out of the ring, but fighting like a maddened bull, Firpo was not able to take advantage of the champion after he climbed (some say, was helped) back in the ring. The Manassa Mauler thereupon hammered *The Wild Bull* to the canvas nine times before ending the fight with a powerful right in the second round.

First American Anarchist, The—See **WARREN, JOSIAH.**

First American Negro Martyr, The—See **ATTUCKS, CRISPUS.**

First Automobile Bandit, The—See **STARR, HENRY.**

First Dark Horse, The—See **POLK, JAMES K.**

First English Victim of Aviation, The—See **ROLLS, CHARLES STEWART.**

First Gentleman of San Fransisco, The—See **RALSTON, WILLIAM CHAPMAN.**

First Gentleman of the Land—See
ARTHUR, CHESTER A.

First Great Protestant, The—See
SAVONAROLA, GIROLAMO.

First Great Racer, The—See
**ROBERTSON, GEORGE
HEPBURN.**

First Grenadier of France, The—See
**LA TOUR D'AUVERGNE,
THEOPHILE MALO CORRET DE.**

First Historian of America, The—See
ANGHIERA, PIETRO MARTIRE.

First Lady of Bendix—See
CUNNINGHAM, MARY.

*First Lady of Hollywood: IRENE
DUNNE (1904–   ), GREER
GARSON (1908–   ), NORMA
SHEARER (1904–1983)*

Never loath to hand out sobriquets wholesale, Hollywood bestowed the title *First Lady of Hollywood* (or *The Screen*) at about the same time to Greer Garson, Irene Dunne and Norma Shearer.

First Lady of Talk, The—See
WALTERS, BARBARA.

*First Lady of the American Stage,
The*—See **HAYES, HELEN.**

First Lady of the Jail, The—See
SCOFFEL, KATHERINE.

First Lady of the Revolution, The—See
WARREN, MERCY OTIS.

*First Lady of the World, *—See
WILSON, EDITH BOLLING.

First Lyrist of France, The—See
RONSARD, PIERRE DE.

First Mama—See **FORD, BETTY.**

First Mannequin—See **REAGAN,
NANCY.**

*First Martyr of the Revolution,
The*—See **SNYDER, CHRISTOPHER.**

*First of the Beautiful People,
The*—See **NAST, CONDE.**

*First of the British Periodical
Essayists, The*—See **STEELE,
RICHARD.**

First of the Nixon Men—
See **HALDEMAN, H. R.**

First Shakespeare, The—See
MARLOWE, CHRISTOPHER.

First Woman in Congress, The—See
RANKIN, JEANETTE.

First Woman in Space, The—See
TERESHKOVA, VALENTINA.

FISCHER, ROBERT JAMES
(1943–   )

Bobby Fischer, an American grand master of chess, has borne such nicknames as *The Boy Robot, The Corduroy Killer* and *The Sweatshirt Kid,* all reflecting his total devotion to the game and lack of other interests.

FISH, ALBERT *(1870–1936)*

Harmless-looking Albert Fish, an elderly house painter in New York City, molested more than 400 children and murdered and ate at least 15 of them. Because of his appearance, Fish was labeled by the press *The Gentle Cannibal.* He was executed in 1936.

FISHER, HENDRICK *(1697–1779)*

A fiery political colonial leader in colonial New Jersey, Hendrick Fisher was the equal of Sam Adams of Massachusetts in demanding independence from England, and he became known as *The Samuel Adams of New Jersey.*

FITZGERALD, A. ERNEST
(1927–   )

Heralded by the press as *The Pentagon Whistle Blower,* A. Ernest Fitzgerald was dismissed from his job as a civilian budget analyst for the U.S. Air Force for telling Congress about billions of dollars wasted by the military. He was subsequently reinstated. The sobriquet "whistle blower" was later applied to other government employees who exposed excessive costs or other scandals.

FITZGERALD, JOHN F. *(1863–1951)*

The founder of a political dynasty, the Kennedys, John F. Fitzgerald became the boss of the democratic party in Boston at the beginning of the 20th century. His trademark song was "Sweet Adeline," which he sang in his "honey-sweet voice," giving birth to the nickname *Honey Fitz.* When his namesake, and grandson, John Fitzgerald Kennedy, became president in 1960, he named the presidential yacht *The Honey Fitz* in his honor.

FITZGERALD, WILLIAM THOMAS
(1759–1829)

William Thomas Fitzgerald, a rather inferior English poet, was squelched by William Cobbett as *The Small-Beer Poet.*

FITZ-WALTER, ROBERT *(fl. early 13th century)*

Robert Fitz-Walter led the forces demanding redress from King John of England. The result was the issuance of the Magna Carta. He was hailed as *The Marshal of the Army of God* at Runnymede in 1215.

Five Cent Cigar Marshall—See
MARSHALL, THOMAS RILEY.

520% Miller—See **MILLER,
WILLIAM F. "520%."**

Fixer, The—See **ROTHSTEIN,
ARNOLD.**

Flaccus, Quintus Horatius—See
HORACE.

Flatterer, The—See BOILEAU-
DESPREAUX, NICHOLAS.

FLAUBERT, GUSTAVE (1821–1880)

French novelist Gustave Flaubert, noted for his objective and detailed realism, especially in *Madame Bovary,* won the designation *The Master of Naturalism.* Flaubert's extreme meticulousness of phrasing using the *mot juste,* or "exact word," contrasts sharply with the more loosely written works of his great English contemporaries Dickens and Thackeray.

Flea—See LEE, FITZHUGH.

Flea of Conventions, The—See
FOLSOM, ABIGAIL.

FLEMING, PAUL (1609–1640)

Seventeenth century poet Paul Fleming was called *The Anacreon of Germany* for his many sweet and exquisite love songs, regarded as comparable to the works of the great Greek poet. Also a composer of hymns, he was likened to his English Cavalier contemporary Robert Herrick and called *The Herrick of Germany.* Indeed, his sacred songs probably achieved an intensity that Herrick never matched.

Fleshy Poet, The—See SWINBURNE, ALGERNON.

FLETCHER, HORACE (1849–1919)

The man who "Fletcherized" America, Horace Fletcher warned that "nature will castigate those who don't masticate." What *The Great Masticator,*

as he became known, meant was that every bite of food had to be chewed at least 40 times, and preferably up to 70 times, before being swallowed. He claimed the food would then "swallow itself" and dissolve into nothingness. Even milk and fruit juices were to be chewed, and millions of Americans followed his instructions, among them Upton Sinclair, John Harvey Kellogg and William James. In time mastication ran its course (James quit, saying, "It nearly killed me"), and it appears that only the chewing gum industry profited from the fad.

FLETCHER, JOHN (1576–1625)

Poet and dramtist John Fletcher has been accorded such designations as *The Muses' Darling* and *A Limb of Shakespeare,* the latter by John Dryden.

FLORINDA (fl. early 18th century)

Because King Roderick of the Goths violated Florinda, her father, St. Julian, turned traitor in an ensuing war between the Moors and the Goths and induced the Moors to invade Spain. Roderick was killed at Xeres in 711, and the unfortunate Florinda was thereafter celebrated as *The Helen of Spain.*

Flower of Poets, The—See
CHAUCER, GEOFFREY.

Flower of Quakerism, The—See
MOTT, LUCRETIA.

FLOYD, CHARLES ARTHUR "Pretty Boy" (1901–1934)

Public enemy Charles Arthur Floyd hated the nickname *Pretty Boy,* saddled on him by Oklahoma neighbors in his youth and later picked up by numerous whorehouse inmates when he was an adult criminal. In fact, he killed at least two gangsters partly because they baited him with the term. Even as he lay riddled with FBI bullets in an Ohio corn field in 1934, he was angered by agents who referred to him as *Pretty Boy Floyd*. With almost his final words, he snarled, "I'm Charles Arthur Floyd!" (See also Introduction.)

FLUDD, ROBERT (1574–1637)

British physician-philosopher Robert Fludd delved into so many different fields of research in philosophy, mathematics and medicine that he was styled *The Searcher*.

Flute Player, The—See PTOLEMY XI.

Flying Angel, The—See LAWLER, DEBBIE.

Flying Dutchman, The—See WAGNER, HONUS.

Flying Highwayman, The: WILLIAM HARROW (?–1763)

A notorious British criminal, William Harrow was known as *The Flying Highwayman*, for his habit of avoiding pursuers by leaping his horse across fences when making an escape. He was finally caught and hanged on March 28, 1763.

Flying Monk, The—See JOSEPH OF COPERTINO.

Flying Mouth, The—See BAILEY, F. LEE.

FLYNT, LARRY (1942–   )

Facing serious criminal charges in two states, *Hustler* magazine publisher Larry Flynt announced he had become a born-again Christian, a process he insisted had nothing to do with his legal cases but which was aided to some extent by President Jimmy Carter's sister, evangelist Ruth Stapleton. "I begged forgiveness for hurting anyone, and I asked God to get into my life," Flynt announced. "Ruth didn't convert me—I just happened to be with her when it happened. Jesus stood right there in front of me. It happened and it changed by life." Not completely, however. He said, "Yes, I am a born-again Christian. But I am going to continue publishing pornography, and anybody who doesn't like it can go kiss a rope. I still believe in what we are doing. Women have got to lose their hang-ups about displaying their bodies." It is perhaps not surprising that Flynt's best-known nickname today is *The Born-again Pornographer*.

Foaming Fudge—See BROUGHAM, HENRY PETER, LORD.

Fog—See PHILLIPS, MARK.

Foghorn Funston—See FUNSTON, EDWARD H. "Foghorn."

FOIX, GASTON DE (1489–1512)

A brilliant young French general, Gaston de Foix won the honorific title *The Thunderbolt of Italy* after his smashing victory over the Spaniards at Ravenna on April 11, 1512. However, he was killed in pursuit of the ragged enemy a short time later.

FOKINE, MICHEL (1880–1942)

Russian-born choreographer Michel Fokine, who created "The Dying Swan" for Pavlova, greatly influenced the development of modern ballet by incorporating music, mime, costume and scenery into dance.

FOLSOM, ABIGAIL (1792–1867)

Because she was a gadfly member of the American Anti-Slavery Society and always determined to speak her mind forcefully, Abigail Folsom was affectionately nicknamed *The Flea of Conventions* by Ralph Waldo Emerson.

FONDA, JANE (1937–   )

U.S. actress and controversial political activist Jane Fonda has evoked strong pro and con feelings since the time of the Vietnam War protests. Supporters have called her the *The Non-Stop Activist;* enemies have denounced her as *The Rottenest American* and *Hanoi Jane.* Others have preferred *Mr. Fonda's Baby Jane.*

Foot Eazer, The—See SCHOLL, WILLIAM.

Football's "Old Man River"—See STAGG, AMOS ALONZO.

FOOTE, HENRY STUART (1804–1880)

During a famous 1848 debate in the Senate concerning slavery, Sen. Henry Stuart Foote of Mississippi told Sen. John P. Hale of New Hampshire that if he ever came to Mississippi he would surely be hanged. Adding he would eagerly lend a hand, Foote thereafter was celebrated in the South and despised in the North as *Hangman Foote.*

FOOTE, SAMUEL (1722–1777)

English comedian and dramatist Samuel Foote was celebrated in his time as *The English* or *Modern Aristophanes* for his unbounded humor. He was also referred to as *Beau Nasty,* a reflection of his personal appearance characterized by clothing soiled with snuff and the remains of past meals. A contemporary reported, "In his young days, and in fluctuation of his finances, he walked about in boots, to conceal his want of stockings, and that, on receiving a supply of money, he expended it all upon a diamond ring, instead of purchasing the necessary articles of hosiery."

FORAKER, JOSEPH E. (1846–1917)

A fiery political figure, Gov. Joseph B. Foraker of Ohio was famed for his inflammatory talk and actions. In 1887 he refused to follow the call of President Grover Cleveland to return to southern states flags captured during the Civil War. Foraker announced, "No rebel flags will be surrendered while I am governor," a statement that won him the sobriquet *Bloody Shirt Foraker.*

FORBES, CHARLES R. (1877–1952)

A World War I hero and member of the "Ohio Gang" under President Warren Harding, Col. Charles R. Forbes went to prison for frauds running into the millions of dollars while he was in charge of the Veterans Bureau. When the depredations became known, his sobriquet *The Veteran's Friend* took on a different meaning.

Forces' Sweetheart, The—See LYNN, VERA.

FORD, ARTHUR A. (1896–1971)

American clergyman and spirit medium Arthur A. Ford was, to his believers certainly, *The Man Who Talked with the Dead.*

FORD, BETTY (1918–)

During husband Gerald Ford's White House years, confirmed CB operator Betty Ford nicknamed herself *First Mama* for the citizens band set.

FORD, CLARA (1865–1950)

The wife of Henry Ford, Clara Ford was nicknamed *The Believer* because of her complete faith in everything her husband did. The one time she disagreed was when she begged him to end his resistance to unions in the 1930s to avert bloodshed. Ford finally bent to her wishes.

FORD, FORD MADOX (1873–1939)

Ford Madox Ford, the English novelist, was "so fat and Buddhistic and nasal," according to British novelist and essayist Norman Douglas, that even his friends dubbed him *An Animated Adenoid.* Poet Robert Lowell referred to him as *Master, Mammoth Mumbler.*

FORD, GERALD R. (1913–)

Gerald Ford, the 38th president of the United States, was instantly dubbed *Mr. Clean* on succeeding to the office after the resignation of Richard Nixon, who had been stained by the Watergate scandal. Also called *Mr. Middle America,* Ford enjoyed few upbeat nicknames. He was called *Poor, Dull Jerry* by Alice Roosevelt Longworth, *Dumb-Dumb* by the Rev. Duncan Littlefair of his hometown of Grand Rapids, Mich., and *A Big St. Bernard* by his high school classmates. Even Ford's self-proclaimed *A Ford, Not a Lincoln* could hardly be classified as a stirring retort to critics.

FORD, JOHN (1895–1973)

A winner of five Academy Awards, director John Ford became almost a father figure to many of his male stars and picked up several nicknames in the process. He was *Pappy* to Henry Fonda, *Boss* to Jimmy Stewart and *Coach* to John Wayne.

Ford, Not a Lincoln, A—See FORD, GERALD R.

FORD, ROBERT NEWTON (1860–1892)

Bob Ford, the turncoat who murdered Jesse James for reward money, was celebrated in song and saying as *The Dirty Rotten Coward Who Shot Mr. Howard,* the latter being the cover name used by James at the time he was killed.

FORD, WHITEY (1928–)

Long-time New York Yankee baseball pitcher Whitey Ford was known to teammates as *The Chairman of the Board* because he was the take-charge pitcher in showdown situations. Manager Casey Stengel said that if his life ever depended on his team winning a game, he'd want Ford to pitch.

Foreign Office's Charlie McCarthy, The— See BEVIN, ERNEST.

Forgotten Man, The—See
BRADDOCK, JAMES J.

FORMAN, DAVID (1745–1797)

An American rebel who was notorious for his cruelty to Tories in New Jersey, David Forman was nicknamed *Devil David*, even by staunch supporters of the Revolution. He died in 1797 aboard a British privateer, which had captured the ship he was traveling on.

Fornicator, The—See **BURNS, ROBERT.**

FORRESTAL, JAMES V. (1892–1949)

The first secretary of defense of the United States and a noted supporter of Cold War policies, James V. Forrestal was nicknamed *The Cabinet Judas* within the Truman administration. It was discovered that when Thomas E. Dewey appeared certain to win the 1948 presidential election, Forrestal had carried on negotiations with the candidate to maintain his post in a Republican administration. After Truman was reelected, he dismissed Forrestal, who shortly thereafter, committed suicide, the victim of a deteriorating mental condition.

Founder of Analytic Geometry, The—See **DESCARTES, RENE.**

Founder of Danish Literature, The—See **HOLBERG, LOUIS, BARON DE.**

Founder of Modern Socialism, The—See **MARX, KARL.**

Founder of the Critical Philosophy, The—See **KANT, IMMANUEL.**

Founder of the French Theatre, The—See **ROTRON, JEAN DE.**

Founding Father, The—See **KENNEDY, JOSEPH P.**

Fountain, The: ANTHONY MORENO (?)

During the 1960s Spanish gypsy Anthony Moreno became the greatest welfare cheat in the world by inventing 197 fictitious French families and 3,000 children and collecting all the appropriate benefits. Fleeing to Spain, he became a gypsy folk-hero nicknamed *El Chorro*, or *The Fountain*, because of the limitless flow of funds he garnered—an estimated $6,440,000. He was last reported to be living in comfort, without extradition worries under Spanish law.

Fourth Musketeer, The—See **DUMAS, ALEXANDER, PERE; FAIRBANKS, DOUGLAS.**

FOWLER, ORSON SQUIRE (1809–1897)

Few quacks in the field of 19th century phrenology could match the activities of Orson Squire Fowler, who, completely lacking any training in medicine, physiology or science, became known as *The Great Gun of Phrenology in America*. He operated New York's most thriving "examination clinic" for the "reading of heads" and offered a detailed personality analysis and advice for clients. For those residing outside New York, he offered an assessment by mail if they sent along "a good daguerrotype.'' Fowler numbered Mark Twain among his thousands of patrons and told him he had an ''underdeveloped mirthfulness faculty.''

FOX, CHARLES JAMES (1749–1806)

An English Tory statesman turned Whig, Charles James Fox was nicknamed *The Man of the People* for supporting many liberal positions, including complete freedom for Ireland, the end of the slave trade, political freedom for Catholics and Dissenters, support for the French Revolution, a commission government for India and the end of coercive policies against the American Colonies. His Tory opponents labeled him *Carlo Khan* and charged that a bill he had introduced concerning the East Indies was aimed at allowing him to establish a personal dictatorship there.

Fox, The—See VAN BUREN, MARTIN.

FOXE, FANNE (1936–)

Argentine-born stripper Fanne Foxe won nationwide fame as *The Tidal Basin Bombshell* in 1974 after she jumped into Washington's tidal basin during a wild drinking spree with Rep. Wilbur D. Mills, Arkansas Democrat and chairman of the House Ways and Means Committee, and others. Police had to fish her out of the water at 2 AM. The ensuing scandal forced Mills from Congress and sent Fanne on a triumphal tour of the nation's bump-and-grind circuit.

Foxy Harry—See DAUGHERTY, HARRY M.

FOYT, A. J. (1935–)

Professional racing car driver A. J. Foyt is nicknamed *The Houston Hurricane* and *The Hard-Nosed Demon of the Ovals*. The latter probably says it all by indicating how much of an opening in the lanes he will give an opponent.

FRANCE, CLAUDE DE (1499–1524)

Claude de France, daughter of Louis XII and wife of Francis I, was so ugly and lame that she was facetiously referred to in French court circles as *La Bonne Reine*, or *The Handsome Queen*.

France's Greatest Detective—See BERTILLON, ALPHONSE.

France's Henry Ford—See RENAULT, LOUIS.

Franchise, The—See ABDUL-JABBAR, KAREEM.

FRANCIS, KAY (1905–1968)

Kay Francis, a notoriously tightfisted film actress, was known in Hollywood as *Hetty Green*, after the infamous millionairess-miser.

FRANCIS I OF FRANCE (1494–1547)

While fighting many futile wars in an attempt to become the Holy Roman emperor, Francis I of France was also a Renaissance monarch and the patron of Leonardo da Vinci, Benvenuto Cellini, Andrea del Sarto and Rabelais, among others. He was called *The Father of Letters*.

FRANCO, FRANCISCO (1892–1975)

Francisco Franco, or *El Caudillo (The Chief)*, who became dictator of Spain in 1936 when he overthrew the republic, was also referred to as *The Enduring Fascist*. His caution during World War II, not to mention his broken promises to enter the conflict, permitted him to survive both Hitler and Mussolini.

FRANK, LEO (1884–1915)

Perhaps the most shameful anti-Semitic lynching in American history was that of Leo Frank, a young Atlanta, Ga., businessman convicted of the rape-murder of a 14-year-old girl who worked in his pencil factory. His death sentence was commuted to life because of mass protests in the North. By granting the reprieve, Georgia governor John Slaton committed political suicide, since local public opinion was violently against Frank, who was called *The Jew Monster* by the public and much of the southern press. Finally, an angry mob broke into the prison where Frank was being held, took him on a 175-mile ride to the murdered girl's hometown and lynched him there. Today there is little doubt that Frank was innocent of the murder.

FRANKLIN, BENJAMIN (1706–1790)

An American of almost limitless abilities, Benjamin Franklin was a revolutionary, statesman, scientist, inventor, publisher, philanthropist and philosopher, and as such had literally dozens of nicknames. He was *Poor Richard*, after *Poor Richard's Almanack*, which he published, and the *Father of* many things, from the *Mail Order Catalog* to the *Stove* to the *Continental Congress*. Accolades ranged from *The American Socrates* and *America's Newton* to the no less apt *Jolly Imbiber*.

FRANTIZIUS, PETER VON (?–1968)

Operating an establishment called Sports, Inc., Chicago gun dealer Peter von Frantizius came to be regarded as Al Capone's regular supplier of weaponry. Dubbed by the press *The Armorer of Gangland,* he furnished machine guns and other firearms that figured in many of the most spectacular gang killings of the 1920s. Once pressed to explain the sale of six machine guns to Capone mobsters, he blandly informed a coroner's jury that he had assumed they were for the Mexican government to put down revolutionaries.

FRATIANNO, JIMMY "the Weasel" (1913–   )

Mafioso Jimmy Fratianno, the highest-ranking mob figure ever to "turn" and testify against important crime leaders, was nicknamed *The Weasel*. The term was one of endearment in the underworld, however, and went back to his youthful fruit-stealing days in Cleveland's Little Italy, when he demonstrated, to the admiration of onlookers, how he could outrun pursuing policemen.

Fraud President, The—See HAYES, RUTHERFORD B.

Fraumark Bear-Girl (c. 1767)

One of the few recorded cases of a female living in the wild was the *Fraumark Bear-Girl*, who was captured near Fraumark, Hungary in 1767. Two hunters shot her bear companion and subdued her after she attacked them. It was obvious she had lived with bears since infancy, and she appeared to be about 18 years old. Treated as a freak, she was finally incarcerated in an insane asylum because she would rip off clothes given her and eat only tree bark and raw meat.

FRAZIER, WALT "Clyde" (1945–   )

A professional basketball player with the New York Knicks, Walt Frazier was nicknamed *Clyde*, after Clyde Barrow of the 1930's crime-couple Bonnie Parker and Clyde Barrow. Considered the court's premier "thief" at stealing the basketball, as such Frazier was actually far slicker than his nick-namesake.

Free Born John—See LILBURNE, JOHN.

FREDERICK II, ELECTOR OF BRANDENBURG (1413–1471)

Only 27 on his accession, Frederick II, elector of Brandenburg, was deemed by many of his subjects to be inexperienced and pliable, but he demonstrated that he could react quickly against anyone taking liberties with him by sternly "biting off" their machinations. Hence he was called *Iron Tooth*.

FREDERICK III OF GERMANY—See Handsome, The.

FREDERICK IV OF AUSTRIA (1384–1439)

Long a captive of Holy Roman emperor Sigismund, Frederick IV of Austria suffered degradation unmatched by any other Austrian prince. Held virtual prisoner in Constance and under threat of imminent severe treatment, he was devoid of supporters and virtually deprived of the necessities of life. Called *The Pennyless*, Frederick finally regained power and, partially through the seizure of estates of nobles who had opposed him, accumu-

lated a rich treasury. However, until the end of his days he never lost his sobriquet of misfortune.

FREDERICK V, ELECTOR PALATINE (1569–1632)

The irresolute Frederick V, Elector Palatine, was a confirmed Calvinist who took the crown of Bohemia in 1619. His opponents, the Jesuits, mocked him as a *Snow King* or *Winter King*, meaning one who would survive the cold months on the throne but vanish at the first rays of the spring sun. They were right: Frederick was defeated at White Hill, west of Prague, and lost both Bohemia and his hereditary dominions.

FREDERICK AUGUSTUS, DUKE OF YORK (1763–1827)

Frederick Augustus, duke of York, the second son of King George III, became known as *The Soldiers' Friend* while commander of the British troops in the Low Countries during the French Revolution. He abolished the system of favoritism and the weighing of soldiers' political beliefs for military promotions.

Frederick of Thought, The—See LESSING, GOTTHOLD EPHRAIM.

FREDERICK THE GREAT (1712–1786)

Alaric-Cotin, a nickname first bestowed on Frederick the Great by Voltaire, paid homage to the Prussian ruler for both his military genius and his appreciation of letters. The original Alaric was a famous 5th century Visigoth king, and the abbe Charles Cotin a poet. Some might find the allusion to Cotin not totally complimentary because he is best celebrated for his mediocrity.

Frederick the Greatest—See WILLIAM II, KAISER.

FREDERICK WILLIAM IV OF PRUSSIA (1795–1861)

In what may be regarded, in a manner of speaking, as one of the first product endorsements by royalty, Frederick William IV of Prussia was nicknamed *Clicquot* since he was strongly partial to that brand of champagne.

Frederick's of Hollywood— See MELLINGER, FREDERICK N.

Freeway Killer, The—See BONIN, WILLIAM.

FREISLER, ROLAND (?–1945)

The president of the Third Reich's People's Court, which tried the Hitler assassination conspirators and other German dissidents, Roland Freisler ran the rankest sort of justice system and acted as both prosecutor and judge. The accused were hardly permitted to defend themselves before he sentenced them to death. Hitler affectionately nicknamed Freisler *Our Vishinsky*, referring to the Soviet prosecutor in the notorious Moscow trials of the 1930s. Freisler died in an American bombing raid near the end of the war while the court was in session trying desperately to claim more victims.

FREMONT, JOHN C. (1813–1890)

Because of his many discoveries as an explorer of the American West, John C. Fremont was dubbed *The Pathfinder of the West*. In 1856 he became the first presidential candidate of the new Republican Party. Although he was defeated, he later became known as *The Pathfinder for Lincoln*.

French Angel, The—See DU BARTAS, SALUSTIUS.

French Aristophanes, The—See MOLIERE.

French Chaucer, The—See MAROT, CLEMENT; RONSARD, PIERRE DE.

French Devil, The—See BART, JEAN.

French Erasmus Darwin, The—See BOISJOLIN, JACQUES FRANCOIS.

French Fenimore Cooper, The—See GLOUX, OLIVIER.

French Homer, The—See LA FONTAINE, JEAN DE.

French Justinian, The—See REMI, PHILIPPE DE.

French Lope de Vega, The—See HARDI, ALEXANDRE.

French Michelangelo, The—See PUGET, PIERRE.

French Pindar, The—See DINEMANDY, JEAN.

French Raphael, The—See BOUCHER, FRANCOIS; LE SUER, EUSTACE.

French Ripper, The: JOSEPH VACHER (1869–1898)

Joseph Vacher, a tramp who roamed the French countryside begging for food from farmers, slaughtered at least seven women and four youths. His method was reminiscent of England's Jack the Ripper during the previous decade, and the unknown killer was called *The French Ripper*. Discovered when he was arrested for molesting a woman, Vacher confessed the series of murders and was executed after leading "alienists" found him normal. These same experts asked to have his severed head for further study.

French Ritson, The—See RIVE, JEAN JOSEPH.

French Roscius, The—See TALMA, FRANCOIS JOSEPH.

French Tibullus, The—See DEFORGE, EVARISTE DESIRE.

French Whore Lover, The—See CRANE, STEPHEN.

FRENEAU, PHILIP (1752–1832)

Often considered the first professional U.S. journalist, Philip Freneau was also a poet and was dubbed *The Poet of the American Revolution* for his satirical verse, which attacked the British and upheld the right of rebellion. His poems of this era are typified by "The British Prison Ship."

FRERON, ELIE-CATHERINE (1719–1776)

Nineteenth century French critic Elie-Catherine Freron was noted for his acidulous comments,

which moved Voltaire to refer to him at first as *The Poor Devil*. Voltaire then modeled a thinly disguised character after him named *Frelon,* i.e., The Wasp, in his play *L'Ecossaise.* Freron's portrayal as a hack writer and a spy who would do anything dirty for money prompted literary circles to commonly call him *The Wasp.* However, other writers, who perhaps had more to fear from the critic than Voltaire, preferred a stronger sobriquet, *The Serpent.*

Fretting Frog, The—See COLBERT, CLAUDETTE.

Fried Chicken King, The—See SANDERS, "Colonel" HARLAND.

FRIEDAN, BETTY (1921–   )

Although the sobriquet can hardly be considered accurate, Betty Friedan is nonetheless deserving of being called *The Mother of the Feminist Movement in America.* She was vital in reviving the feminist movement and in galvanizing other women into action. As she has put it, "This whole society could erupt in one great wave of boredom. As for me, I'm very unbored. I'm nasty, I'm bitchy, I get mad. But, by God, I'm absorbed in what I'm doing."

Friend, The—See WINGATE, ORDE CHARLES.

Friend of Helpless Children, The—See HOOVER, HERBERT.

Friend of Presidents, The—See SULLIVAN, MARK.

Friend of Sinners, The—See HAWTHORNE, NATHANIEL.

Friend of the Jews, The—See
GRANT, ROBERT.

Friend of the People, The—See
JEFFERSON, THOMAS.

FRITH, MARY—See Moll Cutpurse.

FROEBEL, FRIEDRICH (1782–1852)

German scholar Friedrich Froebel founded the first kindergarten in Blankenburg in 1836, in the belief that educational play and activity for pre-school children gave them a tremendous advantage in later learning. He thus became known as *The Father of the Kindergarten,* although he was considered a bit of an old fool by local burghers for romping in the fields with children. Although Prussia banned the kindergarten from 1851 until 1860, Froebel's place in educational history remained secure, as young teachers influenced by him spread the kindergarten idea throughout the world.

Frogman—See HENRY, CLARENCE "Frogman."

Frogman Spy, The—See CRABB, LIONEL.

FROISSART, JEAN (1337–c. 1401)

The French chronicler of the 14th century, Jean Froissart has since been dubbed *The Walter Scott of the Middle Ages.* But some observers, especially in France, have called him *The Valet of Princes* and accused him of displaying his personal gratitude to many persons by distorting the facts of his history. Most, however, reject the sobriquet, as unwarranted.

Front Man for Traitors, A—See
MARSHALL, GEORGE C.

FROST, ROBERT (1874–1963)

The U.S. poet who won four Pulitzer Prizes, Robert Frost wrote mostly about rural New England in a traditional form but with a colloquial style. He was labeled *The Voice of New England.*

Frothy General, The—See
SANTERRE, ANTOINE JOSEPH.

FRY, ELIZABETH (1780–1845)

English reformer and humanitarian Elizabeth Fry fought to improve the lot of prisoners and lunatics, especially women, and she was nicknamed *The Female Howard,* after the man who preceded her in such work. John Howard had devoted his life and a good part of his personal fortune to correcting inhumane prison conditions.

Fucking Bastard, That—See
KENNEDY, JOHN F.

Fuddle-Duddle Trudeau—See
TRUDEAU, PIERRE ELLIOTT.

Fuehrer of America, The—See
KUHN, FRITZ.

FUGGER, JAKOB, II—See Jakob the Rich.

Fugitive from the Camp of Victory, The—See ORWELL, GEORGE.

FULBRIGHT, J. WILLIAM (1905–)

A senator from Arkansas for 30 years, J. William Fulbright was a defender of congressional prerogatives in foreign relations and a frequent critic of presidents, even those of his Democratic party, especially Lyndon Johnson, whom he criticized for his handling of the Vietnam War. In 1946, following the great Republican sweep, Fulbright suggested that President Harry Truman name Sen. Arthur H. Vandenberg, senior Republican on the Senate Foreign Relations Committee, secretary of state and then resign. In that way, Fulbright said, the party with the greatest current popular support would have the power and responsibility to govern. The salty Truman responded by awarding Fulbright the nickname *Senator Halfbright*.

FULTON, ROBERT (1765–1815)

Although he has come down to us as *The Father of the Steamboat,* Robert Fulton was referred to by friends as *Quicksilver Bob* because, as an employee of a smithery producing government arms, he had a habit of appropriating large amounts of quicksilver for his personal experiments.

Fum the Fourth—See GEORGE IV OF ENGLAND.

FUNSTON, EDWARD H. "Foghorn" (1836–1911)

A representative from Kansas during the 1880s and 1890s, Edward H. Funston became known as *Foghorn Funston* for his loud and booming voice, which often drowned out a foe's words in a debate on the House floor.

Furioso, Il—See ROBUSTI, JACOPO.

Furious Visarion—See BELINSKY, VISARION GRIGORYEVICH.

FURMAN, RICHARD (1755–1825)

The American clergyman Richard Furman was called *The Boy Preacher* because he was a leading pulpit orator who attracted huge audiences in 1775, when he was only 19. The sobriquet remained with him until he died in 1825 at the age of 70.

FURUSETH, ANDREW (1854–1938)

The long-time president of the International Seamen's Union in America, Andrew Furuseth was often called *Abraham Lincoln of the Sea*. He was instrumental in securing passage of the 1915 Seamen's Bill, commonly referred to as the seamen's emancipation act, which greatly improved the working and safety conditions of commerical sailors.

G

Gabby—HARTNETT, CHARLES "Gabby."

Gabriel Grave-Digger—See HARVEY, GABRIEL.

GABRIELLI, TRIFONE (1470–1549)

The Venetian scholar Trifone Gabrielli was called *The Socrates of His Age* for both his learning and high ethical standards.

Gadfly, The—See LONGWORTH, ALICE LEE ROOSEVELT.

Gaelic Homer, The—See OSSIAN.

GAGE, PHINEAS P.—See **Crowbar Man, The.**

GAGE, THOMAS (1721–1787)

Thomas Gage, the British general and colonial governor of Massachusetts, drew the wrath of many colonists for quartering British troops and was decried as *The Father of the Quartering Act* and *Lord Boston.*

GAINHAM, JOHN—See **Bishop of Hell, The.**

GAITSKELL, HUGH (1906–1963)

During the factional battles that erupted within Britain's Labor Party after World War II, Aneurin Bevan labeled party leader Hugh Gaitskell *The Desiccated Calculating Machine.*

GALANTE, CARMINE (1910–1979)

Considered to have been one of the most ruthless and brutal of U.S. Mafia leaders, Carmine Galante was known as *The Cigar* because he was seldom without one. In fact, when he was murdered at a restaurant in a 1979 gangland "hit," he had a cigar in his mouth. After the assassination it was said in the underworld that the "cigar problem" had been solved.

GALEN, CLAUDIUS (131–c. 200)

Greek physician and medical writer Claudius Galen became famous for his practice in Rome, where he was court physician to Emperor Marcus Aurelius. He gained the designation *The Father of Experimental Physiology* for his medical texts, which retained their virtually undisputed authority until the 1700s.

GALENTO, ANTHONY "Two-Ton Tony" (1909–1979)

Italian-American professional boxer and wrestler Tony Galento was nicknamed *Two-Ton Tony* because of his rotund shape, which brought his boxing ability into question. He eventually battled—with disastrous results—heavyweight champion Joe Louis. A saloon man, he was also known as *The Battling Barkeep,* a calling perhaps more attuned to his abilities. Galento later became highly successful in the show business world of professional wrestling.

GALIANI, FERDINAND (1727–1788)

An Italian abbe who boasted he had never wept in his life, Ferdinand Galiani claimed he had even remained tearless at the deaths of his parents, his sister and a number of friends. He was nicknamed *The Little Machiavelli.*

GALL, FRANZ JOSEPH (1758–1828)

German physician Franz Joseph Gall was hailed as *The Father of Phrenology,* a theory that was greatly exploited by charlatans who pretended to read an individual's character and future potential from cranial bumps. Gall's idea fell into complete disrepute by the beginning of the 20th century.

Gallant Pelham, The—See PELHAM, JOHN.

Galliard, The—See JOHNSTONE, WILLIAM.

GALLO, JOSEPH "Crazy Joe" (1929–1972)

Joseph Gallo was a Brooklyn underworld figure known to rival mafiosi as *Crazy Joe* because he was considered "flaky" and hard to deal with. Moreover, unlike other Mafia men, he showed a willingness to work with black gangsters. A gentlemen's agreement within the Mafia forbids any "rub-outs" in lower Manhattan's Little Italy, but an exception was made for *Crazy Joe*. He was murdered while celebrating his birthday at a restaurant there.

Galloping Dick: RICHARD FERGUSON (?–1800)

A notorious highwayman who terrorized the English countryside, Richard Ferguson was commonly referred to as *Galloping Dick*. He was arrested and summarily hanged at Aylesbury on April 4, 1800.

Galloping Ghost, The—See GRANGE, HAROLD EDWARD "Red."

GALLOWAY, JAMES "Bad News" (1887–1950)

A member of the St. Louis Cardinals baseball team in the early 1900s, Jim Galloway was nicknamed *Bad News* when he had worked as a telegrapher before making it to the big leagues. During those early years, whenever he needed an excuse to leave work to play in a semipro game, Galloway arranged to have a coworker send him a phony wire saying a relative had gotten sick, injured or had passed on. Because he received so many of these ill tidings, *Bad News Galloway* seemed to be truly under an evil star.

GANDHI, MOHANDAS "Mahatma" (1869–1948)

The great Indian political leader-holy man Mohandas Karamchand Gandhi, who led the nationalist movement that freed India from British rule, was known to his people as *Mahatma*, or *Great Soul*. He was also called *The Father of India*. To the British and to Winston Churchill in particular, he was *The Seditious Fakir*. Gandhi was assassinated in 1948 by an anti-Muslim fanatic.

Gandhi of Japan, The—See KAGAWA, TOYOHIKO.

Gandhi of Sicily, The—See DOLCI, DANILO.

Gangbuster, The—See DEWEY, THOMAS E.

Gangdom's Favorite Florist—See O'BANION, DION.

Gangster's Nightmare, The—See MCCLELLAN, JOHN.

GARDNER, ORVILLE (fl. 1850s)

Mid-19th century American professional boxer Orville Gardner shocked his many fans when he turned ardent temperance advocate. He was toasted thereafter as *Awful Gardner*.

GARDNER, ROY—See Escaping Professor, The.

GARFIELD, JAMES A. (1831–1881)

James A. Garfield, the 20th president of the United States, was called *The Preacher President* and *The Teacher President* because he had studied in a seminary and held various teaching posts before the Civil War. Although he was left-handed (the first such president) he could write equally well with his right hand, an aptitude that earned him the sobriquet *The Ambidextrous Chief Executive*. In fact, some insisted he could simultaneously write classical Greek with his left hand and classical Latin with his right. Before being elected president he was criticized by opponents as *The Available Man*, meaning he was available for any chore and was most pliable to handling. As one said, "Garfield has an interest everywhere . . . but in the Kingdom of Heaven." After his assassination Garfield, like Lincoln, was called, *The Martyr President*.

GARIBALDI, GIUSEPPI (1807–1882)

Italian patriot Giuseppe Garibaldi is often accorded the sobriquet *The Liberator of Italy*, but his more common name among the Italian people was *El Capitano des Popolo*, or *The People's Captain*.

GARLAND, JUDY (1922–1969)

After tragic years that included suicide attempts and addiction to alcohol and amphetamines, for-mer child star Judy Garland died of an overdose, bearing at the end the nickname *Little Dorothy Lost*. The reference was to her greatest role, little Dorothy in the *Wizard of Oz*.

GARNER, JOHN NANCE "Cactus Jack" (1869–1967)

A longtime U.S. congressman and vice president during Franklin Roosevelt's first two terms, John Nance *Cactus Jack* Garner was also nicknamed *The Sage of Uvalde*, after his home community in Texas. Perhaps the most famous of his sage observations was that the vice presidency is "not worth a bucket of warm spit."

GARNIER, ROBERT (1534–1590)

Trained for the law, Robert Garnier deserted that field for poetry. Because his works, at least in his time, were considered the equal of Sophocles and Euripedes, he was dubbed *The Father of French Tragedy*.

GARRETT, PAT (1850–1908)

Famed as the lawman who ambushed and killed Billy the Kid, Pat Garrett was known as *Big Casino* in his pre-lawman days when he was a most adept gambler. It was then that he formed his first acquaintance with a young Billy the Kid, who stuck to him so closely that he was called Little Casino. Garrett gained nationwide fame in 1881 for killing Billy the Kid but in New Mexico he was called, with a certain disdain, *The Kid's Killer*. He was denied renomination to the sheriff's office later the same year.

GARRICK, DAVID (1717–1779)

Regarded as the greatest English actor of all time, David Garrick was nicknamed *The Silver-tongued* and *The English Roscius,* after the great Roman slave-actor. Garrick, who played no less than 17 Shakespearean roles, is buried in Westminster Abbey at the foot of Shakespeare's statue.

GARRISON, WILLIAM LLOYD (1805–1879)

Ardent abolitionist William Lloyd Garrison was called *The Father of Abolitionism.* The first issue of his famous antislavery journal, *Liberator,* published in 1831, contained his famous announcement: " . . . I am in earnest—I will not equivocate—I will not excuse—I will not retreat a single inch—AND I WILL BE HEARD.'' Thus he was also nicknamed *I Will Be Heard Garrison.*

GARSON, GREER—See First Lady of Hollywood.

Gas—See DARWIN, CHARLES.

Gascon Moses, A—See DU BARTAS, SALUSTIUS.

Gaseous Cassius—See ALI, MUHAMMAD.

Gashed, The—See HENRI II, DUKE OF GUISE.

GASSION, JEAN, COMTE DE (1609–1647)

A skilled French general, Jean, Comte de Gassion, was considered to be one of the bravest officers in French history. Pitiless in battle and holding a contempt for life, he seemed worthy of only one sobriquet, *La Guerre,* or war itself. When he was killed at the siege of Lens in 1647, a contempo-

rary wrote, "In gaining a hamlet, France lost a hero.''

Gatekeeper, The—See KRIPALANI, JIWATRAM BHAGWANDAS.

GATES, HORATIO (1728–1806)

American Revolutionary War general Horatio Gates was simultaneously referred to as *The Hero of Saratoga* and *Granny Gates.* Although the English forces under Burgoyne surrendered to Gates at Saratoga, there were many who considered Gates' military moves to have been more befitting an old lady, and they called him *Granny Gates,* giving credit for the victory to several talented subordinates.

GATES, JOHN W. "Bet-a-Million" (1855–1911)

The great industrialist and barbed-wire entrepreneur John W. Gates was an incurable gambler who won the nickname *Bet-a-Million Gates* when he once tried to place a million-dollar bet on a horse—and caused bookmakers to run for cover. He was occasionally called *The Big Stiff* by con men, who sometimes fleeced him on bets but not very often. Gates beat wealthy playboy John Drake, the son of the former governor of Iowa and the founder of Drake University, out of $11,000 on a bet over whose piece of bread dunked in coffee would attract the most flies. What young Drake didn't know was that *Bet-a-Million* had put six spoons of sugar in his cup.

Gator Lover, The—See BALL, JOE.

GAY, JOHN (1685–1732)

English poet, dramatist and wit John Gay was called *The Orpheus of Highwaymen* because so much of his work celebrated the doings of the underworld. Actually his highly popular *The Beggar's Opera* and its sequel *Polly* were barbed satires of the contemporary political and social scenes, especially aimed at Sir Robert Walpole and the court of George II.

Gaylord the Greaser—See PERRY, GAYLORD.

GEBEL-WILLIAMS, GUNTHER (1934–)

German animal trainer and circus performer Gunther Gebel-Williams, regarded as today's most accomplished and daring lion trainer, has been nicknamed *The Lord of the Ring*.

GEHRIG, LOU (1903–1941)

One of the few baseball nicknames not based on tenuous sports-page hype belonged to first baseman Lou Gehrig, who was called *The Iron Horse*. He set a major-league record by playing 2,130 consecutive games as a New York Yankee. He died at age 38 of a rare spinal disease that bears his name. While Gehrig became a legend in his own time, he was addressed rather differently by teammates, who reflected on his lead-weighted attributes and called him *Biscuit Pants*.

General Booth—See BOOTH, WILLIAM AND CATHERINE.

General of General Motors, The—See DURANT, WILLIAM CRAPO.

General Swagger—See BURGOYNE, JOHN.

General Who Never Lost a Battle, The—See ZHUKOV, GEORGI.

General with Three Long Legs, The—See CHANG CHUNG-CH'ANG.

Generalissimo of the Open Shop, The—See OTIS, HARRISON GRAY.

Geneva Bull, The—See MARSHALL, STEPHEN.

GENGHIS KHAN (c. 1162–1227)

The Mongol conqueror Temujin was given the sobriquet Genghis Khan, or *Precious Warrior*. The name summed up his ability, which was to conquer but not rule. His empire disintegrated within a generation of his death.

Genius of Romance, The—See HAWTHORNE, NATHANIEL.

Genius of the Soil, The—See LYSENKO, TROFIM D.

Genius on a Low Budget—See KRAMER, STANLEY.

GENKER, CHARLIE ''Monkey Face'' (fl. early 20th century)

A colorful fixture in Chicago prostitution circles for several decades, Charles Genker, better known as *Monkey Face Genker*, was the terror of brothel customers. His duty was to see that the girls did not dawdle with customers, and Genker, whose countenance and bounciness matched that of his jungle cousins, would scamper up a door and peek through the transom to make sure business was proceeding with all deliberate speed. Regular customers would hurry indeed to avoid seeing *Monkey Face.*

Gentle Boy, The—See
HAWTHORNE, NATHANIEL.

Gentle Cannibal, The—See **FISH, ALBERT.**

Gentle Don, The—See **BRUNO, ANGELO.**

Gentle General, The—See **LEE, ROBERT E.**

Gentle Guru of the Flower People—See **GINSBERG, ALLEN.**

Gentleman in Search of a Man-Servant, A—See **THACKERAY, WILLIAM MAKEPEACE.**

Gentleman Johnny—See
BURGOYNE, JOHN.

Gentleman of Oxford, A—See
SHELLEY, PERCY BYSSHE.

Gentleman Pirate, The: STEDE BONNET (c. 1670–1718)

Major Stede Bonnet was called *The Gentleman Pirate,* a misnomer since he was the bloodthirsty sort. Having read numerous tales of how pirates were supposed to behave, he actually made prisoners walk the plank, something few buccaneers ever did. His nickname apparently derived from his early life as a gentleman of leisure who came from a good family and had a proper education. In middle age, he suddenly deserted his estate on the island of Barbados for the pirate life. One biographer assures us he "was driven to it by a nagging wife." (See also Lafitte, Jean.)

GEOFFREY IV OF ANJOU—See
Plantagenet.

GEORGE, HENRY (1839–1897)

U.S. economist and author Henry George was so shocked by the inequalities of wealth in New York City that he sought to find a way to redistribute wealth through a single tax. Called *The Single Taxer,* he ran on a reform ticket for mayor in 1886 and came quite close to winning.

GEORGE, PRINCE OF DENMARK (1653–1703)

Out of sheer exasperation King James II of England bestowed the nickname *Est-il possible? (Is it possible?)* on Prince George of Denmark, his son-in-law and the husband of the future Queen Anne. The sobriquet was born during the Revolution of 1688, when the prince shook his head and uttered the French phrase with each successive report of military desertions brought to the king.

GEORGE I OF ENGLAND (1660–1727)

The first Hanoverian king of England, George I came there from Germany with little knowledge or interest in the country. An indication of this was his suggestion that St. James Park be turned into a turnip ground. He was thus nicknamed *The Turnip-hoer*.

GEORGE III OF ENGLAND
(1760–1820)

King George III of England was disparagingly referred to by American colonists as *German Georgie*, an allusion to his Hanoverian heritage. In England he was more commonly known as *Farmer George* because of his interest in agriculture and the fact that he actually earned a profit from a farm near Windsor. Some used the term less flatteringly as a description of the monarch's simple appearance and manners.

GEORGE IV OF ENGLAND
(1762–1830)

A profligate, exceedingly unpopular English king, George IV was dubbed by Lord Byron *Fum the Fourth*, a disparagement of the entire Hanoverian line. George set aside his first marriage in 1785 and married his cousin, Princess Caroline of Brunswick, whom he mistreated so much that she left him, winning herself public sympathy. He was further disparaged by the nickname *Fat Adonis of Forty*, later amended to *Fifty*.

Georgia Fire-Eater, The—See **TOOMBS, ROBERT.**

GERGUSON, HARRY—See **Romanoff, "Prince" Michael.**

German Borgia, The—See **HAHN, ANNA.**

German Cid, The—See **HERMANN.**

German Dickens, The—See **HACKLAENDER, FRIEDRICH WILHELM.**

German Georgie—See **GEORGE III OF ENGLAND.**

German Horace, The—See **RAMLER, CHARLES WILLIAM.**

German Milton, The—See **KLOPSTOCK, FRIEDRICH GOTTLIEB.**

German Plato, The—See **JACOBI, FRIEDRICH HEINRICH.**

German Pliny—See **GESNER, KONRAD VON.**

German Princess, The—See **CARLETON, MARY.**

German Voltaire, The—See **GOETHE, JOHANN WOLFGANG VON.**

GERONIMO (1829–1909)

While the white man gave the Apache chief Goyathlay the name of Geronimo, the Indians called him *Goyakla*, or *One Who Yawns*. It was certainly a deceptive nickname, considering his fighting prowess. During World War II the name

Geronimo became the battle cry of U.S. Army paratroops.

Gertrude Stein of the Musical Underground, The—See KAUFMAN, MURRAY.

GESNER, KONRAD VON (1516–1565)

The noted Swiss scholar and naturalist Konrad von Gesner won the accolades *The Modern Pliny* and *The German Pliny* for his *Historia Animalium,* considered to be the most thorough and learned work on animals up to that time.

GETTY, JOHN PAUL, III (1957–   )

The grandson of J. Paul Getty, the billionaire oilman, John Paul Getty III was the victim of a sensational 1973 kidnapping in Italy. A ransom demand for $2.9 million was made to his grandfather, who at first did not pay, apparently because he felt the plot was a hoax engineered by the teenager to gain funds to continue his life as *The Golden Hippie*. When the kidnappers cut off the boy's ear and mailed it to a newspaper, along with a photo of his mutilated head, Getty paid the money and his grandson was released.

GHIBBES, JAMES ALBAN (1616–1677)

In his own eyes James Alban Ghibbes, the poet laureate of Leopold, emperor of Germany, was aptly called *The Horace of His Age,* since Ghibbes fashioned the nickname himself.

GIANCANA, SAM "Moony" or "Momo" (1908–1975)

Although he rose to the top echelon of the Chicago syndicate before being assassinated, Sam Giancana was considered by police, press and fellow gangsters as having an erratic personality. In fact he was rejected for military service as ''a consitutional psychopath'' and therefore often called *Moony*. He did not appreciate the nickname and fellow mobsters altered it slightly to *Momo* and made it a term of affection.

Giant of Literature, The—See JOHNSON, SAMUEL.

GIBSON, JANE—See Pig Woman, The.

GIBSON, JOHN *(fl. 1760s)*

Col. John Gibson of western Virginia is generally believed to have been the embodiment of what American Indians called Long Knife or Knives. During a battle Gibson beheaded a chief with a swift stroke of his sword and became known thereafter to the Indians as the *Long Knife Warrior*. In time all whites bearing swords were called Long Knives.

GIBSON, JOSH *(1911–1947)*

Never permitted to play in white baseball, Josh Gibson was denied the opportunity to prove he may have been the greatest slugger in the game. He nonetheless was called *The Black Babe Ruth*.

GIGANTE, VINCENT *(1926–   )*

A blubbery 300-pound gangster who failed to kill top mobster Frank Costello in a 1957 attempt, Vincent Gigante was nicknamed *The Chin* because he had several quivering chins. Described by a witness to the shooting, *The Chin* was hied off to the country by the mob to lose weight. When finally he walked into a New York police station to surrender a few months later he had shed about 100 pounds and even the cause of his nickname had vanished. The witness couldn't identify him and he was released.

Giggles—See ZELL, HARRY VON.

GILBERT, CASS (1859–1934)

American architect Cass Gilbert was dubbed *The Father of the Skyscraper* because he designed the tallest buildings of his era, including the Woolworth Building in New York City. He also designed the Supreme Court Building in Washington, D.C., and a number of state capitols.

GILBERT, JOHN (1895–1936)

The career of famous U.S. silent-screen star John Gilbert faltered when he appeared in his first talkie and spoke in a high, squeaky voice. His voice sounded better in his second film, but by then the damage had been done. His public, which had once called him *The Great Lover,* referred to him as *The Great Squeaky Lover.* It is part of Hollywood lore that MGM mogul Louis B. Mayer deliberately had sound engineers play havoc with the troublesome Gilbert's voice so the studio could be rid of him.

GILBERT, JOHN (1817–1897)

English painter and illustrator Sir John Gilbert has been called *The Scott of Painting,* after Sir Walter Scott, the Scottish writer of epic historical romances.

GILLIS, LESTER J.—See Nelson, George "Baby Face."

GILPIN, BERNARD (1517–1583)

Bernard Gilpin was called *The Apostle of the North* for spreading Protestant doctrine in Scotland. Because of his great efforts to alleviate the suffering of the improverished, he was also labeled *The Father of the Poor.*

GINSBERG, ALLEN (1926–   )

American hippie poet Allen Ginsberg, who achieved fame in 1956 with the publication of *Howl,* has been called *The Gentle Guru of the Flower People.*

GINTER, LEWIS (1824–1897)

Union general officer Lewis Ginter gained the nickname *The Fighting Commissary* from his superiors because they were unable to keep him from joining in combat during the Civil War. Whenever the opportunity arose he dropped his official duties to engage in battle.

GIORGIONE DE CASTELFRANCO (c. 1478–1510)

Because he was perhaps equally talented at playing the lute, Venetian painter Giorgione was called *The Artist with Brush and Lute.* Among the few of his paintings that remain are ''Sleeping Venus'' and ''The Tempest.'' When Giorgione died of the plague in 1510, Titian, about the same age, finished a number of his paintings.

GIOVANNI, DOMENICO DI
(1403–1448)

Italian satirist Domenico di Giovanni worked in his father's barber shop in Florence, where the wits of the town gathered to hear *The Rhyming Barber* recite his latest verses. They were then carried throughout the city.

Girl Gershwin, The—See SUESSE, DANA.

Girl in the Hansom Cab, The—See PATTERSON, NAN.

Girl on the Red Velvet Swing, The—See THAW, EVELYN NESBIT.

GIRTY, SIMON (1741–1818)

A frontiersman and scout, Simon Girty deserted the American cause in the Revolutionary War after being fired by the Continental Congress for "ill behavior." In the pay of the British, he led Indian bands against settlements in western Pennsylvania, where his sadistic treatment of white captives included burning at the stake. Feared as *The Great Renegade* and *The White Savage*, he continued his activities after the war in the Ohio country, trying to keep out American settlers. Near the end of the century, he was forced to flee to Canada, where the British granted him land. One of William Henry Harrison's objectives in invading Canada in 1813 was to bring back *The Great Renegade*, an effort that proved unsuccessful.

GI's General, The—See BRADLEY, OMAR N.

GI's Own Songwriter, The—See LOESSER, FRANK.

GISH, LILLIAN (1896–   )

Since she could and often did consume carrots by the pound, American film actress Lillian Gish was nicknamed *Carrots*.

Give 'em Hell Harry—See TRUMAN, HARRY S.

GLADSTONE, WILLIAM (1809–1898)

A four-time prime minister of Great Britain, William Gladstone was known in political circles as *The Grand Old Man*. He also actively sought to reform "ladies of the night" and often prowled London's Soho area seeking them out. He brought them to his home in an effort to reform them and convince them to enter a home he had founded for former prostitutes. In a play on his name, he was called *Old Glad-eye* by enemies and the observation was made that he tended to select the prettier harlots. Although gossip had it that he engaged in sex with many of the women, Gladstone did have some success in his rehabilitation efforts.

Glamour Boy—See MOUNTBATTEN, LORD LOUIS.

Glamour Boy of the Race Drivers, The—See REVSON, PETER.

GLASS, CARTER "Sound Money"
(1858–1946)

Virginia senator Carter Glass served a total of 42 years in both houses of Congress, where he became known as *Sound Money Glass* for drafting the bill that provided for the Federal Reserve System. He was also known in the Senate as *The Snapping Turtle* due to his quick displays of temper when opposed.

GLEASON, JACKIE (1916–   )

Because he perenially dominated television ratings in his time slot during the earlier years of television, comic Jackie Gleason was nicknamed *Mr. Saturday Night* in the trade.

GLEASON, PATRICK JEROME (c. 1830s–1901)

The mayor of Long Island City, N.Y., in the 1880s, Patrick Jerome Gleason was dubbed *Battle Axe Gleason* because he fought the encroachment of the Long Island Railroad on city property by chopping down the railroad fence, gates and ticket office that the company had erected across Front Street.

Glitterati Tiny Terror, The—See CAPOTE, TRUMAN.

Gloomy Dean, The—See INGE, WILLIAM RALPH.

Gloomy Gus—See NIXON, RICHARD M.

Glorious Iceberg, The—See SUTHERLAND, JOAN.

Glory of Netherland, The—See ERASMUS, DESIDERIUS.

Glory of Scotland, The—See OSSIAN.

Glory of the Priesthood, The—See ERASMUS, DESIDERIUS.

GLOUX, OLIVIER (1818–1883)

The French-American frontiersman and author Olivier Gloux was referred to as *The Dumas of the Indians* and *The French Fenimore Cooper.*

GLUCK, CHRISTOPH WILLIBALD VON (1714–1787)

An important composer of German operas, Christoph Willibald Gluck was called *The Hercules of Music* for uniting music more closely with poetry and giving new importance to the overture. His work was based on simplicity and did much to check the over-ornamentation of the Italian style.

Glutton of Literature, The—See MAGLIABECCHI, ANTHONY.

Goat, The—See WOOLF, VIRGINIA.

Goat Gland Brinkley—See BRINKLEY, JOHN RICHARD "Goat Gland."

Goat of the Wets, The—See VOLSTEAD, ANDREW J.

God—See CRIPPS, STAFFORD; GRIFFITH, D.W.

God of Whiggish Idolatry, The—See BROUGHAM, HENRY PETER, LORD.

Goddess of Health, The—See
HAMILTON, EMMA LYONS,
LADY.

GODFREY, ARTHUR (1903–1983)

Radio and television personality Arthur Godfrey was dubbed *The Huck Finn of Radio* by comedian Fred Allen for his homey yet sly wit. However, *The Old Redhead,* as he preferred to call himself, was often not as folksy as all that and was noted for his live-telecast firing of cast members. In 1953 a trade publication, *Broadcasting-Telecasting,* complained of "the deification of Arthur Godfrey" and said, "it is only a matter of time before the second syllable of Godfrey will be forgotten."

GODFREY, HOLLEN (fl. 1860s)

Grizzled old Indian fighter and settler Hollen Godfrey was known to his Indian foes as a brave and daring opponent, and they dubbed him *Old Wicked*. He defended his sod house on the Platte Plains in Colorado with such stubborn effectiveness that they dubbed it Fort Wicked.

Godfrey the Courageous: GODFREY III OF BRABANT (1142–1190)

Duke Godevaart, or Godfrey III of Brabant (Belgium) was only three months old when he succeeded his father to the throne. As such he was also head of the army and, when war broke out immediately after his accession, required to lead his troops into battle. His cradle was strapped between two trees on the battlefield by his nurse, and he was credited with the day's victory and celebrated thereafter as *Godfrey the Courageous* or *The Cradle Duke*.

God-given, The—See CHAMBORD, COMTE DE.

Godless Anne Royall—See ROYALL, ANNE NEWPORT.

Godless Regent, The—See PHILIPPE II, DUKE OF ORLEANS.

God-like, The—See WEBSTER, DANIEL.

GODOY, MANUEL DE (1767–1851)

Although he was only an impoverished royal court guardsman, Manuel de Godoy became prime minister and virtual dictator of Spain, thanks to his love affair with the sexually compulsive Queen Maria Louisa. The queen, who totally dominated her husband, Charles IV, quickly promoted Godoy—some 16 years her junior—and even gave him the title Prince of the Peace. The Spanish populace was hardly enthralled with Godoy, who had reached the pinnacle of power at the age of 25, and they referred to him as *The Sausage Man*. Some said the sobriquet arose from the fact that Godoy's home province, Extremadura, was famed for its sausages, but there have been more earthy explanations. Eventually dethroned, the royal couple fled into exile with Godoy, continuing their infamous menage in Italy. After the royal couple's death within three months of each other in 1819, Godoy lived out his years in extreme poverty, ending up in Paris, where Louis Philippe granted him a small pension.

God's Cousin—See MACARTHUR, DOUGLAS.

God's Englishman—See CROMWELL, OLIVER.

God's Instrument—See SWEDENBORG, EMANUEL.

GOEBEL, WILLIAM (1856–1900)

Although Kentucky legislator William Goebel was credited with much reform legislation as a Democratic state senator, he was called *Dictator Goebel* for his high-handed tactics. Nowhere was this more evident and provocative than in the manner in which he secured the nomination for governor in 1899 through alteration of rules and steamroller tactics. The result was a spirited, gunshot-filled, contested election and Goebel's murder on Jan. 30, 1900. Goebel did gain his goal, however: The legislature declared him the legally elected governor before his death.

GOERING, HERMANN (1893–1946)

The No. 2 Nazi in Germany after Hitler, Hermann Goering enjoyed far less respect with the German people than with other important personages. He was often referred to as *The Fat One,* especially later in World War II, when his Luftwaffe proved incapable of stopping British and U.S. bombing raids. In Allied countries he was referred to as *The Sawdust Caesar.*

GOETHE, JOHANN WOLFGANG VON (1749–1832)

German poet, playwright and prose writer Johann Wolfgang von Goethe was nicknamed by admirers *The Prince of Poets, Der Meister,* or *The Master,* and *The German Voltaire.* Carlyle took exceptions to the last sobriquet since, he said, "Goethe is all, or the best of all, that Voltaire was, and he was much that Voltaire did not dream of." While studying law at Wetzlar, Goethe was called *Goetz von Berlichingen, the Honest.* He explained in his autobiography: "To every one a name with an epithet was assigned. Me they called 'Goetz von Berlichingen, the Honest.' The former I earned by the attention to the gallant German patriarch, the latter by my upright affection and devotion for the eminent men with whom I became acquainted."

Goetz of the Iron Hand: GOETZ VON BERCHLINGEN (1480–1562)

German fedudal knight Goetz von Berchlingen is remembered as *Goetz of the Iron Hand.* He lost his right hand when a cannon shot split the hilt of his sword and drove one of the halves through his arm. Berchlingen calmly turned his horse with his good hand and rode back to camp, where he was treated by a surgeon. Fitted with an iron hand designed for him, *Goetz of the Iron Hand* continued going to war for another 58 years.

Goetz von Berlichingen, the Honest— See GOETHE, JOHANN WOLFGANG VON.

GOFF, JOHN W. (1848–1924)

As counsel for the Lexow Committee that investigated New York City police corruption in 1893 and 1894, John W. Goff was regarded by the force as its worst enemy, and officers dubbed him *The Saintlike S.O.B.* Goff's work was credited with cleaning up the force and doing much to advance the career of Theodore Roosevelt. Goff later became a distinguished state justice.

Gold Humbug, The—See BENTON, THOMAS HART.

GOLDBERG, ARTHUR (1908–   )

As legal counsel to the CIO, Arthur Goldberg was dubbed *The Labor Architect* for helping to bring about the merger of the Congress of Industrial Organizations with the American Federation of Labor.

GOLDBERG, RUBE (1883–1970)

U.S. cartoonist and author Rube Goldberg, whose zany contraptions made his name synonymous with anything ludicrously complicated, was celebrated as *The Wizard of Wacky Inventions*. He won the Pulitzer Prize in 1948.

Goldbrick Cassie—See CHADWICK, CASSIE.

GOLDEN, MATILDA "Goldie" (1902–   )

Matilda Golden, more commonly referred to as *Goldie,* was the secretary of showman Florenz Ziegfeld. She was awarded what was apparently the highest accolade available to a woman in that field: *The Last Virgin on Broadway.*

Golden Bear, The—See NICKLAUS, JACK.

Golden Greek, The—See ONASSIS, ARISTOTLE SOCRATES.

Golden Hippie, The—See GETTY, JOHN PAUL, III.

Golden Holden—See HOLDEN, WILLIAM.

Golden Nose—See BRAHE, TYCHO.

Golden Rule Fellow, That—See STEFFENS, LINCOLN.

Golden Rule Jones—See JONES, SAMUEL M. "Golden Rule."

Golden Tonsil, The—See DAY, DORIS.

Golden-Tongued, The—See MENOT, MICHAEL.

GOLDKETTE, JEAN (1900?–1962)

U.S. jazz great Jean Goldkette was nicknamed *The Father of Sweet Jazz* because of his distinctive musical interpretations.

GOLDONI, CARLO (1707–1793)

Italian dramatist Carlo Goldoni was nicknamed *The Moliere of Italy* because he exhibited many of the traits and opinions of the noted French writer, including a sympathetic delineation of women and a certain acrimony toward the nobility.

GOLDSMITH, OLIVER (1728–1774)

Oliver Goldsmith—*Goldy* to some—the English poet, novelist and dramatist noted for his humorous style was called *The Inspired Idiot* by detractors for what they considered to be his frequent blunders and absurdities.

Goldsmith of the Bar, The—See BURROWES, PETER.

GOLDWATER, BARRY M. (1909–   )

Few candidates for president of the United States conjured up more fear than Arizona Republican senator Barry M. Goldwater during the 1964 election campaign. Considered to be far to the right, he was referred to by opponents and others disturbed by what he might do in office as *Beelzebub M. Goldwater* and *The Monster from Arizona*. Consequently he went down to disastrous defeat, and Lyndon Johnson was elected. Ironically, Ronald Reagan, elected in 1980, shared many of Goldwater's views but came across to the public as ''a nice guy'' rather than a ''kook.''

Golf Bag Sam—See HUNT, ''Golf Bag'' SAM.

GONGORA, LUIS Y ARGOTE (1561–1627)

Determined to justify the nickname *The Wonderful*, Spanish poet Luis y Argote Gongora sought to produce something completely new and unheard of in poetry. By and large, his efforts did not meet with critical acclaim, and *The Wonderful*'s verses were said to be ''of the most pedantic and tasteless description.'' Perhaps for this perverse reason he retained his nickname.

Good Badman, The—See BASS, SAM.

Good Bishop, The—See BELSUNCE, HENRI FRANCOIS.

Good Citizen, The—See SCHUSTER, ARNOLD.

Good Clerk—See HENRY I OF ENGLAND.

Good Duke Humphrey—See HUMPHREY, DUKE OF GLOUCESTER.

Good Gray Poet, The—See WHITMAN, WALT.

Good Guy of OPEC, The—See YAMANI, SHEIKH AHMED ZAKI.

Good News Tonight Man, The—See HEATTER, GABRIEL.

Good Provider, The—See HEINZ, HENRY J.

Good Queen Bess—See ELIZABETH I OF ENGLAND.

Good Scholar—See HENRY I OF ENGLAND.

Good Starr, The—See STARR, HENRY.

GOODYEAR, CHARLES (1800–1860)

U.S. inventor Charles Goodyear devised the vulcanized rubber process which effectively got the rubber industry off the ground. After his death he was referred to as *Rubber's Good Year*. He died a pauper.

Goosey Goderich—See ROBINSON, FREDERICK.

GORDON, CHARLES GEORGE (1833–1885)

Celebrated as *Chinese Gordon*, British general Charles George Gordon became a national hero for his military exploits in China from 1859 to 1865. Killed in the 1885 siege of Khartoum in the Sudan, he was also referred to as *Gordon of Khartoum*. His death angered the British public and caused the Gladstone government to fall.

GORDON, VIVIAN (1899–1932)

The victim in one of New York City's gaudiest murder cases, Vivian Gordon was a prostitute-madam whose trusty "little black books" revealed much about political corruption in the city and provided the impetus for the famed Seabury Investigations. The press labeled her *The Broadway Butterfly*, a sobriquet used a decade earlier for another sexy murder victim, Dot King. The Gordon murder was never solved, but there was much speculation that powerful political forces were behind it.

Gordon, Waxey: IRVING WEXLER (1889–1952)

Waxey Gordon, born Irving Wexler, was one of the nations's top bootleggers in the 1920s and a millionaire many times over. His nickname *Waxey* was given to him back in his days as a youthful pickpocket, for his ability to slip a wallet out of a mark's pocket as though it were coated with wax.

Gordon of Khartoum—See GORDON, CHARLES GEORGE.

GORE, THOMAS PRYOR (1870–1949)

Thomas Pryor Gore was called *The Blind Savant* because he was especially learned although blind. The first sightless member of the U.S. Senate, he represented Oklahoma from 1907 to 1921 and from 1931 to 1936.

Gorgeous George: GEORGE RAYMOND WAGNER (1915?–1963)

One of the most show business-oriented of U.S. professional wrestlers, George Raymond Wagner was nicknamed *Gorgeous George* because of his lovely blond locks. It was said the name was first shouted at him by female wrestling fans.

Gorgeous Hussy, The—See EATON, MARGARET O'NEILL.

Gorilla Murderer, The: EARLE LEONARD NELSON (1892–1928)

Earle Leonard Nelson was a Bible-loving sex killer who was called *The Gorilla Murderer* for the sadistic way he killed at least 20 landladies in the United States and Canada. At the peak of his activities, in 1926, he tried to average one killing every three weeks. Finally captured, he was hanged in Canada.

Gossip, The—See TRISTAN L'ERMITE.

GOSSMANN, KLAUS—See Midday Murderer, The.

GOUGH, JOHN BARTHOLOMEW (1802?–1866)

Nineteenth century English-American temperance advocate John Gough was often parodied as *The Apostle of Cold Water*.

GOULD, JOE (1889–1957)

Nicknaming himself *Professor Sea Gull* (because he said he'd mastered their language) and *The Hot*

Shot Poet from Poetville, Joe Gould was one of the most colorful bohemians and brilliant raconteurs ever to grace New York's Greenwich Village. His greatest "work" was *Oral History,* which he claimed was taller than himself and weighed more than his 100 pounds. The manuscript probably was never written, although he quoted from it extensively while cadging drinks. One of his more famous lectures, supposedly from *Oral History* and delivered from atop tables at Village parties, was "Drunk as a Skunk, or How I Measured the Heads of Fifteen Hundred Indians in Zero Weather." Actually, Gould had done just that in 1915 on a scientific research expedition for the Carnegie Institute, leading him to conclude that Indians should run the country, and whites be sent to reservations. Perhaps his most fitting nickname was bestowed on him by poet and critic Horace Gregory, who dubbed him *The Pepys of the Bowery.*

Governess, The—See BERNSTEIN, THEODORE.

Governor Moonbeam—See BROWN, JERRY.

GOWER, JOHN (c. 1320–c. 1402)

English poet John Gower was dubbed *Moral (Morall) Gower* by Chaucer, who regarded Gower as one of the few men capable of correcting his verses.

GRABLE, BETTY (1916–1973)

U.S. screen star Betty Grable was in her heyday labeled *The No. 1 Pinup Girl,* and pinup pictures of her were in such demand among GIs during World War II that she was also called *The Soldier's Inspiration.* She was so often dubbed *The Worst Actress of the Year* in college campus publications,

however, that this became a permanent nickname as well.

GRACE, WILLIAM RUSSELL (1832–1904)

William Russell Grace, the English-American merchant and ship owner, was nicknamed *The Master of the Multi-national Enterprise* for having fashioned the prototype for this century's international corporations.

GRAHAM, BILLY (1918–   )

Southern Baptist evangelist William Franklin Graham, better known as Billy Graham, has been called many things, including *Mr. Christian, Moses,* and his self-proclaimed *Citizen of Heaven.* Perhaps his most colorful sobriquet dates back to his youthful sermonizing in Florida, when he was called *The Preaching Windmill* because of his exuberant arm flailing. Graham has in recent years greatly reduced the windmilling as well as his penchant for Kelly-green suits and hand-painted ties.

GRAHAM, GEORGE (1675–1751)

Illustrious English watchmaker George Graham, who apprenticed under Thomas Tompion, the so-called Father of Clockmaking, was called *Honest George* as a tribute to his skill. In his time a watch that lost a mere hour a day was considered to be of high quality, but Graham produced far more accurate, or honest, watches. (See also Tompion, Thomas.)

GRAHAM, SYLVESTER (1794–1851)

The Reverend Sylvester W. Graham, the originator of the graham cracker, was the most dedicated apostle of bowel regularity in the United States, crusading against such evils as meat-eating, rum and white bread. Having a large following of Grahamites, including Thomas Edison, J. H. Kellogg and Horace Greeley, he was dubbed *The Peristaltic Persuader* by newspapers. Also called *The Poet of Bran Meal and Pumpkins,* Graham irritated bakers when he accused them of adulterating their white bread with plaster of Paris, chalk and pipe clay. In Boston in 1841 a lynch mob of bakers broke through police barriers around Graham's hotel seeking to string him up. They were routed finally by a squad of Grahamites who shoveled slaked lime on the mob from second-floor windows.

Grammatical Cur, The—See
GRONOVIUS, JAMES.

Grammatical Cynic, The—See
SCIOPPIUS, GASPAR.

Grand Corrupter, The—See
WALPOLE, ROBERT.

Grand Old Lady of Opera, The—See
SCHUMANN-HEINK, ERNESTINE.

Grand Old Lady of the German Theater, The—See DURIEUX, TILLA.

Grand Old Lady of the Movies, The—See DRESSLER, MARIE.

Grand Old Man—See GLADSTONE, WILLIAM.

Grand Old Man of the Aw Shucks School, The—See STEWART, JAMES.

Grand Persuader, The—See
STRAUSS, ROBERT S.

Grandfather of Yale Rowing, The—See
SHEFFIELD, GEORGE ST. JOHN.

Grandma Flapper—See HOPPER, EDNA WALLACE.

Grandmother of Boston, The—See
PEABODY, ELIZABETH PALMER.

Grandmother of the Gray Panthers, The—See KUHN, MARGARET "Maggie."

GRANGE, HAROLD EDWARD "Red" (1903–)

Red Grange, considered by many the greatest football player of all time, had his day of days as an Illinois junior when his school played Michigan. Considered a conference championship match-up and most likely a close contest, the game opened with Grange running back the kickoff 95 yards for a touchdown. After that he scored on runs of 67, 56, and 40 yards. In all he racked up five touchdowns and 402 yards rushing. The game more than any other established his nickname *The Galloping Ghost.*

Granite Woman, The—See SNYDER, RUTH.

Granny Gates—See GATES, HORATIO.

Granny Hayes—See HAYES, RUTHERFORD B.

GRANT, ROBERT (1785–1838)

After failing in his efforts to have the House of Commons remove civil restrictions placed on Jews, Robert Grant at least received a sobriquet both his friends and many of his foes could agree on: *The Friend of the Jews*.

GRANT, ULYSSES S. (1822–1885)

Civil War general Ulysses S. Grant gained his most famous sobriquet *Unconditional Surrender Grant*, in February 1862, when the commander of the besieged Confederate garrison at Fort Donelson requested terms for a possible surrender. Grant's answer was blunt: "Sir: Yours of this date proposing Armistice and appointment of Commissioners, to settle terms of Capitulation is just received. No terms except unconditional and immediate surrender can be accepted. I propose to move immediately upon your works. I am sir, very respectfully, Your obt. svt. U.S. Grant, Brig. Gen." In the North Grant was called, among other honorifics, *The Great Hammerer, The Hero of Fort Donelson*, and *The Hero of Appomattox*. Surprisingly, even the Confederate press treated him kindly when it came to nicknames, most being a switch on *Unconditional Surrender*. These included *Union Safeguard, Uniformed Soldier, Unprecedented Strategist, Unquestionably Skilled, Uncle Sam*, and *United States*, the last two having been also assigned to him earlier by cadets at West Point. Union soldiers, not quite as laudatory of his military methods, called him *Butcher Grant* because his strategies usually resulted in considerable casualties to his command. *Useless Grant* was a sobriquet born during his Ohio youth and revived during his postwar presidency by political enemies. He was also denounced as *The American Caesar* by those who feared he intended to run for a third term and continue what they considered to be tyranny.

Grant's Conscience: JOHN A. RAWLINS (1831–1869)

Throughout the Civil War, John A. Rawlins served as adjutant general to Ulysses S. Grant. A well-known foe of liquor—his wife supposedly died of alcoholism—Rawlins, it was said, was primarily assigned to prevent Grant from returning to his old drinking habits. Whether this was true or not, Grant's enemies bestowed on Rawlins the nickname *Grant's Conscience*.

Grapefruit King, The—See HARRIS, JAMES ARMSTRONG.

GRASSO, ELLA (1919–1982)

As a woman running for governor of Connecticut, Ella Grasso was not exempt to political sobriquets from foes, although the practice may have sunk to a new low when she was called *Smella Ella*.

GRATTAN, HENRY (1746–1820)

Perhaps the most eloquent and ablest of 18th century Irish patriots, Henry Grattan ardently championed independence and successfully led moves to free the Irish Parliament from British control and obtain the right to vote for Catholics. He was hailed as *The Patriot of Humanity* not only by the Irish but by Americans as well, then also seeking their independence from England.

GRAUPNER, JOHANN CHRISTIAN GOTTLIEB (1767–1836)

German-born musician-composer Johann Christian Gottlieb Graupner was hailed as *The Father of American Orchestral Music* because of his important contributions to the field and his founding of the Philharmonic Society. He was also dubbed *The Father of Negro Songs* for introducing such songs in 1799 as a form of theatrical entertainment. He impersonated a black man and sang "The Gay Negro Boy" to his own accompaniment on the banjo.

GRAY, CHARLES (1729–1807)

British general Sir Charles Gray became known to American Revolutionary soldiers as *No Flint* because of his fondness for the bayonet assault.

GRAY, FINLY HUTCHINSON (1864–1947)

A colorful Democratic congressman from Indiana, Rep. Finly Hutchinson Gray was known to his colleagues as *The Hoosier Shakespeare.* In manners and elegance of dress, he seemed to have stepped from one of the Bard's plays.

GRAY, GILDA (1901–1959)

Polish-born Broadway dancer Gilda Gray, generally credited with inventing the "shimmy-dance" of the 1920s, was dubbed *The Mother of the Shimmy.*

GRAY, JUDD (1893–1928)

With his lover Ruth Snyder, Judd Gray perpetrated one of the most sensational murders in the United States during the 1920s, by bludgeoning, chloroforming and strangling her husband in the couple's bedroom. Gray became known as *The Dumb Bell Murderer,* not simply because he had used a sash

weight in the killing but because Mrs. Snyder (called "The Granite Woman") exercised considerable influence over him. After authorities uncovered numerous love letters in which Snyder referred to Gray as *Lover Boy,* that became his tabloid nickname until the pair's execution in 1928. (See also Snyder, Ruth.)

GRAY, L. PATRICK (1920–)

L. Patrick Gray, FBI director during the Watergate scandal, was referred to as *The Big Clown* by President Richard M. Nixon during conversations with his Oval Office associates.

GRAY, THOMAS (1716–1771)

The best known English poet of his day, Thomas Gray was hailed as *The Torre of Poetry,* an interesting allusion since Torre is largely unknown today. Torre was famed at the time for his fireworks displays at Marylebone Gardens, London.

***Gray Eminence, The*—See HOWE, LOUIS; KROCK, ARTHUR; TREMBLEY, JOSEPH DE.**

***Gray Ghost, The*—See MOSBY, JOHN SINGLETON.**

***Greasy Thumb*—See GUZIK, JAKE "Greasy Thumb."**

***Great American Bluenose, The*—See COMSTOCK, ANTHONY.**

***Great American Condenser, The*—See WOOD, JOHN B.**

Great American Rascal, The—See
BURR, AARON.

Great American Traveler, The—See
PRATT, DANIEL.

Great Assassin, The—See
ABDUL-HAMID II.

Great Astrologer, The—See ABU
YUSUF ALKENDI.

Great Bastard, The—See ANTOINE
DE BOURGOGNE.

Great Bullet-Head, The—See
CADOUDAL, GEORGES.

Great Commoner, The—See
BARNARD, JOHN; PITT, WILLIAM
(the elder).

Great Communicator, The—See
REAGAN, RONALD.

Great Compromiser, The—See CLAY,
HENRY.

Great Dissenter, The—See HOLMES,
OLIVER WENDELL, JR.

Great Eater, The—See COMESTOR,
PETER.

Great Eater of Graye's Inn, The—See
MARRIOTT, JOHN.

Great Elder Statesman, A—See
REAGAN, RONALD.

Great Emancipator, The—See
LINCOLN, ABRAHAM.

Great Eye, The—See SCHUYLER,
PHILIP JOHN.

Great Father at Detroit, The—See
CASS, LEWIS.

Great Financier, The—See
SHERMAN, JOHN.

Great God Pan, The—See
WORDSWORTH, WILLIAM.

*Great Gun of Phrenology in America,
The*—See FOWLER, ORSON
SQUIRE.

Great Hammerer, The—See GRANT,
ULYSSES.

Great Harlot, The—See PIUS VI,
POPE.

Great Impostor, The—See DEMARA,
FERDINAND WALDO, JR.

Great John L., The—See SULLIVAN,
JOHN L.

Great Khan of Wall Street, The—See
MORGAN, JOHN PIERPONT.

Great Land Pirate, The—See
MURREL, JOHN A.

Great Liberal, The—See WHEELER,
BURTON K.

Great Lover, The—See VALENTINO,
RUDOLPH.

Great Man, The—See ROCKNE,
KNUTE.

Great Masticator, The—See
FLETCHER, HORACE.

Great Moralist, The—See JOHNSON,
SAMUEL.

Great Mouthpiece, The—See
FALLON, WILLIAM J.

Great Naturalist, The—See DARWIN,
CHARLES.

Great Nullifier, The—See CALHOUN,
JOHN C.

Great Objector, The—See HOLMAN,
WILLIAM STEELE.

Great Pan, The—See VOLTAIRE.

Great Poet-Sire of Italy, The—See
DANTE ALIGHIERI.

*Great Preserver of Pope and
Shakespeare, The*—See
WARBURTON, WILLIAM.

Great Profile, The—See
BARRYMORE, JOHN.

Great Rehabilitator, The—See
BRYANT, PAUL WILLIAM
"Bear."

Great Renegade, The—See GIRTY,
SIMON.

Great Repealer, The—See BARTON,
BRUCE.

Great Rogue, The—See MURREL,
JOHN A.

Great Romantic, The—See HUGO,
VICTOR.

Great Shakespeare Forger, The—See
IRELAND, WILLIAM HENRY.

Great Sopper, The—See BEDA,
NOEL.

Great Soul—See GANDHI,
MOHANDAS "Mahatma."

Great Sow, The—See ISABELLA OF
BAVARIA.

Great Squeaky Lover, The—See
GILBERT, JOHN.

Great Stone Face, The—See
SULLIVAN, EDWARD VINCENT.

Great Survivor, The—See HUSSEIN,
ABDUL IBN, KING OF JORDAN.

Great Unknown, The—See SCOTT,
WALTER.

Great White Devil, The—See VAN
CORTLANDT, PHILIP.

Great White Hope, The—See
JEFFRIES, JAMES J.; WILLARD,
JESS.

Great Whore, The—See BOLEYN,
ANNE.

Great Witch of Balwery, The:
MARGARET AIKEN (*fl. late 17th*
century)

Margaret Aiken, a Scottish woman accused of
witchcraft, was labeled *The Great Witch of
Balwery*. She saved her own life by informing on
others.

Great Wolf, The—See TRYON,
WILLIAM.

Greatest, The—See ALI,
MUHAMMAD.

Greatest Gallant of His Time,
The—See SUCKLING, JOHN.

*Greatest Hog Caller East of the
Rockies, The*—See KAUFMAN,
MORRIS.

Greatest Italian of Them All, The—See
PONZI, CHARLES.

*Greatest Mathematician of the Age,
The*—See NEUMANN, JOHN VON.

*Greatest Medical Detective of the
Century, The*—See SPILSBURY,
BERNARD HENRY.

*Greatest Painter of Antiquity,
The*—See APELLES.

*Greatest Unread English Author,
The*—See JONSON, BEN.

GREB, HARRY (*1894–1926*)

The great world's middleweight boxing champion
Harry Greb was called *The Human Windmill* by
awed sports writers both for his fighting style and
his incredible stamina—it was common knowledge
that Greb often entertained young ladies in his
dressing room before a fight.

GREELEY, HORACE (*1811–1872*)

The founder of the *New York Tribune*, Horace
Greeley set unusually high standards for his
newspaper and was thus called *The Prince of
Journalists*. On launching the publication he
promised to bar from its pages ''the unmoral and
degrading Police Reports, Advertisements, and
other matters which have been allowed to disgrace

the columns of our leading Penny Papers.'' Pledging to render the *Tribune* "worthy of the beauty approved of the virtuous and refined, and a welcome visitant to the family fireside,'' he favored the organizing of labor, a free land policy ("Go West, young man, go west!''), the abolition of slavery, and Lincoln's policies. Having little interest in current styles, he habitually wore a high-topped white hat, which made him always stand out in a crowd and earned him the nickname *Old White Hat*. In the latter part of his life he became known as *The Sage of Chappaqua*, after his farm where he adjourned on weekends. He ran for the presidency in 1872 as a Liberal Republican but was defeated by Ulysses S. Grant and died a few weeks later.

GREEN, EDDIE (c. 1900–1934)

Gangster Eddie Green, one of the most vital members of John Dillinger's criminal gang in the 1930s, was nicknamed *The Jug Marker*. His job was to find out which bank to rob and when, learning how much money would be on hand and how the institution's security system operated. When he was shot by FBI agents in 1934, the loss to the Dillinger gang was enormous; some experts noted the outfit lost its steerage.

GREEN, HENRIETTA "Hetty" (1834–1916)

An eccentric who increased her family fortune from $5 million to over $100 million, Hetty Green was known as *The Witch of Wall Street*. She was a miser who wore rags and lived in fleabag hotels. Once Hetty tried to get free medical treatment for her son's infected knee, but when her identity was learned and payment was demanded, she took the child away without treatment. Later his leg had to be amputated.

Green, Hetty—See FRANCIS, KAY.

GREENBERG, DAVID—See Batman and Robin.

GREENE, NATHANAEL (1742–1786)

Although raised as a Quaker, Nathanael Greene became one of America's most accomplished generals of the Revolutionary War. Because he refused to obey entreaties by those of his faith opposed to war, he was nicknamed *The Fighting Quaker*—and excommunicated.

GREENFIELD, ELIZABETH TAYLOR (1808–1876)

A leading black singer of the 19th century in both the United States and England, Elizabeth Taylor Greenfield was nicknamed *The Black Swan*. Born into slavery in Mississippi, she was given her freedom and educated by her mistress because of her beautiful voice.

GREENHOW, ROSE O'NEAL (1817–1864)

A member of pre-Civil War Washington society, Rose Greenhow was able to provide the Confederate leadership with much valuable information including, allegedly, the Union plans for the first battle of Bull Run. Her activities were eventually exposed, and she and her daughter were imprisoned in the Old Capital Prison and then sent south. Branded *Rebel Rose* in the North, she continued her work for the Confederacy abroad until drowned trying to run the Union's naval blockade.

GREGORY OF TOURS (544–595)

For his 10 books of Frankish history—the first attempt at French historiography—Gregory of Tours was dubbed *The Herodotus of Barbarism* and *The Father of Frankish History.*

GREGORY THE GREAT (c. 540–604)

Born a patrician Roman, Gregory became mayor of Rome at the age of 30 and then resigned to become a Benedictine monk. Elevated to pope in 590, he was to win the lasting sobriquet *Rome's Greatest Pope* for his many good works, such as assisting the poor. His writings are classics of ascetical literature. The title he took for himself was *Servus Servorum Dei,* or *The Servant of the Servants of God,* the servants being the bishops.

Gretch the Wretch—See YOUNG, LORETTA.

GRETRY, ANDRE (1741–1813)

The celebrated Belgian operatic composer Andre Gretry has often been called *The Moliere of Music* for what has been described as "the essentially French bent of his genius."

GREY, LADY JANE (1537–1554)

Pushed onto the British throne by the duke of Northumberland, who prevailed upon Edward VI to bequeath her the crown, Lady Jane Grey was a reluctant monarch. Ousted by Edward's sister Mary, who enjoyed popular support, Lady Jane was arrested after only nine days on the throne and beheaded on Tower Green, to be remembered thereafter as *The Queen of Nine Days.*

Grey-Eyed Man of Destiny, The—See WALKER, WILLIAM.

GRIFFITH, D. W. (1875–1948)

Never hesitant about going to excess in its accolades, Hollywood conferred upon pioneer motion picture producer and director D. W. Griffith a simple enough tribute: *God.* This did not alter the fact that Griffith was relatively unemployable for the last two decades of his life.

Grim Chieftain, The—See LANE, JAMES HENRY.

Grim Reaper, The—See STOCKMAN, DAVID A.

GRIMES, BURLEIGH (1894–   )

As one of the most prolific hurlers of a pitch that has since been outlawed, Burleigh Grimes was dubbed *The Last of the Spitball Pitchers,* a sobriquet that proved to be most inaccurate.

Grocer, The—See HEATH, EDWARD.

GROLIER, JEAN (1479–1565)

A noted French patron of literature who financed many writers, Jean Grolier gained the honorific *The Maecenas of Book-Lovers,* after the Roman patron of Horace and Virgil. Gathering the most precious books available from the great cities of Europe, he built one of the finest personal libraries in existence. To this day one of a bibliomaniac's fondest dreams is to possess a uniquely bound book from Grolier's library.

GRONOVIUS, JAMES (1645–1716)

James Gronovius, a Dutch antiquary, was called *The Grammatical Cur* because of his caustic criticisms of those whose ideas he rejected. Some Italian contemporaries dubbed him *Grunnovius,* to liken him to animals who grunt, as expressed by the word *grunnire,* to grunt.

Gross, The—See DOUGLAS, JAMES.

GROSSMAN, GUSTAVUS (1746–1796)

Like both Schiller and Kotzebue, Gustavus Grossman was dubbed *The Shakespeare of Germany.* And like the Bard of Avon, he was an actor and writer. It was in part through his acquaintanceship with dramatist and poet Gotthold Lessing that he turned to dramatic composition and produced several very successful pieces for the German theater. Imprisoned for political offenses in 1796, he died shortly thereafter.

GROSVENOR, CHARLES HENRY (1833–1917)

A 10-term Republican congressman from Ohio around the turn of the century, Charles Henry Grosvenor was dubbed by colleagues *Old Figgers* because of his regular, extremely accurate predictions on upcoming elections.

GROTIUS, HUGO (1583–1645)

The Dutch humanitarian thinker Hugo Grotius became known as *The Father of International Law* for the publication of his famous treatise "On the Right of War and Peace" in 1625. While his supporters have since claimed that Grotius put international law on a "scientific" basis, the fact is that he constructed a grandiose "law of nature" which is superior to the so-called sovereignty of states. His form of international law did not attempt to abolish war but merely to limit it to those conceived to be "just." According to his plan, the occupations of peace would come to be regarded as more rational than war and war, believed to be the highest expression of sovereignty, would in turn lose its prestige. It has yet to happen.

GROTO, LUIGI (1541–1585)

The sobriquet *The Blind Poet* was applied to the 16th century Italian dramatist and poet Luigi Groto. In the following century it was applied to John Milton. (See also Milton, John.)

GROVER, MARTIN—See Ragged Lawyer, The.

GROZA, LOU "the Toe" (1924–   )

A premier football defensive lineman and placekicker, Lou Groza was able to last an almost unheard-of 22 years in the professional ranks. He was of course dubbed *The Toe.*

Grunnovius—See GRONOVIUS, JAMES.

Guardian of Civil Service, The—See RAMSPECK, ROBERT.

Guardian of Mankind, The—See AKBAR THE GREAT.

GUARDIOLA, SANTOS (1810–1862)

One of Central America's most cruel military strongmen during the 19th century, Gen. Santos Guardiola was noted for his harsh treatment of civilians and enemies. Labeled *The Tiger of Central America,* he declared himself president of Honduras in February 1856 and ruled until his death in 1862.

GUDERIAN, HEINZ (1888–1953)

German strategist Gen. Heinz Guderian proved the value of the tank in the Nazis fast-moving *blitzkrieg* attacks of World War II. He scored brilliant successes early in the war in Poland and France and was nicknamed *Swift Heinz,* a name Hitler often called him. By late 1941, however, *Swift Heinz*'s military star was in decline, and he was dismissed for warning Hitler that advanced positions in Russia could not be maintained in the winter months. Later restored to duty, he argued fiercely with Hitler and was dismissed from duty again.

Guerre, La—See GASSION, JEAN, COMTE DE.

GUEST, EDGAR A. (1881–1959)

U.S. newpaperman and poet Edgar A. Guest was called *The Poet of the Plain People.* The appropriateness of the sobriquet is best illustrated by the fact that Guest was the only poet ever quoted by Edith Bunker on television's "All in the Family."

GUIDARELLI, GUIDARELLO (fl. 16th century)

A fearless 16th century Italian soldier, Guidarello Guidarelli was sculpted in marble by his contemporary Tullio Lombardo and preserved for the ages. The fabled fighter began to receive his greatest acclaim about three and a half centuries later, however, when the superstition developed that women who kissed the reclining statue, on display at the Academy of Fine Arts in Ravenna, would marry happily. It has been estimated that since the late 1800s about five million women have kissed Guidarelli's marble lips, so that the statue's mouth has acquired a faint reddish glow. The soldier is now known as *The Most Kissed Man in the World.*

GUILLEMIN, ROBERT—See Sidewalk Sam.

GUIMARD, MADELEINE (1743–1816)

A famed dancer of the French opera during the reign of Louis XVI, Madeleine Guimard was nicknamed *The Spider* because of her incredible thinness.

GUINAN, TEXAS (1884–1933)

One of the high points of Broadway night life during Prohibition, brassy blonde Mary Louise Cecilia Guinan, better known as Texas Guinan, was called *The Queen of the Speakeasies.* She was famous for greeting big-spending visitors to her nightspot with "Hello, Sucker!" In her earlier years, Tex, fresh off a ranch near Waco, Texas, was a genuine lady gunslinger who made several Hollywood westerns as *The Female Bill Hart.* But she found her true calling in Manhattan's fun-loving booze traps during the supposedly dry era. A good sport about being arrested, she often had the band strike up "The Prisoner's Song" when the revenuers arrived to haul her away.

GULBENKIAN, NUBAR SARKIS (1896–1972)

Eccentric Iranian oil millionaire Nubar Gulbenkian was known as *The Last of the Big Spenders*, a name that, while technically not accurate, was appropriate because of the opulence and grandeur of his lifestyle.

GULLY, JOHN (1783–1863)

Perhaps the greatest success in the history of British pugilism was the career of heavyweight champion John Gully, known to fans as *Poor Gully*. In 1805 reigning champion Henry Pearce visited Gully, a butcher boy and his childhood friend, in debtors' prison. Gully asked to spar a bit with his old chum and proceeded to give him quite a lathering. When the news of the one-sided battle leaked out, Fletcher Reid, a gambler who hated Pearce, paid Gully's debts and put him in training to fight Pearce. During the match, however, Pearce stopped Gully in a brutal battle. The following year Pearce retired and Gully claimed the title, which he kept until retiring from boxing in 1809 to open a tavern with his ring profits. The business prospered and he bought a string of race horses, twice winning the English Derby. Several other rich stakes added to his fortune, and he eventually became a member of Parliament. When *Poor Gully* died in 1863, he left an estate estimated at more than $1 million.

Gumshoe, The—See HUNTER, WHITESIDE GODFREY.

GUNNESS, BELLE (1860–?)

Belle Gunness, one of America's most prolific mass murderers, slaughtered at least 14 suitors from 1901 to 1908 on her farm near La Porte, Ind., for loot ranging from $1,000 to $20,000 per victim. Actually, her victim toll may have been 42 suitors, a couple of legal husbands, three of her own children and an unknown woman whose corpse she had tried to use as a stand-in for herself in a fire. For years the hunt for the woman now known as *The Bluebeard of La Porte* was pressed without success.

Guru of LSD, The—See LEARY, TIMOTHY.

GUTENBERG, JOHANN (c. 1396–1468)

German printer Johann Gutenberg is called *The Father of Printing* for being the first to print from movable type. Actually, movable type had been invented earlier in Korea, although the Western development was a completely independent one. However, many experts now believe the first European to use movable type was Laurens Janszoon Koster, a Dutchman.

Guttersnipe, The—See PEGLER, WESTBROOK.

GUYER, ULYSSES SAMUEL (1863–1943)

An ardent Prohibitionist from Kansas, Rep. Ulysses Samuel Guyer was nicknamed *The Kansas Dry* and *The Dry Wind* because even after national Prohibition had ended, he perennially introduced bills to outlaw the sale and drinking of alcoholic beverages in the District of Columbia.

GUZIK, JAKE "Greasy Thumb" (1885–1956)

Jake Guzik, a long-time devoted aide to gangster Al Capone, was known as *Greasy Thumb* because he peeled off so many bills from his huge bankroll—to pay off Chicago politicians and policemen—that he could never get the inky grease off his thumb. Actually, the nickname was first applied to Jake's older brother, Harry, who played the same pay-off role for the syndicate, especially in vice enterprises. When Harry died, Chicago newspapermen could not bear the thought of losing so colorful a moniker, and they transferred it to brother Jake, who deserved it even more.

GUZMAN, JACOBO ARBENZ
(1913–1971)

Guatemalan president Col. Jacobo Arbenz Guzman became known as *The Red Colonel* after expropriating American property and opening relations with communist nations. He was deposed by a U.S.-backed invasion.

GWYN, ELEANOR "Nell"
(1650–1687)

Mistress to the Merry Monarch, Charles II of England, Eleanor "Nell" Gwyn was only 14 when plucked by his highness from the Drury Lane Theater, where she had been performing, to share the royal bed. Unlike many other mistresses, she enjoyed great public popularity and was generally cheered when passing by in her carriage. She was hailed as *The Beautiful* or *Witty* and disparaged *The Protestant Whore*. The king never tired of Nell, who remained faithful to him and bore him two sons. As he lay dying, Charles II whispered to his brother, "Let not poor Nelly starve." He did not.

Gyp the Blood: HARRY HORROWITZ
(1889–1914)

Harry Horrowitz, better known as *Gyp the Blood*, had a sobriquet unusually apt in that it captured the two great joys of his life: stealing and violence.

Always ready to take on a murder-for-hire, *Gyp the Blood* was enormously strong and boasted he could break a man's back by bending him across his knee, a feat he performed on numerous occasions, one with a stranger just to win a $2 bet. He also loved bombing assignments, explaining, "I likes to hear de noise." He went to the electric chair with three others for the 1912 murder of a notorious gambler on orders from Lt. Charles E. Becker of the New York police.

H

HAAKON II OF NORWAY
(1147–1162)

Haakon II, the young king of Norway, was nicknamed *Herdebred,* or *Broad Shouldered.*

HAAKON IV HAAKONSSON OF NORWAY (1204–1263)

Haakon IV Haakonsson, king of Norway, was nicknamed *The Old* and lived to the ripe old age of 59, a remarkable achievement for Norwegian rulers of that era. Haakon V, who succeeded to the throne at the age of about 45, was accorded the same sobriquet but died within a very short time.

HAAKON V MAGNUSSON OF NORWAY (1270–1319)

Haakon V Magnusson, king of Norway, was called *Haalegg,* or *Longlegs.*

HAARMANN, FRITZ (1879–1925)

Fritz Haarmann, a German mass murderer in post-World War I Germany, butchered perhaps as many as 50 boys and young men and sold their flesh in the form of sausages or as horse meat. *The Ogre of Hanover,* as he came to be known, did right by his neighbors, who assumed the bones he gave them to make soup came from animals. He was beheaded in 1925.

Habeas Corpus Howe—See HOWE, WILLIAM F.

HABER, JOYCE (c. 1931–   )

Syndicated gossip columnist Joyce Haber has been nicknamed *Hollywood's No. 1 Voyeur* and described by *Time* magazine as "more intelligent, more accurate—and more malicious—than her predecessors." In one of her more famous exchanges, she described actress and singer Julie Andrews as "boredom in rowdy bloom." The usually restrained Miss Andrews retorted, "She needs open-heart surgery and they should go in through her feet."

HACKENSCHMIDT, GEORGE (1877–1968)

Called *The Russian Lion,* Estonian-born heavyweight wrestler George Hackenschmidt gained such popularity in the United States that many men appropriated the nickname of Hack for themselves, among them Hack Wilson, the celebrated baseball home run hitter.

HACKET, JOHN—See Begging Bishop, The.

HACKLAENDER, FRIEDRICH WILHELM (1816–1877)

Friedrich Wilhelm Hacklaender, a popular German author and a contemporary of Britain's Charles Dickens, was designated *The German Dickens* because his works had a similar range of pathos and humor, although not the same social import.

HAFIZ, MOHAMMED (?–1388?)

Mohammed Hafiz, the Persian poet, philosopher, divine and grammarian, has often been described as *The Persian Anacreon,* after the illustrious lyric poet of ancient Greece. He was frequently referred to in his own time as *Sugar-Lip* because of the mellifluousness of his verses.

HAGLER, "Marvelous" MARVIN (1952?–   )

The resistance to "hype" in sports nicknames was exemplified in 1982 by the frustrating attempts of boxer Marvin Hagler to become known as *Marvelous* Marvin Hagler. The ABC television network stated that if he wanted to be called Marvelous, "let him go to court and have his name changed." Hagler did precisely that and is now legally known as *Marvelous* Marvin Hagler.

HAGUE, FRANK "I Am The Law" (1876–1956)

The political boss of Jersey City, N.J., Mayor Frank Hague was nicknamed *I Am The Law Hague,* after a famous boast of his. When the CIO attempted to unionize city workers in 1938, Hague, claiming "I am the law," loosed his police force on the union agents and "deported" the "CIO Reds." In the end, the federal courts reined Hague in, and his political machine thereafter headed toward oblivion.

HAHN, ANNA (1906–1938)

A native of Germany who immigrated to the German section of Cincinnati, Ohio, Anna Hahn poisoned a number of well-off elderly men after either marrying them or becoming their nurse-companion. *The German Borgia,* as she was labeled when apprehended, would appropriate each victim's wealth after killing him and then move on to the next one. She was executed in 1938.

HAIG, ALEXANDER M. (1924–   )

U.S. general Alexander M. Haig was nicknamed *The New Haldeman* when he replaced H. R. Haldeman as President Richard Nixon's White House chief of staff during the death throes of that administration. Later, as President Ronald Reagan's secretary of state in 1981, Haig was whimsically designated *In Charge Haig* when he announced, immediately after Reagan was shot by a would-be assassin, "I am in charge here." A wave of "in-charge" jokes swept through political circles, such as the one that had Haig going to the Vatican to see the Pope, only to find him out. Haig immediately announced, "I am in charge here."

HAILE SELASSIE (1891–1975)

Born Ras Tafari Makonnen, Haile Selassie was emperor of Ethiopia from 1930 to 1974, when he was overthrown by a military coup. Among his official titles was *The Lion of Judah.* His tenacity won him the title *The Conquering Lion* from adversaries who believed he had "jaws like a lion."

Hair Buyer, The—See HAMILTON, HENRY.

HALDEMAN, H. R. (1926–   )

During President Richard Nixon's administration, presidential aide H. R. Haldeman had several nick-names bestowed on him by the press and others, including *First of the Nixon Men, Nixon's Alter Ego,* and *The Lickety-Split Technician.* Among political insiders, however, and even within the president's own party, he was best known as *Rasputin* or *The Iron Chancellor.* The latter was a reference to the autocratic manner he used to control access to the president as well as to his Germanic background. Haldeman and two other members of the Nixon high command, John Ehrlichman and Henry Kissinger, also of Germanic background, were accused of comprising a "Berlin Wall" around the president. Kissinger called his two compatriots *The Praetorian Guard.* Others referred to them as *The Katzenjammer Kids.*

HALDEMAN-JULIUS, EMANUEL (1889–1951)

Emanuel Haldeman-Julius, who published the "Little Blue Books"—cheap paperback reprints of classics—was called *The Book Doctor* for the ways he increased sales, generally by altering the titles. Thus Theophile Gautier's novel *Golden Fleece* went from an annual U.S. sale of 600 copies to 50,000 under the title *The Quest for a Blonde Mistress.* Victor Hugo's play *Le Roi s'amuse,* or *The King Amuses Himself,* was going nowhere until Haldeman-Julius changed it to *The Lustful King Enjoys Himself.* Cashing in on the how-to trend, he turned Thomas De Quincey's *Essay on Conversation* into a bestseller as *How To Improve Your Conversation.* *The Book Doctor* dismissed criticisms of his methods by pointing out they brought great literature to the masses.

HALE, SARAH JOSEPHA (1788–1879)

Author and editor Sarah Josepha Hale, who wrote "Mary Had a Little Lamb," was dubbed *The Mother of Thanksgiving.* Her writings in *The Lady's Book,* a magazine of which she was literary editor, prompted President Abraham Lincoln to proclaim Thanksgiving a national holiday in 1864.

Half-Hanged Smith: JOHN SMITH (c. 1705)

A habitual English criminal who took a hiatus to serve as a sailor and soldier, John Smith returned to his wicked ways as a civilian. He was captured and sentenced to hang at Tyburn on Dec. 12, 1705. Smith was hanging for 15 minutes when a horseman galloped up with a royal pardon, based on his military service. Cut down and revived, he became a celebrity as *Half-Hanged Smith*. Much later it was learned the reprieve had been faked by his friends.

HALL, ABRAHAM OAKLEY (1826–1898)

The mayor of New York during its most corrupt period, Abraham Oakley Hall was a key member of the Tweed Ring, along with Tammany boss William Marcy Tweed, City Comptroller Richard B. "Slippery Dick" Connolly and Chamberlain Peter B. Sweeney. Typically, he once okayed the payment of $1,826,000 for plastering a municipal building, a job that should have cost no more than $50,000. Ensuring his political position by ethnic appeals to voters, Hall was nicknamed *Mayor Von O'Hall* because he so successfully wooed the Irish and Germans. A dapper dresser, he was also dubbed *The Elegant One* and *Elegant Oakley*.

HALL, EDWARD WHEELER (1881–1922)

When the Rev. Edward Wheeler Hall, a New Jersey minister, was murdered with Mrs. Eleanor Mills, a member of the choir of his church, he was nicknamed *Babykins* by the press. The name had turned up often in the pair's love letters, which the tabloids of the day felt obliged to publish for their readers. The Rev. Hall's widow was tried for the crime but acquitted. It was estimated that more words were written about the 1920s trial than any other criminal case up to that time.

HALL, GUS (1920–   )

The general secretary of the Communist Party in the United States, Gus Hall is often called *The Chauffeured Communist,* since he is driven to work each day by a chauffeur. Having been convicted under the Smith Act of conspiracy to overthrow the government, Hall is prohibited from operating a motor vehicle by New York state law.

HALL, WESTON B. (1886–1948)

Weston "Bert" Hall, one of the founders of the World War I Lafayette Escadrille, was called *The Pilot of Fortune*. The group was a squadron of American volunteer fliers who fought for the French. Hall was one of only a few original members to survive the war.

HALLECK, HENRY WAGER (1815–1872)

Having written a book on military science and translated the works of French military theorists, Union general Henry W. Halleck believed in "going by the book" in fighting the Civil War. Thus he often failed to follow up victories in the field with a quick pursuit, prompting his troops to call him *Old Brains* for his lack of initiative. In 1864 he was removed as commander in chief and relegated to the post of chief of staff under Gen. Ulysses S. Grant.

HAMILCAR (c. 270–228 B.C.)

Hamilcar, the Carthaginian general and father of Hannibal, was nicknamed *Lightning* to describe how rapidly he marched his forces and how fiercely he attacked.

HAMILTON, ALEXANDER (1755–1804)

Alexander Hamilton authored the *Federalist Papers* with James Madison and thus was called *The King of the Feds.* He was also referred to as *The Father of the Tariff,* since he saw such levies as an excellent way to raise revenues, and *Alexander the Coppersmith,* because, as the first secretary of the Treasury, he introduced the coining of copper one-cent pieces. A formidable public figure and debater, he was additionally called *The Little Lion.* An extramarital love affair with Mrs. Maria Reynolds threatened his political career, and his foes referred to him as *The Adulterer.* But Hamilton made a full confession of his misdeeds in a best-selling pamphlet—which is often described as the first American "true confession" story—and won the public's forgiveness, as well as that of Mrs. Hamilton, and the derogatory sobriquet faded away.

HAMILTON, EMMA LYONS, LADY (1761–1815)

Emma Lyons, later to become Lady Hamilton and the mistress of Horatio Nelson, was in the 1780s known as *The Goddess of Health,* having presided over the "celestial bed" of sex charlatan Dr. James Graham. Graham's Temple of Health and Hymen in London was finally closed down by the authorities, who called it nothing more than a glorified brothel.

HAMILTON, HENRY (c. 1730–1796)

Perhaps the most hated Briton on the American frontier during the Revolutionary War was Henry Hamilton, who, as lieutenant governor of Detroit, organized and financed Indian raids on settlements. He was universally said to have paid bounties for American scalps taken in these raids and was con-

temptuously dubbed *The Hair Buyer.* When he was captured in 1779, Thomas Jefferson, then governor of Virginia, refused him the courtesies of his rank and had him shackled in irons and thrown into a cramped, foul dungeon. To Hamilton's protests, Jefferson responded that the treatment was "justified on the general principle of national retaliation." Hamilton was freed in a prisoner exchange in 1781.

HAMILTON, JANET (1795–1873)

Janet Hamilton, a 19th century Scottish poet whose verses have been compared with those of Burns, was called *The Peasant Poetess* and, after she went blind at the age of 60, *The Blind Poetess.* Being illiterate, she dictated her earlier verses to her children until, at the age of 50, she managed to teach herself to write, although not well. She possessed a remarkable memory and was able to continue composing poems after her blindness, once again dictating her verses.

HAMILTON, WILLIAM "Single-Speech" (1729–1796)

An 18th century member of Parliament, William Hamilton became noted in English politics as *Single-Speech Hamilton* because his maiden speech proved highly successful. Unfortunately, it proved to be his last notable one.

HAMMARSKJOLD, DAG (1905–1961)

The highly respected secretary general of the United Nations from 1953 until his death in 1961, Dag Hammarskjold was called *The Curator of the Secrets of 62 Nations.* Awarded the Nobel Peace Prize posthumously, he was credited with building the prestige of the UN and establishing its independence from the United States.

HAMMER, ARMAND (1898–   )

The wheeling-and-dealing head of Occidental Petroleum, Armand Hammer has been called *The Salesman Deluxe* and *The Russian Connection* for his ability to strike deals with almost any sort of government, including Libya's right and left regimes as well as that of the USSR. In his Brooklyn school days he was nicknamed *Arm & Hammer*— after a brand of baking soda—by other children who knew nothing of the hero of Dumas' *Camille,* after whom he was actually named.

Hammer, The—See CHARLES MARTEL.

Hammer and Scourge of England, The—See WALLACE, WILLIAM.

Hammer of the Heretics, The—See AUGUSTINE, ST.; FABER, JOHANN.

Hammer of the Monks, The—See CROMWELL, THOMAS.

Hammer of the Scots, The—See Edward Longshanks.

Hammerer, The—See MACCABEE, JUDAS.

HAMMOND, JAMES H. (1807–1864)

Few senators of the immediate antebellum South offended the beliefs of abolitionists and northern liberals more than James H. Hammond of South Carolina. In a provocative address to the Senate, he declared that in every society there had to be people of unskilled abilities worthy of doing only menial labor. He defined such people as "the mudsill of society" and thus was thereafter labeled *Mudsill Hammond.*

HAMPTON, HOPE (1897–1982)

Hope Hampton, film actress, opera singer, and socialite, enjoyed her greatest fame as a first nighter on Broadway and at the Metropolitan Opera. Called *Miss First Nighter* and *The Duchess of Park Avenue* (for the opulent town house she maintained on New York's Park Avenue for more than half a century), she created a sensation when she swept into a theater garbed in high-fashion gowns and furs. Frequently, the curtain was held if she was late arriving. In her last years first nights began losing appeal for her, however, and she was shocked to see a young woman in dungarees at the opera. "Glamour is finished," she announced. "I don't want my picture in the papers next to a girl with jeans on." She never again attended an opening night at the Metropolitan.

HANCOCK, JOHN (1737–1793)

American patriot and Revolutionary War leader John Hancock was derided by the British and their sympathizers as *King Hancock* because he lived in a grand manner and had armed servants much like a king's guard. They also called him *King of the Smugglers* and charged that his revolutionary ardor sprang from his desire to avoid taxation on his imports. The British soldiers sang of him as *Old Mother Hancock:*

Old Mother Hancock, with a pan
  All crowded full of butter,
Unto the lovely Georgius [Washington] ran,
  And added to the splutter.

Patriots countered all this with one sobriquet, dubbing Hancock *The Yankee Doodle Dandy.*

HAND, LEARNED (1872–1961)

Widely acknowledged as "the greatest living judge in the English-speaking world," Learned Hand was a U.S. district court judge for 15 years, prior to serving on the U.S. court of appeals from 1924 until his retirement in 1951. During that time he authored more than 2,000 opinions. While some legal experts disputed the accolades heaped on him, the press nicknamed Hand *The Tenth Justice of the Supreme Court,* a measure of the impact his decisions had on the High Court, as well as a form of criticism for a political system which did not elevate him to that body.

Hand and Pen of the Congress, The— See THOMPSON, CHARLES.

Handcuff King, The—See HOUDINI, HARRY.

HANDEL, GEORGE FREDERICK (1685–1759)

German-born British composer George Frederick Handel was dubbed by Mozart *The Thunderbolt* for his enormous output. Never surpassed in vocal composition, especially choral, he produced over 40 operas, 23 oratorios, songs, and chamber, harpsichord and sacred music. His works include *The Messiah, Israel in Egypt, Samson, Joshua, Judas Maccabaeus* and *The Water Music.*

Handsome, The: FREDERICK III OF GERMANY (1286–1330), PHILIP I OF CASTILE (1478–1506)

Several rulers have been doted over by their subjects and called *The Handsome.* By and large there is general agreement that the most deserving of the title were Frederick II, king of Germany, and Philip I, king of Castile.

Handsome Frank—See PIERCE, FRANKLIN.

Handsome Mediocrity, The—See FILLMORE, MILLARD.

Handsome Queen, The—See FRANCE, CLAUDE DE.

Handsome Swordsman, The—See MURAT, JOACHIM.

HANDWERKER, NATHAN (1891?–1974)

A Polish-American restaurateur who operated Nathan's, the most famous hog dog stand in New York's Coney Island, and indeed in all America, Nathan Handwerker was called *Mr. Coney Island.* Few knew him by any other name than just Nathan.

HANDY, W. C. (1873–1958)

W. C. Handy, the black jazz musician and composer who wrote "St. Louis Blues," "Memphis Blues," "Mr. Crump," and many more, was nicknamed *The Father of the Blues.* Because he could not find a publisher for many of his early works, he had to publish them himself. Some critics have called Handy presumptuous for accepting the title *The Father of the Blues* since many of his songs were sung long before he wrote them down and had them copyrighted. However, Handy never claimed that many of his compositions were original.

Hanging Judge, The—See
NORBURY, EARL OF.

Hanging Parker—See PARKER,
ISAAC C.

Hangman Foote—See FOOTE,
HENRY STUART.

Hangman Heydrich—See
HEYDRICH, REINHARD.

Hangman of Lyons, The—See
BARBIE, KLAUS.

HANKS, O. C. "Deaf Charley"
(1863–1902)

A member of the outlaw Wild Bunch headed by
Butch Cassidy, Camilla, or O. C., Hanks was
known as *Deaf Charley Hanks* to the outfit, especially after dispatching a passenger who had gotten the drop on him during a train robbery. When
the man cocked his gun behind Hanks and, in a
low hiss, ordered him to drop his weapon, Hanks
instead turned and shot the man down. He had
whispered in the outlaw's deaf right ear, and Hanks
simply had not heard the command or the gun being
cocked.

Hanoi Jane—See FONDA, JANE.

HANSON, ROGER WEIGHTMAN
(1827–1863)

As a strict disciplinarian and a believer in drills
and weapon inspections, Confederate brigadier
general Roger W. Hanson became known to the

men of the famed Kentucky, or Orphan, Brigade
as *Old Flintlock*. A typical antebellum duelist, Hanson had been wounded in the leg, which remained
stiff for the rest of his life. The condition gave
rise to his also being called *Bench-leg*.

HANTZ, ROBERT—See Batman and
Robin.

Happiest Among Mortals, The—See
BOONE, DANIEL.

Happy Hooker, The: XAVIERA
HOLLANDER (?–   )

An Indonesia-born Dutch prostitute and madam
in New York during the 1960s, Xaviera Hollander
has become famous by the nickname used as the
title of a book about her career, *The Happy Hooker*.

Happy Talker, The—See CAVETT,
DICK.

Happy Warrior, The—See
HUMPHREY, HUBERT H.;
ROOSEVELT, THEODORE; SMITH,
ALFRED E.

Happy Warrior of Squandermania,
The—See LLOYD GEORGE,
DAVID.

Hard Cider Harrison—See
HARRISON, WILLIAM HENRY.

HARDI, ALEXANDRE (1560–1631)

Because his prodigious output rivaled that of his
Spanish counterpart, dramatist Alexandre Hardi

was designated *The French Lope de Vega.* It has been estimated that his theatrical productions numbered 600, and some say the figure was higher. However, only 34 remain. Hardi could write 2,000 lines in a 24-hour period and was able to finish a play and have it performed within three days. Alas, he was also described as *A Shakespeare Without Genius.*

HARDIE, KEIR *(1856–1915)*

Keir Hardie, leader of the Independent Labor Party in England, the forerunner of the British Labor Party, was nicknamed *Don't Keir Hardie* for his many idiosyncrasies, such as insisting on wearing a cloth cap to the House of Commons.

HARDIN, BENJAMIN *(1784–1852)*

A representative from Kentucky for several terms from 1815 to 1837, Benjamin Hardin was noted as *The Terror of the House* because of his acerbity in debate, in an era when harshness of tone was often considered the norm.

HARDING, FLORENCE DEWOLFE *(1860–1924)*

The wife of President Warren Harding, Florence DeWolfe Harding was a cold, imperious woman rather feared by her husband as well as his entire Ohio gang of cronies, who dubbed her *The Duchess.*

HARDING, WARREN G. *(1865–1923)*

Warren G. Harding, the 29th president of the United States, was taunted by the nickname *Nigger* as an Ohio youth because neighbors suspected that his dark complexion was caused by mixed ancestry. At the 1920 Republican convention, he was dubbed *Everybody's Second Choice* after long sessions in

the original "smoke-filled room." Since corruption made his administration a disaster, Harding won no glorious sobriquets. Woodrow Wilson called him *Bungalow Mind,* and William Allen White, *He-harlot* because of the ease with which he could be used. Harding's father perhaps gave the best comment on this characteristic: "If you were a girl, Warren, you'd be in the family way all the time. You can't say no."

Hard-Nosed Demon of the Ovals, The—See FOYT, A. J.

HARDY, OLIVER—See Fiddle and the Bow, The.

HARE, WILLIAM—See Body Sellers, The.

HARE, WILLIAM HOBART *(1838–1909)*

The missionary bishop of the Episcopal Church in Sioux country for more than 30 years, William Hobart Hare was called *The Apostle to the Sioux Indians.* If all the Sioux were not impressed by his religious teachings, they did respect his riding ability, calling him *Swift Bird* for the speed with which he rode to carry out his devoted work.

HARGRAVES, DICK *(1824–c. 1881)*

Famed on the Mississippi riverboats of the pre-Civil War period as *The Honest Gambler,* Dick Hargraves was an Englishman who hit the river at the age of 16, won $30,000 in a poker game and went on to a fabulous career as a card player noted for never cheating. He accumulated some $2 million from gambling and was the object of attention by many women, single and married, over whom he fought several duels. Regarded along the Mississippi as a traitor for serving as a major in the Union Army during the Civil War, he never returned after the conflict but retired to Colorado, where he died of tuberculosis.

Harlequin—See HARLEY, ROBERT.

HARLEY, ROBERT (1661–1724)

English statesman Robert Harley, first earl of Oxford, was known to political foes as *Robin the Trickster* and *Harlequin*. The latter sobriquet may have been used first by Sarah Jennings Churchill, the duchess of Marlborough, who said that Harley's consistently awkward motions betrayed ''a turbulent dishonesty.'' Harley was also known as *The King of Book-Collectors*. The year before his death the government purchased his library—which included 400,000 pamphlets and 8,000 manuscripts—and established the Harleian Collection of the British Museum.

HARLOW, JEAN (1911–1937)

Known to the public as *The Platinum Blonde* and *The Blonde Bombshell*, film actress Jean Harlow was affectionately known by all Hollywoodians as just plain *Baby*.

HARNETT, CORNELIUS (1723–1781)

As much a firebrand for the American Revolution in his own state as Sam Adams was in Massachusetts, Cornelius Harnett was dubbed by both the colonists and the British *The Samuel Adams of North Carolina*.

HARNEY, WILLIAM SELBY—See Military Humboldt, The.

Harold Skimpole—See HUNT, LEIGH.

Haroun-al-Roosevelt—See ROOSEVELT, THEODORE.

Harrington, Happy Jack (fl. 1870–1890)

Legendary whoremaster *Happy Jack Harrington* ran some of the bawdiest places on San Francisco's Barbary Coast, when not periodically being saved by missionaries. Acclaimed *The Beau Brummel of the Coast,* he was once described as ''invariably attired in the height of fashion. His favorite costume consisted of a high-crowned plug hat, beneath which his hair was puffed out in curls; a frock coat, a white shirt with a ruffled bosom, a fancy waistcoat, and cream- or lavender-colored trousers so tight that he looked as though he had been melted and poured into them. His principal adornment and greatest pride, however, was his silky brown mustache, which was so long that he could tie its ends under his chin.'' With such a stunning appearance he did not have trouble attracting women to his enterprises.

HARRIOT, THOMAS (1560–1621)

Mathematician and astronomer Thomas Harriot was nicknamed *The Universal Philosopher* because of his accomplishments in so many fields. His innovations in algebra were later adopted by Descartes and men of letters hailed his interpretations of Homer. At the age of 25 Harriot visited Virginia and composed at least a partial alphabet of the language of the Indians there.

HARRIS, ARTHUR ''Bomber'' (1892–   )

The foremost Allied exponent of area bombing during World War II, Sir Arthur Harris, head of the British Bomber Command, was known as *Bomber Harris*. The nickname proved to be less than fortuitous after the war, when the subject of mass bombings became unpopular with politicians. *Bomber Harris'* request for a special medal in recognition of his military service was denied.

HARRIS, BENJAMIN (c. 1673–1716)

English bookseller Benjamin Harris is known as *The Father of American Newspapers* because he published the first one, *Public Occurrences, Both Foreign and Domestic,* in Boston in 1690. The newspaper was ordered suppressed by the Massachusetts Bay Colony governor and council for, among other things, mentioning the king of France and the Mohawk Indians with less than total repugnance.

HARRIS, FRANK (1854–1931)

Irish-born author Frank Harris considered himself aptly nicknamed *The Sexpert* and had Lloyd's of London insure for $150,000 his card file of 2,000 women he claimed to have seduced during his sexual career. This may explain why he was also called *The Man Who Was Never Asked Back,* presumably by irritated husbands.

HARRIS, JAMES ARMSTRONG (1847–1921)

A pioneer in establishing the orange industry in Florida by improving the quality and flavor of the fruit, James Armstrong Harris was dubbed *The Orange King.* Harris more rightfully was called *The Grapefruit King* for doing so much to win that fruit's acceptance by consumers in the North.

HARRIS, JOEL CHANDLER (1848–1908)

One of the few authors to become identified with a character he created, Joel Chandler Harris wrote a series of celebrated tales about animals as told to the fictional Uncle Remus, an old black man. Harris himself was nicknamed *Uncle Remus,* and mail so addressed was delivered to him in his native Georgia.

HARRIS, MAC (1854–1947)

Born a slave, Mac Harris went on to win a fortune and become known as *The Black King of the Gamblers* and *The Dictator of Beale Street,* in Memphis, Tenn. However, he ended his years in poverty.

HARRISON, BENJAMIN (1833–1901)

Benjamin Harrison, the 23rd president of the United States, was called *The Son of His Grandfather,* since President William Henry Harrison was his grandfather. When it was suggested that he enter politics and run for governor of Indiana, Harrison showed only a slight interest and for that reason was called *Kid-Gloves Harrison.* The sobriquet took on another meaning for certain capital wags after Harrison became president and electricity was installed in the White House. The Harrisons were so fearful of the new system that they often would not touch the switches and left the White House lights burning all night. Because Harrison opposed restrictions on Chinese immigration, he gained the nickname of *Chinese Harrison.* Theodore Roosevelt, who greatly disliked him, came up with the sobriquet *The Timid Old Psalm-singing Indianapolis Politician.*

HARRISON, WILLIAM HENRY (1773–1841)

William Henry Harrison, the ninth president of the United States and the first to die in office, was called *The Farmer President* and *Log Cabin Harrison* because of his rural background. He gained the sobriquets *The Hero of Tippecanoe* and *Old*

Tippecanoe for defeating the Indians at the Battle of Tippecanoe in 1811. In recognition of his victories as a major general during the War of 1812, he was dubbed *The Washington of the West*. During the Log Cabin and Hard Cider Campaign of 1840, he was called *Hard Cider Harrison*, as he ignored the issues and was portrayed as a simple man of the frontier, happiest just sipping cider in his log cabin, as contrasted with President Martin Van Buren, who was pictured as a foppish dandy. The Whigs composed this song for their hero:

> Let Van from his cooler of silver drink wine
> And lounge on his cushioned settee;
> Our man on his buckeye bench can recline
> Content with hard cider is he!

HARROUN, RAY (1879–1968)

Ray Harroun, U.S. automotive engineer, inventor and racing car driver, won the first Indianapolis 500 and was nicknamed *Lady's First*.

HARROW, WILLIAM—See Flying Highwayman, The.

Harry the Hop—See HOPKINS, HARRY L.

Harry Twitcher—See BROUGHAM, HENRY PETER, LORD.

HARTNETT, CHARLES "Gabby" (1900–1972)

Since he gabbed almost incessantly both on and off the field, baseball catcher Charles Hartnett was nicknamed *Gabby*. His chatter could be very distracting to opposing batters.

HARVEY, GABRIEL (c. 1545–1630)

English writer, pamphleteer, and poet Gabriel Harvey was the object of a bombardment of sobriquets

from the acid pen of satirist Thomas Nash. Nash often called him *The Homer of His Age*, but lest this be taken as other than jesting invective, consider some of Nash's other barbs, which have become classics of English literary feuds: *This Mud-Born Bubble, This Vain Braggadocio, Silly Quirko* and *Gabriel Grave-Digger*. This last epithet was occasioned by the fact that Harvey wrote a caustic satire about Robert Greene after the latter's death. Nash countered by accusing Harvey of continually attacking the dead.

HARVEY, PAUL (1918–   )

A leading U.S. radio commentator for many years, Paul Harvey has been nicknamed *The Voice of the Silent Majority*, in part a reflection of the fact that his popularity is greater in the heartland than in large cities, especially those of the East.

HASKINS, HESTER JANE—See Jane the Grabber.

Hatchet Face—See ROOSEVELT, ELEANOR.

Hatchet Man with a Sense of Humor, A—See LASKY, VICTOR.

HATFIELD, BAZIL MUSE (1870–?)

Much like Johnny Appleseed, who promoted the planting of apple trees, Bazil Muse Hatfield traveled about Texas and other states planting and giving out persimmon seeds wherever he went and becoming known as *Johnny Simmonseed*.

HATFIELD, CHARLES M. (1876–1958)

Perhaps the most famous U.S. rainmaker of his day, Charles M. Hatfield, alias *The Moisture*

Accelerator, collected considerable sums of money from municipalities for allegedly creating rain, notably in Los Angeles during the drought of 1905. His stormiest experience, however, occurred in 1916 in San Diego, where he was offered $10,000 to fill the reservoirs with water. Nine days after he began, the deluge hit and overshot the mark. The Morena Reservoir filled to its 18 billion gallon capacity for the first time and spilled over, causing a major flood. When a second storm produced record rains, 12 deaths and property damage in the millions, the city council refused to pay *The Moisture Accelerator,* on the grounds he had submerged the city instead of just washing it down.

Hatpin Mary *(fl. 1940s–1950s)*

Hatpin Mary was an unidentified female fan who made a name for herself on the U.S. wrestling scene in the 1940s and 1950s. She would bring down the house by taking vengeance on the "villain" wrestler of a match by sticking his rump with her hatpin.

HATTON, CHRISTOPHER (1540–1591)

Sir Christopher Hatton, chancellor of England under Queen Elizabeth I, won the monarch's favor for his graceful movements at court balls and was nicknamed *The Dancing Chancellor.* Some opponents of Sir Christopher unfairly attributed his political advancement from an obscure country squire solely to his dancing.

Hawaiian Musikmeister, The—See BERGER, HENRY.

Hawaiian Pineapple King, The—See DOLE, JAMES DRUMMOND.

HAWKINS, BENJAMIN (1754–1816)

A North Carolina senator and Indian agent, Benjamin Hawkins was nicknamed by Indians *The Beloved Man of the Four Nations* because they trusted him implicitly. During his commission as an agent in Georgia, Alabama and Mississippi, from 1795 to 1812, "his Indians"—the Choctaws, Chickasaws, Cherokees and Creeks—scrupulously maintained the peace.

HAWKWOOD, JOHN (?–1394)

One of the most famous soldiers of his time, Sir John Hawkwood was known as *Needle John* because he had started life as a tailor before turning to the battlefield. Said to be able to direct a lance with the accuracy of a needle, he was one of the highest-paid English mercenaries of the 14th century.

HAWTHORNE, NATHANIEL (1804–1864)

U.S. novelist and short story writer Nathaniel Hawthorne was called *The Genius of Romance* and, after his story of that title, *The Gentle Boy.* In it he described a sensitive youth totally devoid of malice, and people who knew the author well said he was simply drawing his own portrait. A lasting tribute was given at his funeral by James Freeman Clarke, who called Hawthorne *The Friend of Sinners* for his classic studies of wrongdoers.

HAYAKAWA, SAMUEL I. (1906–   )

A scrappy Japanese-American semantics professor, Samuel I. Hayakawa leaped to national prominence in the 1960s as president of San Francisco State College for his strong stand against politically dissident students and faculty. Affectionately dubbed by right wingers *The Samurai Scholar* and regarded as refreshingly outspoken, he was elected to the U.S. Senate in 1976. During his term, however, he was an embarrassment in Congress, where his nickname became *Sleepin' Sam,* a reference to his penchant for dozing off during proceedings. Faced with an extremely low standing in the polls, he decided not to stand for reelection in 1982.

Haydn's Wife—See BOCCHERINI, LUIGI.

HAYES, HELEN (1900–   )

Renowned actress Helen Hayes is often referred to as *The First Lady of the American Stage.*

HAYES, LUCY (1831–1889)

For refusing to serve liquor or wine but only soft drinks with fruit juices in the White House, First Lady Lucy Hayes became known as *Lemonade Lucy.* Her teetotaling undoubtedly furnished further impetus to those who referred to President Rutherford B. Hayes as Granny Hayes.

HAYES, RUTHERFORD B. (1822–1893)

Rutherford B. Hayes, the 19th president of the United States, was subjected to a number of epithets following his disputed, if not stolen, victory over Samuel J. Tilden in the 1876 election. Among these were *The Fraud President, His Fraudulency, Boss Thief,* and *Rutherfraud B. Hayes.* In office he was also referred to as *Granny Hayes* due to his fussy manners, although the term really ap-

pears to have been coined by his Republican party bosses, who became exasperated by his insistence on ethical standards of political conduct.

HAYNAU, JULIUS JAKOB VON (1786–1853)

Austrian general Julius Jakob von Haynau was dubbed *The Hyena of Brescia* for his massacres of rebels in Brescia in 1849.

HAYNE, PAUL HAMILTON (1830–1886)

Because his poetry glowingly reflected the environment and customs of Dixie, 19th century U.S. poet Paul Hamilton Hayne was dubbed *The Poet Laureate of the South.*

HAYS, MARY LUDWIG—See Pitcher, Molly.

HAYS, WILL H. (1879–1954)

A former chairman of the Republican National Committee and postmaster general under President Warren Harding, Will H. Hays became the czar of Hollywood morals when he was chosen to head the hastily organized Motion Picture Producers and Distributors of America in 1922 following a string of movieland scandals. Stars found their private lives spied on and nicknamed their new guardian *Hays Fever.* Tied in 1928 to a number of shenanigans committed by Harding's Ohio Gang, Hays was accused in the Senate of taking $260,000 in "gifts" and "loans" from Harry "Teapot Dome" Sinclair in gratitude for pushing Harding into the White House. The tormented stars thereafter called him *Shifty Hays,* but he remained in office and in 1934 promulgated the so-called Hays Code, to keep watch over morals depicted on the motion picture screen.

Hays Fever—See HAYS, WILL H.

HAYWARD, HARRY T.
(c. 1865–1895)

Harry T. Hayward gained fame in the annals of crime as *The Hypnotic Plotter* for murdering his fiancee, Kitty Ging, by "remote control" in 1894 for her insurance money. Minneapolis police learned that Hayward had recently taken a course in hypnotism and had used the technique on a simple-minded handyman to get him to murder the woman. Hayward meanwhile established a perfect alibi by attending the opera. It was never clear how much of the handyman's act was controlled by hypnotic powers and how much simply by a stronger will, but in any event Hayward hanged while the actual killer got a lesser sentence.

HEAD, EDITH *(1907–1981)*

Edith head, one of Hollywood's leading fashion designers, was famed as *The Doctor* because of her ability to make stars look entirely different in various roles through wardrobe alone. She won eight Academy Awards for costume design and was nominated 27 other times.

HEADLEY, JOEL TYLER
(1813–1897)

Although enormously successful as a 19th century author of historical and biographical works, Joel Tyler Headley was extremely superficial in thought, and his facts were often questionable. Edgar Allan Poe labeled him *The Autocrat of the Quacks*.

HEARST, PATRICIA *(1954–   )*

Heiress and granddaughter of William Randolph Hearst, Patricia Hearst became a kidnap victim and then willing associate of the Symbionese Liberation Army and was known by the nickname of *Tania,* after a female Cuban revolutionary comrade of Che Guevara who had died in Bolivia.

HEARST, WILLIAM RANDOLPH
(1863–1951)

The controversial newspaper and magazine magnate William Randolph Hearst won his chief nickname, *The Lord of San Simeon,* because of his baronial private life. San Simeon, his estate in California, cost an estimated $60 million, half of which went into the rebuilding of a colossal Spanish castle overlooking the Pacific. When he died, Hearst bequeathed the building to the University of California, which declined the gift as being too expensive to maintain. The state finally took it over and opened it as a public park.

Heartthrob of the 1980s, The—See MOORE, DUDLEY.

HEATH, EDWARD *(1916–   )*

The prime minister of Great Britian in the early 1970s, Edward Heath was dogged by double-digit inflation, threatened strikes by coal miners and strong opposition to England's entry into the Common Market, which he supported and ultimately negotiated. On account of this latter position, Heath was disparagingly referred to as *The Grocer*. When Margaret Thatcher succeeded him as leader of the Conservatives, she was called The Grocer's Daughter.

HEATTER, GABRIEL *(1890–1972)*

U.S. radio news announcer and analyst Gabriel Heatter, who at one time during World War II attracted a nightly audience of 120 million listeners, carried two seemingly incongruous nicknames: *The*

Voice of Doom and *The Good News Tonight Man*. The latter sprang from his opening words, "Ah—there's good news tonight," which became a national catch phrase. However, he delivered his broadcasts in such a deep, oratorical manner or wailing that he was tabbed *The Voice of Doom*.

HEBER, REGINALD (1783–1826)

English prelate Reginald Heber, who became bishop of Calcutta, was dubbed *The Christian Atticus*. He is best remembered for the hymn "From Greenland's Icy Mountains."

HEBER, RICHARD (1773–1833)

The great English book collector Richard Heber was nicknamed *The Magnificent Heber*. The tribute was not solely for his library—whose partial sale required 144 days— but for his wine cellar as well, described as "so superior to all others in the world."

Hedda Hopper of the Criminal Courts, The—See ROOT, GLADYS TOWLES.

HEDGEPETH, MARION C. (?–1910)

Described by the Pinkertons as "one of the really bad men of the West," Marion C. Hedgepeth was a multiple killer and train robber who was nicknamed *The Debonair Bandit* because of his modish dress and his effect on women. In 1906 he was granted a pardon for a train robbery conviction mainly through the agitation of women-dominated committees. They called him a "friend of society" because his information to police led to the capture of H. H. Holmes, a mass murderer of women. Hedgepeth was shot dead during a robbery in Chicago in 1910.

HEFNER, HUGH M. (1926–   )

Hugh M. Hefner, the publisher of *Playboy* magazine and proprietor of the Playboy "Bunny" nightclubs, has been nicknamed *Mr. Playboy of the Western World* and *Boss of the Bunny Empire*.

HEGEL, GEORG WILHELM FREDERICK (1770–1831)

German idealist philosopher Georg Hegel was called *The Philosopher of the Absolute*. His system influenced such later movements as Marxism, existentialism, positivism, and analytical philosophy.

He-harlot—See HARDING, WARREN G.

HEINECKEN, CHRISTIAN HEINRICH (1721–1726)

Child prodigy Christian Heinrich Heinecken won fame in 18th century Germany as *The Infant of Lubeck*. He was said to have mastered the entire history of the Bible at the age of two and to have been totally fluent in French and Latin at three. He died at the age of five.

HEINRICH, EDWARD OSCAR (1881–1953)

Solving an estimated 2,000 major and minor crimes in his laboratory over a 45-year span, criminologist Edward Oscar Heinrich was dubbed by the press *The Edison of Crime Detection*. As the nation's first all-around scientific investigator, he convinced police departments throughout the country that the microscope was more potent than the blackjack in solving mysteries.

HEINZ, HENRY J. (1844–1919)

H. J. Heinz, the U.S. American food packer, was said to have relished the nickname bestowed upon him by the media: *The Good Provider.*

Heir to Barnum's Mantle, The—See TODD, MIKE.

HEITLER, MIKE "de Pike" (?–1931)

A remarkable old brothel keeper of indeterminate age, Mike *de Pike* Heitler was for many years a foremost figure in Chicago commercialized vice operating at the low end of the financial ladder, which made him a piker or, in the venacular, *de Pike.* He sat by a cash register at his famous joint at Peoria and West Madison and rang up 50 cents each from men lined up at the foot of the stairs. As a girl came down the stairs with a customer, Heitler handed her a brass check redeemable for 25 cents later and she took the next man upstairs.

HELD, ANNA—See Hourglass Girl, The.

Helen of Spain, The—See FLORINDA.

HELLMAN, WALTER (1916–   )

American Walter Hellman, the world's checker champion, could hardly escape the sobriquet *The Bobby Fischer of Checkers.*

Hellmuth the Taciturn—See MOLTKE, HELLMUTH KARL BERNHARD VON.

HEMINGWAY, ERNEST (1899–1961)

Novelist, short story writer and journalist Ernest Hemingway was *Papa* to many and *The Spokesman for the Lost Generation* to admirers. Famed for his terse, understated style, Hemingway was not admired by all, however. Author Max Eastman called him *False Hair on the Chest.*

HEMPHILL, JOSEPH "Single Speech" (1770–1842)

As a young representative from Pennsylvania, Joseph Hemphill gave his maiden speech before the House in opposition to the repeal of a judiciary act. Although he was the only member of the opposition, he swayed the chamber to his point of view, over the sentiments of all other speakers. For this novel accomplishment he became known as *Single Speech Hemphill* and was regarded as one of Congress' most persuasive orators.

HENDERSON, FLETCHER (1898–1952)

Benny Goodman, The King of Swing, credits much of his success to arranger Fletcher Henderson, known as *The Big Band's Black Man.* In the 1930s Henderson originated the "big band sound" that catapulted Goodman to musical fame.

HENIE, SONJA (1912–1969)

Norwegian ice skater, Olympic gold medalist and later U.S. movie star, Sonja Henie was called *The Symphony on Silver Skates.*

HENLEIN, PETER (fl. early 16th century)

It is difficult to ascribe the title *The Father of the Watch* to one person with any degree of certainty.

However, most experts give that honor to a young German locksmith Peter Henlein, or Heinlein, Henle or Hele, as his name appears in various records. In 1511 the *Cosmographia Pomponii Melae*, published in Nuremberg, Henlein's home, stated: "Every day finer things are being invented. Peter Hele, still a young man, has constructed a piece of work which excited the admiration of the most learned mathematicians. He shapes many-wheeled watches out of small bits of iron, which run without weights for forty hours, however they may be carried, in pocket or chemisette." Still, the accolade may not have been deserved since a number of Italian watches are believed to date back to the mid-15th century.

HENLEY, JOHN (1692–1756)

English preacher and eccentric John Henley, noted for lectures in which he criticized many eminent figures, was in turn ridiculed with such labels as *The Cain of Literature* and *Orator Henley*. Pope, vicious at criticism himself, called him *The Zany of His Age*.

HENRI, DUKE OF GUISE (1550–1588)

French statesman and general Henri, duke of Guise, gained considerable popularity among the people of France during the reign of the dissolute King Henry III (The Man Milliner) and was often called *The People's King*. Out of jealousy Henry III had the duke assassinated in 1588, a fate the monarch himself suffered the following year.

HENRI II, DUKE OF GUISE (1614–1664)

Henri II, duke of Guise, was called *Le Balafre,* or *The Gashed,* on account of a huge scar he got from a sword cut at the battle of Dormans.

HENRY, CLARENCE "Frogman" (1937–   )

Rock-'n'-roll singer Clarence Henry picked up the nickname *Frogman* when he recorded his first hit, "Ain't Got No Home." One of the three voices he used on the recording sounded like that of a frog, and the *The Frogman* tag stuck.

HENRY, JOHN (?–1873)

A black railroad worker noted for his extraordinary strength, John Henry inspired legends after he died while working on the construction of the Big Bend Tunnel in Virginia. He was celebrated as *The Negro Paul Bunyan,* but the legends told of him had deeper meaning, reflecting the last stand of manual workers against the inevitable coming of the machines of progress.

HENRY, PATRICK (1736–1799)

Virginia lawyer Patrick Henry was aptly nicknamed *The Voice of the Revolution*. His famous declaration, "Give me liberty or give me death," galvanized the forces of rebellion against the British crown.

HENRY, PRINCE (1594–1612)

The popular son of the unpopular king of England James I, Prince Henry was regarded as having the mark of greatness, since he possessed an equal grasp of warfare, art, music, literature, and morality. When he died at the age of 18, he was regarded as *Our English Marcellus*. Disraeli wrote that Henry "was wept by all the muses, and mourned by all the brave in Britain."

HENRY I OF ENGLAND (1068–1135)

Henry I of England, the youngest son of William the Conqueror, won the crown by repelling an invasion by his brother Robert, duke of Normandy, in 1101. He was nicknamed *Beauclerc,* or *Good Scholar* or, more precisely, *Good Clerk.* The term was not meant demeaningly, however, since clerk-like abilities were then a rare commodity. They stood *Beauclerc* in good stead in the organized expansion of royal administration.

HENRY II, KING OF GERMANY AND HOLY ROMAN EMPEROR (972–1024)

A most pious prince and a favorite of the Church, Holy Roman Emperor Henry II was said to be more fit for a cloister than the throne. Called *The Saint* and *St. Henry,* he built many religious houses, the most famed being the great Strasbourg cathedral.

HENRY II OF ENGLAND—See Henry Curmantle.

HENRY III OF FRANCE (1551–1589)

King Henry III of France was nicknamed *The Man Milliner* because he much preferred to spend his time devising new fashions in dress than minding affairs of state.

HENRY V OF ENGLAND (1387–1422)

Henry V of Monmouth, who ascended the English throne in 1413, restored domestic peace by settling difficulties with the Church. Turning to Europe, he reopened the Hundred Years War and scored a string of unbroken successes, including great victories at Agincourt and in the conquest of Normandy. For his triumphs he was hailed as *The English Alexander,* especially since, like the Macedonian conqueror, he was stopped only by an early death.

HENRY V OF GERMANY (1081–1125)

King Henry V of Germany was called *The Parricide,* for while he did not kill his father, he drove him from the throne and forced his abdication.

HENRY VI OF ENGLAND (1421–1471)

Henry VI of England was aptly nicknamed *The Martyr King* during and after his unfortunate reign. Crowned both king of England and France as a baby, his rule was marred by the rebellion of Jack Cade, the disastrous conclusion of the Hundred Years War and the War of the Roses. Imprisoned in 1460, he acknowledged Edward IV of York as monarch the following year. Freed, he fled to Scotland, only to be captured and imprisoned in the Tower of London. Restored to the throne in 1470 by Warwick (The King-maker), he reigned only briefly as Warwick's pawn and was murdered in 1471, probably by Gloucester.

HENRY VI OF GERMANY (1163–1197)

Nicknamed *The Cruel* for terrorizing his subjects and torturing prisoners, King Henry VI of Germany was ultimately excommunicated by the Pope. The captor of Richard the Lion Hearted, he used the ransom gained for freeing him to launch an invasion of Sicily, where he also committed innumerable acts of cruelty. He was finally poisoned by his wife, who was of Sicilian birth.

HENRY VII OF ENGLAND (1457–1509)

Henry VII of England defeated Richard III in 1485 to become the first Tudor king. He won the sobriquet *The English Solomon* for the shrewd ways he forced loyalty from rebellious nobles, eliminating their private armies and uniting the houses of York and Lancaster. He made peace with Scotland in 1499, marrying his daughter Margaret to James IV of Scotland.

HENRY VIII OF ENGLAND (1491–1547)

Henry VIII of England may have been rather fickle about his many wives, divorcing some and beheading two, but *Bluff King Hal,* as he was called, was initially the most devoted of husbands. He first married Catherine of Aragon, his brother's widow, and grew to love her deeply. He even wore her initials on his sleeves at jousts and nicknamed himself *Sir Loyal Heart.* When Catherine failed to produce a male heir by 40 and was worn out by unproductive pregnancies, Henry divorced her, and *Sir Loyal Heart* lived no more.

Henry Curtmantle: HENRY II OF ENGLAND (1133–1189)

Henry Curtmantle, or Henry II of England, was awarded his surname due to the short coat, or curtmantle, which he introduced to court. The curtmantle, falling only to the knees, proved especially useful in riding and hunting, and the fashion spread rapidly in English society.

Henry Ford of Aviation, The—See PIPER, WILLIAM T.

Henry of Navarre: HENRY IV OF FRANCE (1553–1610)

Henry of Navarre, or Henry IV of France, was known as *Mon Soldat,* or *My Soldier,* and *The King of Brave Men* because of his great military leadership.

Henry the Fowler: HENRY I OF GERMANY (876–936)

Henry I, king of Germany, was nicknamed *The Fowler* because he was fowling with a hawk on his wrist when notified of his election to the throne. According to some accounts, he was more interested in the sport than in his new throne.

Henry the Impotent: HENRY IV OF CASTILE (1425–1474)

Henry IV of Castile was called *The Impotent* even after the birth of his daughter Juana. The Cortes strongly questioned the child's legitimacy, suspecting the father to be a close friend of the king. Henry was driven from the throne in 1464 but was restored when his successor died the following year. He solved the problem of succession by adopting as his heiress his half-sister Isabella.

Henry the Morgue—See MORGENTHAU, HENRY, JR.

Henry the Navigator: PRINCE HENRY OF PORTUGAL (1394–1460)

Prince Henry of Portugal, the younger son of King John I, was nicknamed *Henry the Navigator,* although he made no great voyages of his own. However, he greatly encouraged science and geographical discovery, and expeditions he sent out rounded Cape Bojador in 1433 and discovered the Azores, Madeira, the Senegal, and other places. It was *The Navigator*'s impetus that led to Portuguese ventures to the Indies and the New World after his death. Henry turned his home at Sagres into a library and clearing house for information about discoveries, map changes and improvements and innovations in shipbuilding.

Henry the Warlike: HENRY II OF FRANCE (1519–1559)

Henry II of France was known somewhat puckishly as *Henry the Warlike* because he was a monarch much given to safe pleasures. It must be noted, however, that he died in a tournament joust.

HERBERT, GEORGE (1593–1633)

English poet George Herbert was dubbed *The Sweet Singer of the Temple* for his religious poems, which were published a short time after his death in a volume called *The Temple of Sacred Poems and Private Ejaculations*.

Hercules Mary—See PROMITIS, MARY.

Hercules of Music, The—See GLUCK, CHRISTOPH WILLIBALD VON.

Hercules Secundus—See COMMODUS, LUCIUS AELIUS AURELIUS.

Heretic, The—See BRUNO, GIORDANO.

Heretic King, The—See IKHNATON.

HEREWARD (fl. c. 1070)

A noted English outlaw and patriot, Hereward was called *The Wake* because of his ability never to be caught off guard in defense of Ely against the Normans. He was further immortalized in *Hereward the Wake,* an 1866 novel by Charles Kingsley.

HERING, CONSTANTINE (1800–1880)

Drawing on the work of German physician Samuel C. F. Hannemann, who invented the system of medical therapy known as homeopathy, Constantine Hering brought the "science" to the United States and became *The Father of Homeopathy in America*. He founded the North American Academy of the Homeopathic Healing Art in Allentown, Pa. Homeopathy holds that a disease is curable by drugs producing effects similar to the symptoms of the illness and that the effect of drugs increases if they are given in minute doses. By the turn of the century, there were more than 12,000 practicing homeopaths in the United States and millions of patients who swore by homeopathy's results. Now, however, the practice has been drastically reduced in size as an independent movement and it is merely one method among several therapeutic systems.

HERMANN (?–21)

Hermann, the liberator of his land from Rome and perhaps the greatest hero of the era, comes down to us as *The German Cid*, the subject still of many ballads and historic lays.

Hermit of Grub Street, The—See WELBY, HENRY.

Hermit of La Ripaille, The—See AMADEUS VIII, FIRST DUKE OF SAVOY.

Hero Calley—See CALLEY, WILLIAM.

Hero Husband, The—See WANDERER, CARL.

Hero of Appomattox, The—See GRANT, ULYSSES S.

Hero of Chappaquiddick, The— KENNEDY, EDWARD M.

Hero of Charleston, The—See LEE, CHARLES.

Hero of Fort Donelson, The—See GRANT, ULYSSES S.

Hero of Fort Sumter, The—See ANDERSON, ROBERT.

Hero of Many a Well-Fought Bottle, The—See PIERCE, FRANKLIN.

Hero of New England, The—See STANDISH, MILES.

Hero of Saratoga, The—See GATES, HORATIO.

Hero of Sumter, The—See BEAUREGARD, PIERRE GUSTAVE TOUTANT.

Hero of the Crater, The—See MAHONE, WILLIAM "Little Billy."

Hero of the Hundred Battles, The—See NELSON, HORATIO.

Hero of the Marne, The—See JOFFRE, JOSEPH JACQUES CESAIRE.

Hero of the Nile, The—See NELSON, HORATIO.

Hero of Tippecanoe, The—See HARRISON, WILLIAM HENRY.

HERODOTUS (c. 484 B.C.–c. 430 B.C.)

The Greek historian Herodotus, remembered often as *The Father of History,* is, all the same, nicknamed *The Father of Lies* for including material in his works without a total regard for truth. His histories have been criticized as being more anecdotal and less factual than they should have been. By contrast the historian Thucydides is noted for such qualities as accuracy and narrative ability, characteristics that did not qualify him for any lasting sobriquet.

Herodotus of Barbarism, The—See GREGORY OF TOURS.

Heroin Kingpin, The—See RICORD, AUGUST.

Heroine of Bald Mountain, The—See MORROW, "Pegleg" ANNIE.

Hero-Sergeant of Fredericksburg, The—See KIRKLAND, RICHARD R.

Herrick of Germany, The—See FLEMING, PAUL.

HERSHEY, LEWIS B. (1894–1977)

Gen. Lewis B. Hershey, director of the Selective Service Systems under six presidents, oversaw the drafting of almost 15 million men in three wars. He was nicknamed *The Oldest Soldier,* since he was the oldest military man on active duty when he retired in 1973, a term that was used disparagingly by protestors during the Vietnam War.

HERSHEY, MILTON S. (1857–1945)

Obviously, no sobriquet other than *The Chocolate King* could apply to Milton S. Hershey, unless it was *The Father of the Hershey Bar.*

HERVEY, JOHN (1696–1743)

The 18th century English politician and writer John Hervey was ridiculed by his literary enemies as *Lord Fanny* because of his effeminate habits, including the use of cosmetics—a practice he adopted because of his poor physical health. The sobriquet was coined by Alexander Pope, who resented Lord Hervey's friendship with Mary Wortley Montagu, and it was used savagely by Horace Walpole.

HESS, RUDOLPH (1894–   )

The number 3 man in the Nazi Party, Rudolph Hess shocked the world by flying to Britain in 1941 in a deluded hope of arranging a settlement to end World War II. His act presented an embarrassing situation to the Nazis, who solved their dilemma by publicly referring to him as *Mad Rudi,* indicating he had suffered "hallucinations traceable to World War injuries." Privately, Hitler did not accept such excuses for Hess and ordered that he be shot out of hand if he ever came into German custody.

Hessian Wolf-Boy (?–1344)

In the German kingdom of Hesse in 1344, hunters captured a strange boy, judged to be somewhere between 7 and 12 years old, who had apparently survived most or all of his life in the wild. Dubbed the *Hessian Wolf-Boy,* he slept at night in holes in the ground and appeared to have been brought food by wolves. He ran on all fours and was capable of leaping great distances. He did not survive long in human captivity, apparently reacting badly to a steady diet of cooked food instead of the raw meats he was used to.

HEYDRICH, REINHARD (1904–1942)

A high official in the Gestapo, Reinhard Heydrich was the administrator of concentration camps and head of the Reich Central Security Office. As such he was feared as the Nazi specialist in terror and referred to as *Hangman Heydrich.* He was assassinated by Czech patriots.

HEYNE, CHRISTIAN GOTTLOB (1729–1812)

Certainly one of the most prolific scholars, Christian Gottlob Heyne of Germany edited or translated a great number of Greek and Latin classics as well as writing several volumes of essays. He also reviewed no less than 7,500 books in the *Gottinger Gelehrten Anzeigen,* of which he was the director, earning the sobriquet *The King of Critics.*

HHH—See HUMPHREY, HUBERT H.

HICKOK, JAMES BUTLER "Wild Bill" (1837–1876)

James Butler Hickok was originally nicknamed *Duck Bill* because of his long nose and protruding lip, and only as his reputation as a western gunfighter and his list of victims grew did it become more common—and more prudent—to call him *Wild Bill*.

Hickory Solomon—See SOLOMON, MOSES.

HIGGINS, EUGENE (1874–1958)

Known perhaps in too limiting a sense as *The Millet of America,* Eugene Higgins was compared with the French painter of peasant life Jean Francois Millet because he too painted rural scenes. However, Higgins also produced many realistic portraits of sailors, slum people and refugees that were equally impressive.

HIGGINSON, STEPHEN (1770–1834)

Stephen Higginson, a steward of Harvard University in the early 19th century, was often referred to as *The Man of Ross,* an allusion to the original bearer of the sobriquet, John Kyrle of Ross, Herefordshire, England. Kyrle was a man of great benevolence and was thus eulogized by Pope. Higginson too was famous for his many charitable works.

High Pressure Lee—See TREVINO, LEE.

High Tax Harry—See TRUMAN, HARRY S.

High-Born Demosthenes, The—See William the Silent.

Highland Mary: MARY CAMPBELL AND MARY MORISON (fl. late 18th century)

Lovers of Scottish poet Robert Burns, Mary Campbell and Mary Morison shared the nickname *Highland Mary.* The bawdy bard had many other lovers, of course, but none were also named Mary, or the sobriquet would have been further subdivided.

HILL, DAVID BENNETT (1843–1910)

A governor of New York in the 1880s, David Bennett Hill was dubbed *Young Hickory,* after Andrew Jackson (Old Hickory), because he believed just as earnestly, and perhaps even more so, in the wholesale use of the spoils system.

HILL, JOE (1879–1915)

Joe Hill, the Swedish revolutionist, U.S. labor leader and songwriter, was found guilty of murder in Utah on exceedingly flimsy evidence and was executed by a firing squad. Because he became an inspiration to the labor movement and his songs survived him, he was called *The Man Who Never Died.*

HILL, JOHN (1716–1775)

English author and critic Sir John Hill had so many more enemies than friends that in time publishers would agree to publish his works only if they were done anonymously. He was often referred to as *The Cain of Literature* and *The Janus-Faced Critic*. Fielding dubbed him *A Paltry Dunghill;* poet Christopher Smart preferred *The Universal Butt of All Mankind*.

HILL, ROWLAND *(1772–1843)*

Second in British popularity only to Wellington after the Battle of Waterloo, Viscount Rowland Hill was hailed as *The Waterloo Hero* for his gallantry in action. Although his horse was shot from under him and he was wounded in five places and believed dead by his troops, Hill rejoined them and was in the thick of action until the final shot.

HILL, VIRGINIA *(1918–1966)*

Labeled *The Queen of the Mob* during the U.S. Senate's Kefauver Committee hearings into organized crime in the early 1950s, Virginia Hill did not really deserve the title. She played no important role in formulating criminal policy but was trusted implicitly as a ''bag lady,'' transporting huge sums of money for the mob, including deposits for Swiss banks. She gained this trust from many criminal big shots because she had slept with them, leading some crime reporters to insist that the most accurate nickname for her was *The Bride of the Mafia*.

Himmler of Russia, The—See BERIA, LAVRENTI P.

Hippie, That—See HUSTON, TOM CHARLES.

Hippieland's Court Chemist—See STANLEY, AUGUSTUS OWSLEY.

HIPPOCRATES *(c. 460–357 B.C.)*

Called *The Father of Medicine,* the Greek physician Hippocrates is credited with works on epidemics, diet and public health that were used in the teaching of medicine for hundreds of years. It must be noted that his writings appear to have been done by various hands. He is of course the reputed author of the Hippocratic oath, which defines the obligations and duties of a physician.

HIPPONAX *(fl. 6th century B.C.)*

The Greek iambic poet Hipponax was banished from Ephesus for his verses taunting the tyrants there. He became known as *The Father of Parody*.

His Accidency—See ARTHUR, CHESTER A.; FILLMORE, MILLARD; JOHNSON, ANDREW; TYLER, JOHN.

His Chain Gang Excellency—See TALMADGE, EUGENE.

His Fraudulency—See HAYES, RUTHERFORD B.

His Rotundity—See ADAMS, JOHN.

His Royal Rudeness—See EDWARD, PRINCE OF ENGLAND.

Historian Who Never Wrote a Book, The—See ACTON, JOHN EMERICH EDWARD DALBERG-ACTON, LORD.

HITCHCOCK, ALFRED (1899–1980)

English film director Alfred Hitchcock viewed with disfavor his nicknames *The Portly Master of the Involuntary Scream* and *The Cherubic Master of Suspense* as "lacking a leanness of style." Many film critics agreed that the descriptions had a pomposity Hitchcock's films avoided.

HITCHCOCK, THOMAS, JR. (1900–1944)

One of the foremost polo players in the world, Tommy Hitchcock, Jr., was nicknamed *The Babe Ruth of Polo*. A lieutenant colonel commanding a U.S. fighter plane force during World War II, he was killed in a plane crash in England in 1944.

HITLER, ADOLF (1889–1945)

The head of Nazi Germany, Adolf Hitler was referred to disparagingly as *The Little Napoleon* and *The Little Dictator* early in his career, when he was thought not to be the menace Napoleon had been. He was also given the Napoleonic sobriquet *The Little Corporal,* since he had served as a corporal in the Bavarian army in World War I and was short in stature. The Allies, especially Churchill, referred to him as *The Paperhanger,* although there is no evidence he ever engaged in such an occupation. The most telling lampoon was *Schickelgruber,* the family name of his father's mother, which was used by foes in Vienna to point up the fact that Hitler was the son of a bastard (although his father had won the right to be known by *his* father's family name, Hitler). Secretly, the anti-Hitler plotters of the July 1944 bomb attempt on his life and several earlier attempts that had gone awry, referred to him as *The Buffoon.* The term apparently was first used in 1936 by Claus von Stauffenberg, the colonel who eventually planted the bomb in the 1944 bunker assassination attempt.

HOBBES, THOMAS (1588–1679)

English philosopher Thomas Hobbes was called *The Atheist* and *The Mighty Leviathan* for his materialistic approach to matters of human nature, of which he took a pessimistic view. In his *Leviathan* he argued for an absolutist government to avoid the destruction of man. His admiring companions referred to him as *The Bear* because he swore ferociously when his views were challenged. Aubrey writes in his *Letters* (vol. ii.): "The witts at Court were wont to bayte him; but he would make his part good, and feared none of them. The King would call him the Beare: Here comes the Beare to be bayted."

***Hobbes Inverted*—See HUME, DAVID.**

HOCH, JOHANN (1855–1906)

A Chicago mass murderer of women, Johann Hoch was dubbed *Bluebeard Hoch* some 15 years before Frenchman Henri Landru was nicknamed after the eternal Bluebeard. In many respects Hoch was more deserving of the title. He was known to have bigamously married some 55 women and murdered somewhere between 15 and 25, with other estimates ranging much higher. Landru's total was only 10.

***Hockey Enforcer, The*—See SCHULTZ, DAVE "the Hammer."**

HOFER, ANDREAS (1767–1810)

Tyrolese patriot Andreas Hofer, who headed the insurrection of 1809, was to become known as *The*

Wallace of Switzerland because, like the Scottish national hero, he was noted for his courage and met death at an early age.

HOFFMAN, ABBOTT "Abbie" (1936–   )

In his more activist civil rights days, Abbott "Abbie" Hoffman was often called *George Metesky*, which was the real name of New York's notorious Mad Bomber.

HOFFMAN, DUSTIN (1937–   )

U.S. screen actor Dustin Hoffman, rather short in stature, is known as *The Little Big Man*, after one of his hit movies.

HOFMANNSTHAL, HUGO VON (1874–1929)

During his lifetime Austrian poet and dramatist Hugo von Hofmannsthal was called *The Poet of a Doomed Austria* for seeking to recreate the culture of a disintegrating empire doomed to extinction. Even his libretti for the operas of Richard Strauss, such as *Der Rosenkavalier,* must be judged in that light—the works of a preserver.

HOGAN, FRANK S. (1902–1974)

The district attorney of Manhattan, New York City for more than three decades, Frank S. Hogan was dubbed *Mr. District Attorney* after a popular radio and television program, but the sobriquet was actually a tribute to his absolute incorruptibility. He successfully prosecuted a long string of racketeers, gangsters and corrupt city officials.

HOGARTH, WILLIAM (1697–1764)

English painter and engraver William Hogarth attempted to win recognition as an important painter, but his canvasses were overshadowed by his skilled, satiric engravings, which exposed the hypocrisy and degeneration of English society. He was called *The Juvenal of Painters,* after the Roman satirist, and *A Fielding Among Painters* and *A Lillo Among Painters,* since he captured both the comedy and tragedy of the low life. His enemies referred to him as *The Pensioned Dauber* after he accepted the position of the king's sergeant painter, and, even more caustically, as *The Beautifyer.* The latter was in disagreement with his subject matter and his thesis that a curve is the most natural and pleasing line.

Hogarth, Jr.—See KENT, ROCKWELL.

HOLBERG, LOUIS, BARON DE (1685–1754)

Louis de Holberg is considered to be *The Founder of Danish Literature.* As perhaps the wittiest and most accomplished writer of light comedy of his time, he was also called *The Danish Moliere* after the French comic dramatist, and *The Danish Plautus,* after the Roman writer of comedy.

Hold That Line—See BLANTON, THOMAS LINDSAY.

HOLDEN, WILLIAM (1918–1981)

Movie actor William Holden, who soared to stardom in *Golden Boy,* was nicknamed *Golden Holden.* However, that label came more often to refer to the fact that he was for many years Hollywood's top-grossing actor.

HOLLADAY, BENJAMIN
(1819–1887)

One of the leading transportation entrepreneurs of the American West, Benjamin Holladay was known as *The Stagecoach King,* a sobriquet with much of the same negative connotation as those applied to later railroad robber barons, such as Jay Gould and James J. Hill. Holladay was noted for driving competitors out of business by lowering prices (and even staging "Indian" raids) and then, having achieved a monopoly, raising rates to unheard-of levels.

HOLLAND, HENRY FOX, LORD
(1773–1840)

British politician George Fox, later Lord Holland, was known to his friends as *The Sly Fox* but to his foes as *Lord Bluster.*

HOLLAND, PHILEMON (1551–1636)

Regarded in his time as one of the foremost and most productive translators of Greek and Latin classics into English, Philemon Holland was referred to in literary circles as *The Translator-General.*

HOLLANDER, XAVIERA—See Happy Hooker, The.

Hollow Earth Symmes—See SYMMES, JOHN CLEVES "Hollow Earth."

Hollywood's Melancholy Blonde—See NOVAK, KIM.

Hollywood's No. 1 Voyeur—See HABER, JOYCE.

Hollywood's Straightest Straight-Shooter—See ROGERS, ROY.

HOLMAN, JAMES (1787–1857)

A British naval lieutenant who lost his eyesight in 1812, James Holman later gained fame as *The Blind Traveler* for writing books on travel and sightseeing.

HOLMAN, WILLIAM STEELE
(1822–1897)

Although no official count was ever kept, 19th century representative William Steele Holman of Indiana was popularly held to have cast more no votes against appropriation bills than any other member of the House. He was thus dubbed *The Great Objector.*

HOLMES, H. H. (1858–1896)

Herman Webster Mudgett, alias H. H. Holmes, was probably the greatest mass killer in American history, having in the early 1890s murdered an estimated 40 to 200 women in a three-story "torture hotel" he built in Chicago at the corner of Wallace and Sixty-third Street. The building was found to contain many torture chambers and air-proof "asphyxiation" rooms. Holmes, who was hanged in 1896, was known as *The Monster of Sixty-third Street.*

HOLMES, OLIVER WENDELL, JR.
(1841–1935)

Oliver Wendell Holmes, Jr., long-time U.S. Supreme Court justice, fearlessly served the liberal cause in famous dissenting opinions, for which he gained the nickname *The Great Dissenter.*

HOLTZMAN, ELIZABETH
(1942–   )

Elizabeth Holtzman won the nickname *Liz the Lion Killer* by unseating long-time Brooklyn representative Emanuel Celler from his House seat. She enhanced her reputation for toughness during President Richard Nixon's impeachment hearings. She lost a 1978 race for the Senate but made a political comeback in 1981 by defeating the candidate of the Brooklyn Democratic machine for district attorney.

Holy Horatio—See ALGER, HORATIO, JR.

Holy Hylan—See HYLAN, JOHN F. "Honest John."

Holy Johnson—See JOHNSON, JAMES.

Holy Satyr, The—See RASPUTIN, GRIGORI EFIMOVICH.

Holy Terror from Texas, The—See MCCLENDON, SARAH.

Home Run Baker—See BAKER, JOHN "Home Run."

Homer of Ferrara, The—See ARIOSTO, LUDOVICO.

Homer of His Age, The—See HARVEY, GABRIEL.

Homer of Painting, The—See RUBENS, PETER PAUL.

Homer of Portugal, The—See CAMOENS, LUIS.

Homer of the Franks, The—See ANGILBERT.

Homer of 20th Century Mythology, The—See LEE, STAN.

Homicide Hank—See ARMSTRONG, HENRY.

Honest, The—See INNOCENT VIII, POPE.

Honest Abe—See LINCOLN, ABRAHAM.

Honest Dictator, The—See BREZHNEV, LEONID.

Honest Gambler, The—See HARGRAVES, DICK.

Honest George—See GRAHAM, GEORGE.

Honest Hero of the Black Sox Scandal, The—See KERR, RICHARD H.

Honest Jack—See FELTON, JOHN.

Honest King, The—See VICTOR EMMANUEL II OF ITALY.

Honey—See WALKER, WILLIAM.

Honey Fitz—See FITZGERALD, JOHN F.

Honie-Tongued—See SHAKESPEARE, WILLIAM.

HOOD, JOHN BELL (1831–1879)

Confederate general John Bell Hood became notorious as *Butcher Hood* in the later stages of the Civil War, even to his own men, because he sacrificed so many soldiers in his campaigns.

Hoodlum Priest, The—See CLARK, CHARLES DISMAS.

HOOK, SIDNEY (1902–)

Professor emeritus of philosophy at New York University, Sidney Hook is recognized as one of America's most influential, if controversial, thinkers. He is often called *The American Socrates*.

HOOKER, JOSEPH "Fighting Joe" (1814–1879)

Early in the Civil War, Gen. Joseph Hooker, the commander of a Union division, engaged the enemy at the Battle of Williamsburg, and a press account was wired back to various newspapers in the North with the headline "Fighting—Joe Hooker." This was quickly transformed into *Fighting Joe Hooker,* a nickname he never lost. However, he has been more lastingly connected with a different sort of nickname that refers to other activities. Among his troops the general was famed for the many women callers to his tent. In time they were referred to leeringly as "Hooker's women," and over the years the term "hooker" came to mean prostitute.

Hoosier Shakespeare, The—See GRAY, FINLY HUTCHINSON.

HOOVER, HERBERT (1874–1964)

The 31st president of the United States, Herbert Hoover had been considered a strong leader prior to the Depression, which began during his term of office. He had emerged as the strongman in cabinets under previous presidents and was called *The Chief.* For his relief work following World War I, he was dubbed *The Friend of Helpless Children* and *The Man of Great Heart.* However, during the Depression he became an object of ridicule, reinforced by his incredible statements, such as this 1931 comment to newspaper reporters: "What our country needs is a good big laugh. If someone could get off a good joke every ten days, I think our troubles would be over." Hoover also inspired a number of nicknames for other things. The shantytowns of the unemployed poor people became Hoovervilles; old newspapers wrapped around themselves for warmth were Hoover Blankets; rabbits shot for food were Hoover Hogs; broken-down cars pulled by mules were Hoover Wagons; shoe soles with holes were Hoover Soles; and empty pockets turned inside out were Hoover Flags.

HOOVER, J. EDGAR (1895–1972)

FBI Director J. Edgar Hoover was caustically nicknamed *The Master of Deceit* within certain ranks of the FBI, especially those agents and officials involved in the research, editing and writing of the book *Masters of Deceit,* an anti-Communist study that bore Hoover's name as author. They were incensed that Hoover kept the royalties for himself rather than giving them to charity or to a fund for the agents in general, and they were even more annoyed at being forced to listen to Hoover's complaints that the income from the book raised his tax bracket. According to William C. Sullivan, the former No. 3 man in the bureau, the joke went, *"Masters of Deceit,* written by the Master of Deceit who never even read it."

HOPE, BOB *(1903–   )*

Comedian Bob Hope was born Leslie Townes Hope, and, perhaps with an eye to his potential, his classmates called him *Hope-Les.*

Hope-Les—See HOPE, BOB.

HOPITAL, MICHEL DE L' *(1505–1573)*

Regarded as one of the most virtuous men in 16th century France, Michel de l'Hopital was called in his time *A Second Cato the Censor,* after that virtuous Roman statesman. Opposing the establishment of the Inquisition, he gave up his post as lord chancellor so as not to aid the king and queen mother in their campaign against reformers.

HOPKINS, HARRY L. *(1890–1946)*

Harry L. Hopkins, presidential assistant to Franklin D. Roosevelt, was known to the White House staff and to Roosevelt as *Harry the Hop.* Political detractors labeled him *A Combination Machiavelli, Svengali and Rasputin,* and *The Backstairs Intriguer.*

HOPKINS, JOHN *(1663–1732)*

One of the most denounced financial speculators in England, London merchant John Hopkins rapaciously acquired wealth through some rather dubious stock speculations, earning him the designation *Vulture Hopkins.* He made a considerable fortune out of the so-called South Sea Bubble.

HOPKINS, MATTHEW *(fl. c. 1645)*

A pretended discoverer of witches, in the mid-17th century, Matthew Hopkins whipped up witch-hunting in England to its worst excesses and won for himself the sobriquet *Witchfinder General.*

HOPKINS, SAMUEL *(1721–1803)*

If not the first advocate in America of abolishing the slave trade, Samuel Hopkins was probably the first effective one. His personal campaigning in 1774 secured the passage of a law in the Rhode Island Colony that forbade the importing of slaves and won him the accolade *The Father of Abolition.* In 1785, largely through his agitation, another law was passed declaring the children of slaves born after March 1 of that year to be automatically free.

HOPKINSON, FRANCIS *(1737–1791)*

Noted for his satires, American Revolutionary War leader Francis Hopkinson was called *One of the People* and *A Lover of Candour.* He designed the American flag.

HOPPER, EDNA WALLACE *(?–1959)*

The star of the great 1900 American stage hit *Floradora,* Edna Wallace Hopper became *The Eternal Flapper* and *Grandma Flapper* decades later because of the way she remained beautiful and up-to-date. Her age became a national guessing game. When she died in 1959, it was estimated that she was somewhere between 85 and 99.

HOPPER, EDWARD *(1882–1967)*

Edward Hopper, the famous American realist painter, was nicknamed *The Painter of Loneliness* because a sense of silence and isolation pervades his works. Some have speculated his loneliness was fueled by a lack of success early in his career. Indeed, from 1900 to 1923, Hopper sold only two paintings.

HORACE *(65–8 B.C.)*

The Roman poet Horace was more correctly named Quintus Horatius. As he grew more corpulent he became known as *Quintus Horatius Flaccus,* or *Quintus Horatius the Flabby.*

Horace of France, The—See **RONSARD, PIERRE DE.**

Horace of His Age, The—See **GHIBBES, JAMES ALBAN.**

HORROWITZ, HARRY—See Gyp the Blood.

Horse Emperor, The—See **CALIGULA.**

Horse Face—See **FERNANDEL.**

Horseback Harry—See **SMITH, HARRY.**

Horse-Kruger—See **KRUGER, FRANZ.**

HORTHY, MIKLOS VON NAGYBANYA *(1869–1957)*

Miklos von Nagybanya Horthy commanded the Austro-Hungarian fleet in World War I and subse- quently ousted the Bela Kun regime as the so-called *Admiral on Horseback.* He served as regent of Hungary from 1920 to 1944.

Hostess with the Mostes', The—See **MESTA, PEARL.**

Hot—See **CARTER, JIMMY.**

Hot Shot Poet from Poetville, The—See **GOULD, JOE.**

Hot Stove Jimmy—See **QUINN, JAMES ALOYSIUS.**

Hotcake Baron, The—See **CHILDS, WILLIAM.**

Hotspur—See **PERCY, HENRY.**

Hotspur of Debate, The—See **STANLEY, LORD.**

HOUBRAKEN, JAKOB *(1698–1780)*

Eighteenth century painter and engraver Jakob Houbraken, a contemporary of the English artist and satirical engraver William Hogarth, worked in a style that earned him the sobriquet *The Dutch Hogarth.*

HOUDINI, HARRY *(1874–1926)*

Hungarian-born U.S. magician and illusionist Harry Houdini was commonly nicknamed *The Handcuff King,* even though manipulating his hands free was one of his easier tricks. He was also called *The King of the Escapologists,* making astounding escapes from obviously secure prison cells and, while handcuffed, from boxes chained all around and submerged in a tank of water.

Houdini in the White House, The—See ROOSEVELT, FRANKLIN D.

Hound of Hell, The—See LEO X, POPE.

Hourglass Girl, The: ANNA HELD (1873–1918)

Anna Held, the glamorous star of the Ziegfeld Follies, was dubbed *The Hourglass Girl* because of her 18-inch waist. It was said that her rigorous diet and extremely tight corsets contributed to her death at an early age.

HOUSTON, SAMUEL (1793–1863)

Having played a vital role in the fight with Mexico that led to the establishment of the Republic of Texas, Sam Houston won the honorific *The Father of Texas*. The Indians, however, were not so high-minded in their assignment of nicknames, using more elementary criteria. To them Houston was *Big Drunk*.

HOUSTON, TEMPLE (1860–1905)

Colorful Oklahoma lawyer Temple Houston, the son of Texas patriot Sam Houston, was nicknamed *Rattlesnake Houston* because he habitually wore a necktie made of the reptile's skin.

Houston Hurricane, The—See FOYT, A. J.

HOW, JAMES EADS (1868–1930)

An heir to the Eads bridge-building family fortune, James Eads How was left a quarter of a million dollars by his mother, but refused to touch it. Believing it was immoral to live on money he had not earned, he traveled about the country on foot, seeking whatever work he could find and winning the nickname *The Millionaire Hobo*.

HOWARD, JOHN (1726–1790)

John Howard, the British reformer and penologist, became shocked at prison conditions while serving as high sheriff of Bedfordshire, and devoted his life and fortunes to improving the lot of prisoners and the poor and suffering in general. Gaining the popular nickname *The Philanthropist*, he traveled throughout England and Europe on his mission and also studied prison and hospital ships. He died of fever in Russia during one of his trips.

HOWARD, OLIVER OTIS "Bible-Quoting" (1830–1909)

Oliver Otis *Bible-Quoting* Howard was often called *The Christian General*, mainly for his Bible-thumping humanitarian work while directing the Freedmen's Bureau. However, he failed to transfer his energetic efforts on behalf of blacks to the Indians of the West. Although he was enlightened in his treatment of the Chiricahua Apache, he was brutal toward the Nez Perce. The Indians also called him *The Christian General* but found his religious fervor often disconcerting. Once, approaching an Apache council, Howard suddenly dropped to his knees in loud prayer, causing the Apaches to flee, angered that a man would come among them and start making "bad medicine."

HOWE, JOHN (1630–1705)

Puritan clergyman John Howe won his nickname *The Puritan Plato* from Oliver Cromwell, whom he served as domestic chaplain.

HOWE, LOUIS (1871–1936)

The lifetime aide to President Franklin D. Roosevelt, Louis Howe became known as *The Gray Eminence* because his position as secretary to FDR gave him enormous power. The relationship was similar to that of Father Joseph de Trembley—the original Gray Eminence—to Cardinal Richelieu in 17th century France.

HOWE, SAMUEL GRINDLEY (1801–1876)

An educator, social reformer, abolitionist and revolutionary, Samuel Grindley Howe was known as *The Lafayette of the Greek Revolution* for helping the Greeks and serving as a surgeon from 1824 to 1831 during Greece's fight for liberation from the Turks. He contributed funds and raised money in the United States to aid starving people and founded a colony on the isthmus of Corinth for political exiles. He was active in the United States prison reform and in the education of mentally retarded, blind and deaf-mute children. With Julia Ward Howe, his wife, he was a secret supporter of abolitionist John Brown. At one time he was imprisoned in Poland for aiding revolutionary forces there.

HOWE, WILLIAM F. (1828–1906)

One of America's great shyster lawyers, William F. Howe gained notoriety during the Civil War as *Habeas Corpus Howe* because he secured the discharge of literally hundreds of Union soldiers under habeas corpus proceedings by claiming they had been drunk when induced to enlist. Later the partner of Little Abe Hummel in the notorious firm of Howe and Hummel, he was famed for winning the acquittal of some of the worst criminals with his histrionic tactics, which included sobbing or whatever other heart-tugging approach would best sway the jury. He was referred to as *Crying Howe*.

Howell of the Horse Shoes—See HOWEL-Y-PEDOLAU, SIR.

HOWELLS, WILLIAM DEAN (1837–1920)

U.S. novelist and editor William Dean Howells, a champion of realism in literature, was dubbed *The Father of Realism*. Among the writers he influenced were Hamlin Garland, Stephen Crane and Mark Twain.

HOWEL-Y-PEDOLAU, SIR (c. 1284–?)

Sir Howel-y-Pedolau, a Welsh knight and foster brother of Edward II, was nicknamed *Howell of the Horse Shoes* for his ability to break or straighten horseshoes with his bare hands.

Howlin' Wolf (1910–1976)

Howlin' Wolf, born Chester Arthur Burnett, gained his nickname because of his distinctive howl in his music. Regarded by many as the greatest of the bluesmen, he ultimately became a bridge between the blues of the 1940s and the rock and roll of the 1950s. He has also been labeled *A Walking Encyclopedia of the Blues*.

HOY, WILLIAM E. "Dummy" (1862–1961)

A deaf-mute who became an outstanding major league baseball player around the turn of the century, William E. Hoy frequently led his league in walks and stolen bases. He was often baited by opposing fans who called him *Dummy Hoy*. The insult failed to rattle him because, as he noted, he couldn't hear it.

HOYLE, EDMOND (1672–1769)

Famed still today by the phrase "according to Hoyle," Edmond Hoyle codified the rules of card and board games, such as backgammon. In his day he was best known as *The Father of Whist* for having systematized the game in *The Short Treatise* (1742).

HUBER, FRANCOIS (1750–1831)

Francois Huber, a noted Swiss naturalist, went blind early in life because of constant study, but he nevertheless continued his scientific research, with the assistance of his wife. He became famous as *The Blind Naturalist*.

Huck Finn of Radio, The—See GODFREY, ARTHUR.

Huckster of the Tabernacle, The—See SUNDAY, BILLY.

HUDLUN, ANNA ELIZABETH (fl. 1870s)

Black social worker Anna Elizabeth Hudlun was probably the greatest heroine of the Chicago Fire of 1871, as well as another major conflagration in 1874. Offering food, shelter, and other assistance to a huge number of victims, she became known as *The Fire Angel* and *Chicago's Grand Old Lady*.

HUDSON, JEFFREY (1619–1682)

Called *Lord Minimus*, English dwarf Jeffrey Hudson first came to fame in the court of Charles I. At the age of 30 he measured only 18 inches tall but later grew to a height of 42 inches. Unlike most midgets he led an adventurous life, being held prisoner at various times by Flemish and Barbary pirates and, briefly, at the age of 60, by the English on charges of conspiracy. He was immortalized on canvas by the Flemish painter Van Dyck.

HUGGINS, JOHN RICHARD DESBORUS (fl. early 1800s)

Probably the most famous barber during the early years of the United States, John Desborus Huggins was a professional hairdresser and wigmaker who called himself *Empereur du Frisseurs and Roi du Barbieres*. He was certainly worthy of his nickname *The Knight of the Comb*, having attracted a wealthy clientele of ladies and gentlemen—mostly Federalists and aristocrats—in New York and traveled as far as Philadelphia, Boston and New Haven to tend to their wants. As barbers have since then, he took strong political positions. He was famed for his attacks on Thomas Jefferson and his democratic notions, which greatly pleased his clients but brought down on his pomaded head the wrath of Tammany Hall worthies. Brom Martling, an early sachem of Tammany, once publicly rope-whipped *The Knight of the Comb* for his outspoken views on political subjects.

HUGHES, CHARLES EVANS (1862–1948)

Charles Evans Hughes, the American jurist and politician who lost the 1916 presidential election to Woodrow Wilson in a tight contest, was dubbed *The Bearded Iceberg* because he rarely exhibited strong emotions. Lawyers said that while he was on the Supreme Court it was difficult to anticipate how he would vote.

HUGHES, HOWARD *(1905–1976)*

The great industrialist, financier and recluse Howard Hughes had a strong desire to live in total privacy, perhaps even greater than his desire to make money. He was called *The Billionaire Recluse* and *The Bashful Billionaire,* reflecting a trait that made possible writer Clifford Irving's classic hoax of a Hughes "autobiography."

HUGO, VICTOR *(1802–1885)*

French novelist, dramatist and poet Victor Hugo stood in the forefront of the Romantic movement and was called *The Great Romantic.* The sobriquet was also applied to his personal life, however, for he carried on love affairs with literally hundreds of women. His most famous mistress, Juliette Drouet, estimated he had had affairs with at least 200 women between 1848 and 1850. In addition, he was known as *The Indefatigable Egotist* and exhibited his conceit by emblazoning his walls with the motto *Ego Hugo,* or *I, Hugo.*

Huguenot Pope, The—See MORNAY, PHILIPPE DE.

Human Buzzsaw—See ARMSTRONG, HENRY.

Human Polar Bear, The—See BRICKNER, GUSTAVE A.

Human Vacuum Cleaner, The—See ROBINSON, BROOKS.

Human Windmill, The—See GREB, HARRY.

Humanity Dick—See MARTIN, RICHARD.

Humble and Colossal Pissarro, The—See PISSARRO, CAMILLE.

HUME, DAVID *(1711–1776)*

Reducing knowledge to simple sensory experiences, Scottish philosopher and skeptic David Hume gained the sobriquet *Hobbes Inverted* because his beliefs thoroughly conflicted with those of Thomas Hobbes, the English materialist philosopher.

HUME, JOSEPH *(1777–1855)*

Because he constantly predicted ruin and disaster for his country, English politician Joseph Hume was dubbed *Adversity Hume* by detractors, William Cobbett being the first to use the name.

HUME, PAUL *(1915–   )*

The music critic for the *Washington Post* during the Truman era, Paul Hume earned the enmity of the president when he wrote a scathing review of daughter Margaret Truman's attempt to launch a career as a concert singer. In a much-publicized letter to Hume, Truman dubbed him *An Eight-ulcer on a Four-ulcer Job,* a nickname which stuck to him thereafter, as did the president's threat: "I have never met you, but if I do you'll need a new nose and plenty of beefsteak and perhaps a supporter below." While in some quarters Truman's words were viewed as demeaning to presidential dignity, many Americans appreciated his total devotion to his family, and it was felt the incident greatly aided his successful run for election in 1948.

Hump, The—See HUMPHREY, HUBERT H.

HUMPERDINCK, ENGELBERT
(1854–1921)

Noted German composer Engelbert Humperdinck was called *The Modern Wagner* because he was a worshipful disciple of the earlier master and composed his opera *Hansel und Gretel* in Wagner's style. Humperdinck was also a skillful orchestrater of Wagner, particularly of *Parsifal*.

HUMPHREY, DUKE OF GLOUCESTER (1391–1447)

Humphrey, duke of Gloucester, a noted book collector and patron of learning, became known as *Good Duke Humphrey* for these qualities. He donated the books for which the library of Balliol College, Oxford was founded.

HUMPHREY, HUBERT H.
(1911–1978)

A former U.S. senator, vice president and Democratic candidate for president in 1968, Hubert H. Humphrey was affectionately known as *The Hump*, *HHH* and *The Happy Warrior*. In his high school days he was nicknamed *Pinky* because his skin had a pink tint and he sunburned easily.

Hunk, The—See MATURE, VICTOR.

HUNT, E. HOWARD (1918–   )

The author of many spy novels and a former CIA agent, convicted Watergate defendant E. Howard

Hunt was nicknamed *The Compulsive Spy* since, in both fact and fiction, Hunt seemed to have a need to be involved in undercover work. He was also called *The Master Storyteller*, not solely in reference to his writing.

HUNT, "Golf Bag" SAM (?–1956)

One of the Capone mob's great "blazers," *Golf Bag Sammy* Hunt was an inventive hit man who carried automatic weapons concealed in his golf bag when on murder assignments.

HUNT, LEIGH (1784–1859)

British poet and essayist Leigh Hunt is barely remembered today for his poems, but as a journalist he exerted a powerful influence in his time. His sobriquet for George IV, The Fat Adonis of Fifty, landed him in jail for a time, and he himself was dubbed *The Jove of the Modern Critical Olympus*. He was also called *Harold Skimpole*, after the character in Charles Dickens' *Bleak House*. Hunt's friends, if not Hunt himself, saw in the unflattering portrait of Skimpole much of Hunt. Hunt finally protested to Dickens, who apologized to him.

HUNTER, BOBBY LEE (1950–   )

U.S. pugilist Bobby Lee Hunter, a former convict turned professional boxer, was dubbed by the press *The Fighting Con*.

HUNTER, WHITESIDE GODFREY
(1841–1917)

A turn-of-the-century congressman and political leader in Kentucky, Whiteside Godfrey Hunter seemed to organize and run the Republican political machine with iron discipline. There was so little dispute that it was said he had to be wearing rubber overshoes, and thus he was called *The Gumshoe*.

HUNTINGTON, C. P. (1821–1900)

U.S. railroad builder C. P. Huntington was at times disparaged as *Nailed-down Huntington* by detractors for his robber-baron image, created by his famous saying: "What is not nailed down is mine. Whatever I can pry loose is not nailed down."

Hurricane, The—See MIRABEAU, COMTE DE.

Hurricane Bella—See ABZUG, BELLA.

Hurricane Jackson—See JACKSON, THOMAS "Hurricane."

Hurry-up Henry—See KAISER, HENRY J.

HUS, JOHN (1369–1415)

Bohemian religious reformer and martyr John Hus was excommunicated for translating the writings of another reformer, English religious leader John Wycliffe, into Czech, but he continued to preach. He was ordered to the Council of Constance and an imperial safe conduct pass guaranteed his return to Bohemia, but instead he was put on trial and burned at the stake. He was designated *The Czech Forerunner of Protestantism*.

HUSSEIN, ABDUL IBN, KING OF JORDAN (1935–)

King Hussein, the pro-western monarch of Jordan, is known as *The Great Survivor* for having maintained his throne since 1953 despite the turbulent politics of the Near East.

HUSTON, TOM CHARLES (1941–)

The hatred of FBI chief J. Edgar Hoover for Tom Charles Huston was limitless. Huston authored the controversial secret Huston Plan that would have coordinated the nation's intelligence operations under the direct control of the Nixon White House. The Huston Plan would have authorized opening the mail and burglarizing the homes of private citizens and generally stepping up domestic spying. Hoover saw in Huston an aggressive young man who was a threat to his power, and he was particularly incensed by Huston's two-inch sideburns. Thus it became common within the top echelon of the FBI to refer to Huston as *That Hippie*. At interagency intelligence conferences, Hoover refused to call Huston by his correct name and deliberately used wrong ones, such as Hoffman or Hutchinson.

HUTCHESON, MAURICE A. (1897–1983)

Maurice Hutcheson, who succeeded his father, William L. "Big Bill" Hutcheson, in 1952, as president of the United Brotherhood of Carpenters and Joiners of America for two decades, was nicknamed *Maurice the Silent* within the executive council of the AFL-CIO. He often sat through debates without a word as the 28 other members of the council argued heatedly, the prime reason being that, like his father, he was a Republican among a horde of Democrats and thus had nothing to say on political matters.

HUTTON, BARBARA—See Poor Little Rich Girl.

HUXLEY, THOMAS HENRY
(1825–1895)

British naturalist Thomas Huxley was the strongest supporter of the theory of evolution advanced by his close friend Charles Darwin. Because he often carried the Darwinian banner in scientific debates, especially against Bishop Samuel Wilberforce, Huxley became known as *Darwin's Bulldog*. He once wrote to Darwin, in anticipation of a confrontation, "I am sharpening my beak and claws." As a marine biologist of considerable merit, the tall, thin Huxley was called *Stork* by his friends.

Hyena in Petticoats, The—See
WOLLSTONECRAFT, MARY.

Hyena of Brescia,The—See **HAYNAU,
JULIUS JAKOB VON.**

HYLAN, JOHN F. "Honest John"
(1868–1938)

One of the more inept of New York City's mayors, John F. *Honest John* Hylan became known as *Holy Hylan* after he "solemnly swore" to the populace in 1922 that there was no crime wave in the city. He further asserted, "The police are fully able to meet and compete with the criminals."

Hypnotic Hippie, The—See **MANSON,
CHARLES M.**

Hypnotic Plotter, The—See
HAYWARD, HARRY T.

Hypocrite in Public Life, A—See
WASHINGTON, GEORGE.

I

I, Hugo—See **HUGO, VICTOR.**

I Am The Law Hague—See
HAGUE, FRANK.

I Don't Care Girl, The—See
TANGUAY, EVA.

I Will Be Heard Garrison—See
GARRISON, WILLIAM LLOYD.

Iago—See **RIBBENTROP,
JOACHIM VON.**

IBARRURI, DELORES (1895–   )

A much-celebrated Spanish Communist who was active against Franco during the country's civil war, Delores Ibarruri was called *La Pasionaria,* or *The Passionate One.* At the end of the war she fled to the Soviet Union, returning to Spain in 1976 when the Communist Party was legalized by King Juan Carlos.

IBRAHIMA—See Slave Prince, The.

Ice King, The—See **MORSE,
CHARLES WYMAN; TUDOR,
FREDERIC.**

Ice Princess, The—See **KELLY,
GRACE.**

Ice Queen, The—See BURFORD, ANNE M. (GORSUCH).

Icebanks—See FAIRBANKS, CHARLES W.

Iceberg, The—See ADAMS, SHERMAN; LANDRY, TOM.

Idol of the Mob, The—See WILKES, JOHN.

Ike—See EISENHOWER, DWIGHT DAVID.

IKHNATON (*c. 1388–1358 B.C.*)

Known as *The Heretic King,* Ikhnaton, pharaoh of Egypt, shook the country's institutions to its roots during his 17-year reign. He was Egypt's first monotheist, its first known idealist and its first exponent of internationalism. Renouncing new military campaigns, he instead spent defense funds on the building of new temples of Aton, the name of his new religion. Angered by his policies, the country's military leaders forced the pharaoh to divide his power with them. When Ikhnaton died in 1358 B.C., his new religious temples were dismantled, and his name was virtually expunged from Egyptian history. *The Heretic King*'s unknown tomb was not found until 1907.

Imbecile, The—See JANE OF CASTILE.

Impartial Hand, The—See JOHNSON, SAMUEL.

Impeachment Thomas—See THOMAS, J. PARNELL.

Imperial Machiavelli, The—See TIBERIUS CAESAR.

Imperial Peacock of Park Avenue, The—See BONAPARTE, CHARLES JOSEPH.

Impious Buffoon, The—See SWIFT, JONATHAN.

Impressionist Printmaker, The—See PISSARRO, CAMILLE.

In Charge Haig—See HAIG, ALEXANDER M.

Incorruptible, The—See ROBESPIERRE, MAXIMILIEN FRANCOIS MARIE ISIDORE DE.

Incorruptible Sherlock Holmes of America, The—See WOOLDRIDGE, CLIFTON.

Incredible Detective, The—See BURNS, WILLIAM J.

Indecrat, The—See KYLE, JAMES HENDERSON.

Indefatigable Egotist, The—See HUGO, VICTOR.

Indian, The—See PARKER, ELY
SAMUEL.

Indian's Friend, The—See
McLAUGHLIN, JAMES;
WILLIAMS, ROGER.

Indy's First—See HARROUN, RAY.

Inevitable General, The—See
WESTMORELAND, WILLIAM C.

*Infamous Harlot of the North,
The*—See ELIZABETH PETROVNA,
EMPRESS OF RUSSIA.

Infant Casanova, The—See
RIMBAUD, ARTHUR.

Infant of Lubeck, The—See
HEINECKEN, CHRISTIAN
HEINRICH.

Infant Roscius, The—See BETTY,
WILLIAM HENRY WEST.

Infidel Jefferson—See JEFFERSON,
THOMAS.

INGE, WILLIAM RALPH
(1860–1954)

English theologian William Ralph Inge, the long-
time dean of St. Paul's Cathedral, explored the
mystical aspects of Christianity and was noted for
his pessimism, which gained him the sobriquet *The
Gloomy Dean.*

INGERSOLL, ROBERT G.
(1833–1899)

Robert G. Ingersoll, lawyer, politician, lecturer,
soldier and agnostic, found his political career cut
short because of his views on religion. Nicknamed
The Fighting Atheist, he became very unpopular
for his attacks on the Bible but nonetheless had a
profound impact on popular thought in his era.

In-I-Go Jones—See JONES,
EDWARD.

INNOCENT VIII, POPE (1432–1492)

Pope Innocent VIII became known as *The Honest*
because he was the first pope to acknowledge publicly his illegitimate children.

Innocent Sheriff, The—See
PLUMMER, HENRY.

Inquisitor of Atheists, The—See
NAIGEON, JACQUES ANDRE.

Insects' Homer, The—See FABRE,
JEAN HENRI.

Insolent, The—See CAFARELLI.

Inspired Idiot, The—See
GOLDSMITH, OLIVER.

Instant Genius—See REINER,
CARL.

Intellectual Eunuch, The—See
CASTLEREAGH, ROBERT
STEWART.

Inventive Wizard, The—See
WESTINGHOUSE, GEORGE.

*Inventor of the Public Enemies,
The*—See LOESCH, FRANK J.

Inventor of the Snowmobile, The—See
DELOREAN, JOHN ZACHARY.

Inventor of the Telephone, The—See
AMECHE, DON.

Invincible Stonewall—See JACKSON,
THOMAS JONATHAN "Stonewall."

IRELAND, WILLIAM HENRY
(1777–1835)

Nineteen-year-old William Henry Ireland came to
fame when he supposedly found in an English
country manor an awesome Shakespearean trea-
sure trove, which contained a new version of *King
Lear,* a fragment of *Hamlet,* love letters by the
bard to his mistress and, best of all, two completely
unknown Shakespearean plays, *Henry II* and
Vortigern, the latter a romance of the Saxon
conquest. Scholars who examined the find were
ecstatic, and in 1796 *Vortigern* was staged at the
Drury Lane Theatre. However, considerable doubts
about Ireland had already been stirred, and by the
end of the performance the audience was screaming
its disdain. Within a year Ireland confessed he had
forged the entire find, and he was thereafter labeled
The Great Shakespeare Forger.

Irish Plato, The—See BERKELEY,
GEORGE.

IRNERIUS (fl. 12th century)

When the Pandects of Justinian were unearthed at
Amalfi in 1137, Irnerius, the German, was the
first to lecture on them, gaining the sobriquet *The
Lamp of the Law.*

Iron Butt—See NIXON, RICHARD M.

Iron Butterfly, The—See
MACDONALD, JEANETTE.

Iron Chancellor, The—See
BISMARCK, OTTO VON;
HALDEMAN, H. R.

*Iron Chancellor of Prohibition,
The*—See BOOLE, ELLA A.

Iron Czar, The—See NICHOLAS I
OF RUSSIA.

Iron Duke, The—See SULLY,
MAXIMILIEN DE BETHUNE, DUC
DE; WELLINGTON, ARTHUR
WELLESLEY, FIRST DUKE.

Iron Hand, The—See TONTI, HENRI
DE.

Iron Horse, The—See GEHRIG,
LOU.

Iron Lady, The—See THATCHER, MARGARET.

Iron Magnolia, The—See CARTER, ROSALYNN.

Iron Mistress, The—See SHREWSBURY, COUNTESS OF.

Iron Poet, The—See OVERBURY, THOMAS.

Iron Shirt: POHIBITQUASHO (?–1858)

A renegade Comanche chief, Pohibitquasho was nicknamed *Iron Shirt* by Texans because he went into battle protected by a suit of Spanish torso armor, a precaution that saved his life on a number of occasions. He died in May 1858 in a battle with 100 Texas Rangers, when a bullet passed between the plates of his hip armor.

Iron Tooth—See FREDERICK II, ELECTOR OF BRANDENBURG.

Iron Victim, The—See MOLLOY, "Indestructible" MIKE.

Ironclad Outlaw, The—See KELLY, NED.

Ironsides—See CROMWELL, OLIVER.

Irreverent Mr. Mencken, The—See MENCKEN, HENRY LOUIS.

IRVIN, LESLIE L. (1895–1966)

For developing the modern parachute, Leslie L. Irvin was accorded the designations *Sky Hi Irvin* and *The Edison of American Parachute Design.*

IRVING, WASHINGTON (1783–1859)

Among the many sobriquets applied to essayist and historian Washington Irving was *The Addisonian,* given because his work was considered close in literary merit to Joseph Addison's. He was also called *The American Goldsmith* because his prose style was said to match the charm of Oliver Goldsmith's. He earned the accolade *The Father of American Literature* for being the first American man of letters recognized internationally.

IRWIN, JAMES B. (1930–   )

James Irwin, one of the astronauts who landed on the moon on the Apollo 15 flight, said that walking on the moon had been a religious experience, during which he had "felt the presence of God." He retired from the space program shortly thereafter and, labeling himself *The Moon Missionary,* hit the evangelical circuit.

Is It Possible?—See GEORGE, PRINCE OF DENMARK.

ISABELLA OF BAVARIA (1360–1435)

Isabella of Bavaria, the highly unpopular consort of Charles VI of France, was dubbed *The Great Sow* because of her dissolute lifestyle.

ISABELLA I OF CASTILE AND ARAGON (1451–1504)

With her husband, Ferdinand II, Isabella I ruled over Castile and Aragon and was patron to Christopher Columbus. She was called *The Catholic* for her role in reestablishing the Inquisition.

ISABELLA OF FRANCE (1292–1358)

Isabella of France, the adulterous wife of Edward II of England, invaded England with the powerful Mortimers and brought about the death of her husband's advisors, Hugh Despenser and his father. In 1327, she killed her husband by thrusting a hot iron into his bowels. That act won for Isabella the awesome title *The She-Wolf of France.* She was immortalized by Thomas Gray in *The Bard:*

    She-wolf of France, with unrelenting fangs
    That tear'st the bowels of thy mangled Mate.

ISABELLA OF VALOIS (1389–1409)

Isabella of Valois, or France, was called *The Little Queen* because her marriage contract to wed Richard II of England was signed when she was just seven years old. Richard died when she was 10, and she then married Charles, count of Angoulême, a renowned poet. She died at the age of 20.

ISHI (c. 1862–1916)

In August 1911 a strange Indian was found crouching against the fence of a corral outside a slaughterhouse near Oroville, Calif., too terrified or perhaps unable to defend himself against a pack of wild dogs that had cornered him there. At first called *The Wild Man of Oroville,* he was in time identified by scientists as Ishi, the last survivor of the Yana Indians, a tribe that had lived in the foothill country of Mt. Lassen for thousands of years.

The Yanas had made little cultural advances since the time of their Stone Age ancestors and, starting with the California gold rush of 1849, they were being systematically destroyed by organized parties of settlers, professional trackers, and Indian bounty hunters. By 1864 there were perhaps 2,000 Yanas still alive; by the end of 1865 there were no more than 50; by 1911, only one.

While being studied by anthropologists, Ishi was put on the payroll of the University of California as a janitorial assistant at $25 a month, half of which he saved. He learned to handle his own money, shop for food and cook in the white man's style. He taught whites the Yana ways and led expeditions deep into what had been wild Yana country. *The Last Stone Age Man in the United States,* as he was then known, died in 1916, having contracted tuberculosis, a disease passed on by the white man.

ISOCRATES (436–339 B.C.)

Isocrates, the Athenian orator and teacher of rhetoric, died of grief on hearing of the outcome of the Battle of Chaeronea, which was to doom Grecian liberty. He was nicknamed *Old Man Eloquent* centuries later by Milton.

Israel's Patton—See EYTAN, RAFAEL.

It Boy, The—See COOPER, GARY.

It Girl, The—See BOW, CLARA.

Italian Nightingale, The—See CATALANI, ANGELICA.

Italian Pindar, The—See CHIABRERA, GABRIELLO.

***Italy's Greatest Tenor*—See CARUSO, ENRICO.**

***Itinerant Evangelist for Peace, The*—See PAGE, KIRBY.**

ITURBIDE, AGUSTIN DE (1783 or 1784–1824)

Agustin de Iturbide is in many respects logically nicknamed *The Napoleon of Mexico* since he started off as a revolutionary and then made himself emperor.

Ivan Moneybag: IVAN I OF MOSCOW (?–1340)

Ivan I, grand duke of Moscow, was known as *Ivan Moneybag* because he brutally extracted taxes and kept strict accounts on all funds.

Ivan the Terrible: IVAN IV OF RUSSIA (1530–1584)

Ivan IV Vasilievich, grand duke of Moscow and czar of Russia, earned the sobriquet *The Terrible* early in his rule for throwing dogs from rooftops and torturing animals. His reign of terror reached a fever pitch in 1570 when he marched on Novgorod and, in a five-week orgy of violence, killed thousands, including many children heaved into the icy river there. Ten years later he killed his own son in a wild rage.

IVERS, ALICE (1851–1930)

English-born Alice Ivers was one of the few female gamblers of the West who was also an accomplished gunfighter. Nicknamed *Poker Alice,*

she smoked big black cigars and was famed for saying, "I never gamble on Sundays," and "I'll shoot you in your puss, you cheating bastard." In her later years she ran a gambling house-brothel in South Dakota. Found guilty of killing a soldier in her joint in 1920, she got off with probation and a very stern lecture, since she was then 69.

J

***Jack Cade of France, The*—See CAILLET, GUILLAUME.**

***Jack the Giant Killer*—See DILLON, JACK.**

***Jack the Giant-Killer*—See RANDOLPH (OF ROANOKE), JOHN.**

***Jack the Liar*—See REED, JOHN.**

Jack the Ripper (?–   )

Jack the Ripper is the name given to a sadistic murderer of at least five prostitutes in London's East End in 1888. Although he was never identified, intrepid writers over the years have come up with well over a dozen likely suspects. Ironically, the Jack the Ripper murders stirred the Victorian conscience about poverty in the East End.

***Jack-Amend-All*—See CADE, JOHN "Jack."**

Jackie Robinson of Golf, The—See
SIFFORD, CHARLES.

JACKSON, ANDREW (1767–1845)

Andrew Jackson, seventh president of the United
States, was dubbed *Old Hickory* by his soldiers in
the War of 1812 because he was considered ''as
tough as hickory.'' His long string of duels won
for him the sobriquet *The Duel Fighter*. During
his campaigns for the presidency, his foes accused him of being an exterminator of the Indians,
a charge he denied, much against the facts; the
Indians called him *Sharp Knife*. Because of his
strong-willed policies in office, his enemies
derisively referred to him as *King Andrew the
First*. After he finished his two terms Jackson
retired to his estate, the Hermitage, in Tennessee.
There he was called *The Sage of the Hermitage*
by everyone, including his political enemies, who
insisted *The Sage* ruled over his hand-picked
successor, President Martin Van Buren.

JACKSON, FLORA MAE KING—See Baby Flo.

JACKSON, GEORGE PULLEN (1874–1953)

A black American authority on religious folk
songs, George Pullen Jackson was often called
Judge Jackson and, in what some saw a certain
irony, *The Black Giant of White Spirituals*.

JACKSON, HENRY M. (1912–1983)

Sen. Henry Jackson of Washington was nicknamed *Scoop* because of his journalistic background. Generally a liberal on most social issues,
he was at the same time, coming from a defense-
oriented state, a hawk on most military matters.

He was thus also called *The Last of the Cold War
Liberals*.

JACKSON, JOHN "Gentleman Jack" (1769–1845)

One of the most loved men in English history,
Gentleman Jack Jackson was a rarity among late
18th century boxers in that he was a college
graduate, an intimate of royalty and a friend of
aristocrats and poets. The Prince of Wales was often at ringside when *Gentleman Jack* defended his
heavyweight crown. Retiring in 1795, Jackson, despite having a medical degree, opened a boxing
school that boasted among its pupils the poet Lord
Byron, who dubbed Jackson *The Emperor of
Pugilism*. For many years, by royal command,
Jackson displayed his boxing prowess at exhibitions for visiting royalty, including the king of Prussia and the czar of Russia.

JACKSON, REGGIE (1946–   )

Star baseball player Reggie Jackson is known as
Mr. October because of his seemingly inevitable
heroics near the conclusion of the pennant race and
the World Series, when he has a knack for coming up with dramatic home runs.

JACKSON, THOMAS "Hurricane" (1931–1982)

A leading heavyweight boxing contender in the
1950s, *Hurricane* Jackson was so nicknamed because he swarmed his opponent, ignored defense
and gave the crowd the violence it craved. After
several such fights against skilled opponents,
Hurricane was left incapable of further fighting and
had to be kept out of the ring for his own good. For
a time, in later years, he was a down-and-out
shoeshine man and finally a not unprosperous
taxi driver. He died as the result of injuries
received when he was hit by a car as he stepped
out of his cab.

JACKSON, THOMAS JONATHAN "Stonewall" (1824–1863)

One of the most famous Confederate generals, Thomas J. Jackson gained his best known nickname in combat at the first battle of Bull Run. As his Confederate forces were being driven back upon Jackson's brigade, Gen. Bernard E. Bee is alleged to have said: "There is Jackson, standing like a stone wall. Let us determine to die here, and we will conquer. Follow me." Thus both Jackson and his brigade became known to posterity as *Stonewall*. Many claim that Bee was actually condemning Jackson for not coming to his support, but this will never be known for certain since Bee was killed shortly afterwards.

Jackson, a man of awkward appearance, strange manners and fanatical religious beliefs, earned the sobriquet *Tom Fool Jackson* from his students at the Virginia Military Institute. He was also called *Old Blue Light,* a reference to his alleged religious bigotry. In the end, however, Jackson is remembered in the heroic cut as *Stonewall, Invincible Stonewall,* and *The Sword of the Confederacy.* (See also Introduction.)

JACKSON, WILLIAM L. "Mudwall" (1825–1890)

A second cousin of the famous Confederate general Stonewall Jackson, William Lowther Jackson was also a Confederate general officer. However, his field accomplishments never came close to those of his more illustrious relation, and in a play on the latter's nickname, he was disparagingly referred to as *Mudwall Jackson.* (See also introduction.)

JACOBI, ABRAHAM (1830–1919)

A radical who served two years in prison for high treason in his native Germany, Abraham Jacobi, a medical school graduate, came to America and developed the care and treatment of babies and children into the new science of pediatrics. He was designated *The Father of American Pediatrics.*

JACOBI, FRIEDRICH HEINRICH (1743–1819)

German philosopher Friedrich Heinrich Jacobi was dubbed *The German Plato.* Anti-Kantian, he based his philosophy on faith, belief and feeling, by which, he insisted, truth was immediately revealed in the individual consciousness.

JACOBS, HIRSCH (1904–1970)

U.S. thoroughbred racing trainer Hirsch Jacobs, whose horses often won big races, taking in more than $12 million in purses, even though they were of the cheap, or plater, variety. He was thus known in the turf world as *The Emancipator of the Plater.*

JACOBSON, EDMUND (1888–1983)

U.S. specialist in tension control, Dr. Edmund Jacobson was called *The Father of Progressive Relaxation.* His techniques for reducing muscular activity formed the basis of natural childbirth methods.

Jail Robber, The—See FALLON, WILLIAM J.

Jakob the Rich: JAKOB FUGGER (1459–1525)

The scion of a great commercial, mining and banking family of Augsburg, Jakob Fugger II was perhaps the most powerful money man in Europe in the 15th and 16th centuries. Referred to as *Jakob the Rich,* he became the chief financial backer of a number of emperors, kings, princes and popes, always at enormous interest rates despite the medieval ban on usury. With his important royal connections, *Jakob the Rich*'s business ventures were all highly profitable, bringing an estimated annual return of 54 percent, a figure Wall Street would find awesome. The family fortune is still maintained by his descendants.

JAMES, CLIFTON (1897–   )

British actor and impersonator Clifton James substituted for British General Bernard Montgomery on various occasions during World War II, winning him later fame as *The False Monty.* The hoax confused the Germans about Allied military plans.

JAMES, LORD OF DOUGLAS—See Black Douglas.

JAMES, ROBERT (1896–1942)

Notorious California wife killer Robert James was dubbed by the press *The Rattlesnake Murderer* after he attempted to slay his wife by having her bitten by two rattlesnakes. As a backup he had a black widow spider, but in the end he simply drowned her when the snakebites proved less than lethal.

JAMES I OF ENGLAND (1566–1625)

James I of England, a well-read but rather weak and incapable monarch, was labeled by the Duc de Sully *The Wisest Fool in Europe.* After the appearance of the so-called authorized King James Version of the Bible, his nickname was somewhat broadened to make him *The Wisest Fool in Christendom.*

JAMES I OF SCOTLAND (1394–1437)

James I of Scotland was called *The Orpheus of Scotland* for his talent as a poet and for his ability to play eight different musical instruments. He was held prisoner for the first 18 years of his reign and later was murdered by his nobles.

JAMES II OF ENGLAND (1633–1701)

James II of England was called *The Lion* and *A Second Constantine* in Dryden's poems, but his most common sobriquet was *The Popish Duke.* While duke of York under his brother Charles II, he converted to Catholicism in 1671 and the following year he resigned the post of lord high admiral rather than take an anti-Catholic oath. His sobriquet guaranteed that his reign, which began in 1685, would be a short one, and he was forced to flee to France in 1688 following the Glorious Revolution.

JAMES II OF SCOTLAND (1430–1460)

James II of Scotland was nicknamed *Fiery Face* because one side of his face bore a large red spot.

"James III"—See STUART, JAMES FRANCIS EDWARD.

JAMES V OF SCOTLAND (1512–1542)

James V of Scotland was nicknamed *The King of the Commons* because he protected the poor against oppression by the nobles and mingled freely with the common folk.

James the Conqueror: JAMES I OF ARAGON (1208–1276)

Coming to the throne at the age of five, James I of Aragon was called *The Conqueror* because his reign was marked by almost constant conflict. In a six-year campaign, he conquered the Balearic Islands. He also captured Valencia and, for some two decades, engaged in war with the Moors.

JAMESON, GEORGE (1586–1644)

The 17th century Scottish painter George Jameson, a favorite of George I of England, was nicknamed *The Scottish Vandyke*. He studied in Antwerp under Rubens and was a fellow student of Vandyke.

JANE OF CASTILE (1479–1555)

Jane of Castile, who married Philip the Handsome, archduke of Austria, was called *The Imbecile* after losing her sanity, it was said, because of her husband's neglect.

Jane the Grabber: HESTER JANE HASKINS (fl. 1860s–1870s)

One of the most notorious female procurers of the 19th century, Hester Jane Haskins was so proficient at recruiting young girls into prostitution that she was called *Jane the Grabber*. Prosecuted in a New York "grabber scandal" in 1875, she had until then operated relatively free of police interference—so long as she lured only poorer-class girls into "the life." However, because vice operators needed girls of "refinement" to satisfy their clients, she began recruiting girls from good families, thus bringing down on herself the full fury of the law. She was sent to prison and on her release was rousted from the city.

Janus of the Gothic Revival, The—See PUGIN, AUGUSTUS WELBY NORTHMORE.

Janus-Faced Critic, The—See HILL, JOHN.

Jaunting Carr—See CARR, JOHN.

Jay—See STEELE, RICHARD.

Jazz's Angry Man—See MINGUS, CHARLIE.

JEFFERSON, THOMAS (1743–1826)

Thomas Jefferson, third president of the United States, was accorded a great number of honorifics, such as *The Apostle of Liberty, The Friend of the People, The Pen of the Revolution, The Sage of Monticello,* and *The Philosopher of Democracy.* Quite tall for his time, at 6 feet 2½ inches, he was called *Long Tom,* although today his height would not require him to stoop to pass through a doorway.

His foes dubbed him *Infidel Jefferson,* a term used by the *New England Palladium,* which warned its readers that if he were elected president, "the seal of death is that moment set on our holy religion, our churches will be prostrated, and some infamous prostitute, under the title of goddess of reason, will preside in the sanctuaries now devoted to the worship of the most High." Dedicated abolitionist William Cullen Bryant called him *Philosophist* for his relationship with his slave girl Sally Hemmings. John Adams, before his later reconciliation with Jefferson, decried what he regarded as his "ambitiousness" and denounced him as *Oliver Cromwell.*

JEFFRIES, JAMES J. (1875–1953)

Jim Jeffries, world heavyweight boxing champion from 1899 to 1905, was nicknamed *The California Hercules*. He retired from the ring in 1905 but was talked into returning five years later to retrieve the title from the first black champion, Jack Johnson, earning the appellation *The Great White Hope*. The "battle of the century" took place in Reno, Nevada., in an atmosphere of racial hatred, with the crowd applauding wildly as the band played "All Coons Look Alike to Me." However, Johnson administered a fearsome beating to Jeffries before the fight was stopped in the 15th round. (See also Willard, Jess.)

JELLICOE, JOHN RUSHWORTH (1859–1935)

Although British Admiral John Rushworth Jellicoe commanded the fleet at the Battle of Jutland in World War I, after which Germany no longer challenged England's mastery of the sea, he generally received less than unqualified acclaim, being called *The Sailor with a Flawed Cutlass*. One critic said he "fought to make a German victory impossible rather than a British victory certain," and Winston Churchill described him as "the only man on either side who could lose the war in an afternoon."

Jelly Roll Morton—See MORTON, FERNINAND JOSEPH "Jelly Roll."

Jemmy—See MADISON, JAMES.

JENNER, BRUCE (1949–   )

When Bruce Jenner won the gold medal for the decathalon at the Montreal Olympics in 1976, the press immediately dubbed him *The Olympics' In-*

stant Millionaire. Jenner proved to be as shrewd a businessman as he was a talented athlete. "The whole ballgame," he said "is to preserve your credibility and not do something that makes you look like a fool. I don't want to end up like Mark Spitz." Various endorsements and stints as a TV pitchman soon had Jenner collecting an estimated half a million dollars a year.

JENNINGS, AL (1864–1961)

Few nicknames irritate historians of the American West more than *The Last of the Western Outlaws,* given to Al Jennings as the result of a lurid profile of his career in the *Saturday Evening Post*. One historian called Jennings' outlaw rampage "the shortest and funniest on record," since it lasted only 109 days in 1897. Joined by one of his brothers and three saddle bums, Jennings abandoned two proposed train holdups before the gang finally pulled off a successful one that netted them $60 each—and sent Jennings to prison for seven years. With a record like that it is hardly surprising *The Last of the Western Outlaws* wound up with a Hollywood career.

JENNINGS, SARAH (1660–1744)

As adviser to Queen Anne of England, Sarah Jennings, duchess of Marlborough, was so powerful that politicians referred to her as *Queen Sarah* and *The Viceroy*. The Whigs depended on her to maintain their power, and as the wife of John Churchill, she could make or break careers. She finally lost favor with the queen and was forced to retire to private life. Thereafter the same politicians who had previously curried her favor called her *Old Sarah*.

JENSEN, JAMES A. "Dinosaur Jim" (1918–   )

American archaeologist James A. Jensen is called *Dinosaur Jim* for having discovered both the world's largest and smallest dinosaurs. His findings are viewed as confirming the theory of continental drift.

JENYNS, SOAME (1704–1789)

For daring to attack Samuel Johnson after his death, English writer and wit Soame Jenyns was thereafter disparaged by Johnson's literary supporters as *A Little Ugly Nauseous Elf.*

Jersey Lily, The—See LANGTRY, LILY.

Jersey Slick—See TICHENOR, ISAAC.

Jester, The—See LINCOLN, ABRAHAM.

Jesuit, That—See PENN, WILLIAM.

Jew Monster, The—See FRANK, LEO.

Jew-Baiter Number One—See STREICHER, JULIUS.

Jewish Dickens, The—See ASCH, SHOLEM.

Jewish Florence Nightingale, The—See SZOLD, HENRIETTA.

Jewish Plato, The—See JUDAEUS, PHILO.

Jingle Money Smith—See SMITH, JAMES MONROE "Jingle Money."

Joan Makepeace: QUEEN JOAN OF SCOTLAND (1321–1362)

After she married David II, king of Scotland, when she was seven and he was five, Queen Joan of Scotland was labeled *Joan Makepeace* because her marriage was one of the requirements for a peace settlement reached in 1328. She was also called *Joan of the Tower* since she was born in the Tower of London.

Joan of Arc of the Modern Religious World—See UTLEY, ULDINE.

JOAN OF KENT (1328–1385)

Joan, the wife of England's Black Prince (Edward, Prince of Wales, son of Edward III) and mother of Richard II, was called *The Fair Maid of Kent* not only because she was considered "the fairest lady in all the kingdom" but "the most amorous" as well.

Joan of the Tower—See Joan Makepeace.

JOANNA LA LOCA (1479–1555)

An imbecile, Joanna la Loca, the daughter of Ferdinand and Isabella of Spain, was nicknamed *Crazy Jane.*

JOFFRE, JOSEPH JACQUES CESAIRE (1852–1931)

Commander-in-chief of the Allied forces at the start of World War I, Marshal of France Joseph

Jacques Cesaire Joffre was hailed as *The Hero of the Marne*. By the end of 1916, however, Joffre, forced to struggle with military politics and jealousy, saw his command split up.

JOHANN, ELECTOR OF BRANDENBURG *(fl. 1486–1499)*

Johann, Elector of Brandenburg, was noted for his eloquence and called *The Cicero of Germany*.

JOHN, DUKE OF BURGUNDY *(c. 1370–1419)*

John, duke of Burgundy, assassinated the duke of Orleans in 1407, gaining the nickname *The Fearless*. He himself was assassinated 12 years later.

JOHN III OF POLAND *(1624–1696)*

John Sobieski, John III of Poland, was nicknamed *The Wizard* by the Tatars because he scored such incredible victories that they became convinced he possessed supernatural powers.

JOHN XII, POPE *(938?–964)*

Considered by many the wickedest pope of all, John XII gained the sobriquet *The Christian Caligula* because of his gambling, insatiable sexual appetites, and his use of the Roman mob to maintain power. Deposed by the antipope Leo VIII, he regained power in 964 but was murdered by enemies that year.

JOHN CHRYSOSTOM, ST. *(c. 347–407)*

A celebrated father of the Greek Church and patriarch of Constantinople, John Chrysostom—his surname meaning golden mouth—was considered one of the most ardent preachers and was nicknamed *The Thirteenth Apostle*.

JOHN FREDERICK, DUKE OF SAXONY *(?–1532)*

John Frederick, duke of Saxony, joined the reformers of the Church, and, as a friend of Martin Luther, appointed professors of his persuasion to Wittenberg University. He was called *The Second Parent of the Reformed Church*.

John Lackland: JOHN OF ENGLAND *(1167–1216)*

King John of England was called *John Lackland* because, unlike the other three sons of Henry II and Eleanor of Aquitaine, he received no fiefs in England or France. The French nicknamed him *Dollheart* (as contrasted to his brother, who was called Richard the Lionhearted) because he fled the siege of La Roche-aux-Moines in 1214, despite having the advantage of superior numbers.

JOHN OF AUSTRIA, DON *(1547–1578)*

G. K. Chesterton dubbed fabled soldier Don John of Austria, the brother of King Philip II of Spain, *The Last Knight of Europe* because he considered him the epitome of a dying breed. In the largest naval battle of the century in the Mediterranean, Don John destroyed a great fleet of Turkish warships, freeing hundreds of Christian captives used as galley slaves.

John O'Cataract—See NEAL, JOHN.

John Partridge—See PAGE, JOHN.

JOHN PAUL I, POPE (1912–1978)

Although he lived only 33 days as pope, John Paul I survived long enough to win the sobriquet *The Smiling Pope.*

John (Jean) the Good: JOHN II OF FRANCE (1319–1364)

John II of France was mockingly called *The Good* because he was a thoroughly bad king whose reign was marked by looting of the treasury and oppression of the people. Defeated by the Black Prince (Edward, Prince of Wales, son of Edward III) in the Battle of Fortiers in 1356, he died in England after being unable to raise his ransom money.

John Wayne of the Football World, The— See BRYANT, PAUL WILLIAM "Bear."

Johnny Appleseed: JOHN CHAPMAN (1768 or 1774–1845)

John Chapman, who became famous along the frontier as Johnny Appleseed, followed his chosen vocation in life of planting and caring for apple trees and nurseries from the Allegheny Mountains to central Ohio—and beyond. He sold thousands of seedlings to pioneers and gave others away to those who could not afford them.

Johnny Shiloh—See CLEM, JOHN LINCOLN.

Johnny Simmonseed—See HATFIELD, BAZIL MUSE.

JOHNSON, ADAM R. "Stovepipe" (1834–1922)

A Confederate raider under John M. Morgan, Adam R. Johnson was renowned for his resourcefulness. In his most famous exploit, he faked having cannon power by mounting pieces of stovepipe on the running gear of an old wagon. This ruse netted him the capture of Newburgh, Ind., and the nickname *Stovepipe Johnson.*

JOHNSON, ANDREW (1808–1875)

As a U.S. senator, Andrew Johnson became known as *The Father of the Homestead Act* since he had framed and was largely responsible for the passage of the Homestead Bill in 1862. Succeeding to the presidency on the assassination of Abraham Lincoln, he was referred to as *His Accidency,* even more venomously than John Tyler had been when he became the first vice president to replace a president who had died in office. The radical Republicans of the North referred to Johnson as *King Andy* because he opposed any changes in the Constitution that would have prevented representatives and senators of southern states from resuming their seats in Congress after the Civil War. Similarly, they dubbed him *Sir Veto* for vetoing so many bills dealing with Reconstruction. His archenemy in Congress, Thaddeus Stevens, called him *The Unfortunate, Unhappy Man.*

JOHNSON, CLAUDIA ALTA TAYLOR— See Johnson, Lady Bird.

JOHNSON, HEWLETT (1874–1966)

The dean of Manchester from 1924 to 1931 and later of Canterbury, Hewlett Johnson was nicknamed *The Red Dean* because of his advocacy of socialism and his friendship toward the Soviet Union.

JOHNSON, J. MONROE "Rowboat" (1878–1964)

The assistant secretary of commerce of the United States during the 1930s, J. Monroe Johnson later served as chairman of the Interstate Commerce Commission and near the end of World War II, director of the Office of Defense Transportation. He never escaped the nickname *Rowboat Johnson,* pinned on him in 1937, when a congressional investigating committee sought to find out why the Commerce Department was not enforcing the law on sprinkler regulations aboard ships. Monroe made the unfortunate observation that his "knowledge of maritime affairs was limited to rowboats."

JOHNSON, JAMES (1836–1917)

Nigerian bishop James Johnson was dubbed *The Pioneer of African Nationalism,* but both foes and supporters referred to him as *Holy Johnson*—with differing inflections.

Johnson, Lady Bird: CLAUDIA ALTA TAYLOR JOHNSON (1912–   )

The wife of U.S. president Lyndon B. Johnson, Claudia Alta Taylor Johnson became far better known as *Lady Bird* after the family cook described her as looking as "purty as a lady bird."

JOHNSON, LYNDON BAINES (1908–1973)

Lyndon B. Johnson, who became the 36th president of the United States after the assassination of John F. Kennedy, was inevitably dubbed *The Accidental President.* Early in his political career in Texas, he gained the nickname of *Landslide Lyndon* for having won the Democratic senatorial primary in 1948 by 87 votes—an election that critics of Johnson have charged was rife with fraud. Kennedy spoke of his vice president as *A Riverboat Gambler.* As the Johnson administration pursued both the Vietnam War and the Great Society, he was referred to as *Johnson the Tough* and *Johnson the Nice.* Because of the criticism heaped on him for his prosecution of the war, he dubbed himself *The Most Denounced Man in the World.*

JOHNSON, SAMUEL (1709–1784)

Dr. Samuel Johnson, the English lexicographer, poet, essayist, playwright and wit, was heaped with accolades, including *The English Socrates, The Giant of Literature, The Literary Colossus,* and *The Great Moralist.* He was also called *The Impartial Hand,* although many consider his most important work, *The Lives of the English Poets,* to be brilliant but one-sided and especially harsh on Milton and Gray.

JOHNSON, WALTER (1887–1945)

Walter Johnson, the great baseball fireball pitcher of the Washington Senators, was nicknamed *The Big Train* because of the blinding speed of his pitches, which in the early part of the century represented the ultimate in made-made velocity. Had he pitched in more recent years, a sportswriter has opined, he would have been called Jet Johnson.

JOHNSON, WILLIAM "Pussyfoot" (1862–1945)

One of the most colorful "drys" of Prohibition-era in America, William Eugene Johnson became known as *Pussyfoot Johnson* years earlier for his stealth of movement when tracking lawbreakers as a special officer in Indian Territory.

Johnson the Nice—See JOHNSON, LYNDON BAINES.

Johnson the Tough—See JOHNSON, LYNDON BAINES.

*Johnson's Zany—*See **BOSWELL, JAMES.**

JOHNSTON, JAMES A. (1876–1958)

The first warden of Alcatraz, James A. Johnston was described in the press of the day as ''tough but kindly.'' To the prisoners, however, he was known as *Saltwater Johnston* because they regarded him as bitter as saltwater. Eventually, and often against Johnston's desires, the hard rules he established were eased by federal prison authorities, until Alcatraz was finally closed in the 1960s, the general acknowledgment being that a ''supertough'' prison was an unworkable concept.

JOHNSTON, JOHN ''Liver Eating'' (1826?–1900)

One of the most colorful of western trappers and mountain men, John Johnston waged a four-decade war against the Crow Indians in what is now Wyoming after they killed his young and pregnant Chinook Indian wife. Not satisfied with merely dispatching his foes, he developed the odd peccadillo of cutting out and eating their livers. No one ever figured out why he did so; it was not a custom rooted in any white man's or Indian tribe's lore. However, other whites simply allowed Johnston his pastime and settled for calling him *Liver-Eating Johnston.* His habit—which reached a toll of an estimated 250 to 300 victims—never caused him any trouble with the rest of society, and he was utilized by the U.S. Army as a scout and served as a lawman in several communities. In the late 1880s, now along in years, Johnston made peace with the Crow, who even took him into the tribe as a blood brother. It was, other whites theorized, an act of self-preservation by the Indians.

*JOHNSTON, VELMA—*See **Wild Horse Annie.**

JOHNSTONE, WILLIAM (fl. 16th century)

A noted 16th century freebooter, William Johnstone was a celebrated hero of Scottish song and called *The Galliard,* a term for a lively, gay and dissipated character.

*Jolly Imbiber, The—*See **FRANKLIN, BENJAMIN.**

JONES, CHARLES COLCOCK (1831–1893)

The distinguished 19th century historian of Georgia, Charles Colcock Jones was designated *The Macaulay of the South.*

JONES, CHARLES JESSE ''Buffalo'' (1844–1919)

The man most responsible for the near extinction of the buffalo, hunter Charles Jesse *Buffalo* Jones underwent a transformation in 1875 and began setting up sanctuaries for the animals. In the 1880s he captured 58 buffalo calves and put them on his Kansas ranch to breed. It is believed that most of the animals alive today trace back to the efforts of *Buffalo Jones.* In 1902 the ex-buffalo hunter was made warden of Yellowstone National Park.

JONES, EDWARD (1822–?)

The original *Palace Prowler,* Edward Jones intruded in Buckingham Palace almost a century and a half before Michael Fagan, the 1982 palace pest, slipped into Queen Elizabeth II's bedroom. Jones broke into the palace at least four times, and so captured Britain's imagination, he was nicknamed *In-I-Go Jones.* When first apprehended in 1838, he was found wandering through the palace covered with soot (he had apparently climbed in through a chimney). Being only 15, he was sent away with a reprimand. American novelist James Fenimore Cooper was so taken by the exploit he wanted to import Jones to the United States as a "typical example of British enterprise" but the boy's parents vetoed the idea.

In 1840 Jones again was found in the palace, hiding under a settee next to Queen Victoria's bedroom. Entering through an open window, he had stolen a meat pie from the larder and had hidden for two days in an attic. This time he was jailed for three months. As soon as he got out, he went straight back to the palace but was caught by a night watchman. He served three more months and subsequently made a fourth attempt. On being apprehended, he was "encouraged" to enlist in the Royal Navy, and no more was heard of *In-I-Go* after that.

JONES, INIGO (1573–1651)

Inigo Jones studied architecture in Italy and later introduced the Palladian style of architecture to England, winning the title of *The English Palladio,* the latter being a celebrated 16th century Italian architect called the Architect of Reason. Jones prepared designs for the palace at Whitehall.

JONES, JOHN P. (1829–1912)

A senator from Nevada from 1863 to 1893, John P. Jones was considered one of the West's greatest advocates of the common people. Called *The Nevada Commoner,* he enjoyed tremendous support from miners.

JONES, JOHN PAUL (1747–1792)

The Scottish-American naval hero of the Revolutionary War, John Paul Jones was called *The Bayard of the Sea,* after the 16th century French military hero Pierre du Terrail, Chevalier de Bayard, whose daring in battle he matched. Later in France and Russia, Jones became known to ladies at court as *The Agreeable Sea Wolf* for his boudoir daring, which became legendary.

JONES, SAMUEL M. "Golden Rule" (1846–1904)

A Toledo, Ohio manufacturer in the 1890s, Samuel M. Jones gained the sobriquet *Golden Rule Jones* because, instead of posting restrictive rules around the plant, he tacked up copies of the Golden Rule: "Whatsoever ye would that men should do to you, do even so to them." As a result the factory enjoyed what was described as an unparalleled harmonious relationship between employer and employees.

JONES, WILLIAM (1726–1800)

The founder of *The British Critic,* English clergyman and theological writer William Jones authored a number of works defending the doctrine of the Trinity and was thus dubbed *Trinity Jones.*

JONSON, BEN (c. 1573–1637)

Elizabethan poet and playwright Ben Jonson was known by such sobriquets as *The English Horace* and, sadly, *The Greatest Unread English Author.* However, the most fitting was *Rare Ben Jonson,* since he remained one of a kind, even after death. Jonson was buried standing up in Westminster Abbey to save on the cost of grave space.

JOPLIN, SCOTT (1868–1917)

By the age of 14, black jazz great Scott Joplin was playing piano in cafes, saloons and whorehouses and gaining renown for his syncopated rhythms, which at first were called "ragged time." Not until a half century after his death did he gain the acknowledgment of white Americans as *The King of the Ragtime Composers,* however, for writing such famous rags as "Maple Leaf Rag" and "The Entertainer," which became the theme for the hit movie *The Sting.* Never achieving the accolades or financial rewards the public heaped on other musical greats, Joplin died in a New York mental hospital, not long after his ragtime opera *Treemonisha,* which dealt with black freedom, flopped.

JORGENSEN, CHRISTINE (1927–)

In 1950 George Jorgensen became Christine Jorgensen, the first American to undergo a sex-change operation in Denmark, and was celebrated in the sensational press and in nightclub jokes as *The Lad Who Became a Lady.* In the 1970s she was quoted as saying, "Twenty years ago I met with almost complete hostility. Today there's almost complete comprehension."

JOSEPH OF COPERTINO, ST. (1603–1663)

Giuseppe Desa, later to be known as St. Joseph of Copertino, became famous as *The Flying Monk* because of his remarkable levitations during ecstatic religious states. In February 1651 Johann Friedrich, duke of Brunswick, traveled to the village of Copertino—located in the heel of Italy—in the hope of witnessing one of Joseph's miraculous flights. On two successive days, while in the midst of saying Mass, Joseph rose in the air in a kneeling position and then moved slowly backward and forward. The duke was so awed he renounced the Lutheran faith and turned Catholic. Joseph was sainted in 1767.

Josiah of England, The—See EDWARD VI OF ENGLAND.

Jove of the Modern Critical Olympus, The—See HUNT, LEIGH.

Jovial Toper, The—See MAPES, WALTER.

JOYCE, WILLIAM—See Lord Haw Haw.

JOYEUSE, ANNE DE (1561–1587)

Because of his influence over King Henry III, Anne de Joyeuse was known in the French court as *The King's King.*

JUDAEUS, PHILO (c. 20 B.C.– c. 40 A.D.)

Philo Judaeus, a Hellenistic Jewish philosopher of Alexandria, was honored as *The Jewish Plato.*

Judas—See FERGUSON, ROBERT.

Judas of the West, The—See CLAY, HENRY.

JUDD, WINNIE RUTH (1909–)

For 40 years Winnie Ruth Judd, perpetrator of the grisly murder and dismemberment of two young women in Arizona in 1931, was the darling of newspaper headline writers, who dubbed her *The Tiger Woman.* The sobriquet derived from the violent temper she displayed at her original trial and her seven prison escapes, one of which lasted seven years. For a long time the thought of *The Tiger Woman* on the loose sent chills through millions of American newspaper readers, but when she was paroled in 1971, oddly, no one much cared.

Judge Gripus—See YORKE, PHILIP.

Judge Jackson—See **JACKSON, GEORGE PULLEN.**

Jug Marker, The—See **GREEN, EDDIE.**

JULIAN (331–363)

Reared a Christian, the Roman emperor Julian, Flavius Claudius Julianus, was dubbed *The Apostate* when he cultivated pagan learning and culture and announced his conversion in 361. However, he did not engage in any systematic persecutions of Christians, and he died in a war with the Persians.

JULIAN, GEORGE WASHINGTON (1817–1899)

One of the founders of the Free Soil Party in 1848, George Washington Julian was deprecated as *The Orator of Free Dirt* by those opposed to such a policy and as *The Apostle of Disunion* by pro-slavers since he favored abolition. Both groups agreed the logical sobriquet for him was *Wooly-head.*

JULIUS II, POPE (1443–1513)

A pope whose reign was given over almost entirely to political and military efforts to reestablish sovereignty over papal lands, Julius II was dubbed *A Second Mars,* after the god of war.

JUNG, CARL GUSTAV (1875–1961)

Swiss pioneer psychologist and psychiatrist Carl Jung, who created the terms "extrovert," "introvert" and "inferiority complex," developed the theory that stressed human drive toward religion rather than toward sex. He was dubbed *The Father of Analytic Psychology.*

JUNOT, ANDOCHE (1771–1813)

Napoleon nicknamed Andoche Junot, one of his most daring and impetuous generals, *The Tempest.*

Just, The—See **ARISTIDES.**

Justice Department Waterboy—See **REHNQUIST, WILLIAM.**

Justice Greedy—See **MICHELL, FRANCIS.**

Juvenal of Chivalry, The—See **MOLK, HEINRICH VON.**

Juvenal of Painters, The—See **HOGARTH, WILLIAM.**

Juvenile Lead, The—See **EDEN, ANTHONY.**

K

Kaffir King, The—See **BARNATO, BARNETT ISAACS "Barney."**

KAGAWA, TOYOHIKO (1888–1960)

Japanese Christian convert and social reformer Toyohiko Kagawa renounced his wealthy Buddhist origins and worked for the poor in pre-World War

II Japan. He opposed the 1936 war against China as well as World War II and preached peace. He was imprisoned briefly and ordered by the Tojo government to stop all writings and preaching about the war. Called *The Gandhi of Japan,* he was a leader in the postwar democratic movement in Japan.

KAHN, ALBERT *(1869–1942)*

German-American architect and engineer Albert Kahn was called *The World's No. 1 Industrial Architect* for sparking the revolution in the construction of industrial plants. His crowning achievement was the Ford aircraft plant at Willow Run.

KAISER, HENRY J. *(1882–1967)*

American industrialist Henry J. Kaiser won the accolade *Hurry-up Henry* during World War II when, although he was new to shipbuilding, he nonetheless had his yards turn out vessels with amazing speed, including a 10,500-ton liberty ship built in four days and 15 hours.

Kaiser Bill—See WILLIAM II, KAISER.

KALAKAUA, DAVID: KING OF HAWAII *(1836–1891)*

Because of his penchant for the good and happy life, David Kalakaua, king of Hawaii, was known as *The Merry Monarch,* a nickname previously accorded Charles II, the Restoration king of England. Perhaps a better identification of Kalakaua, reflecting the tragedy of a dying era, was *The Last King of Paradise.*

KALIDASA *(fl. 5th century)*

Kalidasa, the Hindu dramatist and poet, has been designated *The Shakespeare of India.*

KALTENBORN, H. V. *(1879–1965)*

H.V. Kaltenborn, a long-time radio news commentator for CBS, was often referred to as *The Dean of Commentators* and, more picturesquely, *Columbia's Gem of the Ozone.*

KALTENBRUNNER, ERNST *(1902–1946)*

Austrian Nazi leader Ernst Kaltenbrunner, the successor to Hangman Heydrich as chief of German security, was said to have been the only man his superior, Heinrich Himmler, feared. Himmler secretly nicknamed him *The Callous Ox.*

KAMEHAMEHA I, KING OF HAWAII *(1758?–1819)*

Kamehameha I, king of Hawaii, was known as *The Napoleon of the Pacific* after he gained control of northern Hawaii and conquered a number of other islands.

KANG-WANG *(1098–1152)*

The reign of Kang-wang, the third ruler of China's Thow dynasty, was so tranquil that he was called *The Peaceful.* We are told that not a single person was put to death or imprisoned during his rule.

Kansas Dry, The—See GUYER, ULYSSES SAMUEL.

Kansas' Senator at Large—See WHITE, WILLIAM ALLEN.

KANT, IMMANUEL *(1724–1804)*

Although he led in most respects an isolated existence, German philosopher Immanuel Kant was one of the foremost thinkers of the Enlightenment, and his influence, if somewhat on the wane, probably extended further than that of any other thinker of modern times. For trying to reconcile two previously divergent trends in philosophy—the empiricism of Hume (who, Kant said, had aroused him from dogmatic slumbers) and rationalism—he was called *The Founder of Critical Philosophy*.

Oddly, this worldly man of thought never traveled more than 40 miles from Konigsberg, refusing all appointments elsewhere and finally obtained the chair of logic and metaphysics at the University of Konigsberg at the age of 46. A bachelor, Kant followed an incredibly meticulous and unswerving routine in his personal life. After being awakened at 5 a.m. by his manservant, he studied for two hours, lectured at the school for two more, and then returned to his studies until his midday meal, the only regular one of the day. From 4 to 5 in the afternoon he walked, regardless of the weather, and spent the evening in lighter reading until retiring at 10 p.m. He was such a creature of habit that the citizens nicknamed him *The Timepiece of Konigsberg* because, it was said, they could set their watches by him. Kant's restricted life did not isolate him from worldly affairs, however, and he supported both the American and French revolutions.

KAPLAN, NATHAN—See Kid Dropper.

KARAMZIN, NICHOLAS MIKHAELOVITCH (1765–1826)

Russian poet, novelist and historian Nicholas Mikhaelovitch Karamzin was often designated *The Russian Livy*, after the Roman historian.

KARPIS, ALVIN "Creepy" (1907–1979)

Public Enemy No. 1 Alvin Karpis long bore the nickname *Creepy* because of his sallow, dour-faced and sinister looks. On the run from the FBI before his capture in 1936, Karpis grew even more creepy, thanks to a botched plastic surgery operation to change his face.

KARRAS, ALEX "Tippy Toes" (1935–   )

One of professional football's most feared defensive linemen, Alex Karras was euphemistically called *Tippy Toes* because there were few things more awesome for a ball carrier to see than Karras bearing down on him. More appropriately, Karras was said to waddle in like a duck—or rather like a *Mad Duck*.

Katzenjammer Kids, The—See EHRLICHMAN, JOHN; HALDEMAN, H.R.

KAUFMAN, GEORGE S. (1889–1961)

In an era when gangsters were starting to be labeled "public enemy no. 1" and so on, playwright George S. Kaufman became famous throughout the nation as *Public Lover No. 1* when the contents of the "scandalous" diary of actress Mary Astor became public knowledge. A publisher offered $10,000 for a photograph of Kaufman in gym trunks or a swimming suit, and the writer fled Hollywood when subpoenaed to appear at Miss Astor's divorce trial. After the case was settled and Kaufman was able to return to California, he is reputed to have asked every woman he pursued, "Do you keep a diary?"

KAUFMAN, HENRY (1927–   )

Perhaps the most noted "interest-rate bear" in Wall Street circles, Henry Kaufman, an economist for Solomon Brothers, was dubbed in the 1970s and early 1980s *Dr. Doom* for his predictions of ever higher interest rates.

KAUFMAN, MORRIS (1911?–   )

Regarded by many as the foremost square-dance caller in United States, Morris Kaufman was duly awarded the accolade *The Greatest Hog Caller East of the Rockies*.

KAUFMAN, MURRAY (1921?–1982)

Disc jockey Murray Kaufman, better known as *Murray the K,* formed a friendship with the Beatles during their first U.S. tour and boosted them so incessantly that he was soon dubbed *The Fifth Beatle.* His hard-driving style made him the nation's best known DJ in the 1950s and early 1960s, and he was also tabbed *The Gertrude Stein of the Musical Underground.* He was eventually fired for featuring such controversial protests singers as Joan Baez and Richie Havens.

KEARNEY, DENIS (1847–1907)

A rabble-rousing Irish labor agitator, Denis Kearny organized the Workingmen's Party in California and for a time enjoyed considerable power. He was called *The Sandlot Orator* because he held many meetings in vacant or construction lots, running mainly on a platform whose theme was "The Chinese must go!" to protect American jobs. He was instrumental in forcing through a law that suspended Chinese immigration to the United States.

KEARNY, PATRICK—See Trash Bag Murderer, The.

KEARNY, PHILIP "One-Armed Phil" (1815–1862)

U.S. general Philip Kearny was known as *One-Armed Phil* to his men after losing his arm in the Mexican War. His enemies, the Mexicans and later the Confederates, referred to him as *The One-Armed Devil*.

KEATON, JOSEPH FRANCIS "Buster" (1895–1966)

The famous comedian Joseph Francis Keaton got the nickname *Buster* at the age of six months while touring with his show-business parents in a tent show. The boy fell down some stairs and another member of the company, magician Harry Houdini, said, "What a buster!"

KEATS, JOHN (1795–1821)

After his death English poet John Keats was poetically accorded the nickname *Adonais* by Shelley, who compared his untimely demise to that of Adonis. Rather less enthusiastic was Lord Byron, who dubbed him *A Tadpole of the Lakes* and attacked his "piss-a-bed poetry."

KEITEL, WILHELM (1882–1946)

Chief of the German high command during World War II, Gen. Wilhelm Keitel achieved his powerful status by fawning over Hitler and never disagreeing with him. Even German generals who flitted back and forth in their support of Hitler regarded Keitel as a craven sycophant, and a popular wordplay on his name was *Lakeitel,* meaning *Lackey.*

KEITH, MINOR COOPER (1848–1929)

Railroad builder, Minor Cooper Keith, the founder of the United Fruit Company, became the dominant capitalist in several Caribbean nations and was called by boosters and critics alike *The Emperor of the Caribbean*.

KELLEMS, VIVIEN (1896–1975)

A virulent protester of U.S. Internal Revenue Service tax policies, Vivien Kellems was noted for refusing even to withhold income tax deductions from her employees' paychecks and for thoroughly rattling officials about how to handle her. She was in exasperation referred to simply as *The Connecticut Tax Lady.*

KELLEY, WILLIAM DARRAGH (1814–1890)

Pennsylvania representative William Darragh Kelley was called *The Father of the House* because he held his seat from 1860 to 1890 and became the oldest member in length of service. He was more importantly known as *Pig Iron Kelley,* not favorably in all quarters, for his unyielding service to the development of his state's iron and steel industry.

KELLY, ALVIN "Shipwreck" (1885–1952)

Flamboyant stuntman and flagpole sitter Alvin Kelly was nicknamed *Shipwreck Kelly* because he allegedly had been a sailor shipwrecked 32 to 62 times (Kelly seldom told the same story twice). More likely the sobriquet went back to his boxing days when he was known as *Sailor Kelly.* He spent so much time stretched out on the canvas that the fans chanted, ''The sailor's been shipwrecked again.''

KELLY, GEORGE R. "Machine Gun" (1895–1954)

Machine Gun Kelly was purely a product of the press, the FBI and, most importantly, his wife, who succeeded in converting a small-time blunder-

ing bootlegger named George R. Kelly into the feared public enemy of the 1930s. Determined to make him a somebody in crime, his ambitious wife, Kathryn, gave him a machine gun as a birthday present and made him practice shooting walnuts off fence posts. She distributed spent shells from his gun in underworld haunts as ''souvenirs from my husband, *Machine Gun Kelly.*'' The record showed that although he did pull a kidnapping and took part in several minor bank robberies, Kelly never killed anyone or even fired his weapon in anger at anyone.

KELLY, GRACE (1929–1982)

Movie star Grace Kelly, who later became Princess Grace of Monaco, was known in Hollywood for her aloofness and was nicknamed *The Ice Princess.* Robert Cummings, who starred with her in *Dial M for Murder* in 1954, once recalled, ''I think she said no more than 50 words to me outside the script. Long before we thought of her being a princess, the hairdressers would refer to her as 'the ice princess.' Unlike Ann Sheridan, Doris Day, Loretta Young, she wouldn't sit and talk. She was very private, like Ingrid Bergman.''

KELLY, "Honest" JOHN (1821–1886)

A leading 19th century Tammany Hall politician and grafter, John Kelly was so dishonest that journalists, in biting irony, dubbed him *Honest John Kelly.*

KELLY, "Honest" JOHN (1856–1926)

A leading U.S. gambler, John Kelly was nicknamed *Honest* John Kelly and reputed never to have run a crooked gambling house operation. His sobriquet traced back to 1888 when, as a baseball umpire, he refused a $10,000 bribe to favor one team over another in an important game. Thereafter he was the darling of big gamblers, who trusted him to be the dealer in games in which tens of thousands of dollars rode on the turn of a card.

KELLY, JOSEPH "Bunco"
(1838–1934)

Among the most notorious shanghaiers in American history, Joseph Kelly, operating in Portland, Ore., turned thousands of men into unwilling seamen, selling duped or drugged men to crew-short sea captains. His nickname *Bunco* derived from a particularly double-dealing trick whereby he toted on board a victim wrapped in a blanket and deposited him directly into a bunk, explaining the man was drunker than any sailor he'd ever seen. The captain would pay Kelly his standard $50 fee and discover only when out to sea that he had been slipped a cigar store Indian instead of a drunken sailor.

KELLY, MICHAEL J.—See Ten Thousand Dollar Beauty, The.

KELLY, NED (1854–1880)

An Australian outlaw and folk hero, Ned Nelly was considered a Robin Hood figure by small Irish farmers in their struggle against big landowners. He became celebrated as *The Ironclad Outlaw* because he clanged into battles with police wearing armor made of hammered-out plowshares. Finally shot by police firing at his unprotected legs, Kelly was captured and hanged.

Kelly, Shanghai (1835–?)

One of the two famous shanghai specialists named Kelly, *Shanghai Kelly* is known only by his nickname. The most prolific practitioner of his craft

on San Francisco's Barbary Coast, he once filled orders from two ships for 90 seaman in one day. Renting a paddle-wheel steamer for what he said was his birthday party, he charged an admission price for unlimited liquor and beer and pulled out as soon as he had 90 men aboard. The drinks of course were drugged, and when all the celebrants fell into a stupor, *Shanghai Kelly* pulled up to the two vessels and passed over the victims. He continued his nefarious practices until the late 1800s, when he faded from view.

KENNEDY, CRAMMOND
(1842–1918)

At the age of 14 Crammond Kennedy was delivering religious sermons in New York and was being called by the press *The Boy Preacher*. In 1861, before he was 19, he was ordained a chaplain in the Union Army.

KENNEDY, EDWARD M.
(1932–   )

The incident that resulted in the nicknames *The Chappaquiddick Chicken, The Hero of Chappaquiddick,* and *The Coward of Chappaquiddick* was undoubtedly the single most important reason preventing Edward M. "Ted" Kennedy from winning the Democratic presidential nomination in 1976 and 1980.

KENNEDY, JOHN F. (1917–1963)

The 35th president of the United States, John F. Kennedy felt the name of Jack was unbefitting his office and specifically asked newsmen not to use it. He suggested that JFK was shorter and told a more complete message in a headline. During his early Senate days, Kennedy dated a dazzling parade of Hollywood starlets and debutantes and became known as *Washington's Gay Young Bachelor*. His political enemies continued to use the term after his marriage to Jacqueline Bouvier. It is said that Richard Nixon referred to him as *That Fucking Bastard*—especially after one of the Kennedy-Nixon television debates, for Kennedy's use of notes. Nixon in that debate spoke of the dignity of the presidency.

KENNEDY, JOHN PENDLETON (1795–1870)

A 19th century U.S. cabinet officer, educator and editor, John Pendleton Kennedy developed what some regarded as a habit for altering his position on various matters, which won him the sobriquet *Solomon Secondthoughts*.

KENNEDY, JOSEPH P. (1888–1969)

Joseph P. Kennedy, the American business executive and U.S. ambassador to England, was referred to as *The Founding Father* because he sired a political clan of three sons, John, Robert and Edward. Often accused of thinking Hitler was right during the war, he was dubbed *A Chamberlain-umbrella Policy Man*. Lyndon Johnson used the sobriquet often during the 1960 primary campaign.

KENNEDY, ROBERT F. (1925–1968)

Former U.S. attorney general and senator Robert F. Kennedy, generally referred to as Bobbie or Bobby, was assigned the initials RFK to pair with JFK, those of his brother John F. Kennedy. Teamster union president Jimmy Hoffa called him *Poison Snake,* while President Lyndon Johnson, perhaps even more venomously, always referred to him as *The Little Shit*.

KENT, JAMES (1763–1847)

James Kent, an American jurist and writer on legal subjects, had a profound impact on U.S. law in the 19th century and won the accolade *The American Blackstone*. Extremely conservative, Kent was an ardent legal opponent of Jacksonian policies, which he felt would destroy the federal government. He was elected to the Hall of Fame for Great Americans in 1900 but is little remembered today.

KENT, ROCKWELL (1882–1971)

Prolific landscape and graphic artist Rockwell Kent, also known for his espousal of leftist political causes, was nicknamed *Hogarth, Jr.,* for his style of painting.

KERR, RICHARD H. (1893–1963)

Chicago baseball pitcher Dickie Kerr emerged from the sport's worst scandal in 1919 as *The Honest Hero of the Black Sox Scandal*. During that year's World Series he pitched brilliantly and won two games while several of his White Sox teammates went about losing games to Cincinnati. In fact *The Honest Hero* did so well that Eddie Cicotte, a pitcher in on the fix, got jealous and won a game he was supposed to lose.

KERR, ROBERT S. (1896–1963)

Oilman Bob Kerr, a senator from Oklahoma, was a magnetic spokesman for the oil and gas interests and wielded so much power in conservative circles that he was dubbed *The Uncrowned King of the U.S. Senate*. The title was one to which Senate majority leader Lyndon Johnson did not take kindly. Among Kerr's most remembered lines was, "I'm against any deal I'm not in on."

KERRIGAN, JAMES (?–1903)

An Irish coal miner in Pennsylvania, Jim Kerrigan became the first to inform on the terrorist Mollie Maguires, and because of the damage he did to the organization, he was referred to by the miners as *Powderkeg*.

KESEBERG, LEWIS—See Man-Eater, The.

KESSELRING, ALBERT (1885–1960)

One of the most capable German generals in World War II, Albert Kesselring was called *Smiling Alfred* because he seldom did so. He was sentenced to death for the Ardeatine massacre of hostages in Italy, but the sentence was commuted to life, and he was released from prison in 1952 because of poor health.

Ketch, Jack: JOHN KETCH (?–1686)

John Ketch, a famous English executioner, was nicknamed *Jack Ketch,* which became the sobriquet for a number of hangmen thereafter. Adding to the popularity of the name was its use in the puppet play *Punch and Judy.*

Ketchum, Catacorners (fl. late 19th century).

An otherwise undistinguished miner in the Old West, *Catacorners Ketchum* gained his sobriquet and his claim to fame in folklore due to the depredation of his Bible-quoting partner, who made off with all their nuggets. Ketchum said, "If I ever ketch that sneak he'll get a Bible crammed down his throat, catacorners."

Kewpie Doll Lady, The—See O'NEILL, ROSE.

KEYNES, JOHN MAYNARD (1883–1946)

English economist John Maynard Keynes was designated *The Father of the New Economics* for advancing theories that called for increased gov-ernment participation in economic affairs. According to Keynes, private and public expenditures determined income and employment levels. In his Cambridge University days, he was often twitted as *Snout* for his thin face and long nose.

KHALID (or KHALED) (582–642)

Khalid, the Arab military leader who conquered Syria in the seventh century, was designated *The Sword of Allah.* He was one of the first military men to convert to the new Moslem faith.

KHRUSHCHEV, NIKITA (1894–1971)

Soviet premier Nikita Khrushchev was often referred to as just Nikita, even by his political foes both in and outside the USSR. In Hungary, however, he is still referred to as *The Butcher of Budapest* for the brutal Soviet suppression of the Hungarian uprising of 1956.

Kickback Thomas—See THOMAS, J. PARNELL.

Kid Dropper: NATHAN KAPLAN (1891–1923)

Nathan Kaplan, regarded as the number one racketeer in New York in the early 1920s, was better known by the nickname *Kid Dropper.* He earned the monicker in his youth when he became adept at working the dropped wallet racket, in which a billfold jammed with counterfeit money would be dropped in front of a gullible-looking passerby. Pretending to "find" the wallet, *Kid Dropper* would pick it up and claiming to be in a hurry, offer to sell it to the potential victim, who could return it to the owner for a reward. Naturally, the victim would buy the worthless find, planning to keep all the money.

Kid Sheriff of Nebraska, The—See WEDGWOOD, EDGAR A.

Kid Twist: MAX ZWEIBACH (1882–1908)

One of the top gang leaders in New York in the first decade of the 20th century, Max Zweiback was so shifty that he was known simply as *Kid Twist*. Once, engaged in a battle for the leadership of the great Eastman gang, *Kid Twist* proposed a peace meeting with his rival, Richie Fitzpatrick, to be held in a Greenwich Village dive. As the talks began, the lights went out and a gun blazed. When the police arrived, all they found was *Kid Twist*'s foe dead on the floor, a bullet in his heart and his arms folded on his chest. *Kid Twist* sent flowers to the funeral and wore a mourning band on his sleeve for months thereafter. A later gangster, Abe Reles of Murder, Inc., fame, so admired *Kid Twist* for his deviousness that he adopted his nickname.

Kid-Gloves Harrison—See HARRISON, BENJAMIN.

Kid's Killer, The—See GARRETT, PAT.

KIEFT, WILLIAM (?–1647)

William Kieft, fifth Dutch governor of New Netherland, was noted for his violent temper, a family trait. Kieft was a corruption of the Dutch *Kyver*, meaning scolder or wrangler. Washington Irving reported that within a year of Kieft's taking office "he was universally known as *William the Testy.*"

Kiki: MARIE PRIN (1901–1953)

Marie Prin, better known as Kiki, was a French farm girl who came to Paris at 16 and became perhaps the most beautiful artist's model of her day, toasted as *The Venus of Montparnasse*. She posed for such artists as Kisling, Utrillo, Soutine, Foujita, Cocteau and Man Ray. She later helped support herself as a nightclub entertainer but slowly degenerated in a fog of drink and cocaine. She died alone in a dingy garret room, surrounded by many valuable paintings of her by great artists, works she would not part with.

KILGALLEN, DOROTHY (1913–1965)

Newspaper columnist and television panelist Dorothy Kilgallen was known as *The Voice of Broadway,* the name of her syndicated column. Running items that invited rather heated responses, she was subjected to a number of disparaging sobriquets, such as *The Chinless Wonder,* accorded her by Frank Sinatra.

Kill Cavalry Kilpatrick—See KILPATRICK, HUGH JUDSON.

Killer, The—See RANKIN, JOHN E.

Killer of Killers— See MATHER, "Mysterious" DAVE.

KILPATRICK, HUGH JUDSON (1836–1881)

During the Civil War the standard Union infantryman's barb was, "Did you ever see a dead cavalryman?" This did not apply to the command of Hugh Judson Kilpatrick, however. Because of his poor judgment and tactics at Gettysburg and in the Kilpatrick-Dahlgren raid on Richmond, his force suffered enormous losses and they, obviously referring to the infantry affront, dubbed him *Kill Cavalry Kilpatrick.*

KIMURA, HENRY SEIMATSU (1875–1958)

A leading Japanese Congregationalist minister, Henry Seimatsu Kimura was often called *The Billy*

Sunday of Japan because he equaled, in part, the U.S. revivalist's theatrical mastery of language.

Kinderhook Fox—See VAN BUREN, MARTIN.

KING, DOT: DOROTHY KEENAN
(1894–1923)

A New York playgirl whose murder in 1923 caused social scandal, Dorothy Keenan, better known as Dot King, was nicknamed *The Broadway Butterfly* because of her habit of flitting from one wealthy or, sometimes, gangsterish lover to another. The case was never solved.

KING, MARTIN LUTHER, JR.
(1929–1968)

The leader of the U.S. civil rights movement from the mid-1950's until his death in 1968, Martin Luther King, Jr., was called *The Peaceful Warrior* because of his advocacy of nonviolent resistance. In 1964 he was awarded the Nobel Peace Prize. More militant black leaders disparaged him as *De Lawd*, but such criticisms and opposition to his methods faded after his assassination by James Earl Ray.

KING, WAYNE HAROLD (1901–   )

U.S. jazz musician, bandleader and composer Wayne King was dubbed *The Waltz King* for his slow, dreamy style.

KING, WILLIAM HENRY
(1864–1949)

William Henry King, a long-time Democratic senator from Utah, was labeled *The King of the District* because of the power and influence, sometimes described as dictatorial, he exercised over the District of Columbia. He was chairman of the committee in charge of Washington's municipal matters.

KING, WILLIAM RUFUS
(1786–1853)

Sen. William Rufus King of Alabama, who served as president pro tem in the 1830s, was called *Miss Nancy King* by his friends because he was such "a prim, spare bachelor." Such epithets were considerably more ingenuous then than today.

King, The—See PRESLEY, ELVIS.

King Andrew the First—See JACKSON, ANDREW.

King Andy—See JOHNSON, ANDREW.

King Arthur of the Stage, The—See MACREADY, WILLIAM CHARLES.

King Bark: CHRISTOPHER III OF SWEDEN *(?–1448)*

During famines that hit Sweden in the 15th century, peasants referred to King Christopher III as *King Bark* because they had to mix birch bark with meal to fill their stomachs. The king joined his subjects in the practice.

King Bomba—See FERDINAND II OF THE TWO SICILIES.

King Cohn—See COHN, HARRY.

King Coody—See TANEY, ROGER B.

King Hancock—See HANCOCK, JOHN.

King Herod—See BLACKMUN, HARRY.

King Martin the First—See VAN BUREN, MARTIN.

King of Acid, The—See STANLEY, AUGUSTUS OWSLEY.

King of American Clowns,The—See RICE, DAN.

King of Book-Collectors, The—See HARLEY, ROBERT.

King of Brave Men, The—See HENRY OF NAVARRE: HENRY IV OF FRANCE.

King of Broadway, The—See WINCHELL, WALTER.

King of Chefs and The Chef of Kings, The—See ESCOFFIER, GEORGES AUGUSTE.

King of Comedy, The—See SENNETT, MACK.

King of Critics, The—See HEYNE, CHRISTIAN GOTTLOB.

King of Daredevil Comedy, The—See LLOYD, HAROLD.

King of Dulness, The—See CIBBER, COLLEY.

King of Dunces, The—See CIBBER, COLLEY; THEOBALD, LEWIS.

King of European Guides, The—See FIELDING, TEMPLE.

King of Fashion, The—See POIRET, PAUL.

King of Jazz, The—See WHITEMAN, PAUL "Pops."

King of Kung Fu, The—See LEE, BRUCE.

King of Musical Corn, The—See WELK, LAWRENCE.

King of Painters, The—See PARRHASIUS.

King of Passion Fashion, The—See MELLINGER, FREDERICK N.

King of Poets, The—See RONSARD, PIERRE DE.

King of Psychopharmacology, The—See STANLEY, AUGUSTUS OWSLEY.

King of Reptiles, The—See VILLE, BERNARD GERMAIN ETIENNE DE LA.

King of Sleuthhounds,The—See STIEBER, WILLIAM.

King of Sports Promoters, The—See RICKARD, GEORGE L. "Tex."

King of the Bank Robbers, The—See LESLIE, GEORGE LEONIDAS.

King of the Bath—See NASH, RICHARD "Beau."

King of the Bootleggers—See DWYER, WILLIAM V. "Big Bill."

King of the Border—See SCOTT, ADAM.

King of the Cattle Thieves, The—See AVERILL, JAMES.

King of the Commons—See JAMES V OF SCOTLAND.

King of the District, The—See KING, WILLIAM HENRY.

King of the Escapologists, The—See HOUDINI, HARRY.

King of the Fairies, The—See CROKER, THOMAS CROFTON.

King of the Hobos—See DAVIS, JEFF.

King of the Hollywood Air Devils, The—See MANTZ, (ALBERT) PAUL.

King of the Hotel Thieves, The—See DOTY, SILE.

King of the Jukes, The—See COMO, PERRY.

King of the Keelboatmen, The—See FINK, MIKE.

King of the Missouri, The—See MACKENZIE, KENNETH.

King of the Muckrakers, The—See STEFFENS, LINCOLN.

King of the Naughty Nightie, The—See MELLINGER, FREDERICK N.

King of the New Dealers, The—See MINTON, SHERMAN.

King of the Nudie Movie, The—See MEYER, RUSS.

King of the Pulp Writers, The—See BRAND, MAX.

King of the Quakers—See PEMBERTON, ISRAEL.

King of the Quick Quip, The—See
ALLEN, FRED.

*King of the Ragtime Composers,
The*—See JOPLIN, SCOTT.

King of the Road, The—See PETTY,
RICHARD; TURPIN, DICK.

King of the Smugglers—See
HANCOCK, JOHN.

King of the Stakes Riders, The—See
ARCARO, EDDIE.

King of the Swashbucklers, The:
RALPH FAULKNER (1890–   )

Magnificent swordsman Ralph Faulkner has taught
fencing styles since 1929 to many of the movies'
top adventure actors, including Errol Flynn, Douglas Fairbanks, Jr., and Ronald Colman. He was
still teaching swordplay at the age of 91 and regarded as *The King of the Swashbucklers.*

King of Thieves—See SCOTT,
ADAM.

King of Torts, The—See BELLI,
MELVIN.

King Pym—See PYM, JOHN.

King Roosevelt I—See ROOSEVELT,
THEODORE.

King Wampum—See PEMBERTON,
ISRAEL.

Kingfish, The—See LONG, HUEY.

King-Maker, The—See NEVILLE,
RICHARD.

King's Bishop, The—See SINCLAIR,
WILLIAM.

King's King, The—See JOYEUSE,
ANNE DE.

King's Murderer, The—See
BRADSHAW, JOHN.

KIRCHHOFF, THEODORE
(1828–1899)

As near as anyone to being the poet laureate of
San Francisco, German-born lyric poet Theodore
Kirchhoff was dubbed *The Poet of the Golden Gate*
because so much of his verse described the culture
and scenery of the area.

KIRKLAND, RICHARD R.
(1841–1863)

During the Civil War's bloody Battle of Fredericksburg in 1862, a young sergeant from South
Carolina calmly charged between the lines of
fire to carry water to a large number of wounded men on both sides. For his act of heroism,
he was celebrated in both the Union and the
Confederacy as *The Hero-Sergeant of Fredericksburg.* He was killed in the Battle of Chickamauga
the following year.

Kiss of Death Evelyn: EVELYN
MITTLEMAN (1914–   )

Evelyn Mittleman was not the first to be called
The Kiss of Death Girl, but she won that accolade

as the girl friend of Pittsburgh Phil Strauss, the most prolific killer of Murder, Inc. Since three of her previous lovers had died violently, each the victim of the following one, she gained fame as a jinxed lady. Pittsburgh Phil, her fourth, went to the electric chair in 1941, and *Kiss of Death Evelyn* disappeared from public view.

Kiss of Death Girl, The—See Kiss of Death Evelyn.

KISSINGER, HENRY (1923–)

One of the most controversial U.S. foreign policy experts, Henry Kissinger has admirers and detractors both on the left and right. To his admirers Kissinger is known as *Superhenry*. The left disparages him as *The Sammy Glick of the Cold War* for his alleged rush to power, and the far right, typified by William Loeb's newspaper, the *Manchester Union Leader,* called him *Kissinger the Kike.* Those who wish to attack his German background rather than his Jewishness use the sobriquet *Super Kraut.*

Kissinger the Kike—See KISSINGER, HENRY.

Kitchen Counterfeiter, The—See BUTTERWORTH, MARY.

KITT, EARTHA MAE (1930–)

Black American singer and actress Eartha Kitt has sometimes been called *The Bad Eartha* by those opposing her political stands.

KLOPSTOCK, FRIEDRICH GOTTLIEB (1724–1803)

Friedrich Gottlieb Klopstock was dubbed *The German Milton* for having been greatly influenced by

Paradise Lost and modeling his own *Messiah* on the work. This first modern German epic is today widely regarded as dreary, but some of Klopstock's *Odes* have a tenderness and simplicity that depart from the cold classicism that marked earlier German efforts, and they fully justify his sobriquet.

KNIEVEL, EVEL "Evil" (1938–)

Stunt motorcycle rider Evel Knievel, who has escaped many brushes with death and has also had his woes with the law for alleged acts of violence, won the nickname *Evil Knievel.*

Knight in Buckskin, The—See SMITH, JEDEDIAH.

Knight of Romance, The—See PLEASANTON, ALFRED.

Knight of the Comb, The—See HUGGINS, JOHN RICHARD DESBORUS.

Knight of the Most Honorable Order of Starvation—See LIVINGSTON, WILLIAM.

Knight of the Red Rose, The—See TAYLOR, ALFRED ALEXANDER.

Knight of the White Rose, The—See TAYLOR, ROBERT LOVE.

Knight Without Fear and Blame, The—See BAYARD, PIERRE DU TERRAIL, CHEVALIER DE.

Knitting Hattie—See CARAWAY, HATTIE.

KNOWLES, JOE (1869–1942)

In 1913 Joe Knowles gained fame as *Nature Boy* for allegedly having lived two months in the Maine woods without clothing, food, matches, or weapons. His efforts had been sponsored by a Boston newspaper to boost circulation with his stories of survival. During those eight weeks Knowles' adventures, scratched on birch bark and left in the forks of trees for reporters, did wonders to increase the newspaper's readership. Upon his return, however, an envious newspaper attacked him, claiming his experiences were fabrications. As an example it pointed out that his bearskin robe could not have come from a bear he had trapped because it contained four bullet holes. Eventually, *Nature Boy* confessed his hoax.

KNOX, JOHN (1505–1572)

A previously undistinguished Scottish priest, John Knox took part in a Protestant plot in which the able but dissolute archbishop of St. Andrews was killed and then, for good measure, hanged. Convicted for his part in the episode, Knox was sentenced to serve as a galley slave in the French fleet but escaped after 19 months. He made his way to Geneva, where he studied under John Calvin. Returning to Scotland, he assumed the leadership of the Protestant movement and became known as *The Apostle of the Scottish Reformation*.

KNOX, PHILANDER CHASE (1852–1921)

U.S. attorney general under President William McKinley, Philander Chase Knox was caustically called *Sleepy Phil* by liberal elements who were chagrined by his failure to prosecute big trusts.

KNUTSON, HAROLD (1880–1953)

Minnesotan Harold Knutson, a representative from 1916 to 1948, was referred to as *Anti-War Knutson*

when he was for a time the last surviving member of Congress to have voted against a declaration of war in World War I. However, in 1941 Jeanette Rankin, who served from 1917 to 1919 and had also voted against the war, returned to the House, just in time to cast the lone dissenting vote against a declaration of war in World War II.

KOCH, ILSE (?–1967)

Ilse Koch, the sadistic wife of the commander of the Nazi concentration camp of Buchenwald, became infamous for her life-and-death power over inmates, who nicknamed her *The Bitch of Buchenwald*. One of her murderous peccadilloes was using the tattooed skin of exterminated prisoners as lampshades. She was sentenced to life imprisonment after the war. Her husband's behavior had been so gross that the S.S. itself executed him during the war for "excesses."

Kochleffl—See ROSENTHAL, A. M.

KOENIGSMARK, AURORA (1668–1728)

Aurora Koenigsmark, the German beauty and wit, was designated *The Most Famous Woman of Two Centuries*.

KOERNER, CARL THEODOR (1791–1813)

The youthful Carl Theodor Koerner, whose war songs inflamed the Germans to revolt against Napoleon, was dubbed *The Tyrtaeus of Germany*, after the ancient Greek who so inspired the Spartans.

KOHL, HELMUT (1930–   )

Christian Democrat party leader Helmut Kohl, who became chancellor of West Germany in 1982, was affectionately called by followers *The Black Giant,* an allusion to his towering height and generally somber dress. Usually described as genial, Kohl long detested his predecessor, Social Democrat Helmut Schmidt—his physical and temperamental opposite. He once said of him, "I don't have the complexes my opponent has. I don't need high heels. I have no problems of authority."

KOLB, REUBEN FRANCIS (1839–1918)

Reuben Francis Kolb, an agrarian political leader in Alabama, was the Harold Stassen of his day. He ran unsuccessfully for governor four times, and his political foes dubbed him *Run Forever Kolb,* a play on his initials.

KONARSKY, MATT *(fl. late 1800s)*

One of the most colorful nicknames of the Old West was accorded a grizzled miner named Matt Konarsky in Butte, Mont. He often pecked out two-fingered tunes on pianos at the saloon or in the parlor of his boarding house, and such talent did not go unnoticed. He was immediately labeled *Tchaikovsky* for his musical skills and for being Polish, which was pretty much the same thing as being Russian. One day while Konarsky was putting on his outside clothes in the mine change-room, an Irish fellow miner spotted him wearing a double truss, which with its black rubber pads much resembled a telephone operator's headset. "Lord God," the Irish miner exclaimed, "will ye have a look at the tiliphones on old Tchaikovsky!" Konarsky was thereafter known as *Telephone Tchaikovsky.*

KORETZ, LEO *(1881–1925)*

Few swindlers were treated more affectionately than Leo Koretz, who, before committing suicide

in 1925, took stockholders for millions by offering shares in alleged oil fields in Panama. Investors reaped huge dividends that Koretz avoided paying by allowing them to reinvest their profits in more stock. He was hailed even in the financial press as *The New Rockefeller,* and happy stockholders once held a testimonial for him, unfurling huge banners reading "Lovable Lou . . . Our Ponzi." In time they regretfully learned he really was as great a swindler as Charles Ponzi.

KORNGOLD, ERICH WOLFGANG (1897–1957)

Austrian-born opera composer and two-time winner of Academy Awards for his movie music, Erich Korngold was often, if perhaps excessively, called *The Modern Mozart.*

KOUFAX, SANDY *(1935–)*

Brooklyn and Los Angeles Dodgers pitcher Sandy Koufax, one of the modern era's most effective hurlers, was dubbed by the press *The Man with the Golden Arm.* He pitched four no-hit games, had the National League's lowest earned-run average five years in a row and won the Cy Young Award three times.

KRAMER, STANLEY E. *(1913–)*

U.S. movie producer Stanley Kramer built a reputation on his ability to turn out good motion pictures at low cost, winning for himself the accolade *Genius on a Low Budget.* Perhaps his best example was *High Noon.*

KRASICKI, IGNATIUS *(1735–1801)*

Celebrated Polish poet and man of letters Ignatius Krasicki has been dubbed *The Polish Voltaire.*

KREUGER, IVAR (1880–1932)

Undoubtedly the greatest swindler of modern times, one whose acts even dwarfed those of the likes of Charles Ponzi, Ivar Kreuger was called *The Swedish Match King* because he controlled between one-third and one-half of the world's output of matches. He used his profits to build a larger financial empire through forgery and fraudulent deals, by selling stocks and bonds backed by the revenues of nonexistent companies to some of the supposedly shrewdest banking houses of Europe and the United States. He committed suicide in 1932 when his empire crumbled because of the worldwide depression.

KRIPALANI, JIWATRAM BHAGWANDAS (1889–1982)

A close disciple of Mohandas Gandhi, J.B. Kripalani was often called *The Gatekeeper* because, as Gandhi himself stated, he "made it his aim in life to save me from visitors." It was a process that gave Kripalani enormous personal power. In later years, after Gandhi's death, he became estranged from the Congress Party under Nehru and eventually formed a broad coalition that for a time toppled Nehru's daughter, Indira Gandhi, from power.

KROCK, ARTHUR (1886–1974)

Political columnist Arthur Krock of the *New York Times* was famed as the *Gray Eminence* of the newspaper's Washington bureau. He was known for his unlimited ability to get his way on the publication's political stands, and it was said that his threat to resign prevented the *Times* from switching its presidential endorsement from Eisenhower to Stevenson in 1956. A conservative southerner, Krock often rankled Franklin D. Roosevelt, who referred to him publicly with disdain as *Li'l' Arthur.*

KROGH, EGIL (1939–)

During the Watergate scandal Egil Krogh emerged with the dubious distinction of heading the White House "Plumbers." Because of his "unusual piety" earlier in the Nixon administration, other White House staffers jokingly dubbed him *Evil Krogh.*

KRUGER, FRANZ (1797–1857)

Nineteenth century German portrait painter Franz Kruger gained greater fame as a painter of horses and was dubbed *Pferde-Kruger,* or *Horse-Kruger.*

KRULAK, VICTOR H. "Brute" (1913–)

Marine lieutenant general Victor H. Krulak was not illogically nicknamed *Brute Krulak* despite being only 5 feet-4¾-inches tall. He was regarded as being as scrappy as an ill-tempered terrier.

KRUPP, ALFRED (1812–1887)

Alfred Krupp, the German munitions manufacturer, was called *The Cannon King.* He was the most prominent member of a line of Krupps who together would be called *The Merchants of Death.*

Krupp of the Confederacy, The—See ANDERSON, JOSEPH REID.

KUHLAU, FRIEDRICH DANIEL RODOLPH (1787–1832)

Because he was one of the most productive composers for the instrument, Friedrich Daniel Rodolph Kuhlau was hailed as *The Beethoven of the Flute.*

KUHN, FRITZ (1896–1951)

Fritz Kuhn was the leader of the German-American Bund before World War II and was hailed by his followers as *The Fuehrer of America.*

KUHN, MARGARET "Maggie" (1905–   )

U.S. social worker Margaret "Maggie" Kuhn has been known as *The Grandmother of the Gray Panthers* ever since she organized the group in the 1970s to fight for improved conditions for senior citizens.

KURTEN, PETER—See Monster of Dusseldorf, The.

KWAISULIA (1851–1909)

The Strong Man of the Solomon Islands was the title bestowed on Kwaisulia, Polynesian chief of the Lau.

KYLE, JAMES HENDERSON (1854–1901)

One of the Midwest's most successful independent politicians, James Henderson Kyle was called *The Indecrat* because he sat with the Democrats both in the South Dakota state senate and, from 1893 until his death, in the U.S. Senate. However, he was far to the left of the Democrats on most issues, supporting women's suffrage, working with the Knights of Labor and promoting the political process of initiative and referendum. Within South Dakota he won the votes of Democrats, Republicans and Populists.

L

La Belle Americaine—See MONROE, ELIZABETH KORTRIGHT.

LA FONTAINE, JEAN DE (1621–1695)

Seventeenth century poet Jean de La Fontaine was designated *The Aesop of France* and *The French Homer* by his contemporaries.

LA GUARDIA, FIORELLO H. (1882–1947)

Easily the most colorful mayor in New York City's history, Fiorello H. La Guardia was called *The Little Flower,* a translation of his Italian given name that suited his short stature, and a clear counter point to his fiery personality. In that sense his other nickname—*Butch*—may have been closer to the mark.

La Guerre—See GASSION, JEAN, COMTE DE.

LA MARCK, GUILLAUME DE (1446?–1485)

The famed Belgian soldier Guillaume de la Marck was nicknamed *The Wild Boar of the Ardennes,* according to Sir Walter Scott in *Quentin Durward,* both for his looks and disposition.

LA TOUR D'AUVERGNE, THEOPHILE MALO CORRET DE *(1743–1800)*

A heroic French soldier who gained renown in the wars of 1792–1800, Theophile Malo Corret de la Tour d'Auvergne commanded the "Infernal Column" and refused a promotion to general. Napoleon dubbed him *The First Grenadier of France* and after his death his name was kept on the roll of his company as a mark of tribute. When his name was called, the color sergeant would respond, "Dead on the field of honor."

LA VALLIERE, LOUISE DE *(1644–1710)*

One of Louis XIV's favorite mistresses, Louise de la Valliere, a modest, delicate and slightly lame blonde, was nicknamed *A Little Violet*. Frankly ashamed of her position, la Valliere twice escaped to a convent but was brought back to Versailles by the king, who threatened to have the convent at St.-Cloud set ablaze by his troops unless she was surrendered. Only after Louis become interested in new mistresses did he grant her royal permission to enter a Carmelite convent, where she remained the last 35 years of her life.

LABE, LOUISA *(1526–1566)*

An extraordinary 16th century Frenchwoman, Louisa Labe was a person of many accomplishments. She understood Latin, Spanish and Italian and was an accomplished lutanist and a writer of verses, who was said to have inspired Erasmus and La Fontaine in some of their writings. She was nicknamed *The Aspasia of Lyons* after the Greek courtesan noted for her wit, learning and beauty, although Labe's looks were no more then average. She was sometimes called *Captain Louisa* because

of her skill as a horsewoman in male attire and her courageous performance at the siege of Perpignan. She married Ennomond Perrin, a rope maker from Lyons, and the street where they lived was named, in her honor, *La Belle Cordière,* or *The Beautiful Rope-Maker*.

Labor Architect, The—See **GOLDBERG, ARTHUR.**

Labor Baron, The—See **LEWIS, JOHN L.**

Labor Mayor, The—See **DORE, JOHN FRANCIS.**

Lackey, The—See **KEITEL, WILHELM.**

Lad, The—See **FARINELLI, CARLO BROSCHI.**

Lad Who Became a Lady, The—See **JORGENSEN, CHRISTINE.**

LADD, WILLIAM *(1778–1841)*

One of the leaders of the 1812 U.S. peace movement, which did not carry the day, William Ladd was dubbed *The Apostle of Peace*. He served as head of the American Peace Society for 13 years, until his death in 1841.

Lady Bluebeard of La Porte—See **GUNNESS, BELLE.**

Lady Desperado, The—See **STARR, BELLE.**

Lady in Red, The—See SAGE, ANNA.

Lady Lindy—See EARHART, AMELIA.

Lady with the Hatchet, The—See NATION, CARRY.

Lady with the Lamp, The—See NIGHTINGALE, FLORENCE.

Lady with the Owl, The—See NIGHTINGALE, FLORENCE.

Lafayette of the Greek Revolution, The—See HOWE, SAMUEL GRINDLEY.

LAFFEMAS, ISAAC DE (1587–1657)

Isaac de Laffemas, the rather active public executioner under Cardinal Richelieu, was nicknamed *The Cardinal's Hangman.*

LAFITTE, JEAN (c. 1780–1826)

Lionized in Louisiana ever since he helped Andrew Jackson defeat the British at the Battle of New Orleans in 1815, Jean Lafitte was known as *The Gentleman Pirate.* Although he was granted a full pardon for his past acts of piracy and murder, Lafitte tired of respectable New Orleans life and returned to privateering. Unlike some of his men, however, he refrained from attacking U.S. vessels.

LAING, A. S.—See Mr. Fang.

LAKE, VERONICA (1919–1973)

At the start of her movie career, actress Veronica Lake sported a hairdo that covered one eye, and studio press agents tried to dub her *Cyclops Cinderella.* Not surprisingly, it did not catch on with the public, who preferred calling her *The Peekaboo Girl.* The hairdo became quite the rage and the subject of many jokes. (Bob Hope in allusion to driving with her: "I was stopped by a cop the other night for driving with one headlight.") For a time the style was copied by American women and it was held responsible for a number of industrial accidents by female war workers. In time the style faded, as did *The Peekabo Girl's* career.

LAMARTINE, ALPHONSE (1792–1869)

One of the most harmonious of 19th century French poets, Alphonse Lamartine was credited with producing much pleasing verse. However, he was dubbed *The Narcissus of France* since he could never separate the subject of his verses from that part of France which he admired most—himself.

Lamb Who Strayed from the Fold, The— See CHURCHILL, SARAH.

LAMBERT, GERALD BARNES (1887–1967)

Although Jordan Wheat Lambert had invented Listerine in 1880 as a general purpose mild antiseptic, its sales were unexciting until the 1920s, when his son, Gerald Barnes Lambert, found a way to send sales soaring by capitalizing on one of the nation's greatest social fears. In a frantic but effective advertising campaign, he warned consumers they might be suffering from "halitosis."

Lovers could see their hopes for marriage foundering. Men feared the loss of job promotions. The perils were endless. The public desperately made war on the scourge, and within two years *The Man Who Invented Halitosis* was able to sell out for $25 million and retire at the age of 36. No doubt Lambert would not have been nearly as successful warring against mere bad breath, which is why he cleverly used the Latin word for it.

Lame, The—See ALBERT II, DUKE OF AUSTRIA.

LAMOUR, DOROTHY (1914–   )

Screen actress Dorothy Lamour was nicknamed *The Sarong Girl* because of her many jungle-girl roles set in the South Pacific. During World War II she was called *The Sweetheart of the Foxholes,* although quite a few GIs noted her South Pacific and theirs were quite different.

Lamp of the Law, The—See IRNERIUS.

LANDON, ALFRED M. (1887–   )

Coming out of Kansas in 1936 to run for president against Franklin D. Roosevelt, Alf Landon was touted by Republicans as *The Coolidge of the West.* The idea of a return to Coolidge normalcy during the Great Depression proved to have a disastrous political effect and Landon was swamped in a Roosevelt landslide.

LANDRU, HENRI DESIRE—See Bluebeard.

LANDRY, TOM (1924–   )

Tom Landry, the first and only coach of the Dallas Cowboys of the National Football League, is often described by sportscasters as *The Iceberg* because of his ability to keep a cool exterior whether his team's fortunes rise or fall. The speculation is that if the *Titanic* were raised and collided with Landry, it would again sink.

Landslide Lyndon—See JOHNSON, LYNDON B.

LANE, JAMES HENRY (1814–1866)

Perhaps the most dedicated and determined abolitionist Union general in the Civil War, James Henry Lane was regarded by Confederates as a fierce, uncompromising opponent, and he was called *The Grim Chieftain.*

LANGTRY, LILY (1852–1929)

Born in Jersey, English actress and beauty (some said more the latter than the former) Lily Langtry was hailed as *The Jersey Lily.* She was even more famous for her offstage romantic affairs, including one with Edward, Prince of Wales, later Edward VII.

LANMAN, CHARLES (1819–1895)

Painter Charles Lanman was dubbed by Washington Irving *The Picturesque Explorer of the United States* because he traveled throughout the country and captured on canvas much of the nation's scenery.

LAS CASAS, BARTOLOME DE (1474–1566)

Catholic bishop Bartolome de Las Casas became known as *The Protector of the Indians* in 1517. Alarmed by the suffering of the Central and South

American Indians, who were forced to labor in the mines for the Spaniards and Portuguese, he petitioned Pope Leo X to allow African slaves to be brought in to do the work. The bishop's "mercy plea" came to naught, however, and the Indians continued on their way to mass extinction, and mass enslavement of blacks then began.

LASKY, VICTOR (1918–   )

Right-wing journalist Victor Lasky once estimated he has spent a fifth of his life writing about the Kennedys, including such poorly reviewed but financially rewarding works as *JFK: The Man and the Myth* and *Robert Kennedy: The Man and the Myth*, both of which were published the years each was assassinated. Lasky dubbed himself *A Hatchet Man with a Sense of Humor*, but many of his subjects might disagree.

LASSERAN-MASSENCOME, SEIGNEUR DE MONTLUC (1501–1577)

A noted French marshal, Seigneur de Montluc Lasseran-Massencome was nicknamed *The Royalist Butcher* by the Protestants because of his unrestrained cruelty toward them.

Last Caesar, The—See TRUJILLO, RAFAEL.

Last Cocked Hat, The—See MONROE, JAMES.

Last Cold War Warrior, The—See ULBRICHT, WALTER.

Last English Maecenas, The—See ROGERS, SAMUEL.

Last Genro, The—See SAIONJI, PRINCE KIMMOCHI.

Last Great American Hero, The—See ELLSBERG, DANIEL.

Last King of Paradise, The—See KALAKAUA, DAVID.

Last Knight of Europe, The—See JOHN OF AUSTRIA, DON.

Last Lady of the Land—See TRUMAN, BESS.

Last Man, The—See CHARLES I OF ENGLAND.

Last Minstrel of the English Stage, The—See SHIRLEY, JAMES.

Last of the Barons, The—See NEVILLE, RICHARD.

Last of the Big Spenders, The—See GULBENKIAN, NUBAR SARKIS.

Last of the Big Time Grafters, The—See SULLIVAN, TIMOTHY "Big Tim."

Last of the Cocked Hats, The: JOHN MEASE (1746–1826)

John Mease, who served in the Continental Army directly under George Washington, was known in the final years of his life as *The Last of the Cocked Hats* for wearing the three-cornered hat of the Revolutionary period long after it had gone out of style.

Last of the Cold War Liberals, The— See **JACKSON, HENRY M. "Scoop."**

Last of the Goths, The—See **RODERICK.**

Last of the Great New York Bosses, The—See **DE SAPIO, CARMINE.**

Last of the Incas, The—See **CONDORCANQUI, JOSE GABRIEL.**

Last of the Knights, The—See **MAXIMILIAN I OF GERMANY.**

Last of the Monsters, The—See **PIUS VI, POPE.**

Last of the Platonists, The—See **ERIGENA, JOHN SCOTUS.**

Last of the Samurai, The: HIROO ONODA (1920–   )

Japanese soldier Hiroo Onoda continued a guerrilla war in the Philippines for 29 years after World War II, refusing to believe it was over. He became a national hero in Japan when he returned home in 1974, winning the accolade *The Last of the Samurai*.

Last of the Spitball Pitchers, The—See **GRIMES, BURLEIGH.**

Last of the Tacky Ladies, The—See **MIDLER, BETTE.**

Last of the Western Outlaws, The—See **JENNINGS, AL.**

Last Rider, The—See **MILLER, CHARLES "Bronco Charlie."**

Last Stone Age Man in the United States, The—See **ISHI.**

Last Stuart, The—See **YORK, HENRY BENEDICT MARIA CLEMENT STUART.**

Last Virgin on Broadway, The—See **GOLDEN, MATILDA "Goldie."**

Late Mayor, The—See **WALKER, JAMES J.**

Laughing Killer, The—See **SELZ, JEROME VON BRAUN.**

Laughing Philosopher, The—See **DEMOCRITUS.**

Laundry-Mark Hawkshaw, The—See **YULCH, ADAM.**

Laureate of the Civilized World—See **PETRARCH, FRANCESCO.**

Laureate of the Nursery, The—See **MILLER, WILLIAM.**

***LAUREL, STAN*—See Fiddle and the Bow, The.**

LAURENS, JOHN (1754–1782)

Because of his gallantry and daring in battle, American patriot John Laurens was nicknamed *The Bayard of the Revolution,* being considered the equal of Pierre du Terrail, Chevalier de Bayard, the great French knight of the 16th century. Laurens, angered in 1778 by his commanding officer's "constant personal abuse" directed at George Washington, fought a duel to protect Washington's honor. Like Bayard, Laurens died in combat, at the Battle at Combachee River in South Carolina in August 1782.

LAW, ANDREW BONAR (1858–1923)

The leader of Britain's Conservative Party in the early 1900s and prime minister in 1922–23, Andrew Bonar Law was often savaged by former Liberal prime minister Herbert Henry Asquith, who called him *The Unknown Prime Minister.* After Law's death in 1923, Asquith noted, "It is fitting that we should have buried the Unknown Prime Minister by the side of the Unknown Soldier."

LAW, JOHN (1671–1729)

Scottish financier and speculator John Law was called *The Paper King,* after his notorious Mississippi Bubble, a colossal fraud, based on investing in the Louisiana colony, that gripped France in a frenzy of speculation. *The Paper King* fled the country, which was driven to the edge of financial ruin.

***Law West of the Pecos, The*—See BEAN, JUDGE ROY.**

LAWES, KATHRYN (1885–1937)

Few persons were more worthy of their nicknames than Kathryn Lawes, the wife of Warden Lewis E. Lawes of Sing Sing. She was called *The Angel of Sing Sing* by prisoners because of her many kindnesses to them. When she died in a tragic automobile accident in 1937, the gates of Sing Sing were thrown open and the prisoners were permitted to march without guard to the warden's house a quarter of a mile away to file past her bier. None tried to escape.

***Law-Giver of Parnassus, The*—See BOILEAU-DESPREAUX, NICHOLAS.**

LAWLER, DEBBIE (1951–)

U.S. stunt motorcyclist Debbie Lawler has been nicknamed *The Flying Angel* and, almost inevitably, *The Female Evel Knievel.*

LAWSON, JOHN DANIEL (1816–1896)

Although his elective service was limited to only two years in Congress, John Daniel Lawson was regarded as one of the most faithful members of the New York Republican Party. He was nicknamed *Sitting Bull* because his attendance at each important conference could be counted on. He was a delegate to every national convention of the party from 1868 to 1892 and died shortly before the convention of 1896.

***Lawyer, The*—See BLACKSTONE, WILLIAM.**

LAZAR, IRVING PAUL "Swifty" (1907–   )

Literary agent Irving Paul Lazar was given the nickname *Swifty* by Humphrey Bogart after he closed five major deals in one day.

Lazy, The—See ROSSINI, GIOACCHINO.

LAZZERI, TONY "Push-'em-up" (1903–1946)

Regarded as one of baseball's most dependable hitters for advancing men on base, New York Yankee infielder Tony Lazzeri was invariably called, and expected to be, *Push-'em-up Lazzeri*.

LE SUEUR, EUSTACE (c. 1617–1655)

French painter Eustace Le Sueur was dubbed *The French Raphael*, an accolade to which he was more entitled than was Francois Boucher, who was accorded the same honor in the following century. Boucher was thus labeled almost solely because he was a favorite of Louis XV.

LEA, LUKE (1879–1945)

A Democratic senator from Kentucky, Luke Lea was called *Young Thunderbolt* because of his reputation for concocting daring schemes. In 1918 he was foiled in an attempt to kidnap Kaiser Wilhelm.

Leaden Penciller Willis—See WILLIS, NATHANIEL P.

Leader of the Rat Pack, The—See SINATRA, FRANK.

LEAHY, FRANK (1908–1973)

The famed coach of Notre Dame's football team, Frank Leahy was known as *The Prussian Leprechaun,* in recognition of the fact that despite his reputation as a happy-go-lucky leprechaun, he was a hard-driving taskmaster who demanded disciplined play.

Leaning Tower of Putty, The—See MUNDT, KARL.

Learned Blacksmith, The—See BURRITT, ELIHU.

Learned Cabbage-Eater, The—See RITSON, JOSEPH.

Learned Painter, The—See LEBRUN, CHARLES.

LEARY, TIMOTHY (1920–   )

In 1966 Timothy Leary, a former lecturer at Harvard, announced that his "ultimate aim is to change the spiritual level of the United States and the world" by making LSD (lysergic acid diethylamide) "a new religion." He thus gained the nicknames *The Chemical Messiah, The Supersalesman of the Turned-on Generation* and *The Guru of LSD*. Prison terms, escapes to foreign countries, recapture and, in 1976, a parole followed. By then Leary had turned his back on LSD and its sale had slowed to a mere trickle. Although his former followers denounced him as a "cop informant" and a "paranoid schizophrenic," Leary testified against no one.

Leather Lung Pete: PETE ADELIS (fl. 1940s–1950s)

Nicknamed *Leather Lung Pete*, Pete Adelis was baseball's first and apparently only professional heckler. He started his career in Philadelphia, where he sat in a box behind home plate and needled opposing team players. *Leather Lung* so rattled players that the Philadelphia Athletics took to paying his expenses so he could travel to their road games as their heckling weapon. The New York Yankees later hired him to shake up the opposition. Once, in Brooklyn's Ebbets Field, a player became so upset that he jumped into the stands after *Leather Lung,* ready to commit violence. Adelis escaped, but was thereafter barred from Ebbets Field.

Leatherbreeches—See DILGER, HUBERT CASIMIR ANTON.

LEBRUN, CHARLES (1619–1690)

Noted 17th century French historical painter Charles Lebrun was dubbed *The Learned Painter* because he also authored a number of historical works.

LEBRUN, PONCE-DENIS ECOUCHARD (1729–1807)

Perhaps because he did not receive quite the acclaim to which he felt entitled, French lyric poet Ponce-Denis Ecouchard Lebrun dubbed himself *Lebrun-Pindare,* after the ancient Greek lyric poet Pindar.

Lebrun-Pindare—See LEBRUN, PONCE-DENIS ECOUCHARD.

LEDAIN, OLIVER (?–1484)

Oliver Ledain, the barber of King Louis XI of France and his tool in many intrigues, was nicknamed *The Devil* because of the fear and contempt he inspired.

LEE, ANN (1736–1784)

Religious leader Ann Lee, often referred to as *Mother Lee,* was the driving force behind the growth of the "Shaking Quakers" in England and later in America. Many of her followers regarded her as Christ come back as a woman and referred to her as *Ann the Word,* because she carried back the word of the Son of God.

LEE, BRUCE (1940–1973)

Bruce Lee, the U.S.-born Chinese star of karate movies and TV programs, was nicknamed by ecstatic fans *The King of Kung Fu* and *The Little Dragon.* They have remained loyal to him after his death in 1973, to the extent of resisting Hollywood's efforts to promote any new martial arts superstar to replace him.

LEE, CHARLES (1731–1782)

American Revolutionary War hero Charles Lee was nicknamed *The Hero of Charleston* for his brilliant defense of that South Carolina city against the British in 1776. Earlier, during the days he lived with the Mohawk Indians and became a tribal chief, the Mohawks called him *Boiling Water* because they found his behavior so forceful and temperamental.

LEE, FITZHUGH (1835–1905)

Because he habitually signed military orders "F. Lee," Civil War Confederate general Fitzhugh Lee was referred to as *Flea*.

LEE, GYPSY ROSE (1914–1970)

The multitalented (she was also a writer) strip-teaser Gypsy Rose Lee was often called *The Best Undressed Woman in America*. It should be noted that she learned her craft from Tessie the Tassel-Twirler.

LEE, IVY L. (1877–1934)

Ivy L. Lee, John D. Rockefeller's thousand-dollar-a-month press agent (fabulous pay for the era), was known in the media as *The Public Relations Genius*. The striking miners of Colorado had a different sobriquet for him, *Poison Ivy*. He was held responsible by them for gross misrepresentations in the Ludlow strike of 1913-14. During the strike female supporters of the United Mine Workers were branded prostitutes, and terrible infamies were circulated about Judge Ben B. Lindsey and the committee of miners' wives who went to Washington, D.C., to plead the miners' cause.

LEE, JOHN (1864–1933)

English murderer John Lee escaped death by hanging in 1885 when the trap door of the gallows failed to open on three separate tries, although it worked fine when Lee was not standing on it. Unable to carry out the sentence, the sheriff returned Lee to his cell. The gallows' failure was never satisfactorily explained, and theories ranged from rain having waterlogged the trap door so that it would not open when weight was placed on it, to sabotage

by prisoners who had built the scaffold, to, of course, the Hand of God. Lee's case was debated in the House of Commons and finally his sentence was reduced to life imprisonment. He was released in 1907, and for the next quarter century he toured England and America touted in personal appearances as *The Man They Could Not Hang*.

LEE, MARIA—See Black Maria.

LEE, NATHANIEL (c. 1653–1692)

Nathaniel Lee, an English dramatist and poet whose greatest success was a tragedy, *The Rival Queen*, was called *The Mad Poet* because of his erratic behavior, which was caused by drinking. He spent five years in an asylum and died at the age of 39.

LEE, RICHARD HENRY (1732–1794)

Virginia lawyer Richard Henry Lee was lionized as *The Cicero of the Revolution* for the passion of his oratory in support of independence for the American colonies. Later, because of his opposition to ratification of the Constitution, he was called *The Federal Farmer*, after his *Letters from the Federal Farmer to the Republican*. He later withdrew his opposition to a strong central government and served as a U.S. senator.

LEE, ROBERT E. (1807–1870)

Famed Confederate general Robert E. Lee was affectionately called *Uncle Robert, Marse Robert* and *The Gentle General* by his soldiers and staff. Even a slightly less affectionate nickname, *Old Ace of Spade*, was used more in resigned exasperation than in disparagement, referring to his habitual insistence that his soldiers immediately dig trenches upon occupying a new position.

LEE, STAN (1922–   )

The head of Marvel Comics, Stan Lee created such molders of American culture as Spider-Man and The Fantastic Four and has won for himself the designation *The Homer of 20th-century Mythology*.

LEEK, SYBIL (1917?–1982)

The English astrologer, author and witchcraft advocate Sybil Leek garnered so much publicity during this century for the occult arts that she became known as *The Twentieth Century Witch*.

Lee's War Horse—See LONGSTREET, JAMES.

LEESE, GEORGE (fl. c. 1840s–1850s)

A notorious New York gangster of the mid-19th century, George Leese was sometimes described as a pickpocket—among other nefarious occupations—and won the nickname *Snatchem*. He was described by a contemporary journalist as "a beastly, obscene ruffian, with bulging, bulbous, watery-blue eyes, bloated face and coarse swaggering gait," and his ability at the light-fingered craft was much exaggerated. However, since he never ventured abroad on his criminal forays with less than two revolvers in his belt and a knife in his boot-top, his victims readily conceded that he was a most expert pickpocket.

LEETEG, EDGAR (1904–1953)

Edgar Leeteg, an American artist who lived in Tahiti, was often called *The American Gauguin*.

Legal Killer, The—See ELLIOTT, ROBERT G.

LEHR, LEW (1895–1950)

Radio and newsreel comic Lew Lehr had what can only be described as a "moist" form of humor, leading many of his co-workers to nickname him *Dribblepuss*.

LEIBNITZ, GOTTFRIED WILHELM VON (1646–1716)

Noted German philosopher and scholar Baron Gottfried von Leibnitz was called *The Living Dictionary*, the nickname apparently having been first applied to him by George I of England.

LEIBOWITZ, SAMUEL S. (1893–1978)

Famed defense lawyer and, later, judge Samuel S. Leibowitz achieved his greatest fame in defense of the Scottsboro Boys, nine young blacks who had been accused in Alabama in 1931 of raping two "Southern ladies." Throughout much of the South, including the press of the day, he was commonly called *The New York Jew Nigger Lover*.

LEIGH, VIVIEN (1913–1967)

English actress Vivien Leigh, who rocketed to fame as Scarlett O'Hara in *Gone with the Wind*, was nicknamed on the set of that film *Fiddle-dee-dee* by director Victor Fleming. It reflected the fact that she exhibited the same flightiness as Scarlett, who mouthed the phrase constantly.

LEITZEL, LILLIAN (1893–1931)

One of the greatest circus aerialists of all time, German-born Lillian Leitzel performed throughout

Europe and the United States, earning the tribute *The Queen of the Circus*. She died in Copenhagen as the result of a 29-foot fall when the swivel of her Roman rings broke. She was the first person named to the Circus Hall of Fame.

LEMA, ANTHONY *"Champagne Tony"* (1934–1966)

One of the most exuberant competitors on the U.S. professional golf circuit, Tony Lema became known as *Champagne Tony* for his lavish and sharing celebrations whenever he won major prize money.

LEMKE, WILLIAM (1878–1950)

A representative in Congress from North Dakota from 1933 until his death, William Lemke became known as *Moratorium Bill* after he successfully co-authored a bill in 1935 that suspended mortgage payments on farm property. He ran as the Union Party candidate for president in 1936 but garnered only minor support, including that of right-wing extremists Gerald L. K. Smith, Fr. Charles E. Coughlin and Francis E. Townsend.

Lemonade Lucy—See HAYES, LUCY.

LENIN, NIKOLAI (1870–1924)

Russian revolutionary Vladimir Ilich Ulyanov, better known by the pseudonym Nikolai Lenin, was at 23 already bald and had lined features. Because of these physical characteristics as well as his superior intellectual ability, his fellow revolutionaries called him *Starik,* or *Old Man.* When the czarist secret police first heard this reference to an "old man," they quite understandably did not connect it to a youth in his twenties.

LEO VI, BYZANTINE EMPEROR (866–911)

Byzantine emperor Leo VI was dubbed *The Philosopher.* The sobriquet may be regarded as pure flattery.

LEO X, POPE (1475–1521)

A singularly unpopular Roman pontiff in Germany—even before the agitations of Martin Luther— Pope Leo X, Giovanni de Medici, was often denounced for his lavish lifestyle. When he demanded a subsidy from the German peoples for a crusade against the Turks, it was refused. Called *The Hound of Hell,* he was described as the real enemy of Christianity, rather than the Turks.

Leonardo of the Shoe Trade, The—See WARHOL, ANDY.

Leonidas of America, The—See STARK, JOHN.

Leonidas of Modern Greece, The—See BOZZARIS, MARKOS.

Leonidas Wedell—See WEDELL, H. C.

LEONSKI, EDWARD JOSEPH—See Singing Strangler, The.

LEOPARDI, GIACOMO (1798–1837)

Giacomo Leopardi, the tragic Italian poet, has been credited by critics with composing "some of the most exquisite lyrics in Italian; and some of the saddest utterances on human affairs in any language.'' He has been labeled *A Poet Alone*. At the age of 21 he wrote, ''I was terrified to find myself in the midst of nothingness, myself a nothing.'' Developing a hunchback, he wrote verses that became the product of *A Poet of Sorrow*, and when he died at the age of 37, he had, biographers assure us, never kissed a woman in his life.

LEOPOLD, NATHAN—See Thrill Killers, The.

LEOPOLD II OF BELGIUM (1835–1909)

Leopold II of Belgium had numerous mistresses during his scandalous reign. At the age of 65 he took up a liaison with a 16-year-old prostitute named Caroline Lacroix, an affair that lasted the rest of his life. Caroline, who bore the king two children, called him *Tres Vieux*, or *Very Old*, a nickname that was picked up immediately by the gossips of Europe. The king married her a few days before he died.

Lepke, Louis—See BUCHALTER, LOUIS.

LESLIE, GEORGE LEONIDAS (1838–1884)

Without doubt the greatest bank robber in American history, George Leonidas Leslie was dubbed by the New York City police *The King of the Bank Robbers*. It was estimated that he was the mastermind of 80 percent of all bank thefts in the nation from 1865 until he was murdered by underworld foes in 1884.

LESSING, GOTTHOLD EPHRAIM (1729–1781)

Critic, philosopher and dramatist Gotthold Ephraim Lessing, the outstanding exponent of the German enlightenment, has been dubbed *The Father of German Literature* and *The Frederick of Thought* after the great Prussian ruler. He restored a national character to German literature, which, some critics said, had been ''corrupted and enslaved by French influences.'' Under Lessing the German theater moved from the classical French tradition to the influence of Shakespeare.

Leviathan of Book-Collectors, The—See RAWLINSON, THOMAS.

Lewd Vegetarian, The—See SHELLEY, PERCY BYSSHE.

LEWIS, ED "Strangler" (1890–1966)

One of the greatest wrestlers of all time, Ed Lewis gained his nickname *Strangler Lewis* because of his feared headlock. He worked on the hold constantly, practicing on a dummy head filled with coils and springs.

LEWIS, ESTELLE ANNA BLANCHE ROBINSON (1824–1880)

U.S. poet Estelle Lewis, or Sarah Anna Lewis, was dubbed by Edgar Allan Poe *The Rival of Sappho*. She was more commonly called *The Female Plutarch*, a sobriquet bestowed on her by the French poet Alphonse Lamartine.

LEWIS, JAMES H. (1866–1939)

Considered one of the best-dressed and most mannerly members of the U.S. Senate during the early part of the 20th century, James H. Lewis of Illinois was known to his fellow lawmakers as *The Beau Brummel of the Senate*.

LEWIS, JOHN L. (1880–1969)

As president of the United Mine Workers of America for four decades, John L. Lewis built the organization into one of the most powerful unions in the country. Because of an eloquence of speech and grandiose manner that implied a near-kingly status—and contrasted starkly with the image of his men—Lewis was referred to as *The Labor Baron*.

LEWIS, MERIWETHER (1774–1809)

Moody, introverted and extremely serious, Meriwether Lewis of the Lewis and Clark expedition was nicknamed by friend and foe alike, with differing tones, *The Sublime Dandy*. He was always immaculately dressed, with polished manners and fastidious personal habits and was the articulate member of the expedition. Called "undoubtedly the greatest pathfinder this country has ever known," he died mysteriously at the age of 35, and it has never been ascertained whether it was suicide or murder.

LEWIS, VACH—See Cyclone Louie.

LEWIS, WYNDHAM (1884–1957)

Known for his satiric, often virulent novels and political essays, writer and artist Wyndham Lewis was called *The Father of Vorticism,* for the short-lived art movement that emphasized rhythm based on cubist and futurist doctrines. Poet W. H. Auden dubbed him *That Lonely Old Volcano of the Right.*

Liar Taylor—See TAYLOR, CHEVALIER JOHN.

LIBERACE, GEORGE J. (1911–   )

U.S. violinist and musical leader George Liberace had so much of his pianist brother's fame rub off on him that he was known simply as *Brother George*.

Liberator, The—See BOLIVAR, SIMON; O'CONNELL, DANIEL.

Liberator of Genoa, The—See DORIA, ANDREA.

Liberator of Italy, The—See GARIBALDI, GIUSEPPE.

Library Profession's No. 1 Reference Reviewer, The—See CHENEY, FRANCES NEEL.

Libyan Giant, The—See NASHNUSH, SULAIMAN ALI.

Lickety-Split Technician, The—See HALDEMAN, H. R.

Lifer's Last Hope, A—See MARIS, HERBERT L.

Light of the West, The—See
MAIMONIDES.

Light of the World, The—See
SIGISMUND.

*Lightfoot, Captain: MICHAEL
MARTIN (1775–1822)*

Irish highwayman Michael Martin, better known
as *Captain Lightfoot,* was so named because of
his lightning speed in eluding pursuers. He transferred his transgressions from Ireland and Scotland to America in 1818 and was finally caught
and hanged in 1822 in Massachusetts.

Lightning—See **HAMILCAR.**

*Lightning Pilot, The: HORACE
BIXBY (1826–1912)*

Horace Bixby was in the minds of many the most
accomplished Mississippi River pilot. He was nicknamed *The Lightning Pilot* because his tenacious
memory and instant judgment allowed him to take
packet boats along the river with amazing speed.
In the 1850s Bixby taught Mark Twain the art of
piloting.

LI-HUNG CHANG (1823–1901)

Li-Hung Chang, the foremost Chinese diplomat
of the late 19th century, was known as *The Bismarck of Asia* for his advocacy of the self-
strengthening of China. He joined Chinese Gordon
in suppressing the Taiping Rebellion, became
prime minister of China in 1895 and negotiated
with foreigners during the Boxer Rebellion. In the
United States he became as well known for another achievement, which earned him the sobri-

quet *The Father of Chop Suey.* At a New York
banquet given in his honor in 1894, Li-Hung Chang
was asked to have his private chef contribute one
dish to the feast. Fearing whites would not like
real Chinese food, he had the chef prepare a
stew of meat and vegetables, which he declared
to be "chop suey." Actually the name was a
corruption of the Cantonese *shop sui,* meaning
"odds and ends."

Li'l' Arthur—See **KROCK,
ARTHUR.**

LILBURNE, JOHN (c. 1614–1657)

A famous English republican, John Lilburne was
nicknamed *Free Born John* for his spirited defense
of his rights as a freeborn Englishman before the
Star Chamber. As head of the Levelers, Lilburne
led the republican opposition to Cromwell and
strongly defended his rights and Leveler principles.
He was banished by Cromwell in 1651 but was
later pardoned when he returned to England upon
his conversion to Quakerism.

*LILLIE, BEATRICE GLADYS
(1898–   )*

Canadian-born actress and comedienne Bea Lillie
was dubbed *The Mistress of Sophisticated Slapstick.*

LILLIE, GORDON W. (1860–1942)

U.S. frontier scout and showman Gordon W. Lillie was called *Pawnee Bill* and *The White Chief of
the Pawnees.* Although by the late 19th century
Lillie had turned completely to show business,
there is little doubt he was more entitled to fame
as a genuine western adventurer than were Buffalo Bill Cody and Annie Oakley, who never
had been west of Ohio except on tours. He was

much in demand by the U.S. Army as a scout and interpreter and was trusted fully by Indian tribes, especially the Pawnees, who made him an honorary chief.

Lillo Among Painters, A—See **HOGARTH, WILLIAM.**

LILLY, WILLIAM (1602–1681)

English astrologer and prophet William Lilly has been ridiculed as *The Father of Errors* and *The English Merlin*.

Limb of Shakespeare, A—See **FLETCHER, JOHN.**

Limey Louis—See **MOUNTBATTEN, LORD LOUIS.**

LINCOLN, ABRAHAM (1809–1865)

Abraham Lincoln, 16th president of the United States, presided over the nation during the Civil War and was of course subjected to many nicknames. In addition to being *Honest Abe, The Rail-Splitter* and *The Great Emancipator*, he was savaged by his enemies as *The Buffoon, The Baboon, Caesar, The Jester, Massa Linkum* and *The Tyrant*. We are indebted to *Harper's Weekly* for the following collection: *Filthy Story-Teller, Despot, Liar, Thief, Braggart, Buffoon, Usurper, Monster, Ignoramous, Old Scoundrel, Perjurer, Robber, Swindler, Tyrant, Field-Butcher, Land-Pirate*. Some biographers say *Honest Abe* actually derived from Lincoln's early frequent activities as a judge and referee at cockfights. In 1847, as a freshman congressman from Illinois during the Mexican War, Lincoln challenged President James Polk's claim that the conflict started and the first American blood was spilled on American soil. Lincoln continually demanded to have that so-called spot identified, and his "Spot Resolutions" for more information and his antiwar stand led to his being disparaged as *Spot Lincoln*. The sobriquet helped send Lincoln into political oblivion for several years, and in 1858 it was still used successfully against him by Stephen Douglas in their senatorial race. After his assassination Lincoln became known in the North as *The Martyr President*.

LINCOLN, MARY TODD (1818–1882)

The wife of Abraham Lincoln, Mary Todd Lincoln was known, both before their marriage and during their White House years, as *The She-Wolf* because of her erratic temper.

LINCOLN, ROBERT TODD (1843–1926)

Robert Todd Lincoln, the eldest son of Abraham Lincoln, gained the unwanted sobriquet *The Assassination Witness* for having been nearby when three U.S. presidents were shot. He rushed to Lincoln's side after he was shot in 1865; he was in the Washington train depot in 1881 when James A. Garfield was struck down; and he had just arrived in Buffalo, N.Y., to meet President William McKinley in 1901 when the chief executive was fatally wounded. After that Lincoln studiously avoided the next president, declaring, "There is a certain fatality about Presidential functions when I am present."

LINCOLN, WARREN (1870–1941)

A noted Chicago lawyer in the early 1900s, Warren Lincoln was so successful at getting defendants off that he was called *Scot Free Lincoln*. However, when in 1923 he murdered his wife and his brother-in-law, all his courtroom magic proved to be of no avail. He went to prison for life and died in Joliet in 1941.

LIND, JENNY (1820–1888)

Operatic and oratorio soprano Jenny Lind, born Johanna Maria Lind, was acclaimed for her vocal purity and control and was universally referred to as *The Swedish Nightingale*.

LINDBERGH, CHARLES A. (1902–1974)

Charles A. Lindbergh, the aviator who made the first nonstop solo flight across the Atlantic Ocean, in his *Spirit of St. Louis,* was acclaimed around the world as *Lucky Lindy* and *The Lone Eagle*.

LINDBERGH, CHARLES A., JR. (1930–1932)

The infant son of aviator Charles Lindbergh, The Lone Eagle, Charles A. Lindbergh, Jr. was dubbed *The Little Eaglet* immediately following his birth. The sobriquet was much used after his kidnapping and murder in 1932.

LINDSAY, VACHEL (1879–1931)

U.S. poet Vachel Lindsay, whose favorite themes were American folklore and history, spent a considerable portion of his career as a tramp who traded poems for food, thus gaining the nickname *The Tramp Poet*.

LINDSEY, BEN B. (1869–1943)

A fiery, controversial U.S. judge, Ben B. Lindsey was a reformer friend of youth, an advocate of companionate marriage and a foe of political bosses. His main contribution to law was the founding of the juvenile court system, for which he was designated *The Father of the Juvenile Court*.

Lion, The—See JAMES II OF ENGLAND.

Lion of Judah, The—See HAILE SELASSIE.

Lion of Kashmir, The—See ABDULLAH, MOHAMMAD.

Lion of Malaya, The—See YAMASHITA, TOMOYUKI.

Lion of Sweden, The—See BANIER, JOHAN.

Lioness of Literary Letters, The—See WEST, REBECCA.

Lip, The—See DUROCHER, LEO; SCHMIDT, HELMUT.

LIPPMAN, SALLY—See Disco Sally.

LIPPMANN, WALTER (1889–1974)

Political journalist Walter Lippman so influenced world opinion that he was often called *The Other State Department*.

Literary Bull-Dog, The—See WARBURTON, WILLIAM.

Literary Colossus, The—See JOHNSON, SAMUEL.

Literary Machiavel, The—See
ADDISON, JOSEPH.

Little Beagle, The—See CECIL,
WILLIAM, LORD BURLEIGH.

Little Big Man, The—See
HOFFMAN, DUSTIN.

Little Blue-Cloak, The—See
CHAMPION, EDME.

Little Caesar—See PETRILLO,
JAMES CAESAR.

Little Corporal, The—See HITLER,
ADOLF; NAPOLEON.

*Little Corporal of Unsought Fields,
The*—See MCCLELLAN, GEORGE B.

Little David—See FELTON, JOHN;
RANDOLPH (OF ROANOKE),
JOHN.

Little Dictator, The—See HITLER,
ADOLF.

Little Dorothy Lost—See GARLAND,
JUDY.

Little Dragon, The—See LEE,
BRUCE.

Little Eaglet, The—See LINDBERGH,
CHARLES A., JR.

Little Electra, The—See BYRON,
AUGUSTA ADA.

Little Flower, The—See
LA GUARDIA, FIORELLO H.

Little Giant, The—See DOUGLAS,
STEPHEN.

*Little Giant of Twentieth Century
Music, The*—See STRAVINSKY,
IGOR.

Little Goldilocks—See TEMPLE,
SHIRLEY.

Little Hillock—See CONFUCIUS.

Little Ike—See EISENHOWER,
DWIGHT DAVID.

Little Indian Fighter—See
STANDISH, MILES.

Little King Pepin—See CHANNING,
WILLIAM ELLERY.

Little Lion, The—See HAMILTON,
ALEXANDER.

Little Mac—See MCCLELLAN,
GEORGE B.

Little Machiavelli, The—See
GALIANI, FERDINAND.

Little Magician, The—See VAN BUREN, MARTIN.

Little Man on the Wedding Cake, The—See DEWEY, THOMAS E.

Little Man with the Goatee, The—See ULBRICHT, WALTER.

Little Man with the Smile, The—See LOYOLA, ST. IGNATIUS OF.

Little Marlborough, The—See SCHWERIN, COUNT KURT CHRISTOPH.

Little Master, The—See BEHAM, HANS SEBALD.

Little Miss Poker Face—See WILLS, HELEN.

Little Mother of All the Russians—See CATHERINE THE GREAT OF RUSSIA.

Little Napoleon—See BEAUREGARD, PIERRE GUSTAVE TOUTANT; HITLER, ADOLF.

Little New Dealer, The—See EARLE, GEORGE H., III.

Little Old Lady in Tennis Shoes, The—See CANNON, ISABELLA W.

Little Pale Star from Georgia, The—See STEPHENS, ALEXANDER H.

Little Phil—See SHERIDAN, PHILIP HENRY.

Little Poison—See WANER, PAUL AND LLOYD.

Little Queen, The—See CHAMPDIVERS, ODETTE DE; ISABELLA OF VALOIS.

Little Shit, The—See KENNEDY, ROBERT F.

Little Signor, The—See VICTOR EMMANUEL III OF ITALY.

Little Sure Shot—See OAKLEY, ANNIE.

Little Tramp, The—See CHAPLIN, CHARLES.

Little Ugly Nauseous Elf, A—See JENYNS, SOAME.

Little Violet, A—See LA VALLIERE, LOUISE DE.

Liver-Eating Johnston—See JOHNSTON, JOHN "Liver-Eating."

Livery Muse, The—See DODSLEY, ROBERT.

Living Cyclopedia, The—See
LONGINUS, DIONYSIUS CASSIUS.

Living Dictionary, The—See
LEIBNITZ, GOTTFRIED WILHELM VON.

Living Library, The—See
**MAGLIABECCHI, ANTHONY;
TOUSSAIN, JACQUES.**

Living Pentecost, The—See
**MEZZOFANTI, CARDINAL
GUISEPPE.**

LIVINGSTON, ROBERT R.
(1746–1813)

Because of the quality of his oratory, which greatly aided the cause of the American Revolution, Robert R. Livingston was called *The Cicero of America*. The sobriquet was first bestowed on him by Benjamin Franklin.

LIVINGSTON, WILLIAM *(1723–1790)*

The governor of New Jersey during the Revolutionary War, William Livingston was one of the most hated officials by the British and Tories, who called him *The Spurious Governor* and *The Knight of the Most Honorable Order of Starvation* because of his stern dealings with loyalists. He was the subject of several unsuccessful kidnap attempts.

Liz the Lion Killer—See
HOLTZMAN, ELIZABETH.

Lizzie Schwartzkopf—See **TAYLOR,
ELIZABETH.**

LLOYD, HAROLD *(1893–1971)*

Silent-film comedian Harold Lloyd has been aptly called *The King of Daredevil Comedy* since he personally performed the dangerous stunts in his movies. During one movie shooting, Lloyd lost his right index finger and thumb and thereafter always wore gloves or special prosthetic fingers when before the cameras.

LLOYD GEORGE, DAVID
(1862–1945)

The Liberal British prime minister who led his nation to victory in World War I, David Lloyd George had, as chancellor of the exchequer, pushed through his social insurance program in 1910. While chancellor, he was attacked by the Tories as *The Happy Warrior of Squandermania*, a sobriquet originated by Churchill.

Loaded Dies—See **DIES, MARTIN.**

Loathsome Limey, The—See
MOUNTBATTEN, LORD LOUIS.

Locksmith King, The—See **LOUIS
XVI OF FRANCE.**

Loco Americano—See **WALLACE,
WILLIAM "Big Foot."**

LODGE, HENRY CABOT
(1850–1924)

As the Republican senator from Massachusetts who successfully led congressional opposition to U.S. entry into the League of Nations, Henry Cabot Lodge became known as *The Destroyer of the League of Nations*.

LOEB, RICHARD—See Thrill Killers, The.

LOESCH, FRANK J. *(1853–1944)*

Frank J. Loesch, a venerable corporation counsel and founding member of the Chicago Crime Commission and five times its head, was dubbed by the press *The Inventor of the Public Enemies*. He coined the term while coming up with the idea of a list naming the worst offenders in the Chicago area.

LOESSER, FRANK *(1910–1969)*

Broadway composer Frank Loesser, who scored *Where's Charley, Guys and Dolls* and *The Most Happy Fella,* among others, wrote so many Army-oriented songs that he was called *The GI's Own Songwriter* and *The Army's One-Man Hit Parade.*

Log Cabin Harrison—See HARRISON, WILLIAM HENRY.

Logic-Chopping Machine, The—See MILL, JOHN STUART.

LOISON, LOUIS HENRI, COMTE *(1771–1816)*

Gen. Louis Henri Loison, a French cavalry commander, was nicknamed *Maneta,* or *The Bloody One-Handed.* Despite that inconvenience, as the British poet and novelist Robert Southey observed, "His misdeeds were never equalled or paralleled in the dark ages."

LOLLARD, WALTER *(?–1322)*

Attacking the seven sacraments and the ceremonies of the Catholic Church as priestly inventions, Walter Lollard was to be recognized later as *The Morning Star of the Reformation in Germany.* For uttering such offenses, demanding simplicity of ritual and denouncing temporal possessions as the ruination of the Church, Lollard fell victim to the Inquisition and was burned at the stake in Cologne in 1322. Nevertheless, thousands of his disciples spread his doctrines through Bohemia and Austria, and the Lollard movement became particularly powerful in England.

LOMBARDO, ANTONIO "the Scourge" *(1892–1928)*

One of the craftiest members of the Chicago underworld, Antonio Lombardo was nicknamed *The Scourge* because of the ruthless plots he concocted as Al Capone's *consigliere,* or adviser. He was murdered in 1928, leaving Capone to formulate his own treacheries thereafter.

LOMBARDO, GUY *(1902–1977)*

Bandleader Guy Lombardo was nicknamed *Mr. New Year's Eve* and *The Man Who Owns New Year's* because he seemingly forever held sway over ushering in the New Year on TV. He always insisted that when he went, he was taking New Year's with him.

LONDON, JACK *(1876–1916)*

U.S. author Jack London was nicknamed by admirers *The American Kipling* for his vigorous, skillfully told stories and novels and *The Boy Socialist* for his recurrent Marxian themes, best typified by *The Iron Heel.* On a more personal level, he was labeled *The Stallion* by friends as he moved from one frenzied love affair to another, and biographers have tended to characterize him as "a sexual anarchist."

London Bach—See BACH, JOHANN CHRISTIAN.

London Stout Russell—See RUSSELL, WILLIAM HOWARD.

Lone Eagle, The—See LINDBERGH, CHARLES A.

Lone Lion, The—See BORAH, WILLIAM E.

Lone Wolf of the Senate, The—See MORSE, WAYNE.

Lone Wolf of the Underworld, The—See MILLMAN, HARRY.

Lonely Old Volcano of the Right, That—See LEWIS, WYNDHAM.

LONG, HUEY (1893–1935)

A spellbinding Louisiana governor and later U.S. senator, Huey P. Long was the virtual political dictator of the state until his assassination in 1935. To his worshipers, the southern poor, he was *The Kingfish,* the undisputed master, as he decried their poverty. His foes saw him as just plain *Hooey Long.*

LONG, WILLIAM J. (1866–1952)

U.S. Congregational Church minister William J. Long wrote about nature and animal life for children, including such classics as *Briar Patch Philosophy* and *Wood Folk Comedies,* and was duly dubbed *Peter Rabbit.*

Long Fellow, The—See DE VALERA, EAMON.

Long Knife Warrior—See GIBSON, JOHN.

Long Meg of Westminster
(fl. 16th century)

A madam and procuress, *Long Meg of Westminster* was reputed to be one of England's finest practitioners of the carnal arts during the time of Henry VIII. She was described in a contemporary account of the Tudor Court as a "lusty, bouncing romp."

Long Nosed—See OVID.

Long Tom—See JEFFERSON, THOMAS.

LONGBAUGH, HARRY—See Sundance Kid, The.

LONGFELLOW, HENRY WADSWORTH (1807–1882)

Henry Wadsworth Longfellow has been called *The Children's Poet* because so much of his verse was written for or about children, and because some considered his poetry shallow and sentimental. Many referred to him as *The Poet of the Commonplace* for his ability to bestow beauty on the most common objects and thus inspire the most common lives. Edgar Allen Poe, who was not a total devotee of Longfellow, stated, "He has written brilliant poems, by accident; that is to say, when permitting his genius to get the better of his conventional habit of thinking, a habit deduced from German study."

LONGINUS, DIONYSIUS CASSIUS (c. 213–273)

Athenian Neo-Platonic philosopher Dionysius Cassius Longinus was called *The Living Cyclopedia, The Prince of Critics* and *The Walking Museum,* all tributes to his great learning. Longinus attributed the decline of Athenian letters to the destruction of democracy. He was beheaded following a conspiracy against Rome.

Longlegs—See HAAKON V MAGNUSSON.

LONGSTREET, JAMES (1821–1904)

One of Robert E. Lee's principal subordinates—with Stonewall Jackson—James Longstreet became a very controversial figure in the South. Some charged that his slowness cost the Army of Northern Virginia victory at Gettysburg and that Lee always accompanied Longstreet's column because he needed prodding. However, these charges did not gain wide popularity until after Lee died and Longstreet had joined the Republican Party—treason in the eyes of many Southerners. The fact is that Lee appointed Longstreet his senior ranking general ahead of Jackson, dubbing him *My Old War Horse.* During the war the southern press always affectionately termed him *Lee's War Horse.* It was said that while Lee regarded Jackson's corps as his fast-moving unit, he felt Longstreet's soldiers were the steady troops of his command and that, fittingly, he should travel with them.

LONGWORTH, ALICE LEE ROOSEVELT (1884–1980)

Mrs. Alice Roosevelt Longworth, the eldest daughter of President Theodore Roosevelt, was known in her White House years as *Princess Alice.* A no-torious free spirit, she once created quite a stir by taking pot shots with a pistol at telegraph poles during a long train trip. Forbidden to smoke under the White House roof, Alice took to puffing away on top of the roof. Roosevelt once said, "I can be President of the United States or I can control Alice. I cannot possibly do both." In her later years she was for decades the national capital's leading socialite and was dubbed *Washington's Other Monument* and *The Barbed Tongue.* Famed for her comments on presidents—she knew every one from Benjamin Harrison to Gerald Ford—she called Harding a "slob," Eisenhower a "boob," and Franklin Roosevelt "90 percent mush and 10 percent Eleanor." She also labeled Gerald Ford as "poor, dull Jerry," which caught on as a nickname for Ford. Perhaps her most appropriate sobriquet was *The Gadfly,* a term long used by friends. When she died in 1980 at the age of 96, authorities wanted the family to supply her profession for the death certificate. Knowing nothing about her, the authorities suggested "housewife." However, the family went with "gadfly."

Longy—See ZWILLMAN, ABNER "Longy."

Loquacious Linguist Labor Loves, The—See PERKINS, FRANCES.

Lord All-Pride—See SHEFFIELD, JOHN, DUKE OF BUCKINGHAMSHIRE AND EARL OF MULGRAVE.

Lord Bluster—See HOLLAND, HENRY FOX, LORD.

Lord Boston—See GAGE, THOMAS.

Lord Champion, The—See Cid, El.

Lord Fanny—See HERVY, JOHN.

Lord Haw Haw: WILLIAM JOYCE (1906–1946)

U.S. Nazi radio propagandist William Joyce, who broadcast to England from Hamburg during World War II, was called *Lord Haw Haw* by the British. The nickname took the edge off the false claims Joyce made to try to undermine public morale in Britain.

Lord High Executioner, The—See ANASTASIA, ALBERT.

Lord Minimus—See HUDSON, JEFFREY.

Lord of San Simeon—See HEARST, WILLIAM RANDOLPH.

Lord of the Ring, The—See GEBEL-WILLIAMS, GUNTHER.

Lord Porn: FRANCIS AUNGIER PAKENHAM (1905–)

Francis Aungier Pakenham, earl of Longford, political reformer and at one time leader of the House of Lords, was nicknamed *Lord Porn* because of his campaign in the early 1970s against pornography and what he regarded as a decline of moral standards. He called for a cleansing of films, television and books, a stricter definition of obscenity and the banning of sex education in school unless parents consented.

Lord Strutt—See CHARLES II OF SPAIN.

Lorenzo de Medici of Hungary, The—See CORVINUS, MATTHIAS, KING OF HUNGARY.

Lorenzo the Magnificent—See MEDICI, LORENZO DE.

Lorenzo the Magnificent of the Stage, The—See ZIEGFELD, FLORENZ, JR.

LORING, WILLIAM WING (1818–1886)

Confederate general William Wing Loring was nicknamed *Old Blizzards* because his rallying cry to his men was, "Give them blizzards, boys!" After Appomattox Loring sought other fields of military conflict. He served the Khedive of Egypt for several years and was made a pasha for his efforts. When he returned to the United States in 1879 he was called *Pasha Loring*.

Lost Leader, The—See CANNON, JAMES, JR.; WORDSWORTH, WILLIAM.

Louie the Lightbulb—See EISENBERG, LOUIS.

LOUIS, JOE (1914–1981)

Early in his career Joe Louis, who won the world heavyweight boxing crown in 1937, was dubbed *The Detroit Destroyer,* a name that failed to convey his awesome punching power. After his rematch one-round victory over Max Schmeling in 1938, *The Detroit Destroyer* was no more and Joe Louis became *The Brown Bomber*.

LOUIS III OF THE HOLY ROMAN EMPIRE *(c. 880–928)*

Ill-fated Holy Roman emperor Louis III ascended the throne of Provence in 890 and was crowned emperor in 910. He was deposed by Berengar I of Italy, who had him blinded and sent back to Provence to live out his remaining 23 years as *The Blind Emperor*.

LOUIS IV OF FRANCE *(c. 921–954)*

Louis IV of France was nicknamed *Louis D'Outremer,* or *Louis from Beyond the Seas,* because after the death of his father, Charles III, his mother spirited him to England and the protection of her brother, King Athelstan. The move was necessary to protect him from Rudolph of Burgundy, whom the nobles had elected king of France. Louis returned from his overseas exile in 936 on the death of Rudolph and took the throne.

LOUIS XII OF FRANCE *(1462–1515)*

One of the most popular French monarchs, Louis XII was affectionately known as *The Father of His People*. His reform of the courts and tax laws won him popularity. For a time he conquered Genoa, Milan, Venice and Naples in the Italian wars.

LOUIS XIV OF FRANCE *(1638–1715)*

Louis XIV of France was hailed as *The Sun King* because of both the opulence of his reign and the decadence of his court. His reign represented the high point of the French monarchy in a golden age of advances in engineering, architecture, painting and literature. However, his political policies, marked by his ''I am the state'' absolutism and revocation of the Edict of Nantes, weakened France

through the loss of merchants and workers, who settled elsewhere. By the end of *The Sun King's* rule the sun was setting on an impoverished nation.

LOUIS XVI OF FRANCE *(1754–1793)*

After his death by guillotine, Louis XVI of France became a martyr to some. To many others, however, he remained a villain. He was nicknamed *The Baker* after he and his wife Marie Antoinette, gave bread to the hungry mob at Versailles on Oct. 6, 1789. He was also known as *The Locksmith King* because of his hobby of making locks.

Louis from Beyond the Seas—See LOUIS IV OF FRANCE.

LOUIS PHILIPPE I OF FRANCE *(1773–1850)*

Known as *Philippe Egalite* during the French Revolution, Louis Philippe of France joined the Jacobin Club in 1790. In 1793 he plotted to overthrow the Republic by marching on Paris but was thwarted and fled the country. He returned upon the restoration of the Bourbons and took extremely liberal political positions. When the July Revolution broke out in 1830, Louis Philippe stood out as the logical *Citizen King* and was proclaimed monarch of France. During his reign he suppressed the Republicans and Socialists while advancing middle-class interests. He was overthrown by the Revolution of 1848 and fled to England.

Louis the Cruel: LOUIS XI OF FRANCE *(1423–1483)*

Louis XI of France was called *Louis the Cruel* because of the repressiveness of his reign. He was also nicknamed *The Universal Spider* for constantly conducting intrigues to increase his power. He is credited with plotting against the throne while still dauphin and waging war on Burgundy within four years of gaining the crown.

Louis the Desired: LOUIS XVIII OF FRANCE (1755–1824)

King Louis XVIII of France was nicknamed *The Desired* precisely because he was hardly desired by the people. The brother of the beheaded Louis XVI, he claimed the throne after the supposed death of the dauphin in 1795. He was enthroned in 1814, following the fall of Napoleon, but had to flee during the Hundred Days. After he was restored once more, his reign grew steadily more harsh until his death.

Louis the Do-Nothing—See Louis the Sluggard.

Louis the Fat: LOUIS VI OF FRANCE (1081–1137)

One of the most corpulent French kings, Louis VI was known as *Louis the Fat*. In his forties he put on so much weight that he could no longer mount his horse. He was seldom ridiculed, however, because his reign was one of peace and prosperity, and he was accordingly called *Louis the Wide-Awake*.

Louis the Foolish: LOUIS VII OF FRANCE (1120–1180)

King Louis VII of France was called *Le Jeune,* or *The Young,* for having succeeded to the throne at the age of 17. A most inept monarch, he followed a political policy that eventually left Henry II of England with more power in France than he had. He was of course dubbed *Louis the Foolish.*

Louis the Just: LOUIS XIII OF FRANCE (1601–1643)

Louis XIII of France was sarcastically nicknamed *The Just* because he was considered neither upright nor moral. His reign was marked by the excesses of his mother, Marie de Medici, the queen regent, and his minister, Cardinal Richelieu.

Louis the Lion: LOUIS VIII OF FRANCE (1187–1226)

Louis VIII of France won the accolade *Louis the Lion* after he forced John Lackland to flee the siege of La Roche-aux-Moines in 1214, even though the latter enjoyed superior forces. The nickname was a play on the fact that John's brother was called Richard the Lionhearted. By contrast the French dubbed John Lackland Dollheart.

Louis the Pious: LOUIS I OF THE HOLY ROMAN EMPIRE (778–840)

Holy Roman Emperor Louis I, the third son of Charlemagne, was renowned as *Louis the Pious* because of his efforts to reform and purify the clergy and do away with immorality at court.

Louis the Quarreler: LOUIS X OF FRANCE (1289–1316)

Although Louis X of France ruled only about two years, during that short reign he was known as *Louis the Quarreler* because of his frequent disputes with advisers. He even ignored suggestions that he not overindulge in cold wine after becoming overheated playing ball, a practice that may have led to his contraction of pleurisy and death.

Louis the Sluggard: LOUIS V OF FRANCE (966?–987)

Louis V of France was known as *Louis the Sluggard* or *The Do-Nothing* because of his self-indulgence and the fact that he did nothing. He failed even to produce an heir, thus ending the Carolingian succession.

Louis the Well-Beloved: LOUIS XV OF FRANCE (1710–1774)

Louis XV of France was known as *The Well-Beloved* precisely because he was not. Rather he was regarded as a libertine. The king was perceptive enough to see his faults and was famous for observing, "After me, the deluge."

Louis the Wide-Awake—See Louis the Fat.

Louisa—See WALLACE, LEWIS.

Louisiana Ram—See MOUTON, ROBERT L.

Louse in the Locks of Literature, A— See COLLINS, CHURTON.

Lovable Egghead, The—See USTINOV, PETER.

Lovable Lou—See KORETZ, LEO.

LOVEL, LORD—See Rat, Cat and Lovel our Dogge.

Lover Boy—See GRAY, JUDD.

Lover of Candour, A—See HOPKINSON, FRANCIS.

Lover of Mankind, The—See DEBS, EUGENE V.

Loving His Father—See PTOLEMY IV.

LOW, DAVID (1891–1963)

British political cartoonist David Low became so famous as the creator of *Colonel Blimp*—a symbol of unyielding British conservatism—that the name of the character stuck to him as a sobriquet.

LOWDEN, FRANK O. (1861–1943)

A Republican governor of Illinois and a U.S. congressman, Frank O. Lowden was called *The Sage of Sinnissippi*, after the name of his home. It is dubious that the sobriquet was helpful to him in his quest for the Republican presidential nomination in 1920 and 1924.

LOWE, JOSEPH "Rowdy Joe" (1846?–1899)

Joseph Lowe was a western gunman and procurer who in the 20th century would be called *The Lucky Luciano of the Plains*. In his day he was referred to as *Rowdy Joe* because of his antisocial behavior, such as shooting men who tried to take one of his harlots "away from all this." On another occasion, a lawman stopped a fight between *Rowdy Joe* and another man and demanded they apologize to one another. Lowe said to his foe, "Come here. I want to kiss and make up." Then he bit off the end of the man's nose.

LOWE, THADDEUS S. C. (1832–1913)

During the Civil War Professor Thaddeus S. C. Lowe served as the director of the branch of engineers manning the hot air balloons used for observation by the Union armies in the field. He thus gained the nickname *The Father of the U.S. Air Force.*

Lower Case Cummings—See CUMMINGS, E. E.

LOWSHER, JAMES (?–1802)

Known as one of the stingiest men in England during the 18th century, Sir James Lowsher, earl of Lonsdale, was called *Farthing Jamie*. He was noted for patronizing only remote and low-priced eating establishments when visiting London. If a single item on the menu had been raised even a farthing, he would storm from the place never to return.

Loyal Hard Hat, The—See BRENNAN, PETER J.

LOYOLA, ST. IGNATIUS OF (1491–1556)

Crippled for life and hardly ever free of pain after receiving a leg wound from a cannon ball as a combat soldier, the future St. Ignatius, founder of the Society of Jesus, or Jesuits, was known as *The Little Man with the Smile* for his forbearance in accepting his suffering.

LUCCHESE, THOMAS (1903–1967)

A major mafioso in America, Thomas Lucchese became known as *Three-Finger Brown* after losing three fingers in an accident as a youth. He adopted the name from a leading major league pitcher of the same name who had one finger missing. However, when he reached high Mafia standing, he ordered that he never be so addressed.

LUCHAIRE, CORINNE (1921–1950)

French actress Corinne Luchaire was dubbed her country's *No. 1 Woman Quisling* after the Norwegian Nazi collaborator Vidkun Quisling, because of her collaboration with the Nazis in World War II.

LUCIAN (c. 120–c. 180)

The famed Greek writer, satirist and rhetorician Lucian was a major force in the revival of Greek literature under the Roman empire and has been dubbed *The Voltaire of Grecian Literature*. The greatest of the Greek satirists after Aristophanes, he is most famed for his *Dialogues* and *The True History,* the latter recounting an imaginary voyage to the moon, parodying all such contemporary fanciful narratives and serving as a model for Rabelais, Swift and Cyrano de Bergerac.

LUCIANO, CHARLES "Lucky" (1897–1962)

When Charles Luciano became the first underworld figure to be taken for "a ride" and return alive, he was admiringly acknowledged as *Lucky Luciano,* even though he was knife-slashed to the bone on his right cheek, leaving him with a permanently drooping right eye. Who his abductors were has long been in dispute. Luciano told whatever varying story served his interests best: his torturers had been one of two rival gangs or a bunch of rogue cops trying to make him reveal the location of a huge narcotics shipment. Perhaps the most likely version was that he was abducted and mutilated by the family of a cop whose daughter he had dishonored. Since that was hardly heroic, Luciano came up with the "ride" story, which added to his glory in the underworld.

LUCILIUS, CAIUS (c. 180–103 B.C.)

The satirical poet Caius Lucilius has been called *The Father of Roman Satire*. Of him, Dryden wrote that he "to Roman vices did the mirror hold" and "showed worth on foot, and rascals in a coach."

LUCKNER, COUNT FELIX VON (1881–1966)

After the ship under his command, the German raider *Seeadler,* broke through a British blockade to attack Allied shipping during World War I, Count Felix von Luckner was nicknamed *The Sea Devil*. He harassed shipping in the Atlantic and then in the South Pacific before finally being captured in 1917.

Lucky Lindy—See LINDBERGH, CHARLES A.

Lucky Luciano of the Plains, The—See LOWE, Rowdy Joe.

Lucky Swede, The—See ANDERSON, CHARLIE.

LUCRETIUS (c. 96–55 B.C.)

Lucretius (Titus Lucretius Carus), the Roman poet, wrote the six-volume *De Rerum Natura (On the Nature of Things),* commonly regarded as the greatest philosophical poem of antiquity. In recognition of the lasting quality of his work, his countrymen called him *The Sculptor Poet*.

Lucullus—See BERNARD, SAMUEL.

LUDLOW, LOUIS LEON (1873–1950)

A 10-term U.S. representative and an outspoken isolationist, Indiana Democrat Louis Leon Ludlow was nicknamed *Peace Ludlow* for his Ludlow War Referendum Resolution of 1938 and for his naval and arms limitations bills.

Ludwig the Leaper: MARGRAVE OF THURINGIA (1042–?)

Ludwig, an 11th century margrave of Thuringia, became famous as *Ludwig the Leaper* for his daring escape from the castle of Giebichenstein, near Halle, by leaping into the Saale River.

LUETGERT, ADOLPH (1848–1911)

Chicago wife killer Adolph Luetgert became known as *The Sausage-Maker Murderer* because he melted down his wife's body along with meat being prepared for sausage in his food plant. He was caught after her wedding ring, which she had been unable to remove for years, was found in the drain of the vat.

LUKE, FRANK, JR. (1897–1918)

During World War I U.S. fighter pilot Frank Luke, Jr., downed 21 German planes but was nicknamed *The Balloon Buster* for his greater daring in shooting down a number of enemy balloons. This was most hazardous because the balloons were protected at all times by heavy ground fire, which made an attacking plane, rather than the balloon, a "sitting duck." Luke died in 1918 in a ground fight with German troops after his plane was forced down in enemy territory in France.

LUNDY, BENJAMIN (1789–1839)

Recognized as one of the first active abolitionists in America, Benjamin Lundy became known as *Peter the Hermit of the Abolitionist Movement*.

Luscious Lucius—See BEEBE, LUCIUS.

Lusty Stucley—See STUCLEY, THOMAS.

LUXEMBURG, ROSA (1870–1919)

Dubbed *Red Rosa*, German socialist revolutionary Rosa Luxemburg was considered by European governments "the most feared woman" of the early 20th century. Along with Karl Liebknecht she was arrested by German troops in 1919 and shot "while trying to escape."

Lying Nun, The—See MONK, MARIA.

Lying Traveller, The—See MAUNDEVILLE, JOHN.

LYNN, VERA (1916–   )

Certainly the most famous British vocalist during World War II, radio singer Vera Lynn entertained troops within a few miles of combat and was called *The Forces' Sweetheart*.

LYSENKO, TROFIM D. (1898–1977)

A major proponent of what was actually an old idea, Soviet biologist T. D. Lysenko believed in the inheritance of acquired characteristics, in opposition to mainstream biology and genetics. As a protege of Josef Stalin, Lysenko was hailed by the Soviet press as *The Genius of the Soil*. While others denounced him as a fanatical fake, he became director of the Soviet Institute of Genetics, and many leading Russian scientists were driven from their posts and some even jailed or liquidated. *The Genius of the Soil* continued to thrive under Khrushchev but fell from favor with the latter's political demise in 1964. By then the Soviet lag in biology compared to the rest of the world was all too obvious, and Lysenko's hoaxes could no longer be concealed. Supposedly prize cows he had bred were found to be actually nothing more than the result of secret culling, and his experimental trees that grew in barren areas were actually planted in moist soil, unlike the dry ground around them. Lysenko's statues were removed and he lived out his life in secluded retirement, no longer nicknamed *The Genius of the Soil*.

Lysenko of the New World, The—See BURBANK, LUTHER.

MACARTHUR, DOUGLAS (1880–1964)

The many nicknames of U.S. general Douglas MacArthur may be divided into the "I Love Mac" category and the "I Loathe Mac" category. Sobriquets from the former include: *The Beau Brummel of the Army, The D'Artagnan of the A. E., The Napoleon of Luzon, The Magnificent* and *The Voice of God*. Some of the less favorable include: *God's Cousin, Almighty Mac* and *Dugout Doug,* the last being the name given him by GIs in the Pacific during World War II. The allegation was that MacArthur cowered in a tunnel at Corregidor while his men were dying on Bataan. In fact, MacArthur often exposed himself to enemy bombardment as an inspiration to his men.

MACDONALD, JEANETTE
(1907–1965)

Jeanette MacDonald, the popular soprano in many Hollywood movies, and Nelson Eddy, her singing partner, were known as America's Sweethearts. But she had another, less flattering nickname. In the profession, she was referred to as the *Iron Butterfly,* meaning that while she appeared to the public as a performer with the beauty and grace of a butterfly, she was a rather iron-willed person who demanded and usually got her own way.

MACDONALD, RAMSAY (1866–1937)

A Labor Party leader and the first Labor prime minister in British history, Ramsay MacDonald was often savaged by the Conservatives as *The Boneless Wonder,* a phrase originated by Winston Churchill to highlight McDonald's political vascillation and indecisiveness.

MACFADDEN, BERNARR
(1868–1955)

Magazine publisher, health faddist and eccentric Bernarr MacFadden, or *Body Love MacFadden,* as the press delighted in calling him, produced, among other things, a number of publications dedicated to his belief that right living, right diet and right exercise could make any man live to be 125. At his magazine offices he sat at a desk in the middle of the floor while his editors labored above him on balcony levels. At any moment MacFadden might hop up on his desk and lead his editors in

required exercises, and from his vantage point he could spot any slackers. His magazines, especially *Physical Culture,* featured virile males and busty females in scantily clad "classic poses." These were forerunners of "cheesecake" magazines aimed at readers who did not share MacFadden's penchant for physical well-being. He lived to be 86, engaging in parachute jumps shortly before his death.

MCADAM, JOHN L. (1756–1836)

Scottish engineer John L. McAdam revolutionized transportation by inventing the macadam road, made of layers of interlocking stones over a prepared bed. This remarkable accomplishment earned him the honorific *The Colossus of Roads.*

MCADOO, WILLIAM GIBBS
(1863–1941)

As the guiding genius behind the construction of the Hudson Tubes, railroad tunnels under the Hudson River connecting New York and New Jersey, former California senator William G. McAdoo was called *McAdoo Tubes.* During the administration of Woodrow Wilson, McAdoo served as secretary of the treasury and in 1914 married the president's daughter Eleanor, winning the disparaging sobriquet *The Crown Prince* from Republicans.

McAdoo Tubes—See MCADOO, WILLIAM GIBBS.

MCCARTHY, EUGENE (1916–   )

In 1968 U. S. senator Eugene McCarthy of Minnesota forced Lyndon Johnson out of the presidential race by a strong run against him in the New Hampshire Democratic primary. During the campaign he became known as *Clean Gene* because the anti-war youths who worked for him in the campaign took pains to be clean-cut and well-dressed so as to avoid giving the impression that they were "hippie" protesters and their candidate was a radical left-winger.

MCCARTHY, JOSEPH R. (1908–1957)

U.S. senator Joseph R. McCarthy of Wisconsin, whose name became synonymous with militant anti-communism and witchhunt investigations into domestic subversion during the early 1950s, came out of World War II with the nickname *Tail Gunner Joe,* supposedly reflecting his combat record in the Pacific as a Marine lieutenant. However, exposes by columnists Drew Pearson and Jack Anderson destroyed that image. Actually a desk officer, he only went on "milk run bombings" of abandoned Japanese airfields. Nevertheless one credit given *Tail Gunner Joe* by the Associated Press did stand up. He had indeed fired 4,700 rounds of ammunition in one day, the most by any soldier in the war. However, the only target of this awesome shooting display had been foliage, which led his colleagues to put up a huge sign back at the base: SAVE OUR COCONUT TREES. SEND McCARTHY BACK TO WISCONSIN.

McCarty, Henry—See Billy the Kid.

MCCLELLAN, GEORGE B. (1826–1885)

Following the disastrous rout of the Union Army at the First Battle of Bull Run, the Lincoln administration was searching for a hero and a savior. George B. McClellan was the only one to be found. Only 10 days before, his army in Western Virginia had won a minor battle, although credit for the victory should have gone to his subordinate, since McClellan failed to advance as he was supposed to. However, because these details were not known at the time, McClellan, "the hero," was put in charge of the army defending Washington. The press dubbed him *The Young Napoleon,* in anticipation of his future victories. While he proved to be an excellent administrator, reorganizing the disarrayed Bull Run contingent into an effective fighting machine, he was an extremely cautious commander, constantly overestimating the opposition and besieging Lincoln with requests for more troops and supplies. In Washington circles he became known as *Mac the Unready* and *The Little Corporal of Unsought Fields.* Failing to produce the victories demanded of him, he was finally removed from command in late 1862. But in one respect his nickname *The Young Napoleon* was appropriate: he had limitless ambition. He often wrote his wife that his troops, who affectionately called him *Little Mac,* would back him in a move to become dicatator. He entered the race for president in 1864 but was defeated by Lincoln.

MCCLELLAN, JOHN (1896–1977)

Known best to the public for his investigations of organized crime and abuses in the labor movement, U.S. senator John McClellan of Arkansas was called *The Gangster's Nightmare* and *The Man Behind the Frown,* a comment on the dour-faced righteous indignation he exhibited when questioning witnesses.

MCCLENDON, SARAH (1913–   )

Long-time White House reporter Sarah McClendon, known for her incisive, if sometimes emotional, questioning, has been dubbed by her colleagues *The Holy Terror from Texas.*

MCCLINTIC, JAMES V. (1878–1948)

A long-time Democratic congressman from Texas and advocate of a strong Air Force, James V. McClintic was nicknamed *Rivet McClintic* by those who mocked him for insisting that every rivet used in the construction of the dirigible *Akron* be individually inspected and tested. The *Akron* went down in 1933 with the loss of 73 lives.

MCCOY, WILLIAM—See Real McCoy, The.

MCDONALD, MARIE *(1924?–1965)*

Curvacious screen star Marie McDonald was dubbed *The Body* by movie publicists, and the screen colony agreed that the name also covered the full range of her acting abilities.

MCDOUGAL, DAVID STOCKTON *(1809–1882)*

A U.S. naval officer during the Civil War, David McDougal sailed his ship deep in Asiatic waters to hunt Confederate privateers and proved rather unmindful of Japanese territorial waters. When three Japanese naval vessels attacked in July 1863, McDougal's ship put them out of commission and effectively countered land batteries, winning him the nickname *The American Devil* from the Japanese.

MCENROE, JOHN *(1959–)*

U.S. tennis superstar John McEnroe has earned such sobriquets as *Superbrat* and *McTantrum* because of his ill-tempered displays on the court, directed especially against the officials but at times against the audience as well.

MCFARLANE, WILLIAM D. *(1894–)*

A Texas Democratic congressman, William D. McFarlane was tabbed *Anti-McFarlane* because of his opposition to virtually all of President Franklin Roosevelt's New Deal proposals of the 1930s.

MCGOVERN, GEORGE, S. *(1922–)*

Democratic senator George S. McGovern was called *The Master Wrecker* by political foes who felt his presidential campaign against Richard Nixon in 1972 was doomed to failure because of "leftward" tilt.

MCGUFFEY, WILLIAM HOLMES *(1800–1873)*

U.S. educator William Holmes McGuffey was known as *The Creator of the "Eclectic Readers,"* for his six volumes, published between 1836 and 1857, that became the standard 19th century public school texts. Because they sold 122 million copies and shaped the minds of three generations of school children, McGuffey was most deservedly called *The Schoolmaster of Our Nation.*

MCGURN, "Machine Gun" JACK *(1904–1936)*

An Italian gangster and hit man for Al Capone, Jack McGurn, whose real name was James DeMora, was nicknamed *Machine Gun* for his proficiency with the weapon. He adopted the name Jack McGurn because it was part of the underworld prejudice of the day—even among many Italian gangsters—that a real criminal should sport a good Irish name. In addition to his criminal endeavors, he tried his hand at boxing, another field where an Irish monicker was de rigueur.

MCKINLEY, WILLIAM *(1843–1901)*

While a student at Pollard Seminary in Ohio, William McKinley gained the nickname *The Stockingfoot Orator* because the town of Pollard was so muddy that he often discarded his dirty shoes when appearing onstage for school debates. When he became the 25th president of the U.S., McKinley was called *The Napoleon of Protection* for his support of protective tariffs. His campaign manager, Mark Hanna, dubbed him *Prosperity's Advance Agent* because shortly after his election economic conditions greatly improved. Theodore Roosevelt agreed to run as McKinley's vice presidential candidate in 1900 even though he did not think highly of the president, referring to him as *A Chocolate Eclair,* an allusion to what Roosevelt thought was McKinley's lack of backbone in dealing with vested interests.

MCLAUGHLIN, JAMES (1842–1923)

Indian agent James McLaughlin called himself *The Indian's Friend,* an identification that most whites but few Indians accepted. It is clear to historians that the Army used McLaughlin, who was married to a half-breed Santee woman, in its attempts to suppress the remnants of Indian culture. McLaughlin gave the arrest order that resulted in the fatal shooting of Sitting Bull.

MCLEAN, EVALYN WALSH (1886–1947)

Society leader and owner of the Hope diamond, Mrs. Evalyn Walsh McLean was known as *Washington's Cinderella* after her marriage to millionaire playboy Ned McLean. Exceedingly gullible, she was prey to various fortune hunters and con men and was taken for $104,000 by an incredible rogue, Gaston B. Means, who assured her he was in touch with the Lindbergh-baby kidnappers and could arrange the child's ransom. All Mrs. McLean got for her money was an evermore complicated story that was pure fantasy.

MCPHERSON, AIMEE SEMPLE (1890–1944)

Sister Aimee Semple McPherson was America's most successful female evangelist and was hailed by her admirers in the 1920s as *The World's Most Pulchritudinous Evangelist.* Her career started in decline in 1926 when she was supposedly kidnapped. It later developed, to the satisfaction of all but her most unquestioning followers, that what had really taken place was a sexual tryst.

McTantrum—See MCENROE, JOHN.

Mac the Knife—See MACMILLIAN, HAROLD.

Mac the Unready—See MCCLELLAN, GEORGE B.

Macauley of the South, The—See JONES, CHARLES COLCOCK.

MACCABEE, JUDAS (?–160 BC)

Judas Maccabee, who was nicknamed *The Hammerer,* founded a Jewish dynasty after leading a revolt against the Syrian king Antiochus Ephiphanes when he tried to force Greek worship upon the Jews. He was killed in battle eight years later in 160 BC.

MACDONALD, DWIGHT (1906–1982)

Dwight Macdonald, left-wing author, essayist, editor and critic, was noted for his individualism, which prevented him from embracing any particular ideology for long and led to his being dubbed *The One-Man Anti-Communist Left Movement.* Even when he joined the splintered Trotskyite movement, he was known jocularly as a faction of one. Antifascist philosopher Hannah Arendt stated the sentiment somewhat similarly by labeling him *All Dwight.*

MACDONALD, JAMES (1741–1766)

Sir James Macdonald, seventh baronet of Sleat, gained much fame for his learning and grace of manners as a young man. On a tour of the Continent he was welcomed in all the great cities and called *The Scottish Marcellus*. The cardinals of Rome especially lavished attention upon him, but he became ill there and died at the age of 25.

MACDONALD, JOHN A. (1815–1891)

Canada's first and long-time prime minister, John A. Macdonald was adept at delaying issues until somehow the problems solved themselves or quietly disappeared. This procrastination earned from his enemies the lampoon *Old Tomorrow*.

Macher, Der—See SCHMIDT, HELMUT.

Machiavel—See CECIL, WILLIAM, LORD BURLEIGH.

Machine Gun Kelly—See KELLY, GEORGE R. "Machine Gun."

Machine Gun McGurn—See MCGURN, "Machine Gun" JACK.

Machine Gun Molly: MONICA PROIETTI SMITH (1938–1967)

One of the most violent female criminals in recent years, Monica Proietti Smith of Canada was known as *Machine Gun Molly* because of her proficiency with the weapon. Credited with a long string of crimes, *Machine Gun Molly* was killed in a gun battle with police following a holdup in suburban Montreal.

Mack, Connie: CORNELIUS MCGILLICUDDY (1862–1956)

Cornelius McGillicuddy, the fabled long-time baseball manager, got the nickname *Connie Mack* because his name had to be shortened to fit on the lineup sheet or scorecard.

MACKENZIE, KENNETH (1797–1861)

Scottish-American fur trader Kenneth Mackenzie was known as *The King of the Missouri* because, through competitive ruthlessness, he dominated the fur trade on that river and in much of the West. His personal manners were those of an aristocratic martinet and he lived grandly on the frontier, always wearing a uniform.

MACKENZIE, WILLIAM LYON (1795–1861)

A pioneer in the fight to loosen British colonial rule in Canada and the firebrand of the Reformers in Upper Canada, William Lyon Mackenzie was called *The O'Connell of Canada*, after the 19th century Irish patriot Daniel O'Connell. He quite possibly outdid O'Connell in attacking the power elite, crying: "Tories! Pensioners! Placemen! Profligates! Orangemen! Churchmen! Brokers! Gamblers! Parasites! allow me to congratulate you. Your feet are at last on the people's necks."

MACKINTOSH, JAMES (1765–1832)

Sir James Mackintosh, who had written in support of the French Revolution but later accepted a judgeship in India from British prime minister William Pitt, an enemy of that cause, was denounced by Dr. Samuel Parr and his supporters as *The Apostate*.

MACMILLAN, HAROLD (1894–   )

British prime minister from 1957 to 1963, Harold Macmillan became known as *Mac the Knife* following his sacking of seven cabinet ministers in 1962. Liberal Party leader Jeremy Thorpe commented on *Mac the Knife* : "Greater love hath no man than this, that he lay down his friends for his life."

MACON, NATHANIEL (1758–1837)

Recognized as the first patriarch of the U.S. Congress, Nathaniel Macon of North Carolina was accorded the title *The Father of the House*. He served uninterrupted in the House of Representatives and later in the Senate from 1791 through 1828.

MACPHERSON, JAMES (1736–1796)

Eighteenth century Scottish poet James Macpherson published *The Works of Ossian* (1760–63), purported to be actual translations of the poetry of the 14th century Celtic bard, which recounted the heroic adventures of his father, the hero Fion. The poems captured the imagination of Europe and did much to foster the study of folklore in general. They have been the source of much controversy, however, and many scholars now attribute the poems to Macpherson himself. He has therefore been known as *The Sire of Ossian*.

MACREADY, WILLIAM CHARLES (1793–1851)

The eminent English actor William Charles Macready was lionized in his home country as *The King Arthur of the Stage,* but he received a most contrary treatment in the United States. A jealous feud erupted between Macready and the American actor Edwin Forrest. When Macready replaced Forrest in *Macbeth* at the Astor Place Opera House in 1849, anger ran high among New York's Irish population, and a huge mob decided to stop the performance by Macready, denouncing him as *The English Hog*. It did so by hurling rotten eggs, pennies and even chairs onto the stage and tossing papers filled with gunpowder into the chandeliers. Exhorted by Washington Irving, John Jacob Astor and others, Macready tried again on May 10. A hysterical crowd of 15,000 surrounded the theater, and inside, Macready was bombarded with bricks until he fled the stage. The angry mob then set the theater on fire. In the ensuing Astor Place Riots 23 persons were killed and well over 100 injured, and soldiers had to be called in to quell the action. *The English Hog* was smuggled out of the city and taken to Boston, from where he sailed to England, never to return to the United States.

Mad Anne: ANNE HENNIS TROTTER BAILEY (1742–1825)

One of the most remarkable fighting women in American history, Anne Hennis Trotter Bailey received little public acclaim for her heroism other than the nickname *Mad Anne*. Her first husband, Richard Trotter, was killed by Indians in 1774. Seeking to avenge his death, she dressed as a man and joined a military contingent on the Kanawha River in what is now West Virginia. She was a sharpshooter, and as a messenger during the Revolutionary War, she risked her life dozens of times traveling from fort to fort. No thought was ever given to recognizing her acts since they were considered more insane than heroic.

Mad Austrian, The—See BLUDHORN, CHARLES.

Mad Bell—See BELL, WILLIAM.

Mad Bomber, The: GEORGE METESKY *(1903–   )*

During the 1950s a mysterious mad bomber terrorized New York, planting more than 30 homemade bombs in such busy places as train stations and movie theaters, including Radio City Music Hall. Eventually *The Mad Bomber* was caught and identified as George Metesky. After being found criminally insane, he was sent to a mental hospital. In 1973 he was pronounced cured and released.

Mad Cavalier, The—See RUPERT, PRINCE.

Mad Dog of the Bunch, The—See TRACY, HARRY.

Mad Duck—See KARRAS, ALEX.

Mad Fred—See DEEMING, FREDERICK BAILEY.

Mad Jack—See PERCIVAL, JOHN.

Mad Monk, The—See RASPUTIN, GRIGORI EFIMOVICH.

Mad Monk of Massachusetts, The—See DRINAN, ROBERT.

Mad Pittsburgh Playboy, The—See THAW, HARRY W.

Mad Poet, The—See CLARKE, MCDONALD; LEE, NATHANIEL.

Mad Priest, The—See BALL, JOHN.

Mad Rudi—See HESS, RUDOLPH.

Mad Russian, The—See VUKOVICH, WILLIAM.

Mad Shelley—See SHELLEY, PERCY BYSSHE.

Mad Swinburne—See SWINBURNE, ALGERNON.

Madame Deficit—See MARIE ANTOINETTE.

Madame Featherlegs *(fl. late 19th century)*

A Wyoming madam known to posterity only by her nickname *Madame Featherlegs* was so called because of her custom of riding stride-saddle at her Rawhide Buttes "hog ranch" with her long red underwear flapping about her legs, much like chicken feathers.

Madame Killer—See RESTELL, MADAME.

Madame Mustache: ELEANOR DUMONT *(1831–1879)*

One of the most storied gambling ladies and brothel keepers of the Old West, a French woman named Simone Jules, alias Eleanor Dumont, became famous as *Madame Mustache* because of a full mustache she sported, although artists of the day appear to have endowed it with more flowing growth than it really possessed. Her wealth gave her all the lovers she wanted despite her mustache, although they do seem to have decamped with her money with monotonous regularity. She caught up with one of them and shotgunned him to death. *Madame Mustache* committed suicide in Bodie, Calif., in 1879 after being cleaned out by a pair of card sharks.

Madcap Maxie—See BAER, MAX.

MADDOX, LESTER G. (1915–   )

Flamboyant restauranteur and archsegregationist Lester G. Maddox, who was elected governor of Georgia, was nicknamed *Mr. White Backlash*. He later became a nightclub entertainer.

Mademoiselle, La Grande: ANNE, DUCHESSE DE MONTPENSIER (1627–1693)

Anne, Duchesse de Montpensier, the cousin of Louis XIV, was called *La Grande Mademoiselle* by some because of her strength of character and by others because of her wealth and position.

MADER, CHARLEY (fl. 1870s–1880s)

One of the top criminals in New Orleans during the 19th century, Charley Mader was a leading holdup man and killer, a rather remarkable achievement considering his apparent mental capacity. A German, he somehow thought wearing a false Prussian-style beard was a perfect disguise. Indeed, it led to Prussian Charley's unmasking and his imprisonment in the late 1880s.

MADISON, JAMES (1751–1836)

James Madison, fourth president of the United States, was *The Father of the Constitution* and *The Sage of Montpelier*. Since he was only 5 feet 4 inches and weighed less than 100 pounds, Washington Irving dubbed him *A Withered Little Apple-*

john. His popular nickname *Jemmy* was an allusion to his diminutive size as well as his boyish subservience to his mentor Thomas Jefferson.

Madman of Macedonia, The—See ALEXANDER THE GREAT.

Madman of the North—See CHARLES XII OF SWEDEN.

Maecenas of Book-Lovers, The—See GROLIER, JEAN.

Maecenas of His Day, The—See MAZARIN, JULES.

Maecenas of His Time, The—See VISCONTI, GALEAZZO.

Maestro Seducer, The—See STOKOWSKI, LEOPOLD.

Magdalen Smitz—See SMITZ, GASPAR.

Magic Fingers of Radio, The—See DUCHIN, EDWIN FRANK ''Eddie.''

Magical Maker of Mobiles, The—See CALDER, ALEXANDER.

Magical Maker of Stabiles, The—See CALDER, ALEXANDER.

MAGLIABECCHI, ANTHONY (1633–1714)

Italian bibliographer Anthony Magliabecchi was called *The Glutton of Literature, The Living Li-*

brary and *The Devourer of Books*, all tributes to his great learning, and his statements of facts were considered most authoritative. He earned a certain jealous enmity from the duke of Tuscany because virtually all literary visitors to Florence would first seek out Magliabecchi before calling on the duke.

MAGLIE, SAL ''the Barber'' (1917–)

Long-time New York Giants pitcher Sal Maglie was nicknamed *The Barber* because he threw his ''brush-back'' pitch so close to a batter's head that it could almost give him a shave.

Magnanimous, The—See ALFONSO V, KING OF NAPLES, ARAGON AND SICILY.

Magnificent, The—See MACARTHUR, DOUGLAS; MEDICI, LORENZO DE.

Magnificent Giant, The—See MELCHIOR, LAURITZ.

Magnificent Heber, The—See HEBER, RICHARD.

Magnificent Rube, The—See RICKARD, ''Tex'' GEORGE L.

MAGNUS, EARL OF NORTHUMBERLAND (?–1449)

Magnus, earl of Northumberland, was noted for his long red beard and was celebrated by the English as *Magnus Red-beard*. The Scotch derisively called him *Magnus with the Red Mane*.

Magnus Red-beard—See MAGNUS, EARL OF NORTHUMBERLAND.

Magnus the Law Mender: MAGNUS VI OF NORWAY (1238–1280)

A rarity at the time, King Magnus VI of Norway was a monarch of peace, bringing an end to the Scottish War three years after he ascended the throne in 1266. Magnus then turned his attention to his nation's laws, winning the sobriquet *Magnus the Law Mender*.

Magnus with the Red Mane—See MAGNUS, EARL OF NORTHUMBERLAND.

MAGRUDER, JEB STUART (1934–)

Because of the eagerness he showed for performing dirty tricks during the Nixon Administration's Watergate affair, Jeb Stuart Magruder, special assistant to President Richard Nixon, became known, particulary in college circles, as *The Brown-Nose of the Year*.

MAGRUDER, JOHN BANKHEAD (1810–1871)

Famed for his courtly manners and lavish parties, John Bankhead Magruder was a bon vivant during his tenure as commandant of Fort Adams, R.I., in the pre-Civil War U.S. Army. His fellow officers at the fort dubbed him *Prince John*. After a mixed career as a Confederate general, Magruder died in Texas in what must have seemed to him abject poverty, considering his princely past.

MAHANEY, JACK—See American Jack Sheppard, The.

MAHARAJ JI, GURU (1959–   )

Much of young "hip" society has embraced the young Indian guru Maharaj Ji and accepted his claims of being a true avatar. Rennie Davis, who was a leading activist against the Vietnam War, once said, "I would cross the planet on my hands and knees to touch his toe." However, others have been less impressed with his religion, noting his $100,000 town house in London, his private jets and yachts, his telex machines and his airline stewardess bride. In Detroit a nonbeliever smacked him in the face with a shaving-cream pie, but perhaps the greatest insult of all comes from the holymen of the Upper Ganges, who refer to him simply as *That Fat Boy.*

Mahatma, The—See RICKEY, BRANCH.

MAHONE, WILLIAM "Little Billy" (1826–1895)

At 5 feet 5 inches and less than 100 pounds, *Little Billy Mahone* was one of the smallest Confederate generals. In addition to that sobriquet, his men called him *Skin and Bones.* When Mahone was severely wounded at the Second Battle of Bull Run, the governor of Virginia tried to break the news gently to the general's wife. To calm her fears, the governor told her that it was only a flesh wound. Hearing this, Mrs. Mahone screamed, "The General hasn't any flesh!" Mahone recovered to gain yet another nickname, *The Hero of the Crater,* for his bravery during the Battle of the Petersburg Crater in July 1864.

MAIMONIDES (1135–1204)

Spanish-born Moses ben Maimun, or Maimuni, better known as Maimonides, was probably the most renowned Jewish scholar, writer and philosopher of the Middle Ages and was referred to as *The Light of the West.*

Malagrida—See SHELBURNE, LORD.

MALEDON, GEORGE (1834–1911)

During the late 19th century in Fort Smith, Ark., it was said that Isaac Parker, the famous Hanging Judge, sentenced men to death and his hangman, George Maledon, suspended sentence. *Suspended Sentence Maledon* hanged almost all the 88 men Parker doomed, and boasted to the press, "I never hanged a man who came back to have the job done over."

MALHERBE, FRANCOIS DE (1555–1628)

Francois de Malherbe established new cannons of French poetry that would set the norm for the next few centuries, becoming *The Father* (and some might sat The Dictator) *of Modern French Poetry* and *The Purist of Language.* He stripped away all newly contrived Greek and Latin words and banned the use of foreign idioms and provincial expressions in favor of the refined language of an educated Parisian. Under his rules one line of verse could not run into another and a word ending in a vowel could not be followed by one starting with a vowel.

MALLON, MARY—See Typhoid Mary.

MALTHUS, THOMAS ROBERT (1766–1834)

English economist Thomas Malthus, in his *An Essay on the Principle of Population* in 1798, declared it was a "law of nature" that population must increase faster than the means of subsistence, so that working men could never earn more than the barest essentials. He insisted that famine, war, and pestilence were necessary to keep the population in check; later he allowed that birth control might be somewhat helpful. For his theories he was dubbed *The Economic Pessimist*. Other authorities later found that his analysis contained grave flaws and that, as a ''classical'' economist, he was functioning merely as a conscious or unconscious mouthpiece for the rising industrialists, who could use his theories to explain that they bore no guilt for the suffering of the masses since it was the ''law of nature'' that caused the latter's plight.

MAMOUN (786–833)

As a youth, Mamoun, the seventh caliph of the Abassides, had as his friends the foremost men of science, including Greeks as well as Persians, and during his 20-year reign made Baghdad a resort for poets, philosophers and mathematicians regardless of race or creed. He had many books translated into the Arabic and became known as *The Father of Arabic Literature* and *The Augustus of Arabic Literature*.

Man, The—See BILBO, THEODORE GILMORE.

Man Behind the Frown, The—See MCCLELLAN, JOHN.

Man Burner, The: ISOM PRENTICE ''Print'' OLIVE (1840–1886)

During the 1800s Isom Prentice *''Print''* Olive best typified the big western rancher who was a law unto himself. He believed he had a God-given right to punish cattle rustlers himself, generally shooting, hanging and, after dousing them with whiskey, burning them. For such outrages Olive was referred to as *The Man Burner*. Sent to prison for one such homicidal outrage, he was freed after spending

$250,000 for a new trial, which was never held because the witnesses had vanished. Olive was finally shot dead in a gunfight in 1886, inspiring some biographers to bestow on him a new sobriquet— *Out of Print Olive*.

Man from Missouri, The—See TRUMAN, HARRY S.

Man in the Iron Mask, The (?–1703)

The sobriquet *The Man in the Iron Mask* was given to a mysterious prisoner ordered jailed by King Louis XIV of France in 1669. His face was concealed with a mask, not of iron but of black velvet stiffened with whalebone. Even his death was kept a secret by Louis XIV and later by Louis XV. Various theories of his identity spread, including, quite naturally a standard rumor that he was the real Louis XIV, kept in prison while his illegitimate half-brother ruled. On one occasion Louis XV said he would have freed *The Man in the Iron Mask* if he were still alive; on another occasion, he declared, ''No one has yet told the truth and all conjectures are false.''

Man in the Padded Room, The—See REID, WALLACE ''Good Time Wally.''

Man in the Straw Hat—See CHEVALIER, MAURICE.

Man in the Zoo, The: OTA BENGA (1881–1916)

Early in the 20th century a young Congolese Pygmy named Ota Benga suffered a fate in America that never would have been permitted in later years, gaining the nickname *The Man in the Zoo*. Explorer Samuel Verner brought him to the United States in 1904 for the St. Louis Exposition.

Benga was later given by the explorer to William Hornaday, director of the Bronx Zoo in New York. Hornaday displayed the 4-foot 11-inch Benga in a cage, together with an orangutan named Dohong and a parrot. It was the first time that a human being was exhibited in a cage in any American zoo. Much of the black community protested the exhibition, as did a number of clergymen, although the latter were more concerned about what they saw as a plot to prove the Darwinian theory than about the sinfulness of caging a man. Finally, under threat of legal action by blacks, Benga was allowed out of his cage, but strutting about the zoo in a white suit, he continued to draw tourists and still slept in the primate house. Eventually the situation became so scandalous that Benga was taken out of the zoo as a ward of a succession of individuals and institutions. Unhappy in the United States but without funds to return to Africa, he committed suicide in 1916.

Man Milliner, The—See HENRY III OF FRANCE.

Man of a Thousand Faces, The—See CHANEY, LON.

Man of Blood, The—See CHARLES I.

Man of Blood and Iron, The—See BISMARCK, OTTO VON.

Man of December, The—See NAPOLEON III.

Man of Destiny, The—See CLEVELAND, GROVER.

Man of Great Heart, The—See HOOVER, HERBERT.

Man of Independence, The—See TRUMAN, HARRY S.

Man of Iron, The—See WALESA, LECH.

Man of Mutinies, The—See BLIGH, WILLIAM.

Man of Ross, The—See HIGGINSON, STEPHEN.

Man of Sedan, The—See NAPOLEON III.

Man of Sin, The—See CROMWELL, OLIVER.

Man of Steel, The—See ORIGEN.

Man of the People, The—See FOX, CHARLES JAMES.

Man on Horseback, The—See BOULANGER, GEORGES ERNEST JEAN MARIE.

Man on the Ledge, The: JOHN WARDE (1912–1938)

The man who committed the most publicized suicide in American history, John Warde was called *The Man on the Ledge* for the 11 hours he stood on the 17th-floor ledge of New York's Gotham Hotel, rejecting pleas to come back inside. Huge crowds flooded the area, press photographers and newsreel cameramen captured the event on film and radio broadcasters carried live minute-by-minute reports for the rest of the nation. It was estimated the media spent $100,000 to cover the incident for a Depression-wracked nation. In the end *The Man on the Ledge* plunged to his death.

Man They Could Not Hang, The—See LEE, JOHN.

Man Uptown, The—See ROTHSTEIN, ARNOLD.

Man Who Ate Democrats. The: ALFRED PACKER (1842–1907)

A mountainman prospector and guide, Alfred Packer was convicted of cannibalism and the murder of five men after they were trapped in heavy snows in the Colorado high country in 1873. He became celebrated in story and song as *The Man Who Ate Democrats,* a title accorded him by his trial judge, who cried, "Packer, you depraved Republican son of a bitch, there were only five democrats in Hinsdale County, and you ate them all!"

Man Who Banned the Corset, The— See POIRET, PAUL.

Man Who Broke a Thousand Chains, The—See BURNS, ROBERT ELLIOTT.

Man Who Broke the Bank at Monte Carlo, The: CHARLES WELLS (1841–1926)

A roundish, bearded, bald little cockney, a swindler named Charles Wells arrived in Monte Carlo in July 1891, and though he did not break the bank, he wiped out one of the tables. The table

closed down until it was replenished with 100,000 francs. Wells broke it a second, a third, and fourth time. In 11 hours he broke the bank 12 times. His phenomenal streak continued for two more days, and at one point he won 23 out of 30 spins of the wheel. His winnings were well over one million francs. A few months later Wells returned to the casino and repeated his feat. Although the casino had detectives watch him, experts checked the wheel and croupiers interrogated, no evidence of fraud was discovered. Other gamblers charted Wells' plays in an effort to find his system. They never did and Wells became part of gambling folklore. He was known by the title of a tune written in his honor, "The Man Who Broke the Bank at Monte Carlo." In 1892 Wells broke a table's bank six more times, and then suddenly he started to lose—and lose and lose. Rich friends in England wired him more money and still he lost. Wells retired from casino gambling and spent his remaining years in various swindles that sent him to prison a number of times. He died in poverty in 1926. Near the end of his life he admitted his great winning streak had not been based on any system or scam and had been nothing more than sheer luck.

Man Who Came to Dinner, The—See WOOLLCOTT, ALEXANDER.

Man Who Hated Sherlock Holmes, The—See DOYLE, ARTHUR CONAN.

Man Who Invented Halitosis, The—See LAMBERT, GERALD BARNES.

Man Who Knew the Fairies, The—See YEATS, WILLIAM BUTLER.

Man Who Never Died, The—See HILL, JOE.

Man Who Owns New Year's, The—See **LOMBARDO, GUY.**

Man Who Reared 50 Million Kids, The—See **SPOCK, BENJAMIN M.**

Man Who Shot Dillinger, The—See **PURVIS, MELVIN.**

Man Who Stole Portugal, The—See **REIS, ARTURO ALVES.**

Man Who Talked with the Dead, The—See **FORD, ARTHUR A.**

Man Who Was Never Asked Back, The—See **HARRIS, FRANK.**

Man Who Was Sherlock Holmes, The—See **DOYLE, ARTHUR CONAN.**

Man with the Golden Arm, The—See **KOUFAX, SANDY.**

Man with the Orchid-Lined Voice, The—See **CARUSO, ENRICO.**

Man with the Sling, The—See **RANDOLPH (OF ROANOKE), JOHN.**

Man with Two Lives, The—See **BRODIE, WILLIAM.**

Man Without a Skin, The—See **CUMBERLAND, RICHARD.**

Manassa Mauler, The—See **DEMPSEY, JACK.**

Manassa Slacker, The—See **DEMPSEY, JACK.**

MANDELBAUM, FREDERICKA "Marm" (1818–1894)

Fredericka Mandelbaum, one of the America's most successful fences, was known to members of the underworld as *Marm* because she was like a mother to any crook who was honest with her.

Man-eater, The: LEWIS KESEBERG (181?–1895)

Lewis Keseberg was a survivor of the ill-fated Donner Party, a California-bound wagon train caught in the mountain snows in 1846. Like many others he survived by cannibalism. Of the 89 emigrants in the party, only 45 were found alive by rescuers. Charged with six murders, Keseberg denied killing the victims, insisting they had died of starvation or exposure to the elements, but he admitted cooking and eating their flesh. He was freed by the court, but the name of *Man-eater* followed him the rest of his days, and children would cry after him, "Stone the Man-eater."

Mango, the King of the Pickles: JOHN MYTTON (1796–1834)

It has been said that Squire John Mytton was the most besotted Englishman in history, having started to drink at the age of 10 and averaging eight quarts of port a day for many years. Because of his capacity for alcohol, he was dubbed *Mango, the King of the Pickles*. This tolerance for alcohol hardly produced upright behavior in Mytton, who was constantly falling from his horse, driving his carri--

age at breakneck speed through the streets and occasionally insisting on riding a brown bear.

MANKIEWICZ, JOSEPH (1909–   )

U.S. writer and film director Joseph Mankiewicz, a notedly hard taskmaster, has long been nicknamed *Monkeybitch,* a play on his name originated by F. Scott Fitzgerald.

MANSON, CHARLES H. (1934–   )

The murderous leader of a "hippie family" in California in the 1960s, Charles Manson directed his followers, mostly girls, to commit a total of seven brutal murders, including that of actress Sharon Tate. Because of his strong influence over his followers, the press labeled Manson *The Hypnotic Hippie.*

MANTZ, PAUL (1903–1965)

Racing and motion picture stunt pilot Paul Mantz was known as *The King of the Hollywood Air Devils.*

MAPES, WALTER (1150–1196)

The medieval German poet Walter Mapes is often remembered as *The Anacreon of the Twelfth Century,* after the famous lyric poet of ancient Greece. However, Mapes was even more celebrated for his dedicated drinking songs, the best known of which, "The Jovial Priest's Confession," was translated into English by Leigh Hunt and won for Mapes the sobriquet *The Jovial Toper,* or drunkard.

MARCANTONIO, VITO (1902–1954)

A pro-Soviet U.S. representative from New York from 1934 to 1936 and 1938 to 1950, Vito Marcantonio was nicknamed *Firebrand* by both friend and foe, because of his fiery support of labor rights bills, some said, or because of his radicalism, others said.

Marcel Marceau of Television, The— See SKELTON, RED.

Marcher, The—See CHAVEZ, CESAR.

MARCOS, IMELDA (1931?–   )

Imelda Marcos, the wife of Filipino dictator Ferdinand Marcos, has won the nickname *The Evita of the Orient.* A beauty contest winner—Miss Manila of 1953—she is considered the equal in beauty of another political wife, Evita Peron. However, Evita Peron's hold on her masses was undoubtedly greater than that of her oriental counterpart on the Filipino population, whom her husband, Ferdinand Marcos, ruled for years with the aid of martial law.

Mare of Flanders, The—See ANNE OF CLEVES.

Marginal Prynne—See PRYNNE, WILLIAM.

MARIA LOUISA, QUEEN OF SPAIN (1751–1819)

Maria Louisa, queen of Spain during the French Revolution, scandalized the courts of Europe and her own normal-minded countrymen by her long string of infidelities, for which she was lampooned as *Dona Juana,* after the legendary Spanish libertine Don Juan. She recruited sexual playmates from the ranks of the royal bodyguard and elevated one of them, Manuel de Godoy, 16 years her junior, from guardsman to prime minister and virtual dicatator of Spain. (See also Godoy, Manuel de.)

MARIA THERESA, ARCHDUCHESS OF AUSTRIA (1717–1780)

Archduchess Maria Theresa of Austria was called *The Mother of Her Country* because of the rapid growth of prosperity and population that took place during her reign. An absolutist monarch, moralist and mother, she married off her daughters in the interests of Austria, sending Marie Antoinette off to France as the wife of Louis XVI. While she encouraged the arts and sciences and protected trade, she also abolished the game laws and the right of sanctuary. Her so-called Chastity Police was formed to counter her husband's infidelities, and nowhere on the Continent were laws against sex more strictly enforced. A performer on the stage who happened to bare an ankle or midriff was certain to be hauled off to jail; border patrols rifled mailbags for smutty books and pictures; and any woman walking unescorted through the streets of Vienna risked being sent to a rehabilitation camp for prostitutes.

Marian Doctor, The—See DUNS SCOTUS, JOHN.

MARIE ANTOINETTE (1755–1793

Gay, frivolous and extravagant, daughter of Archduchess Maria Theresa, Marie Antoinette, of Austria, was the highly unpopular wife of Louis XVI of France, who like her husband went ot the guillotine in October 1793. Known as *The Austrian Wench,* Marie had a number of uncomplimentary nicknames, especially *Madame Deficit,* an expression of the public perception of her responsibility in driving the country to near bankruptcy. She was also called *The Baker's Wife* (Louis was *The Baker)* after the royal couple gave bread to the angry mob at Versailles on Oct. 6, 1789. The attribution to her of the comment "Let them eat cake," in a response to the demands of a populace starving for bread—whether true or not—typified the ill-feeling toward her. (See also Reagan, Nancy.)

MARION, FRANCIS (c. 1732–1795)

A brilliant tactician of backwoods guerrilla warfare, American Revolutionary War general Francis Marion was called, in exasperation, *The Swamp Fox* by the British. The British were ill-equipped for the swamp warfare Marion subjected them to in South Carolina. His daring in combat also won him the title *The Bayard of the South,* after the courageous 16th century French military leader.

Marionette Emperor, The—See MAXIMILIAN.

MARIS, HERBERT L. (1880–1960)

A Philadelphia lawyer whose work formed the basis of a television series called "Lock-Up," Herbert L. Maris brought about the release of at least 500 unjustly convicted persons during a 50-year career. In all Pennsylvania prisons he was known as *A Lifer's Last Hope,* and succeeded in freeing many innocent men and women. He believed that the validity of the convictions of "fully twenty percent of those in our prisons is extremely doubtful."

MARIUS, CAIUS (155–86 BC)

Driven from Rome in 88 BC, Caius Marius, a leading general, returned the following year and, with Cinna, captured the city, winning the honorific *The Third Founder of Rome.*

MARKEL, LESTER (1894–1977)

Lester Markel, long-time editor of the Sunday department of the *New York Times,* was an autocratic boss whom staffers dubbed *The Sun King* since he guarded his domain just as zealously as an earlier Sun King, Louis XIV, who said, "I am the State."

MARKHAM, EDWIN (1852–1940)

In 1899 Edwin Markham, a relatively unknown poet published "The Man with the Hoe," which warned that kingdoms and kings and all men of great economic power were facing a terrible reckoning in "the silence of the centuries." The poem brought Markham instant fame and the title *Poet Laureate of Labor*. It had so great an appeal to the masses that it was translated into 30 languages.

Marlborough, Duchess of—See JENNINGS, SARAH.

Marlborough, Duke of—See CHURCHILL, JOHN.

MARLOWE, CHRISTOPHER (1564–1593)

According to scholarly consensus, Christopher Marlowe was "the only English playwright who might have given Shakespeare serious competition." He was nicknamed posthumously *The Second Shakespeare,* and there is a minority who would call him *The First Shakespeare,* claiming he survived his so-called murder in 1593 and hired for a stipend, a dull-witted actor, William Shakespeare, to lend his name the author of Marlowe's subsequent works. It is a minority theory.

Marm—See MANDELBAUM, FREDERICKA "Marm."

MAROT, CLEMENT (1484–1544)

The literary progress of poet Clement Marot may be measured by his progession of nicknames. Since he had been for a time valet de chambre to Francois I of France, he was dubbed *The Valet Poet*. As he gained esteem at court, he was called *The Poet of Princes*. Finally he won acclaim as *The French Chaucer*.

MARQUEZ, LEONARDO (c. 1820–?)

A 19th century Mexican general who was regarded as even crueler than Santa Ana, Leonardo Marquez gained the fearsome nickname *The Tiger of Tacubaya* after his massacre of a large number of prisoners at Tacubaya in April 1859.

MARRIOTT, JOHN (fl. early 17th century)

Recognized as one of the great gluttons of his day, John Marriott was nicknamed after a pamphlet about his feeding habits, *The Great Eater of Graye's Inn*. He was also called *The Cormorant,* after the large, voracious aquatic bird of the same name.

Marse Robert—See LEE, ROBERT E.

MARSH, SYLVESTER "Crazy" (1803–1884)

In the late 1850s Sylvester Marsh garnered the nickname *Crazy Marsh* when he came up with the apparently impossible scheme of building a railroad to the top of New Hampshire's Mount Washington, the towering peak of the White Mountains. Despite incredible hardships, both engineering and financial, and considerable ridicule, he completed the project in 1869. Thereafter *Crazy Marsh* became a phrase of admiration.

Marshal Forwards—See BLUCHER, GEBHARD LEBERECHT VON.

Marshal of the Army of God, The—See FITZ-WALTER, ROBERT.

MARSHALL, GEORGE C. (1880–1959)

U.S. Army chief of staff in World War II and later secretary of state under President Harry Truman, George C. Marshall was often denounced by the postwar far right as *A Front Man for Traitors,* a nickname coined by Republican senator William Jenner of Indiana. Certainly, most people did not agree, and Marshall, who authored the Marshall Plan for postwar European relief, was awarded the Nobel Peace Prize in 1953.

MARSHALL, JOHN (1755–1835)

The distinguished chief justice of the U.S. Supreme Court, John Marshall was nicknamed *Silver Heels,* a sobriquet given to him during the Revolution because he ran fast races with men under his command. Marshall raced in stocking feet in blue socks with white heels, and he reputedly always won.

MARSHALL, STEPHEN (1600–1666)

English churchman and pamphleteer Stephen Marshall was a devoted follower of John Calvin, the French Protestant leader who spread his teachings from Geneva, and, as perhaps Calvin's most leather-lunged exponent in England, was accorded the sobriquet *The Geneva Bull.*

MARSHALL, THOMAS RILEY "Five Cent Cigar" (1854–1925)

One of the least qualified vice presidents in U.S. history was Thomas Riley Marshall, who served under Woodrow Wilson. He was a happy-go-lucky gladhander best remembered for coining the phrase, "What this country needs is a good five cent cigar," thus immortalizing himself as *Five Cent Cigar Marshall.* He often said he liked being vice president because he had "no responsibil-ities." When Wilson fell severly ill, and he was reminded he might inherit the position, Marshall buried his head in his hands and was unable to speak.

MARSHALL, THURGOOD (1908–   )

Thurgood Marshall, who in 1967 became the first black Supreme Court justice, had for years handled civil rights cases, often for little or no compensation, and gained the appellation *Mr. Civil Rights.*

Martial Macaroni, That—See BURGOYNE, JOHN.

MARTIN, ALEXANDRE—See Albert the Workingman.

MARTIN, JAMES GREEN (1819–1878)

Despite having lost his right arm at the Battle of Churubusco in the Mexican War, James Martin insisted on fighting against the Union during the Civil War. His Confederate comrades nicknamed him *Old One Wing.*

MARTIN, LUTHER (1748–1826)

A representative from Maryland to the Constitutional Convention in 1787, Luther Martin, an absolute Federalist, refused to sign the document. In exasperation Thomas Jefferson labeled him *The Federal Bull-dog,* and through the years Martin aligned himself with the Federalists in opposition to Jefferson.

MARTIN, MICHAEL—See Lightfoot, Captain.

MARTIN, RICHARD (1754–1834)

Richard Martin, a member of Parliament, fought for the passage of a bill, later known as Martin's Act, to protect animals, which in 1824 led to the formation of the Royal Society for the Prevention of Cruelty to Animals. For this he won the nickname *Humanity Dick* from the prince regent. Martin went to great lengths to see the law was obeyed and even hauled abused animals into court. His sobriquet became a mark of derision to many, as cartoonists and poets lampooned him and the press sneered at him. Still, the sobriquet was one deserved as an accolade. Martin's humanity was not restricted to animals. He was a Protestant who fought for the civil rights of Roman Catholics in Ireland and opposed the death penalty for such crimes as forgery, and he was a landlord who provided pensions to widows and orphans on his estate.

MARTIN, BISHOP OF TOURS, ST. (316–397)

St. Martin, bishop of Tours, was often hailed as *The Apostle of Gaul* for resisting the persecution of heretics and seeking to win adherents through examples of self-denial and charity.

Martin Van Ruin—See VAN BUREN, MARTIN.

Martyr King, The—See HENRY VI OF ENGLAND.

Martyr of the Renaissance, The—See DOLET, ETIENNE.

Martyr President, The—See GARFIELD, JAMES A.; LINCOLN, ABRAHAM.

Martyr to Science, The—See BERTHOLLET, CLAUDE LOUIS, COUNT.

MARVELL, ANDREW (1621–1678)

Andrew Marvell, an English satirist and influential member of the House of Commons, remained firm in his opposition to Charles II, refusing promotions and bribes. He was nicknamed *The British Aristides*, after the Greek statesman and general who despite many victories was ostracized from his native Athens.

Marvellous Boy, The—See CHATTERTON, THOMAS.

Marvelous—See HAGLER, "Marvelous" MARVIN.

Marvelous Marv—See THRONEBERRY, MARV.

MARX, ADOLPH ARTHUR "Harpo" (1888–1964)

More than those of his equally famous brothers, Groucho and Chico, *Harpo*'s nickname can be dismissed as a show business title, referring to his harp playing. However, it should be noted that his friends and acquaintances always used his nickname when talking to him. Somehow his real name, Adolph, seemed rather unfitting.

MARX, HERBERT "Zeppo" (1901–1979)

The origin of the nickname *Zeppo* remains clouded. In his last years brother Groucho insisted it came from the word "zeppelin," and he at times mentioned the crash of the zeppelin *Hindenburg* in Lakehurst, N.J., in 1937. Clearly, Groucho had his dates mixed up since Zeppo had his nickname decades before that tragedy, and the explanation need not be taken seriously. On other occasions Groucho said simply that the nickname had something to do with zeppelins, but he could not recall what. Others have insisted the nickname was a corruption of the Zippo lighter, but there is no credible evidence to support that theory.

MARX, JULIUS "Groucho"
(1890–1977)

Unlike most show business personages, whose nicknames are professional "hypes," Julius Marx got his nickname, *Groucho*, before entering show business. An inveterate poker player, he carried his cash in a "grouch bag," or G-string, and was thus dubbed *Groucho*. The sobriquet eventually carried over to the Marx Brothers act.

MARX, KARL (1818–1883)

Although German philosopher, political economist and communist theorist Karl Marx is today most often referred to as *The Founder of Modern Socialism,* he was more commonly called *The Moor,* a reference to his swarthiness, by contemporaries.

MARX, LEONARD "Chico"
(1887–1961)

Chico, the piano-playing member of the Marx Brothers comedy team, gained his nickname as a youth because of his prowess as a "chicken hunter," the then current description of a wolf. His brothers were awed by his success with the "chickies," hence *Chico.*

MARX, MILTON "Gummo"
(1897–1977)

Gummo, the least active of the Marx Brothers comedy team, obtained his nickname as a sickly child who caught cold so often that Mama Marx took to sending him forth wearing rubbers—rain or shine.

MARY I—See Bloody Mary.

MARY OF MODENA (1658–1718)

The second wife of England's ill-fated James II, Mary of Modena shared her husband's unpopularity with the people. Because of this sentiment, her subsequent life of exile in France and the fact that all five of her children by James died at a young age, she was nicknamed *The Queen of Tears.*

MASACCIO, TOMMASO "Bad Tom"
(1401–1428)

In a nickname perhaps more befitting a mafioso, Tommaso Masaccio, a noted Italian Renaissance painter, was called *Bad Tom Masaccio* by his contemporaries. Like many other artists of his day, his religious paintings were hardly reflective of his wild private life.

MASANIELLO—See Seven Days' King, The.

MASON, STEVENS THOMSON
(1811–1843)

Stevens Thomson Mason became known as *The Boy Governor* for his rapid advance politically before he had reached his mid-twenties. He was secretary of the Michigan Territory at the age of 19 and at 24 was named its first governor.

Massa Linkum—See LINCOLN, ABRAHAM.

Massachusetts Madman, The—See ADAMS, JOHN QUINCY.

MASSENA, ANDRE (1758–1817)

Andre Massena, a much-celebrated marshal of France, scored such a string of military triumphs in Italy, Switzerland, Germany and Poland that he was dubbed *The Favored Child of Victory*.

MASSILLON, JEAN BAPTISTE (1663–1742)

One of the finest orators of the pulpit, Jean Baptiste Massillon was dubbed *The Cicero of France*.

MASSINGER, PHILIP (1584–1640)

English playwright Philip Massinger was commended by such sobriquets as *Our Mercury* and *Apollo's Messenger*. Since his plays often included barbs that disturbed the cream of society, such as those in his comedy *A New Way to Pay Old Debts*, there was sore need for a derogatory nickname as well, and he was labeled *The Sot*, indeed a rather pale complaint against writers of that day.

Master, The—See Cid, El; GOETHE, JOHANN WOLFGANG VON.

Master, Mammoth Mumbler—See FORD, FORD MADOX.

Master Maker of the Queer, The—See BECKER, CHARLES.

Master of Deceit, The—See HOOVER, J. EDGAR.

Master of Dirty Tricks, The—See COLSON, CHARLES W. "Chuck."

Master of Light and Violence, The—See CARAVAGGIO, MICHAELANGELO MERISI DA.

Master of Naturalism, The—See FLAUBERT, GUSTAVE.

Master of Paradox, The—See CHESTERTON, G(ILBERT) K(EITH).

Master of the Epithet, The—See PEGLER, WESTBROOK.

Master of the Multi-National Enterprise, The—See GRACE, WILLIAM RUSSELL.

Master of the Nations, The—See TARTINI, GUISEPPE.

Master of Undergraduate Humor, The—See SHULMAN, MAX.

Master of Violence, The—See PECKINPAH, SAMUEL.

Master Storyteller, The—See HUNT, E. HOWARD.

Master Wrecker, The—See MCGOVERN, GEORGE S.

MASTERSON, WILLIAM BARCLAY "Bat" (1853–1921)

The nickname of the legendary western gunman *Bat Masterson* has been erroneously ascribed to the fact that he carried a "bat," or walking stick, which he used as a club or secret repository for a small gun. However, he did not carry a walking stick until his later days as a gambler; the sobriquet actually dated back to his youth. He coined it himself because he could not stand his given name—Bartholemew—which he subsequently also changed to William Barclay. Masterson gained another nickname during his days as a lawman in Dodge City, Kan., with Wyatt Earp. Together they became known as *The Fighting Pimps* since they spent most of their time as gunslingers, procurers and card sharks who preferred taking gratuities from vice operators to enforcing various statutes aimed at curbing their activities.

Mastiff Cur, The—See WOLSEY, THOMAS.

MATHER, "Mysterious" DAVE (1845–?)

One of the strangest killers in the Old West, *"Mysterious"* Dave Mather, a cold-blooded gunman, seems to have been a descendant of New England's Cotton Mather. He was called *Mysterious* because he was involved in so many illegal enterprises while at other times, or perhaps concurrently, serving as a lawman. Noted in many towns where he wore a badge as a *Killer of Killers*—at times in the service of Wyatt Earp, among others—Mather also committed several merciless killings without a badge.

MATHEWSON, CHRISTY (1880–1925)

New York Giants pitcher Christy Mathewson was known as *Big Six,* after the city's Big Six fire company, which was considered the champion in its field. He was so well known by the nickname that mail addressed with nothing but a large "6" was delivered to him.

MATHIAS, THOMAS JAMES (1750–1835)

English writer Thomas James Mathias, author of *The Pursuits of Literature*, was savaged by Stratford Canning, in his poem *New Morality,* as *The Nameless Bard*. The poet John Wolcot had a still more cutting name for him—*That Miserable Imp*.

MATTHEWSON, WILLIAM "Buffalo Bill" (fl. 1860s)

A government scout, William Matthewson became a hero in Kansas during the drought of 1860, when he killed vast number of buffaloes and had the meat sent to starving settlers around Wichita. He was lionized as *Buffalo Bill* and appears to have been the original possessor of that nickname.

Matty Van—See VAN BUREN, MARTIN.

MATURE, VICTOR (1916–   )

When early in Victor Mature's movie career Hollywood studio press agents were trying to come up with a suitable nickname for him, female fans beat them to it, dubbing him *The Hunk*.

MAUNDEVILLE, JOHN (1300–1372)

Because accounts of the voyages of Englishman Sir John Maundeville were filled with so many wondrous incidents, skeptics referred to him as *The Lying Traveller*.

MAUPASSANT, GUY DE (1850–1893)

French author Guy de Maupassant was nicknamed *The Tireless Frenchman* by those who knew of his sexual capacity.

Maurice the Silent—See HUTCHESON, MAURICE A.

MAXIMILIAN: FERDINAND MAXIMILIAN JOSEPH (1832–1867)

In 1864 Austrian archduke Maximilian accepted the crown of the ill-conceived and highly unpopular Mexican Empire, which was created by Napoleon III of France. When the French pulled out in 1867, Maximilian, disparaged as *The Marionette Emperor,* was doomed. He died before a firing squad on orders from Mexican president Benito Juarez.

MAXIMILIAN I OF GERMANY (1459–1519)

Maximilian I of Germany was sometimes referred to as *The Last of the Knights,* a rather generous sobriquet. More fitting was that of *Il Pochi Danari,* or *The Pennyless,* bestowed on him by the Italians because, although his possessions were greater than those of any kaiser before him, he was constantly expending fortunes on warfare and thus was

forced to beg for additional funds. He married off his sons and grandsons for money or territory and always used the payments for his own ends.

Maximum John—See SIRICA, JOHN J. "Maximum John."

Mayer's Sundial—See RAPF, HARRY.

MAYHEW, THOMAS (1593–1682)

Thomas Mayhew, who settled Martha's Vineyard and became its governor, was called *The Patriarch of the Indians* for his constant efforts to befriend them and convert them to Christianity. During the bloody Indian uprising known as King Philip's War, Mayhew's colony was spared from attack by the Indians because of his previous relationship with them.

Mayor Von O'Hall—See HALL, ABRAHAM OAKLEY.

Maypole, The—See SCHULENBURG, EHRENGARD MELUSINA VON DER.

MAYS, WILLIE (1931–)

The great centerfielder for the New York Giants, Willie Mays picked up the nickname *Say Hey* in 1951 when, upon entering the big leagues, he found it difficult to remember other player's names. Being unsure, he would yell, "Say, hey!" to catch a player's attention. The tag stuck to him while he played winter ball in Puerto Rico, where the fans even dropped *"Oye, mira!"* (literally, *"Hey, look!"*)—the Spanish equivalent of *Say Hey* —to chant the nickname in English every time he came to bat.

MAZARIN, JULES: GIULIO MAZARINI (1602–1661)

The protege of Cardinal Richelieu, Italian-born French cardinal Jules Mazarin, tutor and first chief minister to Louis XIV, controlled France from Richelieu's death in 1642 until his own death in 1661, save for the period of the Fronde uprising. Considered most avaricious and niggardly, Cardinal Mazarin gathered a fortune in books, and his 40,000-volume library was regarded as the most extensive and splendid France had ever seen, earning him the title *The Maecenas of His Day,* after the Roman patron of literature.

Mazarin of Letters, The—See ALEMBERT, JEAN LE ROND D'.

MBOYA, THOMAS JOSEPH (1930–   )

Kenyan labor leader Tom Mboya has been dubbed by the press *Africa's Angry Young Man.*

Meanest Gambler in New York, The: ALBERT J. ADAM (1844–1907)

The policy king of New York in the late 1800s, Albert J. Adams became known as *The Meanest Gambler in New York* because he rigged the numbers results and then bet heavily with other operators so that he could drive them out of business and take over their shops.

MEANS, GASTON BULLOCK (1880–1938)

Perhaps the greatest rogue ever to operate near the center of power in Washington, D.C., Gaston B. Means was for a time the number two man in the Bureau of Investigation, the forerunner of the FBI.

His frauds were so outrageous that he became known as *The Munchhausen in Modern Dress,* after the fictional Baron Munchhausen, the German spinner of tall tales. During the Harding administration, he took bribes from bootleggers, allegedly for Secretary of the Treasury Andrew Mellon, whom he described to the underworld as a multi-millionaire who always wanted more. After serving a prison sentence for a number of scams, he wrote a scandalous best-seller, *The Strange Death of President Harding,* which inferred that Mrs. Harding poisoned her husband. He later died in prison after swindling a gullible society woman out of $104,000 with the claim that he could ransom the kidnapped Lindbergh baby.

MEANY, GEORGE (1894–1980)

U.S. labor leader George Meany helped reunite the labor movement by reconciling his AFL with the CIO, but he never thought much of his nickname *The Silver-haired Statesman of American Labor,* much preferring that of *The Proud Plumber.* His pride operated on two levels: he was proud of never having had to strike in his years as a plumber and of his working-class origins. He once observed: "I say plumbers, in a good many cases, are more important than lawyers. You can put millions of people in a great city and get along without lawyers; but you couldn't get them in there without plumbers. So I must warn you never to underestimate the importance of a plumber. In fact, I know anyone who has ever got a bill from a plumber doesn't underestimate them."

MEASE, JOHN—See Last of the Cocked Hats, The.

Meat Loaf: MARVIN LEE ADAY (1949–   )

The heavyweight rock singer *Meat Loaf* received his nickname (now his legal name) in the seventh grade, when at 5 feet 2 inches he already weighed 240 pounds.

Meddlesome Friar, The—See
SAVONAROLA, GIROLAMO.

Medfly, Johnny (fl. late 20th century)

California's 1981 war against the tenacious Mediterranean fruit fly produced an apparent perverse new enemy, a hoaxer nicknamed *Johnny Medfly,* who was suspected of clandestinely "salting" detection traps with dead flies to create false evidence of infestation.

MEDICI, LORENZO DE (1449–1492)

Lorenzo de Medici, or *Lorenzo the Magnificent,* became the ruler of Florence at the age of 20. Well versed in the classics and a poet and writer, he founded the University of Pisa and, as a munificent patron of literature and art, contributed greatly to the revival of the humanities, winning the additional sobriquet *The Father of Letters.*

MEDWICK, JOE "Duckie Wuckie" (1911–1975)

St. Louis Cardinal star outfielder Joe Medwick lost his original nickname—*Mickey*—when he gained a new one—*Duckie Wuckie*—after a sportswriter overheard some female baseball fans at a swimming pool observe that he swam like a duck.

MEEK, "Colonel" JOSEPH L. (1810–1875)

One of the most colorful trappers and mountainmen of the West, Joseph L. Meek was noted for exaggerating his many adventures. Thus it was fitting that despite an on-again, off-again military career during which he never reached a rank higher than that of major, he was always referred to as *Colonel.*

MEESE, EDWIN, III (1931–   )

White House counselor to President Ronald Reagan, Ed Meese is often referred to as *Easy Ed* because of his seemingly easy-going nature. He is also called *No Problem Meese* because of his frequent use of the phrase.

MEHEMET ALI (c. 1769–1849)

Mehemet Ali, the 19th century pasha (governor) of Egypt, was the first of the latter-day Egyptian rulers to seek a major role for his domain in Europe and Asia Minor. Energetic and intelligent, he attempted to reform the Egyptian state in the Western pattern, with an efficient army and navy, and was accorded the sobriquet *The Peter the Great of Egypt.* His efforts to subjugate Greece in the 1820s and the Ottoman Empire the following decade were thwarted only through the combined resistance of the European powers.

MEHTA, ZUBIN (1936–   )

Born in India, Zubin Mehta was named musical director of the Los Angeles Symphony in 1962, and Californians immediately dubbed him *Zubie Baby.* This reflected his good looks, youth and above all his reputation as a ladies' man.

MEIER, SALLY (1928–   )

California animal lover and protector of stray cats, Sally Meier has been designated *The Cat Lady of San Francisco.*

Melancholy Jacques, The—See
ROUSSEAU, JEAN JACQUES.

MELANCHTHON, PHILIPP:
PHILIPP SCHWARZERT
(1497–1560)

German religious reformer and collaborator of Martin Luther, Philipp Melanchthon was called by Luther *The Teacher of Germany* because he spread Luther's doctrines throughout that land.

MELCHIOR, LAURITZ (1890–1973)

Danish opera singer and actor Lauritz Melchior was known throughout his career as *The Magnificent Giant*.

MELLINGER, FREDERICK N.
(1914?–   )

U.S. fashion designer and retailer who founded Frederick's of Hollywood, Frederick Mellinger became the nation's leading seller of such exotic clothing as inflatable bras, crotchless panties and falsies for just about every part of a woman's anatomy. He was dubbed, among other things, *The King of Passion Fashion* and *The King of the Naughty Nightie*.

MELLON, ANDREW W. (1855–1937)

U.S. financier and secretary of the treasury from 1921 to 1931, Andrew W. Mellon was popularly, although perhaps not accurately, dubbed *The World's Second Richest Man,* after J. P. Morgan.

Memory for All Seasonings, A—See
CONRAD, JOHN.

Memory Thompson—See
THOMPSON, JOHN.

Memory Woodfall—See WOODFALL, WILLIAM.

MENCKEN, HENRY LOUIS
(1880–1956)

U.S. author, journalist, editor and critic H. L. Mencken was a pioneer excoriator of the American "booboisie" (a combination of "boob" and "bourgeosie") attacking organized religion, business and many other institutions. He had numerous nicknames, including *The Sage of Baltimore, The Irreverent Mr. Mencken* and, probably the one he liked best, *The Disturber of the Peace*.

MENDES-FRANCE, PIERRE
(1907–1982)

A politician who tilted at windmills, former French premier Pierre Mendes-France was often referred to as *Monsieur Quixote*. During World War II he escaped from Vichy and joined the Resistance at its lowest point. After De Gaulle came to power, he attacked Gaullism, scorning its authoritarianism. Perhaps his most hopeless battle was to get a nation of wine imbibers to switch to milk.

MENGELE, JOSEF (1911–   )

Auschwitz concentration camp doctor Josef Mengele is regarded to be one of the major Nazi war criminals still at large. He was known to concentration camp prisoners as *The Angel of Death* because of his ghoulish "medical experiments" and his authority to decide who lived and who died. In all, he is believed responsible for the deaths of 400,000 people. In the 1970s he was known to be living in Paraguay under government protection.

MENKEN, ADAH ISAACS
(1835–1868)

Considered one of the most shocking and daring females of the Victorian era, U.S. actress Adah Isaacs Menken won fame as *The Naked Lady* for her seminude stage appearances in the United States and Europe. Actually she wore a skin-tight body stocking and would be considered tame by 20th century standards. A more accurate nickname for her was *The Enchanting Rebel*. No ordinary sexpot, she had an intelligence and wit that made her the mistress and confidante of many of the leading literary figures of the 19th century, including Bret Harte, Mark Twain, Algernon Swinburne and Alexandre Dumas *pere*. She died at the age of 33, almost certainly of complications resulting from venereal disease.

MENOT, MICHAEL (1440–1518)

The noted French preacher Michael Menot was called, with biting sarcasm, *The Golden-Tongued* by those who regarded his sermons as oozing with grossness and buffoonery.

Mephistopheles Merck—See MERCK, JOHANN HEINRICH.

Mephistopheles of Politics, The—See BURR, AARON.

MERCATOR, GERARDUS
(1512–1594)

Known as *The Father of Modern Geography,* 16th century Flemish mathematician, cartographer and geographer Gerardus Mercator was greatly responsible for freeing mapmakers from the misconceptions that stemmed from the work of Ptolemy, a second-century Egyptian who for centuries had been regarded as the final authority on geographical knowledge.

Merchant of Death, The—See KRUPP, ALFRED.

MERCK, JOHANN HEINRICH
(1741–1791)

The 18th century German author Johann Heinrich Merck was called *Mephistopheles Merck* for the savageness of his criticism. Among his victims was Goethe, who wrote: "Mephistopheles Merck here did me, for the first time, a great injury. When I communicated the piece to him, he answered, 'You must write hereafter no more such trifles: others can do such things.' "

MERKLE, FRED "Bonehead"
(1888–1956)

By making possibly the saddest mistake in baseball history, Fred Merkle cost the New York Giants the pennant in 1908. As a runner on first base in the last of the ninth inning, in a key game against the Chicago Cubs, he failed to touch second base as the winning run scored from third. The opposing second baseman noticed Merkle had failed to run out the play and called for the ball—even as the crowd swarmed onto the field—and stepped on second. The umpire ruled Merkle out and the game was called a tie. It was later replayed, and the Cubs won it and the pennant. Through a long career, thereafter, Merkle could not shake the nickname *Bonehead* bestowed on him by vociferous fans.

MERRICK, DAVID (1912–   )

U.S. theatrical producer David Merrick has been dubbed by the press *The Barnum of Broadway*.

MERRICK, JOHN—See Elephant Man.

Merry Andrew: ANDREW BORDE (1500–1549)

A former English monk turned physician and eccentric, Andrew Borde became famous for attending markets and fairs "where he would make humorous speeches, couched in such language as caused mirth." He was dubbed *Merry Andrew* for his antics, which did not always please the authorities, who locked him up many times for such offenses as stocking his home with numerous long-residing prostitutes. In time the nickname was applied to any buffoon or clown.

Merry Monarch, The—See CHARLES II; KALAKAUA, DAVID.

MESMER, FRANZ ANTON (1734–1815)

It has lately become the vogue to consider Franz Anton Mesmer, *The Father of Animal Magnetism,* more than just a quack occult healer and charlatan. The Austrian physician devised a method of stroking patients with magnets to cure them of various ailments. He even carried a little magnet in a pouch around his neck and took to "magnetizing" flowers and trees. Although he was elected to Bavaria's Academy of Sciences, he was finally forced to leave Austria for France, where, having discarded the use of magnets for a new "animal magnetism," he became wealthy affecting many cures. In the process he acquired such believers as Marie Antoinette, Montesquieu and Lafayette. Mesmer was clearly a man ahead of his time. He understood he was the "animal" in his animal magnetism but assumed the magnetism was supernatural. Actually he was one of the first to treat patients by the use of hypnotism, although he did not understand that his so-called magic wand and seancelike setting had a hypnotic effect on a number of people. Judged an impostor by a scientific commission, which was appointed by King Louis XVI, and included Benjamin Franklin, Mesmer fell from favor and died in obscurity. A century later Freud and others would profit from his work.

Messenger of Allah, The—See MUHAMMAD, ELIJAH.

MESTA, PERLE (1889–1975)

Perle Mesta was the foremost unofficial hostess in Washington, D.C., during the 1940s and was a particular favorite of President Harry Truman, who named her envoy to Luxembourg. She was called *The Hostess with the Mostes'* and was the inspiration for a Broadway musical, *Call Me Madam.*

METESKY, GEORGE—See Mad Bomber, The.

Metesky, George—See HOFFMAN, ABBIE.

Methodist Pope, The—See CANNON, JAMES, JR.

Met's Second Caruso, The—See TUCKER, RICHARD.

Metternich of His Age, The—See POBEDONOSTSEV, KONSTANTIN.

Mexican Firecracker, The—See VELEZ, LUPE.

***Mexican Midget, The*—See ZARATE, LUCIA.**

***Mexican Spitfire, The*—See VELEZ, LUPE.**

***Mexico's Charlie Chaplin*—See CANTINFLAS.**

MEYER, RUSS *(1922–   )*

Motion picture director and producer Russ Meyer is considered one of the trailblazers of pornographic movies in the United States and has been called *Mr. X* and *The King of the Nudie Movie*, although his pioneering work in the 1970s amounts to rather tame stuff today.

MEZZOFANTI, GUISEPPE *(1774–1849)*

Cardinal Guiseppe Mezzofanti, an Italian linguist, was credited, according to various sources, with being able to speak 50 or 58 languages and was nicknamed *The Living Pentecost*. Byron called him *A Walking Polyglot*.

MICHAEL III, EMPEROR OF THE EAST *(c. 839–867)*

Byzantine emperor Michael III was nicknamed *The Drunkard*, a rather mild appellation considering his depravities, as described in Gibbon's *Decline and Fall of the Roman Empire*.

MICHELANGELO *(1475–1564)*

The famous Italian Renaissance painter, sculptor, architect and poet Michelangelo was called *The Divine Madman* because he would seclude him-self in meditation for long periods before under-taking any project.

***Michelangelo of Battle-Scenes*—See CERQUOZZI, MICHAEL ANGELO.**

***Michelangelo of the Lyre, The*—See PALESTRINA, GIOVANNI PIERLUIGI DA.**

***Michelangelo of the Middle Ages, The*—See CAMBIO, ARNOLFO DEL.**

MICHELL, FRANCIS *(fl. c. 1620)*

Few men of business were savaged as much as Francis Michell and Giles Mompesson, who to-gether were granted the infamous patent to manu-facture gold and silver lace. In his play *A New Way to Pay Old Debts* Philip Massinger dubbed Michell *Justice Greedy*, a name he could not thereafter escape. (See also Mompesson, Giles.)

***Michigan's Co-Ed Murderer*—See COLLINS, JOHN NORMAN.**

***Midas of the Mutual Funds, The*—See CORNFELD, BERNARD.**

***Midas of the Rockies, The*—See STRATTON, WINFIELD SCOTT.**

Midday Murderer, The: KLAUS GOSSMANN *(1941–   )*

A strange German mass murderer in the 1960s, Klaus Gossmann shot a number of his victims in the Nuremberg area at exactly noon so that church bells would cover the noise. While still uniden-tified, he was dubbed *The Midday Murderer*.

Gossmann was captured and imprisoned for life in 1967.

MIDLER, BETTE (1944–   )

Zany pop singer Bette Midler gave herself, rather proudly, the nickname *The Last of the Tacky Ladies.*

Mid-Victorian Modern, The—See BUTLER, SAMUEL.

Mighty Bambino, The—See Ruth, Babe.

Mighty Leviathan, The—See HOBBES, THOMAS.

Mighty Medicine Man, The—See POWELL, DAVID FRANKLIN.

Milan Bach—See BACH, JOHANN CHRISTIAN.

MILBURN, WILLIAM HENRY (1823–1903)

A blind Methodist minister, William Henry Milburn was for many years an itinerant minister generally known as *The Blind Preacher.* He later served as chaplain of the U.S. Senate and House of Representatives.

Military Humboldt, The: WILLIAM SELBY HARNEY (1800–1889)

Gen. William Selby Harney, perhaps the most traveled and utilized American military officer, was dubbed *The Military Humboldt,* after the peripatetic German geographer and explorer. He led numerous expeditions against the Seminoles in Florida

and the western Indians (once he was called back from a European vacation to lead a campaign against the Sioux), distinguished himself in the Mexican War, had confrontations in Kansas with settlers opposing federal authority and was barely prevented from hanging Brigham Young in a confrontation with the Mormons in Utah. Ironically, he received no active command during the Civil War because he was suspected of having Confederate sympathies, and was retired in 1863.

MILL, JOHN STUART (1806–1873)

English economist and philosopher John Stuart Mill was called by admirers *The Logic-Chopping Machine.*

MILLER, CHARLES "Bronco Charlie" (1849–1955)

Born in a covered wagon, colorful Charlie Miller was a dispatch rider, U.S. Army scout, stagecoach driver and Wild West showman. Considered one of the West's foremost bronco busters, he picked up the moniker of *Bronco Charlie.* He served as a pony express rider at the age of 11, receiving an arrowhead wound for his efforts. When he died in 1955 at the age of 105, Miller was known as *The Last Rider,* the final survivor of those daring men.

MILLER, DAISY ORR (1877–1955)

Long-time president of Animal Protective Union, Daisy Orr Miller gained an international reputation as *The Dog Detective* for her efforts to retrieve lost and stolen canines.

MILLER, EDWARD ABRAHAM "Bozo" (1909–   )

Accorded the sobriquet *The World's Greatest Trencherman,* Edward Abraham "Bozo" Miller has been known to eat as many as 25,000 calories a day. Undefeated in eating contests since 1931, he downed 27 two-pound pullets at Trader Vic's in San Francisco in 1963.

MILLER, JAMES P. "Deacon Jim" (1866–1908)

An enigmatic westerner who never smoked, drank or cursed, James P. Miller was such a devout churchgoer he was nicknamed *Deacon Jim*. Possibly his only failing was that he was a professional killer. Estimates of the number of persons he killed vary from 15 to 40. He is suspected of having engineered the 1908 murder of Pat Garrett, the former sheriff who killed Billy the Kid. He was lynched after one of his victims lived long enough to focus suspicion on him.

MILLER, JOAQUIN (1841–1913)

U.S. poet Joaquin Miller impressed his generation with the flamboyance and picturesqueness of his Wild West verse and his enormous output. His poetry was marked by much dash and fire, if little profundity. Called *The Oregon Byron* and *The Poet of the Sierras,* he is remembered for little other than his "Christopher Columbus."

MILLER, JOE (1684–1738)

Josias or Joseph Miller was a Shakespearean actor who became famous in 18th century England as *The Father of Jests* following the posthumous publication of *Joe Miller's Jest Book or, The Wits Vade-Mecum,* etc. Actually, according to some sources, Miller never cracked a smile. When he died in 1738, leaving his family destitute, his tavern friends decided to put out a collection of jokes and claim they had been told by Miller; all the revenues were to go to support his widow and children. The book, the first of its kind, was assembled by John Mottley, a very minor playwright.

The 247-joke volume became a best-seller, and Joe Miller's reputation as a joke teller, rather than Mottley's, became part of history.

MILLER, WILLIAM (1810–1872)

Nineteenth century Scottish poet William Miller, author of "Wee Willie Winkie," was dubbed *The Laureate of the Nursery.*

MILLER, WILLIAM F. "520%" (1874–?)

A lowly Brooklyn, N.Y., bookkeeper named William F. Miller became one of America's biggest swindlers by claiming he had a stock market system that would pay off at 10 percent interest per week. Becoming famous as *520% Miller,* he was able to make good on his claims as long as more and more suckers handed over their money. Before the bubble burst, Miller had milked his victims for at least $1 million—and perhaps much more.

Millet of America, The—See HIGGINS, EUGENE.

MILLIGAN, MAURICE M. (1884–1959)

The U.S. attorney for the Western District of Missouri from 1924 to 1945, Maurice M. Milligan gained the nickname *Missouri's Tom Dewey,* after the racket-busting New York prosecutor. Milligan convicted 259 members of the Tom Pendergast political machine in Kansas City, Mo., in 1936 and sent Pendergast to prison for income tax invasion.

Million Dollar Slugger from the Five-and-Ten-Cent Store, The—See WILSON, LEWIS "Hack."

Millionaire Hobo, The—See HOW, JAMES EADS.

Millionaire Sheriff, The—See BAKER, ANDERSON YANCEY.

Millionaire Streetwalker, The: WATERFORD JACK (1840–?)

A common Chicago streetwalker in the 1870s identified only as Waterford Jack was dubbed, even in the respectable press of the day, *The Millionaire Streetwalker* because she often told police of her plan to retire when she had accumulated $30,000, which in that day and in her circle was certainly enough to make her the equivalent of a millionaire. Press reports noted that in 1877 she was up to $22,000, and when she faded from sight in 1880, it was generally, and happily, assumed she had reached her goal.

MILLMAN, HARRY (1910–1937)

The reputed leader of the notorious Purple Gang, Detroit mobster Harry Millman was called *The Lone Wolf of the Underworld* since he supposedly had no close relationships with criminals who served under him. He could have used a friend in November 1937 when he became the victim of an underworld rub-out.

MILORADOWITCH, MICHAEL (1770–1820)

Regarded as one of Napoleon's most capable opponents, Michael Miloradowitch was called *The Russian Murat,* after Bonaparte's daring marshal. It was a sobriquet the French emperor grudgingly acknowledged, if he did not originate.

MILTON, JOHN (1608–1674)

The sobriquet *The Blind Poet* was applied in the 16th century to Italian poet and dramatist Luigi Groto and in the following century to John Milton, the celebrated English poet. Milton wrote many of his classics, including *Paradise Lost,* after he went totally blind in 1652. He was also called *The British Homer*.

MIND, GOTTFRIED (1768–1814)

Renowned for his portraits of cats, the Swiss painter Gottfried Mind was dubbed *The Raphael of Cats.*

MINER, WILLIAM "Old Bill" (1847–1913)

Old Bill Miner received the nickname *Old* very early in his career as a western stagecoach and train robber because of his premature look of age. He lived up to the label by remaining an active outlaw for half a century, pulling his last train robbery in 1911 and breaking out of prison three times over the next two years until his death in 1913. Caught waist-deep in swamp water with bloodhounds baying at him, he told his captors: "Boys, I guess I'm getting too old for this sort of thing."

Minerva—See MONTAGU, MARY WORTLEY.

Ming the Merciless—See MORSHEAD, LESLIE.

MINGUS, CHARLIE (1924–1979)

Generally credited as the greatest bass player in jazz, Charlie Mingus was outspoken in his anger over racial discrimination in the United States and was nicknamed *Jazz's Angry Man*. He claimed jazz as "the American Negro's tradition. . . .White people don't have a right to play it." This did not prevent Mingus from often having white musicians in his bands. They were, as he put it, "colorless."

Minstrel of the Border, *The*—See SCOTT, WALTER.

MINTON, SHERMAN (1890–1965)

Because he was perhaps the most ardent supporter in Congress of the policies of President Franklin D. Roosevelt, Indiana senator and later Supreme Court justice Sherman Minton was called *The King of the New Dealers*. He was regarded as the administration's "point man" in attempts to get other lawmakers to support New Deal programs.

MIRABEAU, COMTE DE: HONORE GABRIEL RIQUETTI (1749–1791)

The great orator of the French Revolution, Comte de Mirabeau was referred to as *The Hurricane* because of his stormy eloquence.

MIRABEAU, VICOMTE DE: ANDRE BONIFACE LOUIS RIQUETTI (1754–1792)

Andre Boniface Louis Riquetti, Vicomte de Mirabeau and a brother of the great orator Honore Gabriel Riquetti, Comte de Mirabeau, was given the nickname *Mirabeau-Tonneau*, or *Barrel-Mirabeau*, because of his rotundity. It was said his drinking capacity equaled the speaking capacity of his more famous brother.

Mirabeau of the Mob, *The*—See DANTON, GEORGES JACQUES.

Miracle of Nature, *The*—See CHRISTINA OF SWEDEN.

Miracle of Our Age, *The*—See SIDNEY, PHILIP.

Miraculous Child, *The*—See CHAMBORD, COMTE DE.

MIRANDA, CARMEN (1913–1955)

Portuguese-born singer-dancer Carmen Miranda, who came to Hollywood from Brazil in 1939, was originally dubbed by press agents *The Brazilian Bombshell*. She picked up a more descriptive sobriquet, *The Brazilian Bonanza*, in 1945 when she was listed as the only woman in the United States with an annual earned income of more than $200,000.

Miserable Imp, *The*—See MATHIAS, THOMAS JAMES.

Misleader of the Papacy, *The*—See BONIFACE VIII, POPE.

Miss Dimples—See TEMPLE, SHIRLEY.

Miss First Nighter—See HAMPTON, HOPE.

Miss Frigidaire—See EVERT LLOYD, CHRIS.

Miss Nancy—See WILLIAMS, TENNESSEE.

Miss Nancy King—See KING, WILLIAM RUFUS.

Missouri's Tom Dewey—See MILLIGAN, MAURICE M.

Mrs. Clean of Pornographic Movies—See CHAMBERS, MARILYN.

Mrs. President—See ADAMS, ABIGAIL.

Missy—See WALKER, WILLIAM.

Mr. Agony—See ANTHONY, JOHN J.

Mr. America—See COOPER, ALICE.

Mr. Big—See ROTHSTEIN, ARNOLD.

Mr. Black Labor—See RANDOLPH, A. PHILIP.

Mr. Boston—See FIEDLER, ARTHUR.

Mr. Broadway—See COHAN, GEORGE M.

Mr. Christian—See GRAHAM, BILLY.

Mr. Civil Rights—See MARSHALL, THURGOOD.

Mr. Clean—See DEAN, JOHN W.,III; FORD, GERALD; REAGAN, RONALD; RICHARDSON, ELLIOT L.; ROCKEFELLER, NELSON.

Mr. Coney Island—See HANDWERKER, NATHAN.

Mr. Democrat—See RAYBURN, SAM.

Mr. District Attorney—See HOGAN, FRANK S.

Mr. Economy—See BYRD, HARRY F.

Mr. Fang: A. S. LAING (fl. mid–19th century)

Mr. Fang, best remembered as a Dickens character in *Oliver Twist,* was the name applied to a magistrate of the Hatton Garden Police Office, A. S. Laing. The real-life *Mr. Fang* was notorious for his arrogant and often abusive treatment of defendants and witnesses and was finally forced to resign.

Mr. Fonda's Baby Jane—See FONDA, JANE.

Mr. Gold—See SINCLAIR, JAMES E.

Mr. Kink—See DEKKER, ALBERT.

Mr. Kisskiss Bangbang—See CONNERY, SEAN.

Mr. L.S.D.—See STANLEY, AUGUSTUS OWSLEY.

Mr. Middle America—See FORD, GERALD.

Mr. Music Master—See WELK, LAWRENCE.

Mr. New Year's Eve—See LOMBARDO, GUY.

Mr. Nommo—See NIMMO, ROBERT P.

Mr. October—See JACKSON, REGGIE.

Mr. Playboy of the Western World—See HEFNER, HUGH M.

Mr. Pops—See FIEDLER, ARTHUR.

Mr. Relaxation—See COMO, PERRY.

Mr. Republican—See TAFT, ROBERT A.

Mr. Sam—See RAYBURN, SAM.

Mr. Saturday Night—See GLEASON, JACKIE.

Mr. Solid Man—See CRABB, CHRISTOPHER COLUMBUS.

Mr. Untouchable—See BARNES, LEROY "Nicky."

Mr. Warmth—See RICKLES, DON.

Mr. White Backlash—See MADDOX, LESTER G.

Mr. Wonderful—See DAVIS, SAMMY, JR.

Mr. X—See MEYER, RUSS.

Mistletoe Politician—See VAN BUREN, MARTIN.

Mistress of Sophisticated Slapstick, The—See LILLIE, BEATRICE GLADYS.

MITCHEL, JOHN PURROY (1879–1918)

John Purroy Mitchel, who was later to become a reform mayer of New York City, was nicknamed by the underworld—or at least its more educated lawyers—*Torquemada* for his actions as a special investigator of the Manhattan borough president's office. Because he rooted out many criminal elements, they accused him of conducting a witchhunt in the manner of the 15th century Spanish theologian and grand inquisitor, Tomas de Torquemada.

MITCHELL, JOHN N. (1913–   )

U.S. attorney general under President Richard Nixon and later Nixon's campaign manager, John

N. Mitchell went to prison for his involvement in the Watergate scandal, and was labeled by some Nixon supporters *The President's Worst Friend*. It was of course inevitable that in liberal circles a play on words converted the sobriquet into *The Worst President's Friend*.

MITCHELL, MARTHA *(1918–1976)*

The wife of President Richard Nixon's attorney general John N. Mitchell, Martha Mitchell was continually covered by the media because of her outspokenness and sometimes outrageous comments. She criticized liberals, urged "discipline" for Vietnam War protesters and called for suppression of the press if it continued to reveal government secrets. Within a week of the Watergate break-in, she was on the phone to the press laying the blame on President Nixon for "all the dirty things that go on." Among the nicknames given her were *The American Mouth of the Year* and *The Mouth That Roared*.

MITCHELSON, MARVIN *(1928–   )*

Top U.S. divorce lawyer Marvin Mitchelson was nicknamed *The Paladin of Paramours* after his success in establishing the "palimony" principle in the Lee Marvin-Michelle Triola Marvin case. The idea of paying alimony to an unwedded mate has been called The Marvin Doctrine, not after actor Marvin but rather lawyer Mitchelson.

Mitred Ass, The—See POTIER, AUGUSTIN.

Mitred Dulness—See PARKER, SAMUEL.

MITTLEMAN, EVELYN—See Kiss of Death Evelyn.

MNESARETE *(c. 4th century B.C.)*

The Greek hetaera Mnesarete was nicknamed *Phryne,* meaning "Toad," because of her complexion, despite which she has been described as the most lovely prostitute of all time. Since the 4th century B.C. *Phryne* has been a synonym for courtesan.

Modern Aristophanes, The—See FOOTE, SAMUEL.

Modern Cervantes, The—See PEREDA, JOSE MARIA DE.

Modern Jonah, A—See BARTLEY, JAMES.

Modern Lucretia Borgia, The—See STRUCK, LYDIA.

Modern Marco Polo, The—See RIPLEY, ROBERT.

Modern Mercury, A—See ROOSEVELT, JAMES.

Modern Messalina, The—See CATHERINE THE GREAT OF RUSSIA.

Modern Mozart, The—See KORNGOLD, ERICH WOLFGANG.

Modern Pliny, The—See GESNER, KONRAD VON.

Modern Wagner, The—See
HUMPERDINK, ENGELBERT.

Modest Little Man, The—See
ATTLEE, CLEMENT RICHARD.

Modest Merit—See **THACKERAY,
WILLIAM MAKEPEACE.**

MOHAMMED (c. 570–632)

Mohammed, the founder of Mohammedanism, or
Islam, was called *The Camel-driver of Mecca,*
his early occupation, and *The Apostle of the
Sword,* owing to his enforcement of Islamic faith
at sword point.

*MOHAMMED AHMED
(c. 1841–1885)*

Mohammed Ahmed claimed to be the Mahdi,
who in the Moslem faith would be the last leader
of the faithful to be sent by Allah to earth to establish peace and justice. He overran the East Sudan
and captured Khartoum in 1881. He established
an empire but died in 1885, thereby joining a long
list of pretender Mahdis and becoming known as
The False Prophet.

Moisture Accelerator, The—See
HATFIELD, CHARLES M.

*MOLIERE: JEAN BAPTISTE
POQUELIN (1622–1673)*

The great comic dramatist Moliere, who used a
wide range of styles from high comedy to sheer
farce to ridicule the hypocrisy and pretensions of
the bourgeoisie, won the accolades *The French*

Aristophanes, after the renowned Greek dramatist and author of many satirical comedies, and *The
Anatomist of Humanity.*

Moliere of Italy, The—See **GOLDONI,
CARLO.**

Moliere of Music, The—See
GRETRY, ANDRE.

MOLINEAUX, TOM (1784–1818)

Tom Molineaux, a black, became the first American to fight for the heavyweight championship in
England. A slave in Virginia, he won a fight
against a bully from a neighboring plantation, and
his owner was so pleased that he gave Molineaux
his freedom and paid his way to England so that
he could try professional boxing. Known as
Molineaux the Moor, he won eight fights and then
in 1810 met the defending champion, Tom Cribb.
The increasing animosity between England and the
United States, which erupted in the War of 1812,
coupled with Molineaux's skin color led to his
being baited as *The Yankee Nigger.* For the first
30 rounds of the contest, Molineaux gave Cribb a
frightful beating, but in the 31st round he slipped
and banged his head against a ring post. Two
rounds later a groggy Cribb knocked him out. It
was later discovered Molineaux had fractured his
skull in the fall against the post. The following
year the pair met again, before a record crowd of
40,000, but Molineaux had not regained his health
and was a mere shadow of his former self. The
American was knocked out in the 11th round.
Punch-drunk, Molineaux fought a few minor battles thereafter before drifting into oblivion. He died
in 1818 in an army barracks in Ireland. *The Yankee Nigger* is now in the Boxing Hall of Fame.

Molineaux the Moor—See
MOLINEAUX, TOM.

MOLK, HEINRICH VON
(c. 12th century)

Not too much is known of Heinrich von Molk, one of Germany's earliest and most bitter satirists, but he was some sort of lay brother in his native Molk on the Danube. This did not prevent him from attacking the corruption typifying the clergy of his time. He also attacked the laity, merchants and peasants. However, having spent his early years in some chivalrous capacity, he reserved his most savage cuts for the princes and knights of the period, and he was dubbed *The Juvenal of Chivalry,* after the famous Roman satirist.

Moll Cutpurse: MARY FRITH
(1584–1659)

Englishwoman Mary Frith, better known by her nickname *Moll Cutpurse,* often dressed as a man when abroad on her pickpocketing or highway-lady ventures. When caught, she had accumulated enough wealth to buy her way out of prison. Among her other distinctions is the claim that she was the first woman to use tobacco.

MOLLOY, "Indestructible" MIKE
(1872–1933)

An undistinguished barfly who achieved post-humous notoriety as *Indestructible Mike* and *The Iron Victim,* Mike Molloy survived an incredible series of attempts on his life by a four-man insurance murder ring in New York City. Molloy was fed poisoned clams and sardines and gin spiked with antifreeze; gotten drunk and dumped naked in a snowbank in a park; and run down by a taxi hired for that purpose. But through it all, *Indestructible Mike* thrived. Finally the plotters abandoned all attempts at subterfuge and killed Molloy by knocking him out and running a hose from a gas jet into his mouth. A false death certificate led to the capture of the four murderers, and they were convicted and executed.

Molly—See SAMPSON, DEBORAH.

MOLOTOV, VYACHESLAV M.
(1890–   )

Few Soviet leaders irritated Western officials more than Foreign Minister V. M. Molotov, who was nicknamed *Stone-Ass* by President Franklin D. Roosevelt at the Yalta Conference because he could sit hour after hour at a meeting repeating the same position.

MOLTKE, HELLMUTH KARL BERNHARD VON *(1800–1891)*

Prussian field marshal Hellmuth Karl Bernhard von Moltke, considered the creator of the modern German army and the father of modern military strategy, was nicknamed *Hellmuth the Taciturn.* Fluent in several languages, he never betrayed himself or said more than he intended in any of them.

Momo—See GIANCANA, SAM "Moony" or "Momo."

MOMPESSON, GILES *(fl. 1620)*

An English patent, which drew criticism, gave Giles Mompesson and Francis Michell the exclusive right to produce gold and silver lace. Macauley described it as "the most disgraceful of all patents in English history." Mompesson became known as *Sir Giles Overreach,* a sobriquet accorded him in a play of the day by Philip Massinger. (See also Michell, Francis.)

Monarch of Mastication, The—See
WRIGLEY, WILLIAM, JR.

MONK, MARIA (1817–1849)

One of the most infamous impostors of her time, a young girl named Maria Monk became a heroine to American Protestants fearful of popery when *The Awful Disclosures of Maria Monk* was published in 1836. The book purported to reveal the shocking behavior of priests and nuns that she had witnessed as a novice and a nun. Eventually her charges were proved to be fakes, and she became known as *The Lying Nun,* although many still believed her and her book is available today.

Monkey Face—See **GENKER,
CHARLIE "Monkey Face."**

Monkey Gland Man, The—See
VORONOFF, SERGE.

Monkeybitch—See **MANKIEWICZ,
JOSEPH.**

MONMOUTH, JAMES, DUKE OF (1649–1685)

The natural son of King Charles II of England and captain-general in the king's army, James, duke of Monmouth, was hailed by his admirers as *The Protestant Duke* and the legal claimant to the throne. This put him in contrast to the duke of York and future James II, Charles II's brother, who was known as The Popish Duke, having openly converted to Catholicism. Monmouth had been raised a Catholic but later embraced the Protestant faith. When James II ascended the throne in 1685, Monmouth led a military campaign to seize power but was quickly captured and beheaded.

MONROE, ELIZABETH KORTRIGHT (1768–1830)

The wife of future president James Monroe, Elizabeth Kortright Monroe was, during her husband's ambassadorship in Paris, highly popular with the French people, who called her *La Belle Americaine.*

MONROE, JAMES (1758–1831)

During his administration James Monroe, fifth president of the United States, was called *The Era-of-Good-Feeling President* because, with the Federalist Party in a state of collapse, he had little opposition, especially when he ran for reelection in 1820. When touring the country while in office, he wore a Revolutionary Army officer's uniform complete with a cocked hat, which earned him another nickname: *The Last Cocked Hat.*

Monsieur New York (fl. mid-19th century)

The identity of New York's official hangman in the mid-19th century was a well-kept secret, and he was referred to in the press as simply *Monsieur New York.* In the 1880s a newspaper revealed that he lived with his family in New York City near the East River in the vicinity of 125th Street and that he belonged to the Methodist Church. Thereafter, around the time of an execution many a family man in the area made sure he appeared in public to prove he was not *Monsieur New York.*

Monsieur Quixote—See **MENDES-
FRANCE, PIERRE.**

Monster from Arizona, The—See
GOLDWATER, BARRY M.

Monster of Dusseldorf, The: PETER KURTEN (1883–1931)

Peter Kurten became infamous as *The Monster of Dusseldorf,* Germany for killing nine little girls and then sexually abusing them. He was the subject of Fritz Lang's classic film *M,* which brought Peter Lorre to stardom. Kurten, captured after one of his intended victims got away, was executed in 1931. His last wish was that he could hear his blood spurting when his head was cut off.

Monster of Nature, The—See VEGA, LOPE DE.

Monster of Sixty-Third Street—See HOLMES, H. H.

MONTAGU, MARY WORTLEY (1690–1762)

English poet and letter writer Lady Mary Wortley Montagu was celebrated as *Minerva* for her reply to Voltaire's attack on Shakespeare. Disraeli would later write of "the Minerva . . . whose celestial spear was to transfix the audacious Gaul." Alexander Pope for a time addressed her complimentarily as *Sappho,* but as was often his wont, he was later to use the sobriquet most disparagingly, comparing "Sappho's di'monds with her dirty smock" and viewing "A Sappho at her toil's greasy task."

MONTBARS (fl. 1645)

Seventeenth century French pirate Montbars, the most feared buccaneer on the Spanish Main, was called *El Exterminador,* or *The Exterminator,* for his merciless ferocity. He turned pirate after his uncle, with whom he had been very close, was

killed by Spaniards, and for many years Montbars ravaged Spanish colonies and shipping. His ultimate fate is unknown.

MONTIFAUD, MARC DE (fl. 1830s)

Marc de Montifaud, the author of many erotic works, including *Entre Messe et Vepres,* became known as *The Boccaccio of the Nineteenth Century,* after the 14th century Italian author.

MONTMORENCI, FRANCOIS HENRI (1628–1695)

Francois Henri Montmorenci, duke of Luxembourg, was dubbed *le Tapissier de Notre-Dame,* or *The Upholsterer of Notre Dame,* because he sent back more than 100 captured flags to be hung on the walls of the cathedral as was the custom of the time.

MOODY, DWIGHT LYMAN (1837–1899)

The first nationally known U.S. religious revivalist, Dwight Lyman Moody preached what he called "the Old Fashioned Gospel" and founded the famed Moody's Bible Institute in Chicago in 1889. Called by his enthusiastic followers *The Worker in Souls,* he attracted huge crowds during tours of the United States and England.

MOODY, JOSEPH "Handkerchief" (1700–1753)

Early in his life, Rev. Joseph Moody of York, Me., suffered a strange self-imposed ordeal after he accidentally shot a youthful friend to death. As a token of his remorse he thereafter wore a silk handkerchief over his face and was labeled *Handkerchief Moody.*

Moon Maniac, The: DeWITT CLINTON COOK (1920–1941)

By the age of 20 DeWitt Clinton Cook had committed 300 burglaries and numerous attacks on women in California—all during periods of a full moon. He was labeled *The Moon Maniac* even before he was caught. Although Cook was regarded as perhaps the classic example of "moon madness," the jury was unimpressed by such an insanity defense and sent him to the gas chamber in 1941 for the murder of a young college coed.

Moon Missionary, The—See IRWIN, JAMES B.

Moonlight Murderer of Texarkana, The *(fl. 1946)*

In 1946 a total of three men and two women were murdered in small towns at the Texas-Arkansas border, all on nights when there was a full moon. The killer, nicknamed *The Moonlight Murderer of Texarkana*, was never found, although just after the last slaying a man resembling the description of the killer committed suicide by throwing himself in front of a speeding train.

Moony—See GIANCANA, SAM "Moony" or "Momo."

Moor, The—See MARX, KARL.

MOORE, CLEMENT CLARKE *(1779–1863)*

Credited with having provided the first definitive description of the modern American Santa Claus in his poem "A Visit from St. Nicholas," Clement Clarke Moore has since been known as *The Father of Santa Claus*. He is buried in Trinity Church Cemetery in New York, and every Christmas Eve children gather at his grave and read aloud his poem and tribute to Santa Claus.

MOORE, DUDLEY *(1935–   )*

British comedian Dudley Moore, long called *Cuddly Dudley,* has been converted, almost mystically some might say, into *The Heartthrob of the 1980s.*

MOORE, THOMAS *(1779–1852)*

Irish poet and wit Thomas Moore has been called *The Bard of Erin* and *Anacreon Moore,* the latter because he translated Anacreon into English and also wrote many poems in the same style. To many of his contemporaries, however, he was *Trumpet Moore* because he constantly praised himself.

Moral Censor of China, The—See CONFUCIUS.

Moral Gower—See GOWER, JOHN.

Moral Steam Engine, The—See CLARKSON, THOMAS.

MORAN, GEORGE "Bugs" *(1893–1957)*

One of Chicago's zaniest and deadliest gangsters, George Moran, the last leader of the anti-Capone O'Banion gang, was called *Bugs* because of his flaky behavior. He was, for example, privileged to be the first member of the gang to put a bullet in the head of a horse "executed" by the boys after it had thrown and killed their celebrated compatriot Nails Morton in a riding mishap.

MORAN, JOSEPH PATRICK
(1895–1934)

Dr. Joseph Patrick Moran was known as *The Underworld's Family Doctor,* often traveling with the public-enemy gangs of the 1930s so as to be immediately available to take care of gunshot wounds. One night in 1934 Doc Moran was with the Barker-Karpis gang when he got drunk, his usual state, in an Ohio nightclub and told several mobsters: "I have you guys in the palm of my hand. One word from me and your goose is cooked." The boys took him right out and put him at the bottom of Lake Erie.

MORAN, THOMAS B. "Butterfingers"
(1892–1971)

A practicing dip for 65 years and the acknowledged *King of the Pickpockets* most of that time, Thomas B. Moran felt the nickname *Butterfingers* was a misnomer. He complained to interviewers it was slanderous, considering his some 50,000 successful dips against only 60 arrests. Actually the sobriquet was complimentary, in that he could "slide in and out of a pocket like pure butter."

MORATIN, LEANDRO FERNANDEZ
(1760–1828)

The celebrated Spanish dramatist Leandro Fernandez Moratin is known in his country as *The Spanish Moliere.*

Moratorium Bill—See LEMKE, WILLIAM.

MORELLET, ANDRE (1727–1819)

French satirist Andre Morellet was a steadfast champion of the oppressed. His close friend Voltaire nicknamed him *Mords les,* or *Bite 'em,* to emphasize his eagerness to defend the cause of justice regardless of the opposition and personal danger involved.

MORELLO, PIETRO—See Clutching Hand, The.

MORENO, ANTHONY—See Fountain, The.

MORENZ, HOWARD WILLIAM "Howie" (1902–1937)

Long-time hockey great Howie Morenz, who played mostly for the Montreal Canadians, was nicknamed *The Canadian Comet* and *The Babe Ruth of Hockey* and was later the runaway winner of a 1950 Canadian press poll to name the outstanding hockey player of the half century. He broke his leg in a game in 1937 and died of resulting complications.

MORGAN, JOHN PIERPONT
(1837–1913)

U.S. financier and business tycoon, indeed one of the most powerful men in the world, J. Pierpont Morgan became known as *The Great Khan of Wall Street.* Accumulating a fortune before the concept of big business was even understood, Morgan by the early 1900s controlled huge sums of money and credit, the railways, major industries, indeed, a large part of the U.S. economy. The House Committee on Banking and Currency in 1912 uncovered evidence that "Morgan men" held 341 directorships in 112 companies. In his personal life Morgan lived in a style befitting a *Great Kahn,* with an enormous art collection, a splendid town house, a great country home, a huge steam yacht. Once when a man asked the price of a steam yacht,

Morgan said, "Anybody who even has to think about the cost had better not get one."

MORGAN, LEWIS HENRY
(1818–1881)

The title *The Father of American Anthropology* has been bestowed on Lewis Henry Morgan, who is credited with having made, in the mid-19th century, the first scientific study of the social and political structure of the American Indians. He was adopted into the Iroquois and Seneca tribes.

MORGANA—See Baseball's Kissing Bandit.

MORGENTHAU, HENRY, JR.
(1891–1967)

U.S. secretary of the treasury from 1934 to 1945, Henry J. Morgenthau was one of the prime planners of the New Deal as well as wartime and postwar domestic and international economic policy. He was considered excellent at his job but, shy and reserved, a disaster at public relations, leading President Franklin Roosevelt to call him *Henry the Morgue*.

MORISON, MARY—See Highland Mary.

MORNAY, PHILIPPE DE
(1549–1623)

Long-time leader of the French Huguenots, Philippe de Mornay survived the Massacre of St. Bartholomew in 1572 and later became a trusted adviser of the king of Navarre. Because of the power he wielded, he was called *The Huguenot Pope*.

Morning Star of Song, The—See CHAUCER, GEOFFREY.

Morning Star of the Reformation, The—See WYCLIFFE, JOHN.

Morning Star of the Reformation in Germany, The—See LOLLARD, WALTER.

MORPHY, PAUL CHARLES
(1837–1884)

Considered by many the outstanding genius of chess in the 19th century, American Paul Charles Morphy has been called *The Pride and Sorrow of Chess,* having been the chess world's brightest and darkest light. Even today whenever a brilliant coup is performed by a grand master, it is often described as "a bit of Morphy." Traveling to Europe in the 1850s, Morphy defeated all masters of rank who played him and returned in triumph to the United States in 1859. However, finding that few players were as chivalrous in their play as himself, he suddenly gave up chess. Morphy sank into melancholia and blamed his unsuccessful career as a lawyer on his having been a leading chess player. People, he said, would not trust their legal matters to a man known to be the foremost in another endeavor. He died at the age of 47.

MORRELL, ED (1871–1946)

A convict celebrated in *The Star Rover* by Jack London and called *The Dungeon Man of San Quentin,* Ed Morrell was known as possibly the most tortured man in American penal history. When he won a pardon in 1908, he became a national hero and a prison reformer for the rest of his life.

MORRIS, ROBERT "Bobby the Treasurer" (1734–1806)

Known throughout the American Revolution as *Bobby the Treasurer* because he arranged the financing of supplies for the Continental armies, Declaration of Independence signer Robert Morris was so esteemed that he was asked to become the first secretary of the treasury; he declined. Although he has been lastingly dubbed *The Financier of the American Revolution* and *The Patriot Financier,* Morris ended up impoverished and, in 1798, was sentenced to three years in debtors prison, owing some $3 million.

MORROW, "Pegleg" ANNIE (1860?–1935)

Western pioneer and prostitute Annie Morrow gained the sobriquet *Pegleg Annie* as well as that of *The Heroine of Bald Mountain.* Suffering from possibly fatal frostbite, she was, in the western tradition, tied down and her feet were amputated above the ankles by Tug Wilson, using a jackknife and an ordinary meat saw. Pegleg survived to become one of the most storied practitioners of her craft.

MORROW, "Prairie Dog" DAVE (1837–1893)

One of the most colorful western characters, buffalo hunter and sometime badman Dave Morrow was nicknamed *Prairie Dog Dave* supposedly because he added to his income by catching prairie dogs and selling them to tourists in Dodge City at $5 a pair. A better tale about the origin of the nickname is provided by historian James D. Horan, who quotes a contemporary of Morrow, George Bolds, relating how Morrow was caught out on the prairie by two bandits who tortured him to re-

veal the location of a sum of money he had just received in a cattle deal. Before Dave could get away, the outlaws had whittled down his ears to get him to talk. "In the Long Branch Saloon that night," Bolds said, "someone mentioned that Dave, with his pointed, nicked ears, looked like a prairie dog, and the nickname stuck. That's the way most nicknames were born—they got the fancy of the boys in the saloon and no matter what you did or how much you threatened, there was no changing it." The trouble with this version is that it occurred some time in 1878 or 1879, when Bolds himself first arrived in Dodge City, and there are references to *Prairie Dog Dave* in Kansas newspapers several years before the alleged ear-cropping.

MORSE, CHARLES WYMAN (1856–1933)

An unscrupulous businessman, Charles Wyman Morse was called *The Ice King* after he established the Consolidated Ice Co. in New York City, having forced most of his competitors out of business by cutting prices. He then doubled the price of ice. A governmental investigation revealed that Morse had awarded stock in his company to a number of leading municipal officials. That caper led to the use of the term "ice" as a synonym for graft.

MORSE, SAMUEL F. B. (1791–1872)

U.S. inventor Samuel F. B. Morse was dubbed *The Father of the Telegraph* for developing the first practical telegraph in 1840, with substantial aid from Joseph Henry. Because he was a portrait painter of considerable renown, Morse was also dubbed *The American Leonardo.*

MORSE, WAYNE (1900–1974)

A long-time independent-minded senator from Oregon, Wayne Morse was called *The Lone Wolf of the Senate* and, by his enemies, *The Wrecker,* especially after he bolted the Republican Party.

MORSHEAD, LESLIE *(1889–1959)*

World War II Australian general Leslie Morshead, who developed a reputation in North Africa and Borneo as a tough and able commander of tough and able troops, was dubbed by his men *Ming the Merciless.*

MORTON, FERDINAND JOSEPH *"Jelly Roll" (1885–1941)*

Pianist, composer and combo leader *Jelly Roll Morton* gained his nickname for his composition "Jelly Roll Blues," an important and unique contribution to jazz music.

MORTON, OLIVER *(1823–1877)*

A 19th century senator from Indiana, Oliver Morton was noted as one of the chamber's most forceful speakers. Because he was paralyzed, he generally addressed the Senate while seated and was thus called *Sitting Bull.* However, when really exercised by a political matter, he would pull himself erect with the aid of two canes and so excoriate his opponents that they referred to him as *The Devil on Two Sticks.*

MORTON, WILLIAM THOMAS GREEN *(1819–1868)*

U.S. dentist William Thomas Green Morton, the first to patent and publicize the use of ether as an anesthetic, was elevated to the rank of near deity during his lifetime and was called *The Father of Etherization* and *The Father of Anesthesia.*

MOSBY, JOHN SINGLETON *(1833–1916)*

Civil War Confederate colonel John S. Mosby exhibited an uncanny ability to slip through Union lines and wreak havoc on the enemy. On one occasion, with only 29 men Mosby managed to ride more than 25 miles through the federal lines and return with a Union general and 100 other prisoners, without the loss of a single man. This kind of exploit earned Mosby the title of *The Gray Ghost* for his ability to strike and vanish into the countryside. Following Lee's surrender, Mosby disbanded his command rather than surrender it.

Moses—See GRAHAM, BILLY.

Moses of America, The—See WISE, ISAAC MAYER.

Moses of Her People, The—See TUBMAN, HARRIET.

MOSSLER, CANDACE *(1914–1976)*

Candy Mossler was acquitted of one of the most scandalous and brutal murders of the 1960s, that of her millionaire husband, although much of the public continued to consider her guilty and accorded her such facetious designations as *Wife of the Year* and *Widow of the Year.*

Most Celebrated Author on the Planet, The—See BREZHNEV, LEONID.

Most Denounced Man in the World, The—See JOHNSON, LYNDON B.

Most Famous Woman of Two Centuries, The—See KOENIGSMARK, AURORA.

Most Happy Fellow, The—See REAGAN, RONALD.

Most Impudent Man Living, The—See WARBURTON, WILLIAM.

Most Kissed Man in the World, The—See GUIDARELLI, GUIDARELLO.

Most Learned of the Romans, The—See VARRO, MARCUS TERENTIUS.

Most Unending Ass in Christendom, The—See SPENCER, HERBERT.

MOSTEL, SAMUEL JOEL "Zero" (1915–1977)

Since the academic achievements of comedian Samuel Joel Mostel were near zero, the story goes, his classmates dubbed him *Zero Mostel*.

Mother Courage—See ABZUG, BELLA.

Mother Douglas (?–1761)

Known only as *Mother Douglas,* a notorious 18th century English procuress was famed for her house "at the north-east corner of Covent Garden." Foote immortalized her as Mrs. Cole in his play *The Minor*.

Mother Lee—See LEE, ANN.

Mother of All the Doughboys—See SCHUMANN-HEINK, ERNESTINE.

Mother of Believers, The—See AYESHA.

Mother of Hadassah, The—See SZOLD, HENRIETTA.

Mother of Her Country, The—See MARIA THERESA.

Mother of Level Measurement, The—See FARMER, FANNIE MERRITT.

Mother of Monarchs, The: MARIE-LAETITIA RAMOLINO (1750–1836)

A Corsican-born woman, Marie-Laetitia Ramolino became known as *The Mother of Monarchs*. From her union with Carlo Buonaparte, assessor of the royal court of Ajaccio, she had 13 children; three became kings, two queens and one an emperor. The most famous was Napoleon, emperor of France. The others were Joseph, king of Spain; Jerome, king of Westphalia; Louis, king of Holland; Elisa, queen of Toscana; and Maria Annunciata Caroline, queen of Naples. Lower ranks were achieved by Lucien, prince of Canino, and Marie Pauline, duchess of Guastalla. By the time *The Mother of Monarchs* died in 1836, she had witnessed the complete eclipse of her royal progeny.

Mother of Thanksgiving, The—See **HALE, SARAH JOSEPHA.**

Mother of the Feminist Movement in America, The—See **FRIEDAN, BETTY.**

Mother of the Kindergarten, The—See **BLOW, SUSAN ELIZABETH.**

Mother of the Salvation Army, The—See **BOOTH, WILLIAM AND CATHERINE.**

Mother of the Shimmy, The—See **GRAY, GILDA.**

Motivation Mentor, The—See **PACKARD, VANCE.**

MOTT, JAMES W. *(1883–1945)*

Six-term Republican representative from Oregon James W. Mott was nicknamed *Tonguepoint Mott* by his colleagues because of his persistent efforts to expand the naval base at Tongue Point in his home state.

MOTT, LUCRETIA *(1793–1880)*

U.S. abolitionist and Quaker preacher Lucretia Mott was known as *The Flower of Quakerism* because she was one of the first women in America to spread that faith. Because of her early work in aiding runaway slaves, she was to gain fame as *The Advance Agent of Emancipation.*

MOULAY ISMAIL *(1672–1727)*

The last Sharifian emperor of Morocco and the father of 888 children, Moulay Ismail was called *The Bloodthirsty* for his mass killings.

MOUNT, BESSIE *(or JOHN)* *(fl. 1930s–1940s)*

A brothel proprietor in Oxnard, Calif., Bessie Mount was known as *The Respected Madam of Oxnard* until it was discovered that she was a man, whose real name was John Mount. Bessie-John found the trade more profitable and herself-himself more trusted by customers if she-he was a woman.

Mountain Brutus—See **TELL, WILLIAM.**

Mountain of Egotism and Selfishness, That—See **WILSON, WOODROW.**

MOUNTBATTEN, LORD LOUIS *(1900–1979)*

Lord Louis Mountbatten earned several nicknames during his World War II service as supreme commander of the Southeast Asia theater, especially from his second-in-command, U.S. general Joseph "Vinegar Joe" Stillwell, and the rest of his American staff members. Living up to his reputation for caustic comments, Vinegar Joe generally referred to Mountbatten as *Limey Louis, Curly Lashes, Glamour Boy* and, especially, *The Loathsome Limey.* However, as the war progressed and Stilwell grew to appreciate Mountbatten's skills as a strategist, the general dropped the nicknames.

Mountebank in Criticism, A—See **WARBURTON, WILLIAM.**

Mouth, The—See COSELL, HOWARD.

Mouth of the South, The—See TURNER, TED.

Mouth That Roared, The—See MITCHELL, MARTHA.

MOUTON, ROBERT L. *(1892–)*

When Louisiana politician Robert L. Mouton entered the U.S. House of Representatives, he could hardly expect not to be called *Louisiana Ram* by his colleagues since his surname in French means sheep.

MOZART, WOLFGANG AMADEUS *(1756–1791)*

The *Wunderkind* composer Wolfgang Amadeus Mozart was often called *The Raphael of Music*.

Mud-Born Bubble, This—See HARVEY, GABRIEL.

Mudwall Jackson—See JACKSON, WILLIAM LOWTHER.

MUELLER, HEINRICH "Gestapo" *(1896–)*

As chief of the Gestapo, Heinrich Mueller, better known as *Gestapo Mueller,* is among today's most hunted Nazi war criminals. He was presumed killed in 1945, but in 1963 an examination of the skeleton in his grave determined that it was not Mueller's. In the mid-1970s, he was reported to be residing in Argentina.

MUHAMMAD, ELIJAH *(1897–1975)*

A Detroit automobile assembly-line worker, Elijah Poole, better known as Elijah Muhammad, founded the Nation of Islam, or Black Muslim movement. Accorded the sobriquet *Messenger of Allah,* he preached that the salvation of the black people in the U.S. required the formation of an autonomous state.

Mummy, The—See TRIPPE, JUAN.

Munchhausen in Modern Dress, The—See MEANS, GASTON BULLOCK.

Munchhausen of the West, The—See CROCKETT, DAVY.

MUNDT, KARL *(1900–1974)*

A long-time congressman and senator from North Dakota, Republican Karl E. Mundt was a staunch anti-communist during the McCarthy period. His foes, not impressed with his abilities, called him *The Leaning Tower of Putty.*

MURAT, JOACHIM *(1771–1815)*

A daring French marshal, king of Naples and brother-in-law of Napoleon, Joachim Murat was a cavalry leader who helped bring the French emperor many triumphs. Napoleon called him *le Beau Sabreur,* or *The Handsome Swordsman,* and *The Dandy King,* because of his fondness for gaudy dress and display.

***Murat of America, The*—See WHEAT, CHATHAM ROBERDEAU.**

***Murdering Sexton, The*—See PIPER, THOMAS W.**

MURIETA, JOAQUIN (c. 1830–1853 or 1878)

Known as the greatest desperado of the Gold Rush days in California, Joaquin Murieta may or may not have been a composite of several Mexican bandits. In any event, the gringos considered him a bloodthirsty outlaw while the oppressed Mexicans, driven from the best gold claims, viewed him as a fighter against a foreign invader and called him *El Patrio,* or *The Patriot.* In 1853 American possemen brought in a pickled head that was supposed to be Murieta's but the Mexican version is that he escaped capture and lived out his days farming in Sonora.

MURPHY, AUDIE (1924–1971)

Audie Murphy, the most honored U.S. soldier of World War II and later a movie star, was nicknamed by his combat buddies *Baby Murphy* because of his almost cherubic appearance.

MURPHY, CHARLES F. (1858–1924)

New York Tammany Hall leader Charles F. Murphy was known as *Silent Charley* because he used few words in exercising his political power. In the early 1900s Murphy was a target of the Hearst newspapers, which dubbed him *The Black Hand* and *The Colossus of Graft.* Then in 1906 William Randolph Hearst received the Democratic gubernatorial nomination and such sobriquets, at least in Hearst's papers, ceased. It was left for a poetical journalist of the day to set into verse the burial of the nicknames:

> So I lashed him and I thrashed him in my hot reforming zeal,
> Then I clasped him to my bosom in a most artistic deal.

MURPHY, FRANCIS (1836–1907)

Francis Murphy, a reformed drunkard, gained the nickname *The Apostle of Temperance* for his years of effort promoting the Christian Temperance Movement. A saloon keeper, he became an alcoholic and a pauper and was frequently arrested for drunkenness. While in prison in 1870 he converted to Christianity and on his release composed a total-abstinence pledge, which he signed and got others to sign. It read: "With malice toward none and charity to all, I, the undersigned, do pledge my word and honor, God helping me, to abstain from all intoxicating liquors as a beverage, and that I will, by all honorable means, encourage others to abstain." It became the official pledge of the National Christian Temperance Union.

MURPHY, JOHN "Bear-Tracks" (fl. late 19th century)

An enduring lore of Nevada mining days relates how a miner named Johnny Murphy got his nickname *Bear-Tracks* after a winter of romancing a foreman's wife. The husband returned home unexpectedly, forcing Murphy to leap out the window on all fours and scamper off with his clothes in hand. The foreman demanded to know who had been with his wife. When she insisted no one had, he said, "Well, what are them tracks there then?" pointing to the ground. She replied, "Them? Them's bear tracks."

***Murray the K*—See KAUFMAN, MURRAY.**

MURREL, JOHN A. (1794–?)

Unmatched in American history as a creator of grandiose plans, John A. Murrel became known as *The Great Rogue* and *The Great Land Pirate*. He actually planned to establish an underworld empire by fomenting a slave rebellion in New Orleans, Nashville, Memphis, Natchez and other cities while hundreds of criminal confederates siezed power and established the capital of his new domain in New Orleans. The plot collapsed because of informers and Murrel was arrested before the start of the uprising. Although outbreaks occurred in Nashville, Memphis, and Natchez, they were suppressed by authorities who had been alerted. In Tennessee 20 slaves and 10 whites were hanged for their part in the conspiracy. Murrel served 10 years in prison; when he emerged, his mind was broken. At the time he was last seen, in the 1840s, he was a derelict in the Gut, the red-light district of Memphis.

Muscles—See WANER, PAUL AND LLOYD.

Muse of the Stomach, The—See BRILLAT-SAVARIN, ANTHELME.

Muses' Darling, The—See FLETCHER, JOHN.

Music Man of the 1970s, The—See BACHARACH, BURT.

Musical Giant, The—See STRAVINSKY, IGOR.

Mussolini of Music, The—See PETRILLO, JAMES CAESAR.

Mussolini's Boy—See POUND, EZRA.

Mutt and Jeff of Murder, The—See ANSELMI AND SCALISE.

My Eyes and Ears—See ROOSEVELT, ELEANOR.

My Old War Horse—See LONGSTREET, JAMES.

My Soldier—See HENRY OF NAVARRE.

Mystery Man of Europe, The—See ZAHAROFF, BASIL.

MYTTON, JOHN—See Mango, King of the Pickles.

N

NABOKOV, VLADIMIR (1899–1977)

Vladimir Nabokov was denounced by some critics and self-appointed book censors as *The Writer of the Repulsive* for his 1958 novel *Lolita*, the story of a nubile "nymphet," and the character's name has now entered the language as a synonym for a young female sex object. Nabokov was rather amused by the angry reactions the book evoked. "I rather dislike little girls," he said.

NADER, RALPH (1934–)

Ralph Nader first won public recognition by charging that a number of automobiles produced in Detroit were unsafe. His charges forced a huge number of recalls and the cancellation of certain models, and he has since been nicknamed, among other things, *The People's Lawyer* for his consumer advocacy. The names applied to him in Detroit are of course unprintable.

NAIGEON, JACQUES ANDRE (1738–1810)

French freethinker Jacques Andre Naigeon was dubbed *The Inquisitor of Atheists* because of his own intolerance.

Nailed-Down Huntington—See HUNTINGTON, COLLIS POTTER.

NAISMITH, JAMES (1861–1939)

Credited with originating the game of basketball, James Naismith, a Canadian-American professor of physical education, has been dubbed *The Father of Basketball*.

Naked Lady, The—See MENKEN, ADAH ISAACS.

NAMATH, JOSEPH "Joe" (1943–)

Perhaps the most colorful of all professional football players in recent years, Joe Namath was nick-named *Broadway Joe* for his image as a carefree, high-living playboy.

Namby Pamby—See PHILIPS, AMBROSE.

Namby-Pamby Willis—See WILLIS, NATHANIEL P.

Nameless Bard, The—See MATHIAS, THOMAS JAMES.

NAPOLEON (1769–1821)

Napoleon Bonaparte had many nicknames. He was referred to—affectionately by the French and disdainfully by his enemies—as *The Nightmare of Europe, The Corsican General*, and *The Little Corporal*. The English called him *Boney* and *Tiddy-Doll*. When banished to Elba, Napoleon told his followers he would "return with the violets." "Violet" became his adherents' code word. "Do you like violets?" they would ask. An answer of merely *"Oui"* meant nothing, but *"Eh Bien"* indicated the respondent was a supporter. Napoleon returned to the Tuileries in Paris on March 20, 1815, when the violets were in full bloom. The violet became the flower of the Hundred Days, but after Waterloo it became foolhardy and dangerous to wear a violet or even to express admiration for the flower. He was also known as *Corporal Violet*.

NAPOLEON II (1811–1832)

The son of Napoleon in whose behalf Bonaparte abdicated, Napoleon II was no more than a titular emperor. His sobriquets generally tended to be diminutives, such as *The Eaglet* and, simply *The*

Son of the Man. In 1940 Hitler had his remains brought from Vienna and reinterred in the Invalides near his father's tomb.

NAPOLEON III: LOUIS NAPOLEON
(1808–1873)

Louis Napoleon, later Napoleon III of France, nephew of Napoleon Bonaparte, was nicknamed *The Prisoner of Ham,* a fortress where he was held captive for six years, from 1840 to 1846, after plotting to succeed his uncle as emperor of France. After his escape from Ham, he was dubbed *Badinguet,* the name of a Moor in whose guise he slipped away. Victor Hugo, who was exiled upon Louis Napoleon's coup d'etat, continued to propagandize against him, calling him *Tom Thumb* and *Napoleon the Little.* Louis, who had also gained the sobriquet *The Man of December* for his coup in that month, later found himself ignominiously known as *The Man of Sedan* because he surrendered to Germany after the Battle of Sedan in September 1870.

Napoleon of Crime, The—See **WORTH, ADAM.**

Napoleon of Liverpool Finance, The—See **RANGER, MORRIS.**

Napoleon of Luzon, The—See **MACARTHUR, DOUGLAS.**

Napoleon of Mexico, The—See **ITURBIDE, AGUSTIN DE.**

Napoleon of Opera, The—See **SPONTINI, GASPARO.**

Napoleon of Oratory, The—See **PITT, WILLIAM (the elder)**

Napoleon of Promoters, The—See **RICKARD, "Tex" GEORGE L.**

Napoleon of Protection, The—See **MCKINLEY, WILLIAM.**

Napoleon of Slavery—See **CALHOUN, JOHN C.**

Napoleon of the Pacific, The—See **KAMEHAMEHA I.**

Napoleon of the Stump, The—See **POLK, JAMES K.**

Napoleon of the West, The—See **BURR, AARON.**

Napoleon the Little—See **NAPOLEON III.**

Narcissus of France, The—See **LAMARTINE, ALPHONSE.**

NASH, RICHARD "Beau"
(1674–1761)

Richard Nash, better known as *Beau Nash,* could be described simply as a gambler and a dandy, but he was much more. He was also master of the ceremonies at Bath and did much to turn it into one of the world's most fashionable spas, winning for himself the sobriquet *King of the Bath.* He played a large role in changing England's manners and mores, establishing rules for balls and assemblies and ending the customs of wearing swords and boots in public places. It was *Beau Nash* as much as anyone who caused the custom of dueling to fall out of fashion.

NASH, THOMAS *(1567–1601)*

English novelist, dramatist and pamphleteer Thomas Nash was often called *Pierce Penniless* after his pamphlet *Pierce Penniless, His Supplication to the Devil,* a remarkable depiction of the plight of the free-lance writer in Nash's day. Admirers called him *Our English Rabelais,* but writer Gabriel Harvey, with whom he feuded, provided a number of venomous sobriquets, such as *The Second Leviathan of Prose, The Very Baggage of New Writers* and *The Only Unicorne of the Muses.*

NASH, WALTER *(1882–1968)*

New Zealand minister of finance and later prime minister, Sir Walter Nash was dubbed *The Architect of the Welfare State* because of the wide scope of social programs he instituted.

NASHNUSH, SULAIMAN ALI *(1943–   )*

Dubbed *The Libyan Giant* by the press, Sulaiman Nashnush stood at 8 feet 0.4 inches when he underwent an operation to halt his growth.

NASMYTH, PATRICK *(1787–1831)*

The 19th century Scottish landscape painter Patrick Nasmyth was often called *The Scotch Hobbema.* His style was very reminiscent of the Dutch landscape painter Meindert Hobbema.

NASSER BEN HARETH *(c. 6th century)*

During the time of the prophet Mohammed, Nasser Ben Hareth was an Arabian merchant who traveled extensively, especially in Persia, and returned to tell numerous fables of other lands. In fact it was said that many Arabs found Nasser's tales far more interesting and beautiful than the narrations of Mohammed. Nasser was subjected to Mohammed's curse and to this day mention of Nasser's name draws the contempt of the prophet's true believers. Nevertheless, Nasser has come down as *The Aesop of Arabia.*

NASSER, GAMAL ABDEL *(1918–1970)*

The first president of Egypt, Gamal Abdel Nasser led a successful coup d'etat against King Farouk in 1952 and thereafter became known as *The Strong Man of Egypt.* Despite his loss of the 1967 war to Israel, he continued to enjoy the support of the Egyptian masses until his death, although he had to bear the unwanted sobriquet of *The Conquered Hero.*

Nasser's Poodle—See SADAT, ANWAR.

NAST, CONDE *(1874–1942)*

U.S. publisher Conde Nast was dubbed *The First of the Beautiful People* because of the type of magazines he published.

NAST, THOMAS *(1840–1902)*

German-born Thomas Nast became *The Father of American Political Cartoonists* for his powerful cartoons in *Harper's Weekly* depicting political corruption. He created the Republican Elephant and the Democratic Donkey as political symbols, graphically covered the Civil War and whipped up public support and interest in Garibaldi's Risorgimento campaign. On the lighter side, he portrayed Santa Claus flying through the air in his sleigh pulled by reindeer. However, his greatest fame stemmed from his exposure of the Tweed Ring, which earned him the sobriquet *The Crime Fighter*.

NASTASE, ILIE "Nasty" (1946–   )

Because of his on-court temper tantrums, Rumanian tennis star Ilie Nastase is called *Nasty Nastase*.

Nathan—See HANDWERKER, NATHAN.

Natick Cobbler, The—See WILSON, HENRY.

NATION, CARRY (1846–1911)

The saloon-busting Carry Nation became famous as *The Lady with the Hatchet* as she traveled about the country axing up saloons in her crusade against alcohol. Actually she had three trusty hatchets, dubbed Faith, Hope and Charity. In the early 20th century miniature Carry Nation hatchets became big sellers.

Nation Builder, The—See WEIZMANN, CHAIM.

Nation's Toughest Television Reporter, The—See WALLACE, MIKE.

Nature Boy—See KNOWLES, JOE.

Navarre of the American Revolution, The—See BUTLER, THOMAS.

Nazim of Necromantic Nudity, The—See TODD, MIKE.

NEAL, JOHN (1793–1876)

U.S. novelist and poet John Neal was nicknamed *John O'Cataract,* in the words of contemporaries, "on account of his impetuous manners." Neal grew to appreciate the name and adopted it later as a pseudonym.

Nebraska Fiend, The—See RICHARDS, STEPHEN LEE; STARKWEATHER, CHARLES.

Needle John—See HAWKWOOD, JOHN.

Negro, The—See NINO, PEDRO ALONSO.

Negro Moses, The—See TUBMAN, HARRIET.

Negro Paul Bunyan, The—See HENRY, JOHN.

Negro Sappho, The—See WHEATLEY, PHILLIS.

NEHRU, JAWAHARLAL "Pandit" (1889–1964)

Second only to Mahatma Gandhi in winning the adoration of a cult figure in India, Jawaharlal

Nehru was affectionately known as *Pandit,* or *Wise Man,* by his followers. He went to prison nine times between 1921 and 1945 during the struggle for independence from British rule.

NELSON, EARLE LEONARD—See Gorilla Murderer, The.

NELSON, GEORGE "Baby Face" (1908–1934)

While he had a baby face, Lester J. Gillis was the most vicious and homicidal of all the public enemies. He discarded his real name as too "sissy" and insisted on being called "Big George" Nelson, an outrageous demand considering his entire 5 feet 4 3/4 inches. Thus he became *Baby Face Nelson* to the underworld—behind his back only.

NELSON, HORATIO (1758–1805)

One of Britain's most popular and successful fighting men, Horatio Nelson was celebrated as *The Hero of the Hundred Battles* and *The Hero of the Nile,* after his 1798 victory that stranded Napoleon and his French army in Egypt. Nelson died during the Battle of Trafalgar, his greatest triumph.

Nemesis of Kinky Hair, The—See WALKER, SARAH BREEDLOVE.

Nero of Germany, The—See WENCESLAS VI OF BOHEMIA.

NESS, ELIOT (1902–1957)

The famed federal law officer who harassed the Capone mob in the late 1920s and early 1930s, Eliot Ness was nicknamed by the underworld *The Untouchable* because he could not be bought, a rare quality for a law officer in that era. He carefully selected nine federal agents to help him and they became known as *The Untouchables*.

NESTOR (c. 1054–c. 1114)

Nestor, a monk of Kiev-Petchersk, has been designated *The Father of Russian History* since much of that nation's early events are recorded in his narratives.

Nestor of English Authors, The—See ROGERS, SAMUEL.

Nestor of the Confederacy, The—See STEPHENS, ALEXANDER H.

NEUMANN, JOHN VON (1903–1957)

Hungarian-born mathematician John Von Neumann, who developed the mathematical science of "game theory" in 1928, was often designated *The Greatest Mathematician of the Age.* He later worked on the hydrogen bomb and was a member of the U.S. Atomic Energy Commission.

Nevada Commoner, The—See JONES, JOHN P.

Nevada's Master Pimp—See CONFORTE, JOSEPH.

Nevada's Third Senator—ADAMS, EVA B.

Never Fail Burns—See BURNS, WILLIAM J.

NEVILLE, RICHARD (c. 1428–1471)

Richard Neville (or Nevil), earl of Warwick, was nicknamed *The King-maker* for his role in raising two men to the English throne. His influence was vital in first securing the crown for his cousin, Edward of York, against whom he later turned because of Edward's intrigues. He released Henry VI from prison, a move that led to Henry's restoration to the throne. Warwick was killed at Barnet by the forces of Edward. The earl of Warwick is also known as *The Last of the Barons,* that being the title of Lord Lytton's novel that tells his story.

New England Burns—See WHITTIER, JOHN GREENLEAF.

New England Cicero, The—See WEBSTER, DANIEL.

New Haldeman, The—See HAIG, ALEXANDER M.

New Rockefeller, The—See KORETZ, LEO.

New World Superman, The—See PERON, JUAN.

New York Jew Nigger Lover, The—See LEIBOWITZ, SAMUEL S.

New Ziegfeld, The—See TODD, MIKE.

NEWMAN, SARAH JANE—See Skull, Sally.

Newspaper Detective, The—See WHITE, ISAAC DEFOREST "Ike."

NEWTON, ISAAC (1642–1727)

Perhaps the greatest scientific mind ever, Sir Isaac Newton has been dubbed, with perhaps some understatement, *The Priest of Nature.*

NEY, MICHEL (1769–1815)

One of Napoleon's greatest marshals, Michel Ney was dubbed by the emperor after *The Bravest of the Brave.*

NHAT CHI MAI (?–1967)

Nhat Chi Mai, a young Vietnamese university student who immolated herself in Saigon during the height of the Vietnam War, is now remembered by the sobriquet she used to sign the letters and poems she left behind: *The One Who Burns Herself for Peace.* Her most famous verse is:

> I offer my body as a torch
> to dissipate the dark
> to waken love among men
> to give peace to Vietnam.

NICHOLAS I OF RUSSIA (1796–1855)

Nicholas I of Russia was known as *The Iron Czar* because as emperor he immediately and mercilessly crushed an uprising aimed at establishing a constitutional monarchy. Thereafter he ruled the country by strict censorship and police repression.

NICKLAUS, JACK (1940–   )

U.S. professional golfer Jack Nicklaus is nicknamed *The Golden Bear* but referred to affectionately by many players on the tour circuit as *Ohio Fats*, for obvious reasons.

Nigger—See HARDING, WARREN G.

Nigger Jack—See PERSHING, JOHN JOSEPH.

Night Mayor, The—See WALKER, JAMES J.

NIGHTINGALE, FLORENCE (1820–1910)

The first and most famous of the war nurses, Florence Nightingale became known as *The Lady with the Lamp* to the grateful wounded in the Crimean War as she inspected the wards at night carrying a lamp. She and her 37 nurses reduced the death rate of wounded soldiers from 40 percent to two percent. She was later sometimes affectionately nicknamed *The Lady with the Owl* because she carried a pet owl in her pocket whenever she traveled.

Nightingale of a Thousand Songs, The—See SADI, MOSLEHEDIN.

Nightmare of Europe, The—See NAPOLEON.

NILSSON, BIRGIT (1918–   )

The great soprano Birgit Nilsson, considered by many the greatest interpreter of Wagnerian roles in the late 20th century, has gained the nickname *Daughter of the Gods,* a fitting extension of the Wagner themes.

NIMMO, ROBERT P. (1922–   )

The first chief of the Veterans Administration under President Ronald Reagan, Robert P. Nimmo used blunt-edged means to cut back programs and tighten eligibility requirements, leading veterans to dub him *Mr. Nommo,* as in "you don't deserve no mo'."

NIMZOWITSCH, ARNOLD (1886–1935)

Latvian chess master Arnold Nimzowitsch was known as *The Stormy Petrel of the Chess World* and more recently as *The Bobby Fischer of His Day.*

NINO, PEDRO ALONSO (1468?–1505)

A young Spanish navigator, Pedro Alonso Nino, nicknamed *El Negro,* or *The Negro,* sailed with Columbus and is believed to have been the first black in the New World. Although Africans were being brought to Europe as slaves at the time, Nino was a free man.

NIXON, PATRICIA (1912–   )

During her White House days First Lady Pat Nixon was called *Plastic Pat* by some because of her desire for privacy. In a 1982 television appearance former president Richard Nixon brought up the question of whether the press created myths about first ladies and cited his wife's nickname as an example—or perhaps, as some suggested, just in case some viewers were not aware of the sobriquet.

NIXON, RICHARD M. (1913–   )

Richard M. Nixon, 37th president of the United States, was named after Richard the Lion-Hearted. In his youth the nickname ''Dick'' was never used. His mother recalled, ''I always called him Richard.'' An item in his Whittier High School newspaper reads: ''Nothing is funnier than to call Richard Nixon 'Nicky' and watch him bristle.'' At Duke Law School Nixon was known as *Iron Butt* and *Gloomy Gus*. But of course his most famous sobriquet was *Tricky Dick*. It was first used by a small southern California newspaper, the *Independent Review,* in 1950 during Nixon's campaign for the U.S. Senate against Helen Gahagan Douglas, a liberal Democrat he dubbed The Pink Lady in an attempt to link her to communist causes. Years later, in 1968, Nixon commented on the nickname: ''They still call me 'Tricky Dick.' It's a brutal thing to fight. The carefully cultivated impression is that Nixon is devious. I can overcome the impression in one way only: by absolute candor.''

Nixon's Alter Ego—See HALDEMAN, H. R.

Nixon's Nixon—See AGNEW, SPIRO T.

No Flint—See GRAY, CHARLES.

No Problem Meese—See MEESE, EDWIN, III.

Noble Savage, The—See BOONE, DANIEL.

NOGUCHI, THOMAS (1927–   )

Glamorized as the inspiration for the TV series ''Quincy,'' Los Angeles medical examiner Thomas Noguchi was hailed as *The Coroner of the Stars*. He was demoted by officials in 1982 for what was described as ''a litany of horrors'' in office, including sensational comments about the deaths of film stars William Holden and Natalie Wood and allegations that he prayed for jumbo jets to crash.

No-Hit Nolan—See RYAN, NOLAN.

Nonentity with Side Whiskers, A—See ARTHUR, CHESTER A.

No-Nick Shave Man, The—See SCHICK, JACOB.

Non-Organization Man, The—See DELOREAN, JOHN ZACHARY.

Non-Stop Activist, The—See FONDA, JANE.

Non-Violent Singer, The—See BAEZ, JOAN.

NORBURY, EARL OF: JOHN TOLER (1745–1831)

The earl of Norbury, chief justice of the Common Pleas in Ireland in the 1820s, was called *The Hanging Judge* because he sentenced so many persons to the gallows. He was in the habit of carrying on a jocular banter with the defendants while imposing the death penalty.

NORTH, JOHN—See South's Most Crooked Gambler, The.

Northern Dante, The—See OSSIAN.

Northern Herodotus, The—See STURLASON, SNORO.

NORTON, JOSHUA—See Norton I, Emperor of the United States.

Norton I, Emperor of the United States: JOSHUA A. NORTON (1819–1880)

One of the oddest characters in American history, Joshua A. Norton proclaimed in 1859 that the California Legislature had chosen him *Emperor of the United States,* and as *Norton I* he was perhaps San Francisco's best known citizen for 21 years. He wore a blue military uniform with gold-plated epaulets given him by U.S. Army officers and, carrying a cane and umbrella, he promenaded the downtown streets greeting his subjects. San Franciscans humored him and the Board of Supervisors even appropriated funds for him when he was in need of a new uniform. *Norton I* ate free in whatever restaurant, lunchroom or saloon that struck his fancy, and whenever he was short of ready cash, he issued 50-cent bonds, which he sold to his subjects. Merchants and banks also honored his 50-cent checks. When he died in 1880, 10,000 mourners lined the funeral route.

Nosey Parker—See PARKER, MATTHEW "Nosey."

NOVAK, KIM (1933–   )

Actress Kim Novak, a notorious recluse, has been dubbed *Hollywood's Melancholy Blonde.*

No. 9653—See DEBS, EUGENE V.

No. 1 Brain Truster—See ROSENMAN, SAMUEL I. "Sammy the Rose."

No. 1 Pinup Girl— See GRABLE, BETTY.

No. 1 Woman Quisling—See LUCHAIRE, CORINNE.

Nun of Amherst, The—See DICKINSON, EMILY.

Nun of Kent, The—See BARTON, ELIZABETH.

Nurse of Antiquity, The—See CAMDEN, WILLIAM.

Nutcracker Man (c. 1,748,000 B.C.)

Perhaps the earliest nickname, admittedly applied some 1.75 million years after the subject's death, was that of *Nutcracker Man,* given by anthropologists Louis and Mary Leakey to the long-departed owner of a big-jawed skull found in 1950 in Tanzania. They dubbed him *Nutcracker Man (Zinjanthropus boisei)* because of his big teeth.

O

OAKLEY, ANNIE (1860–1926)

A genuine markswoman, Annie Oakley was nicknamed *Little Sure Shot* by Sitting Bull. She was also called *America's Sweetheart* and idealized as the archetypal western girl, even though she had never been west of Ohio except on tours. Her shooting of card targets gave rise to the use of the term "Annie Oakley" for any kind of pass that is punched full of holes, much as she perforated her targets with bullets.

OASTLER, RICHARD (1789–1861)

English reformer Richard Oastler earned the sobriquet *The Factory King* because of his success at changing so many labor laws; his efforts led to an improvement of child labor conditions, the introduction of the 10-hour day and various other reforms. He even managed to keep up his campaign in a weekly publication while he was imprisoned for debt.

OATES, TITUS (1649–1705)

A man described as a "slimy, perverted moron," Titus Oates swore away the lives of innocent Englishmen with forged evidence in the so-called 1678 Popish Plot, an alleged plan by Jesuits to assassinate King Charles II and massacre Protestants. His evidence was believed and Oates was hailed as *The Savior of His Country*. The sobriquet continued to be used, derogatorily, after Oates was convicted of perjury in 1689. He was imprisoned but later pardoned by William of Orange.

O'BANION, DION (1892–1924)

While Dion O'Banion was denounced by a police chief as *Chicago's Arch Criminal*, the press and public, almost affectionately, nicknamed him *Deanie* and *Gangdom's Favorite Florist*. The killer of at least 25 men, O'Banion ran a florist shop, and Chicagoans saw the humor of his not only taking part in the city's gang wars but making a profit by supplying the flowers for one lavish gangland funeral after another.

OBERON, MERLE (1911–1979)

Tasmanian-born actress Merle Oberon was known as *Queenie* by her schoolmates in Calcutta because of her regal bearing. The aura carried over to Hollywood, where she was called *The Princess*.

O'Berta, Dingbat: JOHN OBERTA (1892–1930)

A bootlegger and killer who wanted to turn "legit," John Oberta sought respectability in politics and became a Republican committeeman in Chicago's corrupt political scene during the 1920s. He then moved on to such offices as alderman and state senator. Since his bailiwick turned strongly Irish, the Polish Oberta simply changed his name to *O'Berta* and spoke with a thick brogue whenever he addressed Irish groups. His nickname *Dingbat* derived from a character in a popular comic strip who was considered to be almost as "nutty" as the juvenile-minded Oberta. *Dingbat O'Berta* was the victim of a gangland slaying in 1930.

OBERTA, JOHN—See O'Berta, Dingbat.

OBICI, AMADEO (1877–1947)

A penniless 19-year-old immigrant from Oderzo, Italy, Amadeo Obici went into business in the United States roasting peanuts, which he sold for five cents a bag. He formed the Planters Peanut Company in 1906 and became *The Peanut King of America*.

Obsessive Poisoner, The—See YOUNG, GRAHAM.

O'CAROLAN, TURLOCH (1670–1738)

A renowned Irish minstrel, Turloch O'Carolan was nicknamed *The Orpheus of the Green Isle*. He traveled with a harp from door to door and was supposedly the last of the wandering musical bards.

OCHS, ADOLPH S. (1858–1935)

Publisher of the *New York Times* from 1896 until his death in 1935, Adolph S. Ochs was given the sobriquet *The Watchdog of Central Park* for his efforts to ensure that the park remained a place of recreation for the city's residents.

O'CONNELL, DANIEL (1775–1847)

Perhaps not really deserving of the sobriquet *The Liberator,* Irish political leader Daniel O'Connell failed in his efforts to free Ireland from British rule, but did force London to accept the Emancipation Act of 1829, allowing Roman Catholics to hold office and sit in Parliament.

O'Connell of Canada, The—See MACKENZIE, WILLIAM LYON.

Official Greeter of New York City, The—See WHALEN, GROVER A.

Ogre of Hanover, The—See HAARMANN, FRITZ.

OH, SADAHARU (1940–   )

Japanese baseball slugger Sadaharu Oh, who has hit over 800 home runs, is known as *The Babe Ruth of Japan*.

O'HARA, JOHN (1905–1970)

U.S. novelist and short-story writer John O'Hara, who depicted the mores of upper-middle class America in the 20th century, was accurately nicknamed *The Voice of the Hangover Generation*.

O'HARA, MAUREEN (1921–   )

Because of her unseemly gait as a child, red-haired screen star Maureen O'Hara was nicknamed *Baby Elephant*. This did not prevent her from growing up to become *The Queen of Technicolor*.

Ohio Fats—See NICKLAUS, JACK.

Ohio Gong, The—See ALLEN, WILLIAM "Fog Horn."

OLAV II OF NORWAY (995–1030)

King Olav II of Norway was known by two rather diverse sobriquets, *The Tiger* and *The Saint*, the former for his severity and the latter for his extreme piety. He perhaps proved the aptness of both when he caught himself absentmindedly whittling wood on the Sabbath. In contrition he completely burned off his whittling hand.

Old, The—See HAAKON IV HAAKONSSON OF NORWAY.

Old Ace of Spades—See LEE, ROBERT E.

Old Beeswax—See SEMMES, RAPHAEL.

Old Blizzards—See LORING, WILLIAM WING.

Old Blood and Guts—See PATTON, GEORGE S., JR.

Old Blue Light—See JACKSON, THOMAS JONATHON "Stonewall."

Old Brains—See HALLECK, HENRY WAGER.

Old Buena Vista—See TAYLOR, ZACHARY.

Old Commoner, The—See STEVENS, THADDEUS.

Old Daddy—See TUBMAN, WILLIAM V. S.

Old Dutch Cleanser—See BLANKENBURG, RUDOLPH.

Old Figgers—See GROSVENOR, CHARLES HENRY.

Old Flintlock—See HANSON, ROGER WEIGHTMAN.

Old Forty-Eight Hours—See DOUBLEDAY, ABNER.

Old Fox, The—See WASHINGTON, GEORGE.

Old Fuss and Feathers—See SCOTT, WINFIELD.

Old Gimlet Eye—See BUTLER, SMEDLEY DARLINGTON.

Old Glad-Eye—See GLADSTONE, WILLIAM.

Old Glory—See SWANSON, GLORIA.

Old Grog—See VERNON, EDWARD.

Old Hair-and-Teeth—See SHAW, GEORGE BERNARD.

Old Hickory—See JACKSON, ANDREW.

Old Ironsides—See STEWART, CHARLES.

Old Jack's Commissary General—See BANKS, NATHANIEL PRENTISS.

Old Jube—See EARLY, JUBAL ANDERSON.

Old Jubilee—See EARLY, JUBAL ANDERSON.

Old Man—See LENIN, NIKOLAI.

Old Man Eloquent—See ADAMS, JOHN QUINCY; COLERIDGE, SAMUEL TAYLOR; ISOCRATES.

Old Man Stratton—See STRATTON, WINFIELD SCOTT.

Old Mortality—See SMITH, WILLIAM HENRY.

Old Mortality of Pictures, The—See VERTUE, GEORGE.

Old Mother Hancock—See HANCOCK, JOHN.

Old One Wing—See MARTIN, JAMES GREEN.

Old Pap—See PRICE, STERLING.

Old Parr—See PARR, THOMAS.

Old Pretender, The—See STUART, JAMES FRANCIS EDWARD.

Old Rosy—See ROSECRANS, WILLIAM STARKE.

Old Rough and Ready—See TAYLOR, ZACHARY.

Old Rowley—See CHARLES II OF ENGLAND.

Old Sarah—See JENNINGS, SARAH.

Old Shoe—See WILSON, THORNTON ARNOLD.

Old Sink or Swim—See ADAMS, JOHN.

Old Skedad—See PRICE, STERLING.

Old Tippecanoe—See HARRISON, WILLIAM HENRY.

Old Tomorrow—See MACDONALD, JOHN A.

Old Two-to-Ten—See BAKER, HOWARD, JR.

Old Usufruct—See TILDEN, SAMUEL J.

Old Veto—See TYLER, JOHN.

Old White Hat—See GREELEY, HORACE.

Old Wicked—See GODFREY, HOLLEN.

Old Wig, The—See BACH, JOHANN SEBASTIAN.

Old Wigs—See DUNSTAN, JEFFREY.

Old Wrinkle-Boots—See WILLIS, BROWNE.

Oldest Soldier, The—See HERSHEY, LEWIS B.

OLDHAM, JOHN (1653–1683)

English poet John Oldham, whose verses were often savagely satirical, was labeled *The English Juvenal,* after the famous Roman satirist.

Ole Redhead, The—See GODFREY, ARTHUR.

OLIVE, ISOM PRENTICE "Print"—See Man Burner, The.

Oliver, Laurence—See OLIVIER, LAURENCE.

Oliver Cromwell—See JEFFERSON, THOMAS.

OLIVIER, LAURENCE (1907–   )

English stage and movie actor Sir Laurence Olivier suffered the loss of the second "i" in his name because of Humphrey Bogart, who insisted on always calling him *Laurence Oliver.* Bogie held that Olivier sounded "phony."

Olympics' Instant Millionaire, The—See JENNER, BRUCE.

OMAR I (c. 581–644)

Omar I, second Mohammedan caliph, had been an adviser to Mohammed and Abu Bekr, the first caliph after whose death he served for 10 years. He was designated *The Emperor of Believers* and *The Commander of the Faithful,* a title continued by succeeding caliphs. He conquered Syria, Palestine, Egypt and Persia. Omar I was assassinated by a Persian slave.

OMAR KHAYYAM (1048?–1122?)

Since the Persian poet, astronomer and mathematician Omar Khayyam's nickname was *The Tentmaker* (i.e., Khayyam), he was probably the son of a tentmaker. During his lifetime he made his mark in several fields, including law, history, medicine, mathematics and astronomy—but not poetry. That fame did not descend upon him until the English Victorian poet Edward FitzGerald made his free and creative translation of *The Rubaiyat* in 1859.

ONASSIS, ARISTOTLE SOCRATES (1906?–1975)

A Greek refugee from oppression in Turkey, Aristotle Socrates Onassis was making 25 cents an hour as a telephone operator in Buenos Aires in 1922. He saved his limited funds, entered the tobacco import business and became a millionaire before the age of 25. Famed as *The Golden Greek,* he was estimated to be worth more than half a billion dollars by 1968, primarily in oil tankers, and had garnered what some considered his greatest prize, Jacqueline Bouvier Kennedy, his second wife.

One of the People—See HOPKINSON, FRANCIS.

One of the Seven Humbugs of Christendom—See ELGAR, EDWARD WILLIAM.

One Price—See STEWART, ALEXANDER T.

One Who Burns Herself for Peace, The—See NHAT CHI MAI.

One Who Yawns—See GERONIMO.

One-Armed Devil, The—See KEARNY, PHILIP "One-Armed Phil."

One-Leg Paget—See PAGET, HENRY WILLIAM "One-Leg."

One-Legged Governor of New Netherlands—See STUYVESSANT, PETER "Wooden Leg."

One-Man Anti-Communist Left Movement, The—See MACDONALD, DWIGHT.

One-Man-One-Vote Chandler—See CHANDLER, WALTER.

One-Take Astor—See ASTOR, MARY.

One-Take Van Dyke—See VAN DYKE, W. S.

O'NEILL, ROSE *(1874–1944)*

Rose O'Neill, the creator of the Kewpie Doll, was quite logically nicknamed *The Kewpie Doll Lady.* The royalties from her design brought her $1.4 million.

O'NEILL, THOMAS P. "Tip," JR. *(1912–   )*

House of Representatives speaker Thomas P. O'Neill, Jr., gained his nickname *Tip* from a 19th century baseball player named O'Neill who was famed for foul-tipping pitches.

O'NEILL, WILLIAM O. "Buckey" *(1860–1898)*

An Arizona lawman of considerable courage, William O. O'Neill—called *Buckey* for his habit of "bucking" the faro tables—fought with Theodore Roosevelt's Rough Riders in the Spanish-American War, winning the sobriquet *Teddy's Terror*. He distinguished himself in a number of engagements before being killed by a sniper on San Juan Hill.

Onionhead—See PERICLES.

Only Unicorne of the Muses, The—See NASH, THOMAS.

ONODA, HIROO—See Last of the Samurai, The.

Oomph Girl, The—See SHERIDAN, ANN.

OPITZ, MARTIN (1597–1639)

Admirers of German writer and poet Martin Opitz called him *The Father of German Poetry* and *The Restorer of German Poetry* for the beauty and metrical smoothness of his work, which they considered far superior to the material produced by his predecessors. However, his poetry lacked imagination, vigor and above all originality, and he was no more than a pale imitator of the Italian poets. Although he was called *The Dryden of Germany,* and is sometimes so listed in modern texts, the appellation was meant to be ironic; as one critic put it, Opitz "bears no resemblance to the Glorious John."

OPPENHEIMER, J. ROBERT (1904–1967)

The physicist who directed the development of the atomic bomb, J. Robert Oppenheimer is known as *The Father of the Atom Bomb.* In 1953 the federal government, alleging that Oppenheimer was a security risk, stripped him of his security clearance. Ten years later he was awarded the Atomic Energy Commission's $50,000 Enrico Fermi Award.

Orange King, The—See HARRIS, JAMES ARMSTRONG.

Orange Peel—See PEEL, ROBERT (The Younger).

Orator Henley—See HENLEY, JOHN.

Orator of Free Dirt, The—See JULIAN, GEORGE WASHINGTON.

Orator of Secession, The—See YANCEY, WILLIAM L.

Orator of the Human Race, The—See CLOOTZ (or CLOOTS), JEAN BAPTISTE.

Orchid Man, The—See CARPENTIER, GEORGES.

Oregon Byron, The—See MILLER, JOAQUIN.

Organizer of Victory—See CARNOT, LAZARE NICOLAS MARGUERITE.

Oriental Homer, The—See SADI, MOSLEHEDIN.

ORIGEN (c. 185–253)

Because of his tireless efforts on behalf of the faith, Origen, a Greek father of the Church, was nicknamed *The Man of Steel.*

Original I-Want-to-Be-Alone Woman, The—See ADAMS, MAUDE.

Original Robinson Crusoe, The—See SELKIRK, ALEXANDER.

Original Swinger, The—See WEISSMULLER, JOHNNY.

ORPHEUS (pre-9th century B.C.?)

A Greek poet named Orpheus, who lived before Homer, has been awarded the accolade *The Father of Poetry;* however, many, including Aristotle, have doubted whether he ever existed. As a result, the sobriquet has been applied to Homer as well.

Orpheus of Arabia, The—See ABU NASR MOHAMMED AL FARABI.

Orpheus of Highwaymen, The—See GAY, JOHN.

Orpheus of Scotland, The—See JAMES I OF SCOTLAND.

Orpheus of the Green Isle, The—See O'CAROLAN, TURLOCH.

ORWELL, GEORGE (1903–1950)

British satirical novelist and literary critic George Orwell, author of *1984* and *Animal Farm,* was called *The Fugitive from the Camp of Victory* for his general pessimism and his embrace of Trotskyism over Stalinism as the inheritor of Leninism.

OSBORNE, GEORGE O. (1845–1926)

One of the early enlightened prison wardens in the United States, George O. Osborne, *The Father of Prison Reform* inaugurated in the late 19th century several revolutionary reforms at New Jersey State Prison, including schools with practical courses for convicts and an improved parole system. He was perhaps the first warden to eliminate such dehumanizing practices as striped uniforms, shaved heads, the ball and chain and "dark cells," or dungeons.

OSBORNE, JOHN (1929–)

During the 1950s and 1960s English playwright and screenwriter John Osborne, who leaped to fame with his play *Look Back in Anger,* became the leader of the Angry Young Men of the British

theater and was himself known as *The Angry Young Man.*

OSCAR OF THE WALDORF: OSCAR MICHEL TSCHIRKY (1866–1950)

Oscar Michel Tschirky, the maitre d'hotel at New York's Waldorf-Astoria, was best known as *Oscar of the Waldorf.* He has been credited with the creation of the Waldorf Salad.

OSSIAN (c. 4th century)

The ancient bard Ossian, claimed by both Scotland and Ireland, has been called *The Glory of Scotland, The Gaelic Homer, The Celtic Homer* and *The Northern Dante.* One critic stated that Ossian "draws often from his phantoms cries more human and more heart-rending than those of the heroes of Homer." However, some scholars believe certain works attributed to Ossian really belong to 18th century Scottish poet James Macpherson. (See Macpherson, James.)

Ostrich—See UPDIKE, JOHN.

Other Eye of Florence, The—See CAVALCANTI, GUIDO.

Other State Department, The—See LIPPMANN, WALTER.

OTIS, HARRISON GRAY (1837–1917)

Because of his antipathy toward organized labor, Gen. Harrison Gray Otis, former military officer and publisher of the *Los Angeles Times,* was called *The Generalissimo of the Open Shop.* During the early years of the 20th century Otis was responsible for Los Angeles being called "the scabbiest town on earth." Labor-management strife there was marked by bombings and mass firings of union men. Otis traveled about the city with a small cannon strapped to the running board of his car.

OTTO III OF THE HOLY ROMAN EMPIRE (980–1002)

One of the most ambitious rulers of the Holy Roman Empire, Otto III was referred to as *The Wonder of the World* because of his intellect. Otto III planned to make Rome the center of a new world empire, but he died at the age of 22, his dream unfulfilled.

Otto the Mad: OTTO OF BAVARIA (1848–1926)

King Otto of Bavaria was totally insane when he succeeded to the throne in 1886. Kept under constant guard, *Otto the Mad* was permitted to exercise what he considered his royal prerogative of shooting a peasant every morning. His guards indulged him by giving him a gun loaded with blanks while one of them disguised himself and hid in the bushes on the lawn. When Otto spotted his victim, he would fire and the man would keel over on hearing the shot.

Our Bitter Patriot—See DREISER, THEODORE.

Our English Marcellus—See HENRY, PRINCE.

Our Grover—See CLEVELAND, GROVER.

Our Lady of Mercy—See TALLIEN, MADAME.

Our Mercury—See MASSINGER, PHILIP.

Our Nazi—See BRAUN, WERNER VON.

Our Pindar—See COWLEY, ABRAHAM.

Our Vishinsky—See FREISLER, ROLAND.

Out of Print Olive—See Man Burner, The.

Outlaw Doc, The—See BELL, TOM.

OVERBURY, THOMAS (1581–1613)

Imprisoned in the Tower of London at the instigation of Lady Frances Howard, the poet Sir Thomas Overbury was subjected to an incredible 100-day murder diet that included nitric acid, arsenic, hemlock, ground diamonds and mercury. Although the diet was enough to kill off a score of men, he survived until finally his guards were bribed to kill him with an injection of a powerful corrosive. When the facts were revealed Sir Thomas posthumously became known as *The Iron Poet*.

Overland Man, The—See SUTHERLAND, JOCH BAIN "Jock."

OVID (43 B.C.–17 A.D.)

In the case of Ovid, the renowned Roman poet, one word was worth a thousand pictures: Ovid's surname was *Naso,* or *Long Nosed*.

OWEN, JOSHUA THOMAS
(1821–1887)

Because of his supposed Irish origins, Union General Joshua Thomas Owen was nicknamed *Paddy*. It did no good to try to correct this misapprehension, especially among Irish soldiers, and the fallacy remained with Owen throughout his military career despite the fact that he was born in Wales, not Ireland.

OWEN, ROBERT *(1771–1858)*

Welsh manufacturer, educator and pioneer in the co-operative movement, Robert Owen has been dubbed *The Father of British Socialism*. Although his immediate utopian projects failed, Owen's ideas have long influenced socialist and co-operative movements.

P

P.T. Barnum of Sports, The—See **PYLE, CHARLES C. "Cash and Carry."**

P.X. Millionaire, The— See **WOOLDRIDGE, WILLIAM O.**

Pacific, The—See **AMADEUS VIII, First Duke of Savoy.**

Pacific Cyclone, The—See **SMITH, HOLLAND M. "Howling Mad."**

Pacifist Absolutist, The—See **BISHOP, CORBETT.**

PACKARD, VANCE *(1914–   )*

U.S. journalist Vance Packard, author of a number of popular sociological books, gained the nickname *The Motivation Mentor* after the publication of his best-selling book *The Hidden Persuaders*.

PACKER, ALFRED—See **Man Who Ate Democrats, The.**

Paddy—See **OWENS, JOSHUA THOMAS.**

PAGANINI, NICCOLO *(1782–1840)*

Widely regarded as the greatest violinist of all time, Niccolo Paganini began making public performances at the age of 11. He held almost hypnotic sway over audiences and was often called *The Devil* because it was felt he must have been in league with Satan to perform so brilliantly.

PAGE, JOHN *(1744–1808)*

John Page, Revolutionary War patriot and then a member of Congress and governor of Virginia, was referred to by friends as *John Partridge* because of his interest in astronomy. Partridge, who was born exactly a century before Page, was perhaps the most famous English astrologer and almanac producer of his day.

PAGE, KIRBY *(1890–1957)*

Evangelist preacher for the Disciples of Christ, U.S. pacifist Kirby Page was nicknamed *The Itinerant Evangelist for Peace*.

PAGET, HENRY WILLIAM "One-Leg" (1768–1854)

At the Battle of Waterloo, Henry William Paget, first marquess of Anglesey and a cavalry officer, was standing with Wellington in the midst of the conflict, when he suddenly announced, "By God, sir, I have lost my leg!" Wellington glanced over and replied, "By God, sir, so you have," and continued giving commands. Paget's severed leg was later buried in a coffin in a garden at Waterloo and he was thereafter known as *One-Leg Paget*.

Painless Parker: EDGAR RUDOLPH RANDOLPH PARKER (1872–1952)

Brooklyn-born dentist Edgar Rudolph Randolph Parker was nicknamed *Painless Parker* and *The Great Tooth Tycoon*. He turned dentistry into show business, employing showgirls and circuses, practicing his trade on sidewalks and legally adopting the name *Painless* as he built a chain of dental offices on the West Coast.

Painter for Millionaires, The—See RIVERA, DIEGO.

Painter of Limited Color, The—See WHISTLER, JAMES ABBOTT McNEILL.

Painter of Limited Comment, The—See WHISTLER, JAMES ABBOTT McNEILL.

Painter of Loneliness, The—See HOPPER, EDWARD.

Painter of Presidents, The—See STUART, GILBERT.

Painter of the Graces, The—See APPIANI, ANDREA; BOUCHER, FRANCOIS.

PAKENHAM, FRANCIS AUNGIER—See Lord Porn.

Palace Prowler, The—See FAGAN, MICHAEL.

Paladin of Paramours, The—See MITCHELSON, MARVIN.

PALESTRINA, GIOVANNI PIERLUIGI DA (1526–1594)

Italian musician and composer Giovanni Pierluigi da Palestrina set a pattern for Roman Catholic sacred music that has remained virtually unchanged. He was accorded the sobriquet *The Michelangelo of the Lyre*.

PALMER, DANIEL D. "Fish" (1845–1913)

The founder of the Palmer School of Chiropractic, a foremost institution of its type, Daniel D. Palmer was nicknamed *Fish* by friends because early in life he collected and studied goldfish bones. Later he switched to human bones, made spinal adjustments and began an osteopathic practice. As his fame grew, he started the Palmer School in 1898.

Paltry Dunghill, A—See HILL, JOHN.

Pancho Villa's Butcher—See FIERRO, RODOLFO.

Panic of 1837, The—See VAN BUREN, MARTIN.

Papa—See HEMINGWAY, ERNEST.

Papa Doc—See DUVALIER, FRANCOSIS.

Paper King, The—See LAW, JOHN.

Paperhanger, The—See HITLER, ADOLF.

Paper-Sparing Pope—See POPE, ALEXANDER.

Pappy—See FORD, JOHN.

Paraguayan Connection, The—See RICORD, AUGUST.

Pardoning Governor, The—See SMALL, LEN.

PARE, AMBROISE (1510–1590)

Sixteenth century French doctor Ambroise Pare became known as *The Father of Modern Surgery*. He made notable advances in the treatment of wounds and generally improved standards of cleanliness in surgical procedures.

PARKER, BONNIE—See Bonnie and Clyde.

PARKER, DOROTHY (1893–1967)

U.S. author, playwright and critic Dorothy Parker was celebrated as *The Deadly Asp* for her cutting wit. A case in point occurred when Clare Boothe Luce met her in a doorway and said, "Age before beauty." Parker glided past, responding, "Pearls before swine."

PARKER, EDGAR RUDOLPH RANDOLPH—See Painless Parker.

PARKER, ELLIS (1873–1940)

A New Jersey county detective, Ellis Parker gained worldwide fame because of his ability to solve murder mysteries, 226 out of 236, winning the accolade *The Cornfield Sherlock*. He ruined his career, however, by abducting and torturing an innocent man he thought was responsible for the Lindbergh baby kidnapping. Parker went to prison for six years and died there.

PARKER, ELY SAMUEL (1828–1895)

A sachem of the Seneca tribe in upstate New York named Donehogawa became an engineer and adopted the name Ely Samuel Parker. He befriended Ulysses S. Grant while the latter was a civilian. At the start of the Civil War he applied for a commission in the Union Army but, as an Indian, was turned down. Eventually, with Gen. Grant's intercession, he became a staff officer, and Grant's military secretary. At the end of the war Parker wrote out the terms of Lee's surrender at Appomattox, and he was made a brigadier general, the highest rank of any Indian in the Union Army. Because of Parker's visibility on Grant's staff, the members of the Union Army called him simply *The Indian*, not necessarily with affection.

PARKER, ISAAC C. (1838–1896)

The U.S. version of The Hanging Judge was Isaac C. Parker, better known simply as *Hanging Parker,* who presided in the federal court at Fort Smith, Ark. and had jurisdiction over Indian Territory (now Oklahoma) from 1875 until 1896. Although he sent 88 men to the gallows (84 other defendants he condemned were saved by higher court reviews) it was said that often Parker wept while a sentence was being carried out.

PARKER, MATTHEW "Nosey" (1504–1575)

Archbishop of Canterbury during the early reign of Queen Elizabeth I, Matthew Parker was noted for being overinquisitive about church matters, a habit that won him the label *Nosey Parker.* Oddly, he was notoriously shy about all other subjects.

PARKER, SAMUEL (1640–1687)

Dr. Samuel Parker, a one-time stern Puritan who became the favorite of England's James II and bishop of Oxford, was often denounced as *Mitred Dulness* because of his boring sermon.

PARNELL, CHARLES STEWART (1846–1891)

Irish leader in the House of Commons and a champion of home rule, Charles Stewart Parnell so dominated the nationalist movement in his country that he was labeled *The Uncrowned King of Ireland.* He lost his support near the end of his life because of his involvement in a scandal with a colleague's wife.

PARR, THOMAS (1483?–1635)

An English peasant, Thomas Parr, was reputed to have survived to the age of 152 and was known as *Old Parr.* He lived through the reigns of 10 kings and queens of England and was painted by Vandyke and Rubens. Parr was buried in Westminster Abbey.

PARRHASIUS (c. 400 B.C.)

Recognized as one of the greatest painters of antiquity, the Greek artist Parrhasius never had any doubts about his status. He bestowed himself the sobriquet *The King of Painters.*

Parricide, The—See HENRY V OF GERMANY

Parsley Peel—See PEEL, ROBERT (the elder).

Parson's Emperor—See CHARLES IV OF THE HOLY ROMAN EMPIRE.

Pasha Loring—See LORING, WILLIAM WING.

Passionaria, La—See IBARRURI, DELORES.

Passionate One, The—See IBARRURI, DELORES.

Passionate Skeptic, The—See RUSSELL, BERTRAND

PASTOR, TONY (1837–1908)

Actor and manager Tony Pastor became known as *The Father of the Music Hall* in the United States. His Tony Pastor's Opera House in New York brought in talent from London, and he was the discoverer of many important American performers, among them Lillian Russell.

PASTORIUS, FRANCIS DANIEL (1651–1719)

Francis Daniel Pastorius, who in 1864 founded Germantown, Pa., is best remembered as *The Pennsylvania Pilgrim,* from Whittier's poem of the same name.

PATHE, CHARLES (1863–1957)

A founder of the French motion picture industry, Charles Pathe is best remembered as *The Father of the Newsreel.*

Pathfinder, The—See FREMONT, JOHN C.

Pathfinder for Lincoln, The—See FREMONT, JOHN C.

Pathfinder of the West, The—See FREMONT, JOHN C.

PATIN, GUY (1601–1672)

A well-known 17th century physician, wit and freethinker, Guy Patin was called *The Rabelaisian Doctor.* His mode of dress consisted of boots, hose, doublet, cloak, collar and hat all in conflict with one another. It was Patin's method of protest against vanity and fashion.

PATINO, SIMON I. (1862–1947)

A Spanish-Indian peasant, Simon I. Patino developed the world's richest tin mine and became a near billionaire. Because of his tremendous economic and political power, he was called *The Tin King of Bolivia.*

PATMAN, WRIGHT (1893–1976)

U.S. Representative Wright Patman served in the House from 1928 to 1976 and sponsored the legislation that created the Small Business Administration. An opponent of concentrated economic power, he particularly fought against chain store formations and was nicknamed *Anti-chain-store Patman.*

Patriarch of the Indians, The—See MAYHEW, THOMAS.

Patriot, The—See MURIETA, JOAQUIN.

Patriot Financier, The—See MORRIS, ROBERT "Bobby the Treasurer."

Patriot of Humanity, The—See GRATTAN, HENRY

Patron Saint of Dry Sundays—See ROOSEVELT, THEODORE.

PATTEN, GEORGE WASHINGTON
(1808–1882)

A soldier in the Union Army during the Civil War, George Washington Patten wrote a book of poetry, entitled *Voices of the Border,* that told of the common soldier's life. It became extremely popular with the troops and Patten was dubbed *The Poet Laureate of the Army.*

PATTERSON, JOSEPH MEDILL
(1879–1946)

Newspaper publisher Joseph Medill Patterson is known as *The Father of the Tabloid,* having founded the *New York Daily News,* the first successful tabloid in the United States.

PATTERSON, NAN (1882–?)

Broadway Florodora Girl and accused murderess, Nan Patterson was labeled *The Girl in the Hansom Cab* after the shooting death of her married lover, Caesar Young, in a hansom cab on Broadway in 1904. The prosecution contended she had pulled a gun and shot him, but Nan insisted he had produced the gun and shot himself out of despondency because he had to leave her. Three all-male juries failed to convict the beautiful defendant, and she finally went free, for a time enjoying an acting career billed as *The Girl in the Hansom Cab.* She faded into obscurity when theatergoers decided she had no real talent, which may or may not have been relevant as to the question of whether or not she had been acting at her trials.

PATTON, GEORGE S., JR.
(1885–1945)

One of the most flamboyant military men of World War II, U.S. general George S. Patton, Jr.,

was known as *Two-Gun Patton* because he wore two pearl-handled pistols. He was also known as *Old Blood and Guts,* a name that was not often appreciated by the average soldier, many of whom felt Patton willingly sacrificed men to gain his objectives. The GI play on the sobriquet was "our blood and his guts."

Patton in Pinstripes—See
STEINBRENNER, GEORGE.

Paul Jones of the South—See
SEMMES, RAPHAEL.

Paul Revere of Ecology, The—See
COMMONER, BARRY.

Pawnee Bill—See **LILLIE,
GORDON W.**

Payroll Bess—See **TRUMAN, BESS**

PEABODY, ELIZABETH PALMER
(1804–1894)

Because of her many cultural contributions to Boston, Mass., Elizabeth Palmer Peabody was called *The Grandmother of Boston.* She sought reforms in education and in 1860 founded the first kindergarten in Boston. Her famous bookstore was a rendezvous for the leading figures of the Transcendental movement and other intellectuals of the day.

Peace Ludlow—See **LUDLOW, LOUIS
LEON.**

Peaceful, The—See **KANG-WANG.**

Peaceful Warrior, The—See **KING, MARTIN LUTHER, JR.**

Peanut—See **CHIANG KAI-SHEK.**

Peanut King of America, The—See **OBICI, AMADEO.**

Peanut Man, The—See **CARVER, GEORGE WASHINGTON.**

Peanut Politician, The—See **CARTER, JIMMY.**

Peanuts—See **TRUMAN, JOHN ANDERSON.**

Pearl King of the World: LEONARD ROSENTHAL (1872–1955)

Leonard Rosenthal virtually monopolized the wholesale pearl business in Paris before World War II and was nicknamed *Pearl King of the World.*

PEARSON, DREW (1898–1969)

Muckraking Washington columnist Drew Pearson was accorded many sobriquets, almost all of the disparaging ones by victims of his exposes. Thus he was called *The Rasputin of Our Society* (first by Sen. Thomas Dodd) and *The Polecat of Journalism* (by Rep. James Mott). Many called him *Pearson-the-sponge,* as Sen. Theodore Bilbo explained, ''because he gathers slime, mud and slander from all parts of the earth and lets them ooze out through his radio broadcasts and through his daily contribution to a few newspapers which have not found him out.'' During World War II, Pearson's exposes of military fiascoes and waste

and profiteering in the war effort brought demands that Gen. George C. Marshall have him prosecuted for alleged violations of national security. Marshall vetoed the idea, noting that Pearson was the country's *Best Inspector General.*

Pearson-the-Sponge—See **PEARSON, DREW.**

PEARY, MARIE AHNIGHITO (1893–)

After Arctic explorer Robert Peary married Josephine Diebitsch, she insisted on accompanying him on an expedition. In 1893 their daughter, Marie Ahnighito, was born in Greenland, at that time the farthest north any white child had been born. She was celebrated first by the Eskimos and then by all Americans as *The Snow Baby.*

Peasant Bard, The—See **BURNS, ROBERT.**

Peasant Poet of Northamptonshire, The—See **CLARE, JOHN.**

Peasant Poetess, The—See **HAMILTON, JANET.**

Peasant Pope, The—See **PIUS X, POPE.**

PECKINPAH, SAMUEL (1925–)

Because of his attempts to raise screen mayhem to the level of an art form, Hollywood director Sam Peckinpah has been designated *The Master of Violence.* Some producers have used the nickname, only partially in jest, to portray Peckinpah's reaction when someone tries to enter his set while he is shooting.

Pedestrian, The—See WESTON, EDWARD PAYSON.

Pedro the Cruel: PEDRO, KING OF CASTILE *(1334–1369)*

Pedro the Cruel, king of Castile, was so labeled because of the many murders he perpetrated to maintain power. He was finally murdered by his brother Henry II, who succeeded him.

Peekaboo Girk, The—See LAKE, VERONICA.

PEEL, ROBERT *(the elder)* *(1750–1830)*

The father of the more famous Sir Robert Peel (the younger), Sir Robert Peel (the elder) was a cotton manufacturer noted for a parsley pattern on his fabrics that became the rage in Britain and won him the sobriquet *Parsley Peel*. His son became known as Orange Peel for a far different reason. (See also Peel, Robert [the younger].)

PEEL, ROBERT *(the younger)* *(1788–1850)*

Sir Robert Peel (the younger) was referred to as *Orange Peel* since, as chief secretary for Ireland, he was partial to the Protestants, or Orangemen, and opposed Catholic emancipation, a position he altered in 1729 when he put through the Emancipation Bill. He also established the London Metropolitan Police Force, and its members have since been called Peelers or Bobbies, after their founder.

Pegleg Annie—See MORROW, "Pegleg" ANNIE.

PEGLER, WESTBROOK *(1894–1969)*

Right-wing columnist Westbrook Pegler, who won the 1941 Pulitzer Prize for his expose of labor union corruption, was dubbed *The Angry Man of the Press* and *The Master of the Epithet*. A measure of the latter "ability" was his giving First Lady Eleanor Roosevelt the nickname Hatchet Face. One of the few who could match Pegler invective for invective was President Harry Truman, who labeled him *The Guttersnipe*.

Peking's Man for All Seasons—See CHOU EN-LAI.

PELE *(1940–   )*

Probably the most famous athlete in the world, soccer star Pele led the Brazilian national team to three World Cup championships. He later joined the New York Cosmos, where he was credited with doing more than any other person to popularize the game in the United States. It has been said that millions of people around the world can identify the nickname *The Black Pearl* more readily than any other sobriquet, including, for instance, The Little Corporal.

PELHAM, JOHN *(1838–1863)*

During the Battle of Fredericksburg in 1862, Confederate major John Pelham, already known as *The Boy Major* because he was only 23, was in command of the horse artillery. As Union troops prepared to advance on the right flank, Pelham volunteered to advance two of his guns and open fire on them. A Union shell quickly put one gun out of action, but Pelham kept moving his remaining gun to different positions and maintained his fire, even when 24 Union artillery pieces concentrated on his lone Napoleon gun. Despite repeated urging to retreat, Pelham held his position. Gen.

Robert E. Lee, observing the action, said, "It is glorious to see such courage in one so young!" Lee described the young artillerist as "gallant," and Maj. Pelham became famed as *The Gallant Pelham*. Only when he was running short of ammunition did Pelham retreat. In March 1863 Lee promoted Pelham to the rank of lieutenant colonel, but he was fatally wounded in action before the appointment reached him.

PELLEY, WILLIAM DUDLEY (1890–1965)

The U.S. leader of the pro-Nazi Silver Shirt Legion of America, William Dudley Pelley was referred to before World War II by some and during the war by many as *Smelly Pelley*.

PEMBERTON, ISRAEL (1715–1779)

One of the wealthiest merchants in colonial times, Israel Pemberton of Pennsylvania was called *King of the Quakers* and *King Wampum* for the large sums he expended in philanthropic pursuits. Much of his funds were spent to promote peaceful relations with the Indians.

Pen of the Revolution, The—See JEFFERSON, THOMAS.

Penciller Willis—See WILLIS, NATHANIEL P.

Penman of the American Revolution, The—See DICKINSON, JOHN.

PENN, WILLIAM (1644–1718)

Because of his role in the founding and settling of the original colony in Pennsylvania, William Penn was designated *The Father of Pennsylvania*. Rather ludicrously Quaker Penn was later dubbed *That Jesuit* for preaching in favor of James I and his Declaration of Indulgence.

PENNI, GIOVANNI FRANCESCO (1488–1528)

Italian painter Giovanni Francesco Penni handled all the domestic concerns of Raphael, the famous Renaissance artist and was thus nicknamed *Il Fattore,* or *The Steward*. He was also one of Raphael's principal assistants and worked on the cartoons of the Arazzi. After Raphael's death, Penni did his own frescos as well as several oils that drew high praise. Few, however, have survived.

Pennsylvania Pilgrim, The—See PASTORIUS, FRANCIS DANIEL.

Pennyless, The—See FREDERICK IV OF AUSTRIA: MAXIMILIAN I OF GERMANY.

Pensioned Dauber, The—See HOGARTH, WILLIAM.

Pentagon Whistle Blower, The—See FITZGERALD, A. ERNEST.

Penurious Parliamentarian, The—See ELWES, JOHN.

People's Attorney, The—See BRANDEIS, LOUIS D.

People's Captain, The—See GARIBALDI, GIUSEPPE.

People's Cherce, The—See
WALKER, FRED "Dixie."

People's King, The—See **HENRI,**
DUKE OF GUISE.

People's Lawyer, The—See **NADER,**
RALPH.

People's President, The—See
CLEVELAND, GROVER.

Pepin the Short: PEPIN, KING OF
THE FRANKS (714–768)

Pepin the Short, king of the Franks and father of
Charlemagne, was aptly named, being only 4½
feet tall. To compensate, he carried a sword six
feet long, and history tells us he was a mighty
swordsman.

PEPPER, CLAUDE (1900–   )

A liberal Democrat from Florida, Claude Pepper
has picked up nicknames of right-wing invective,
the most common being *The Red Pepper*. In what
is regarded as one of the dirtiest political campaigns
of the 20th century, Pepper was defeated by George
Smathers in the 1950 Democratic senatorial primary in Florida. Smathers denounced Pepper as a
"known extravert" who "practiced celibacy" before marriage. If that wasn't shocking enough to
rural voters, it was further revealed that Pepper
had a sister who was a "thespian" and a brother
who was a "practicing homo sapiens." *The Red
Pepper* was soundly trounced in that election. In
1962 he was elected to the House of Representatives, where he has continued to serve.

Pepys of His Age, The—See
BOURDEILLE, PIERRE DE.

Pepys of the Bowery, The—See
GOULD, JOE.

PERCIVAL, JOHN (1779–1862)

One of the most daring U.S. naval officers during
the War of 1812, John Percival was known to his
comrades as *Roaring Jack*. The British tended to
call him *Mad Jack*.

PERCY, HENRY (1364–1403)

Henry Percy, eldest son of the first earl of Northumberland, was given the nickname *Hotspur*
because of his valor in battles along the Scottish
border, which made him a hero to knights and
common soldiers alike. Shakespeare immortalized
his virtues in *King Henry IV. Hotspur* was killed
at the Battle of Shrewsbury in 1403.

PEREDA, JOSE MARIA DE
(1833–1906)

Spanish novelist Jose Maria de Pereda has often
been referred to as *The Modern Cervantes*.

Perfect Female, The—See **ANNE,**
PRINCESS OF ENGLAND

Perfect Witness, The—See
SPILSBURY, BERNARD HENRY.

PERICLES (c. 490–424 B.C.)

The great Athenian statesman Pericles was nicknamed *Schinocephalus*, or *Onionhead*, because of
his elongated or peaked head which he usually
concealed with a helmet.

Peristaltic Persuader, The—See
GRAHAM, SYLVESTER.

Perjured Lover, The—See **SWIFT,
JONATHAN.**

PERKINS, CHARLES NELSON
(1936–   )

Australian civil rights activist and social welfare director Charles Nelson Perkins has gained the sobriquet *Australia's Martin Luther King*.

PERKINS, FRANCES *(1882–1965)*

Secretary of Labor Frances Perkins was considered to be among the most liberal members of the President Franklin Roosevelt's various cabinets and was particularly unmindful of political attacks on her, winning such sobriquets as *Fearless Frances* and *The Loquacious Linguist Labor Loves*.

PERKINS, GEORGE W. *(1862–1920)*

Because he was the foremost financial backer of Theodore Roosevelt's Bull Moose Party, banker George W. Perkins was nicknamed *Dough Moose*.

Pernicious Germ, A—See **DE MARIA,
ALFRED T.**

PERO NINO, DON *(c. late 14th century)*

One of the most celebrated examples of medieval chivalry, the Spanish knight Don Pero Nino was famed for his incredible feats of survival. In one battle an arrow "knit together his gorget and his neck," but he continued to fight with "several lance stumps . . . still in his shield and it was that which hindered him most." Then a bolt from a crossbow "pierced his nostrils most painfully whereat he was dazed, but his daze lasted but a little time." He continued to press the enemy and received a number of sword blows, which "sometimes hit the bolt embedded in his nose making him suffer great pain." When the battle ended, his shield "was tattered and all in pieces; his sword blade was toothed like a saw and dyed with blood . . . his armor was broken in several places by lance-heads of which some had entered the flesh and drawn blood, although the coat was of great strength." With perhaps a measure of understatement, Pero Nino was nicknamed *The Unconquered Knight*.

PERON, EVA *(1919–1952)*

The second wife of Argentine strongman Juan Peron, Eva Peron, better known as Evita, was far more popular with the people than her husband. She was idolized by the "shirtless ones" as *Saint Evita*. The Argentine unions were shocked and angered after her death in 1952 when the pope refused a request that she be canonized.

PERON, JUAN *(1895–1974)*

When Juan Peron first came to power in Argentina in 1946, he was nicknamed *The New World Superman*. However, his reign lasted only until 1955, three years after the death of his wife, Evita, whose hold on the public was greater than his own. He was overthrown in 1955 and sent into exile. He returned to become president in 1973 but without the enormous powers he had previously wielded.

PERRY, GAYLORD *(1938–   )*

In a baseball era when the illegal spitball pitch is more closely watched for than at any time in the past, Gaylord Perry is regarded as the master of the craft. He is called *THE Spitball Pitcher* and *Gaylord the Greaser*. In 1982, after 21 years in the major leagues, Perry, pitching for the Seattle Mariners, was ejected from a game for throwing a spitball. The media immediately dubbed him *The Ancient Mariner,* not so much in reference to his team or his 43 years as to the moistness of his pitch.

Persecutor, The—See RAWSON, EDWARD.

PERSHING, JOHN JOSEPH *(1860–1948)*

One of the more sanitized nicknames was *Black Jack,* given to U.S. general John Joseph Pershing during World War I. There was considerable effort then to attribute his sobriquet to a general dourness of disposition, but it actually referred back to Pershing's days commanding black troops in the 10th Cavalry. At that time he was known as *Nigger Jack,* indicating not merely racial bias but the belief that officers took such commands because they led to more rapid promotions. As Pershing became better known, a strenuous effort was necessary to re-dub him *Black Jack.*

Persian Anacreon, The—See HAFIZ, MOHAMMED.

Pete Doughsmell—See ROZELLE, PETE.

PETER (c. 1812)

Peter, an infamous Calabrian bandit chieftain, was referred to by the Italian people as *The Emperor of the Mountains*.

Peter Porcupine—See COBBETT, WILLIAM.

Peter Rabbit—See LONG, WILLIAM J.

Peter the Great—See ROZELLE, PETE.

Peter the Great of Egypt, The—See MEHEMET ALI.

Peter the Hermit of the Abolitionist Movement—See LUNDY, BENJAMIN.

Peter the Mad: PETER III OF RUSSIA (1728–1762)

The husband of the future Catherine the Great of Russia, Czar Peter III was a childlike emperor who in his short reign became known as *Peter the Mad*. He much preferred playing with toy soldiers than ruling his people. He was deposed by Catherine, who had herself declared empress. Most probably at Catherine's instigation, *Peter the Mad* was strangled by Aleksei Orlov, brother of her lover, Grigori Orlov. The Orlov brothers were lavishly rewarded by the grateful Catherine.

PETIOT, MARCEL (c. 1897–1946)

A medical doctor and member of the French Resistance, Dr. Marcel Petiot appears to have been the leading private mass murderer during World War II, killing, by his own count, 63 persons. While he claimed they were Nazi collaborators, most were actually rich Jews seeking a way out of France, which *The Super Bluebeard,* as he was called after being caught, offered them. They came to his Paris home with their valuables to enter his escape pipeline, but instead of smuggling them out of the country, Dr. Petiot murdered them and incinerated the bodies in his furnace, keeping their valuables. He was guillotined after the war.

PETRARCH, FRANCESCO (1304–1374)

For several centuries the Italian scholar and poet Petrarch, whose work served as a model for Italian literature, held the titles *Laureate of the Civilized World, The Prince of Italian Poets* and *The Father of Humanism.* Those less enthused about his worth have generally preferred S. W. Singer's *The Tuscan Imp of Fame.*

PETRILLO, JAMES CAESAR (1892–   )

President of the American Federation of Musicians, James Caesar Petrillo, an Italian American, was so tough in his union bargaining demands that he was nicknamed *Little Caesar* and *The Mussolini of Music.*

PETRONIUS, CAIUS (?–c. 66 BC)

Caius Petronius, the Roman writer, was famous as the organizer of Emperor Nero's revels. He was called *Petronius Arbiter* because Nero relied on his judgment and would not wear a new fashion until Petronius had approved it. More recently he has been called *A Roman Beau Brummel.* Eventually, because the intrigues of Nero's court, Petronius fell from favor and, realizing his fate was sealed, committed suicide.

Petronius Arbiter—See PETRONIUS, CAIUS.

Petticoat Pet—See VAN BUREN, MARTIN.

Petticoat Rustler, The—See RICHEY, ANNIE BYERS.

PETTY, RICHARD (1937–   )

U.S. racing driver Richard Petty is acknowledged to be *The King of the Road.*

PETTY, WILLIAM (1623–1687)

One of the most accomplished men of 17th century England, William Petty, a statistician, political economist, physician and musician, was hailed as *The Universal Genius.* Among his accomplishments were serving as a professor of anatomy at Oxford, a professor of music at Gresham College and a physician with the English army in Ireland. In 1663 he invented a double-bottomed ship.

PEZZA, MICHELE (1760–1806)

An Italian bandit or revolutionary, depending on one's viewpoint, Michele Pezza was nicknamed *Fra Diavolo* or *Brother Devil.* He led a force of Bourbon partisans from 1799 to 1806, when he was hanged at Naples.

PFEIFFER, JANE CAHILL—See Attila the Nun.

PFIESTER, DORIS (1912–1982)

An elderly Loveland, Ohio woman, Doris Pfiester, became famous as *The Valentine Lady* for remailing Valentines for thousands of people in 50 states as well as 30 countries around the world. She placed her "Loveland" postmark on Valentine cards and notes people wished re-mailed to loved ones.

Philadelphia Lady, The—See
ANDERSON, MARIAN.

Philadelphia's Jean Valjean—See
BURKE, WILLIAM.

*Philadelphia's Murdering Faith
Healer*—See BOLBER, MORRIS.

Philanthropist, The—See HOWARD,
JOHN.

PHILIP I OF CASTILE—See
Handsome, The.

PHILIP V OF SPAIN (1683–1746)

Philip V, King of Spain, was nicknamed *Philip
Baboon* by his enemies, especially the English,
who also called Louis XIV of France, Philip's
grandfather, Lewis Baboon. Philip's attempt to
gain the Spanish throne resulted in the War of the
Spanish Succession which ended with his recognition as king but resulted in the loss of many
possessions, including Gibraltar, to England.

Philip Baboon—See PHILIP V OF
SPAIN.

Philip the Daring (or the Hardy):
PHILIP III OF FRANCE *(1245–1285)*

Unlike his crusader father, Louis IX, Philip III of
France was anything but fearless and adventurous
and was thus contemptuously called *Philip the
Daring* or *Philip the Hardy*.

*Philip the Fair: PHILIP IV OF
FRANCE (1270–1314)*

King Philip IV of France was ironically nicknamed
Philip the Fair. His rule was unsavory and ruthless,
typified by financial double-dealing and bloodshed,
such as in the destruction of the Order of the
Knights Templar.

*Philip the Good: PHILIP, DUKE OF
BURGUNDY (1396–1467)*

Philip, duke of Burgundy, was the true founder
of the Burgundian state from which modern Belgium and Holland originated. In his private life
he sired a large number of illegitimate children and
had concurrent mistresses in various parts of his
realm, causing the bishop of Tournai to denounce
his "weakness of the flesh." Such denunciation
was of small consequence to his subjects, who
called him *Philip the Good,* a tribute to the fact
that he made his nation perhaps the most prosperous in the Western world. Under his rule court life
during the Middle Ages reached its apogee in lav-
ishness and extravagance.

*Philip the Lucky: PHILIP VI OF
FRANCE (1293–1350)*

Philip VI of France was one of the most luckless
of French rulers, his reign being marked by con-
flicts with Edward III of England, eventually leading to the Hundred Years War. In irony, he was
dubbed *Philip the Lucky*.

*Philip the Magnanimous: PHILIP II
OF FRANCE (1165–1223)*

Philip II of France, in addition to being a strong
and warlike king, was also noted for his selfish-

ness. With a touch of Gallic humor, he was dubbed *Philip the Magnanimous*.

Philip the Prudent (or the Great): PHILIP II OF SPAIN (1527–1598)

Philip II, king of Spain, who was very popular with his people, was celebrated as *Philip the Great* or *Philip the Prudent*. Philip's prudence perhaps failed him when he allowed the Spanish Armada to sail against England in 1588. Although the monarch spent many hours on his knees in prayer, the Armada was defeated and later destroyed by storms.

PHILIPPE II, DUKE OF ORLEANS (1674–1723)

Philippe II, duke of Orleans and regent of France during the minority of Louis XV, was called *The Godless Regent* because he believed in no religion. He was, however, obsessed with astrology.

Philippe Egalite—See LOUIS PHILIPPE I OF FRANCE.

PHILIPPE JOSEPH, DUC D'ORLEANS (1747–1793)

Philippe, duc d'Orleans, an ambitious intriguer and, like King Louis XVI of France, a member of the House of Bourbon, at first managed to survive the fall of the monarchy by joining the Jacobins. After he renounced his hereditary titles, he was nicknamed for a time *Egalite,* or *Citizen Equality*. As a newly converted democrat at the Convention, he invited the contempt of much of the rest of the world by voting for the death of Louis XVI. His vote, however, did not save him from the guillotine later.

Philippe the Amorous: PHILIPPE I OF FRANCE (1052–1108)

Philippe I, king of France, was dubbed *Philippe the Amorous* after he divorced his wife Berthe to claim Bertrade, who was already married to Foulques, count of Anjou. Centuries later, Henry VIII of England eagerly cited Philippe's case as a precedent for his first divorce.

PHILIPS, AMBROSE (1671–1749)

Playwright and poet Ambrose Philips, who took part in literary feuds with Henry Carey and Alexander Pope, was dubbed *Namby Pamby*. Carey invented the nickname as a play on Philips' name, and Pope applauded it as one suited to his "eminence in the infantile style."

PHILLIPS, MARK (1948–   )

According to the more gossipy elements of the British press, Capt. Mark Phillips, a commoner who married Princess Anne in a glittering Westminister Abbey ceremony in 1973, is known among members of the Royal Family as *Fog*. It is said that they mean a rather thick one.

Philologos—See BAILEY, NATHAN.

Philos—See DARWIN, CHARLES.

Philosopher, The—See LEO VI, BYZANTINE EMPEROR; SERMENT, LOUISE ANASTASIE DE.

Philosopher of China, The—See CONFUCIUS.

Philosopher of Democracy, The—See JEFFERSON, THOMAS.

Philosopher of Disenchantment, The—See SCHOPENHAUER, ARTHUR.

Philosopher of Ferney, The—See VOLTAIRE.

Philosopher of the Absolute, The—See HEGEL, GEORG WILHELM FREDERICK.

Philosopher of the Arabs, The—See ABU YUSUF ALKENDI.

Philosophist—See JEFFERSON, THOMAS.

Phoenix of His Age, The—See ABU YUSUF ALKENDI.

Phrasemaker, The—See WILSON, WOODROW.

Phryne—See MNESARETE.

PHYSICK, PHILIP SYNG (1768–1857)

Dr. Philip Syng Physick, a Philadelphia surgeon, is justifiably known as *The Father of American Surgery* for his improved surgical techniques and the instruments he developed. Somewhat less impressive is his nickname *The Father of Soda Pop*. It must be said that when he commissioned a chemist to invent carbonated water, he thought it would have health-giving properties for his patients. While others later added flavorings, Physick is remembered as the father of the brew.

PIAZZA, "Countess" WILLIE V. (fl. 1895–1917)

One of New Orleans' most famous madams during the heyday of the Storyville red-light district, *"Countess"* Willie V. Piazza was noted, in the city that gave birth to the blues, as *The Countess Who Cures the Blues*. *The Countess* also uttered the immortal words, "The country club girls are ruining my business!"

Picaroon—See BALLANTYNE, JOHN.

Picasso of Children's Books, The—See SENDAK, MAURICE.

Picayune Butler—See BUTLER, BENJAMIN.

PICHEGRU, CHARLES (1761–1804)

A French general, Charles Pichegru, gained the epithet *The Savior of His Country* for, upon being summoned to Paris, suppressing the insurrection of April 1795. He was soon overshadowed by another "savior," Napoleon.

PICKFORD, MARY (1893–1979)

Canadian-born screen actress Mary Pickford, who continued to play the role of a forlorn child in dozens of movies even after she became an adult, was *America's Sweetheart* to the movie-going public.

Pictorial Historian of Aboriginal America, The—See CATLIN, GEORGE.

Picturesque Explorer of the United States, The—See LANMAN, CHARLES.

Pied Piper of Boston, The—See PONZI, CHARLES.

Pied Piper of Contentment, The—See COUE, EMILE.

Pied Piper of Murder, The—See UNRUH, HOWARD.

PIERCE, FRANKLIN (1804–1869)

President Franklin Pierce's nickname was as undistinguished as his political abilities. His friends called him *Purse,* an uninventive play on his name. A vain and colorful dresser, Pierce, 14th president of the United States, was called *Handsome Frank.* Although known to be at least a semi-alcoholic, he was not saddled with an alcohol-related sobriquet until the opposition Whigs described him during the 1852 campaign for president as *The Hero of Many a Well Fought Bottle.* His selection as presidential candidate after 48 deadlocked ballots had startled the nation and prompted to Sen. Stephen Douglas to quip "Hereafter, no private citizen is safe."

PIERCE, JANE MEANS APPLETON (1806–1863)

Certainly the most withdrawn of all America's First Ladies, Jane Pierce never appeared in public dur-

ing the first two years of husband Franklin Pierce's term as president. In mourning over the death of their only surviving son, 11-year-old Benny, in a railway accident in 1853, two months before the inauguration, she was referred to by the press as *The Shadow in the White House.* Mrs. Pierce wore mourning clothes the rest of her life.

Pierce Penniless—See NASH, THOMAS.

Pig Iron Kelley—See KELLEY, WILLIAM DARRAGH.

Pig Woman, The: JANE GIBSON *(1870–1930)*

The star witness in the sensational Hall-Mills murder trial in the 1920s, Jane Gibson was labeled *The Pig Woman* because she raised Poland China pigs in the New Brunswick, N.J., area. Dying of cancer, she testified from a hospital bed that was brought into the courtroom. She told of hearing and seeing part of the events at the time of the murders in the dead of night and then riding off in terror on her mule, but all the defendants she linked to the crime were acquitted.

PIGNATARI, FRANCISCO "Baby" or "Piggy" (1916–1971)

Brazilian industrialist and one-time international playboy Francisco Pignatari was nicknamed *Baby* for his youthful charms. Some gossip columnists informed their readers, however, that quite a few society husbands referred to Pignatari as *Piggy.*

Pillar of Doctors, The—See CHAMPEAUX, WILLIAM DE.

Pillar Saint, The: ST. SIMEON STYLITES (388?–459)

Called *The Pillar Saint,* St. Simeon Stylites was the first of a group of hermits who exhibited devotion to God by isolating themselves for years atop pillars during the 5th and 6th centuries. In Syria entire desert tribes were converted to Christianity after flocking to pay Simeon homage for his incredible ordeal of suffering atop a pillar of 60 feet high, where he remained for the better part of 36 years. He was discovered dead in 459, his body in a position of prayer. By the end of the 6th century, there were no more followers of *The Pillar Saint.*

Pilot of Fortune, The—See HALL, WESTON B.

PINDAR (c. 522–443 B.C.)

Although only his 44 *Epinicia (Odes to Victory)* have come down to us in complete form, they are more than enough to justify the nickname *The Theban Lyre* for Pindar, the great lyric poet of ancient Greece.

Pindar of France, The—See RONSARD, PIERRE DE.

Pindar of Italy, The—See CHIABRERA, GABRIELLO.

PINGREE, HAZEN S. "Potato" (1840–1901)

Around the turn of the 20th century, Hazen S. Pingree served simultaneously as governor of Michigan and mayor of Detroit. He won the nickname *Potato Pingree* for starting the potato patch mania that resulted in the conversion of vacant urban lots into vegetable gardens throughout the country. Faced with huge unemployment during his mayorality, Pingree turned over unused city land to the unemployed to raise potatoes on.

Pink Lady, The—See DOUGLAS, HELEN GAHAGAN.

PINKERTON, ALLAN (1819–1884)

The 19th century Scottish-American detective Allan Pinkerton was nicknamed by criminals *The Eye* because of his agency's "We never sleep" trademark showing an open eye. Eventually his nickname was transferred to private detectives in general and they were called private eyes.

Pinky—See HUMPHREY, HUBERT H.

Pint-a-Day Davis—See DAVIS, JEFF.

PINTO, FERNAO MENDES (c. 1509–1583)

A Portuguese adventurer and traveler in the East whose tales were not always reliable, Fernao Mendes Pinto was nicknamed *The Prince of Liars.* First to use the term was Cervantes.

Pioneer of African Nationalism, The— See JOHNSON, JAMES.

Pioneer of Fistic Science, The—See SPRING, TOM.

Pious, The—See ALBERT IV, DUKE OF AUSTRIA; ANTONINUS.

Pipe, The—See FENWICK, MILLICENT.

PIPER, THOMAS W. (1849–1876)

A sex murderer of women and young girls in Boston during the 1870s, church sexton Thomas W. Piper held the city in a grip of terror that was unmatched until the rampage of the Boston Strangler 90 years later. Caught after the body of a girl was found in the church where he worked, Piper became noted as *The Murdering Sexton*. He was hanged in 1876.

PIPER, WILLIAM T. (1880–1970)

William T. Piper, who developed the Piper Cub airplane, was dubbed *The Henry Ford of Aviation*.

PISSARRO, CAMILLE (1830–1903)

French impressionist painter Camille Pissaro, famed for his paintings of the boulevards of Paris, Rouen street scenes and Normandy landscapes, was designated *The Impressionist Printmaker*. Paul Cezanne, grateful for Pissarro's aid in his development, called him *The Humble and Colossal Pissarro*. In his later years Cezanne, when agreeing to show his work, insisted on being identified in catalogues as "Paul Cezanne, pupil of Pissarro."

Pitcher, Molly: MARY LUDWIG HAYS (1754–1832)

At the Battle of Monmouth in 1778, during the Revolutionary War, as many men dropped of heat prostration as of gunshot wounds. Among those who fell was artillery sergeant John Hays. His wife, Mary, who had followed him to camp and to battle, sprang into action at his gun and then seized a pitcher to bring water to other artillerymen and the wounded during the heat of battle, gaining the nickname *Molly Pitcher*. After the war *Molly Pitcher* buried two husbands and worked as a servant until 1822, when Pennsylvania granted her a $40 a month pension in commemoration of her wartime heroism.

Pitchfork Ben—See TILLMAN, BENJAMIN RYAN.

PITT, WILLIAM (the elder) (1708–1778)

English statesman William Pitt, later earl of Chatham, was nicknamed *The Great Commoner* because he was a commoner rather than a peer. He was also referred to as *The Napoleon of Oratory* and spoke eloquently for a conciliatory British policy toward the American colonies.

PITT, WILLIAM (the younger) (1759–1806)

The younger William Pitt, who was the equal of his father as an orator and a statesman, was called *The Bottomless Pit* because of his extreme thinness, although political foes saw his speeches as endless and thus bottomless.

PITTMAN, KEY (1872–1940)

A former Gold Rush miner in Alaska, Key Pittman served as Democratic senator from Nevada from 1913 until his death in 1940. He was nicknamed *The Voice of Silver* for successfully sponsoring a law, called the Pittman Act, that authorized the coinage of silver.

Pittsburgh Phil: HARRY STRAUSS (1908–1941)

Harry Strauss, better known by his chosen nickname of *Pittsburgh Phil,* was the most prolific killer of Murder, Inc., definitely linked by authorities to 56 hired slayings. As far as is known, he had never been in Pittsburgh but took the name of *Pittsburgh Phil,* the sobriquet of a noted gambler, just because it sounded "exotic."

PIUS VI, POPE (1717–1798)

As Disraeli was to note, no pope was more vehemently attacked by any Protestant pen than Pope Pius VI was by a poet scorned. Pius accepted a volume of verse by the Italian poet Monti by quoting some lines of Metastasio and noting to Monti that "no one nowadays writes like that great poet." Monti, furious over this slight, was finally able to vent his rage freely when the French carried off Pius VI from Rome, acording the Pontiff such vicious sobriquets as *The Great Harlot* and *The Last of the Monsters.*

PIUS IX, POPE (1792–1878)

Pope Pius IX became known as *The Prisoner of the Vatican* in 1870 when he was deprived of his temporal possessions and ordered to stay in the Vatican by the Italian Nationalists.

PIUS X, POPE (1835–1914)

Because of his impoverished background, Pope Pius X was called *The Peasant Pope.* When as Cardinal Patriarch of Venice he was called to conclave in Rome on the death of Leo XIII in 1903, he had to borrow money for train fare from a Jewish friend. Nevertheless he was elected pope and launched one of the most influential pontificates in modern times.

Pixie of Gasoline Alley, The—See SACHS, EDWARD.

Plant Inventor, The—See BURBANK, LUTHER.

Plantagenet: GEOFFREY IV OF ANJOU (1113–1151)

Since he was fond of wearing a sprig of the broom plant, or *planta genista,* in his cap, Geoffrey IV of Anjou was nicknamed *Plantagenet.* Although nicknames of rulers are seldom inherited his son, who became Henry II of England, was known as the first of the *Plantagenets,* and the nickname was applied to the rest of the dynasty.

Plastic Historian, The—See DAVIDSON, JO.

Plastic Pat—See NIXON, PATRICIA.

Platinum Blonde, The—See HARLOW, JEAN.

Plato: ARISTOCLES (427?–347 B.C.)

The Greek philosopher Aristocles became more famous to Athenians by his nickname, *Plato,* meaning "broad-shouldered."

Plato of the Eighteenth Century, The— See VOLTAIRE.

Playboy—See REED, JOHN.

Playboy Mayor, The—See WALKER, JAMES J.

Playboy of the Piano, The—See RUBINSTEIN, ARTUR.

Playful—See POCAHONTAS.

PLEASANTON, ALFRED (1824–1897)

As commander of the cavalry of the Union Army of the Potomac, Alfred Pleasanton was hardly a shining success, having particularly failed in the Antietam campaign to breach the screen set by Jeb Stuart to protect the Confederate Army. Lacking first-hand intelligence observations, Pleasanton deluged his superiors with reports based on mere speculation and hearsay. Confederate historians, later reading his inaccurate reports, labeled him *The Knight of Romance*.

PLENKHANOV, GEORGI (1857–1918)

A founder along with Lenin of the Russian Social Democratic Labor Party, and the leading exponent of theoretical Marxism, Georgi Plekhanov was called *The Father of Russian Marxism*. He maintained that position of respect with the Bolsheviks even when he sided with the Mensheviks after the 1905 Revolution.

Plotter, The—See FERGUSON, ROBERT.

Plow 'Em Under Wallace—See WALLACE, HENRY A.

Plumber, The—See DURKIN, MARTIN P.

Plumed Knight, The—See BLAINE, JAMES G.

Plumed Knight of the Confederacy, The—See STUART, JAMES EWELL BROWN "Jeb."

PLUMMER, HENRY (1837–1864)

In addition to discharging his official duties, Sheriff Henry Plummer, an inspiration for numerous plots of western novels and movies, headed an outlaw gang that ravaged Montana in the early 1860s, killing at least 102 persons. The gang members were called Innocents because whenever any of them was taken into custody for wrongdoing, Plummer would find him innocent of the charge and release him. *The Innocent Sheriff* and many of his confederates were finally lynched.

Po' Ol' Country Lawyer, The—See ERVIN, SAMUEL JAMES, JR.

POBEDONOSTSEV, KONSTANTIN (1827–1907)

The principal minister of both Czars Alexander III and Nicholas II of Russia, Konstantin Pobedonostsev, a total reactionary, was nicknamed *The Metternich of His Age*, perhaps a disservice even to that Austrian prince. Pobedonostsev held legislative bodies in total contempt, and the existence of a free press was inconceivable to him. Not only chief minister but also head of the Orthodox Church, he suppressed many sects and made any attempt to convert a member of the Orthodox Church a criminal offense. Priests hearing confession were required to report all signs of political untrustworthiness. Pobedonostsev also persecuted many minorities, such as Poles, Finns and Jews. Concerning the Jews, Pobedonostsev stated his plan to convert one-third to Christianity, force another third to flee Russia and starve the rest to death. He fomented numerous pogroms, and he is said to have been the one person responsible for the policy that resulted in New York City gaining the largest Jewish population of any city in the world.

Pocahontas: MATOAKA
(c. 1595–1617)

Pocahontas was actually the nickname for the Indian princess Matoaka. She was given the name *Pocahontas,* meaning *Playful,* by her tribe. When she married John Rolfe and moved to England, she became Rebecca Rolfe.

Pocket Dictator, The—See **DOLLFUSS, ENGELBERT.**

Poet Alone, A—See **LEOPARDI, GIACOMO.**

Poet Laureate of His People, The—See **DUNBAR, PAUL LAURENCE.**

Poet Laureate of Labor, The—See **MARKHAM, EDWIN.**

Poet Laureate of New England, The—See **WHITTIER, JOHN GREENLEAF.**

Poet Laureate of the Army, The—See **PATTEN, GEORGE WASHINGTON.**

Poet Laureate of the South, The—See **HAYNE, PAUL HAMILTON.**

Poet Married to Nature, The—See **CLARE, JOHN.**

Poet Naturalist, The—See **THOREAU, HENRY DAVID.**

Poet of a Doomed Austria, The—See **HOFMANNSTHAL, HUGO VON.**

Poet of Bran Meal and Pumpkins, The—See **GRAHAM, SYLVESTER.**

Poet of Nature, The—See **WORDSWORTH, WILLIAM.**

Poet of Princes, The—See **MAROT, CLEMENT.**

Poet of Sorrow, A—See **LEOPARDI, GIACOMO.**

Poet of the American Revolution, The—See **FRENEAU, PHILIP.**

Poet of the Commonplace, The—See **LONGFELLOW, HENRY WADSWORTH.**

Poet of the Confederacy, The—See **RYAN, ABRAM JOSEPH.**

Poet of the Future, The—See **RONSARD, PIERRE DE.**

Poet of the Golden Gate, The—See **KIRCHHOFF, THEODORE.**

Poet of the Plain People, The—See **GUEST, EDGAR A.**

Poet of the Potboiler, The—See **CAIN, JAMES M.**

Poet of the Sierras, The—See **MILLER, JOAQUIN.**

Poet of the Slaves, The—See **ALVES, CASTRO.**

Poet of Violence, The—See **CHANDLER, RAYMOND.**

Poet Wordy—See **WORDSWORTH, WILLIAM.**

Poetical Charlatan, This—See **WORDSWORTH, WILLIAM.**

Poet's Parasite, The—See **WARBURTON, WILLIAM.**

Poet's Poet, The—See **SPENSER, EDMUND.**

POHIBITQUASHO—See **Iron Shirt.**

POIRET, PAUL (1879–1944)

French fashion designer Paul Poiret was accorded the title *The King of Fashion* and *The Man Who Banned the Corset*.

Poison Ivy—See **LEE, IVY L.**

Poison Snake—See **KENNEDY, ROBERT F.**

Poisoned Mushroom, That—See **CIANO, COUNT GALEAZZO.**

Poker Alice—See **IVERS, ALICE.**

Poker Bride, The—See **China Polly.**

Poker Charley—See **FARWELL, CHARLES B.**

Polecat of Journalism, The—See **PEARSON, DREW.**

Polish Voltaire, The—See **KRASICKI, IGNATIUS.**

Political Parasite, This—See **WORDSWORTH, WILLIAM.**

Political Thor, A—See **FARLEY, JAMES A.**

POLK, JAMES K. (1795–1849)

James K. Polk, 11th president of the United States, became known as *The First Dark Horse* because he was the surprise nominee of the Democratic Party over several better known candidates. His nomination was largely engineered by Andrew Jackson, and for that reason and his continuation of Jackson's expansionist policies he was called

Young Hickory. Polk, a most effective orator, was also nicknamed *The Napoleon of the Stump*.

Pontius Pilate—See BLACKMUN, HARRY A.

PONZI, CHARLES (1877–1949)

The classic swindler Charles Ponzi was called *The Pied Piper of Boston* for swindling thousands of Americans out of millions of dollars. Many of his Italian-American victims continued to believe in him when he was hauled before official hearings to explain his financial schemes, and viewing the investigation as anti-foreigner bias, they hailed him as *The Greatest Italian of Them All*. Most of his victims lost their entire investments, and Ponzi went to prison and was later deported.

Poobah of Popularizers, The—See ADLER, MORTIMER.

Pooh-Bear—See BRADY, JAMES.

POOLE, WILLIAM (?–1855)

U.S. murderer and political gangster Bill Poole was labeled *Bill the Butcher* by the 19th century press. He was by vocation a butcher but deserved the nickname just as much for his gangster activities.

Poor, Dull Jerry—See FORD, GERALD R.

Poor Devil, The—See FRERON, ELIE-CATHERINE.

Poor Gully—See GULLY, JOHN.

Poor Little Rich Girl: BARBARA HUTTON (1912–1979) GLORIA VANDERBILT (1924–   )

Too good a sobriquet to be used only once, the nickname *Poor Little Rich Girl* was bestowed by the press and public on two heiresses, Barbara Hutton and Gloria Vanderbilt. Barbara Hutton, heir to the F.W. Woolworth fortune, was married seven times and was plagued by ill health and unhappiness. Gloria Vanderbilt, heir to a considerable portion of the Vanderbilt fortune, drew sobs from the press because in 1941 she was receiving a piddling $1,200 a month from the family estate.

Poor Man's Counsellor, The—See CLARK, ABRAHAM.

Poor Man's Friend, The—See COUZENS, JAMES.

Poor Matt—See ARNOLD, MATTHEW.

Poor Richard—See FRANKLIN, BENJAMIN.

POPE, ALEXANDER (1688–1744)

English poet and satirist Alexander Pope became the literary dictator of his age, achieving financial independence with his translations of Homer's *Iliad* and *Odyssey*. He was called *The Bard of Twickenham*, having lived in that town the last 26 years of his life. Those literary contemporaries who felt the sting of his scathing invective were more apt to call him *The Wasp of Twickenham*. *The Wasp* relished the nickname and noted:

> Yes, I am proud; and must be proud, to see
> Men not afraid of God afraid of me.

Another sobriquet for Pope was *Paper-Sparing Pope,* coined by Swift because a large portion of the manuscripts for his versions of the *Iliad* and *Odyssey* were written on the backs of old letters.

POPE, JOHN (1822–1892)

During the Civil War, Union general John Pope gained the nickname *Saddle-Bag John* when asked, while on the move, where his headquarters would be, he responded, "In the saddle."

Pope, The—See SINATRA, FRANK.

Pope of Art, A—See RUSKIN, JOHN.

Pope of Geneva, The—See CALVIN, JOHN.

Pope of Philosophy, The—See ARISTOTLE.

Popish Duke, The—See JAMES II OF ENGLAND.

Popish Midwife, The—See CELLIER, ELIZABETH.

Pops—See ZUKOR, ADOLPH.

Pork Baron, The—See ARMOUR, PHILIP D.

PORTER, COLE (1893–1964)

U.S. composer and lyricist Cole Porter, born in Peru, Ind., known for the sophistication of his work, was nicknamed *The Elegant Hoosier Tunesmith* and *The Adlai Stevenson of Songwriters*.

PORTER, DAVID DIXON (1813–1891)

In command of the Mississippi Squadron during the Civil War, Union admiral David Dixon Porter launched numerous raids and foraging expeditions along the banks of the Mississippi and its tributaries. The confederate press branded him *The Thief of the Mississippi,* and planters burned their cotton and other crops to keep them from falling into Porter's hands.

Portly Master of the Involuntary Scream, The—See HITCHCOCK, ALFRED.

Portrait Painter of Presidents, The—See STUART, GILBERT.

Portuguese Maecenas, The—See EMANUEL THE FORTUNATE.

Portuguese Nostradamus, The—See BANDARRA, GONCALO ANNES.

Postman Poet, The—See CAPERN, EDWARD.

Post-Mortem Poet, The—See WHITMAN, WALT

POT, PHILIPPE (1428–1494)

The shrewd, glib prime minister of Louis XI of France (The Universal Spider), and a vital player in the monarch's intrigues, Philippe Pot was nick-named *Cicero's Mouth.*

Potato King, The—See SHIMA, GEORGE.

Potato Mayor, The—See SHANK, SAMUEL L.

Pothouse Peggy—See EATON, MARGARET O'NEILL.

POTIER, AUGUSTIN (?–1650)

Upon the death of King Louis XIII, Augustin Potier, bishop of Beauvais, was one of the leaders of The Importants, a political group that opposed Cardinal Mazarin, and when the latter was forced from Paris, Potier became minister. He proved particularly inept, however, and lasted but a few months, his detractors labeling him *The Mitred Ass.*

POTTER, JOHN FOX "Bowie Knife" (1817–1899)

A three-term representative to Congress from 1857 to 1863, John Fox Potter of Wisconsin was challenged to a duel by Rep. Roger Pryor of Virginia. Potter agreed and used his prerogative to choose bowie knoves as weapons. Pryor immediately withdrew his challenge to Potter, who thereafter was widely known as *Bowie Knife Potter.* It should be noted he was never again challenged to a duel.

POUND, EZRA LOOMIS (1885–1972)

U.S. expatriate poet and World War II fascist propagandist Ezra Pound was often called *Mussolini's Boy.* He denied the sobriquet, saying, "I only saw the bastard once."

Powderkeg—See KERRIGAN, JAMES.

POWELL, DAVID FRANKLIN (1847–1906)

As a frontier doctor and U.S. Army surgeon, David Franklin Powell was known to both whites and Indians in Wyoming and Colorado as *The Mighty Medicine Man* because he treated the two groups with equal efficiency. During a period of hostility between settlers and Indians, Dr. Powell, then an Army surgeon, went into an Indian encampment and vaccinated the whole tribe, thereby stopping a smallpox epidemic. For this act the Indians gave him a white beaver robe and named him *White Beaver,* that being the tribe's sacred animal.

POWELL, JAMES ROBERT (1814–1883)

James Robert Powell, the pioneer developer of Birmingham, Ala., was called the *Duke of Birmingham* because of the vast economic, social and political influence he exerted in the planning, building and developing of the city.

POWELL, JOHN (1808–1870)

The beau ideal of the Mississippi riverboat gamblers of the antebellum period, John Powell was considered one of the few honest gamblers on the river and was called *The Shining Knight of the Poker Table.* A close friend of Andrew Jackson and Stephen A. Douglas, he parlayed his winnings into a considerable fortune through profits from a horse farm in Tennessee, real estate in St. Louis and various holdings in New Orleans. He gambled constantly, never with a hint of scandal, until suddenly his luck deserted him just before the Civil War. He lost all his holdings and died in 1870 in extreme poverty. His change of fortune has become a legend of the Mississippi.

POWERS, JOHN "Shorty" (1922–1980)

NASA Control announcer John *Shorty* Powers was almost as famous as the U.S. astronauts who were launched into space in the 1960s, when he became *The Voice of the Astronauts.*

PRADO, KATIE (1882–1957)

A most peripatetic U.S. madam, Katie Prado earned herself a sobriquet wherever she established her business. She was *The Belle of New York, The Queen of the Bowery, The Voice of the St. Louis Fair* ("Welcome, Boys!") and *The Toast of the Barbary Coast.* She was also called *Diamond-Tooth Lil,* as much an advertisement for her prosperity as for the state of her dentures.

Praetorian Guard, The—See **EHRLICHMAN, JOHN; HALDEMAN, H.R.**

Prairie Dog Dave—See **MORROW, "Prairie Dog" DAVE.**

PRATT, DANIEL (1809–1887)

An eccentric who traveled around the United States living on handouts and lecturing to college students and other audiences, Daniel Pratt was known as *The Great American Traveler.* In the era of television he might have made it as a stand-up monologist.

Preacher President, The—See **GARFIELD, JAMES A.**

Preaching Windmill, The—See **GRAHAM, BILLY.**

Preaching Woman, The—See **SPRAGUE, ACHSA W.**

Precious Warrior—See **GENGHIS KHAN.**

Prelate of Resistance: JULES-GERAUD SALIEGE (1870–1956)

The Roman Catholic archbishop of Toulouse, Jules-Geraud Saliege, who was arrested by the Nazis in 1942 for protesting the deportation of Jews, won the title *Prelate of Resistance.*

Presbyterian Ulysses, The—See **ARCHIBALD, MARQUIS OF ARGYLE.**

Preserver, The—See **PTOLEMY I.**

Preserver II, The—See **PTOLEMY VIII.**

President Nixon's Hired Gunslinger—See **REHNQUIST, WILLIAM.**

President-Maker, The—See **DAUGHERTY, HARRY M.**

Presidentress of the U.S.—See **WILSON, EDITH BOLLING.**

President's Other Friend, The—See **ABPLANALP, ROBERT H.**

President's Worst Friend, The—See
MITCHELL, JOHN N.

PRESLEY, ELVIS (1935–1977)

Singer Elvis Presley was nicknamed *Elvis the Pelvis* because of his lower-body gyrations on stage. In Florida in 1955 police ordered him to perform without moving, and when he made his television debut on the "Ed Sullivan Show," he was seen only from the waist up. By his early twenties he was acknowledged as *The Father of Rock 'N' Roll* and *The King*.

Presto—See **SWIFT, JONATHAN.**

Pretender, The—See **CLEVELAND, GROVER.**

PRICE, STERLING (1809–1867)

Although affectionately dubbed *Old Pap* or *Old Dad* by his men, Sterling Price was not one of the Confederacy's premier generals. His record of frequent retreats led Unionist newspapers to declare that "as a racer he has seen few equals for his weight," and they lengthened his nickname to *Old Skedad*, as in "skedaddle."

Pride and Sorrow of Chess, The—See
MORPHY, PAUL CHARLES.

Priest of Nature, The—See **NEWTON, ISAAC.**

Prime Minister of the Underworld—
See **COSTELLO, FRANK.**

Prince Arthur—See **ARTHUR, CHESTER A.**

Prince Charming—See **FAROUK I.**

Prince John—See **MAGRUDER, JOHN BANKHEAD; VAN BUREN, JOHN.**

Prince of Alchemy, The—See
RUDOLPH II OF THE HOLY ROMAN EMPIRE.

Prince of All the Russias—See
ROMANOFF, "Prince" MICHAEL.

Prince of Coxcombs, The—See
CHARLES JOSEPH, PRINCE DE LIGNE.

Prince of Cranks, The: IGNATIUS DONNELLY (1831–1901)

A fiery nonconformist who dominated several third-party movements, Ignatius Donnelly was known as *The Prince of Cranks*. In 1892 he electrified the Populist Party convention as he ticked off what the political establishment of the day regarded as "lunatic planks," including demands for a graduated income tax, an eight-hour working day, direct election of senators and woman's suffrage. Outside the political sphere founded Nininger City, a utopian city of culture in the agrarian West; set forth theories of Atlantis as the cradle of civilization; asserted that Sir Francis Bacon was the author of Shakespeare's plays; and rivaled Jules Verne in his predictions of the future. But his main mark remained political, as he told his Populist followers, "We have performed work which will affect the politics of this country for the next fifty years."

Prince of Critics, The—See
LONGINUS, DIONYSIUS CASSIUS.

Prince of Darkness, The—See
CARSON, JOHNNY.

Prince of Destruction, The—See
TAMERLANE (or TIMUR or
TIMOUR).

Prince of Diplomatists, The—See
TALLEYRAND-PERIGORD,
CHARLES MAURICE DE.

Prince of Grammarians, The—See
APOLLONIUS OF ALEXANDRIA.

Prince of Humbugs, The—See
BARNUM, PHINEAS T.

Prince of Hypocrites, The—See
TIBERIUS CAESAR.

Prince of Italian Poets, The—See
PETRARCH, FRANCESCO.

Prince of Journalists, The—See
GREELEY, HORACE.

Prince of Liars, The—See PINTO,
FERNAO MENDES.

Prince of Losers, The—See COOK,
FREDERICK A.

Prince of Macaronies, The—See
BUSSY, GEORGE.

*Prince of Negro Songwriters,
The*—See BLAND, JAMES A.

Prince of Painters, The—See
APELLES.

Prince of Peace, The—See
CARNEGIE, ANDREW.

Prince of Poets, The—See GOETHE,
JOHANN WOLFGANG VON.

Prince of Quarrellers, The—See
BEAUMARCHAIS, PIERRE
AUGUSTIN CARON DE.

Prince of Satirists, The—See SACHS,
HANS.

Prince of Showmen, The—See
BARNUM, PHINEAS T.

Prince of Story-Tellers, The—See
BOCCACCIO, GIOVANNI.

*Prince of the American Theater,
The*—See COHAN, GEORGE M.

Prince of the New Pharisees, The—See
BONIFACE VIII, POPE.

Prince of Wails, The—See RAY,
JOHNNY.

Prince of Whales, The—See
ARBUCKLE, ROSCOE "Fatty."

Prince of Wits, The—See
**CHESTERFIELD, PHILIP DORMER
STANHOPE, LORD.**

Prince Rupert of the Confederacy—See
**STUART, JAMES EWELL BROWN
"Jeb."**

Princess—See **OBERON, MERLE.**

Princess Alice—See **LONGWORTH,
ALICE LEE.**

Prisoner of Chillon, The—See
BONNIVARD, FRANCOIS DE.

Prisoner of Ham, The—See
NAPOLEON III.

Prisoner of the Vatican, The—See
PIUS IX, POPE.

Prisoner's Friend, The—See **BEAL,
ABRAHAM.**

Private John—See **ALLEN, JOHN M.**

Pro Golf's Beau Brummel—See
SANDERS, DOUGLAS.

Professional Radical, The—See
ALINSKY, SAUL D.

Professor Sea Gull—See **GOULD,
JOE.**

PROMITIS, MARY (fl. 1920s–1930s)

Mary Promitis, a leading dancer during the dance marathon craze of the 1920s and 1930s, was nicknamed *Hercules Mary* for her stamina.

Prophet Against Empire, The—See
BLAKE, WILLIAM.

Prose Burns of Ireland, The—See
CARLETON, WILLIAM.

Prosperity Robinson—See
ROBINSON, FREDERICK.

Prosperity's Advance Agent—See
MCKINLEY, WILLIAM.

*Protector and Defender of Humanity,
The*—See **BECCARIA, MARCHESE
DE.**

Protector of the Indians, The—See
LAS CASAS, BARTOLOME DE.

Protestant Duke, The—See
MONMOUTH, JAMES, DUKE OF.

Protestant Pope, The—See
CLEMENT XIV, POPE.

Protestant Whore, The—See **GWYN,
NELL.**

Proto Rebel, The—See
**QUEENSBURY, WILLIAM, DUKE
OF.**

Proud Duke, The—See SEYMOUR, CHARLES, DUKE OF SOMERSET.

Proud Plumber, The—See MEANY, GEORGE.

Prussian Charley—See MADER, CHARLEY.

Prussian Leprechaun, The—See LEAHY, FRANK.

Prussian Pindar, The—See WILLAMOW, JOHANN GOTTLIEB.

PRYNNE, WILLIAM *(1600–1669)*

The English Puritan pamphleteer William Prynne was hailed by his friends as *The Brave Jersey Muse* and *William the Conqueror*. Even Charles II, mindful of the 10 imprisonments Prynne had been subjected to by various parties, dignified him with the sobriquet *The Cato of the Age*. Less charitable was John Milton, who contemptuously referred to him as *Marginal Prynne*.

PTOLEMY I *(c. 367–283 B.C.)*

The founder of the Macedonian dynasty in Egypt, Ptolemy I developed Alexandria, his capital, into the world's leading city. He established many museums and libraries, gaining the sobriquet *Soter*, or *The Preserver*.

PTOLEMY II *(309–246 B.C.)*

Ptolemy II, king of Egypt, was nicknamed *Philadelphus*, or *The Brotherly*, because his reign was generally peaceful. He built his kingdom into a great sea power, commercial center and leader of Hellenistic culture. He is generally credited with having the Hebrew Bible translated into Greek by 70 scholars.

PTOLEMY III *(c. 282–211 B.C.)*

Ptolemy III, who reigned as king of Egypt from 246 to 211 B.C., was dubbed *Euergetes*, or *Benefactor*, for while he extended his kingdom to Babylon and Susa by conquest, he also sponsored learning and art and was famed for the many temples he built.

PTOLEMY IV *(c. 244–203 B.C.)*

Ptolemy IV, king of Eygpt, was called *Philopater*, or *Loving His Father*, for his honoring of Ptolemy III as well as other great men of the past. He also built a temple to honor Homer. A vacillating sovereign, he was easily influenced by his court favorites.

PTOLEMY VII *(c. 184–116 B.C.)*

Ptolemy VII, king of Egypt, was nicknamed *The Benefactor* for his good works. However, the populace also referred to him as *Physcon*, or *Fat Paunch*.

PTOLEMY VIII *(?-81 B.C.)*

Ptolemy VIII was dubbed *Soter II*, or *The Preserver II*, after Ptolemy I, who was called *The Preserver* for his fostering of art and learning. it proved a poor identification for Ptolemy VIII, who for a time was forced into exile and whose reign was marked by constant internal upheaval.

PTOLEMY XI *(97?-51 B.C.)*

The father of Cleopatra, Ptolemy XI, a despotic, drunken tyrant whose perhaps one redeeming feature was a love for music, was called *The Flute Player*. That saving grace did not prevent his overthrow in a general rebellion, but the Romans forcibly returned him to the throne.

***Public Energy Number One*—See ROOSEVELT, ELEANOR.**

***Public Lover No. 1*—See KAUFMAN, GEORGE S.**

***Public Relations Genius, The*—See LEE, IVY L.**

***Puck of Commentators, The*—See STEEVENS, GEORGE.**

***PUGET, PIERRE* (1622–1694)**

A noted 17th century French painter, Pierre Puget was equally skilled as a sculptor, architect and engineer and was thus designated *Le Michel-Ange francais,* or *The French Michelangelo.*

***PUGIN, AUGUSTUS WELBY NORTHMORE* (1812–1852)**

English architect Augustus Welby Northmore Pugin has been celebrated as *The Janus of the Gothic Revival,* after the Roman god of gates and doorways. Kenneth Clark has observed, "His buildings look back to the picturesque past, his writings look forward to the ethical future."

***PULITZER, JOSEPH* (1847–1911)**

Publisher Joseph Pulitzer exerted a profound influence on American journalism, for which he was dubbed *The Father of Modern American Journalism*. However, most sobriquets accorded him tended to be exceedingly disparaging, especially those from rivals in the profession. James Gordon Bennett called him *A Selfish Vulgarian* and Charles Dana *This Dick Turpin of Journalism,* after the notorious English highwayman. Theodore Dreiser referred to him as *A Disease-demonized Soul.*

***PULLER, LEWIS B. "Chesty"* (1898–1971)**

U.S. Marine Corps Lewis B. Puller was nicknamed *Chesty* originally because of his bulldog stance. Later the sobriquet referred to his much decorated chest, as he collected every medal of valor awarded by the United States save for the Medal of Honor.

***Puma, The*—See VILLA, PANCHO.**

***Punch*—SULZBERGER, ARTHUR OCHS.**

***Purest Figure in History, The*—See WASHINGTON, GEORGE.**

***Purist of Language, The*—See MALHERBE, FRANCOIS DE.**

***Puritan Pepys, The*—See SEWALL, SAMUEL.**

***Puritan Plato, The*—See HOWE, JOHN.**

***Puritan Poet, The*—See WHITTIER, JOHN GREENLEAF.**

***Purse*—See PIERCE, FRANKLIN.**

PURVIS, MELVIN (1903–1960)

Perhaps the most colorful of all FBI agents, Melvin Purvis was renowned as *The Man Who Shot Dillinger* even though he never fired his gun when the reigning public enemy No. 1 was killed outside a Chicago movie theater. However, he directed the trap, and stepped up to Dillinger and pointed him out to other agents and policemen.

Push-'em-up—See LAZZERI, TONY "Push-'em-up."

PUSHKIN, ALEXANDER (1799–1837)

Generally hailed as the greatest of Russian poets, Alexander Pushkin is often described as *The Russian Byron*. Like the fiery Lord Byron, Pushkin often expressed his political in his poetry. He was exiled to southern Russia and much of his writings were subject to prior censorship. His masterpiece, the narrative poem *Eugene Onegin*, depicts the Byronic hero of the century—cynical, bored, melancholy, in love and out of love, breaking hearts, dueling. Like Byron, Pushkin died young, a dueling victim.

Pussyfoot Johnson—See JOHNSON, WILLIAM "Pussyfoot."

PYLE, CHARLES C. "Cash and Carry" (1881–1939)

C. C. Pyle, better known as *The P.T. Barnum of Sports* and *Cash and Carry* (a play on his initials) *Pyle,* concocted some of the weirdest sports events of the early 20th century, such as the famous Bunion Derby of 1928, a 3,000-mile footrace from Los Angeles to Madison Square Garden in New York. Initially generating wide public interest, it took some 84 days to complete and turned into a public joke. Newspapers started referring to the promoter as *Corn and Callous Pyle,* and by the conclusion of the marathon, Pyle had lost between $75,000 and $100,000 with only 4,000 fans attending the conclusion of the contest. He was more successful in other endeavors, however. Pyle organized the first professional tennis tour, his success leading to the formation of the U.S. Professional Lawn Tennis Association.

PYM, JOHN (1584–1643)

The English Puritan statesman John Pym, a virulent anti-Catholic and antimonarchist, led the parliamentary opposition to Charles I. His strength and influence as a parliamentary leader led to the nickname *King Pym,* an allusion not lost on Charles I, who tried vainly to have him arrested.

PYRICUS (4th century B.C.)

Pliny dubbed the ancient Greek painter Pyricus *The Ryparographer*. The word comes from the Greek meaning "nasty," which Pliny found fitting since Pyricus devoted his talent to producing gross and ridiculous pictures.

Python—See DENNIS, JOHN.

Q

QADDAFI, MUAMMAR (1942–   )

Because of his web of expansionist and terrorist activities, Libyan leader Muammar Qaddafi is known both inside and outside the Arab world as *The Spider of Tripoli*.

Quack in Commentatorship, A—See **WARBURTON, WILLIAM.**

Quaker Martyr, The—See **DYER, MARY.**

Quaker Soldier, The—See **BIDDLE, CLEMENT.**

QUANTRILL, WILLIAM CLARKE (1837–1865)

A Confederate guerrilla leader who raided border states during the Civil War, William Quantrill was labeled an outlaw by Union authorities. His most vicious act was the sacking of Lawrence, Kansas, where he and his men murdered 180 men, women and children and burned most of the town. Before he was killed in 1865, he was designated *The Bloodiest Man in American History,* a title that could possibly be contested only by his aide, Bloody Bill Anderson.

Queen Anne of Wyoming—See **RICHEY, ANNIE BYERS.**

Queen Dick—See **CROMWELL, RICHARD.**

Queen Elizabeth's Merlin—See **DEE, JOHN.**

Queen Marie—See **DRESSLER, MARIE.**

Queen of Disco, The—See **TRUDEAU, MARGARET.**

Queen of Hearts, The—See **ELIZABETH, ELECTRESS PALATINE.**

Queen of Hell's Kitchen, The: **BATTLE ANNIE** *(fl. early 1900s)*

A notorious female tough known simply as Battle Annie was the leader of what was probably the first major female gang in America. Called *The Queen of Hell's Kitchen* by the press, Battle Annie bossed a band of 50 to 100 female sluggers who served in the labor wars of the time. Her women would appear on a strike scene posing as the wives of either strikers or strikebreakers and scratch, bite and claw the men on the other side.

Queen of Nine Days, The—See **GREY, LADY JANE.**

Queen of Queens, The—See **CLEOPATRA.**

Queen of Rock 'n' Rouge, The—See **COOPER, ALICE.**

Queen of Tears, The—See **MARY OF MODENA; SCHRODER-DEVRIENT, WILHELMINE.**

Queen of Technicolor, The—See **O'HARA, MAUREEN.**

Queen of the American Stage, The—See **DUFF, MRS. MARY.**

Queen of the Barbary Coast—See **WALL, TESSIE.**

Queen of the Blues, The—See **WASHINGTON, DINAH.**

Queen of the Bowery, The—See **PRADO, KATIE.**

Queen of the Circus, The—See **LEITZEL, LILLIAN.**

Queen of the Comstock, The—See **BULETTE, JULIA C.**

Queen of the Mob, The—See **HILL, VIRGINIA.**

Queen of the Red Lights—See **SILKS, MATTIE.**

Queen of the Speakeasies—See **GUINAN, TEX.**

Queen Poisoner—See **STRUCK, LYDIA.**

Queen Sarah—See **JENNINGS, SARAH.**

Queen Victoria's Favorite Composer— See **ELGAR, EDWARD WILLIAM.**

Queenie—See **OBERON, MERLE.**

QUEENSBURY, WILLIAM, DUKE OF (?–1695)

William, duke of Queensbury, was dubbed *The Proto Rebel* because he was the first Scotsman to take part in the Glorious Revolution of 1688.

Quentin the Eagle—See **ROOSEVELT, QUENTIN.**

QUERNO, CAMILLO (?–1528)

Poet Camillo Querno, who sang his verses for Pope Leo X, was called *The Antichrist of Wit* by the foes of the de Medici pope.

Quicksilver Bob—See **FULTON, ROBERT.**

QUINN, JAMES ALOYSIUS (?–1924)

One of the more colorful corrupt Chicago politicians of the early 20th century, James Aloysius Quinn was nicknamed *Hot Stove Jimmy,* an identification he achieved early in his career for being ''so crooked he'd steal a hot stove.''

QUISLING, VIDKUN (1887–1945)

The Norwegian Nazi collaborator Vidkun Quisling, who was executed in 1945, was called *The Betrayer of Norway* by his people. The rest of the world made his surname a sobriquet for anyone who was a traitor to his nation.

R

Rabbi of Swat, The—See **SOLOMON, MOSES.**

RABELAIS, FRANCOIS
(c. 1490–1553)

Because of the biting humor of his writings, often bordering on burlesque, the French author and humanist Francois Rabelais was labeled *The Father of Ridicule*.

Rabelaisian Doctor, The—See PATIN, GUY.

RACINE, JEAN (1639–1699)

The French tragic poet Jean Racine was accorded the sobriquet *The Virgil of the French Drama* by an admiring Sir Walter Scott.

Radar Brain, The—See CROISET, GERARD.

Radical Prophet of American Youth, The—See DYLAN, BOB.

Radio Priest, The—See COUGHLIN, CHARLES E.

Rag Smith—See SMITH, EDMUND.

Ragged Lawyer, The: MARTIN GROVER (1811–1875)

A 19th century New York attorney, Martin Grover was known as *The Ragged Lawyer* because he often appeared in court dressed in shabby and old clothes. He knew that such an appearance often elicited sympathy for his client from the jury, whose members would feel the defendant was at a disadvantage having such a defender. The Grover technique was later used with even greater effectiveness by Clarence Darrow.

Ragged Stranger, The (?–1920)

A Chicago murder victim identified only as *The Ragged Stranger* was at first considered to be a heartless murderer who killed pregnant Mrs. Ruther Wanderer in 1920 in the hallway of her home and then was himself shot dead by his victim's husband, Carl Wanderer. Wanderer was for a time lionized as a hero until it was discovered that he had committed the murders, luring the *The Ragged Stranger* to his home from a skid row area with the promise of a job. (See Wanderer, Carl.)

Railroader's Railroader, The—See WHITE, WILLIAM.

Rail-Splitter, The—See LINCOLN, ABRAHAM.

Rake of Piccadilly, The—See DOUGLAS, WILLIAM.

RALSTON, WILLIAM CHAPMAN
(1826–1875)

William Chapman Ralston became the leading citizen of San Francisco and, as its leading banker, financed many of the city's major buildings, including the famous Palace Hotel, as well as many factories, mills and theaters. He was one of the big investors, some say plunderers, of the Comstock Lode and also backed many unwise ventures, including what turned out to be a "salted" diamond mine. Eventually his institution, the Bank of California, had to shut its doors because of Ralston's financial excesses, and shortly thereafter he was found drowned, most likely a suicide victim. Nonetheless through the years Ralston has retained the sobriquet *The First Gentleman of San Francisco*.

Ramblin' Ron—See REAGAN, RONALD.

RAMLER, CHARLES WILLIAM
(1725–1798)

A noted German writer and translator, Charles William Ramler translated many of the odes of Horace and published them with several original imitations of them, gaining the sobriquet *The German Horace*.

RAMOLINO, MARIE-LAETITIA—See Mother of Monarchs, The.

RAMSAY, ALLAN (1686–1758)

Scottish poet Allan Ramsay, celebrated for his pastoral comedy "Gentle Shepherd," was called *The Scottish Theocritus* for having written what some considered "the first genuine pastoral after Theocritus." Theocritus was a Greek pastoral poet who lived in the 3rd century B.C.

RAMSPECK, ROBERT (1890–1972)

A long-time chairman of the Civil Service Committee of the U.S. House of Representatives, Georgia representative Robert Ramspeck was nicknamed *The Guardian of Civil Service* because he was responsible for much of the legislation that extended and protected benefits for federal employees. He later served as chairman of the U.S. Civil Service Commission.

RANDOLPH, A. PHILIP (1889–1979)

U.S. black labor leader A. Philip Randolph, who organized the Brotherhood of Sleeping Car Porters in 1925 and prevailed upon President Franklin Roosevelt in 1941 to issue a fair-employment practices executive order, was designated *Mr. Black Labor*. He also provided the initial impetus for the massive 1963 civil rights march on Washington, D.C., and was dubbed *The Father of the Civil Rights Movement*.

RANDOLPH (OF ROANOKE), JOHN (1773–1833)

Virginia politician and congressman John Randolph (of Roanoke) was nicknamed *Little David, Jack the Giant-killer* and *The Man with the Sling* because in debates he tended to pose as David and cast his opponent in the role of Goliath. To his supporters he was also *The Sage of Roanoke*, but his foes preferred the sobriquet *The Father of Lies*. Rhode Island congressman Tristam Burges once commented on the widely held belief that Randolph was impotent by rejoicing "that *The Father of Lies* can never become The Father of Liars."

Randy Andy—See ANDREW, PRINCE.

RANGER, MORRIS (?–1883)

English speculator Morris Ranger was designated *The Napoleon of Liverpool Finance* because it was said he moved his capital as fast as Napoleon moved his armies.

RANKIN, JEANETTE (1880–1973)

Montana pacifist, suffragist and champion of woman's rights, Jeanette Rankin was, as her sobriquet indicated, *The First Woman in Congress*. She was also the only member of Congress to vote against entry into both World War I and World War II, and she later opposed the Vietnam War as well.

RANKIN, JOHN E. (1882–1960)

U.S. representative John E. Rankin of Mississippi, a notorious white supremacist, was called *The*

Killer for his virulent attacks on blacks, Jews and liberals. His supporters called him *T.V.A. Rankin* because he co-authored the bill that created the Tennessee Valley Authority.

RANN, JOHN—See Sixteen-String Jack.

RAPF, HARRY (1880–1949)

Veteran film producer and vice president of Metro-Goldwyn-Mayer Harry Rapf, who had a large nose, was savaged behind his back in the industry as *Mayer's Sundial.*

RAPHAEL (1483–1520)

The great Italian Renaissance painter Raphael was nicknamed *"Il Divino,"* or *The Divine One,* but according to some biographers, his private life could hardly be considered saintly. He was known to have a passion for the sensual and has been credited with a large number of affairs. It was said he used several of his lovers as models for his Madonnas.

Raphael of Cats, The—See MIND, GOTTFRIED.

Raphael of Domestic Art, The—See WILKIE, DAVID.

Raphael of England, The—See REYNOLDS, JOSHUA.

Raphael of Music, The—See MOZART, WOLFGANG AMADEUS.

Raphael of the Parc-aux-Cerfs, The—See BOUCHER, FRANCOIS.

Rare Ben Jonson—See JONSON, BEN.

RASPUTIN, GRIGORI EFIMOVICH (c. 1871–1916)

Given the name *Rasputnik,* meaning libertine, by fellow villagers, Grigori Efimovich Rasputin was a Russian peasant monk who preached debauchery as a means of repentance and salvation. Known as *The Mad Monk* and *The Holy Satyr,* he exercised great influence over the Empress Alexandra, wife of Czar Nicholas II, who credited him with healing her son, a hemophiliac. Rasputin's behavior at court, affecting political policy and luring women (some said hypnotically) into his bedroom, which he called "the holy of holies," resulted in his assassination by a group of noblemen.

Rasputin—See HALDEMAN, H. R.; SALISBURY, HARRISON.

Rasputin of Our Society, The—See PEARSON, DREW.

Rat, The: HANS SCHAARSCHMIDT (c. 1907)

Hans Schaarschmidt, an obscure German convict, made one of the most amazing prison escapes. Kept in a cell in an old fortress-jail in Gera, Germany, with window bars made of heavy wooden crossbeams, he nightly chewed through the bars until he finally reached freedom. When he was captured sometime later, it was noticed that his front teeth had been ground down to the gum line, and the press quickly dubbed him *The Rat.* Because of *The*

Rat's exploits, German authorities launched a program to replace wooden bars with steel ones in all prisons.

Rat, Cat and Lovel Our Dogge: RICHARD RATCLIFFE (?–1485); WILLIAM CATESBY (?–1485); and LORD LOVEL (?–1487)

One of the most famous and, at times, celebrated nickname rhymes of the 15th century was that penned about the associates of England's Richard III, Sir Richard Ratcliffe, William Catesby and Lord Lovel:

> The Cat, the Rat and Lovel our Dogge
> Rulen all England under an Hogge.

The rhyme (often altered in general usage to the order listed in the heading) cost its author, William Collingborne, his life.

Ratcatcher—See DARWIN, CHARLES.

RATCLIFFE, RICHARD—See Rat, Cat and Lovel Our Dogge.

Rattlesnake Dick: RICHARD BARTER (1834–1859)

Although few outlaws in the Old West were as incompetent as Richard Barter, he won great fame as *Rattlesnake Dick,* with perhaps almost as many dime novels written about him as about Wild Bill Hickok. Apparently the fact that he was an Englishman operating in the West was sufficient to make him exotic. *Rattlesnake Dick* masterminded only one important robbery, that of $80,000 in gold from a California mule train. However, he failed to carry out his role in the caper because he got drunk and was arrested trying to steal some mules. He was shot dead in 1859 shortly after pulling off a $20 stagecoach robbery.

Rattlesnake Houston—See HOUSTON, TEMPLE.

Rattlesnake Murderer, The—See JAMES, ROBERT.

RAWLINS, JOHN A.—See Grant's Conscience.

RAWLINSON, THOMAS (1681–1725)

One of England's most colorful bibliomaniacs, Thomas Rawlinson was called *Tom Folio* and *The Leviathan of Book-Collectors.* The four rooms he maintained as living quarters were so jammed with books that his bed had to be placed in the hallway. He later moved into a large house, which he soon filled from basement to attic with books. It took 18 auctions over 12 years to dispose of all his holdings.

RAWSON, EDWARD (1615–1693)

Although persecution of religious dissenters in 17th century America was most severe, Edward Rawson, secretary of the Boston Colony from 1650 to 1686 and one of the founders of the Old South Church, was nicknamed *The Persecutor* for his exceptionally harsh and determined persecution of Quakers.

RAY, JOHNNY (1927–   )

U.S. pop singer Johnnie Ray, whose singing style seemed at times like crying and who had a hit song called "Cry" in the early 1950s, was nicknamed *The Prince of Wails* in England.

RAYBURN, SAM (1882–1961)

Responsible for passage of a large portion of the New Deal legislation and speaker for all but four years from 1940 to 1961, Sam Rayburn was known affectionately as *Mr. Sam* in recognition of his 48 years of service in the House of Representatives and *Mr. Democrat* for the power he wielded.

Razor, The—See TOJO, HIDEKI.

REAGAN, NANCY (1923–   )

Linked perhaps more than most U.S. first ladies to the political policies of her husband, Nancy Reagan gained the sobriquet *Marie Antoinette*. It was an allusion to her desire for lavish living while at the same time President Ronald Reagan was perceived by many to be callous in his attitude toward the poor. Because of her extensive and expensive wardrobe, Mrs. Reagan also received the nickname *First Mannequin*.

REAGAN, RONALD (1911–   )

A movie actor who turned to politics, Ronald Reagan was called, early in his elective career, *Mr. Clean* and *The Most Happy Fellow*, the latter an allusion to his infectious smile, which proved an effective campaign weapon. Elected president of the U.S. over Jimmy Carter by a large margin in 1980, Reagan was dubbed *The Great Communicator,* a reputation enhanced by his ability to deliver a prepared message with consummate skill, especially in gaining public support for his economic program. However, by late 1982, near the middle of his term, Reagan was being disparaged by reporters, even those of newspapers with long-standing Republican leanings, as *Ramblin' Ron* for his frequently inaccurate or meandering comments in off-the-cuff conversations or during press conferences. On a more partisan basis, after his election Reagan was disparaged as *Reagan Hood* by opponents who claimed his policies were aimed at taking from the poor to give to the rich. Possibly the most cutting nickname, one that did not catch on, was coined by former Texas governor John R. Connally, who opposed Reagan for the 1980 Republican nomination. He called the aging Reagan *A Great Elder Statesman*. Not surprisingly, after Reagan's victory Connally's role in his administration proved miniscule. Because of his persistent efforts at building up America's nuclear arsenal, Reagan was tagged *Ronald Ray Gun* by antinuclear weapons forces.

Reagan Hood—See REAGAN, RONALD.

Real Dr. Jekyll and Mr. Hyde, The—See BRODIE, WILLIAM.

Real McCoy, The: WILLIAM MCCOY (1877–1948)

U.S. bootlegger and rumrunner, Capt. William McCoy was the founder of Prohibition's Rum Row, the flotilla of ships that remained outside U.S. waters until it was safe to make a run to shore with contraband liquor. He was nicknamed *The Real McCoy* because he offered unadulterated booze. Eventually the phrase was applied to all "good stuff."

Rebel Governor, The—See TRUMBULL, JONATHAN.

Rebel of Salem, The—See WILLIAMS, ROGER.

Rebel of Seventh Avenue, The—See CASSINI, OLEG.

Rebel Rose—See GREENHOW, ROSE O'NEAL.

Red—See COOLIDGE, CALVIN.

Red Baron, The—See RICHTHOFEN, BARON MANFRED FREIHERR VON.

Red Colonel, The—See GUZMAN, JACOBO ARBENZ.

Red Dean of Canterbury, The—See JOHNSON, HEWLETT.

Red Eminence, The—See RICHELIEU, CARDINAL.

Red Pepper, The—See PEPPER, CLAUDE.

Red Priest, The—See VIVALDI, ANTONIO.

Red Professor, The—See SUSLOV, MIKHAIL.

Red Rosa—See LUXEMBURG, ROSA.

Redeemed Captive, The—See WILLIAMS, JOHN.

Red-Headed Kid from Wheeling, The—See REUTHER, WALTER P.

Red-Nosed Princess, The—See ELIZABETH, PRINCESS OF THE PALATINE.

REED, JOHN *(1887–1920)*

U.S. war correspondent, poet and revolutionary John Reed came from a wealthy family of high social standing and was a graduate of Harvard. Light-hearted, tall and handsome, he became at the same time a cultural hero of the new radical bohemians in the United States, who dubbed him *Playboy*. He gained great prominence for his coverage of the exploits of Pancho Villa, World War I and the Russian Revolution of 1917, becoming a personal friend of Lenin. Back in the United States he was indicted for sedition, but the jury split on the verdict. Reed continued to be attacked from the right and the left, being called *A Soviet Saint* by the right and *Jack the Liar* by the Communist Party, because he was a member of the rival Communist Labor Party. Indicted once more, Reed fled the United States and returned to Russia, where he died of typhus on Oct. 19, 1920.

REED, THOMAS B. *"Czar"* *(1839–1902)*

The Republican speaker of the House of Representatives in the late 19th century, Thomas B. Reed was dubbed *Czar Reed* for the way he altered House rules whenever necessary to push GOP programs along. Foes also tabbed him *The Terrible Turk* since he was noted for being a terror when he did not get his way.

Reformed Pugilist, The—See BENDIGO.

Reformer of Astronomy, The—See COPERNICUS, NICHOLAS.

REHNQUIST, WILLIAM (1924–   )

When he was an important aide to Attorney General John Mitchell, future Supreme Court justice William Rehnquist had a string of sobriquets, ranging from *The Brains of the Justice Department* to *Justice Department Waterboy* and *President Nixon's Hired Gunslinger*.

REID, WALLACE "Good Time Wally" (1892–1923)

One of the top leading men of silent films, including *The Birth of a Nation,* Wallace Reid was celebrated as *Good Time Wally* until his health and career were wrecked by liquor and morphine. He was placed at the head of movie czar Will Hays' list of "unsafe" Hollywood personalities, but his blacklisting hardly mattered. *The Man in the Padded Room,* as Reid was called by then, died in a sanitarium in January 1923.

REINER, CARL (1922–   )

Television comedian and writer, Carl Reiner is called *Instant Genius* by his colleagues, their recognition of him as one of the funniest spontaneous comedy writers in the field.

REINHARDT, AD (1914–1967)

An abstract expressionist painter, Ad Reinhardt was called *The Black Monk* because he developed a painting style that reduced form and color to a minimum.

REIS, ARTURO ALVES (1896–1955)

Armed with forged documents which authorized a London firm that printed money for the Bank of Portugal to supply him with 500-escudo banknotes, allegedly for the Portuguese colony of Angola, Arturo Alves Reis used the funds to become one of the most powerful financiers of the country and was dubbed *The Man Who Stole Portugal*. Finally exposed in 1925, Reis attempted to use his funds to buy up a majority interest in the Bank of Portugal and almost succeeded. He served 15 years in prison and ended his life penniless.

RELES, ABE (1907–1941)

The most famous underworld informer in the history of American crime, Abe Reles was a leading member of Murder, Inc., a group of professional killers who worked for organized crime. His testimony sent many top mobsters to the electric chair. From the time he started informing until his death in a mysterious plunge from a 6th-floor Brooklyn hotel room window while under police guard, Reles was called *The Singing Canary*. Thereafter, he was known by the underworld and the press as *The Canary Who Couldn't Fly*.

Rembrandt of the Comic Strip, The— See CANIFF, MILTON.

Rembrandt of the West—See REMINGTON, FREDERIC.

REMI, PHILIPPE DE (?–1296)

Until the appearance of Montesquieu some 4½ centuries later, Philippe de Remi was regarded as France's greatest source of legal knowledge and was thus called *The French Justinian,* after the Roman emperor of the East who was responsible for the codification of Roman law, legislative records and legal opinions.

REMINGTON, FREDERIC
(1861–1909)

U.S. artist and war correspondent Frederic Remington readily earned the sobriquet *The Rembrandt of the West* for his paintings and sketches of cowboys, Indians, soldiers and, especially, equestrian subjects.

RENAULT, LOUIS (1877–1944)

Automobile manufacturer Louis Renault was hailed as *France's Henry Ford,* a reputation that was severely damaged during World War II because of his collaboration with the Nazis. He died in 1944 while awaiting trial by a Free French court.

Resolute Doctor, The—See BACON, JOHN.

Respectable Madam of Oxnard, The—See MOUNT, BESSIE (OR JOHN).

Respectable Radical, The—See THOMAS, NORMAN M.

RESTELL, MADAME (1812–1876)

One of the most notorious personages in New York, indeed *The Wickedest Woman in the City,* Ann Trow Lohman, better known as Madame Restell, was described in the press of the day as *Madame Killer.* She was the city's top abortionist, and when she ventured forth in her carriage, street youths followed her shouting: "Yah! Your house is built on babies' skulls!" In another era *Madame Killer* would have been regarded less an abortionist than a purveyor of contraceptives and an operator of an undercover maternity hospital and abortion center. She committed suicide because of an estrangement with her grandchildren after the famous vice crusader Anthony Comstock raided her establishment.

RESTIF, NICOLAS EDME
(1734–1806)

French writer of popular fiction Nicolas Edme Restif's literary standing was best exemplified by his nicknames *The Rousseau of the Gutter* and *The Voltaire of Chambermaids.*

Restoration Rogue, The—See DANGERFIELD, THOMAS.

Restorer of German Poetry, The—See OPITZ, MARTIN.

Restorer of Parnassus, The—See VALDES, JUAN MELENDEZ.

Restorer of Science in Germany, The—See STURM, JOHANN CHRISTOPH.

Restorer of the Roman Empire, The—See AURELIAN.

REUTHER, WALTER P. (1907–1970)

Labor leader Walter P. Reuther was dubbed *The Red-Headed Kid from Wheeling,* it was said, by auto executives in the 1930s who could not believe that so young a worker could be responsible for so much of the drive for unionization of the auto industry.

Revolutionary in Pearl-Gray Gloves, The— See BLUM, LEON.

REVSON, PETER (1939–1974)

Cosmetic heir Peter Revson was nicknamed *Champagne Peter* and *The Glamour Boy of the Race Drivers*. He was killed in a driving accident in 1974.

REYNOLDS, JOSHUA (1723–1792)

Although upon his return to England from study in Italy many of his early paintings were sneered at by other artists and critics, Sir Joshua Reynolds became the most celebrated portrait painter in his country and was thus dubbed *The Raphael of England*.

RHETT, ROBERT B. (1800–1876)

One of the most persistent of secessionist advocates, Robert B. Rhett of South Carolina cherished his sobriquet *The Father of Secession* but was bitterly disappointed when he was not picked to be the first president of the Confederacy.

Rhinoceros Ziska—See ZISKA, JOHN.

Rhyming Barber, The—See GIOVANNI, DOMENICO DI.

Ribald Priest, The—See SWIFT, JONATHAN.

RIBBENTROP, JOACHIM VON (1893–1946)

The foreign minister of the Third Reich, Joachim von Ribbentrop was hailed by Hitler, with considerable exaggeration, as *The Second Bismarck*. Even within the Nazi hierarchy the accolade was too much, and Ribbentrop (who obtained the "von" by having an aristocratic aunt adopt him) was referred to as *Iago*.

RICCA, PAUL "the Waiter" (1897–1972)

For some four decades after the fall of Al Capone in 1931, Paul Ricca was regarded as one of the most powerful mobsters, and perhaps the most important one, heading the Chicago syndicate. He was called *The Waiter* initially because for a very brief period upon his arrival in the United States in 1920—as a fugitive wanted for murder in Italy—he had worked as a waiter. However, the reason the nickname stuck throughout his lifetime was that he constantly cited the occupation of waiter in testimony at immigration hearings to prove he was a worthwhile citizen.

RICE, DAN (1823–1900)

Nicknamed *The King of American Clowns* in the 19th century, Dan Rice achieved such popularity that he was boomed for the Republican presidential nomination in 1868. Rice thought he could win and, with a valid political program, gained the support of a number of newspapers. In the end Ulysses S. Grant defeated him, the only clown, or professional one at least, ever to seek the office of president.

RICE, GRANTLAND (1880–1954)

One of America's greatest sportswriters, Grantland Rice was rightfully known during the Golden Age of Sports as *America's Homer* because he could view every game as an epic struggle. "The drama of sport," he once wrote, "is a big part of the drama of life and the scope of this drama is endless. Sport has its triumphs and its tragedies, its great joys and heavy sorrows with more spectacular effect than most dramas may ever know." He dubbed the Notre Dame backfield of 1924-25 the Four Horsemen and was the first to call Jack Dempsey the Manassa Mauler. He also probably composed the most quoted, and misquoted, lines of verse about sports:

When the Last Great Scorer comes
To mark against your name,
He'll write not "won" or "lost"
But how you played the game.

Rich, The—See CRASSUS, MARCUS LICINIUS.

RICHARD, MAURICE (1921–   )

Maurice Richard, one of the greats of professional hockey, was labeled by the press *The Rocket* and *The Babe Ruth of Hockey*.

RICHARD III OF ENGLAND (1452–1485)

Richard III of England, the duke of Gloucester, took the throne after denouncing the claim of his nephews, the young Edward V and his brother, as illegitimate and having them murdered. He was called *Crookback* for the obvious reason and *The Boar* for his countenance.

Richard the Lion Hearted: RICHARD I OF ENGLAND (1157–1199)

Richard I of England gained his sobriquet *Richard the Lion Hearted* because of his valor in battle.

RICHARDS, STEPHEN LEE (1856–1879)

Labeled *The Nebraska Fiend*, mass murderer Stephen Lee Richards killed at least nine persons in the Lincoln, Neb., area during the 1870s. The same sobriquet was applied to Charles Starkweather, who engaged in a similar murder spree in the same locality almost 80 years later, also claiming nine victims. (See Starkweather, Charles.)

RICHARDSON, ELLIOT L. (1920–   )

U.S. attorney general at the beginning of the Watergate investigation, Elliot L. Richardson was labeled *Mr. Clean* after he was driven out of office in the so-called Saturday Night Massacre by President Richard Nixon for refusing to fire Watergate special prosecutor Archibald Cox. Richardson maintained he could not ethically dismiss Cox as Nixon had ordered.

RICHARDSON, SID (1891–1959)

A colorful, free-wheeling independent oilman, Texan Sid Richardson was reputedly the third richest man in the United States when he died. In his day he was a confidant of Lyndon Johnson, hired a young lawyer named John Connally and, more than anyone else, bankrolled his friend Dwight Eisenhower into the presidency. He was known as *The Billionaire Bachelor,* and when asked why he had never married, he replied that women "are all wantin' a landing field, but mine's fogged in."

RICHELIEU, CARDINAL: ARMAND JEAN DU PLESSIS (1585–1642)

Cardinal Richelieu, the famous French cardinal-statesman who controlled much of Louis XIII's foreign and domestic policy, was called *Eminence Rouge,* or *The Red Eminence* or *The Red Cardinal,* because he wore a red habit, which was unique for the time. (See also Trembley, Joseph de.)

Richest Man in Canada, The—See BRONFMAN, SAMUEL.

RICHEY, ANNIE BYERS
(c. 1891–1921)

Western tales to the contrary, Annie Byers Richey was the first and only woman ever convicted of cattle rustling in the United States, and her conviction occurred in the 20th century, in 1919. True, a few other females, such as the storied Cattle Kate Watson, were strung up for alleged rustling offenses, but none ever had the benefit of a trial. Annie Richey was a popular cowgirl in Lincoln County, Wyo., and long before her troubles with the law she was dubbed by cowboys *Queen Anne of Wyoming* because she could do all the demanding work of the range and yet "she sits her saddle like a queen." After her arrest she was known as *The Petticoat Rustler*. Although convicted and sentenced to serve one to six years in prison, she died mysteriously of poisoning without ever serving time. The popular belief was that she was murdered by a confederate who wished to ensure her silence.

RICHMOND, BILL (1763–1829)

Bill Richmond, a black, was the first American to gain any kind of athletic renown in other countries. When he was very young, Richmond won a number of fights, staged by Gen. Earl Percy of the British Army, against British soldiers. When Richmond was 14, Percy took him back to England, where he achieved fame as *The Black Terror*. Richmond won many fights over the years but was denied full recognition because many leading boxers refused to meet him. Finally in 1805 he faced Tom Cribb, then the leading contender for the heavyweight championship. However, Richmond was then 42 years old, compared with Cribb's 24, and the older man was knocked out in 90 minutes.

RICHTHOFEN, BARON MANFRED FREIHERR VON (1892–1918)

With a record of 80 downed Allied planes, Manfred Freiherr von Richthofen was the most successful air ace of World War I. Baron von Richthofen became a national hero in Germany, where he was called *The Red Baron* because of the maroon Albatross one-seater he flew. On April 21, 1918 he was shot down and killed either by an RAF plane or Australian ground fire.

RICKARD, "Tex" GEORGE L.
(1870–1929)

A flamboyant gambler and boxing promoter, Tex Rickard was called *The King of Sports Promoters* and *The Napoleon of Promoters*. He was also dubbed *The Magnificent Rube,* for while he was capable of garnering fortunes, he was equally capable of losing them on harebrained schemes. He promoted the first million-dollar gate, the Jack Dempsey-George Carpentier fight, and the first two-million dollar gate, the Jack Dempsey-Gene Tunney rematch. Known as a man of his word in a field where ethics were virtually nonexistent, Rickard was largely responsible for both Dempsey and Tunney being able to retire as wealthy men. And little-remembered, washed-up fighters could count on Rickard's aid. He never refused money to a former fighter, even if he suspected he was being conned, and many widows of fighters received support from him.

RICKEY, BRANCH (1881–1965)

Baseball executive Branch Rickey, famous for making shrewd trades and successfully breaking the major league color barrier by putting Jackie Robinson in the starting line-up of the Brooklyn Dodgers, was nicknamed *The Mahatma*. A baseball writer happened to read John Gunther's description of Mahatma Gandhi as "an incredible combination of Jesus Christ, Tammany Hall and your father." Since Rickey was shrewd, religious, devious and paternal, it was decided the name fitted Rickey perhaps even better.

RICKLES, DON (1926–)

Because his comic style is based on insult, directed at other performers as well as the audience, comedian Don Rickles has been dubbed by his fellow comics *Mr. Warmth*.

RICKOVER, HYMAN G. (1900–)

More than anyone else, U.S. admiral Hyman G. Rickover was responsible for the development of the atomic submarine and was properly dubbed *The Father of the Atomic Submarine*. He supervised the construction of the USS *Nautilus* and helped develop the first full-scale U.S. nuclear power plant. Rickover was forced into retirement at 83 by the Reagan administration.

RICORD, AUGUST (c. 1911–)

August Ricord, notorious French heroin smuggler operating in Paraguay, is often referred to as *The Heroin Kingpin* and *The Paraguayan Connection*.

RIEGELS, ROY "Wrong Way" (1909–)

A defensive lineman for the University of California football team, Roy Riegels became a household word after the 1929 Rose Bowl, in which he picked up a Georgia Tech fumble and raced 69 yards—in the wrong direction—before finally being tackled by a teammate on his own two-yard line. Tech scored a safety on the next play and the two points proved to be the margin of victory, making Riegels the goat of the game. Thereafter he was known as *Wrong Way Riegels*.

RIGGS, BOBBY (1918–)

Former U.S. singles and Wimbleton champion Bobby Riggs, who in recent years built up a repu-

tation as a tennis hustler, was dubbed *The Chicken Plucker*. Because of his unbounded self-esteem, the press also labeled him *The White Muhammad Ali*.

Right Reverend New Dealer, The—See RYAN, JOHN A.

RIIS, JACOB AUGUST (1849–1914)

Danish-born U.S. journalist and social reformer Jacob Riis wrote stories for the *New York Tribune,* and books about the plight of New York City's slum dwellers around the turn of the century that aroused public opinion, winning the sobriquet *The Father of Slum Clearance*.

RILEY, JAMES "Butt" (1848–?)

A San Francisco tough in the 1860s and 1870s, James Riley was generally referred to as *Butt Riley* or *King of the Hoodlums*. The possessor of an extremely hard skull, he was a vicious gangster who often butted robbery victims into submission. On raids of Chinese opium houses, he always butted the doors down. Other criminals were loathe to battle him but would eagerly join in his planned capers. Finally a would-be victim found a sure answer to Riley's thick skull and shot him. *The King of the Hoodlums* survived, but his health and stamina were ruined, and he soon degenerated into a run-of-the-mill thug, no longer to be feared. He later disappeared from the San Francisco scene.

RIMBAUD, ARTHUR (1854–1891)

One of the most promising poets of the French Symbolist movement, Arthur Rimbaud was known as *The Infant Casanova* because of his homosexual liaisons as a teenager, especially with the poet Paul Verlaine. Young Rimbaud was the domineering force in the affair, although Verlaine later shot him in the hand and went to prison for two years for the crime. Thereafter Rimbaud, who spurned a reconciliation with Verlaine when the latter was released, completely abandoned poetry in his early twenties and spent most of the rest of his short life as a mercenary adventurer.

Ringlets—See CUSTER, GEORGE ARMSTRONG.

RIPLEY, ROBERT (1893–1949)

Oddity collector Robert Ripley was called *The Believe-It-or-Not Man,* after the title of his cartoon column. He was also known as *The Modern Marco Polo* because of his wide travels in search of the unusual and bizarre. But his favorite nickname was *The Biggest Liar in the World,* which was how many readers addressed contributions to his column, all of which were delivered to him. It should be noted that nothing was used as a "Believe-It-or-Not" feature until it was authenticated.

RIPON, MARQUESS OF (1827–1909)

Besides being an important British statesman in the late 19th century, the Marquess of Ripon achieved the reputation of being the greatest hunter of all time. Between 1867 and 1900, according to his secretary's hunting expedition records, he shot 270,728 animals—everything from birds to rhinoceros—an average of 216 animals a week. Over his lifetime he undoubtedly killed a half million animals, and his monumental slaughter brought him the facetious sobriquet *The Animal Lover.* He was shooting birds on his estate in 1909 when he dropped dead at the age of 82.

RISKO, JOHNNY (1902–1953)

A leading heavyweight boxer in the 1920s and 1930s, Johnny Risko was called *The Rubber Man* for his indefatigability.

RITSON, JOSEPH (1752–1803)

An expert on ancient literature and poetry, Englishman Joseph Ritson was so vicious in his criticism of many poets of his day that he was dubbed *Sycorax,* or "demon." A man of narrow views, he was called *Anti-Scot* because he hated the very name of Scotsman. Still Sir Walter Scott was able through bland courtesy to cull from Ritson much of his valuable store of knowledge of antiquary topics. In jest Scott referred to him as *The Learned Cabbage-Eater,* a sobriquet that disarmed vegetarian Ritson.

Rival of Sappho, The—See LEWIS, ESTELLE ANNA BLANCHE ROBINSON.

RIVE, JEAN JOSEPH (1730–1791)

One of the great bibliographers of all time, Abbe Jean Joseph Rive was librarian to the Duc de la Valliere, a most prolific book collector. He was known as *The Bull-Dog of la Valliere* because the duke would trot him out to settle literary disputes, saying, "Gentlemen, I'll let loose my bull-dog." Rive was caustic in his criticisms of others and was famed for his gross abuse of leading characters of the day in his *Chasse aux Bibliographes.* Likened to a contemporary, English antiquary Joseph Ritson, who was as full of bile in his criticisms, Rive was often called *The French Ritson.*

RIVERA, DIEGO (1887–1957)

A Mexican muralist and supporter of communism, Diego Rivera was most famous for his painting of Lenin in New York's Radio City, which was ordered destroyed by Nelson Rockefeller. Nevertheless he was often castigated and dropped from membership by the Mexican Communist Party. He was dubbed *The Painter for Millionaires* in party publications. Finally readmitted to the party in 1955, he proceeded to embarrass it by embracing religion.

Riverboat Gambler, A—See JOHNSON, LYNDON B.

Rivet McClintic—See MCCLINTIC, JAMES V.

RIVLIN, ALICE MITCHELL (1931–)

As founding director of the Congressional Budget Office, Alice Rivlin has regularly offered economic predictions that are more pessimistic than those propounded by various presidents, infuriating in turn Richard Nixon, Gerald Ford, Jimmy Carter and Ronald Reagan and winning for herself the sobriquet *The Bearer of Bad News*. It must be observed that Mrs. Rivlin's predictions have generally been the more accurate.

RIZZO, FRANK L. (1920–)

Frank L. Rizzo, long-time police chief and then mayor of Philadelphia, was hailed by law enforcement hardliners as *The Toughest Cop in America*. Civil rights advocates were extremely critical of his tactics, citing as one example a case in which 10 Philadelphia policemen broke their nightsticks over a prostrate black man and Rizzo's comment that "it's easy to break some of these nightsticks nowadays."

Roaring Jack—See PERCIVAL, JOHN.

ROBERT I, DUKE OF NORMANDY (?–1035)

Robert I, duke of Normandy, was called *Robert the Devil* by his foes because of both his daring

and cruelty. He himself preferred, and thus was called by many, *Robert the Magnificent*.

ROBERT II, DUKE OF NORMANY—See Curthose.

Robert the Devil—See ROBERT I, DUKE OF NORMANDY.

Robert the Hermit (?–1832)

One of the most famous hermits in American history, *Robert the Hermit* of Massachusetts was buffeted by the fates. Born to an African mother and a white man in New Jersey, he was a bonded slave who bought his freedom, only to be tricked and shipped to a foreign slave market. He finally escaped and made his way back to America. Discriminated and forced to separate from the woman he married, he finally withdrew from society and lived for many years in a hermitage near the Washington Bridge at Seekonk, Mass., refusing thereafter to communicate with other people.

Robert the Magnificent—See ROBERT I, DUKE OF NORMANDY.

Robert the Pious: ROBERT II OF FRANCE (970?–1031)

Robert II, king of France, was called *Robert the Pious* even though he was constantly incurring papal displeasure because of his attitudes on his marriages and sex in general. A contemporary chronicler described him as "a man of excellent, honest and great piety, the ornament of clerks, the nourisher of monks, the father of the poor, the assiduous server of the true God, a king not only of people but even of their morals." This last attribute was illustrated one day when the king was on his way to church and passed two lovers embracing too enthusiastically in full view of passersby. Without a word *Robert the Pious* covered them with his cloak and continued on to attend Mass.

ROBERTSON, GEORGE HEPBURN (1885–1955)

George Hepburn Robertson, pioneer automobile racing driver who won the Vanderbilt Cup in 1908, is remembered as *The First Great Racer*.

ROBESON, PAUL (1898–1977)

Singer, actor and black activist Paul Robeson, who spent much of his adult life willingly and unwillingly outside the United States, was often referred to by certain patriotic types as *The Dark Cloud* for his left-wing activities. The nickname was originally bestowed on him by admiring sportswriters during his college days at Rutgers, where he was a four-letter athlete and an All-American football player before going on to fame in the artistic world.

ROBESPIERRE, MAXIMILIEN FRANCOIS MARIE ISIDORE DE (1758–1794)

Robespierre, the famed leader of the French Revolution, was known as *The Incorruptible* as he doomed all he thought deserving during the Reign of Terror until he himself, facing enemies on all sides in the Convention, went to the guillotine.

Robespierre Marat Fitzthunder—See **SHAW, GEORGE BERNARD.**

Robin Hood of Texas, The—See **BASS, SAM.**

Robin Hood of the Forest, The—See **ALLEN, ETHAN.**

Robin the Trickster—See **HARLEY, ROBERT.**

ROBINSON, BROOKS (1937–)

During his career long-time third baseman for the Baltimore Orioles Brooks Robinson was considered to be the best at that position and was admiringly called *The Human Vacuum Cleaner*.

ROBINSON, FREDERICK (1782–1859)

A member of Parliament, Frederick Robinson became known as *Prosperity Robinson* when he boasted in a speech in 1825 of the great prosperity Britain was enjoying. Almost immediately a financial crisis followed. Robinson, later Viscount Goderich, was also called *Goosey Goderich* in derision of his abilities as a statesman.

ROBINSON, MRS. MARY DARBY— See Fair Perdita.

ROBINSON, "Sugar" RAY (1920–)

Regarded by many experts as pound-for-pound the greatest boxer of all time, Ray Robinson, former welterweight and middleweight champion, was nicknamed *Sugar* after a sportswriter, awed by his ring artistry, described him as "The sweetest fighter . . . sweet as sugar."

ROBUSTI, JACOPO (1518–1594)

An accomplished Venetian painter, Jacopo Robusti was nicknamed *The Thunderbolt of Painting* and *Il Furioso* because he turned out his works at a furious pace.

Rock of Notre Dame, The—See ROCKNE, KNUTE.

ROCKEFELLER, JOHN D. (1839–1937)

Billionaire John D. Rockefeller accumulated incredible profits by ruthlessly crushing his competition in the oil-refining business, but he always insisted his wealth came from God. The tag *"God-gave-me-my-money"* Rockefeller was pinned on him by his detractors and stuck even in later years when he turned into America's greatest philanthropist, giving away an estimated $550 million. Nevertheless a number of charities refused to accept what they regarded as Rockefeller's tainted money.

ROCKEFELLER, NELSON (1908–1979)

Nelson A. Rockefeller, long-time governor of New York and vice president under Gerald Ford, was well known as just plain *Rocky*. Because he was a millionaire and thus judged by the public to be immune to graft-taking, he was often called *Mr. Clean*. Right-wing Republicans who bridled at his big-spending programs referred to him as *The Spendthrift of Albany*. during his years as governor.

Rocket, The—See RICHARD, MAURICE.

ROCKNE, KNUTE (1888–1931)

Knute Rockne, the famed football coach of Notre Dame, was nicknamed by the press *The Rock of Notre Dame* and *The Great Man*.

Rocky—See ROCKEFELLER, NELSON.

RODERICK (c. 710)

Roderick, the last king of the West-Gothic kingdom of Spain in the early 8th century, was called *The Last of the Goths*. He was immortalized 11 centuries later in Robert Southey's poem "Roderick, the Last of the Goths."

RODGERS, JAMES CHARLES "Jimmy" (1897–1933)

Destined to become *The Father of Country Music*, with record sales exceeding 20 million, James Charles "Jimmy" Rodgers began singing full time in 1927 only after tuberculosis forced him to quit a succession of jobs as a railroad brakeman. In a whirlwind career, *The Singing Brakeman*, as he was called, turned out one hit record after another until he succumbed to his illness in 1933.

ROEBUCK, JOHN ARTHUR (1801–1879)

English politician John Arthur Roebuck was nicknamed *Tear 'em* by his friends for his fierceness in debates.

ROGERS, GEORGE W. (1898–1958)

In 1934 George W. Rogers became famous as the heroic ship's radioman in the *Morro Castle* disaster who kept sending SOS messages with flames licking at his feet until aid finally arrived. Nineteen years later he was convicted of robbing and murdering an 83-year-old man and his 58-year-old daughter and was dubbed by the press *The Tarnished Hero*. After his death in 1958, researchers turned up considerable evidence that Rogers may well have started the fire aboard the *Morro Castle* which killed 134 people.

ROGERS, ROY (1912–   )

Long-time cowboy movie star Roy Rogers was called *Hollywood's Straightest Straight-Shooter* because no breath of scandal was ever attached to him. He was reputedly as pure as his horse Trigger, and he once said, "When my time comes, just skin me and put me right up there on Trigger, just as if nothing had ever changed."

ROGERS, SAMUEL (1762–1855)

A banker and patron of the arts, Samuel Rogers was called *The Last English Maecenas,* after the Roman patron of Horace and Virgil. An accomplished poet himself, he was also referred to as *The Nestor of English Authors,* after the Homeric hero venerated for his age and wisdom.

ROGERS, WILL (1879–1935)

Humorist, actor and author Will Rogers was considered one of America's foremost homegrown wits. Called *The Cowboy Philosopher,* he was even, for a time, touted for the Democratic presidential nomination.

ROLAND, JEANNE MANON PHILIPON (1754–1793)

The muse of the republicans during the French Revolution, the tragic Madame Roland was called *The Circe of the Revolution.* Her house was used as a meeting place by the republicans for a time. When the Girondists were proscribed, her husband managed to escape from Paris, but during the Reign of Terror, Madame Roland went to the guillotine. She remains famous for her last words, uttered when she paused to contemplate a statue of Liberty that had been erected nearby. "Liberty," she said, "what crimes are committed in thy name."

When her husband heard of Madame Roland's death, he committed suicide.

ROLFE, LOUISE (fl. 1925–1936)

Louise Rolfe, the lady friend of Chicago gangster Machine Gun Jack McGurn, a suspect in the infamous St. Valentine's Day Massacre, was dubbed *The Blonde Alibi* by the press because she insisted McGurn was with her at the time of the killings. When she later retracted the statement, McGurn, who had told the same story, was charged with perjury. McGurn promptly married Louise, thus making it impossible for her to change her story, since a wife may not testify against her husband.

ROLLS, CHARLES STEWART (1877–1910)

British automobile manufacturer, racing driver and pilot Charles Stewart Rolls created, with Sir Frederick Henry Royce, the Rolls-Royce Motor Co. Rolls crossed the English Channel by airplane in 1910 and later that year was killed in the first British airplane crash. Thereafter he was called *The First English Victim of Aviation.*

ROMAN, JOHAN HELMICH (1694–1758)

Swedish violinist and composer Johan Helmich Roman composed Sweden's first instrumental vocal works comparable with the mainstream of European music and was designated *The Father of Swedish Music.*

Roman Beau Brummel, A—See PETRONIUS, CAIUS.

Roman Chaucer, The—See ENNIUS, QUINTUS.

Roman Thucydides, The—See SALLUST, CAIUS CRISPUS.

ROMANOFF, "Prince" MICHAEL: HARRY GERGUSON (1890–1971)

Harry Gerguson was a Hollywood personality and a grand impostor who posed in the 1920s and 1930s as *Prince of All the Russias* and the son of Czar Nicholas II. Although he passed countless bogus checks and pulled innumerable swindles, it was agreed that he was a likable rogue. With the backing of many celebrity friends, the grand impostor opened a Hollywood restaurant in 1940 that became a smashing success, famed for being able to satisfy the most cultivated of palates.

Romeo Coates—See COATES, ROBERT.

Rome's Greatest Pope—See GREGORY THE GREAT, ST.

ROMMEL, ERWIN (1891–1944)

Field Marshal Erwin Rommel, undoubtedly the greatest German Army general in World War II, won acclaim by foe and friend alike as *The Desert Fox* because of his sly maneuvers as head of the Afrika Korps in North Africa.

Ronald Ray Gun—See REAGAN, RONALD.

RONSARD, PIERRE DE (1524–1585)

The French poet Pierre de Ronsard, who introduced a classical element to his country's poetry, was himself placed on a pedestal of near divinity, being hailed as *The First Lyrist of France,*

The French Chaucer, The Horace of France, The King of Poets, The Pindar of France and, perhaps most lavishly, *The Poet of the Future*. While he must be credited with seeing the need to raise French verse above the creeping tone of the allegorical rhymers, he was not *The Poet of the Future,* and his work is largely ignored today.

ROOSEVELT, ELEANOR (1884–1962)

Eleanor Roosevelt, the wife of President Franklin Roosevelt, attracted almost as much adulation and invective as did her husband during their White House years. To her supporters she was *The Assistant President, The World's Most Admired Woman* and *Public Energy Number One,* and to FDR *My Eyes and Ears.* Nazi Germany's Joseph Goebbels, one of her detractors on the far right, nicknamed her *The Figure of Fun* and columnist Westbrook Pegler referred to her as *Hatchet Face*.

ROOSEVELT, FRANKLIN D. (1882–1945)

Franklin D. Roosevelt, or FDR, 32nd president of the United States, was always *That Man in the White House* to his political foes. Others called him *The Houdini in the White House* for the way he dominated Congress, especially in the early years of the New Deal. In 1939 Roosevelt was dubbed *The Sphinx* as he toyed with the press and others about whether or not he would seek a third term.

ROOSEVELT, JAMES (1907–   )

Because he was utilized by his father, President Franklin Roosevelt, for many duties, including for a time those of administrative assistant and press secretary, James Roosevelt was denounced by Republicans as *The Crown Prince of the New Deal,* on the theory that his father was determined to have James succeed him in office. Perhaps a fairer sobriquet was that offered by the news media, which referred to him as *A Modern Mercury* because of all the messages and coordinating information he supplied to the president.

ROOSEVELT, QUENTIN (1897–1918)

President Theodore Roosevelt's aviator son, Quentin Roosevelt was called *Quentin the Eagle.* He died in action in 1918 during World War I.

ROOSEVELT, THEODORE (1858–1919)

Theodore Roosevelt, 28th president of the United States, had many nicknames. The admiring ones included *The Trustbuster,* for his actions against big-business monopolies, *The Happy Warrior* and *The Rough Rider,* the latter for his Spanish-American War activities. Among the negative sobriquets were *Theodore the Meddler,* a Wall Street standby, and *That Damned Cowboy,* given him by Republican National Chairman Mark Hanna. Because he had his hunting rifles equipped with telescopes, western cowboys called him *Telescope Teddy.* In 1912 he was asked about his health and replied, ''I am as strong as a bull moose.'' He was thereafter called *The Bull Moose,* and that became the name of a political party, the ''Bull Moose Party'' (officially the Progressive Party), through which he made an independent run for the presidency. His most colorful nicknames, however, derived from his days as a police commissioner in New York City in the mid-1890s. Because most policemen seldom fulfilled their tours of duty, Roosevelt took to making nocturnal saunters to ferret out delinquent patrolmen. These night patrols delighted the citizenry and he was dubbed *Haroun-al-Roosevelt,* after the caliph of the *Arabian Nights* who stalked Baghdad after dark. However, his popularity vanished when he insisted on enforcing a long-ignored statute forbidding the sale of alcohol on Sundays, and he was labeled *Patron Saint of Dry Sundays* by much of the press. The especially enraged *Evening Journal* of William Randolph Hearst called him *King Roosevelt I.* Most incensed of all were the German voters, who, deprived of their weekend beer fests, for the first time abandoned their Republican allegiance to vote out the reformer rascals and restore Tammany Hall Democrats to power. German voters wanted no *Patron Saint of Dry Sundays* in their city, although they acknowledged that so moral a man deserved higher office, and they subsequently showed no reluctance to vote for Roosevelt when he ran for governor of the state and later for president of the United States.

ROOT, GLADYS TOWLES (1905–1982)

Flamboyant U.S. lawyer Gladys Towles Root was was often dubbed *The Defender of the Damned,* a sobriquet previously applied to Clarence Darrow. Her colorful attire, featuring towering hats and furs, drew as much notice as her legal tactics and won for her the additional nickname *The Hedda Hopper of the Criminal Courts,* after the Hollywood columnist famed for her hats.

ROSE, BILLY (1899–1966)

U.S. theatrical producer and songwriter Billy Rose was nicknamed by critics *The Basement Barnum,* after the renowned circus showman and producer.

Rose Man of Sing Sing—See CHAPIN, CHARLES.

Rose of Cimarron: ROSA DUNN (1878?–?)

Rosa Dunn has often been identified as the fabled *Rose of Cimarron,* the outlaw teenage heroine who in 1893 in the Oklahoma Territory supposedly came to the rescue of her wounded lover, Bitter Creek Newcomb, shielding him with her body from lawmen's bullets and shooting their way to safety. So much for the legend, if it ever happened. If Rosa was the legendary *Rose of Cimarron,* her romance with Newcomb did not have a storybook ending. It is a matter of record that Rosa's brothers shot Bitter Creek dead in 1895 and toted his corpse to town to collect a reward. As for *Rose of Cimarron?* Shortly thereafter she married another.

ROSECRANS, WILLIAM STARKE (1819–1898)

During the Civil War Union soldiers under Gen. William S. Rosecrans nicknamed their leader *Old Rosy,* not simply in a play on his name but an allusion to his red-faced appearance as well.

ROSENBERG, JULIUS (1918–1953) and ETHEL (1915–1953)

Convicted in 1951 of transmitting atomic bomb secrets to the USSR, Julius and Ethel Rosenberg were dubbed *The Atomic Traitors.*

ROSENMAN, SAMUEL I. "Sammy the Rose" (1896–1973)

Judge Samuel I. Rosenman, President Franklin Roosevelt's top speech writer, was nicknamed *Sammy the Rose.* To Roosevelt's opponents the sobriquet meant that Rosenman applied the magic to the New Deal programs "to make them smell sweet." He was also referred to as the president's *No. 1 Brain Truster.*

ROSENTHAL, A. M. (1922–   )

As a rising editor on the *New York Times,* A. M. Rosenthal, who became the executive editor, in-

volved himself in everything. *Times*man Harrison Salisbury dubbed him *Kochleffl,* a Yiddish word for ladle. "That was Rosenthal—the *kochleffl* stirring up the poet," Salisbury said.

ROSENTHAL, LEONARD—See Pearl King of the World.

ROSSER, THOMAS LAFAYETTE (1836–1910)

For his defense of Virginia's Shenandoah Valley during the Civil War, Thomas Lafayette Rosser was called by Confederates *The Saviour of the Valley.* This sobriquet was very difficult for Rosser to live up to despite a number of victories. In 1864 Rosser's command was put to rout at the Battle of Woodstock in a disaster the Union celebrated as the "Woodstock Races." The defeat totally destroyed *The Saviour of the Valley*'s reputation.

ROSSINI, GIOACCHINO (1792–1868)

The great Italian composer Gioacchino Rossini was known in jest as *The Lazy,* especially after he wrote the score for *The Barber of Seville* in eight days. He did much or most of his work lying in bed, and it was said that if a sheet of paper fluttered away, he preferred to write something else rather than retrieve it.

ROTHSTEIN, ARNOLD (1882–1928)

For about 15 years before his murder, Arnold Rothstein was known as the top criminal mastermind in New York City, being dubbed *Mr. Big, The Brain, The Fixer, The Big Bankroll* and *The Man Uptown.* Operating behind the scenes, he bankrolled many of the enterprises of various underworld kingpins, such as Waxey Gordon, Legs Diamond and Lucky Luciano. In the 1920s he was reputed to have had so much political clout that he could fix any bootlegging charge, and in fact during his time, out of 6,902 bootlegging-related cases scheduled for trial in New York courts, 400 never went to trial and 6,074 were dismissed. *The Brain* was also said to have played a role in the 1919 Black Sox baseball scandal, which involved the fixing of that year's World Series. It is known that the plotters came to Rothstein for financing, but whether he gave it or not is unclear. Instead, it is generally believed that he assumed the fixers would succeed, so he simply bet $270,000 on the underdog, Cincinnati, and won $600,000 without taking part in the conspiracy.

ROTRON, JEAN DE (1609–1650)

Jean de Rotron is sometimes called *The Founder of the French Theatre,* although he is better remembered for improvements in the scenery and the general conduct of the stage rather than his dramatic works, which may be described as on the heavy side although still superior to what preceeded them in France.

Rottenest American, The—See FONDA, JANE.

ROUGET DE LISLE, CLAUDE JOSEPH (1760–1836)

As a young officer during the French Revolution, Claude Joseph Rouget de Lisle was dubbed *The Father of the Marseillaise* for composing the French national anthem. The anthem gained its name when it was sung by a group of revolutionaries from Marseilles as they marched into Paris.

Rough on Rats Valentine—See VALENTINE, LEWIS J.

Rough Rider, The—See ROOSEVELT, THEODORE.

Roundsman of the Lord—See COMSTOCK, ANTHONY.

ROUSSEAU, JEAN JACQUES (1712–1777)

French philosopher, novelist and political thinker Jean Jacques Rousseau was called *The Father of Sentiment* for his romantic sensibility expressed in his longing for closeness with nature. He was enormously influential in the rise of romanticism in literature and even music. To friends he was known as *The Melancholy Jacques* because of his morose nature and morbid feelings.

Rousseau of the Gutter, The—See RESTIF, NICOLAS EDME.

Rowboat Johnson—See JOHNSON, J. MONROE "Rowboat."

Rowdy Joe—See LOWE, JOSEPH "Rowdy Joe."

Royal Black Sheep, The—See SNOWDON, LORD.

Royal Martyr, The—See CHARLES I.

Royal Midas, The—See DENNIS, JOHN.

Royalist Butcher, The—See LASSERAN-MASSENCOME, SEIGNEUR DE MONTLUC.

ROYALL, ANNE NEWPORT (1769–1854)

Writer and traveler Anne Newport Royall, noted for her outspoken views, may be considered the first of America's muckrakers, preceding that group of writers by more than half a century. The editor of a small newspaper in Washington, D.C., she specialized in uncovering graft in government. She was, among other things, an anti-Evangelical, a pro-Mason, an exponent of Sunday mail delivery, an advocate of tolerance of Roman Catholics and a supporter of the separation of church and state. Her many foes nicknamed her *Godless Anne Royall.*

ROZELLE, PETE (1926–   )

When Pete Rozelle was named commissioner of the National Football League at the age of 33, he was instantly dubbed by the press *The Child Commissioner.* The media was later to label him *Pete Doughsmell* in derogation of what many regarded as his overzealous attitude toward the financial success of the game. Needless to say, the team owners had a rather different opinion of his performance, dubbing him *Peter the Great.* Many players refer to him as *St. Peter* for what they consider his puritanical position on pro football players' morals.

Rubber Man, The—See RISKO, JOHNNY.

Rubber's Good Year—See GOODYEAR, CHARLES.

RUBENS, PETER PAUL (1577–1640)

Flemish artist Peter Paul Rubens was perhaps the most prolific major painters, turning out an incredi-ble number of masterpieces and becoming, as Delacroix called him, *The Homer of Painting.*

Rubens of Poetry, The—See SPENSER, EDMUND.

RUBINSTEIN, ARTUR (1889–1983)

Polish-American pianist Artur Rubinstein was nicknamed *The Playboy of the Piano.*

RUBINSTEIN, SERGE (1909–1955)

A notorious Russian financier-swindler, Serge Rubinstein made huge fortunes by manipulating U.S. and foreign companies' balance sheets, driving up the price of their stock shares by having them pay dividends they had not earned and then selling them short. With considerable lack of adulation, he was dubbed *The Boy Wonder of Wall Street.* After he was mysteriously murdered in 1955, it was said that the crime would never be solved because there were "too many suspects." The prediction has proved accurate.

RUBIROSA, PORFIRIO (1909–1965)

The international diplomat and playboy Porfirio Rubirosa was called *Toujours Pret,* or *Always Ready,* a sobriquet none of his lovers ever disputed. He ran through several headlined marriages—to Flor de Oro Trujillo, daughter of the Dominican Republic dictator; French actress Danielle Darrieux; tobacco heiress Doris Duke; and dime-store heiress Barbara Hutton—and had numerous scandalous affairs. At the age of 44, he said, "Never again will I marry for money." He didn't. He married a 19-year-old starlet, Odile Rodin, in 1957 and remained happily married until his death in an auto accident.

RUBY, JACK (1911–1967)

Dallas nightclub owner Jack Ruby, who shot and killed Lee Harvey Oswald, the man who assassinated President John F. Kennedy in 1963, was, naturally, dubbed *The Assassin's Assassin.* Many efforts have been made to portray Ruby's murder of Oswald as part of a wider conspiracy.

RUDOLPH II OF THE HOLY ROMAN EMPIRE (1552–1612)

Rudolph II, emperor of the Holy Roman Empire, was called *The Prince of Alchemy* for his support of various alchemists. He was also the patron of astronomers Johannes Kepler and Tycho Brahe.

RUGGLES, JOHN (1789–1874)

A senator from Maine, John Ruggles became known in 1836 as *The Father of the Patent Office* for leading the drive to correct the chaos then existing in the office and creating the Modern Patent Office with its efficient methods of investigating applications.

Run Forever Kolb—See KOLB, REUBEN FRANCIS.

RUNYON, DAMON (1880–1946)

Popular short-story writer and columnist Damon Runyon was often called *The Sentimental Cynic,* or as one critic put it, "the only writer who could sneer and cry at the same time."

RUPERT, PRINCE (1619–1682)

Prince Rupert, the nephew of Charles I of England, was called *The Mad Cavalier* because of his impetuous daring as the leader of the Royalist cavalry during the English Civil War.

Rupert of Debate, The—See STANLEY, LORD.

RUSKIN, JOHN (1819–1900)

Many considered British art critic, social reformer and author John Ruskin snobbish and moralistic to a fault. He set forth his ethical theories of art to offer ideas of order, imitation, beauty, truth and relationship. He saw more beauty in medieval art than in what he called the "pestilent art of the Renaissance." He propounded seven principles of perfect medieval art: sacrifice, truth, power, beauty, life, memory and obedience. Some called him *A Pope of Art,* but others, artists and critics with whom he disagreed, dubbed him *A Torquemada of Aesthetics,* after the first Spanish grand inquisitor.

RUSSELL, BERTRAND (1872–1970)

Bertrand Russell, the British philosopher, essayist and mathematician, was nicknamed *The Passionate Skeptic.* Starting as an idealist, he became a realist and logical atomist. Russell took many controversial stands on public issues. He was arrested during World War I for resisting conscription and in later years he was a most active opponent of the arms race.

RUSSELL, BILL (1934–   )

While the case of Jackie Robinson is most often cited in discussions about bigotry in professional sports, the ordeal of Bill Russell, the great basketball center for the Boston Celtics, was probably more grueling because of the proximity of basketball players to the crowd. The most common sobriquet that greeted him around the National

Basketball Association in his freshman year was *Black Nigger*.

RUSSELL, JOHN *(1740–1817)*

Rev. John Russell of Kilmarnock, Scotland was famed in his day as *Black Russell* both for his dark complexion and his gloomy, intolerant preaching, leading Robert Burns to write of him:

> Black Russell is no spairin:
> His piercing words, like Highlan swords,
>   Divide the joints an' marrow;
> His talk o' Hell, whare devils dwell,
>   Our vera souls does harrow.

RUSSELL, KEN *(1927–   )*

Controversial film maker Ken Russell is often called *The British Orson Welles*. However, a more accurate sobriquet is that of *The Film Maker Who Always Goes Just Too Far*. Typical of him was his selling of the idea of a movie biography of Tchaikovsky to Hollywood backers by describing it as "the story of a homosexual who married a nymphomaniac."

RUSSELL, WILLIAM E. *(1857–1896)*

Elected mayor of Cambridge, Mass., at the age of 28—during an era when younger men were less likely than today to win office—William E. Russell was affectionately referred to as *Billie the Kid* and *The Boy Mayor*.

RUSSELL, WILLIAM HEPBURN *(1812–1872)*

A pioneer in the express delivery business, William Hepburn Russell was called *The Father of the Pony Express,* which he helped form in 1860. Every pony express rider had to sign the following writ-ten oath: "I hereby swear before the great and living God that during my engagement and while I am an employee of Russell, Majors, and Waddell, I will under no circumstances use profane language; that I will not quarrel or fight with other employees of the firm, and that I will conduct myself honestly, be faithful to my duties, and so direct my acts as to win the confidence of my employers, so help me God." The spectacular enterprise went broke in less than two years, presumably more for economic reasons than for violations of the Russell-inspired oath.

RUSSELL, WILLIAM HOWARD *(1820–1907)*

A famous war correspondent sent by the London *Times* to cover the American Civil War, William H. Russell followed the Union Army to Bull Run and reported its subsequent debacle as he himself was caught up in the troops' panicky rout. His account of the North's inglorious actions angered a great many Northerners when it appeared later in the American press. He was caustically derided as *Bombast Russell* and *London Stout Russell*. He received many threatening letters; he was urged not to go out unarmed; and an angry sentinel nearly killed him. Passers-by on the street began taunting him with a nickname that would stick to him for life—*Bull Run Russell*. The next time the Union Army advanced, *Bull Run Russell* was not permitted to accompany it. Russell later covered the Franco-Prussian and Zulu wars, always with the same honest pen.

***Russian Byron, The*—See PUSHKIN, ALEXANDER.**

***Russian Cecil B. De Mille, The*—See EISENSTEIN, SERGEI.**

***Russian Connection, The*—See HAMMER, ARMAND.**

Russian Lion, The—See
HACKENSCHMIDT, GEORGE.

Russian Livy, The—See **KARAMZIN, NICHOLAS MIKHAELOVITCH.**

Russian Marquis de Sade—See
DOSTOEVSKI, FEODOR.

Russian Murat, The—See
MILORADOWITCH, MICHAEL.

Russian Thunderbolt, The—See
TURCHIN, JOHN BASIL.

Russian Voltaire, The—See
SOUMAROKOV, ALEXANDER PETROVITCH.

Russophobist, The—See
URQUHART, DAVID.

RUSTIN, BAYARD (1910–   )

One of the chief organizers of the 1963 March on Washington, black activist Bayard Rustin won renown as *The Socrates of the Civil Rights Movement.*

Ruth, Babe: GEORGE HERMAN RUTH (1894–1948)

Easily the most famous baseball player of all time, George Herman Ruth was nicknamed *The Mighty Bambino* and *The Sultan of Swat* in recognition of his great hitting ability. However, he was most famous as *Babe Ruth,* so much so that many people do not know his real name. A case in point was a woman contestant on a quiz show who gave the wrong answer when asked to give *Babe Ruth's* real name. She said it was *Babe Ruth.* Informed the right answer was George Herman Ruth, she snapped, "That's insane. Everybody knows his name was *Babe Ruth.*" The program was thrown into chaos for a time when she refused to leave the set, implying that she was being robbed. (See also Introduction.)

RUTH, GEORGE HERMAN—See
Ruth, Babe.

Rutherfraud B. Hayes—See **HAYES, RUTHERFORD B.**

RYAN, ABRAM JOSEPH (1840–1886)

A Roman Catholic chaplain in the Confederate Army, Abram Joseph Ryan won the sobriquet *The Poet of the Confederacy.* Among his best remembered poems are "The Conquered Banner" and "The Sword of Robert E. Lee."

RYAN, JOHN A. (1869–1945)

Roman Catholic churchman, writer and social welfare activist noted for his support of the policies of President Franklin Roosevelt, Monsignor John A. Ryan was referred to as *The Right Reverend New Dealer,* with differing emphasis by friend and foe.

RYAN, NOLAN (1947–   )

Baseball pitcher Nolan Ryan, who has pitched several no-hit games, was dubbed *No-Hit Nolan* by the New York press corps as a way of needling the New York Mets for having traded him away.

RYMER, THOMAS (1639–1714)

Thomas Rymer, who founded in English literature what may be considered the classical or French school of criticism, was dubbed *Shakespeare's Critic*. It was meant as a disparagement, or as Disraeli put it, an "unlucky distinction."

Ryparographer, The—See PYRICUS.

S

SABATH, ADOLPH JOACHIM (1866–1952)

Adolph Joachim Sabath was nicknamed *The Dean of the House,* having served 23 terms in Congress as a representative from Illinois, more than any other member to date. He had been elected to his 24th term a few days before his death on Nov. 6, 1952.

SABATH, JOSEPH (1869–1956)

A Chicago Superior Court justice from 1910 to 1952, Joseph Sabath granted an estimated 70,000 to 90,000 divorces, gaining the sobriquet *The Divorce Judge*. He was more proud of the fact that he had reconciled some 10,000 couples.

SACHS, EDWARD (1927–1964)

U.S. professional auto racer Eddy Sachs was nicknamed *The Pixie of Gasoline Alley* and *The Clown Prince of Racing*—for his behavior off the speedway. During races he was known as a safe and reliable driver. In the 1964 Indianapolis 500, rookie driver Dave MacDonald's car hit the wall and burst into flames, and Sachs crashed into it. Both drivers died.

SACHS, HANS (1494–1578)

The 16th century German poet Hans Sachs was dubbed *The Prince of Satirists*. Turning his poetical barbs against much of the establishment, he called the clergy and the jurists "the pests of the nation" and railed against the nobility for ignoring the general good. He supported Luther, and his writings are considered one of the prime movers of the Protestant cause at that time.

Sackbearer—See AMMONIUS.

SADAT, ANWAR (1918–1981)

Anwar Sadat, the Egyptian leader who made peace with Israel, rose from obscurity within the revolutionary movement, dominated by Gamal Abdel Nasser, that overthrew King Farouk. Before Nasser's death Sadat was referred to as *Nasser's Poodle* and *Colonel Yes-Yes,* and many backed him for the presidency because it was thought he could be manipulated. Instead Sadat proved a strongwilled leader who led Egypt in new directions. He was assassinated in 1981.

Saddle-Bag John—See POPE, JOHN.

SADE, MARQUIS DE: DONATIEN ALPHONSE FRANCOIS (1740–1814)

The Marquis de Sade was a handsome little Frenchman who became infamous for his orgies, during which he whipped and sodomized young women, becoming notorious as *The Fanatic of Vice*. He was imprisoned by royal decree and lived out his final years in an asylum. His legacy to the world is the word "sadism."

SADI, MOSLEHEDIN *(c. 13th century)*

One of the foremost poets of Persia, Sheik Moslehedin Sadi, author of the *Gulistan,* was celebrated as *The Nightingale of a Thousand Songs*. Students of literature have dubbed him *The Oriental Homer*.

Sadie the Goat *(c. mid-1800s)*

One of the most fearsome female gangsters in 19th century New York was a ruthless battler known only by her nickname, *Sadie the Goat*. Among other things *Sadie the Goat* was a vicious Hudson River pirate and a skilled night-time mugger. Her method of disabling a victim was to lower her head and butt him goat fashion in the stomach or chest, stunning him to the extent that he could be clubbed unconscious. Sadie was then able to rifle his pockets at her leisure.

SAGE, ANNA: ANA CUMPANAS *(1891–1947)*

A Chicago madam, Anna Sage, born Ana Cumpanas, led public enemy John Dillinger into a fatal FBI ambush outside a Chicago movie theater. She was dubbed *The Lady in Red* because of the outfit she wore as an identification (actually it was orange). She was given the reward money due her and then deported to her native Rumania.

Sage and Serious Spenser—See SPENSER, EDMUND.

Sage of Auburn, The—See SEWARD, WILLIAM.

Sage of Baltimore, The—See MENCKEN, HENRY LOUIS.

Sage of Chappaqua, The—See GREELEY, HORACE.

Sage of Concord, The—See EMERSON, RALPH WALDO.

Sage of Down House, The—See DARWIN, CHARLES.

Sage of Emporia, The—See WHITE, WILLIAM ALLEN.

Sage of Gramercy Park, The—See TILDEN, SAMUEL J.

Sage of Greystone, The—See TILDEN, SAMUEL J.

Sage of Monticello, The—See JEFFERSON, THOMAS.

Sage of Montpelier, The—See MADISON, JAMES.

Sage of Roanoke, The—See RANDOLPH (OF ROANOKE), JOHN.

Sage of Sinnissippi, The—See LOWDEN, FRANK O.

Sage of the Hermitage, The—See JACKSON, ANDREW.

Sage of Uvalde, The—See GARNER, JOHN NANCE "Cactus Jack."

Sage of Walden Pond, The—See THOREAU, HENRY DAVID.

Sage of Wheatland, The—See BUCHANAN, JAMES.

SAILER, TONI (1935–   )

Austrian Toni Sailer, one of the popular skiers in the 1956 Winter Olympics, competed against a fellow skier from his hometown of Kitzbuehl, Anderl Molterer, who was heralded as a top skier. Called The White Blitz from Kitz, Molterer seemingly wrapped up the 1.7-mile giant slalom in a best time of 3 minutes 6.3 seconds. However, Sailer bettered that mark by a full six seconds, and sportswriters hurriedly came up with a new sobriquet: *The Younger Blitz from Kitz.*

Sailor Kelly—See KELLY, ALVIN "Shipwreck."

Sailor with a Flawed Cutlass, The—See JELLICOE, JOHN RUSHWORTH.

Saint, The—See EDWARD VI OF ENGLAND; HENRY II, KING OF GERMANY AND HOLY ROMAN EMPEROR; OLAV II.

Saint Evita—See PERON, EVA.

St. Henry—See HENRY II, KING OF GERMANY AND HOLY ROMAN EMPEROR.

St. Peter—See ROZELLE, PETE.

SAINTE-BEUVE, CHARLES AUGUSTIN (1804–1869)

French author C. A. Sainte-Beuve became known as *The Don Juan of Literature* because he embraced so many ideas and literary idols. Invariably his enthusiasm for a subject cooled to the point of indifference, and he moved on to new thoughts, much as a Don Juan moved from one sexual conquest to another.

Sainte-Beuve of English Criticism, The— See ARNOLD, MATTHEW.

Saintlike S.O.B., The—See GOFF, JOHN W.

SAIONJI, PRINCE KIMMOCHI (1849–1940)

Prince Kimmochi Saionji, Japanese statesman, was called *The Last Genro,* because he was the last Genro, or elder statesman, associated with Emperor Jeiji. As chief adviser to Emperor Hirohito, he was often referred to as *The Westerner* because of his westernizing influence on the Japanese state.

SAKHAROV, ANDREI DMITRIEVICH (1921–   )

Known as *The Father of the Soviet Hydrogen Bomb,* physicist Andrei Sakharov became a leading Soviet political dissident, demanding intellectual freedom in the USSR and advocating nuclear disarmament. He won the Nobel Peace Prize in 1975.

SALADIN (1138–1193)

Saracen warrior and ruler Saladin stemmed the tide of the Western conquest of the East, uniting the Moslem world in a holy war against the Christians. He was pitted against Richard the Lion-Hearted in the Third Crusade. Richard represented the beau-ideal of Christian knighthood and Saladin was his Moslem counterpart. The Christians acknowledged their foe as *The Chivalrous Saracen* and often told the story of Saladin, seeing Richard unhorsed, sending him a charger, saying he would not see so worthy an opponent without a mount. The bishop of Salisbury told Saladin: "If anyone could give your noble qualities to King Richard, and his to you . . . then the whole world would not furnish two such princes." Despite his chivalry Saladin did not waver in his hatred of Christians, urging his people, "Let us purge the air they breathe." He promised to carry the struggle into Europe "until there shall not remain on the face of this earth one unbeliever in God." The Peace of Ramleh in 1192 ended the Crusades, and Saladin died the following year, thus prevented from carrying his holy war into Christian territories.

Sales, Soupy: MILTON HINES (1926–)

Children's TV show comic Soupy Sales was nicknamed *Soupy* as a child because his real name was Milton Hines and his last name sounded like Heinz, the maker of canned soups among other things. When he entered show business, a radio station insisted he change his last name because Soupy Hines sounded like a plug for Heinz.

Salesman Deluxe, The—See HAMMER, ARMAND.

Salic, The—See CONRAD II, KING OF GERMANY AND HOLY ROMAN EMPEROR.

SALIEGE, JULES-GERAUD—See Prelate of Resistance.

SALISBURY, HARRISON (1908–)

In the editorial infighting at the *New York Times,* the newspaper's long-time Moscow correspondent Harrison Salisbury became known as *Rasputin.* As one newsman put it, "Salisbury spent so many years watching who was standing next to Stalin that now *he's* standing next to Stalin!"

SALLUST, CAIUS CRISPUS (85–35 BC)

In his day the great Roman historian Caius Crispus Sallust was celebrated as *The Roman Thucydides.* Many experts in later generations and centuries have felt he far excelled his model.

Saltwater Johnston—See JOHNSTON, JAMES A.

Sam the Torch—See SCARLOW, SAMUEL.

Sammy Glick of the Cold War, The—See KISSINGER, HENRY.

SAMPSON, DEBORAH (1760–1827)

Deborah Sampson, an American soldier in the Revolutionary War, was nicknamed *Molly* by her fellow soldiers because she had no trace of a beard. They did not suspect she was a woman in disguise. After she had been wounded several times, her true identity was revealed and she was honorably discharged. Another nickname, *The Amorous Amazon*, was accorded her because during her service she had been so ardently pursued by the ladies. Highly popular, she lectured widely after the Revolution on the subject of patriotism and the rigors of war. In 1805, following a campaign by her friend Paul Revere, who assured congressmen she was ''a woman of handsome talents, good morals, a dutiful wife and affectionate parent,'' she was granted a pension of $4 a month. The amount was doubled in 1818. Her death in 1827 was attributed to her war wounds.

Samuel Adams of New Jersey, The—See FISHER, HENDRICK.

Samuel Adams of North Carolina, The—See HARNETT, CORNELIUS.

Samurai Scholar, The—See HAYAKAWA, SAMUEL I.

SANCHEZ, ILICH RAMIREZ—See Carlos the Jackal.

SANCHO I OF PORTUGAL (1154–1212)

Portuguese king Sancho I was one of the most peaceful rulers of the Iberian peninsula. The interests and activities of this monarch, described by scribes as a prudent and beneficient ruler, are well summed up in his sobriquet *The City Builder*.

Sand Lot Orator, The—See KEARNEY, DENIS.

SANDBY, PAUL (1725–1809)

English artist Paul Sandby became celebrated as *The Father of English Watercolor*.

SANDERS, CARL (1925–   )

After failing to win the Georgia gubernatorial nomination in 1966 running as an urbane moderate, Jimmy Carter switched his technique in the 1970 race for governor, de-emphasizing his liberal credentials and running against the ''establishment power brokers'' and ''the big-money boys.'' His main opponent was a moderate, urbane and well-groomed former governor, Carl Sanders. Carter nicknamed his natty opponent *Cufflinks Carl*. The unwanted sobriquet stuck to Sanders and he was soundly trounced in a runoff.

SANDERS, DOUGLAS (1933–   )

U.S. professional golfer Doug Sanders, noted for his dapper dress, is called *Pro Golf's Beau Brummel*.

SANDERS, HARLAND "Colonel" (1891–1981)

Harland Sanders, better known as *Colonel Sanders*, was called *The Fried Chicken King*. His secret recipe for fried chicken revolutionized America's fast-food eating habits.

SANTERRE, ANTOINE JOSEPH (1752–1809)

Antoine Joseph Santerre, a general during the French revolution, was dubbed by the people *The Frothy General* since he had previously been a brewer.

SAPERSTEIN, ABE (1901–1966)

Abe Saperstein, founder of the Harlem Globe-trotters comedy basketball team, was dubbed *The Barnum of Basketball*. However, he must be credited with helping to gain the acceptance of black basketball players by professional sports fans, and several players went from his teams to the National Basketball Association.

Sappho—See MONTAGU, MARY WORTLEY.

Sardanapalus of China, The—See CHEOTSIN.

SARGENT, JOHN SINGER (1856–1925)

While he was the most sought-after portraitist of his time in both Europe and the United States, John Singer Sargent was constantly parodied by fellow artist James McNeill Whistler, who dubbed him *A Sepulchre of Dullness and Propriety*.

Sarong Girl, The—See LAMOUR, DOROTHY.

Satchmo—See ARMSTRONG, LOUIS.

Sausage Man, The—See GODOY, MANUEL DE.

Sausage-Maker Murderer, The—See LUETGERT, ADOLPH.

Savior of European Peace, The—See CHAMBERLAIN, NEVILLE.

Savior of His Country, The—See OATES, TITUS; PICHEGRU, CHARLES; WASHINGTON, GEORGE.

Savior of Little Round Top—See WARREN, GOUVERNEUR K.

Savior of the Nations—See WELLINGTON, ARTHUR WELLESLEY, FIRST DUKE OF.

Saviour of the Valley, The—See ROSSER, THOMAS LAFAYETTE.

SAVONAROLA, GIROLAMO (1452–1498)

A Dominican monk reformer who in the late 15th century preached against church and state corruption, Girolamo Savonarola helped break the power of the Medici and became spiritual leader and virtual dictator of Florence. He was denounced by the Vatican as *The Meddlesome Friar*. Finally Pope Alexander VI excommunicated him in 1497. He was charged with heresy, arrested, brutally tortured, subjected to a biased trial and burned at the stake. In later years he was designated as *The First Great Protestant*.

Sawdust Caesar, The—See GOERING, HERMANN.

Say Hey—See MAYS, WILLIE.

SCARLOW, SAMUEL (1888–?)

Russian-born U.S. professional arsonist Sam Scarlow was so admired by the underworld and the police for his abilities that he was dubbed *Sam the Torch*.

SCARNE, JOHN *(1903–)*

Regarded as today's foremost gambling authority, John Scarne is nicknamed *The Virtuous Card Shark* since he does not gamble professionally but instead provides advice to casinos and hotel chains on how to eliminate cheaters.

Scarsdale Diet Doctor, The—See TARNOWER, HERMAN.

SCHAARSCHMIDT, HANS—See Rat, The.

SCHIAPARELLI, ELSA *(1896–1972)*

Italian-French fashion designer Elsa Schiaparelli was dubbed *The Shocking One* for her daring innovations, especially the use of brilliant colors, particularly "shocking pink."

SCHICK, JACOB *(1877–1937)*

Jacob Schick gained fame as *The No-Nick Shave Man* after he invented the electric razor in 1923.

Schickelgruber—See HITLER, ADOLF.

SCHLAFLY, PHYLLIS *(1924–)*

Phyllis Schlafly, the conservative activist architect of the Equal Rights Amendment's defeat in 1982, is referred to as *The Sweetheart of the Silent Majority*. In that role, she announced, following her triumph over the ERA, that her new efforts will be on behalf of other conservative causes, such as a campaign against sex education: "Sex education is a principal cause of teen-age pregnancy." Another of her causes is a fight against a nuclear freeze: "The atomic bomb is a marvelous gift that was given to our country by a wise God."

Schlock Rock's Godzilla—See COOPER, ALICE.

SCHMIDT, HELMUT *(1918–)*

Former West German chancellor Helmut Schmidt was long hailed by supporters as *Der Macher,* or *The Doer*. Opponents tended to speak of him with disdain as *Super Schmidt*. Both friends and detractors felt *The Lip* was an apt nickname for the loquacious politician.

SCHMITT, HARRISON R. *(1935–)*

U.S. astronaut and later Republican senator from New Mexico, Harrison Schmitt was the first scientist to go into space. A geologist, he was labeled by his fellow astronauts *Dr. Rock*.

Schnozzola—See DURANTE, JIMMY.

SCHOLL, WILLIAM *(1882–1968)*

William Scholl, a shoemaker who became America's most famous "foot doctor," was nicknamed *The Foot Eazer,* after the name of his first arch support, one of many products he developed. He once described his personal credo in promoting his wares while walking from shoe store to shoe store: "Early to bed, early to rise, work like hell, and advertise."

Schoolgirl, The—See WILDE, OSCAR.

School-Master Camden—See CAMDEN, WILLIAM.

Schoolmaster in Politics, The—See WILSON, WOODROW.

Schoolmaster of Our Nation, The—See MCGUFFEY, WILLIAM HOLMES.

Schoolmaster of the Republic, The—See WEBSTER, NOAH.

Schoolmaster of Turkey, The—See ATATURK, MUSTAPHA KEMAL.

Schoolmiss Alfred—See TENNYSON, ALFRED LORD.

School-Mistress of France, The—See ALCUIN.

SCHOPENHAUER, ARTHUR (1788–1860)

Arthur Schopenhauer, the German philosopher, held that discord or strife is the basic feature of all human existence. Thus he was designated *The Philosopher of Disenchantment.*

SCHRODER-DEVRIENT, WILHELMINE (1804–1860)

The celebrated 19th century soprano Wilhelmine Schroder-Devrient, who was famous for her inter- pretations of Bellini and Gluck and was said to have inspired Wagner to write music drama, was called *The Queen of Tears* because of her dramatic genius in tragic roles.

SCHULENBURG, EHRENGARD MELUSINA VON DER (1667–1743)

Exceedingly unpopular with the British public, tall and thin Ehrengard Melusina von der Schulenburg, German mistress of George I, was labeled *The Maypole,* which infuriated the British monarch.

SCHULTZ, DAVE "the Hammer" (1949–   )

The most penalized player in U.S.-Canadian hockey history, Dave *"the Hammer"* Schultz, also known as *The Hockey Enforcer,* has long been cited by sports writers as an example of the type of player used by management to build up atten- dance with the promise of violence. The hockey establishment retaliated by barring Schultz from promoting his book on the subject during TV hockey game broadcasts.

SCHULZ, CHARLES M. (1922–   )

Cartoonist Charles M. Schulz, creator of the "Peanuts" comic strip, showed such total immer- sion in cartoons that in childhood he was nick- named *Sparky,* after the horse Sparkplug in the "Barney Google" comic strip, and *The Timid Soul,* from H. T. Webster's feature "Caspar Milque- toast."

SCHUMANN-HEINK, ERNESTINE (1861–1936)

Prague-born Ernestine Schumann-Heink, one of the most beloved members of the Metropolitan

Opera Company, was called *The Grand Old Lady of Opera*. Because of her generous appearances on countless occasions for U.S. troops during World War I, she gained what she said was her proudest nickname, *Mother of All the Doughboys*. Ironically, her sons fought on both sides of the great war, and one on each side died.

SCHURZ, CARL *(1829–1906)*

A political reformer who was appointed secretary of the interior in 1877 specifically to correct matters in the Indian Office, Carl Schurz was nicknamed *Ich-hon,* or *Big Eyes,* by the Cheyenne. Indian chiefs who visited Washington were amazed at how ignorant *Big Eyes* was of Indian affairs and how one with such enormous visual organs could see so little.

SCHUSTER, ARNOLD *(1928–1952)*

A 24-year-old Brooklyn clothing salesman, Arnold Schuster, became known as *The Good Citizen* when he was murdered after he had located a notorious bank robber, Willie "the Actor" Sutton, and caused his capture by police. Schuster's murder was ordered by Mafia leader Albert Anastasia, who had become enraged at the idea of a private citizen turning police informer.

SCHUYLER, PHILIP JOHN *(1733–1804)*

American Revolutionary War general Philip John Schuyler maintained his headquarters in Albany, N.Y. From there he kept close surveillance on British troops in the northern colonies, providing the American cause with much-needed intelligence and gaining for himself the sobriquet *The Great Eye*. However, he later led an unsuccessful expedition into Canada and resigned.

SCHWERIN, COUNT KURT CHRISTOPH *(1684–1757)*

Count Kurt Christoph Schwerin, a German field marshal who scored great victories at the Battle of Mollwitz in 1741 and in the Second Silesian War and the Seven Years' War, gained the nickname *The Little Marlborough* because his methods and record were similar to those of John Churchill, first duke of Marlborough and an English general.

SCIOPPIUS, GASPAR *(1576–1649)*

The German-born 17th century critic Gaspar Scioppius, one of the most formidable critics of his time, was noted for his invective. Born a Protestant, he converted to Catholicism but nevertheless heaped vicious abuse on the Jesuits. He was equally bitter toward the Protestants and especially James I of England, so much so that the attendants of the English ambassador to Spain once attacked and severely wounded him. *The Grammatical Cynic,* as he was called, bragged of the deaths or suicides of opponents that he caused, but by the end of his life he was fearful that he would find no refuge open to him. Disraeli later dubbed him *The Attila of Authors*.

SCOFFEL, KATHERINE *(1875–1926)*

Katherine Scoffel, the 26-year-old wife of the warden of the Allegheny County Jail in Pittsburgh, Pa., and mother of four, frequently brought religion to prisoners in the death cells and was called *The Angel of the Death Cells*. In one of the most storied crime scandals of the early 20th century, she fell in love with Ed Biddle, one of two brothers awaiting execution for murder. She helped the brothers escape and fled with them, but they were trapped by a posse some miles away in Butler, Pa., in a stolen sleigh. Both brothers were shot to death; Katherine survived a suicide-pact bullet wound from Ed Biddle. She was sentenced to two-years imprisonment in the same Allegheny County Jail. The press then referred to her as *The First Lady of the Jail*. For many years thereafter a popular melodrama called *The Biddle Boys* played to capacity houses.

Scorpion Stanley—See STANLEY, LORD.

Scotch Hobbema, The—See NASMYTH, PATRICK.

Scotch What d'ye Call—See BAILLIE, ROBERT.

SCOTT, ADAM (?–1529)

A Scottish robber, Adam Scott of Tushielaw was called *The King of the Border* and *The King of Thieves* because he ravaged the borderland of England and Scotland until he was caught and beheaded in 1529.

SCOTT, WALTER (1771–1832)

Scottish novelist Sir Walter Scott was the recipient of dozens of sobriquets and honorifics, such as *The Father of the Historical Novel, The Minstrel of the Border* and *The Wizard of the North*. He was also called *The Great Unknown* in allusion to his authorship of the Waverly Novels, which was not revealed until 1827. Thrown deeply in debt by the failure of ambitious publishing ventures, Scott is popularly thought to have died of overwork trying to make up the losses with constant writing.

SCOTT, WALTER—See Death Valley Scotty.

SCOTT, WILLIAM LLOYD (1915–   )

Virginia senator William Lloyd Scott made so many eyebrow-raising statements, especially on foreign junkets, that he gained the nickname *The Dumbest Man in Congress*.

SCOTT, WINFIELD (1786–1866)

One of the most able generals America ever produced, Winfield Scott was nicknamed *Old Fuss and Feathers* not so much for any pomposity or his resplendent dress, for which he was famed, but because he followed strict formality and discipline in dealing with his men and staff.

Scott Free Lincoln—See LINCOLN, WARREN.

Scott of Painting, The—See GILBERT, JOHN.

Scottish Homer, The—See WILKIE, WILLIAM.

Scottish Marcellus, The—See MACDONALD, JAMES.

Scottish Sidney, The—See BAILLIE, ROBERT.

Scottish Theocritus, The—See RAMSAY, ALLAN.

Scottish Vandyke, The—See
JAMESON, GEORGE.

Scoundrel Brahms—See BRAHMS,
JOHANNES.

Scourge, The—See LOMBARDO,
ANTONIO "the Scourge."

Scourge of Fanaticism, The—See
SOUTH, ROBERT.

Scourge of Heresy, The—See
TORQUEMADA, TOMAS DE.

Scourge of Home, The—See ZOILUS.

Scourge of Princes, The—See
ARETINO, PIETRO.

Scourge of the Priests, The—See
FAREL, GUILLAUME.

*Scrambler Amongst the Alps,
The*—See WHYMPER, EDWARD.

Screwballs' Boswell, The—See
SMITH, H. ALLEN.

SCUDERI, MADELINE DE
(1607–1671)

Because the works of a 17th century French poet,
Madeline de Scuderi, were considered to be in the
vein of the love poems of Sappho, she was called
The Tenth Muse.

Sculptor Poet, The—See
LUCRETIUS.

Sea Devil, The—See LUCKNER,
COUNT FELIX VON.

Sea Dreamer, The—See CONRAD,
JOSEPH.

Searcher, The—See FLUDD,
ROBERT.

Sebastian the Madman: SEBASTIAN
OF PORTUGAL (1554–1578)

A youthful king whose obsession for military glory
gained him the nickname *The Madman*, Sebastian
of Portugal came officially of age at 14 and
launched a number of military campaigns shortly
thereafter. However, he achieved only fiascos, especially a crushing defeat in North Africa. *The
Madman* was killed and his army destroyed in a
Moroccan campaign in 1578. Remarkably, a legend arose that Sebastian was not dead and would
return to save Portugal, which had fallen under
Spanish rule with his death. A number of pretend-
ers appeared, but none achieved the great military
victories that had eluded *The Madman* during his
short lifetime.

Secesh Cleopatra—See BOYD,
BELLE.

Second Aristotle, The—See
ACHILLINI, ALESSANDRO.

Second Bismarck, The—See
RIBBENTROP, JOACHIM VON.

Second Cato the Censor, The—See
HOPITAL, MICHEL DE L'.

Second Charlemagne, The—See
CHARLES V OF THE HOLY
ROMAN EMPIRE.

Second Constantine, The—See
JAMES II OF ENGLAND.

Second Hogarth, The—See
BUNBURY, HENRY WILLIAM.

Second John—See ADAMS, JOHN
QUINCY.

Second Johnson, The—See
COLERIDGE, SAMUEL TAYLOR.

Second Leviathan of Prose, The—See
NASH, THOMAS.

Second Mars, A—See JULIUS II,
POPE.

*Second Parent of the Reformed
Church, The*—See FREDERICK,
JOHN, DUKE OF SAXONY.

Second Robespierre, A—See
BABEUF, FRANCOIS NOEL.

Second Shakespeare, The—See
MARLOWE, CHRISTOPHER.

Second-Worst Poet, The—See
DENHAM, JOHN.

Seditious Faker, The—See GANDHI,
MOHANDAS "Mahatma."

SEEGER, PETE (1919–   )

Pete Seeger, singer and composer, who has a long
association with radical-left politics, has been
called *The Thomas Jefferson of Folk Music* and
America's Tuning Fork.

Selfish Vulgarian, A—See
PULITZER, JOSEPH.

SELKIRK, ALEXANDER (1676–1721)

A Scottish sailor who was marooned on a Pacific
island for five years, from 1704 to 1709, Alexander Selkirk was used by Daniel Defoe as the model
for *The Life and Strange Adventures of Robinson
Crusoe,* which appeared in 1719. Thereafter Selkirk was called *The Original Robinson Crusoe.*

*SELZ, JEROME VON BRAUN
(1909–   )*

A particularly ghoulish California murderer, Ralph
Jerome von Braun Selz won the designation *The
Laughing Killer* for having murdered his older
lover, a wealthy 58-year-old woman, in 1935 and
giggling constantly as he led authorities to her
body, which he had buried in the mountains. *The
Laughing Killer* announced to reporters he intended
to seek a Hollywood career once the case was out
of the way. He remains behind bars serving a life
sentence.

Semiramis of the North, The—See
CATHERINE THE GREAT OF
RUSSIA.

Semitic Sacrifice, The—See DREYFUS, ALFRED.

SEMMES, RAPHAEL (1809–1877)

One of the most valiant fighters of the Confederate Navy, Raphael Semmes commanded the *Alabama,* the South's first great fighting ship, and effectively harassed much of the Union's commercial fleet. He was hailed in the Confederate press as *Paul Jones of the South.* Aboard ship, however, his crew called him *Old Beeswax* because he had to wax his fierce mustache constantly to try to keep it under control. A 19th century writer stated: "One end of it had a habit of getting up into the neighborhood of his eye while the other pointed toward the ground. When he went upon the quarterdeck to take his daily exercise, his chief occupation as he walked up and down in solemn state was to train his moustache into proper position. But it was endless task, for when he got the right end out of his eye the left end would be elevated, and *vice versa,* and the *Alabama* was sunk before he got them properly balanced."

Senator from Ar-Kansas—See ASHLEY, CHESTER.

Senator Halfbright—See FULBRIGHT, J. WILLIAM.

SENDAK, MAURICE (1928–   )

Possessing a unique style of illustration, U.S. artist Maurice Sendak has been dubbed *The Picasso of Children's Books.*

SENNETT, MACK (1880–1960)

U.S. film producer Mack Sennett, who produced a vast number of two-reel comedies and gave starts to many famous directors and actors, was nick-

named *The King of Comedy* and, perhaps a bit more esoterically, *Father Goose.*

Sentimental Charley—See UTTER, CHARLES H.

Sentimental Cynic, The—See RUNYON, DAMON.

Sentimental Tommy: THOMAS TOWNSEND BUCKNILL (1845–1915)

A leading British judge, Sir Thomas Townsend Bucknill, was known as *Sentimental Tommy* because of his acknowledged tenderheartedness on the bench. When he was forced to pronounce a death sentence, he would do so, as one chronicler noted, "with tears running down his cheeks."

Sepulchre of Dullness and Propriety, A—See SARGENT, JOHN SINGER.

SERMENT, LOUISE ANASTASIE DE (1642–1692)

French poet Louise Anastasie de Serment was accorded the accolade *The Philosopher* for her contributions to the appreciation of literature.

Serpent, The—See FRERON, ELIE-CATHERINE.

Servant of the Servants of God, The—See GREGORY THE GREAT, ST.

SERVICE, ROBERT WILLIAM (1874–1958)

Scottish-born Canadian writer and poet Robert William Service was called *The Canadian Kipling.*

He was best known for his verse, especially "The Shooting of Dan McGrew," which netted him a half million dollars.

Seven Days' King, The: MASANIELLO (?–1647)

A Neapolitan insurrectionist who seized power in 1647, Masaniello became known as *The Seven Days' King* since that was the duration of his reign before he was killed.

72-Cannon Chang—See CHANG CHUNG CH'ANG.

SEWALL, JOSEPH (1688–1769)

One of the early Methodist preachers in America, Joseph Sewall, noted for his theatrical and highly emotional sermonizing, was dubbed *The Weeping Prophet*.

SEWALL, SAMUEL (1652–1730)

In early New England Judge Samuel Sewall kept a diary for 50 years, beginning in 1674. Much prized by historians for its detailed account of New England life, the diary has earned the austere Puritan the sobriquet *The Puritan Pepys,* after the English diarist Samuel Pepys. Of course, Sewall's diary lacks the raciness of Pepys's.

SEWARD, WILLIAM H. (1801–1872)

One of the most ardent antislavers, William H. Seward, who called himself *The Abolitionist of the Abolitionists,* was considered the leading candidate for president until Abraham Lincoln wrested away the Republican nomination. In his later years he was much honored in his hometown of Auburn, N.Y., as *The Sage of Auburn*. It was not so during the war years, however, when he was Lincoln's secretary of state. He was reviled by many for his pro-war views, and a mob once gathered in front of Seward's home and chanted to his wife and daughter: "Burn his house! Burn his house!"

Sex Kitten, The—See BARDOT, BRIGITTE.

Sexpert, The—See HARRIS, FRANK.

SEYMOUR, CHARLES, DUKE OF SOMERSET (?–1748)

Charles Seymour, duke of Somerset, comes down to us as *The Proud Duke* because he never permitted his children to sit in his presence and endeavored to avoid speaking to his servants, ordering them about by signs.

Sforza—See ATTENDOLO, MUSIO.

Shadow in the White House, The—See PIERCE, JANE MEANS APPLETON.

Shah of OPEC, The—See YAMANI, AHMED ZAKI.

SHAHN, BEN (1898–1969)

Lithuanian-born Ben Shahn, a leading U.S. painter and graphics artist, was nicknamed *The American Hogarth*. He worked on Diego Rivera's "Man at the Crossroads" in New York's Rockefeller Center and other paintings commemorating liberal causes, such as those concerning the trials of anarchists Sacco and Vanzetti and labor agitator Tom Mooney.

Shake-scene—See SHAKESPEARE, WILLIAM.

SHAKESPEARE, WILLIAM
(1564–1616)

The complimentary sobriquets for William Shakespeare abound, with certainly the most enduring being *The Bard of Avon,* for the river running through his native Stratford. Less memorable are *The Sweet Swan of Avon,* coined by Ben Johnson, and David Garrick's contribution, *Avonian Willy.* During his lifetime Shakespeare's critical sobriquets ranged from *Honie-Tongued* to *An Upstart Crow.* Somewhat bewildered by Shakespeare's work, the French adopted Robert Greene's nickname for him: *Shake-scene.*

Shakespeare in Petticoats—See **BAILLIE, JOANNA.**

Shakespeare of Divines, The—See **TAYLOR, JEREMY.**

Shakespeare of France, The—See **CORNEILLE, PIERRE.**

Shakespeare of Germany, The—See **GROSSMANN, GUSTAVUS.**

Shakespeare of India, The—See **KALIDASA.**

Shakespeare of Sweden, The—See **STRINDBERG, AUGUST.**

Shakespeare Without Genius, A—See **HARDI, ALEXANDRE.**

Shakespeare's Critic—See **RYMER, THOMAS.**

Shanghai Kelly—See **KELLY, SHANGHAI.**

SHANK, SAMUEL L. (1872–1927)

A former vaudeville actor, Mayor Samuel L. Shank of Indianapolis, Ind., came up with a novel approach to try to force food prices down during his first term, from 1910 to 1913. He began auctioning farm produce, especially potatoes, on the steps of City Hall, winning the sobriquet *The Potato Mayor.*

Sharp Knife—See **JACKSON, ANDREW.**

SHAW, GEORGE BERNARD
(1856–1950)

Irish playwright, journalist, critic and wit George Bernard Shaw wrote "dramas of ideas" that reflected his passion for social reform and thus gained him such sobriquets as *Robespierre Marat Fitzthunder* and *The Wag of Whitehall Court.* His neighbors simply dubbed him *Old Hair-and-Teeth.*

SHEARER, NORMA—See First Lady of Hollywood.

SHEFFIELD, GEORGE ST. JOHN
(1842–1924)

From 1860 until 1924 the history of rowing at Yale University was inextricably linked to George St. John Sheffield, rowing coach and promoter of the sport in general. Starting as a member of the Yale crew, Sheffield enthusiastically promoted rowing through the decades until he was regarded as virtually the leading exponent of the sport in America and was dubbed *The Grandfather of Yale Rowing*.

SHEFFIELD, JOHN, DUKE OF BUCKINGHAMSHIRE AND EARL OF MULGRAVE *(1649–1721)*

Considered by many of his English contemporaries to be the most vain man of his day, John Sheffield, duke of Buckinghamshire and earl of Mulgrave, was dubbed *Lord All-Pride*.

Sheik, The—See VALENTINO, RUDOLPH.

SHELBURNE, LORD: WILLIAM PETTY FITZMAURICE *(1737–1805)*

Statesman Lord Shelburne was nicknamed *Malagrida* by his English political opponents, an allusion to Gabriel Malagrida, an Italian Jesuit missionary who conspired against the king of Portugal.

SHELLEY, PERCY BYSSHE *(1792–1822)*

Perhaps the most radical of the English Romantic poets in his political verse, Percy Bysshe Shelley was called *A Gentleman of Oxford*, a cutting remark for a young man who had been expelled from that institution for his pamphlet *The Necessity of Atheism*. He was also referred to by his foes as *Mad Shelley*, which did little to silence his attacks on government, the church and wealth. He savaged the leaders of the day, writing of Castlereagh, the reactionary leader of the Tories:

> I met murder on the way.
> He had a mask like Castlereagh.

In his poem "England in 1819" he called George III "an old, mad, blind, despised and dying king, the dregs of his dull race, mud from a muddy stream." Byron nicknamed Shelley *Snake* "because of his noiseless gliding movement, bright eyes, and ethereal diet." Shelley did not resent the name; in fact he alluded to it often in his writing. Chances are, though, that he would have resented Charles Kingsley's sobriquet for him, *A Lewd Vegetarian*.

SHEPPARD, MORRIS *(1875–1941)*

A U.S. senator from Texas for 38 years until his death in 1941, Morris Sheppard was called *The Father of the Eighteenth* (Prohibition) *Amendment* because of his unceasing efforts to get it passed and subsequent efforts to prevent its repeal.

SHERIDAN, ANN *(1915–1967)*

Hollywood star Ann Sheridan was nicknamed *The Oomph Girl*, presumably for want of a better way to describe how she filled a sweater.

SHERIDAN, PHILIP HENRY *(1831–1888)*

At only 5 feet 5 inches, Union cavalry general Philip Henry Sheridan was very short even by Civil War standards. His troopers quickly dubbed him *Little Phil*, and the sobriquet was later reenforced by Abraham Lincoln upon meeting the general. The president pointed out he had originally held that cavalrymen should be at least 6 feet 4, but, after having noted Sheridan's accomplishments, Lincoln became convinced that 5 feet 4 would "do in a pinch."

SHERMAN, JOHN *(1823–1900)*

Since he figured prominently in formulating important governmental financial decisions as a member of the House and Senate, from 1855 to 1877, and of two presidential cabinets, John Sherman of Ohio was referred to by the press as *The Great Financier*.

She-Wolf, The—See LINCOLN, MARY TODD.

She-Wolf of France, The—See ISABELLA OF FRANCE.

Shield of Rome—See VERRUCOSUS, QUINTUS FABIUS MAXIMUS.

Shifty Hays—See HAYS, WILL H.

SHIMA, GEORGE (1870–1929)

A penniless Japanese immigrant who came to the United States at the age of 19, George Shima ran up a $15 million fortune through his development of the potato in agriculture, acquiring the sobriquet of *The Potato King*.

SHINBURN, MARK (c. 1833–?)

Considered the most dapper of U.S. bank robbers and described by many police experts of the day as the equal of the renowned thief George Leslie, Mark Shinburn thought himself the superior of his confederates and properly dubbed *The Aristocrat of the Bank Robbers*. Satisfied with accomplishments, he eventually retired to Europe, where with the proceeds of his crimes he bought a title and became known as Baron Shindell of Monaco. His fate is unknown other than he lived in wealthy retirement on both sides of the Atlantic.

Shining Knight of the Poker Table, The— See POWELL, JOHN.

Shipwreck Kelly—See KELLY, ALVIN "Shipwreck."

SHIRLEY, JAMES (1594–1666)

English dramatist James Shirley is often referred to as *The Last Minstrel of the English Stage* because he was the last of the Shakespearean school.

Shocking One, The—See SCHIAPARELLI, ELSA.

SHOLES, CHRISTOPHER LATHAM (1819–1890)

Christopher Latham Sholes obtained the first two patents for his new typewriter in 1868 but, being unable to perfect the machine, sold out to the Remington Arms Company for a mere $12,000. He has nevertheless been credited as *The Father of the Typewriter*.

SHORT, ELIZABETH—See Black Dahlia, The.

Shotgun Man (fl. early 20th century)

Although he was recognized on sight by thousands of residents of Chicago's Little Italy, the identity of the anonymous *Shotgun Man* remained a mystery to the city's police. A hit man for various Black Hand extortion gangs, *Shotgun Man* was known to have killed 15 Italians and Sicilians between Jan. 1, 1910, and March 26, 1911, all by assignment. In March 1911 he assassinated four victims within a 72-hour period, each one at the intersection of Milton and Oak streets. Because of the fear he instilled in victims of the Black Hand gangs, they all paid him well. He disappeared from Chicago at the end of World War I, some claiming he had returned to Italy to live out his days in comfort on his blood money.

SHREWSBURY, COUNTESS OF
(fl. c. 1668)

After his wife ran off with George Villiers, the duke of Buckingham, the 11th earl of Shrewsbury challenged his rival to a duel. Shrewsbury was killed in the fight, unaware of the fact that his wife had been so eager to witness his death that she disguised herself as a page and held the duke's horse during the duel. The title of Buckingham's famous poem "The Iron Mistress" became the countess' sobriquet.

SHULMAN, MAX *(1919–   )*

U.S. humorist Max Shulman has been called *The Master of Undergraduate Humor* and *Cultured Perelman,* after the humorist and feuilletonist S. J. Perelman.

Siamese Twins, The: ENG AND CHANG *(1811–1874)*

Although they were hardly the first to suffer such a malady (see Biddenden Maids, The), Eng and Chang, born in Siam of a Chinese father and a Siamese mother, gave their sobriquet, *The Siamese Twins,* to all future victims of the abnormality. Joined together at birth by a five-inch ligament at their breastbones, they were brought to the United States, where in 1842 they married two normal sisters, Adelaide and Sarah Yates, and fathered a total of 21 children. When one died in 1874, the other survived 2½ hours.

Siddons of America, The—See DUFF, MRS. MARY.

Sidewalk Sam: ROBERT GUILLEMIN *(c. 1939–   )*

U.S. painter and street-corner artist Robert Guillemin is better known as *Sidewalk Sam,* probably the most accomplished of this least permanent art form.

SIDNEY, PHILIP *(1554–1586)*

English author, poet and statesman Sir Philip Sidney, recognized as the model courtier and Renaissance gentleman, was nicknamed *The Miracle of Our Age.* Only after his death in battle against the Spaniards were his literary works printed. They included *Arcadia, Astrophel, Stella* and *The Defence of Poesie,* the last being a prose answer to the bitter attack on English drama and poetry by the Puritan Stephen Gosson.

SIEGEL, BENJAMIN "Bugsy" *(1906–1947)*

The notorious big-time syndicate killer Benjamin Siegel could be the suavest of gentlemen or a raging killer, ready to take on anyone. His double personality led to his nickname *Bugsy,* the use of which could throw him into murderous rage; he is said to have pistol-whipped a number of characters who forgot his name was just plain Ben. Even his mistress, Virginia Hill, clobbered newsmen who referred to her man as *Bugsy.* Siegel was "hit" in 1947 when he went so "bugs" that he thought he could defy the entire crime syndicate from Lucky Luciano, Meyer Lansky and Frank Costello on down.

SIFFORD, CHARLES *(1923–?)*

For breaking the color line on the professional golf tour, black golfer Charlie Sifford won the sobriquet *The Jackie Robinson of Golf.*

SIGISMUND, EMPEROR OF THE HOLY ROMAN EMPIRE *(1361–1437)*

Sigismund, emperor of the Holy Roman Empire, was called *The Light of the World* as a tribute to his enlightened rule and superior intelligence.

Silent Cal—See COOLIDGE, CALVIN.

Silent Charley—See MURPHY, CHARLES F.

Silent Senator, The—See STURGEON, DANIEL.

Silent Smith—See SMITH, JAMES HENRY "Silent."

SILKS, MATTIE (1847–1929)

Dubbed *Queen of the Red Lights,* Mattie Silks was a Denver madam who ran the most fashionable brothel west of Chicago's Everleigh Club. When she retired in the 1920s, she had achieved a sort of dowager status and was much sought after for newspaper interviews and her reflections on the bad good old days.

SILLS, BEVERLY (1929–)

Opera star Beverly Sills picked up her nickname *Bubbles* at birth when she was born with a large bubble of saliva in her mouth.

Silly Billy: WILLIAM FREDERICK, DUKE OF GLOUCESTER (1776–1834); WILLIAM IV OF ENGLAND (1765–1837)

The nickname *Silly Billy,* indicating a lack of intellect, was applied to both William Frederick, duke of Gloucester, the nephew of George III, and to William IV, king of England, Frederick's cousin. It has been a matter of some historical dispute as to who was more deserving of the title.

Silly Duke—See CHURCHILL, JOHN.

Silly Quirko—See HARVEY, GABRIEL.

Silver Dollar West—See WEST, JAMES MARION "Silver Dollar."

Silver Heels *(fl. late 19th century)*

A Colorado mining camp dancehall girl remembered only as *Silver Heels,* an allusion to the shoes she wore, became one of the West's legendary prostitutes with a heart of gold. When smallpox ravaged the camps of Alma and Buckskin Joe, she refused to leave with the other girls and remained to nurse the stricken miners. The disease ruined her looks. The miners remembered her by naming Mount Silver Heels for her. (See also Marshall, John.)

Silver Tongued and Golden Hearted, The—See WILLARD, FRANCES E.

Silver-Haired Statesman of American Labor, The—See MEANY, GEORGE.

Silver-Tongued, The—See GARRICK, DAVID.

Silver-Tongued Spellbinder, The—See DELMAS, DELPHIN MICHAEL.

SIMEON STYLITES, ST.—See Pillar Saint, The.

Simmonseed Johnny—See HATFIELD, BAZIL MUSE.

SIMON, NEIL (1925–)

The prolific writer of Broadway comedies, Neil Simon is called *Doc* by his friends since it was his boyhood ambition to be a doctor.

Simon the Poet—See BUCKNER, SIMON BOLIVAR.

Simple Lombard, The—See CASTEL, GUIDO DI.

SIMPSON, JERRY (1842–1905)

Jerry Simpson, probably the most liked and renowned of Populist leaders in the United States, was often reviled by his opponents as *Sockless Jerry* or *The Sockless Socrates of the Plains*, a false accusation that he wore no socks. He turned that charge to his advantage and won election to Congress from Kansas for several terms. Actually *Sockless Jerry* was no country bumpkin but an extremely shrewd politician, and despite being a poor writer, he was widely read. Had it not been for his Canadian birth, many historians agree, he would have been a strong contender for the presidency.

SIMS, PHILIP (1933–)

Black American psychologist and consumer advocate Philip Sims has been dubbed *The Black Ralph Nader*.

SINATRA, FRANK (1915–)

When he was a teen heartthrob in the 1940s, singer Frank Sinatra was dubbed *The Voice*. Later, as his career broadened to include film acting, he became an important fixture in Hollywood, referred to as *The Pope, The Chairman of the Board,* and *The Leader of the Rat Pack,* a group of performers who acknowledged him as their mentor and leader.

SINCLAIR, HARRY F. "Teapot Dome" (1876–1956)

Millionaire oilman Harry F. Sinclair became known as *Teapot Dome Sinclair* because he spread his oil money around like water inside the Harding administration to win a secret lease to pump the government's Teapot Dome oil reserves in Wyoming. While others went to prison in the case, Sinclair beat the charges, although years later he was sent to jail for having private detectives shadow the jury in one of his trials. Thereafter both Sinclair and his company, the Sinclair Consolidated Oil Corporation, were referred to as *Sinco*.

SINCLAIR, JAMES E. (1940–)

In the 1970s, James E. Sinclair enjoyed a large Wall Street following and made a considerable amount of money as a "gold bug," advocating investment in the precious metal and winning the sobriquet *Mr. Gold*. However, in 1982 he lost that identification by warring against gold investment, calling the metal's price surge from $35 to $887.50 an ounce a once-in-a-lifetime event. To the chagrin of other gold bugs, Sinclair urged investment in Treasury bills and bonds, stock market index futures and industrial metals.

SINCLAIR, WILLIAM (?–1337)

During the battle at Donibristle in 1317 invading English troops routed a force of 500 Scots. In their flight, the Scots met William Sinclair, bishop of Dunkeld, galloping to their aid with 60 horsemen. Denouncing the fleeing soldiers as cowards, he urged them back to battle and, throwing off his bishop's vestments, seized a spear and shouted, "Who loves his king, or his country, follow me!" The fleeing soldiers rallied behind him and defeated the English. When Robert Bruce, or Robert I of Scotland, learned of the bishop's act, he declared that thereafter Sinclair was *The King's Bishop*.

Sinco—See SINCLAIR, HARRY F. "Teapot Dome."

Singing Brakeman, The—See RODGERS, JAMES CHARLES "Jimmy."

Singing Canary, The—See RELES, ABE.

Singing Capon, The—See EDDY, NELSON.

Singing Strangler, The: EDWARD JOSEPH LEONSKI (1918–1942)

Edward Joseph Leonski, an American GI stationed in Australia during World War II, became infamous as that country's *Singing Strangler* for killing three women "to get their voices." Leonski, who had a family history of mental instability, sang in his cell before his execution on Nov. 9, 1942.

Single-Speech Hamilton—See HAMILTON, WILLIAM "Single-Speech."

Single Speech Hemphill—See HEMPHILL, JOSEPH "Single Speech."

Single Taxer, The—see GEORGE, HENRY.

SIPLE, PAUL ALLMAN (1908–1968)

While still in his teens, U.S. boy scout Paul Siple was a member of the first Byrd Antarctic Expedition in 1928 and was dubbed *The Boy Explorer*. He made six subsequent trips.

Sir Giles Overreach—See MOMPESSON, GILES.

Sir Jack Brag—See BURGOYNE, JOHN.

Sir Loyal Heart—See HENRY VIII.

Sir Reverse—See BULLER, REDVERS HENRY.

Sir Tremendous—See DENNIS, JOHN.

Sir Veto—See JOHNSON, ANDREW.

Sire of Ossian, The—See MACPHERSON, JAMES.

SIRHAN, SIRHAN BISHARA (1944–   )

Shortly after Sirhan Bishara Sirhan shot and killed Robert F. Kennedy in Los Angeles's Ambassador Hotel in 1968, leaflets and posters in Arab capitals in the Middle East hailed him as *Sirhan the Commando*. Palestinian commando sources said that in shooting Kennedy, Sirhan was acting on behalf of all dispossessed Palestinians because Kennedy was a supporter of Israel.

Sirhan the Commando—See SIRHAN, SIRHAN BISHARA.

SIRICA, JOHN J. "Maximum John" (1904–)

U.S. District Court Judge John J. Sirica, who achieved fame in the Watergate cases, was known in court circles as *Maximum John* because of his reputation for handing out very stern sentences.

SISK, MILDRED ELIZABETH—See Axis Sally.

Sister of Shakespeare, The—See BAILLIE, JOANNA.

Sitting Bull—See LAWSON, JOHN DANIEL; MORTON, OLIVER.

Sixteen-String Jack: JOHN RANN (?–1774)

A notorious English highwayman and dandy, John Rann became known as *Sixteen-String Jack* because he wore breeches that had eight strings at each knee. Quite a dashing figure, he became very recognizable and was caught and hanged at Tyburn on November 30, 1774.

SKEFFINGTON, WILLIAM—See Father of Scavenger's Daughter, The.

SKELTON, RED (1913–)

Comedian Red Skelton has been called *The Marcel Marceau of Television* because of his pantomime skills.

Skin and Bones—See MAHONE, WILLIAM "Little Billy."

Skinny Wainright—See WAINRIGHT, JONATHAN MAYHEW.

Skull, Sally: SARAH JANE NEWMAN (1813–1867?)

One of the many men Sarah Jane Newman married was named Skull, and because several of her husbands came to a bad end, she was permanently dubbed *Sally Skull*. When one spouse was fished out of the Nueces River in Texas, the popular opinion was that she had drowned him in a barrel of whiskey. In 1867 Sally rode off into the sunset with husband number six, seven or eight, according to various counts, since the suspicions were getting rather pronounced. Some time later the decomposed body of a woman turned up in the direction the couple had last been seen traveling.

Sky Hi Irvin—See IRVIN, LESLIE L.

Slave Prince, The: IBRAHIMA (c. 1762–1829)

In 1788 a slave, newly imported to Mississippi, was called *Prince* because he kept insisting he was of African royal blood. Seventeen years later a physician, Dr. John Cox, recognized him as Ibrahima, a military leader and scholar whose father was the ruler of the Moslem empire of Futa Jallon in West Africa. Ibrahima had saved the doctor's life when he was in Africa. The prince recounted how he had been beaten in battle and sold to slavers sailing to America. Dr. Cox launched a drive to publicize the plight of the man now known as *The Slave Prince*. Even John Quincy Adams appealed for his release. Nevertheless *The*

Slave Prince was not freed until 1827, whereupon he went on a public-appearance tour sponsored by Secretary of State Henry Clay to raise funds to buy the freedom of his wife and children. Finally Ibrahima secured sufficient funds to free them, and in 1829 he and his family sailed to Liberia on their way back home. However, he died later that same year.

Slavery Brundage—See BRUNDAGE, AVERY.

Slayer of the Bulgarians—See BASIL II.

Sleepin' Sam—See HAYAKAWA, SAMUEL I.

Sleepy Phil—See KNOX, PHILANDER CHASE.

Slick Willie—See SUTTON, WILLIE ''The Actor.''

Slippery Sam—See TILDEN, SAMUEL J.

Slogan Smythe—See SMYTHE, J. HENRY.

Sly Fox, The—See HOLLAND, HENRY FOX, LORD.

SMALL, LEN (1862–1936)

Illinois governor Len Small is often regarded as the most corrupt state chief executive in the nation's history. He was nicknamed *The Pardoning Gov-*

ernor, for good reason. In his first three years in office starting in 1921, Small pardoned some 1,000 felons, then speeded up his activities, freeing another 7,000 over the next five years on a strictly cash basis. A Chicago newsman once explained: ''The Republican party machinery of the state was then in the hands of Len Small as governor, Robert E. Crowe as state's attorney of Cook County and William Hale Thompson as mayor of Chicago. . . . When Crowe would convict a wrongdoer, the man could buy a pardon from Small. Then Small and Crowe would split the take and Crowe would go into court for more convictions.'' Small was finally voted out of office in 1928.

Small-Beer Poet, The—See FITZGERALD, WILLIAM THOMAS.

Smella Ella—See GRASSO, ELLA.

Smelly Pelley—See PELLEY, WILLIAM DUDLEY.

Smiling Alfred—See KESSELRING, ALBERT.

Smiling Cobra, The—See AUBREY, JAMES T., JR.

Smiling Jim—See FARLEY, JAMES A.

Smiling Pope, The—See JOHN PAUL I, POPE.

SMITH, ALFRED E. (1873–1944)

A former governor of New York and the Democratic candidate for president in 1928, Alfred E.

Smith was nicknamed *The Happy Warrior*. The term was coined for him by Franklin D. Roosevelt in a speech to the Democratic Convention in 1928 and based on William Wordsworth's poem "Character of the Happy Warrior."

SMITH, BESSIE (1894–1937)

Legendary blues singer of the 1920s and 1930s Bessie Smith transformed the blues into a modern jazz idiom and is considered by many critics one of the greatest and most influential vocalists of the 20th century. Among her many tributes is the nickname *The Empress of the Blues*. Her career collapsed because of alcoholism, and she died as the result of an automobile accident in 1937.

SMITH, EDMUND (1668–1710)

Ever since his Oxford days, the English poet Edmund Smith was known as *Rag Smith* or *Captain Rag* because of his generally slovenly appearance and because his gown was in tatters and always fluttering like rags about him.

SMITH, EDWARD H. "Iceberg" (1889–1961)

A key man in the Allied effort to keep the North Atlantic open to shipping during World War II, Edward H. Smith of the U.S. Coast Guard was called *Iceberg Smith* because of his role in tracking icebergs. As a rear admiral, he had responsibility for keeping the Germans off Greenland so that they could not use it for weather observations to aid U-boat operations.

SMITH, GEORGE JOSEPH (1872–1915)

An English mass killer, George Joseph Smith was nicknamed *The Brides in the Bath Murderer* because he drowned his several wives in bathtubs. Once when he rented a flat that had no tub, he rushed out to buy one and carried it back there to drown his current wife. He was caught when it became evident that his wives had not drowned accidentally but because he had held their heads under the water.

SMITH, H. ALLEN (1907–   )

Humor writer H. Allen Smith has been dubbed *The Biographer of the Dispensable Man* and, by Fred Allen, *The Screwballs' Boswell*.

SMITH, HARRY (1788–1860)

Col. Harry Smith—for whom Harrismith, South Africa was named—gained the sobriquet *Horseback Harry* for riding 600 miles on horseback in six days to save a town besieged by 15,000 natives.

SMITH, HOLLAND M. "Howling Mad" (1882–1967)

Because of his mercurial temper U.S. Marine Corps general Holland M. Smith was called *Howling Mad Smith*. His innovations in modern amphibious warfare in the Pacific during World War II provided him with the additional sobriquet *The Pacific Cyclone*.

SMITH, JAMES HENRY "Silent" (?–1907)

While not a hermit, James Henry Smith was perhaps New York's most reticent multimillionaire. Refusing to discuss his business affairs or his personal background (a "man who locked up his own soul," one acquaintance said), he was dubbed *Silent Smith*.

SMITH, JAMES MONROE "Jingle Money" (1888–1949)

One of the least complimentary sobriquets in the annals of higher education belonged to Louisiana State University president James Monroe Smith, who became known as *Jingle Money Smith*. A wild liver, he absconded to Canada in 1939 with a huge amount of university funds. Captured, he was convicted of embezzling $100,000, although the actual figure was much higher. He was imprisoned until 1946, when he was released because of poor health.

SMITH, JEDEDIAH (1799–1831)

One of the most colorful Western mountainmen, Jedediah Smith was dubbed *The Knight in Buckskin* because, unlike other mountainmen, he was a conscientious Bible reader, when he was not battling Indians, grizzlies and the elements.

SMITH, JEFFERSON RANDOLPH "Soapy" (1860–1898)

Long before he was lynched in Alaskan gold field country, Jefferson Randolph Smith was a notorious swindler in the Old West. He gained the nickname of *Soapy Smith* from an ancient con game in which he would stand on a soap box and inform cowtown suckers that many of the bars of soapy he was selling had a $10 or $20 bill inside the wrapper. Naturally, only Smith's shills ever won money, which would cause them to celebrate most boisterously.

SMITH, JESSE (1871–1923)

U.S. political "fixer" and right-hand man of Harry M. Daugherty, one of President Warren Harding's Ohio Gang cronies, Jesse Smith, was known as *Beau Jess of Washington Court House* for his ability to get things done. His suicide in 1923, sometimes rumored to be murder, was linked with Teapot Dome and other scandals.

SMITH, JOHN—See Half-Hanged Smith.

SMITH, MONICA PROIETTI—See Machine Gun Molly.

SMITH, WILLIAM (1796–1887)

Later to be governor of Virginia, William Smith became a mail contractor in the 1820s and thereafter proved a master at gaining compensation beyond his regular salary for additional services rendered. An inquiry into the Postmaster General's office in 1834 about the matter of his added compensation led to his being dubbed *Extra Billy Smith*.

SMITH, WILLIAM A. "Watertight" (1859–1932)

Few more monumental slips were ever made by a congressman than that uttered by Sen. William A. Smith of Michigan, who headed a Senate inquiry into the 1912 sinking of the *Titanic*. He asked an expert witness: "Why didn't the passengers on the boat go into the watertight compartments and save themselves from drowning?" It had to be pointed out to the senator that even the watertight compartments went to the bottom of the ocean. Never thereafter could he escape being tagged *Watertight Smith*.

SMITH, WILLIAM F. "Baldy" (1824–1903)

Union general William F. Smith was nicknamed *Baldy*, which confused some Civil War scholars since at the time he had, and photographs from much later in his life show him still having, a relatively full crop of hair. It turned out that when he entered West Point in 1841, his hair was somewhat sparse for a youth of his age and his comrades assumed that he undoubtedly would be one of the first in his class to go bald and dubbed him *Baldy*. It did not work out that way.

SMITH, WILLIAM HENRY (1825–1891)

A leading 19th century English Conservative Party politician who held top Admiralty and War posts, William Henry Smith was dubbed *Old Morality* because his ethics were considered beyond reproach.

SMITH BROTHERS: ANDREW SMITH (c. 1831–1895) and WILLIAM SMITH (1831–1913)

Cough drop manufacturers Andrew and William Smith put their bearded pictures on the box of their product and became one of the country's most famous trademarks (Andrew was labeled *Trade* and William, *Mark*). Given credit for putting their home town of Poughkeepsie, N.Y., on the map, they were nicknamed *The Beards That Made Poughkeepsie Famous*.

SMITZ, GASPAR (?–1689)

The 17th century Dutch painter Gaspar Smitz was, with some humor, designated *Magdalen Smitz* because he gained his fame for his painting of noted courtesans.

SMYTHE, J. HENRY (1883–1956)

Often cited as the first "full-time" political slogan writer, J. Henry Smythe produced many famous Liberty and Victory Bond slogans, battle cries and Republican political slogans, gaining for himself recognition as *Slogan Smythe*. Among his creations were: "Lend to Defend!"; "Do Your Bit to Keep It Lit!"; and "Keep Coolidge—He Keeps Faith!"

Snake—See SHELLEY, PERCY BYSSHE.

Snapping Turtle—See FINK, MIKE.

Snapping Turtle, The—See GLASS, CARTER "Sound Money."

Snatchem—See LEESE, GEORGE.

SNELL, HANNAH (1723–1792)

Hannah Snell of Worcester, England, a woman who passed herself off as a British royal marine during the 18th century, took part in a number of battles before her identity was discovered and she was mustered out of service. She then opened a public house in Wapping, where she continued to wear her male attire, gaining fame as *The Female Marine*. During World War II Hannah's nickname was given to a British Wren serving with the Royal Marines.

Snootiest Madam in America, The—See ARLINGTON, JOSIE.

Snout—See KEYNES, JOHN MAYNARD.

Snow Baby, The—See PEARY, MARIE AHNIGHITO.

Snow King, The—See FREDERICK V, ELECTOR PALATINE.

Snow Queen—See ELIZABETH,
ELECTRESS PALATINE.

Snow White—See COHEN,
MICKEY.

SNOWDON, LORD: ANTHONY ARMSTRONG JONES (1930–   )

Even while still married to Princess Margaret of England, photographer Anthony Armstrong Jones, or Lord Snowdon, was called *The Royal Black Sheep,* indicating his lack of acceptance by at least part of the royal family and much of the public.

Snowshoe Thompson: JOHN A. THOMPSON (1827–1876)

Norwegian-born Jon Torsteinson Rui, who Americanized his name to John A. Thompson, after his arrival in the United States won fame in the American West as *Snowshoe Thompson* after he took on the job of mail carrier traversing the Sierras each winter from Placerville, Calif., to Carson City, Nev. He traveled the 90 miles through snowdrifts in below-zero weather with 60 pounds of mail on his back. From 1856 until his death in 1876 he appears never to have lost, destroyed or delivered late any of the mail.

SNYDER, CHRISTOPHER (c. 1755–1770)

A 15-year-old Boston boy, Christopher Snyder, became *The First Martyr of the Revolution* when he was shot to death in 1770. He was one of a group of young boys harassing American importers of British merchandise when Ebenezer Richardson shot into the crowd and killed Snyder. Richardson was branded a murderer by the colonists. After serving two years in prison, he was pardoned by George III.

SNYDER, RUTH (1895–1928)

Ruth Snyder, the most famous murderess of the 1920s, was nicknamed by the press *The Granite Woman.* She and her lover, Judd Gray (she called him "Lover Boy" and he called her "Queenie, my Momsie, my Mommie") were accused of the murder of her husband. So great was the national interest in their case that the press corps at their trial included such diverse figures as D. W. Griffith, Dr. John Roach Straton, Mary Roberts Rinehart, Aimee Semple McPherson, David Belasco, Peggy Hopkins Joyce and no less than Will Durant, then atop the best-seller list with *The Story of Philosophy.* (See also Gray, Judd.)

Soapy—See SMITH, JEFFERSON
RANDOLPH "Soapy."

Soapy Sam—See WILBERFORCE,
SAMUEL "Soapy Sam."

Sober Sue (fl. early 20th century)

During the first decade of the 20th century a woman known only as *Sober Sue* proved to be a huge attraction on Broadway at Hammerstein's Victoria Theatre, which offered $1,000 to anyone who could make her laugh. Even leading comedians of the day failed. Finally they learned they were wasting their talents. *Sober Sue* could never laugh or even smile since her facial muscles were paralyzed.

Social Historian of Cafe Society, The—
See BEEBE, LUCIUS.

Sockless Jerry—See SIMPSON,
JERRY.

Sockless Socrates of the Plains—See
SIMPSON, JERRY.

SOCRATES (c. 471–399 B.C.)

The Greek philosopher Socrates was known at least to his followers as *The Wisest Man in Greece*. Obviously, given his fate, it was not a universal sentiment at the time, nor for that matter in later periods. Thomas Macaulay said of him: "The more I read him, the less I wonder that they poisoned him."

Socrates of His Age, The—See **GABRIELLI, TRIFONE.**

Socrates of the Civil Rights Movement, The—See **RUSTIN, BAYARD.**

Soldiers' Friend, The—See **FREDERICK AUGUSTUS, DUKE OF YORK; WARD, MARCUS L.**

Soldier's Inspiration, The—See **GRABLE, BETTY.**

SOLOMON, MOSES (1900–   )

One of the most skilled Jewish American baseball players of the early 1900s, Moses Solomon was nicknamed *Hickory Solomon* and *The Rabbi of Swat* for his batting ability.

Solomon Secondthoughts—See **KENNEDY, JOHN PENDLETON.**

SOLTYSIK, PATRICIA (1950?–1974)

Although the press focused on Donald DeFreeze as General Field Marshal Cinque, many authorities considered several women members to be superiors within the Symbionese Liberation Army.

Most often so cited was Patricia Soltysik, referred to as *The Female Brain of the SLA*. She died in the group's last desperate shootout with police in Los Angeles.

SOMERS, SUZANNE (1946–   )

Sexy star of the television series "Three's Company," Suzanne Somers was born Suzanne Marie Mahoney. As a teenager, she was so thin she was nicknamed *Bony Mahoney*.

Son of His Grandfather, The—See **HARRISON, BENJAMIN.**

Son of Sam: DAVID BERKOWITZ (1953–   )

Mass-murderer David Berkowitz, who terrorized New York City from July 1976 to August 1977, called himself *Son of Sam* in letters to the press. He was caught in part because of evidence provided by a neighbor, Sam Carr, who was believed to be the "Sam" referred to by *Son of Sam*.

Son of the Devil, The—See **EZZELINO DI ROMANO.**

Son of the Last Man, The—See **CHARLES II OF ENGLAND.**

Son of the Man, The—See **NAPOLEON II.**

SOPHOCLES (c. 495–c. 405 B.C.)

The Greek tragic poet Sophocles won the sobriquet *The Bee* because of his rather stinging comments.

SOREL, AGNES (1400–1450)

Agnes Sorel, the brazen but devoted mistress of Charles VII of France, was called *La Dame de Beaute* in part because of the Chateau de Beaute, which the king had presented her. Sorel's most striking beauty feature was her breasts, said then and later to be the most beautiful of all time. Fully aware of her mammary pulchritude, she introduced the style of "bare to the waist" dresses at court. At times she displayed only one breast, a style captured on canvas by many leading painters of the day. The most famous painting of her is that by Jean Fouquet, who posed her in the irreverent guise of a Madonna feeding a babe with an obviously milkless breast. It has been described as having "a flavour of blasphemous boldness . . . unsurpassed by any artist of the Renaissance."

Sot, The—See MASSINGER, PHILIP.

SOUMAROKOV, ALEXANDER PETROVITCH (1718–1777)

A rather middling Russian poet, Alexander Petrovitch Soumarokov was known to some as *The Russian Voltaire*. It should be noted that the title was self-bestowed.

Souphouse Charlie—See BONAPARTE, CHARLES JOSEPH.

SOUTH, ROBERT (1633–1716)

A noted English divine, Robert South was famed for his bitterness toward Dissenters. His sermons, a mixture of subtle commentary, buffoonery and ingenuity made him a favorite at court, where he was dubbed *The Scourge of Fanaticism*.

Southern Scott, The—See ARIOSTO, LUDOVICO.

South's Avenging Angel, The—See BOOTH, JOHN WILKES.

South's Most Crooked Gambler, The: JOHN NORTH (?–1835)

For years gambling-house proprietor John North was known as *The South's Most Crooked Gambler*. A vindictive mob hanged him on a hill above Vicksburg, Miss., with a "fixed" roulette wheel left tied to his body.

Soviet Saint, A—See REED, JOHN.

SOWER, CHRISTOPHER (1721–1784)

As a dedicated pacifist, German-born clergyman Christopher Sower became one of the most persecuted men during the American Revolution. Both sides viewed him as an enemy, his property was confiscated and he was for a time imprisoned. Despite these tribulations Sower did what he could to help others, including sharing the little food he had with the impoverished families of soldiers. He became known to them as *Der Brod-vater,* or *The Bread-father*.

SPAETH, SIGMUND (1885–1965)

Because his knowledge of music was so extensive, U.S. musicologist, writer and lecturer Sigmund Spaeth was called *The Tune Detective*.

Spanish Horace, The—See ANGENSOLA, BARTOLOMEO LEONARDO DE and LUPERCIO, LEONARDO DE.

Spanish Jack—See SYMMONDS, JOHN.

Spanish Michelangelo, The—See
CANO, ALONZO.

Spanish Moliere, The—See
MORATIN, LEANDRO
FERNANDEZ.

Sparky—See SCHULZ, CHARLES M.

SPEAKER, TRIS (1888–1958)

One of the greatest outfielders in baseball history
and a member of the Baseball Hall of Fame, Tris
Speaker was nicknamed *Spoke,* because when
called on to hit in critical situations, his bat almost always "spoke."

SPENCER, HERBERT (1820–1903)

English naturalist philosopher and the foremost for-
mulator of the doctrines of Social Darwinism, Herbert Spencer was disparaged by his foes, especially
Thomas Carlyle, as *The Most Unending Ass in
Christendom.*

Spendthrift of Albany, The—See
ROCKEFELLER, NELSON.

SPENSER, EDMUND (c. 1553–1598)

For what one critic called "a finer flush in color
of language," poet Edmund Spenser was called
The Rubens of Poetry. Because so many of his celebrated successors acknowledged his greatness and
his inspiration to them he has been dubbed *The
Poet's Poet* and *The Father of the Poets.* Milton
referred to him as *Sage and Serious Spenser.*

SPENSER, HENRY—See Fighting
Prelate, The.

Sphinx, The—See ROOSEVELT,
FRANKLIN D.

Spider, The—See GUIMARD,
MADELEINE.

Spider of Tripoli, The—See
QADDAFI, MUAMMAR EL.

*SPILSBURY, BERNARD HENRY
(1877–1947)*

British pathologist Sir Bernard Spilsbury was
considered one of the world's foremost medical
authorities on murder. Indeed he was called *The
Greatest Medical Detective of the Century.* Within
the legal profession he was known as *The Perfect
Witness,* one who could explain complicated medical theories in lay terms. His stature was so great
that he did not have to limit his answers to the
specific questions but could impartially present all
his findings with complete indifference as to
whether they helped the prosecution or the defense.

*SPINELLI, JUANITA "Duchess"
(1889–1941)*

Juanita Spinelli organized a school in California
to train young men for crime and masterminded
their depredations, which eventually included
murders. Fearing her, most of the youths followed
her instructions to address her as *Duchess,* which
the press later extended to *The Duchess of Death.*
Since she was the first woman ever to be condemned, legally, to death in the state, Duchess
Spinelli became a cause celebre. She was executed
in 1941.

Spiro T. Eggplant—See AGNEW,
SPIRO T.

SPOCK, BENJAMIN M. (1903–   )

U.S. physician, baby care expert and peace movement leader Dr. Benjamin Spock's book *The Common Sense of Baby and Child Care* has sold well over 28 million copies and has been translated into 26 languages. Quite logically he has been called *The Man Who Reared 50 Million Kids*.

Spoke—See SPEAKER, TRIS.

Spokesman for the Lost Generation, The—See HEMINGWAY, ERNEST.

SPONTINI, GASPARO (1774–1851)

Italian nobleman and composer Gasparo Spontini gained the sobriquet *The Napoleon of Opera* in 1805 when the Empress Josephine appointed him her court composer. He was so successful that he was allowed to remain in Paris during the Bourbon restoration.

SPOONER, BATHSHEBA (1746–1778)

Bathsheba Spooner became known as *The Tory Murderess* after she was sentenced to death in Massachusetts in the first capital case tried under American jurisdiction. She, her young American lover and two British Army deserters were convicted of murdering her elderly husband. Highly unpopular because her father was a Tory, Bathsheba, claiming to be pregnant, pleaded ''my belly.'' Under the law such a plea would have blocked her execution. She was examined by a group of male midwives and matrons, who declared her not pregnant. *The Tory Murderess* was hanged amidst continuing speculation about her maternal condition. An autopsy performed after the execution revealed the presence of a male fetus of five to six months. It was all rather politically embarassing.

SPOONER, WILLIAM ARCHIBALD (1844–1930)

William Archibald Spooner, the English Anglican clergyman and educator, was famous for his malaprops and in time was nicknamed *The Father of Spoonerisms*. Some samples include: To a bridegroom, ''It is kisstomery to cuss the bride''; to a student, ''You hissed my mystery class''; to his class, ''the assissination of Sassero'' (for ''the assassination of Cicero''); and during World War I, ''When the boys come back from France, we'll have the hags flung out.'' The scientific term for his speech affliction is metathesis, the transposition of letters or syllables in the words of a sentence, but the ailment is now more generally referred to as spoonerism.

Spoons Butler—See BUTLER, BENJAMIN.

Sporting Blood—See WARNER, JACK L.

Spot Lincoln—See LINCOLN, ABRAHAM.

SPOTSWOOD, ALEXANDER (1676–1740)

Because he sought to develop an iron industry in early 18th century Virginia, Alexander Spotswood, the governor of the colony, was nicknamed *Tubal Cain of America*, after the biblical Tubal-cain, the first artificer in brass and iron.

SPRAGUE, ACHSA W.
(c. 1828–1862)

U.S. trance medium and one of the first popularizers of and lecturers on spiritualism in the United States, Achsa W. Sprague was called *The Preaching Woman* by her enthusiastic audiences.

SPREULL, JOHN (1657–1740)

For his nonconformity Scottish Presbyterian John Spreull was twice tortured and spent so many years in prison at Bass that he became known as *Bass John*. The duke of York described *Bass John* as more dangerous than 500 common people.

SPRING, TOM (1795–1851)

Heavyweight champion English Tom Spring was sneeringly referred to as *Butter* because the public and press regarded him as "the man whose punch cannot dent butter." But as Spring, a master of the left-hand jab, defeated top sluggers, beating their faces to a pulp and then flattening them, the public came to recognize him as one of the marvels of all ring history. He was hailed as *The Pioneer of Fistic Science*.

SPRINGSTEEN, BRUCE (1949–   )

U.S. singer, guitarist and songwriter Bruce Springsteen became in the late 1970s one of the most popular and influential figures in rock music. In the field he is known simply as *The Boss*.

Spunky—See BEAME, ABE.

Spurious Governor, The—See LIVINGSTON, WILLIAM.

Spy of the Cumberland, The—See CUSHMAN, PAULINE.

Squab Poet, The—See DRYDEN, JOHN.

Squaw Man: YUGASIE OR YOGIA
(c. 1840–1938)

In 1878 a Ute Indian brave named Yugasie or Yogia refused to take part in an Indian massacre and as punishment was forced by his tribe to wear squaw clothing and perform squaw work for the rest of his life. He was also required to answer to the name *Squaw Man,* a penalty that lasted 60 years.

Stagecoach King, The—See HOLLADAY, BENJAMIN.

STAGG, AMOS ALONZO
(1862–1965)

The longest serving football head coach, Amos Alonzo Stagg coached a total of 57 seasons, including 41 at the University of Chicago and 14 at College of the Pacific. Celebrated as *Football's "Old Man River,"* he introduced the huddle, the man-in-motion and the end-around play as well as pioneering the forward pass and the T-formation.

Stallion, The—See LONDON, JACK.

STANDISH, MILES (c. 1584–1656)

A leader of the Massachusetts Bay Colony, Miles Standish was nicknamed *The Hero of New England* and *Little Indian Fighter,* a reference to both his courage and his physical stature. Standish found himself ridiculed by that bane of Puritans Thomas Morton, the playboy fur trader who violated the religious tenets of the colony and was finally taken into custody by Standish. After escaping from Standish more than once, Morton took to calling him *Captain Shrimp*.

STANFORD, SALLY (1903–1982)

One of California's most famous madams, Sally Stanford, whose book on her career was made into a television movie, achieved national prominence in 1972 when she was elected to the city council of Sausalito, Calif. Four years later she was elected to a two-year term as mayor. She served as vice-mayor in 1978, and since that seemed such a likely sobriquet for her, in 1980 the council awarded her the title *Vice Mayor* for life.

STANLEY, AUGUSTUS OWSLEY (1935–)

U.S. illegal drug manufacturer and peddler Augustus Owsley Stanley gained such sobriquets as *Hippieland's Court Chemist, The King of Acid, The King of Psychopharmacology* and *Mr. L.S.D.*

STANLEY, LORD (1799–1869)

Because of his brilliant and cutting oratorial skill, Lord Stanley, later the 14th earl of Derby, was known as *The Rupert of Debate,* after Prince Rupert, the political and military leader. Macaulay dubbed him *The Hotspur of Debate,* and Daniel O'Connell labeled him *Scorpion Stanley*.

STANTON, EDWIN M. (1814–1869)

Lincoln's secretary of war, Edwin M. Stanton was the first official in American history to make a practice of doctoring military news, delaying the re-

lease of news unfavorable to the Union and often changing the figures concerning the losses. He became *The Father of the Official Communique*.

Starch Johnny—See CROWNE, JOHN.

STARK, JOHN (1728–1822)

Gen. John Stark, who commanded the colonial forces that held the pass to the bridge over the Walloomsac River at the Battle of Bennington in 1777, was hailed as *The Leonidas of America*. In Stark's accomplishment he emulated Leonidas and his Spartans, who defended the pass of Thermopylae against the Persians in 480 B.C.

STARKWEATHER, CHARLES (1940–1959)

A teenage mass murderer in the 1950s, Charles Starkweather was the second to claim the nickname *The Nebraska Fiend*. Starkweather murdered a total of nine people, thus earning the sobriquet first applied to Stephen Lee Richards, who in the 1870s also killed nine in a murder binge in the same Lincoln, Neb., area. (See Richards, Stephen Lee.)

STARR, BELLE (1848–1889)

Belle Starr was almost entirely a creation of the eastern press, which heralded her as the great *Bandit Queen, Lady Desperado* and *Female Robin Hood*. She was actually no more than a hatchet-faced horse thief, frontier fence and, when those businesses were slow, common whore. But cover after cover on such publications as Richard Fox's *Police Gazette* brought her great fame and a career in Wild West shows in which she probably held up more stagecoaches than she had ever ridden in. Belle was murdered and the press tried to make a case that her death was the result of a falling out between outlaws; most likely she was shot from ambush by her 18-year-old son, whom she was in the habit of horsewhipping.

STARR, HENRY (1873–1921)

The last of the Starrs, a remarkable western American criminal clan that included Tom, Sam and, by marriage, Belle Starr, Henry Starr was known during Indian Territory days in what is now Oklahoma as *The Good Starr,* since he read the classics and neither smoked nor drank—and hardly ever committed crimes. He was sentenced to death by Hanging Judge Parker in 1894 but had the penalty reduced to a prison term on appeal. He was in and out of prison for the next 15 years, winning a number of pardons. In 1921 he was dubbed *The First Automobile Bandit* because he parked his car, instead of tethering his horse, as his forebears had done, just before robbing a bank. Although he may not have been the first to use an auto for this purpose, he was shot to death during his first try.

Staunch Buckingham—See BUCKINGHAM, WILLIAM ALFRED.

Steamboat Sharper, The—See DEVOL, GEORGE.

STEBBINS, GRANT C. (1862–1925)

One of the more legendary oilmen of Oklahoma, Grant C. Stebbins gained the nickname *Dry Hole Stebbins* for drilling 28 dry holes in a row before finally hitting black gold in Tulsa.

Steel Butterfly, The—See YOUNG, LORETTA.

Steel King, The—See CARNEGIE, ANDREW.

STEELE, RICHARD (1672–1729)

English essayist and dramatist Sir Richard Steele, designated *The First of the British Periodical Essayists,* gained his share of political and literary enemies. They nicknamed him *Jay,* meaning, as one of his critics put it, ''a jay who borrowed a feather from a peacock, another from a bullfinch, and another from a magpie; so that Dick is made up of borrowed colors; he borrowed his humor from Estcourt, criticism from Addison, his poetry of Pope, and his politics of Ridpath.''

STEEVENS, GEORGE (1736–1800)

As one of the foremost of Shakespearian commentators, George Steevens could hardly expect to escape the sobriquet *The Puck of Commentators.*

STEFFENS, LINCOLN (1866–1936)

U.S. journalist and reformer Lincoln Steffens was called *The King of the Muckrakers* for his famed exposes of business and political corruption, most notably in his book *The Shame of the Cities.* President Theodore Roosevelt coined the term ''muckraker'' in reference to Steffens in 1906 when he noted ''men with the muckrake are often indispensable to the well-being of society, if they know when to stop raking the muck.'' Some political figures, bewildered by Steffens' incorruptibility, spoke of *That Golden Rule Fellow.*

STEINBRENNER, GEORGE (1930–   )

The owner of the New York Yankees baseball team, George Steinbrenner has been nicknamed

Patton in Pinstripes, since he has been as controversial and autocratic in running the pin-striped team as Gen. George Patton was in commanding the military.

Steinbrenner of the South, The—See TURNER, TED.

Stepfather of His Country, The—See WASHINGTON, GEORGE.

STEPHENS, ALEXANDER H. (1812–1883)

In the period before the American Civil War, Jefferson Davis denounced those congressmen of the South who still supported the Union, labeling Alexander H. Stephens *The Little Pale Star from Georgia.* Stephens changed in time and became vice-president of the Confederacy under Davis, gaining the sobriquet *The Nestor of the Confederacy.*

STERLING, EDWARD (1773–1847)

One of the most forceful and influential writers on the staff of *The Times* of London, Edward Sterling was called *The Thunderer.* Eventually *The Times* itself was accorded the nickname.

STERNE, LAURENCE (1713–1768)

Laurence Sterne, the British author of *Tristram Shandy,* nicknamed himself *Yorick,* after the jester in *Hamlet,* because he enjoyed delighting his friends. The name was to cling to him all the more in death since like Shakespeare's Yorick he too was exhumed—by graverobbers. Two centuries later what was believed to be Sterne's skull was recovered and reburied in a new grave, one with an epitaph that begins, ''Alas, poor Yorick. . . .''

STEVENS, THADDEUS (1792–1868)

One of the most strong-willed American politicians, long-time congressman Thaddeus Stevens of Pennsylvania was called *The American Pitt* for the tenacity with which he held political positions. Because he was violently opposed to the Freemasons and conducted a legislative investigation of them, he was dubbed *The Arch-Priest of Anti-Masonry.* Stevens, who long hated the institution of slavery, maintained his negative attitudes toward the South even after the Civil War. Lame from birth, old and ill, unmarried and cared for only by a faithful black housekeeper, he was referred to by his supporters as *The Old Commoner.*

STEVENS, WALTER (1867–1939)

Walter Stevens, unique among professional hit men in the 1920s, was called *The Dean of Chicago Gunmen* because of his expert techniques and the fact that in his private life he was well-read and an expert on literature. The authorities were convinced he committed at least 60 murders, mostly for high pay (although he did one job for $50 for a friend). Despite his calling, Stevens was a prude, censoring his children's reading material and tearing out pages of books he considered obscene. Under his puritanical standards, his daughters were not allowed to use lipstick or rouge nor wear short skirts. Shocked when someone dared make an attempt on his life, *The Dean* immediately retired from crime.

STEVENSON, ADLAI (1900–1965)

The nickname *Egghead* was invented for Democratic presidential candidate Adlai Stevenson in 1952 by his Republican opponents. Irving Stone, in *They Also Ran,* asserted: ''. . . it persuaded a considerable portion of the American voters that Adlai Stevenson should be an object of derision because he was an eminently cultured and culti-vated man; and it made acceptable General Eisen-hower's tortured English and highly specialized, unintellectual training.''

Steward, The—See PENNI, GIOVANNI FRANCESCO.

STEWART, ALEXANDER (1343–1405?)

Upon being censured by the bishops of Moray and Ross for deserting his wife, Sir Alexander Stewart, Scottish lord of Badenoch, exacted revenge by burning Forres and Elgin in 1390. For these and other excesses he was labeled *The Wolf of Baden-och* and excommunicated.

STEWART, ALEXANDER T. (1803–1876)

A. T. Stewart was America's first great retail merchant, introducing such innovations in New York as the ''cost sale,'' the ''fire sale'' and the ''money back if not satisfied'' policy. He gained the honorific *The Prince of Merchants*. Perhaps his most revolutionary sales innovation was that of establishing the ''one-price'' system in retailing, with the price of all goods clearly marked and firmly held to. In time shoppers came to regard the policy as a wise one for them, protecting them from being heavily overcharged on some items when they failed to haggle wisely. Gratefully, they made *One Price Stewart* a millionaire.

STEWART, CHARLES (1778–1869)

Rear Admiral Charles Stewart, who commanded the *Constitution*, more commonly called *Old Ironsides*, during the War of 1812, was so suc-cessful at capturing British ships that his vessel's nickname was transferred to him as well.

STEWART, JAMES (1908–   )

Hollywood actor Jimmy Stewart is sometimes re-ferred to as *The Grand Old Man of the Aw Shucks School*.

STEWART, JOHN (?–1822)

A famous English traveler nicknamed *Walking Stewart,* John Stewart crossed by foot the United States, India, Arabia, Persia, Abyssinia, Nubia and large sections of Europe. Charles Lamb alludes to ''A 'Walking Stewart!''' in his ''Pindaric Ode to the Tread-Mill.''

STEWART, ''Yellow'' HENRY (c. 1855–1886)

A notorious gang leader and murderer in New Orleans during the late 19th century, Henry Stew-art suffered from malaria and became known as *Yellow Henry*. Since he suspected, correctly, that his malady would shorten his life, he was a mind-lessly brutal criminal who would as soon kill a vic-tim as merely disable him. His gang became known as the Yellow Henrys and remained a potent force until Stewart went to prison in 1883, where he died of malaria three years later.

Sticks—See TWIGGY.

STIEBER, WILLIAM (?–1892)

Considered the founder of the German espionage system, William Stieber was dubbed *The King of Sleuthhounds* by Prince Otto von Bismarck. It was a most innocuous sobriquet for a spymaster who raised the use of vice and perversion for black-mail purposes to a fine art. After the Franco-Prussian War, Stieber boasted he had 40,000 spies in France.

STIEGEL, HENRY WILLIAM "Baron von" (1729–1785)

German-born glassmaker and ironmaster, Henry William Stiegel was nicknamed in America *Baron von Stiegel,* although his only qualifications as a nobleman were enormous wealth and a tendency to live in the lavish style of Old World nobility. While his contributions to glassmaking were enormous, the *Baron* eventually suffered bankruptcy and died in 1785 in extreme poverty.

STILL, WILLIAM GRANT (1895–1978)

Mississippi-born William Grant Still became the first black to conduct a major American orchestra, the Los Angeles Philharmonic, in 1936. Dubbed *The Dean of Black Classical Composers,* his most famous work is "Afroamerican Symphony."

STILWELL, JOSEPH "Vinegar Joe" (1883–1946)

The blunt, outspoken World War II U.S. general Joseph Stilwell was nicknamed *Vinegar Joe* for his abrasive personality. He was caustic in his evaluations of others, including many of the major figures he had to deal with, but overall rather thoughtful and fair. At first he dismissed Lord Mountbatten as that Loathsome Limey, but as he grew to appreciate Mountbatten's abilities as a strategist, he changed that nickname to Our Limey. *Vinegar Joe* never altered his opinion of Chiang Kai-shek, whom he referred to as The Peanut.

STIMSON, HENRY L. (1867–1950)

The nickname for Henry L. Stimson, secretary of state in President Herbert Hoover's cabinet, was *Stimy*. A capital wit noted that it was probably the nearest outbreak of humor in that somber circle.

When Franklin D. Roosevelt named Stimson his secretary of state during World War II, he continued the use of the sobriquet.

Stimy—See STIMSON, HENRY L.

Stocking-Foot Orator, The—See MCKINLEY, WILLIAM.

STOCKMAN, DAVID A. (1946–   )

David A. Stockman, director of the Office of Management and Budget under President Ronald Reagan, was known in Congress as *The Grim Reaper* and *The Young Slasher* because of what some considered his budget-cutting mania.

STODDART, JOHN (1773–1856)

One of the most outspoken editors of *The Times* of London, Sir John Stoddart was so vitriolic in his denunciations of Napoleon and in his other prejudices that he was nicknamed *Doctor Slop.*

STOKOWSKI, LEOPOLD (1882–1977)

The flamboyant English-born orchestra conductor Leopold Stokowski was often referred to as *The Maestro Seducer* because of his many affairs, to which, at least one biographer said, he devoted almost as much time and energy as he did to his music. Stokowski insisted he needed his sexual escapades to stimulate his musical creativity.

STONE, LOUIS—See Winsted Liar, The.

STONE, LUCY (1818–1893)

Lucy Stone, American feminist and reformer, was the first married woman in the United States to insist upon using her maiden name after her marriage, launching a long tradition of "Lucy Stoners" that continues to the present. For this and other offenses, she was subjected to considerable abuse as people ripped down posters advertising her lectures, hurled prayer books at her and burned pepper in the auditoriums where she spoke. Rather than call her Lucy Stone, many insisted on referring to her as the *Wife of Henry Blackwell*.

Stone-Ass—See MOLOTOV, VYACHESLAV M.

Stonewall of the West—See CLEBURNE, PATRICK RONAYNE.

Stork—See HUXLEY, THOMAS HENRY.

Stork, The—See ANDERSEN, HANS CHRISTIAN.

Stormer of Cities—See ATTENDOLO, MUZIO.

Stormy Petrel of the Chess World, The—See NIMZOWITSCH, ARNOLD.

Stovepipe Johnson—See JOHNSON, ADAM R. "Stovepipe."

STRACHEY, LYTTON (1880–1932)

English biographer and member of the Bloomsbury group, Lytton Strachey was called by intimates *The Arch-bugger of Bloomsbury*. Despite his well-known homosexuality, in 1909 he proposed marriage to and was accepted by Virginia Woolf,

who was then Virginia Stephen. He withdrew the offer the next day, however, stating, "I was in terror lest she would kiss me." Still, he salvaged his friendship with Virginia by suggesting to political activist and writer Leonard Woolf that he seek her hand.

Straight Tongue: HENRY BENJAMIN WHIPPLE (1822–1901)

The first Episcopal bishop in Minnesota and a missionary to the Indians, Henry Benjamin Whipple was nicknamed *Straight Tongue* by the Indians because at first he was regarded as having rare qualities for a white man and even for a missionary: honesty, directness and fairness. A later historical judgment concluded that *Straight Tongue* was an accomplished hand at stealing Indian lands.

STRATTON, CHARLES SHERWOOD— See Tom Thumb.

STRATTON, WINFIELD SCOTT (1848–1902)

A U.S. carpenter who struck it rich when he found gold in Cripple Creek, Colo., Winfield Scott Stratton, better known as *Old Man Stratton*, was nicknamed *The Midas of the Rockies*.

STRAUS, NATHAN (1848–1931)

Nathan Straus, who with his brother, Isidor, became an owner of R. H. Macy's department store in New York, initiated the campaign for compulsory pasteurization of milk in 1892 and with his own funds set up stations in slum districts to make milk available to the poor at reduced prices. The poor, noting the subsequent improvement in the health of their babies and growing children, called him *The Baby Savior*.

STRAUSS, FRANZ JOSEF (1915–)

The intensely nationalistic West German politician Franz Josef Strauss, leader of the autonomous Christian Socialist Union, the powerful Bavarian branch of the Christian Democratic Union, is noted for his strident tones and called by both friends and foes *The Bull of Bavaria*.

STRAUSS, HARRY—See Pittsburgh Phil.

STRAUSS, ROBERT S. (1918–)

Texas politician and former chairman of the Democratic National Committee Robert S. Strauss, considered one of the most adept political operatives in the United States, has been dubbed by the press *The Grand Persuader*.

STRAVINSKY, IGOR (1882–1971)

Russian-born composer Igor Stravinsky, noted for his ballets and avant-garde innovations, was dubbed *The Little Giant of Twentieth Century Music* and *The Musical Giant*, which covered both his professional and physical stature.

Street Tyrone Power, The—See TRAVOLTA, JOHN.

STREICHER, JULIUS (1885–1946)

An early Nazi Party member and one of the party's foremost theorists of anti-Semitism, Julius Streicher insisted on being known by the self-proclaimed sobriquet *Jew-baiter Number One*. He was so corrupt, however, that he was expelled from the party in 1940 for misappropriating Jewish property. Found guilty at the Nuremberg war crimes trials, he was hanged, having become convinced, according to William L. Shirer, that all the judges were Jews.

STRINDBERG, AUGUST (1849–1912)

Swedish playwright and fiction writer August Strindberg led such an impoverished and wretched early life and wrote such extremely pessimistic works that he was called *The Bedeviled Viking*. He was also referred to as *The Shakespeare of Sweden*, although his dramas of social criticism were much closer to the works of Henrik Ibsen.

STROHEIM, ERICH VON (1885–1957)

Few Hollywood personalities were subjected to as many whispering campaigns as was actor-director Erich von Stroheim, who was referred to as *The Dirty Hun*, some say at the instigation of film executive Louis B. Mayer. It was often charged that the orgy scenes in many of his films were the real thing, a theory made more credible by the fact that he declared the set off limits even to studio heads.

STRONG, JOHN—See Blind Mechanician, The.

Strong Man of Egypt, The—See NASSER, GAMAL ABDEL.

Strong Man of the Solomon Islands, The—See KWAISULIA.

Strongbow—See DE CLARE, RICHARD.

STROUD, ROBERT F. (1890–1963)

To everyone except federal prison officials, Robert F. Stroud was *The Birdman of Alcatraz,* perhaps the most amazing example of a brutal killer reforming and becoming in his prison cell a bookish world-famous ornithologist. *The Birdman* spent 54 years behind bars for two murders, including that of a prison guard, and pleas for his release by scientists, animal lovers and many supporters were ignored, mainly because of the opposition of federal prison officials still enraged that his death sentence for killing the guard was commuted to life by President Woodrow Wilson. The name *Birdman of Alcatraz* was a misnomer because Stroud conducted his research with birds in Leavenworth. After having served 26 years in prison, he was transferred to Alcatraz but forbidden to take any of his birds with him. At that grim island prison he conducted research without live specimens. Stroud's *Digest on the Diseases of Birds* is still recognized as a classic in its field. He died in 1963.

STRUCK, LYDIA (1833–1879)

A 19th century murderer who poisoned, among others, several of her husbands and children in New York and Connecticut—her murder toll reads eight confirmed, three probables and, according to some estimates, perhaps 31 others—was labeled *Queen Poisoner* and *The Modern Lucretia Borgia.* A pamphlet bearing the latter sobriquet as part of its title was a best-seller in the 1870s.

STRUGHOLD, HUBERTUS (1898–   )

German-born Hubertus Strughold pioneered physiological studies of the effects of high-altitude flying on humans and in 1954 built the first space-cabin simulator to help condition astronauts for outer space travels. He became internationally known as *The Father of Space Medicine.*

STUART, CHARLES EDWARD (1720–1788)

The son of James Francis Edward Stuart, the so-called Old Pretender who unsuccessfully claimed the English throne as *James III,* Charles Edward Stuart was popular among the Scots, who called him *Bonnie Prince Charlie* and supported his fruitless military efforts to put James on the throne, ending in defeat in 1846 at Culloden. Upon his father's death, Charles claimed to be king and was dubbed *The Young Pretender,* but he too was unsuccessful and was forced to live out his days on the Continent, where he led a life of debauchery and drunkenness.

STUART, GILBERT (1755–1828)

Gilbert Stuart painted portraits of many leading Americans of the Revolutionary era, gaining fame as *The Painter of Presidents* or *The Portrait Painter of Presidents.* Six presidents sat for him—the first six, all who took office during his lifetime.

STUART, JAMES EWELL BROWN "Jeb" (1833–1864)

As the commander of Robert E. Lee's cavalry, James Ewell Brown Stuart, or *Jeb,* by combining his initials, was considered the epitome of manliness and soldierly bearing, and he was thus called *The Plumed Knight of the Confederacy.* As the South's foremost cavalry officer, he was also called *Prince Rupert of the Confederacy,* after the military leader Prince Rupert of the English Civil War in the 1640s. During his cadet days at West Point, he was dubbed *Beauty,* as fellow cadet Fitzhugh Lee put it, "to express their idea of his personal comeliness in inverse ratio to the term employed."

STUART, JAMES FRANCIS EDWARD (1688–1766)

The Prince of Wales, James Francis Edward Stuart, claimed the throne as James III as the successor to James II. He was recognized only by his followers and Louis XIV of France but not by the English people. Some detractors called him *The Warming Pan Baby,* charging that he was brought to the bedroom of Mary of Modena, James II's second wife, in a warming pan after her actual child had been stillborn. His attempts to win the throne a failure, James spent his years in exile, being referred to in later life as *The Old Pretender.*

STUART, LYLE (1922?–   )

The controversial U.S. publisher Lyle Stuart is often referred to within the industry as *The Bad Boy of American Publishing.*

STUCLEY, THOMAS (1520–1578)

English adventurer Sir Thomas Stucley was at various times in the service of Elizabeth of England, Henry II of France and Philip II of Spain. He was also involved in the plot to seat Mary Stuart on the throne of England. Stucley, despite his constant change of colors, was rather admired and the subject of a play and many ballads, which celebrated him as *Lusty Stucley.*

Stuffed Prophet, The—See CLEVELAND, GROVER.

Stupid—See BRUTUS, LUCIUS JUNIUS.

STURGEON, DANIEL (1789–1878)

In his 12 years in the U.S. Senate from 1839 to 1851, Daniel Sturgeon established what must have been a record by making only one brief address to the chamber. Not surprisingly, his colleagues called him *The Silent Senator.*

STURLASON, SNORRI (1179–1241)

The great Icelandic historian of the 13th century, Snorri Sturlason has often been designated *The Northern Herodotus.*

STURM, JOHANN CHRISTOPH (1635–1703)

The Bavarian science writer Johann Christoph Sturm did so much to popularize scientific thought in Germany in the 17th century with his compilations of developments in various fields that he gained the title *The Restorer of Science in Germany.*

STUYVESANT, PETER "Wooden Leg" (c. 1610–1672)

Peter Stuyvesant, the famed *One-Legged Governor of New Netherland,* later New York, was one of the favorite subjects of portrait painters of New World personalities. *Wooden Leg Stuyvesant,* as he was also called after he lost a leg in 1644 while attacking the Portuguese island of St. Martin, was immortalized on canvas for years after his death. Someone eventually noticed that certain paintings showed his wooden leg as the right one and others showed it as the left one. Remarkably, there appeared to be no written record indicating which leg he had lost. Finally early in this century his body was exhumed and since then all paintings of *Wooden Leg Stuyvesant* have shown no right one.

Sublime Dandy, The—See LEWIS, MERIWETHER.

Subtle Doctor, The—See DUNS SCOTUS, JOHN.

Suck All Cream—See CLARKE, SAMUEL.

SUCKLING, JOHN *(1609–1642)*

English Cavalier poet, playwright and courtier Sir John Suckling was much esteemed in his day and designated *The Greatest Gallant of His Time*. He is now remembered mainly for a few lyrics, such as "Why so pale and wan, fond lover?" and "When, dearest, I but think of thee."

Sue Mundy: *MARCELLUS JEROME CLARKE (c. 1843–1865)*

Marcellus Jerome Clarke was a cunning Confederate guerrilla whose operations in Kentucky proved a decided embarrassment to the Union forces, which were unable to capture him. One local newspaper editor twitted the Union forces by giving Clarke the nickname of a notorious black *"Sue Mundy"*—Clarke was dark-skinned, slender and long-haired—and criticized them for being unable to capture "him/her." When Clarke was finally apprehended in early 1865, his notoriety was such that he was promptly court-martialed and hanged on no more specific a charge than that he was *Sue Mundy*.

SUESSE, DANA *(1911–   )*

A child-prodigy pianist and composer, Dana Suesse became known for her rapid composition skills writing pop and semiclassical songs and instrumentals. Her talents won her the title *The Girl Gershwin*. She became associated with Paul Whiteman as a composer and pianist.

Sugar—See ROBINSON, "Sugar" RAY.

Sugar Daddy of Big Bankers, The—See BURNS, ARTHUR F.

Sugar-Lip—See HAFIZ, MOHAMMED.

SULLIVAN, ED *(1902–1974)*

U.S. newspaper columnist and television personality Ed Sullivan was called *The Great Stone Face* because of his general lack of charisma. Despite this failing, or perhaps because of it, Sullivan had one of the most successful variety shows on television.

SULLIVAN, JAMES "Yankee": *JAMES AMBROSE (182?–1856)*

Irish-American prizefighter of the 1840s and 1850s, James Ambrose, better known professionally as James Sullivan, gained the nickname *Yankee Sullivan* because of his custom of entering the ring with an American flag draped around his waist.

SULLIVAN, JOHN L. *(1858–1918)*

World heavyweight champion John L. Sullivan was called *The Great John L.* and *The Boston Strong Boy*. He was reputed to be the hardest puncher in boxing history, but it is impossible to sustain the claim since Sullivan fought bareknuckled and later champions wore gloves.

SULLIVAN, MARK *(1874–1952)*

Regarded as the dean of Washington correspondents, Mark Sullivan, columnist for the *New York*

Herald Tribune from 1924 until his death, was nicknamed *The Friend of Presidents*. For historical accuracy many observers would insert the word "Republican" before *Presidents*.

SULLIVAN, TIMOTHY "Big Tim" *(1862–1913)*

New York Tammany Hall leader and congressman Timothy *"Big Tim"* Sullivan was referred to as *The Big Feller* and *The Last of the Big Time Grafters*, the latter being a gross inaccuracy.

SULLY, MAXIMILIEN DE BETHUNE, DUC DE *(1560–1641)*

The Duc de Sully, head of the French treasury under Henry IV, was the great financial "no" man of his era. Put in charge of the disordered and virtually bankrupt royal finances, Sully proved incorruptible as he rooted out tax frauds and stopped all needless expenditures. He was not only able to wipe out the royal deficit but produced a surplus that allowed for debt reduction. The king, and many others, called Sully *The Iron Duke* for his steadfastness of purpose.

Sultan of Swat, The—See Ruth, Babe.

SULZBERGER, ARTHUR OCHS *(1926–   )*

Because he was inseparable from his sister Judy as a child, *New York Times* publisher Arthur Ochs Sulzberger was nicknamed *Punch* by their father. He grew up playing in the hallways of the newspaper and was dubbed by employees, with affection, *The Crown Prince*. Of the two nicknames he has not outgrown the former.

SUMNER, EDWIN VOSE *(1797–1863)*

One of the oldest Union field commanders in the Civil War, Edwin Vose Sumner did not survive the war. It was not a bullet but natural causes that ended his life, although a bullet had once come close. Since it had bounced off his skull, he received the nickname *Bull Head*.

Sun King, The—See ALBERT, PRINCE OF MONACO; LOUIS XIV OF FRANCE; MARKEL, LESTER.

Sundance Kid, The: HARRY LONGBAUGH *(1863–1911?)*

Harry Longbaugh, a member of the West's Wild Bunch, may or may not have died in South America with Butch Cassidy, but there is little dispute that at least initially he was not fond of his nickname *The Sundance Kid*. At first, whenever he was drunk, which was often, he got nasty if someone called him *The Sundance Kid*. Since the name traced back to an 18-month jail term he served as a teenager in Sundance, Wyoming Territory for horsestealing, it was not a sobriquet of which he was particularly proud.

SUNDAY, BILLY *(1863–1935)*

Evangelist Billy Sunday, known for his demonstrative, vividly idiomatic speaking style, was much criticized for making a business, and a very profitable one at that, out of religion. Among the unwanted sobriquets bestowed on him were *The Huckster of the Tabernacle*, *The Untired Business Man of Theology* and *The Charlie Chaplin of the Pulpit*.

Sunday Gentleman, The—See DEFOE, DANIEL.

Super Bluebeard—See PETIOT, MARCEL.

Super Kraut—See KISSINGER, HENRY.

Super Mex—See TREVINO, LEE.

Super Schmidt—See SCHMIDT, HELMUT.

Superbrat—See McENROE, JOHN.

Superhenry—See KISSINGER, HENRY.

Supersalesman of the Turned-on Generation, The—See LEARY, TIMOTHY.

SUSLOV, MIKHAIL *(1902–1982)*

Mikhail Suslov, for years recognized as the Kremlin's top ideologue and preserver of Marxist doctrine, was nicknamed by Western observers *The Red Professor*. The political mentor of President Leonid Brezhnev, Suslov was generally regarded as a "hardliner." He is believed to have orchestrated Nikita Khruschchev's fall from power.

Suspended Sentence Maledon—See MALEDON, GEORGE.

SUTHERLAND, EDWIN H. *(1883–1950)*

U.S. criminologist, author and educator Dr. Edwin H. Sutherland was designated *The Dean of American Criminologists* for his advances in the field of criminology.

SUTHERLAND, JOAN *(1926–   )*

The great Australian operatic coloratura soprano Joan Sutherland has long borne the nickname *The*

Glorious Iceberg. Many observers believe she typifies both the highly positive and somewhat negative characteristics of numerous opera singers: a magnificent voice and rather poor acting ability.

SUTHERLAND, JOCH BAIN "Jock" *(1889–1948)*

Jock Sutherland, the long-time football coach at the University of Pittsburgh, was known as *The Overland Man* for his insistence that the offense play mainly a running game.

SUTTON, WILLIE "The Actor" *(1901–1980)*

Celebrated as the greatest bank robber of modern times, William Sutton became famous as *The Actor* because of the various disguises he used in his holdups—mailman, window cleaner, messenger, bank guard and police officer, among others. Over a 35-year span, *Slick Willie,* as he was often called, got away with over $2 million in spectacular crimes, but at the end of his career he observed how less than slick he really was: he had spent 33 of 43 years from 1926 to 1969, the major portion of his adult life, behind bars.

Swamp Fox, The—See MARION, FRANCIS.

SWANSON, CLAUDE A. *(1862–1939)*

Franklin D. Roosevelt's first secretary of the navy, Claude A. Swanson was nicknamed *Big Navy Claude* for what some thought was the silly idea of increasing, instead of decreasing, the strength of the U.S. Navy during the Great Depression.

SWANSON, GLORIA *(1899–1983)*

Long-time screen actress Gloria Swanson was called *Old Glory* in Hollywood because of her penchant for denouncing those stars whose behavior she did not approve of. She was always greatly interested in nutrition and fashion and was famous for wearing striking female and male-style apparel. This last foible caused Cecil B. DeMille always to refer to her as *Young Fellow*.

Swearing Jack Waller—See WALLER, JOHN.

Sweater Girl, The—See TURNER, LANA.

Sweatshirt Kid, The—See FISCHER, ROBERT JAMES.

SWEDENBORG, EMANUEL (1688–1772)

Swedish philosopher, mystic, prophet, scientist and visionary Emanuel Swedenborg, who claimed to have achieved communication with the dead and with higher planes of being, had a profound influence on psychology, spiritualism and modern occultism. He also claimed that heaven and hell were not places but states. Among those whom he influenced were Coleridge, Blake, Carlyle, Balzac, William James, Lincoln, Emerson, Helen Keller and Jung. His devoted followers called him *The Explorer of the Spirit* and *God's Instrument*.

Swedish Match King, The—See KREUGER, IVAR.

Swedish Nightingale, The—See LIND, JENNY.

Sweet Potato Man, The—See CARVER, GEORGE WASHINGTON.

Sweet Singer of the Temple, The—See HERBERT, GEORGE.

Sweet Swan of Avon, The—See SHAKESPEARE, WILLIAM.

Sweetheart of the Foxholes, The—See LAMOUR, DOROTHY.

Sweetheart of the Silent Majority, The—See SCHLAFLY, PHYLLIS.

Sweetheart of the Soviet Sky, The—See TERESHKOVA, VALENTINA.

Swell-Foot Tyrant, The—See CASTLEREAGH, ROBERT STEWART.

SWIFT, JONATHAN (1667–1745)

Anglo-Irish satirist, poet, clergyman and political pamphleteer Jonathan Swift, the author of *Gulliver's Travels*, was called *The English Rabelais* by some and *The Impious Buffoon* by others. Macaulay, the Whig historian, denounced Swift for going over to the Tories by calling him *The Ribald Priest, The Perjured Lover* and *The Apostate Politician*. Swift was also playfully called *Presto* by the duchess of Shrewsbury when she could not remember his surname. Swift spent his final days in madness, called by some *A Diogenes in an Irish Cabin*.

Swift Bird—See HARE, WILLIAM HOBART.

Swift Heinz—See GUDERIAN, HEINZ.

Swifty—See LAZAR, IRVING PAUL.

SWINBURNE, ALGERNON (1837–1909)

Poet, playwright and critic Algernon Swinburne was a symbol of the mid-Victorian poetic revolt against the era's morals and philosophy, and his work was marked by individual anarchism. For that reason as well as his alcoholism, epilepsy and masochism, he was called by many *Mad Swinburne.* Gilbert and Sullivan popularized another sobriquet for Swinburne when they satirized him as *The Fleshy Poet* in *Patience. Punch* attacked his poetry for its supposed immorality by referring to him as *Swine-born.*

Swine-Born—See SWINBURNE, ALGERNON.

Sword of Allah, The—See KHALID (or KHALED).

Sword of the Confederacy, The—See JACKSON, THOMAS JONATHAN "Stonewall."

Sword of the Revolution, The—See WASHINGTON, GEORGE.

Sycorax—See RITSON, JOSEPH.

SYKES, GEORGE (1822–1880)

The Union commander of a division of regulars at the Battle of Gettysburg, Gen. George Sykes was later shelved by Ulysses S. Grant when the Army of the Potomac was reorganized in 1864. His nickname, *Tardy George,* which dated back to pre-war days, explains the reason for Grant's action. Although an otherwise solid officer, *Tardy George* clearly was incapable of delivering the quick punch that was necessary in offensive operations.

SYMMES, JOHN CLEVES "Hollow Earth" (?–1829)

A veteran of the War of 1812, John Cleves Symmes became famous as *Hollow Earth Symmes* when he developed the theories that the earth was made up of a group of hollow concentric spheres and that one could enter the earth's inner world through holes in the North and South poles. Symmes gained enough support to have a bill introduced in Congress that would have provided funds for an expedition to prove his theory, but while it garnered 25 votes, the proposal failed to win approval. Support for *Hollow Earth Symmes*'s theory continued into the 20th century.

SYMMONDS, JOHN (?–1756)

A notorious Spanish criminal, whose depredations earned him the sobriquet *Spanish Jack,* tried unsuccessfully to hide his identity in England under the name John Symmonds. He was hanged at Maidstone on April 18, 1756.

Symphony on Silver Skates, The—See HENIE, SONJA.

SZOLD, HENRIETTA (1869–1945)

Baltimore-born Henrietta Szold went to Palestine in 1910 to recover from a disappointing love affair. She became immersed in the Zionist cause and was determined to wipe out the poverty and disease prevalent there. She returned to the United States in 1912 to form Hadassah, the Women's Zionist Organization of America. The first medical unit was sent to the Holy Land the following year and she became known as both *The Jewish Florence Nightingale* and *The Mother of Hadassah*.

T

Tadpole of the Lakes, A—See KEATS, JOHN.

TAFT, ROBERT A. *(1889–1953)*

Although he was clearly the voice of Republican Party orthodoxy for many years, the name *Mr. Republican* was not applied to Ohio senator Robert A. Taft until his 1950 senatorial campaign. It was used constantly in Taft's unsuccessful battle with Dwight D. Eisenhower for the Republican presidential nomination in 1952.

TAFT, WILLIAM HOWARD *(1857–1930)*

William Howard Taft, the 27th president of the United States, was nicknamed *The Big Chief;* less a reference to his role as chief executive than an allusion to his corpulence. He weighed 325 pounds when he entered the White House. Theodore Roosevelt, who handpicked Taft as his successor, came to regret the choice and said, "Taft meant well, but he meant well feebly." Later Taft was named to the Supreme Court and Justice Louis Brandeis was to say; "It's very difficult for me to understand how a man who is so good as Chief Justice could have been so bad as President."

Tail Gunner Joe—See MCCARTHY, JOSEPH R.

Tailpipe Johnny—See DINGELL, JOHN D.

TALBOT, FRANCES JENNINGS *(1649–1730)*

The beautiful sister of Sarah, duchess of Marlborough, Frances Jennings married Richard Talbot, who was later made duke of Tyrconnel. When James II was toppled from the English throne, the couple was forced to flee to France, where the duke died. Left impoverished, Frances secretly returned to England and, unable to make contact with her sister, supported herself as a peddler near the Royal Exchange. She wore a long white dress and a white mask and created much attention as the anonymous *White-Milliner*. Finally she received financial aid from her sister and her late husband's estate and was able to live out her years in comfort in Ireland.

Talebearer, A—See BOSWELL, JAMES.

Talent of the Academy, The—See ARISTOTLE.

TALLEYRAND-PERIGORD, CHARLES MAURICE DE *(1754–1838)*

The French statesman Talleyrand was referred to, not always with unqualified admiration, as *The Prince of Diplomatists*. The ability of this one-time bishop, described by some historians as being slippery as an eel, to change sides constantly made it possible for him to serve in the French National Assembly from 1789 to 1791. Although he left

France during the Reign of Terror, he was later accepted in the Directory and for a time served as Napoleon's foreign minister. By 1814, after Napoleon was deposed for the first time, he had made himself acceptable to King Louis XVIII and was his representative at the Congress of Vienna.

TALLIEN, MADAME (1774–1831)

Madame Tallien, the wife of the proconsul of Bordeaux, managed to save many from execution during the French Revolution. Finally arrested herself, she urged Tallien to stop the killings by having Robespierre sent to the guillotine. Her advice was heeded and the Reign of Terror ended. Madame Tallien was lionized as *Our Lady of Mercy,* and whenever she visited the theater, she was greeted by great applause.

Tallu—See BANKHEAD, TALLULAH.

Tallulah's Papa—See BANKHEAD, WILLIAM B.

TALMA, FRANCOIS JOSEPH (1763–1826)

French tragic actor Francois Joseph Talma was dubbed *The French Roscius,* after the Roman slave turned actor. Talma was the first to introduce on the French stage the practice of wearing a costume of the period being portrayed.

TALMADGE, EUGENE "Gene" (1884–1946)

Georgia governor Eugene Talmadge was perhaps the most unreconstructed white supremacist of the 20th century. Among the invectives hurled at him was *His Chain Gang Excellency.*

TAMERLANE (or TIMUR or TIMOUR) (1333?–1405)

Mongol conqueror Tamerlane, or Timur or Timour, a descendant of Genghis Khan, scored great military victories in Russia, Persia, Turkey and India and at his death ruled an area that included large portions of Russia and stretched to the Great Wall of China, a country he was preparing to invade at the time of his death. While he was a brilliant military man and an able administrator, he was noted for his cruelty and nicknamed *The Prince of Destruction.*

TANEY, ROGER B. (1777–1864)

One of the leaders of the pro-war faction that broke away from the Federalist Party in 1812, Roger B. Taney was called *King Coody,* since the group was known as the Coodies. Taney later served as secretary of the treasury under President Andrew Jackson, who appointed him chief justice of the Supreme Court. He authored the Dred Scott decision.

TANGUAY, EVA (1878–1948)

A flamboyant singer and dancer in the early 1900s, Eva Tanguay was most identified with the hit song "I Don't Care" and dubbed *The I Don't Care Girl.*

Tania—See HEARST, PATRICIA.

Tap Dancer, The—See CORBETT, JAMES J. "Gentleman Jim."

Tapissier de Notre-Dame, Le—See MONTMORENCY-BOUTEVILLE, HENRI .

Tardy George—See
SKYES, GEORGE.

Tarnished Hero, The—See **ROGERS, GEORGE W.**

TARNOWER, HERMAN (1910–1980)

The physician who wrote *The Complete Scarsdale Medical Diet,* a best-seller, Dr. Herman Tarnower was of course nicknamed *The Scarsdale Diet Doctor.* He was shot to death in his home in Purchase, N. Y., by his long-time lover, Jean Harris, who was later convicted of second-degree murder.

TARTINI, GIUSEPPE (1692–1770)

One of the most important figures in the history of the violin, Giuseppe Tartini was the son of a wealthy nobleman and was educated in preparation for, in turn, the clergy, the law and the army (where he became a champion fencer.) However, he forsook all those activities to become first violinist in the orchestra of San Antonio in Padua, Italy. Despite extraordinarily low pay Tartini refused to leave that position even after he gained international acclaim for his virtuosity. In 1728 he established a school for the violin in Padua, which drew eager applicants from many countries, gaining Tartini the honorific of his contemporaries as *The Master of the Nations.*

Tarzancito (c. 1928–   )

In 1933 a woodcutter captured a boy of about five years in a jungle in El Salvador. It was speculated that he had lived in the wild since birth, living on raw fish and wild fruit. Because of the similarity of his existence with the fictional Tarzan, the boy was nicknamed *Tarzancito.* Newspaper columnist Ernie Pyle "interviewed" *Tarzancito* and reported that he howled a lot and bit people approaching him. In time *Tarzancito* adapted to human life.

Tattooed Man, The—See **BLAINE, JAMES G.**

TAUSEN, HANS (1494–1561)

Leader of the religious opposition to Catholicism in Scandinavia, Hans Tausen was nicknamed *The Danish Luther.* The monarchs embraced his preachings since one of his prime tenets was that ecclesiastical wealth belonged to the throne.

TAYLOR, ALFRED ALEXANDER (1848–1931)

Alfred A. Taylor gained the sobriquet of *The Knight of the Red Rose,* an allusion to England's War of the Roses, in 1886 in Tennessee because while he sought the governorship as a Republican, his brother, Robert Love Taylor, was the Democratic gubernatorial candidate. Robert won the race. Alfred subsequently served in the U. S. House of Representatives for three terms and finally, after his brother's death, was elected governor in 1920.

TAYLOR, CHEVALIER JOHN (fl. c. 1750)

English occultist Chevalier John Taylor, who published "a romancing account of his life" in the mid-18th century, was so widely disbelieved that he became known as *Liar Taylor.*

TAYLOR, ELIZABETH (1932–   )

Glamorous film star Elizabeth Taylor cannot abide the name "Liz." Among the nicknames bestowed on her by former husbands are *Lizzie Schwartzkopf* (by Mike Todd) and *Fatty* (by Richard Burton).

TAYLOR, JEREMY (1613–1667)

English bishop and theological writer Jeremy Taylor was dubbed by Emerson *The Shakespeare of Divines*.

TAYLOR, ROBERT (1911–1969)

Movie actor Robert Taylor was often called *Beautiful Bob* by his fans and mail so addressed was delivered to him—or so the studio press agents said.

TAYLOR, ROBERT LOVE (1850–1912)

During the gubernatorial race in Tennessee in 1886, Robert Love Taylor was the candidate for the Democrats while his brother, Alfred Alexander Taylor, ran as a Republican. Robert took to wearing a white rose and his brother a red one. Robert thus became known as *The Knight of the White Rose* and his brother The Knight of the Red Rose, allusions to England's War of the Roses. Robert Taylor won the election and served several terms as governor; he was also elected to the U. S. Senate. He died in 1912. In 1920 his brother finally won the governorship.

TAYLOR, ZACHARY (1784–1850)

Zachary Taylor, the 12th president of the United States, gained the nickname *Old Rough and Ready* as a general during the Mexican War because of his sloppy dress, tobacco chewing and colorful cursing. He was also called *Old Buena Vista* not merely because he won a great victory there, with 5,000 men to Santa Anna's 21,000, but because

he refused orders to pull back to Monterey. Taylor felt that Buena Vista was his strongest point of defense and decided to make his stand there. Had he lost that battle he never would have become president.

Teacher of Germany, The—See MELANCHTHON, PHILIPP.

Teacher President, The—See GARFIELD, JAMES A.

Teapot, The—See TOULOUSE-LAUTREC, HENRI DE.

Teapot Dome Sinclair—See SINCLAIR, HARRY F. ''Teapot Dome.''

Tear 'em—See ROEBUCK, JOHN ARTHUR.

Tear Gas West—See WEST, JAMES MARION ''Silver Dollar,'' JR.

Tea-Table Scoundrel, A—See CHESTERFIELD, PHILIP DORMER STANHOPE, LORD.

TEBBETTS, GEORGE ROBERT ''Birdie'' (1909–   )

A star baseball catcher famed for kibitzing with batters, to shake their concentration, George Tebbetts won the nickname *Birdie*. We are indebted to the famous Dizzy Dean for his observation on the subject: ''Most all ballplayers got nicknames, and *Birdie Tebbetts's* is *Birdie* because he's always ahollerin' like a little ole kinairy bird.''

Teddy's Terror—See O'NEILL, WILLIAM O. "Buckey."

Telephones Tchaikovsky—See KONARSKY, MATT.

Telescope Teddy—See ROOSEVELT, THEODORE.

TELL, WILLIAM (fl. c. 1300s?)

The legendary Swiss hero William Tell is supposed to have lived in the early 14th century under Gessler, the tyrannical Austrian governor of Uri. Forced by the tyrant to shoot an arrow through an apple on his son's head, William Tell was imprisoned after he said that had he missed he would have put an arrow through Gessler's heart. Tell escaped his captors and killed Gessler, winning the sobriquet *The Mountain Brutus*.

TELLER, EDWARD (1908–   )

Hungarian-born U.S. physicist Edward Teller was dubbed *The Father of the H-bomb* because of his incessant lobbying for development of the hydrogen bomb. When J. Robert Oppenheimer, The Father of the Atomic Bomb, was investigated by the Atomic Energy Commission, Teller was the only scientist to speak out against Oppenheimer. He insisted Oppenheimer's security clearance should be downgraded because he "interfered" with the rapid development of the hydrogen bomb. Teller also maintained that had Oppenheimer lent his support, the bomb could have been built as early as 1947. In 1964 Teller gained a new nickname when he was parodied as the title character of the movie *Dr. Strangelove, or How I Learned To Stop Worrying and Love the Bomb*. Despite Teller's strenuous objections the sobriquet *Dr. Strangelove* stuck to him. In the early 1980s Teller proposed stationing in space a "small" nuclear bomb whose payload would be delivered by lasers. The proposal reportedly evoked expressions of disbelief from several space technologists.

Tempest, The—See JUNOT, ANDOCHE.

TEMPLE, SHIRLEY (1928–   )

It may be an insight on the state of America during the Great Depression that the child movie star Shirley Temple could be hailed by the public as *The Eighth Wonder of the World*. In retrospect her other nicknames *Little Goldilocks* and *Miss Dimples* seem more appropriate.

Temporizing Statesman, The—See WHITELOCK, BULSTRODE.

Ten Percent Tony—See CERMAK, ANTON J.

Ten Thousand Dollar Beauty, The: MICHAEL J. "King" KELLY (1857–1894)

One of the top baseball players of the 19th century, Michael J. "King" Kelly was sold in 1887 by Chicago to Boston for the incredible sum of $10,000. Kelly was hailed as *The Ten Thousand Dollar Beauty* and there was comment that no athlete was worth that kind of money, a sentiment voiced in the 1980s when some players command salaries above $1 million a year.

Ten-Cent Jimmy—See BUCHANAN, JAMES.

TENNYSON, ALFRED LORD
(1809–1892)

English poet laureate and spokesman for the Victorian age, Alfred Lord Tennyson was often called *The Bard of Arthurian Romance* for his many poems based on the legends of King Arthur. Many of his fellow poets did not treat him kindly. Bulwer dubbed him *Schoolmiss Alfred,* and Ralph Waldo Emerson called him *A Beautiful Half of a Poet.*

***Tenth Justice of the Supreme Court, The*—See HAND, LEARNED.**

***Tenth Muse, The*—See SCUDERI, MADELEINE DE.**

***Tentmaker, The*—See OMAR KHAYYAM.**

TERESHKOVA, VALENTINA
(1937–   )

Soviet female cosmonaut Valentina Tereshkova is known rather somberly in the USSR as *The First Woman in Space* and a bit more joyously as *The Sweetheart of the Soviet Sky.*

TERRANOVA, CIRO *(1891–1938)*

A highly placed Mafia figure in the 1920s and 1930s, Ciro Terranova became extremely rich as *The Artichoke King* by exploiting an Italian culinary tradition. He set up a firm that brought up all the artichokes shipped into New York City and then held them off the market. Underworld informer Joe Valachi explained, with perhaps a bit of admiration: "Being artichokes, they hold; they can keep. Then Ciro would make his own price, and as you know, Italians got to have artichokes to eat."

***Terrible, The*—See URBAN VI, POPE.**

***Terrible Siren, The*—See WOODHULL, VICTORIA.**

***Terrible Ted*—See TURNER, TED.**

***Terrible Turk, The*—See REED, THOMAS B. "Czar."**

Terrible Williamsons, The *(fl. late 20th century)*

Descended from a Scotsman named Robert Logan Williamson, *The Terrible Williamsons,* as they are called in warnings from the police and Better Business Bureaus, are itinerant hustlers who engage in all sorts of home-repair and other gyps. The clan is estimated to be 2,000 strong, but The Williamsons has now become a synonym for all such gyp artists.

***Terror of the House, The*—See HARDIN, BENJAMIN.**

***Terror of the Spanish Main, The*—See DRAKE, FRANCIS.**

***Testy, The*—See KIEFT, WILLIAM.**

***Teutonic James Dean, The*—See BUCHHOLZ, HORST.**

THACKERAY, WILLIAM MAKEPEACE (1811–1863)

Because he satirized 19th century upper- and middle-class life in London, English novelist William Makepeace Thackeray paid the price with a number of unflattering sobriquets, such as *Modest Merit, A Gentleman in Search of a Man-Servant* and *The Cynic Parasite,* the last bestowed on him by Disraeli.

That Man in the White House—See ROOSEVELT, FRANKLIN D.

THATCHER, MARGARET (1925–   )

The rigid leader of the Tories, Margaret Thatcher, who became prime minister of Great Britain in 1979, was called the *Iron Lady,* both by members of her own party and the opposition, in praise of or disdain for her rigid policies. Because of her unwillingness to alter course she gained *Tina,* a new nickname based on one of her favorite phrases: ''There is no alternative.'' Least flattering of all was the sobriquet heaped on her by the Russians for her assertions of Communist aggression: *The Cold War Witch.*

THAW, EVELYN NESBIT (c. 1885–1967)

The woman in question in a famous love-triangle murder case in New York in 1907, Evelyn Nesbit was a former chorus girl who married a rather disturbed heir to a fortune, Harry K. Thaw, after having had a long affair with Stanford White, the best known architect of the day and a corpulent rake. After Evelyn confessed to Thaw that she had swung naked, or near naked, on a red velvet swing in a ''love nest'' kept by White, her enraged husband shot White to death for defiling his marriage—even though the affair had occured prior to the marriage. Naturally, the newspapers promptly labeled Evelyn *The Girl on the Red Velvet Swing* during the sensational trial that followed. (See also Thaw, Harry K; White, Stanford.)

THAW, HARRY K. (1871–1947)

Harry K. Thaw was dubbed *The Mad Pittsburgh Playboy* after he murdered Stanford White, the most famous architect of the day and, as Thaw described in the later trial, ''a despoiler of young girls.'' Thaw was found not guilty on the ground of insanity but was sent to an asylum, from which he escaped. Charged with horsewhipping a teen-age boy, he was recommitted and finally released in 1922. Although *The Mad Playboy* was said to have continued his wild ways until his death, he never again was in trouble with the law.

THAYER, JOHN (1758–1815)

A former U.S. Congregationalist minister, John Thayer converted to Catholicism in Paris in 1783 and in 1790 returned to the United States as a missionary, only to be disdained in New England as *John Turncoat.* His efforts were basically a failure, although he did succeed in holding the first Catholic meetings ever tolerated in New England towns.

THAYER, SYLVANUS (1785–1872)

While he was not the first superintendent of the U.S. Military Academy at West Point, N. Y., Sylvanus Thayer is known as *The Father of West Point* because he instituted a number of reforms that made the academy into a model institution, imitated by other colleges of the period. Before his arrival there had been a number of scandals at West Point. Thayer served at West Point from 1817 to 1833.

THE Spitball Pitcher—See PERRY, GAYLORD.

Theban Lyre, The—See PINDAR.

THEOBALD, LEWIS (1688–1744)

English playwright, translator and Shakespearean critic Lewis Theobald earned the enmity of Alexander Pope by daring to criticize his edition of Shakespeare's works, and promptly became *The King of Dunces*, the satirized hero of Pope's *The Dunciad*. Theobald lived long enough to see a new version of *The Dunciad* appear in 1743, in which he had been replaced by poet Colley Cibber, who stood then at the head of Pope's list of enemies. (See also Cibber, Colley.)

Theodore the Meddler—See ROOSEVELT, THEODORE.

THESPIS (c. 6th century B.C.)

The Athenian poet Thespis is credited with being *The Father of Greek Tragedy* and is said to have been the first to introduce an actor into a role hitherto rendered only by a chorus.

THIBAUT IV (1201–1253)

Thibaut IV, count of Champagne, comes down to us as *The Father of French Poetry* because he introduced into French poetry alternate masculine and feminine rhymes and produced a more tuneful system of meters than had previously been used.

Thief of the Mississippi, The—See PORTER, DAVID DIXON.

Thief Taker, The—See WILD, JONATHAN.

Third Founder of Rome, The—See MARIUS, CAIUS.

Thirteenth Apostle, The—See JOHN CHRYSTOSTOM, ST.

THOM, WILLIAM (1799–1848)

William Thom, the Scottish minstrel, was called *The Weaver Poet* since at the age of 14 he had apprenticed as a hand-loom weaver. Out of work, he traveled from his native Inverary to Aberdeen in search of employment and on the road composed verses, which he sold to people as he passed their homes. His verses attracted much attention in Aberdeen and many were published in the *Aberdeen Herald*. He was brought to London by social leaders, who lionized him during the last six years of his life.

THOMAS, J. PARNELL (1895–1970)

The controversial chairman of the House Un-American Activities Committee during the Alger Hiss and Hollywood investigations in the 1940s, J. Parnell Thomas had in 1939 gained the sobriquet *Impeachment Thomas* for introducing a bill to impeach Frances Perkins, Franklin Roosevelt's secretary of labor. In 1949 Thomas was convicted of fraud and conspiracy charges and went to prison. He was then labeled *Kickback Thomas*.

THOMAS, NORMAN (1884–1968)

The foremost U.S. socialist from the 1920s until his death in 1968, Norman Thomas noted with some amusement that he was not dubbed *The Respectable Radical* until his late years.

THOMAS AQUINAS (c. 1225–1274)

The great Italian theologian Thomas Aquinas won many sobriquets, including *The Angelic Doctor*, *The Eagle of Divines* and *The Father of Moral Philosophy*. In his youth, however, the nickname given him by his school companions was *Dumb Ox*.

Thomas Jefferson of Folk Music, The— See SEEGER, PETE.

THOMAS THE APOSTLE (c. 1st century)

According to the New Testament, Thomas the Apostle, one of the 12 apostles, refused to accept the resurrection of Jesus after the crucifixion, insisting he would not believe until he could see and feel Christ himself. Later, he affirmed his belief and became thus the original *Doubting Thomas*, a nickname used often since then.

THOMPSON, ALVIN CLARENCE— See Titanic Thompson.

THOMPSON, CHARLES (1729–1824)

Charlie Thompson, who from 1774 to 1789 was secretary of the Continental Congress, was nicknamed by its members *The Hand and Pen of the Congress*. He was selected to tell George Washington of his election as president of the United States. Previously, Thompson had served as negotiator with the Delaware and Iroquois Indians and had been dubbed by them *Truth-Teller*.

THOMPSON, DOROTHY (1894–1961)

One of the most widely read U.S. newspaper columnists, Dorothy Thompson, the wife of Sinclair Lewis, was called *Cassandra of the Columnists* and *The Contemporary Cassandra*, especially for her warnings of the Nazi menace, which went unheeded. Those who sought to downplay the significance of her warnings referred to her by a sobriquet that riled the feminists of the day, *The Wife of Sinclair Lewis*.

THOMPSON, JOHN (1757–1843)

An Englishman celebrated for his fantastic memory, John Thompson was called *Memory Thompson* for his ability to read a newspaper during the night and the following day repeat its contents word for word. He also bestowed the nickname *Corner Memory Thompson* after winning a wager by drawing from memory the plan of St. Giles parish, indicating every coach-turning, public pump, stableyard and even the corner shop of every street.

THOMPSON, JOHN A.—See Snowshoe Thompson.

THOMPSON, JOHN T. (1860–1940)

The director of arsenals during World War I, Brig. Gen. John T. Thompson invented the submachine gun, gaining the title *The Father of the Tommy Gun*. Designed as a "trench broom," it was developed too late for use in the war and in the 1920s became more popular with the underworld than with the military. However, it was widely used in World War II.

THOMPSON, WILLIAM HALE "Big Bill" (1869–1940)

Mayor William *Big Bill* Thompson of Chicago first ran for political office in 1900 to win a $50 bet, and won. In 1915 he captured the mayoralty with the biggest plurality ever garnered by a Republican. Over his three terms, interrupted by a reform slate, he was hailed as *Bill the Builder* because of the city's enormous growth. What Thompson was responsible for building is debatable, but his biggest campaign contributor was Al Capone, and during Prohibition he helped keep Chicago the wettest city in the United States. Professor Charles E. Merriman said that under *Bill the Builder*'s reign, "Chicago is unique. It is the only completely corrupt city in America." Thompson was famous for his political know-nothingness, once vowing to "punch King George of England in the snoot" if he appeared in Chicago.

THOREAU, HENRY DAVID (1817–1862)

Known with affection as *The Concord Rebel, The Sage of Walden Pond* and *The Poet Naturalist,* U.S. naturalist, essayist and poet Henry David Thoreau has not been universally acclaimed, some seeing his work as an exercise in self-exaltation and dubbing him *The Fragile Narcissus.*

Three-Fingered Jack *(fl. late 18th century)*

A popular nickname, that of *Three-Fingered Jack,* is all that comes down to us of a notorious black robber who became the terror of Jamaica in the late 1700s. He once avoided apprehension by battling his way out of a trap against great odds, losing only a finger in the process. He was finally tracked down and killed in 1781.

Three-Million-Dollar Freckled Corporation, The—See DAY, DORIS.

Three-Minute Brumm—See BRUMM, GEORGE FRANKLIN.

Thrill Killers, The: NATHAN "Babe" LEOPOLD (1906–1971) and RICHARD "Dickie" LOEB (1907–1936)

Both sons of millionaire families, Richard "Dickie" Loeb and Nathan "Babe" Leopold became infamous as Chicago's *Thrill Killers* for the kidnap-slaying of 14-year-old Bobby Franks, which was merely an experiment to prove they could commit the perfect murder. They were saved from the death penalty by attorney Clarence Darrow.

THRONEBERRY, "Marvelous" MARV (1933–   )

A first baseman for the New York Mets in the early 1960s when the team was at its depths of ineptitude, Marv Throneberry won the nickname of *Marvelous Marv* because he was anything but that. He once chased a runner to second base while the winning run scored from third and on another occasion belted a triple only to be declared out for failing to touch first base. Mets fans took to wearing T-shirts that read "VRAM"—for "MARV" spelled backwards.

Thunderbolt, The—See BEJAZET I, SULTAN OF THE TURKS; HANDEL, GEORGE FREDERICK.

Thunderbolt of Italy, The—See FOIX, GASTON DE.

Thunderbolt of Painting, The—See ROBUSTI, JACOPO.

Thunderer, The—See STERLING, EDWARD.

TIBERIUS CAESAR (42 B.C.–37 A.D.)

Roman emporor Tiberius Caesar was known as *The Prince of Hypocrites* because while he affected a great air of morality, he indulged in immorality and debauchery. Historians were later to label him *The Imperial Machiavelli* for his tyrannial acts, ensuring his rule by ordering the deaths of many of his friends and relatives.

TICHENOR, ISAAC (1754–1838)

A transplanted New Jerseyite, Isaac Tichenor moved to Vermont during the American Revolution and remained there the rest of his life, actively involved in politics. Since New Jersey at the time was considered a place of smooth operators, Tichenor was baited by opponents as *Jersey Slick*. The sobriquet did not seem to do severe damage since he served in the Continental Congress and the Vermont legislature and was governor of Vermont from 1797 to 1809.

Tidal Basin Bombshell, The—See FOXE, FANNE.

Tiddy-Doll—See NAPOLEON.

Tiger, The—See CLEMENCEAU, GEORGES; OLAV II OF NORWAY.

Tiger of Central America, The—See GUARDIOLA, SANTOS.

Tiger of Tacubaya, The—See MARQUEZ, LEONARDO.

Tiger of the North, The—See VILLA, PANCHO.

Tiger Woman, The—See JUDD, WINNIE RUTH.

Tigerheart: CHIN SHI HUANG-TI (246–210 B.C.)

Chin Shi Huang-Ti, the Chinese emperor who built the Great Wall, was known as *Tigerheart* because of the excesses and cruelties that marked his reign. It has been estimated that perhaps a million coolies were buried in the 1,5000-mile-long wall to give it greater strength. Before his death the emperor decreed all his family and kin were to be interred with him alive.

TILDEN, SAMUEL J. (1814–1886)

A leading reformer, Samuel Tilden was instrumental in driving every member of New York's corrupt Tweed Ring out of office and as a result easily won the governorship of the state. His supporters called him *The Sage of Gramercy Park* and *The Sage of Greystone,* where he maintained residences, while cartoonist Thomas Nast castigated him as *Old Usufruct*. Nast, whose cartoons had first exposed the Tweed Ring, felt Tilden has joined in the attack merely to advance politically. During the Hayes-Tilden presidential race of 1876, Tilden's opponents labeled him *Slippery Sam,* rather ironic considering how he was victimized in the vote tally.

TILLMAN, BENJAMIN RYAN (1847–1918)

One of South Carolina's most outspoken political figures, Sen. Benjamin R. Tillman was called *Pitchfork Ben* because of his violent speeches against political foes. It was said that he had to dig up the material he used and spread it with a pitchfork.

Time Traveler, The—See WELLS, H. G.

Timepiece of Konigsberg, The—See KANT, IMMANUEL.

Timid Old Psalm-Singing Indianapolis Politician, The—See HARRISON, BENJAMIN.

Timid Soul, The—See SCHULZ, CHARLES M.

Tin King of Bolivia, The—See PATINO, SIMON I.

Tina—See THATCHER, MARGARET.

Tine-Man—See DOUGLAS, ARCHIBALD, FOURTH EARL OF.

Tippy Toes—See KARRAS, ALEX "Tippy Toes."

TIPTOFT, JOHN (c. 1427–1470)

A scholar and politician, John Tiptoft, the earl of Worcester, became infamous as *The Butcher of England* for his tenure as lord constable under Edward IV. He summarily executed many Lancastrians and other enemies of the king, often having them hanged, drawn and quartered. Upon Henry VI's reclaiming of the throne, *The Butcher* fled, only to be found hiding among herdsmen and promptly beheaded.

Tireless Frenchman, The—See MAUPASSANT, GUY DE.

Titanic Thompson: ALVIN CLARENCE THOMPSON (1892–1974)

A famous, colorful and possibly murderous gambler, con man and golf hustler, Alvin Clarence Thompson gained his underworld moniker *Titanic Thompson* after having survived the sinking of the *Titanic* in 1912. He not only put in the maximum claims for loss of baggage and valuables but obtained the names of nonsurvivors so his fellow con men could file bogus claims.

Titian of Portugal, The—See COELLO, ALONZO.

TITUS (c. 40–81)

Roman emperor Titus Flavius Sabinus Vespasianus proclaimed himself *The Delight of Mankind*. His delightful doings included besieging and sacking Jerusalem and leading a thoroughly dissolute life. He corrected his dissolute ways upon his accession, but then again he only ruled two years.

Tityrus—See CHAUCER, GEOFFREY.

Toast of the Barbary Coast, The—See PRADO, KATIE.

TODD, MIKE: AVROM HIRSCH GOLDBOGEN (1909–1958)

Theatrical promoter-producer Mike Todd, born Avrom Hirsch Goldbogen, had a string of nicknames, including *America's Greatest Showman*,

The Cut-rate Showman, The Heir to Barnum's Mantle, The New Ziegfeld and *The Nazim of Necromantic Nudity.* Todd died in a plane crash in 1958.

Toe, The—See GROZA, LOU "the Toe."

TOJO, HIDEKI (1884–1948)

World War II leader of Japan and later judged to be a war criminal, Hideki Tojo was known in Japanese political circles as *The Razor* because of his ruthless leadership, which brooked no opposition.

Tokyo Rose: IVA D'AQUINO (1916–   )

Born in the United States of Japanese parents, Iva D'Aquino became known as *Tokyo Rose* for her seductive-voiced radio broadcasts aimed at undermining the morale of U.S. servicemen by implying that their women back home were being unfaithful to them. Brought back to the United States, she was convicted of treason and sentenced to 10 years. She was released in 1956 and in 1977 received a presidential pardon.

TOLLER, JAMES (1795–1819)

The Young English Giant, James Toller, who stood 8 feet 1½ inches when he was 18, was a great court favorite and was presented before the king of Prussia and the czar of Russia. He died at the age of 25.

TOLSTOY, LEO (1828–1910)

The great Russian novelist Leo Tolstoy led a troubled life almost from his childhood until his death.

While still a youth, he was nicknamed *Crybaby Leo* by family and friends.

Tom Folio—See RAWLINSON, THOMAS.

Tom Fool Jackson—See JACKSON, THOMAS JONATHAN "Stonewall."

Tom Thumb: CHARLES SHERWOOD STRATTON (1838–1883)

The most famous midget in history, Charles Sherwood Stratton was hired on a short-term contract (after all, what if he started growing?) by Phineas T. Barnum for Barnum's American Museum in New York. Barnum dubbed him *General Tom Thumb,* after the Tom Thumb of the nursery rhymes. At 25 inches and 15 pounds 2 ounces, he proved to be a great success and performed all over the world, entertaining at many royal courts as well as the White House for Abraham Lincoln. Eventually he reached a height of 35 inches. A shrewd businessman, *Tom Thumb* was one of the few to get equitable pay from Barnum, who started him off at a mere $3 a week, and when he retired, he had a mansion, a yacht, a sailing sloop, pedigreed horses and a wife three inches shorter than himself.

Tom Thumb—See NAPOLEON III.

Tomboy with a Voice, The—See DAY, DORIS.

Tombs Angel, The: MARIA BARBERI (1855–?)

The defendant in one of New York's most colorful murder cases during the 1880s, Italian-born Maria Barberi drew considerable sympathy from the newspaper "sob sisters" of the day, then coming to the zenith of their power. Although Maria had come up behind her lover while he sat at a bar and slit his throat with a razor because he refused to marry her, she was hailed as *The Tombs Angel* because among her virtues she lavished great love on her canary, which she was permitted to keep in her "dank, dark cell" in the Tombs. What truly upset most female readers was the possibility that Maria could become the first woman, indeed perhaps the first person, to die in the newly planned instrument of death, the electric chair. Although her guilt was beyond doubt and she was convicted and sentenced to death, the drumbeat of sympathy in the press won *The Tombs Angel* an acquittal on a retrial, after which she took little time leaving the city.

TOMPION, THOMAS (1638–1736)

Although he made important contributions to both clockmaking and watchmaking, Englishman Thomas Tompion has often been wrongfully dubbed *The Father of Clockmaking*. Clocks were in existence long before his birth and watchmaking certainly dates back to 1511 when a German named Peter Hele or Henlein developed the craft.

Tonguepoint Mott—See MOTT, JAMES.

TONTI, HENRI DE (?–1704)

One of the early French explorers of the Mississippi, Henri de Tonti lost one of his hands and replaced it with an iron one, thus gaining the sobriquet *The Iron Hand*, not only from his companions but from the Indians, who were awed over his great might.

TOOMBS, ROBERT (1810–1885)

Robert Toombs, a political ally of Alexander Hamilton Stephens, vice president of the Confederacy, was regarded as one of the most virulent secessionists and was referred to by the press in the North as *The Georgia Fire-eater*.

TORQUEMADA, TOMAS DE (1420–1498)

Tomas de Torquemada, the famous inquisitor-general of Spain and the leading exponent of the Inquisition, was called *The Scourge of Heresy*. Traveling with a bodyguard of 250 men and in constant fear of being poisoned, Torquemada filled the prisons and fed fires throughout Spain with heretics, faithfully serving King Ferdinand, who was jealous of the wealthy Moors and Jews of Castile and alleged that they had embraced Christianity for its privileges and not out of genuine faith. Torquemada was constantly criticized for his severity, but all efforts to remove him failed as each successive pope acknowledged and praised his zeal.

Torquemada—See MITCHEL, JOHN PURROY.

Torquemada of Aesthetics, A—See RUSKIN, JOHN.

Torre of Poetry, The—See GRAY, THOMAS.

Tory Murderess, The—See SPOONER, BATHSHEBA.

Toughest Cop in America, The—See RIZZO, FRANK L.

TOUHY, ROGER "Terrible" (1898–1959)

A powerful bootlegging kingpin and rival of Al Capone, Roger Touhy was called *Terrible Touhy* because of his reputation for cold-blooded killings. His brothers and gang were called the Terrible Touhys. In fact, Touhy never killed anyone and his entire reputation was built on false posturing, to the point of stocking his headquarters with submachine guns borrowed from Chicago-area police (whom he had on his payroll) just to impress visitors. His reputation was enough, however, to earn him a prison term of almost 25 years for a kidnapping he did not commit. He was finally proved innocent and freed.

TOULOUSE-LAUTREC, HENRI DE (1864–1901)

Adolescent accidents stunted the growth of the great French painter Henri de Toulouse-Lautrec. He lived for a considerable time in a brothel, where the inmates, noting that his large male member contrasted with his short stature, promptly dubbed him, rather affectionately, *The Teapot*.

TOUSSAIN, JACQUES (1547–?)

Regarded as the foremost Hellenist of the late 16th and early 17th centuries, French scholar Jacques Toussain was called *The Living Library*.

Tower Murderer, The—See WHITMAN, CHARLES.

Town Crier, The—See WOOLLCOTT, ALEXANDER.

TRACY, HARRY (1876?–1902)

A desperado who rode with Butch Cassidy and the Wild Bunch, Harry Tracy was considered one of the gang's most cold-blooded killers and was nicknamed *The Mad Dog of the Bunch*. Yet despite his reputation and genuinely murderous behavior,

Tracy never had trouble finding women, single or married, who would hide him when he was on the run. As one baffled editorial writer observed just before Tracy was cornered by a posse and shot to death, there was need for a study of this "wild about Harry" syndrome among so many women.

Traitor, The—See ARNOLD, BENEDICT.

Traitor to Freedom, A—See WEBSTER, DANIEL.

Traitorous Hero, The—See ARNOLD, BENEDICT.

Tramp Poet, The—See LINDSAY, VACHEL.

Translator-General, The—See HOLLAND, PHILEMON.

Trash Bag Murderer, The: PATRICK KEARNEY (1949–)

In a five-year span from Christmas Day 1972 until July 1977, Patrick Kearney killed perhaps as many as 28 men in California, cutting them apart and dumping them, wrapped in plastic, along California freeways and roads. Dubbed *The Trash Bag Murderer*, Kearney was never identified until he voluntarily surrendered in 1977. He was sentenced to life imprisonment.

TRAVOLTA, JOHN (1954–)

A 1970s TV teen idol, John Travolta, upon his arrival in Hollywood, was dubbed *The Street Tyrone Power*, an identification reeking of press agents' dedication to the proposition that all screen personalities were made for nicknames.

TREMBLEY, JOSEPH DE (1577–1638)

Father Joseph de Trembley, secretary of Cardinal Richelieu of France, was called *Eminence Grise, The Gray Eminence* or *Gray Cardinal*, since although he was not a cardinal, he exercised much of the power of a prince of the Church through his influence on Richelieu. Richelieu was called *The Red Eminence* because he wore a red habit, most unusual for the era. To distinguish Father Joseph while acknowledging his power, reference was made to Trembley's wearing a gray habit. (See also Howe, Louis.)

Trembling Admiral, The—See DE RUYTER, MICHAEL.

Tremendous Trifle, A—See CHESTERTON, GILBERT KEITH.

TREURNICHT, ANDRIES PETRUS (1921–)

The leader of the far right wing of South Africa's National Party, Dr. Andries Petrus Treurnicht has been noted for his inflexible resistance to any easing of apartheid in his country and as a result has been ridiculed in the English-language press as *Dr. No.*

TREVINO, LEE (1939–)

A nickname that truly represents its referent is that of *High Pressure Lee* for Mexican pro golfer Lee Trevino. He has won so many close matches that he is said to thrive on the pressure. He is also known as *Super Mex.*

Tribune of the People, The—See BABEUF, FRANCOIS NOEL.

Tricky Dick—See NIXON, RICHARD.

Trinity Jones—See JONES, WILLIAM.

TRIPPE, JUAN (1899–)

A founder of Pan American Airways, hard-driving pioneer airline executive Juan Trippe was, in his school days, a very quiet student. In fact his schoolmates nicknamed him *The Mummy.*

TRISTAN L'ERMITE (1405–1493)

Louis XI of France dubbed Tristan l'Ermite, his willing servant, *The Gossip* for always telling him the court secrets of the day.

Tri-State Terror, The—See UNDERHILL, WILBUR.

TROLLOPE, ANTHONY (1815–1882)

English novelist Anthony Trollope has been called *The Dullest Briton of Them All* by Henry James. It is perhaps a double damning sobriquet considering that James himself has been described by William Faulkner as "one of the nicest old ladies I ever met."

TROUSSE, MARQUIS DE LA (?–1648)

The Marquis de la Trousse, an accomplished dueler, is remembered today as *Alcidas,* as he is called in Moliere's *La Mariage Forcee*. While engaging in a duel, he was always the picture of politeness, complimenting his foe and being overwhelmed with sorrow while doing him in—one might say a perfect character for Moliere.

TRUDEAU, MARGARET (1948–   )

While estranged from her husband, Canadian prime minister Pierre Trudeau, Margaret Trudeau started a new life among the "beautiful people" set, which by her own admission was "a culture laced with drugs and sex." Among the more innocuous descriptions of her during this period was *The Queen of Disco*.

TRUDEAU, PIERRE ELLIOTT (1919–   )

The Canadian Parliament has long been noted as one of the most raucous in the Western world and Prime Minister Pierre Trudeau was always credited with holding his own in any expletive-laden debate. However, on one famous occasion he was accused of "mouthing" the ultimate obscenity in the House. Responding to that accusation, Trudeau came up with the explanation that what he'd actually said was, "Fuddle-duddle!" Canadians didn't buy that one but they were amused and enthusiastically took up the call of *Fuddle-duddle Trudeau*.

True Laureate of England, The—See DIBDIN, CHARLES.

TRUJILLO, RAFAEL (1891–1961)

Dictator Rafael Trujillo ruled the Dominican Republic with an iron hand for three decades, a period marked by repression that included official torture and murder. As a result he was called *The Last Caesar*. Trujillo was assassinated in 1961.

TRUMAN, BESS (1885–1982)

As first lady, Bess Truman made a determined effort always to remain out of the limelight, in striking contrast to her predecessor, Eleanor Roosevelt, so much so that in Washington circles Bess was referred to as *The Last Lady of the Land*. Truman himself, who delighted in pretending to be henpecked, lovingly called his wife *The Boss*. When Truman was nominated as vice president, it was widely reported that Mrs. Truman had been on his Senate payroll at $4,500 a year. Truman defended the action, pointing that she had handled his mail and edited the reports of his investigating committee. Nevertheless Clare Boothe Luce taunted Mrs. Truman as *Payroll Bess*. Truman never forgave her for that.

TRUMAN, HARRY S (1884–1972)

Harry S Truman, 33rd president of the United States, was called *The Man from Missouri* and *The Man of Independence*. His most famous sobriquet was *Give 'em Hell Harry* for his attacks on the Republicans in his successful 1948 bid for election. He later said, "Well, I never gave anybody hell; I just told the truth on these fellows and they thought it was hell." Truman's efforts proved superior to the Republicans' tactic of trying to pin the label *High Tax Harry* on him.

TRUMAN, JOHN ANDERSON (1851–1914)

A prosperous Missouri farmer and mule trader, John Anderson Truman was called *Peanuts* by his friends because of his slight stature, which did not inhibit his two-fisted emotionalism in defending his family or personal honor. His son Harry became president of the United States.

TRUMBULL, JONATHAN (1710–1785)

The only colonial governor to cast his lot with the rebels during the American Revolution, Jonathan Trumbull, who served as governor of Connecticut from 1760 to 1783, was denounced by the British and Tories as *The Rebel Governor*. During the War of Independence Trumbull donated a considerable portion of his wealth to the cause.

Trumpet Moore—See MOORE, THOMAS.

Trustbuster, The—See ROOSEVELT, THEODORE.

Truth, Sojourner: ISABELLA VAN WAGENER (c. 1797–1883)

A freed slave, Isabella Van Wagener became a leading 19th century U.S. abolitionist and reformer, preaching emancipation and women's rights. She adopted the sobriquet *Sojourner Truth* as a description of her message.

Truth-Teller—See THOMPSON, CHARLES.

TRYON, WILLIAM (1725–1788)

Known as one of the crueler British colonial governors in America, William Tryon, who governed North Carolina and later New York, was also most vicious in his treatment of the frontier Indians. The Indians called him *The Great Wolf* and the colonists took up that chant during the American Revolution, especially during Tryon's plundering and burning of New Haven, Fairfield and Norwalk, Conn., in 1779.

TSCHIRKY, OSCAR MICHEL—See Oscar of the Waldorf.

Tubal Cain of America—See SPOTSWOOD, ALEXANDER.

TUBMAN, HARRIET (1821–1913)

Abolitionist Harriet Tubman was known as *The Negro Moses* or *The Moses of Her People* because of her Civil War work with the "underground railway," bringing hundreds of slaves to freedom in the North and Canada. Angry Southerners offered huge rewards for her capture without success.

TUBMAN, WILLIAM V. S. (1896–1971)

President of Liberia, Africa's oldest independent republic, William V. S. Tubman won the nickname *Old Daddy* as he held office from 1944 until his death in 1971. He had won his seventh consecutive term two months before he died.

TUCKER, RICHARD (1914–1975)

A long-time Metropolitan Opera tenor and a well-known cantor, Richard Tucker received the ultimate accolade *The Met's Second Caruso*.

TUDOR, FREDERIC (1783–1864)

One of New England's most colorful entrepreneurs, Frederic Tudor, while in his twenties, developed one of Massachusett's most bountiful resources, ice, into a major export item to tropical and semi-tropical countries, bringing, for instance, the ice cream industry to Martinique. Seamen refused to sail with him on his first voyage, fearing the water from 130 tons of ice in the hold would melt and swamp the ship. After Tudor proved his plan was viable, he won the title *The Ice King*. He was not an instant success, however, losing money on many of his enterprises and once being forced into bankruptcy. However, he pioneered so many uses for ice that he eventually became a millionaire.

TUGWELL, REXFORD G. (1891–1979)

As undersecretary of agriculture in President Franklin Roosevelt's cabinet, political economist Rex Tugwell was regarded as one of the most articulate spokesmen for the New Deal and was labeled by the press *The Barrymore of the Brain Trust*.

Tune Detective, The—See SPAETH, SIGMUND.

TURCHIN, JOHN BASIL: IVAN VASILOVITCH TURCHINOFF (1822–1901)

Born Ivan Vasilovitch Turchinoff, John B. Turchin emigrated to the United States prior to the Civil War and during that conflict became its only Russian-born general. For his hard-hitting combat tactics, especially those he displayed at the Battle of Chickamauga, he became known as *The Russian Thunderbolt*. Turchin's wife displayed some of these same qualities, even on occasion leading his regiment in the field when he was ill.

Turncoat, John—See THAYER, JOHN.

Turncoat Opportunist, The—See COX, JACK.

TURNER, LANA (1920–   )

Screen star Lana Turner became known as *The Sweater Girl* after she was "discovered" at a Hollywood drugstore counter filling out a sweater that indicated her well-developed talent.

TURNER, TED (1939–   )

Flamboyant business executive, yacht racer and baseball-club owner Ted Turner is noted for his controversial statements and actions, for which he has been called *Terrible Ted, The Mouth of the South, The Capsize Kid* and *Captain Outrageous*, the last reference to his having skippered the *Courageous* to victory in the 1977 America's Cup yacht race. His additional nickname *The Steinbrenner of the South* is generally disputed by New York sportwriters. Like George Steinbrenner, owner of the New York Yankees, Turner spends heavily acquiring players but does not rage at them when the team loses as Steinbrenner is apt to do.

Turnip-Hoer, The—See GEORGE I.

TURPIN, DICK (1706–1739)

The legendary English highwayman Dick Turpin became known as *The King of the Road* because of his acts of daring, which turned him into a sort of folk hero until he was finally captured in Yorkshire and hanged.

Tuscan Imp of Fame, The—See PETRARCH, FRANCESCO.

Tuscarora John—See BARNWELL, JOHN.

TUTWILER, JULIA STRUDWICK (?–1916)

Because of her achievements in reforming the penal system of Alabama, Julia Strudwick Tutwiler was often designated *The Angel of the Prisons*. She was particularly successful in correcting many of the abuses in the convict-lease system.

T.V.A. Rankin—See RANKIN, JOHN E.

Twentieth Century Moses—See CHAPLIN, CHARLES "Charlie."

Twentieth Century Witch, The—See LEEK, SYBIL.

Two-Ton Tony—See GALENTO, ANTHONY "Two-Ton Tony."

TYLER, JOHN (1790–1862)

The nickname *His Accidency* was first applied to John Tyler upon his succession to the presidency in 1841 on the death of William Henry Harrison; Tyler was the first vice president to do so. Subsequent vice presidents who later became president in the same way were saddled with the same disparaging sobriquet by their political opponents, in both parties. President Tyler was often denounced as *The Executive Ass* and was also called *Old Veto* because he vetoed nine bills during his term, more than any previous one-term president. For this and other reasons of "gross usurpation of power," he became the first president subjected to a serious impeachment attempt. The vote to start impeachment proceedings in the House of Representatives failed in January 1843 by 127 to 83.

Typhoid Mary: MARY MALLON (1868–1938)

Mary Mallon, a cook, became better known as *Typhoid Mary* because she was literally a walking epidemic, the first known human typhoid carrier in the United States, although she was immune to the disease-carrying germs. From 1906 to 1915 while she worked in the New York area, she was responsible for 54 persons contracting typhoid, three of whom died. She evaded capture, changing jobs often and refusing medical treatment when confronted. She was finally captured in 1915 and was committed to a hospital, where she remained until her death in 1938.

Tyrant, The—See LINCOLN, ABRAHAM.

Tyrtaeus of Germany, The—See KOERNER, CARL THEODOR.

TWIGGY: LESLIE HORNBY (1949–   )

English model and sometimes actress Leslie Hornby is better known professionally as Twiggy. Actually Twiggy is a professional name deriving from her youthful nickname *Sticks,* a reference to her gangling thinness.

Twist King, The—See CHECKER, CHUBBY.

Two Gun Hart—See CAPONE, JAMES.

***Two-Edged Knife, The*—See BILBO, THEODORE GILMORE.**

TYTLER, JAMES (1747–1804?)

James Tytler, a Scottish writer and political activist, was the first of his countrymen to ascend in a fire balloon using the plan of Montgolfier. Forced to flee his homeland because of political persecution, *Balloon Tytler* settled in America and continued his balloon experiments until he drowned about 1804.

U

***Udo, Tommy*—See WIDMARK, RICHARD.**

***Ugly Ike*—See EISENHOWER, DWIGHT DAVID.**

ULBRICHT, WALTER (1893–1973)

The autocratic leader of East Germany from 1950 to 1971, Walter Ulbricht guided the nation along strict Stalinist lines and built the Berlin Wall. He was dubbed *The Last Cold Warrior,* and bitter West Berlin humor also identified him as *The Little Man with the Goatee.*

***Ulysses of the Highlands, The*—See CAMERON, EVAN.**

UMAI (?–1801)

Perhaps the most remarkable rabble-rouser in history was Umai of Tinnevelly, India, who, although a deaf mute, was able to inflame crowds in sign language. By the power of the unspoken word *The Deaf and Dumb Demagogue,* as the British called him, incited the Poligar Rebellion, in which thousands died before Umai was caught and executed.

Umberto the Good: UMBERTO I (HUMBERT), KING OF ITALY (1844–1900)

Like his father Victor Emmanuel II, Umberto I, was regarded as one of the better Italian kings. He won the title *Umberto the Good,* because he always sought to identify with the fortunes of his people. When cholera ravished certain parts of the country, Umberto displayed a far greater disdain for his personal health and safety than contemporary leaders or those of more recent times in going among the victims. Most historians agree that he was a most undeserving victim of an assassin's bullet in 1900.

***Uncle Jumbo*—See CLEVELAND, GROVER.**

***Uncle Remus*—See HARRIS, JOEL CHANDLER.**

***Uncle Robert*—See LEE, ROBERT E.**

Uncle Sam: SAMUEL WILSON (1766–1854)

During the War of 1812 Samuel Wilson, a meat packer from Troy, N.Y., supplied beef to the U.S.

Army and later became an inspector of Army supplies, stamping meats he approved of with the initials ''U.S.'' Wilson sported a beard that gave him a fatherly look, and other quartermasters referred to him as *Uncle Sam*. Soon the initials stood for *Uncle Sam,* and in time Wilson's nickname was transferred to the entire U.S. government.

Uncle Walter—See CRONKITE, WALTER LELAND, JR.

Unconditional Surrender Grant—See GRANT, ULYSSES S.

Unconquered Knight, The—See PERO NINO, DON.

Uncrowned King, The—See BLAINE, JAMES G.

Uncrowned King of Ireland, The—See PARNELL, CHARLES STEWART.

Uncrowned King of the U.S. Senate, The—See KERR, ROBERT S.

UNDERHILL, WILBUR (1901–1934)

One of the most successful bank robbers among the public enemies of the late 1920s and early 1930s, Wilbur Underhill robbed literally dozens of small-town banks in Oklahoma, Arkansas and Kansas, becoming known as *The Tri-State Terror*. He victimized perhaps three times as many banks as did Pretty Boy Floyd, another famed gangster operating out of the same Cookson Hills area of Oklahoma. *The Tri-State Terror* finally died after being wounded in a 1,000-bullet gunfight with FBI agents while on his honeymoon.

Underworld's Family Doctor, The—See MORAN, JOSEPH PATRICK.

Underworld's Host, The—See BARBARA, JOSEPH, SR.

Unfair Preacher, The—See BARROW, ISAAC.

Unforgettable Guerrilla, The—See BUNKE, HAYDEE TAMARA.

Unfortunate, Unhappy Man, The—See JOHNSON, ANDREW.

Uniformed Soldier Grant—See GRANT, ULYSSES S.

Union Safeguard Grant—See GRANT, ULYSSES S.

United States Grant—See GRANT, ULYSSES S.

Universal Butt of All Mankind, The—See HILL, JOHN.

Universal Doctor—See ALBERTUS MAGNUS, ST.

Universal Genius, The—See PETTY, WILLIAM.

Universal Man, The—See VINCI, LEONARDO DA.

Universal Philosopher, The—See
HARRIOT, THOMAS.

Universal Spider, The—See Louis the
Cruel.

Untamed Prime Minister, The—See
LAW, ANDREW BONAR.

Unprecedented Strategist Grant—See
GRANT, ULYSSES S.

Unquestionably Skilled Grant—See
GRANT, ULYSSES S.

UNRUH, HOWARD (1921–)

Howard Unruh, who shot 13 people to death during
a 12-minute murder spree in Camden, N.J., in
1949, was dubbed by the press *The Pied Piper of
Murder* because his leisurely rampage soon brought
more than 60 policemen after him. The Pied Piper,
trapped in his own home, meekly surrendered.

*Unsinkable Molly Brown, The
(1867–1932)*

A ditchdigger's daughter whose prospector husband struck it rich in Leadville, Colo., Molly
Brown received nationwide acclaim for her heroism aboard the sinking liner *Titanic* in 1912. Pistol in hand, she enforced the sea's tradition of
women and children first, organized the rowers
and nursed the injured. To reporters asking how
she'd survived, she quipped, "I'm unsinkable."
And so the name *The Unsinkable Molly Brown*
became part of America's folklore.

Untamed Heifer, The—See
ELIZABETH I.

*Untired Business Man of Theology,
The*—See **SUNDAY, BILLY.**

Untouchable, The—See **NESS,
ELIOT.**

UPDIKE, JOHN (1932–)

In his youthful days author John Updike was nicknamed *Ostrich*, an allusion to his looks.

Upholsterer of Notre Dame, The—See
**MONTMORENCI, FRANCOIS
HENRI.**

Upright, The—See **ABU BAKR.**

Upstart Crow, An—See
SHAKESPEARE, WILLIAM.

URBAN VI, POPE (1318–1389)

Pope Urban VI was nicknamed *The Terrible*
because of being what a number of cardinals called
furiosus et melancholicus—or just plain mad. The
charge was hurled by the same cardinals who had
shortly before elected him pope on the presumption
that they could control him. What upset them most
was Urban's refusal to return the papacy to
Avignon, giving rise at the time to an anti-pope,
Clement VII. Since Clement VII was nicknamed
The Butcher of Cesena, there seems to be validity
to the statements of some historians that the reigns
of the two popes marked the simultaneous low
points of the Rome and Avignon papacies.

URQUHART, DAVID (1805–1877)

Perhaps the leading voice in 19th century England against the "Russian menace," David Urquhart was dubbed by politicians and the press as *The Russophobist*. He resigned his post of secretary to the Turkish Embassy in 1835 over opposition to Lord Palmerston's Russian policy and returned to England, where, after being elected to Parliament, he gained fame for his passionate attacks on Palmerston and the Foreign Office.

Useless Grant—See GRANT, ULYSSES S.

USTINOV, PETER (1921–   )

English actor and playwright Peter Ustinov is called within his profession *The Lovable Egghead*.

UTLEY, ULDINE (1912–   )

U.S. religious revivalist Uldine Utley was nicknamed *Joan of Arc of the Modern Religious World* because in her early teens she conducted mass revival meetings and at the age of 14 held a highly successful religious gathering at New York's Madison Square Garden.

UTTER, CHARLES H. (c. late 19th century)

Colorado Charley, as Charles H. Utter was generally known, was Wild Bill Hickok's closest friend and from time to time his business partner. After the latter's murder in 1876 he received the added sobriquet *Sentimental Charley* because he spent considerable sums over the years paying for Hickok's two graves and markers and fighting to prevent his body from being removed from Deadwood, on one occasion for sale to a New York museum agent.

V

VACHER, JOSEPH—See French Ripper, The.

Vacillating King—See CHARLES ALBERT, KING OF PIEDMONT.

Vain Braggadocio, This—See HARVEY, GABRIEL.

VALDEZ, JUAN MELENDEZ (1754–1817)

Because of his influence on the Spanish literature of his day, poet Juan Melendez Valdez of Spain was called *The Restorer of Parnassus,* that symbol of classic Greek poetry.

VALENTINE, LEWIS J. "Night Stick" (1882–1946)

Famed as the toughest and most honest police chief in New York's history, La Guardia-era commissioner Lewis J. Valentine was called *Night Stick Valentine* and *Rough on Rats Valentine,* the latter bestowed by the mayor, to indicate his tough treatment of known hoodlums. In his enthusiastic campaign against slot machines, he personally axed hundreds of them and caused the slot machine king of the time, Frank Costello, to pull his equipment out of New York and ship it to the safe confines of Huey Long's New Orleans.

Valentine Lady, The—See PFIESTER, DORIS.

VALENTINO, RUDOLPH
(1895–1926)

On screen and off screen Rudolph Valentino was known as *The Great Lover* and *The Sheik*. However, his off-camera loves and marital life were rather disappointing, even including an unconsummated marriage, or possibly two.

Valet of Princes, The—See FROISSART, JEAN.

Valet Poet, The—See MAROT, CLEMENT.

VAN BUREN, JOHN (1810–1866)

When his father, Martin Van Buren, was appointed Envoy Extraordinary to the Court of Saint James in 1831, John Van Buren accompanied him as his secretary. He attended a court dinner given by Queen Victoria and in the official court journal was listed on the roster of princes in attendance. The Whig opposition to Andrew Jackson and the elder Van Buren seized on this error and lampooned young Van Buren as *Prince John*. The unwanted sobriquet stuck to him the rest of his life and, some said, greatly inhibited his political career.

VAN BUREN, MARTIN (1782–1862)

Perhaps the most colorfully nicknamed of all U.S. presidents, Martin Van Buren was known to friends as *The Little Magician, Matty Van* and *Kinderhook Fox,* the last an allusion to his home in Kinderhook, N.Y. His foes called him *King Martin the First* since he was the handpicked successor of Andrew Jackson, whom they referred to as King Andrew the First. He was also derisively referred to as *Martin Van Ruin* and *The Panic of 1837* because of the financial disaster of 1837. As a widower he was highly popular with the women in the Washington social set and was called *Mistletoe Politician* and *Petticoat Pet.* When John C. Calhoun dubbed him *The Fox,* he did not do so in admiration, saying, ''He is not of the race of the lion or of the tiger; he belongs to the lower order—the fox.'' When Calhoun was feeling less charitable toward Van Buren, he called him *The Weazel.* Another barb often hurled was that of *Whiskey Van,* since the president was noted for his penchant for high living.

VAN CORTLANDT, PHILIP
(1749–1831)

American soldier, legislator and trader, Philip Van Cortlandt was nicknamed *The Great White Devil* by the Indians of western New York either for his decisive victory over them or for his cunning transactions with them, the origin of the name being a matter of some dispute.

Van Dyck in Little—See COOPER, SAMUEL.

Van Dyck of Sculpture, The—See COYSEVOX, ANTOINE.

VAN DYKE, W. S. (1889–1943)

Film director W. S. Van Dyke, famous for such films as *The Thin Man, Trader Horn* and *Rage in Heaven,* was nicknamed *One-Take Van Dyke* because he was considered Hollywood's fastest director.

VAN LEW, ELIZABETH
(c. 1861–1865)

When Virginia seceded from the Union in 1861, Elizabeth Van Lew, despite being from a prominent Richmond family, did not. In order to cover up her activities as a spy in the Rebel capital, she developed a reputation as an eccentric old maid. Her neighbors, failing to guess her true occupation, adopted the nickname *Crazy Bet* to explain her actions, such as preparing a guest room for Gen. George McClellan when he threatened to capture the city. With this image of a harmless Unionist, *Crazy Bet* was able to become one of the most reliable intelligence sources of the war.

VAN WAGENER, ISABELLA—See Truth, Sojourner.

VANDER MEER, JOHNNY
(1914–   )

Cincinnati Reds baseball pitcher Johnny Vander Meer picked up the nickname *Double No-Hit* for pitching two consecutive no-hit games, a feat unequaled before or since.

VANDERBILT, CORNELIUS
(1794–1877)

Cornelius Vanderbilt quit school at the age of 11 and by the age of 16 was in business for himself, ferrying passengers on a small boat from his native Staten Island to New York City, quickly gaining recognition as *The Commodore*. He entered the steamboat business in his thirties and went on

to become a millionaire, and the name stuck to him the rest of his life. When he died at the age of 82 in 1877, *The Commodore* was the richest man in the country.

VANDERBILT, GLORIA—See Poor Little Rich Girl.

VARRO, MARCUS TERENTIUS
(c. 116 B.C.–c. 27 B.C.)

The renowned Roman author and scholar Marcus Terentius Varro was designated *The Most Learned of the Romans*.

VEECK, WILLIAM LOUIS
(1914–   )

Baseball club owner Bill Veeck became known as *The Clown Prince of Baseball* because he devised stunts and zany entertainment to lure fans to the ball park, even when his teams were firmly ensconced in the cellar. He held drawings and awarded the winners such prizes as a 300-pound block of ice, a swaybacked horse or pigeons—without cages. He invented the "exploding scoreboard" and offered flagpole sitters as entertainment. He once hired a midget, Eddie Gaedel, to serve as a pinch hitter. Gaedel, at 3 feet 7 inches and wearing uniform number 1/8, quite naturally walked in his only appearance at bat and was banned thereafter from baseball by American League president Will Harridge.

Veep—See BARKLEY, ALBEN W.

Veepess, The—See BARKLEY, ELIZABETH JANE RUCKER HADLEY.

VEGA, LOPE DE: FELIX LOPE DE VEGA CARPIO (1563–1635)

Felix Lope de Vega Carpio, Spain's most prolific dramatist, is believed to have written some 1,500 to 2,000 plays and religious dramas, of which 468 survive. So awed was Cervantes of Lope de Vega—who read Latin at the age of five, translated Claudius at 10 and wrote his first four-act play at 12—that he bestowed the nickname of *Monstruo de la Naturaleza,* or *Monster of Nature,* on him.

VELEZ, LUPE (1909–1944)

Fiery actress Lupe Velez possessed a nickname that had special meaning as a Hollywood inside joke. To the public she was promoted as *The Mexican Spitfire* or *Firecracker,* but her nickname *Firecracker* had a different connotation among Hollywood men. She had a habit of finding her way into gentlemen's beds, and while this was not exactly a breach of movieland etiquette, she had the disconcerting habit of "popping off"—like a firecracker pops off—about her affairs.

Venerable, The—See CHAMPEAUX, WILLIAM DE.

Venus of Montparnasse—See KIKI.

VERLAINE, PAUL (1844–1896)

While the combined effect of imagery and sound, feeling and mood make the poetry of Paul Verlaine almost unequaled even within the Symbolist school, the French poet led a life of alcoholism and homosexuality. He was sent to prison for two years after shooting his lover, the teenage poet Arthur Rimbaud. Even his most ardent supporters referred to him as *The Deplorable Verlaine.*

VERNE, JULES (1828–1905)

French novelist Jules Verne has been rightfully designated *The Father of Science Fiction.* He anticipated many scientific advances of later times, including television, submarines, aqualungs and space travel.

VERNON, EDWARD (1684–1757)

Because he introduced grog in the English navy, Adm. Edward Vernon was tabbed *Old Grog.* The word "grog" is believed to have derived from the grogram breeches Vernon wore.

VERRUCOSUS, QUINTUS FABIUS MAXIMUS (?–203 B.C.)

Heralded as *The Shield of Rome,* Quintus Fabius Maximus Verrucosus was Hannibal's leading foe, winning for himself the accolade *Cuncator,* or *The Delayer,* because of his waiting-game strategy of always keeping his army near the forces of Hannibal and harassing them but never attacking. When he was relieved of his command, Hannibal scored his great victory at Cannae.

VERTUE, GEORGE (1684–1756)

George Vertue, an English engraver, spent a lifetime collecting information on pictures and artists for a history of pictures. When he died at the age of 72, his manuscript ran to 40 volumes and he was nowhere near done with his work; he was called *The Old Mortality of Pictures.* Horace Walpole bought Vertue's manuscript and from it wrote his *Anecdotes of Painting.*

Very Baggage of New Writers, The—See NASH, THOMAS.

Very Old—See LEOPOLD OF BELGIUM.

VESEY, DENMARK (1767–1822)

A former South Carolina slave who bought his freedom in 1800 after winning a lottery, Denmark Vesey in 1822 concocted one of the most daring plots for a slave uprising. His plan, to which slaves from up to 100 miles away rallied, called for the rebels to seize Charleston, S.C., and slaughter all slave holders. The uprising, Vesey felt sure, would trigger numerous slave revolts elsewhere. Betrayed by a slave informer, Vesey and scores of his confederates were captured hours before the slated time for the start of the rebellion, and he and 33 others were hanged. Historians later dubbed Vesey *The Black John Brown.*

Veteran's Friend, The—See FORBES, CHARLES R.

Veto Governor, The—See WINSTON, JOHN A.

Vicar of Hell, The—See WOLSEY, THOMAS.

Vice Mayor, The—See STANFORD, SALLY.

Viceroy, The—See JENNINGS, SARAH.

VICTOR EMMANUEL II OF ITALY (1820–1878)

Victor Emmanuel II of Sardinia became king of a united Italy in 1861 with the aid of Garibaldi. An able ruler, he demonstrated a fine hand at diplomacy and was willing to make expedient adjustments to his policies as the times dictated. Since he brought a new sense of ethics to Italian monarchy, unlike the many rulers of smaller domains who sought bargains with foreign powers to strengthen their power, he was called *The Honest King.*

VICTOR EMMANUEL III OF ITALY (1869–1947)

The king of Italy from 1900 until his abdication in 1946, Victor Emmanuel III was referred to as *The Little Signor,* a play on Napoleon's sobriquet The Little Corporal. However, it was clear from the way the nickname was used it reflected the people's anguish over Emmanuel's lacking qualities as a leader, and the nickname became even more disparaging when he was overshadowed by Benito Mussolini after 1922.

VICTORIA OF ENGLAND (1819–1901)

Queen Victoria went into seclusion for many years following the death of her husband Albert, the Prince Consort, in 1861 and was referred to, not always without a measure of exasperation, as *The Widow at Windsor.* Kipling wrote of her in a poem:

> 'A you 'eard o' the Widow at Windsor,
> With a hairy gold crown on 'er 'ead?

VIDOCQ, FRANCOIS EUGENE (1775–1857)

Regarded as the world's first genuine detective and the founder of a new French criminal investigation department, the Surete, Francois Eugene Vidocq was himself a criminal and a galley slave until he started aiding police in underground assignments. Because of his work he was finally made an officer and in 1812 the head of the new Surete. The Paris underworld, which he often penetrated in disguise, fearfully referred to him as *The Wolf*.

VIEUZAC, BERTRAND BARERE DE—See Anacreon of the Guillotine, The.

Viking of Literature, The—See ERASMUS, DESIDERIUS.

Vile Scum on a Pond, A—See CHESTERTON, GILBERT KEITH.

VILLA, PANCHO: DORETA ARANGO (1877–1923)

After an early career of banditry, Pancho Villa (real name Doreto Arango) joined the Mexican Revolution and the opposition to President Victoriano Huerta. He had for years led the federal troops on a merry chase, gaining the nicknames *The Puma* and *The Tiger of the North* because of his ability to outwit the *federales* in the mountain terrain of upper Mexico. Gen. John J. Pershing's failure to capture Villa after a long campaign in Mexico was probably the most frustrating interval in Pershing's career.

VILLE, BERNARD GERMAIN ETIENNE DE LA (1756–1825)

French natural history researcher Bernard Germain Etienne de la Ville became known as *The King of Reptiles* for his classic study *Histoire Naturelle des Reptiles*.

VILLEHARDOUIN, GEOFFROI DE (c. 1160–1213)

Geoffroi de Villehardouin is often called both *The Father of French History* and *The Father of French*

Prose. He was the first French historian to write in the common form of the language and indeed the first noteworthy writer of French prose in general.

VILLENEUVA, ARNARD DE (1238–1314)

The French chemist, theologian and astrologer Arnaud de Villeneuva has been designated *The Father of Chemistry*.

VINCI, LEONARDO DA (1452–1519)

The most versatile genius of the Renaissance and probably of all time, Leonardo da Vinci, the great painter, architect, composer, sculptor, engineer, chemist, astronomer, botanist, physiologist and geologist, among other things, was referred to as *Homo Universale,* or *The Universal Man*.

Vinegar Joe—See STILLWELL, JOSEPH "Vinegar Joe."

Violin, The—See CORTELLINI, CAMILLO.

Virgil of the French Drama, The—See RACINE, JEAN.

Virgin, The—See DAY, DORIS.

Virgin Modesty—See WILMOT, JOHN.

Virgin Queen, The—See ELIZABETH I.

Virtuous Card Shark, The—See
SCARNE, JOHN.

VISCONTI, GALEAZZO (1320–1370)

Galeazzo Visconti, 14th century ruler of Lombardy, was given the nickname *The Maecenas of His Time* because as his patronage of the arts. He was the friend of Petrarch, collected an enormous library and founded the university at Pavia. None of this, however, prevented him from exhibiting the Visconti family's penchant for cruelty, and in his time the "Galeazzo's lent" was used. This system of torture could extend a victim's life for 40 days.

VIVALDI, ANTONIO (1678–1741)

Because of his brillant red hair Antonio Vivaldi, one of the greatest of all Italian composers, was nicknamed *The Red Priest* by the students at the Music Seminary of the Ospizio della Pieta in Venice, where he taught from 1703 to 1740.

VLAD "the Impaler" TEPES (1432–1477)

One of the great folk heroes of Eastern Europe, Vlad Tepes, as prince of Walachia, an area now comprising much of Rumania, bitterly resisted the encroachments of the Ottoman Empire. He became *Vlad the Impaler* because of his method of executing his enemies by impaling them on a wooden stake fixed to the ground. Once he carried his method of killing to horrific levels when several Turkish ambassadors refused to remove their turbans as a sign of respect to him. He had the turbans nailed to their heads. Vlad, who is remembered as a savior to his people and whose name has been given to many villages in Rumania, was killed in an ambush in 1477.

Voice, The—See **SINATRA, FRANK.**

Voice of Broadway—See
KILGALLEN, DOROTHY.

Voice of Doom, The—See **HEATTER, GABRIEL.**

Voice of God—See **MACARTHUR, DOUGLAS.**

Voice of New England, The—See
FROST, ROBERT.

Voice of Silver, The—See **PITTMAN, KEY.**

Voice of the Astronauts, The—See
POWERS, JOHN "Shorty."

Voice of the Hangover Generation, The—See **O'HARA, JOHN.**

Voice of the Revolution, The—See
HENRY, PATRICK.

Voice of the St. Louis Fair, The—See
PRADO, KATIE.

Voice of the Silent Majority, The—See
HARVEY, PAUL.

Voice of the Uprooted, The—See
BERKOWITZ, ITZHAK DOV.

VOLSTEAD, ANDREW J. (1860–1947)

A U.S. representative from Minnesota, Andrew Joseph Volstead was hailed as *The Father of the Volstead Act,* which authorized enforcement of the Prohibition amendment. To many Volstead was a saint, but historian Herbert Asbury, who summarized the effects of his efforts in *The Great Illusion,* disagreed: "The American people . . . had expected to be greeted, when the great day came, by a covey of angels bearing gifts of peace, happiness, prosperity and salvation, which they had been assured would be theirs when the rum demon had been scotched. Instead they were met by a horde of bootleggers, moonshiners, rumrunners, hijackers, gangsters, racketeers, trigger men, venal judges, corrupt police, crooked politicians, and speakeasy operators, all bearing the twin symbols of the Eighteenth Amendment—the Tommy gun and the poisoned cup." After the repeal of Prohibition the unfortunate Volstead was referred to as *The Goat of the Wets.*

VOLTAIRE (1694–1778)

The great French writer of the Enlightenment Voltaire was accorded many sobriquets, including *Dictator of Letters, The Plato of the Eighteenth Century* (by Carlyle), *The Great Pan* and *The Philosopher of Ferney* (where he lived in Switzerland the last two decades of his life). The most derogatory nickname bestowed on him by straightlaced critics was *The Apostle of Infidelity.*

Voltaire of Chambermaids, The—See RESTIF, NICHOLAS EDME.

Voltaire of Grecian Literature, The—See LUCIAN.

Voltaire of the Sixteenth Century—See ERASMUS, DESIDERIUS.

VOLTERRA, DANIELE DA—See Breeches Maker, The.

Von Ehrlichman—See EHRLICHMAN, JOHN.

VOORHIS, JERRY (1900–   )

A five-term Decocrat from California, Rep. Jerry Voorhis was called by Washington's hard-nosed press corps *The Best Congressman West of the Mississippi.* In 1946 he was defeated for reelection by Richard Nixon, becoming Nixon's first political victim in what experts agree was one of the dirtiest campaigns of the century.

VORONOFF, SERGE (1866–1951)

A Russian-born surgeon, Dr. Serge Voronoff became famous in the United States during the 1940s as *The Monkey Gland Man,* claiming he could rejuvenate aging men sexually by transplanting apes' testes to them. Although he charged a minimum of $5,000, he was flooded with clients and performed well over 2,000 operations before his business fell off. Quite simply, rejuvenation did not occur. In addition to their financial losses many of *The Monkey Gland Man*'s patients contracted simian syphilis, which was transmitted along with the animal glands.

VUKOVICH, WILLIAM (1918–1954)

Professional auto racing driver Bill Vukovich, who died in a racing mishap in 1954, was noted for his carefree attitude and called *The Mad Russian.*

Vulture Hopkins—See HOPKINS, JOHN.

W

WADDEL, JAMES (1730–1805)

Like William Henry Milburn, who although blind
was to win renown as a preacher, Irish-born James
Waddel was called *The Blind Preacher*. He was
considered perhaps the most powerful pulpit orator in Virginia.

Wag of Whitehall Court, The—See SHAW, GEORGE BERNARD.

WAGNER, GEORGE RAYMOND— See Gorgeous George.

WAGNER, HONUS (1874–1955)

Few baseball nicknames were as well deserved as
The Flying Dutchman for Honus Wagner, generally acknowledged to be the greatest shortstop in
the history of the game. When he retired in 1917,
he had scored more runs, made more hits and stolen
more bases than any player in the history of the
National League.

WAINRIGHT, JONATHAN MAYHEW (1833–1953)

Gen. Jonathan Mayhew Wainright, generally called
Skinny Wainright, commanded U.S. and Filipino
forces fighting the Japanese on Bataan and Corregidor after Gen. MacArthur's departure in 1942.
His nickname, actually of prewar origins, nonetheless became a symbol of the ordeal, especially
the Bataan ''Death March,'' endured by the American troops taken prisoner by the Japanese.

WAITE, DAVIS HANSON (1825–1901)

The first and only Populist governor of Colorado,
Davis Hanson Waite was strongly pro-labor in an
era of considerable labor-related violence, especially the great Cripple Creek strike of 1894. He
earned the nickname *Bloody Bridles Waite* from a
speech he made about the war ''against oppression and tyranny to preserve the liberties of man.''
He concluded, ''it is better, infinitely better, that
blood should flow to the horses' bridles, rather than
our national liberties should be destroyed.'' Six
years after his death the Western Federation of
Miners erected a granite memorial at his grave site
in Aspen.

Wake, The—See HEREWARD.

WAKSMAN, SELMAN ABRAHAM (1888–1973)

Russian-born U.S. microbiologist Selman A.
Waksman, who won the Nobel Prize in medicine
in 1952 for his study of antibiotics and discovery
of streptomycin, was dubbed *The Father of Wonder Drugs*.

WALESA, LECH (1943–   )

When Lech Walesa, the leader of the Polish independent labor union Solidarity, was imprisoned by
the Polish government in the early 1980s, he became known as *The Man of Iron,* ironically not
first in his native land but in the United States. A
life-sized bust of Walesa unveiled in the heavily
Polish upstate New York steel town of Lackawanna
showed Walesa behind iron bars, which were to
be removed when he was freed.

WALKER, FRED "Dixie" (1910–1982)

Alabama-born *Dixie* Walker became one of the most popular baseball players for the Brooklyn Dodgers in the 1940s and was nicknamed *The People's Cherce*. The Brooklynese accent contrasted sharply with Walker's melodious southern drawl. There are those who said Walker lived up to his nickname *Dixie* when he allegedly demanded to be traded after Jackie Robinson, the first black to play in the major leagues, joined the Dodgers.

WALKER, JAMES J. (1881–1946)

A consummate rogue whom New Yorkers took to their hearts during the Roaring Twenties and Prohibition, Mayor James J. Walker was affectionately referred to as *Beau James* and *The Playboy Mayor* or *Night Mayor* since he was a regular sight in the illegal nightspots of Broadway. He was also dubbed *The Late Mayor* because after a night of carousing he was never on time for appointments at City Hall the next morning. Reporters labeled him *The Wisecracker* since he was fast with a quip. One of his most famous, on a move to censor novels was: "I have never yet heard of a girl being ruined by a book." However, by the time of the Great Depression, he had outlived his own carefree era and was forced to resign during an investigation of corruption.

WALKER, MARY EDWARDS (1832–1919)

A transvestite who heroically served in the Civil War as a nurse treating the sick and wounded and later as a spy and surgeon, Dr. Mary Edwards Walker was awarded the Congressional Medal of Honor (rescinded in 1917 along with 911 others) by President Andrew Johnson. After the war she was notorious for wearing men's clothes and was often arrested. However, she was never prosecuted since a special act of Congress granted her the right to wear trousers. The newspapers referred to her as *America's Self-made Man*. One newspaper noted: "What must be demanded by all who have the interest of the Republic at heart is the refeminization of Dr. Walker. Her trousers must be taken from her—where and how is, of course, a matter of detail." They never were. When she died in 1919, she was buried in her trousers and Prince Albert coat.

WALKER, SARAH BREEDLOVE (1867–1919)

Sarah Breedlove Walker, a black woman, developed a new hair conditioner that straightened tightly curled hair. Initially peddling it from door to door, she soon had her own manufacturing plant in Indianapolis, Ind. When she died in 1919, *The Nemesis of Kinky Hair,* as the financial press tagged her, was a millionaire.

WALKER, WILLIAM (1824–1860)

Ironically the great American adventurer and filibuster William Walker in his youth was called *Honey* and *Missy* by other boys who considered his bearing, manners and interests to be rather effeminate. Walker proved anything but that as he seized power in Nicaragua and proclaimed himself president of the country. The native Indians of the country were awed by his grey eyes since an ancient legend held that a grey-eyed stranger from the North would eventually come to free them of Spanish tryanny. Thus they considered him *The Grey-Eyed Man of Destiny,* a nickname Walker seized upon and ordered his followers to call him. In 1857, however, Walker was toppled from power, and he then made an ill-fated attempt to gain similar authority in Honduras. He was captured and shot Sept. 12, 1860.

Walking Encyclopedia of the Blues, A—See Howlin' Wolf.

Walking Museum, The—See LONGINUS, DIONYSIUS CASSIUS.

Walking Polyglot, A—See MEZZOFANTI, CARDINAL GIUSEPPE.

Walking Stewart—See STEWART, JOHN.

WALL, TESSIE (1869–1932)

Perhaps the most celebrated California madam, Tessie Wall was given the misnomer *Queen of the Barbary Coast*. A rather snooty practitioner of her trade, she always looked down her nose at crude vice areas, such as San Francisco's Barbary Coast. She preferred to maintain her establishments—for instance, the celebrated one at 337 O'Farrell St.—in the district that housed the city's best theaters and restaurants, the Upper Tenderloin. Until she was driven out of business by a reform wave in 1917, her place was always keynoted by an impressive needlepoint placed in the parlor, reading: "If every man was as true to his country as he is to his wife—God help the U.S.A."

WALLACE, HENRY A. (1888–1965)

When Henry Wallace served as President Franklin Roosevelt's secretary of agriculture he won the nickname *Plow 'em Under Wallace* for originating the practice of having surplus crops plowed under to keep farm prices from falling. Wallace served as vice-president during Roosevelt's third term.

WALLACE, MIKE (1918–   )

Using an aggressive form of interviewing, the television newsman Mike Wallace has been called *The Nation's Toughest Television Reporter*.

WALLACE, WILLIAM (c. 1274–1305)

The Scottish patriot Sir William Wallace was nicknamed *The Hammer and Scourge of England* because of his resistance to the forays of Edward I of England (who was himself given the sobriquet The Hammer of the Scots).

WALLACE, WILLIAM "Big Foot" (1817–1899)

A much-storied frontiersman and sometime Texas Ranger, William Wallace was far better known as *Big Foot Wallace,* although many writers have ascribed his nickname to the wrong reason. While he was a hulking, 240-pound, six-footer, Wallace did not have outsized feet. The nickname derived from his futile efforts to track down a renegade Indian named Big Foot (who apparently did have big feet). A wild man, *Big Foot Wallace* was often incarcerated, especially in Mexico. In skirmishing with Mexican troops he once cut down a soldier of a similar stature to himself just to obtain a change of pants. The Mexicans did not call him *Big Foot,* preferring the appellation *Loco Americano*.

Wallace of Switzerland, The—See HOFER, ANDREAS.

WALLER, FATS (1904–1943)

Fats Waller, the great American jazz great—pianist, composer, singer—was described as *The Black Horowitz*. A prolific composer, Fats once estimated he could get four arrangements to a quart of gin.

WALLER, JOHN (1741–1802)

An 18th century Pennsylvanian notorious for hatred and persecution of Baptists, John Waller was a member of a grand jury that indicted a Baptist clergyman for preaching. At the clergyman's trial, the defendant's speech to the jury converted Waller to Baptist beliefs and in time he became a Baptist minister himself. Thus his nicknames *Swearing Jack Waller* and *The Devil's Adjutant,* given him by religionists, fell into disuse.

WALLACE, LEW (1827–1905)

During his military days as a general in the Civil War, Lew Wallace, who wrote the best-selling novel *Ben Hur,* was nicknamed *Louisa* by his soldiers, apparently because of his long hair.

WALPOLE, ROBERT (1676–1745)

The first de facto prime minister of England, Sir Robert Walpole was called *The Grand Corrupter* because of the corrupt means he used to achieve ascendancy in the House of Commons. He went to the Tower of London on a charge of corruption but was later able to return to political life with the rise of the Whigs to power under George I.

Walter Scott of the Middle Ages, The—See FROISSART, JEAN.

WALTERS, BARBARA (1931–   )

U.S. journalist and television interviewer Barbara Walters has been dubbed *The First Lady of Talk.* She is much parodied and has been satirized as *Barbara Wa-Wa,* an allusion in part to her manner of speaking, which some find somewhat babyish.

Waltz King, The—See KING, WAYNE HAROLD.

WANDERER, CARL (1887–1921)

At first Carl Wanderer seemed the hero in Chicago's murderous Case of the Ragged Stranger. His story was that a ragged stranger opened fire on him and his pregnant wife as they entered the darkened vestibule of their home. Wanderer was armed and shot back, killing the intruder, but his wife lay dying as well. For his heroic act he was dubbed by the press *The Hero Husband.* Later, however, newsmen Charles MacArthur and Ben Hecht proved that Wanderer had planned to murder his wife and had arranged for the ragged stranger, a drifter he met in a skid row bar, to come to his home on a promise of a job. The ragged stranger was to be a convenient and dead scapegoat. Carl Wanderer went to the scaffold in 1921, and instead of being called *The Hero Husband,* he became *The Butcher Boy.*

WANER, PAUL (1903–1965) and LLOYD (1906–1982)

Two baseball brother greats, both in the Baseball Hall of Fame, Paul and Lloyd Waner were nicknamed *Big Poison* and *Little Poison* because of their prowess with the bat. Lloyd, often described as the greatest singles hitter in the game, would get on base and brother Paul, a power slugger, would drive him home. Actually, the origin of the sobriquets had nothing to do with batting ability. Lloyd was extremely thin, a trait that had earlier gained him the monicker *Muscles.* One time in New York a fan in the stands shouted in typical Brooklynese that Lloyd was "a little poison," meaning a little person. The nickname stuck and later was given its added meaning.

War Child, The—See WHEELER, JOSEPH "Fighting Joe."

WARBURTON, WILLIAM (1698–1779)

The English prelate, theologian, editor of Pope and controversialist William Warburton engaged in constant intellectual warfare with those who disagreed with his literary tenets. For his dogmatic attitude and his arrogance he was often called *The Literary Bull-dog*. Others preferred *The Most Impudent Man Living* and still others used *The Great Preserver of Pope and Shakespeare,* facetiously, as though Warburton was certain the two bards would perish without him. Add to those such sobriquets as *The Poet's Parasite, A Mountebank in Criticism* and *A Quack in Commentatorship* and the designation of *A Blazing Star,* accorded him by Dr. William Cuming, seems a bit pale. But Cuming noted, "With such a train of quotations as he carries in his tail, and the eccentricity of the vast circuit he takes the vulgar are alarmed, the learned puzzled. Something wonderful it certainly portends, and I wish he may go off without leaving some malignant influence at least among us, if he does not set us on fire."

WARD, LESTER FRANK (1841–1913)

U.S. social scientist Lester Frank Ward, who took all knowledge as his province, was dubbed by admirers *The Yankee Aristotle.* As impassioned reformer, he attacked the Social Darwinists, who held that society should, like nature, be ruled by the law of the survival of the fittest, a position which seemed to give the unregulated capitalist system scientific sanction. Ward was democratic, humanitarian and egalitarian in outlook, calling the masses "the fourth estate" and insisting the slum child held as much promise as the rich child. He urged "social engineering" to better the conditions of the people.

WARD, MARCUS L. (1812–1884)

During the Civil War Marcus L. Ward, a New Jersey businessman, became known as *The Soldier's Friend* for giving up his business and spending his time and money to alleviate as much as he could the situation of the soldiers on the battlefield and of their families at home.

WARDE, JOHN—See Man on the Ledge, The.

Warhawk, The—See CALHOUN JOHN C.

WARHOL, ANDY (1928–   )

Andy Warhol, the leader of the pop art movement of the 1960s, gained the fame for sculptures of Brillo Soap Pad boxes and paintings of soup cans. However, before he became a prominent New York artist, he did highly regarded fashion illustrations for the shoe business and gained the nickname *The Leonardo of the Shoe Trade.*

Warming Pan Baby, The—See STUART, JAMES FRANCIS EDWARD.

WARNER, JACK L. (1892–1978)

Film pioneer Jack L. Warner, noted for being rather tight-fisted with some employees, was an inveterate gambler who could drop thousands of dollars an evening in casinos in Las Vegas or on the Riviera, thus earning the sobriquet *Sporting Blood.*

WARREN, GOUVERNEUR K. (1830–1882)

Gouverneur K. Warren, chief engineer of the Union Army at the Battle of Gettysburg, was credited with an action that quite likely preserved the North's great victory. On the second day of the battle, while checking the security of the left flank, he was shocked to find the vital summit of Little Round Top held only by a handful of his signalmen. Discovering that Confederate troops were moving on the position, he ordered the signalmen to move about and was thus able to give the Confederates the impression that the hill was heavily occupied. In the meantime he rode off to gather up any nearby infantry and bring them back to the hill. Warren gained instant fame as *The Savior of Little Round Top*. Ironically, less than two years later he was removed from command, although later cleared, for a lack of quick action.

WARREN, JOSIAH (1798–1874)

U.S. inventor and reformer Josiah Warren was called *The Father of Anarchy* and *The First American Anarchist*. He was a member of the socialist experiment at New Harmony, Ind., but later turned to his own theory of individual sovereignty.

WARREN, MERCY OTIS (1728–1814)

A leading American author, playwright and poet Mercy Otis Warren was called *The First Lady of the Revolution*. She knew most of the leaders of the Revolution personally and was generally at the center of many of the dramatic events from 1765 to 1789.

Warrior Lady of Latham, The—See DERBY, CHARLOTTE, COUNTESS OF.

WASHINGTON, DINAH (1924–1963)

U.S. singer Dinah Washington was acclaimed *The Queen of the Blues*, although some purists complained she wasted much of her gutsy blues style by adapting it to pop songs.

WASHINGTON, GEORGE (1732–1799)

George Washington, the first president of the United States, received many accolades, including such obvious ones as *The Father of His Country*, *The Deliverer of America*, *The Sword of the Revolution*, *The Atlas of America* and *The Savior of His Country*. His military foe, Lord Cornwallis, called him *The Old Fox*. Both the Americans and the British dubbed him *The American Fabius* because of his tactics of harassing the British troops without joining in a pitched battle, a policy used by the Roman general Fabius against Hannibal. Because he was summoned out of retirement at Mount Vernon in 1798 to take charge of the army when war with France seemed likely, he was called *The Cincinnatus of the West*, after the Roman Cincinnatus who was twice summoned to power from his farm. However, not all his sobriquets were favorable. During his presidency foes, who charged him with tyrannical rule and claimed he had taken over the work and glory of others, referred to him as *The Stepfather of His Country*. Thomas Paine called him *A Hyprocrite in Public Life*, but in later years Gladstone hailed him as *The Purest Figure in History*. A wealth of nicknames could have been provided by Revolutionary War American general Charles Lee, who described Washington as "that dark designing sordid ambitious vain proud arrogant and vindictive knave."

Washington of Colombia, The—See BOLIVAR, SIMON.

Washington of the West—See HARRISON, WILLIAM HENRY.

Washington's Cinderella Woman—See MCLEAN, EVALYN WALSH.

Washington's Gay Young Bachelor— See KENNEDY, JOHN F.

Washington's Other Monument—See LONGWORTH, ALICE LEE ROOSEVELT.

Wasp, The—See FRERON, ELIE-CATHERINE.

Wasp of Twickenham, The—See POPE, ALEXANDER.

Watchdog of Central Park, The—See OCHS, ADOLPH S.

Watcher, The—See CONVERSE, HARRIET.

WATERFORD JACK—See Millionaire Streetwalker, The.

Watergate Guard, The: FRANK WILLS (1948–   )

Frank Wills, the black security guard who discovered the Watergate break-in, won considerable fame as *The Watergate Guard*, but it never brought him much in the way of financial or career rewards, unlike some of the burglars.

Waterloo Hero, The—See HILL, ROWLAND.

WATERS, ETHEL (1897–1977)

The family and friends of Ethel Waters never doubted she would become a famous entertainer, and she was called *Baby Star*. She went on to become a leading jazz singer and a stage, screen and television actress.

Waters, Muddy: MCKINLEY MORGANFIELD (1915–1983)

Muddy Waters, born McKinley Morganfield, the reigning king of Chicago blues for many years, picked up his nickname as a child, having been raised by his grandparents in the center of the Mis-sissippi Delta. One of the most significant influences on modern popular music, he led what was virtually the first electric blues-rock band, and his 1954 blues tune ''Rollin' Stone'' inspired Bob Dylan's ''Like a Rolling Stone.''

Watertight Smith—See SMITH, WILLIAM A. ''Watertight.''

WATERTON, CHARLES (1782–1865)

Charles Waterton, 27th lord of Walton Hall in Yorkshire, England, was dubbed *The Eccentric Explorer* for his many unusual escapades around the world. His most famous exploit occurred on an expedition in British Guiana during which he captured a 10½-foot caiman by riding on its back. He also knocked out a boa constrictor with a powerful punch and climbed the cross of St. Peter's Cathedral in Rome.

WATSON, ELLA—See Cattle Kate.

WAYNE, JOHN (1907–1979)

Western movie star John Wayne was nicknamed *Duke* in his childhood. He owned an Airedale terrier named Duke from whom he was inseparable, and the firemen at the local station started calling him *Duke* after his dog, and the name stuck.

WAYNE, ''Mad'' ANTHONY (1745–1796)

While there is some divergence of opinion as to how Revolutionary War general *Mad* Anthony Wayne got his nickname—Washington Irving insisted it resulted from his reckless courage in battle—the fact remains that his troops gave it to him after the Milestone Battle at Stony Point, N.Y., in 1779. Among the ''mad'' orders Wayne issued was forcing the men to approach the battle with empty muskets and fixed bayonets. The penalty for removing the musket from the shoulder was death, administered on the spot by the nearest officer. In addition Wayne had white slips of paper stuck in each soldier's headdress for identification.

Weasel, The—See CECIL, WILLIAM LORD BURLEIGH; FRATIANNO, JIMMY "the Weasel."

Weaver Poet, The—See THOM, WILLIAM.

Weazel, The—See VAN BUREN, MARTIN.

WEBSTER, DANIEL (1782–1852)

U.S. statesman, orator and lawyer Daniel Webster inspired a number of laudatory nicknames, such as *The Defender of the Union, The New England Cicero, The Expounder of the Constitution* and *The God-like.* However, he was perhaps best known as *Black Dan,* a nickname dating back to his Dartmouth College days that referred to his dark complexion. It was later used vituperatively by angry abolitionists after he supported the Fugitive Slave law. For the same reason supporters of John Quincy Adams dubbed Webster *A Traitor to Freedom.*

WEBSTER, NOAH (1758–1843)

U.S. lexicographer Noah Webster became especially known for his dictionaries of the English language published in 1806, 1807 and 1828 and was renowned in his lifetime as *The Schoomaster of the Republic.* At various times a schoolteacher, newspaper editor and lawyer, Webster found time to write unceasingly on politics, diseases, history and grammar, and his name has become synonymous with "dictionary."

WEDELL, H. C. (1712–1782)

Gen. H. C. Wedell of Prussia was nicknamed *Leonidas Wedell* by a grateful Frederick the Great for his gallant stand at Teinitz in 1744.

WEDGEWOOD, EDGAR A. (1856–1920)

Although educated for a career as a violinist, the teenaged Edgar A. Wedgewood left his native Massachusetts for Nebraska, where, though not yet having reached his majority, he was elected sheriff of Hall County. He gained fame throughout the state as *The Kid Sheriff of Nebraska.* In later years he became a leading attorney in irrigation and mining law and a hero in the Spanish American War and the Philippine insurrection.

WEDGWOOD, JOSIAH (1730–1795)

The greatest figure in the fields of both ornamental and utilitarian ware, English potter Josiah Wedgwood was especially noted for his copies of classical vases. However, he had a number of failures in the pottery business before he was finally recognized as *The Father of the Potteries.*

Weeping Prophet, The—See SEWALL, JOSEPH.

WEILL, AL "Greasy Vest" (1894–1969)

Boxing matchmaker and manager Al Weill sported an unsavory nickname that many sportswriters saw as typifying a most unsavory racket. He was called *Greasy Vest Weill* because of his generally slovenly appearance. Sportswriter Dan Parker probably put it best when he wrote: "In the boxing business he is variously known and with some affection (although his personal popularity is open to grave question) as *The Vest, The Weskit King* and *Greasy Vest*. These sobriquets date back to his salad days when he took his meals on the fly and the fly retaliated by taking his meals on Al. One could always tell then what Weill had been eating over a two-week period." (See also Introduction.)

WEINBERGER, CASPAR (1917–   )

U.S. secretary of defense under Ronald Reagan, Caspar Weinberger took office with the nickname *Cap the Knife,* earned as budget director under Richard Nixon when he was famous for slashing federal programs. However, as an exponent of higher defense spending, he was described by critics as a man whose knife had grown dull and rusty and had "become an arch-representative of the military-industrial complex." He was also disparaged as *Cap the Suitcase* by critics who declared his foreign travels were too often marked by controversial statements that irritated U.S. allies.

WEISS, HYMIE "the Polack" (1898–1926)

Bootlegger, racketeer and later the leader of Chicago's Dion O'Banion North Side gang, Weiss was something of an anomaly since he was *The Polack* and the North Siders were primarily Irish and generally intolerant of other ethnics. Hymie had sterling qualities that were recognized by his mentor O'Banion, being a master of the art of murder and, in fact, the celebrated *Father of the One-Way Ride.* In 1921 one Steve Wisniewski offended the O'Banions by heisting one of their beer trucks. Weiss invited Wisniewski for a drive in the country along Lake Michigan, and Wisniewski never returned. Later, Weiss started an honored underworld tradition by bragging, "We took Stevie for a ride, a one-way ride."

WEISSMULLER, JOHNNY (1904–   )

The best known of all the movie Tarzans, Olympic champion swimmer Johnny Weissmuller is now known as *The Original Swinger.*

WEIZMANN, CHAIM (1874–1952)

A Jewish chemist, scholar and Zionist leader who became the first president of Israel, Chaim Weizmann was designated *The Nation Builder.* His discovery of synthetic acetone aided British arms production during World War I.

WELBY, HENRY (1554–1638)

Eccentric Henry Welby, an Englishman of wealth and high social position, barely escaped being shot by a younger brother during an argument. At the age of 40 he decided to remove himself from all dangers of human intercourse gaining the sobriquet *The Hermit of Grub Street.* He had three rooms constructed—one within another—in which he lived: eating in one, sleeping in the second and using the third as his study. Whenever servants brought him his food, or fixed his bed or cleaned his rooms, he simply moved ahead of them to an unused chamber so that even they never saw his face. Remarkably, he still kept up with events of the world and found ways to decide on objects of charity. *The Hermit of Grub Street* remained in his self-prisonment for the final 44 years of his life.

WELK, LAWRENCE (1903–   )

Orchestra leader and television personality Lawrence Welk is called *Mr. Music Maker* by his fans, and *The King of Musical Corn* by those less entranced with his style. The fact remains that, of all the groups of the Big Band era, *The King of Musical Corn* is one of the few to have survived.

WELLES, ORSON (1915–)

U.S. actor, director, producer and playwright Orson Welles, hailed as *The Boy Genius,* was only 24 years old when he directed and starred in *Citizen Kane,* regarded by many critics as the best American film ever made. Welles himself preferred his self-proclaimed *Your Obedient Servant.*

WELLINGTON, ARTHUR WELLESLEY, FIRST DUKE OF (1769–1852)

It is a misconception that the Duke of Wellington's nickname, *The Iron Duke,* was derived from his firmness and resoluteness in standing up to the military challenge of Napoleon at Waterloo in 1815. Actually, the sobriquet arose from his service as prime minister from 1828 to 1830, during which he reluctantly secured passsage of the critical Catholic Emancipation Act to avoid an Irish civil war. He then rigidly opposed parliamentary reforms until forced to resign. It was the iron shutters he used to protect his home from angry crowds as well as the iron hand he used in conducting military affairs that led to his being called *The Iron Duke* by the press. With his great victory at Waterloo he was dubbed *The Achilles of England, Europe's Liberator, Savior of the Nations* and *The Best of Cut-Throats* (meant rather flatteringly by Byron).

WELLS, CHARLES—See Man Who Broke the Bank at Monte Carlo, The.

WELLS, H. G. (1866–1946)

English novelist and social reformer–philosopher Herbert George Wells was called *The Critic of Progress* for his views on social and political problems. Since he often used the novel form to present his views of imaginative social philosophy by placing them in various societies throughout the past and future ages of man, he was referred to as *The Time Traveler* (after his famous work *The Time Machine*).

WENCESLAS VI OF BOHEMIA (1359–1419)

Wenceslas VI, the wastrel king of Bohemia and emperor of Germany was disparagingly referred to as *The Drunkard* and more commonly as *The Nero of Germany.* He trained a dog so that on signal it would attack anyone he wished, and he murdered his wife in such a manner. It is also probably true that he had his cook roasted alive for preparing a ragout that he did not like. The latter-day Nero was deposed in 1400.

WENHAM, JANE (?–1730)

Jane Wenham, quaint Englishwoman nicknamed *The Wise Woman of Walkern,* in 1712 became the last person tried for witchcraft in England. She was convicted of, among other things, being able to fly, even though the judge, Sir John Powell, noted that as far as he knew there was no law against flying. The outraged jurist successfully got *The Wise Woman* a reprieve from her death sentence and shortly thereafter she was pardoned. The case proved to be a devastating expose of witch-hunters and their methods and virtually ended public belief in the superstition.

WEST, JAMES MARION "Silver Dollar," JR. (1903–1957)

Almost a parody of what a Texas oil millionaire should be like, James Marion West, Jr., was called *Silver Dollar West* for his custom of heaving rolls of silver dollars in the streets and watching people scramble to retrieve them. His standard tip in a restaurant if he approved the service was 80 silver dollars. Evidently impressed by such spending, the Houston police permitted West to travel the streets at night wearing a diamond-encrusted Texas Ranger badge and a .45-caliber pistol. His car, manned by a uniformed police lieutenant, came stocked with a .28-gauge shotgun, a 30-30 rifle, a Tommy gun and a tear gas cannister. For a time he was called *Tear Gas West* after his car was surrounded by playful costumed trick-or-treaters on Halloween night and he loosed the tear gas into their midst as his idea of a playful response.

WEST, REBECCA (1892–1983)

English novelist, journalist and critic Rebecca West was often accorded the title of *The Lioness of Literary Letters*. Some said *The Lioness* was often capable of baring her claws, as in her comment that "Tolstoy was a lousy writer."

Western Star, The—See CLAY, HENRY.

Westerner, The—See SAIONJI, PRINCE KIMMOCHI.

WESTINGHOUSE, GEORGE (1846–1914)

U.S. inventor and industrialist George Westinghouse was called *The Inventive Wizard*, not only for his own inventions—such as the air brake, other important railroad devices and systems for piping gas—but for his grasp of the potentials of others' inventions. He bought Nikola Tesla's patents for alternating current and developed them into the standard form of electricity in the country.

WESTMORELAND, WILLIAM C. (1914–   )

Gen. William C. Westmoreland, who commanded U.S. forces in Vietnam, was nicknamed *The Inevitable General* by his classmates at West Point.

WESTON, EDWARD PAYSON (1839–1929)

Edward Payson Weston gained nationwide fame as *The Pedestrian* after he walked 478 miles from Boston to Washington as his loser's fate in a bet that Lincoln would not be elected president in 1860. At every town along the way, crowds cheered him on and ladies kissed him and bade that their sentiments be passed on to Lincoln at his inauguration. Weston completed his jaunt in 10 days and had enough strength to attend the Inauguration Ball on the evening of his arrival. After that Weston turned professional and won a huge number of walking contests for big money prizes. He won $10,000 in 1867 for a 1,237½-mile trek from Portland, Me., to Chicago in 26 days, an event the newspapers called The Great Pedestrian Feat. He got so far ahead of schedule on that walk that he stopped to address crowds along the way and attend church services. He repeated the same walk in 1907 at the age of 68 and bettered his own mark by 29 hours. In his seventies he won walking contests of up to nearly 4,000 miles.

Wet Star, The—See WILLIAMS, ESTHER.

WHALEN, GROVER A. (1886–1962)

A New York merchant, promoter and official who made an institution out of a civic welcome, Grover A. Whalen was called *The Official Greeter of New York City*. He originated the city's celebrated ticker-tape parades for the famous.

WHEAT, CHATHAM ROBERDEAU (1826–1862)

In 1859 Virginian Chatham Roberdeau Wheat fought with the forces of Giuseppe Garibaldi in the war for Italian independence. Wheat was hailed in Italy as *The Murat of America*, after Napoleon's brilliant cavalry commander, for his leadership of Garibaldi's cavalry. When the American Civil War broke out, Major Wheat returned and organized a Confederate battalion, fighting with distinction until he was killed in action in June 1862.

WHEATLEY, PHILLIS (1753?–1784)

The first black woman poet in America, Phillis Wheatley was taught to read and write by her owners, Boston merchant John Wheatley and his wife, after being brought from Africa when she was about eight years old. She eventually published her *Poems on Various Subjects, Religious and Moral*. The Wheatleys died in 1778 and Phillis was declared a free person. However, sickly and impoverished, she died six years later at the age of about 31. She has since been lionized as *The Negro Sappho*.

WHEELER, BURTON K. (1882–1975)

Early in his Senate career, Democrat Burton K. Wheeler, who gained fame as the Teapot Dome Scandal prosecutor, was nicknamed *The Great Liberal*, that being his political inclination until the advent of the New Deal in 1933. Thereafter he opposed almost all aspects of the New Deal and was one of the greatest isolationists in Congress.

WHEELER, JOSEPH "Fighting Joe" (1836–1906)

Only 26 years old when made a brigadier general in the Confederate Army, Joseph Wheeler was nicknamed *The War Child* by his cavalry troopers. As his reputation and military accomplishments grew he was also called *Fighting Joe Wheeler*. His reputation continued long after the Civil War, *Fighting Joe* being one of only two former Confederate generals who served in the U.S. Army during the Spanish-American War.

Where Does Beares Come In?—See BEARES, JAMES D.

WHIPPLE, HENRY BENJAMIN— See Straight Tongue.

Whiskey Straight—See BOGART, HUMPHREY.

Whiskey Van—See VAN BUREN, MARTIN.

WHISTLER, JAMES ABBOTT MCNEILL (1834–1903)

Expatriate American painter, etcher, author, wit, dandy and eccentric James McNeill Whistler, whose painting was known for its color tones, was dubbed *The Painter of Limited Color*. His style, provocative writings and credo "art for art's sake" greatly upset critic John Ruskin, leading to an explosive battle of words. Whistler was never at a loss in such duels, and the sobriquet *The Painter of Limited Words* could indeed be considered most facetious. His joustings with Ruskin led to a famous courtroom confrontation in a libel action. As celebrated were Whistler's verbal skirmishes with former friend and disciple Oscar Wilde, of whom he once wrote: "What has Oscar in common with Art? except that he dines at our tables and picks from our platters the plums for the pudding he peddles in the provinces. Oscar—the amiable, irresponsible, esurient Oscar—with no more sense of a picture than the fit of a coat, has the courage of the opinions . . . of others!" In time *Limited Words* drew back from most verbal frays: "I'm lonesome. They are all dying. I have hardly a warm personal enemy left."

WHITE, BYRON RAYMOND "Whizzer" (1917–)

A former college and professional football star, Byron White was nicknamed *Whizzer* for his ability both as a player and a Rhodes scholar. When he was appointed to the Supreme Court by President John Kennedy, capital wits commented that The Nine Old Men had now been converted into Eight Old Men and a *Whizzer*.

WHITE, ISAAC DEFOREST "Ike" (1864–1943)

Isaac DeForest *Ike* White was for many years the *New York World*'s ace crime reporter. He solved so many cases that had baffled the police, he was nicknamed *The Newspaper Detective*.

WHITE, JOHN (1590–1645)

The English Protestant theologian John White was nicknamed *Century White* from his acerbitic work, *First Century of Scandalous Malignant Priests*.

WHITE, STANFORD (1853–1906)

Stanford White, U.S. architect and New York rake was called *The Builder* because he was considered to be the most distinguished architect of his day, with some 50 elegant buildings and monuments in the city alone, including the magnificent Washington Square Arch, to his credit. He was murdered by a jealous husband, Harry K. Thaw, in 1906. When details of White's sexual escapades with Thaw's wife, before the couple was married, and with other young girls became known, White's nickname was extended to *The Builder and The Beast*. (See also Thaw, Evelyn Nesbit; Thaw, Harry K.)

WHITE, WILLIAM (1897–1967)

Chief executive officer or president of a number of U.S. railroads, William White was considered so thoroughly knowledgable about rail transport that he was nicknamed by his contemporaries *The Railroader's Railroader*.

WHITE, WILLIAM ALLEN (1868–1944)

Journalist and author William Allen White became nationally famous as editor of the Emporia, Kan., *Gazette* for his pungent editorial comments. He was an acknowledged spokesman for progressive-brand Republicanism. He was hailed as *The Sage of Emporia,* and Kansans, many of whom did not fully agree with him, spoke of him as *Kansas' Senator at Large,* although he never succeeded in winning elective office.

White Beaver—See POWELL, DAVID FRANKLIN.

White Chief of the Pawnees, The—See LILLIE, GORDON W.

White Flower, The—See DANTE ALIGHIERI.

White House Fireman, The—See EHRLICHMAN, JOHN.

White House Hatchet Man, The—See COLSON, CHARLES W. "Chuck."

White Knight, The—See AGNEW, SPIRO T.

White Man's Negro, The—See
FETCHIT, STEPIN.

White-Milliner, The—See TALBOT,
FRANCES JENNINGS.

White Muhammad Ali,—See RIGGS,
BOBBY.

White Savage, The—See GIRTY,
SIMON.

WHITELOCKE, BULSTRODE (1605–1676)

Bulstrode Whitelocke was a member of the "Long Parliament" that defied Charles I of England, a counsel at the impeachment of Buckingham and a leading figure in bringing the charges against Stafford. However, when he later refused to take part in the trial against the king, he was sneeringly referred to by the followers of Oliver Cromwell as *The Temporizing Statesman.*

WHITEMAN, PAUL "Pops" (1891–1967)

Bandleader Paul *Pops* Whiteman was dubbed *The King of Jazz* for introducing the musical form to ballrooms and concert halls, giving it an acceptance it had not had before.

WHITMAN, CHARLES (1942–1966)

Mass murderer Charles Whitman is forever etched in the memory of the citizens of Austin, and the students of the University of Texas as *The Tower Murderer.* In August 1966 the 24-year-old Whitman turned the college campus into a shooting gallery from atop a 307-foot observation deck, killing

18 and wounding 30 others in an hour and a half. Police finally made it up the barricaded tower and shot Whitman to death.

WHITMAN, WALT (1819–1892)

Called by his admirers *The Good Gray Poet,* Walt Whitman also had his detractors. Novelist D. H. Lawrence popularized the sobriquet *The Post-mortem Poet,* adding: "This poet with the private soul leaking out of him all the time. All his privacy leaking out in a sort of dribble, oozing into the universe."

WHITTIER, JOHN GREENLEAF (1807–1892)

John Greenleaf Whittier was accorded such honorifics as *The Poet Laureate of New England, The Puritan Poet* and the one that best satisfied his ambition, *New England Burns*—after Scottish poet Robert Burns—but "without glorifying lawless passion," according to Walter Fuller Taylor.

WHYMPER, EDWARD (1840–1911)

English mountain climber Edward Whymper was called *The Conqueror of the Matterhorn* after he led the first successful scaling of the Matterhorn near the village of Zermatt, Switzerland. Four members of the party died in the descent. Whymper had previously failed six times to climb the Matterhorn and had been called *The Scrambler Amongst the Alps.*

Wickedest Man in New York, The: JOHN ALLEN (c. 1830–?)

Although he had three brothers who were ministers and he himself had trained at the Union Theological Seminary, John Allen became the notorious operator of an infamous New York dance hall-brothel featuring 20 girls famed for wearing bells on their ankles and little else. His desertion of the ministry for the ways of depravity won for Allen the nickname of *The Wickedest Man in New York,* which he professed not to understand since, unlike his competitors, he furnished each of the cubicles where his girls entertained customers with a Bible and other religious tracts. When Allen vanished from the scene in the late 1860s, at which time his wealth was estimated at an impressive $100,000, there were rumors he had undergone a complete reformation and taken up the cloth.

Wickedest Man in the World, The—See CROWLEY, ALEISTER.

Wickedest Woman in the City, The—See RESTELL, MADAME.

Wide Mouth—See BOONE, DANIEL.

WIDMARK, RICHARD (1916–)

Movie actor Richard Widmark was nicknamed *The Young Man with a Sneer* after his screen debut as a smirking pathological killer who pushes a little old lady in a wheelchair down a flight of stairs in *Kiss of Death.* For some time, newcomer Widmark was better known by the name of the character he portrayed, *Tommy Udo,* than by his professional name.

Widow at Windsor, The—See VICTORIA, QUEEN.

Widow of the Year—See MOSSLER, CANDACE.

WIENER, NORBERT (1894–1964)

U.S. mathematician Norbert Wiener was dubbed *The Father of Automation.* He coined the term

"cybernetics" to cover the system of communication and control within and among animals, machines and organization, on which much of automation is based.

Wife of Henry Blackwell—See STONE, LUCY.

Wife of Sinclair Lewis, The—See THOMPSON, DOROTHY.

Wife of the Year—See MOSSLER, CANDACE.

WILBERFORCE, SAMUEL "Soapy Sam" (1805–1873)

Samuel Wilberforce, bishop of Winchester, was an English clergyman noted for his ability to calm tempers during serious political disputes, an attribute that won him the sobriquet *Soapy Sam.* He was fond of claiming that while he often got into hot water, he emerged from the situation with clean hands.

WILCOXSON, BOBBY RANDELL "One-Eye" (1929–)

One of the most efficient, if brutal, bank robbers of recent vintage, Bobby Randell *One-Eye* Wilcoxson was nicknamed *The John Dillinger of the 1960s.* He planned his robberies meticulously and on one occasion "cased" a bank job so thoroughly he befriended the bank guard and had coffee with him. From his conversation with the guard, Wilcoxson decided that the man would very likely start shooting if there was a holdup attempt. Thus when Wilcoxson and his gang hit the bank, he immediately shot the guard dead. Indeed, his sobriquet might be considered libelous to Dillinger, who killed only when his own life was in imminent danger. Wilcoxson was captured, convicted and confined to life imprisonment.

WILD, JONATHAN (c. 1682–1725)

Jonathan Wild was England's most remarkable criminal mastermind, who also betrayed other criminals for the reward on their heads. Called *The Thief Taker,* he turned in all criminals, including old accomplices, unless they joined his own underworld organization. A dandy, he maintained an office in London and a country estate, each with a large staff of servants, and deceived the authorities for a number of years. He was exposed and hanged in 1725. Henry Fielding, the author of *Tom Jones,* wrote a whimsical biography of Wild and called him *The Great Man.*

Wild Bill—See HICKOK, JAMES BUTLER "Wild Bill."

Wild Boar of the Ardennes, The—See LA MARCK, GUILLAUME DE.

Wild Boy of Aveyron, The (c. 1783–1823)

In 1800 hunters in the forests of Aveyron, France, found a boy of about 17 who had apparently lived alone in the woods since infancy. Efforts were made to introduce him to human society, but he repeatedly attempted escape. Whenever a human approached he growled and bared his teeth. He finally adjusted to his new life, although when *The Wild Boy of Aveyron* died in 1823 at the approximate age of 40, he had learned to say only three words.

Wild Bull of the Pampas, The—See FIRPO, LUIS ANGEL.

WILD HORSE ANNIE: VELMA JOHNSON (1912–1977)

For almost three decades Velma Johnson led the fight to halt the slaughter of wild horses that roamed the West, becoming famous to supporters and critics as *Wild Horse Annie.*

Wild Man of Oroville, The—See ISHI.

WILDE, OSCAR (1854–1900)

Witty, sophisticated Anglo-Irish playwright Oscar Wilde was celebrated as *The Apostle of Aestheticism* when, at the height of his popularity in 1895, he was convicted of homosexuality and sentenced to two years' imprisonment. However, as early as 1882, while Wilde was on a triumphant speaking tour in the United States, the less inhibited elements of the American press referred to him as *The Schoolgirl,* an allusion to his mannerisms and mode of dress.

WILKES, JOHN (1727–1797)

A conspicuous leader of the English Radicals of the 18th century, John Wilkes championed the cause of the American colonies and gathered a large following both in England and among the revolutionaries of America. On the floor of the House of Commons in 1775, he declared, "I consider it my duty no less strenuously to defend the rights of America than of England, and I feel an equal indignation against the oppressors of our fellow subjects whether at home or on the other side of the Atlantic." Some observers felt that Wilkes took savage delight in baiting George III, and he was labeled *The English Brutus* and *The Idol of the Mob.*

WILKIE, DAVID (1785–1841)

Since so many paintings by the Scottish artist David Wilkie depict home subjects, he was designated *The Raphael of Domestic Art.*

WILKIE, WILLIAM (1721–1772)

Scottish poet William Wilkie, author of *The Epigoniad,* has been called *The Scottish Homer.*

WILLAMOW, JOHANN GOTTLIEB (1736–1777)

Johann Gottlieb Willamow, seeking to glorify Frederick the Great in poetry as a great monarch, heroic figure and wise man, produced a dithyrambic style more heavy-handed, it seemed to many critics, than elevated and wild. Thus his sobriquet *The Prussian Pindar,* a reference to the great Greek lyric poet, appears excessive.

WILLARD, FRANCES E. (1839–1898)

U.S. educator and reformer Frances E. Willard, elected to the Hall of Fame for Great Americans in 1910, was world president of the Women's Christian Temperance Union. Her admirers called her *The Silver Tongued and Golden Hearted.*

WILLARD, JESS (1883–1968)

After boxer Jack Johnson became the first black to win the heavyweight title by knocking out Tommy Burns in 1908, shocked white fans began a long search for *The Great White Hope* to recapture the crown. Even the aging ex-champ Jim Jeffries was hauled out of retirement, but Johnson beat him. Finally in 1915 another *Hope,* Jess Willard, a plodder out of Kansas with little grounding in scientific boxing, took on Johnson in Havana, Cuba. Although Johnson easily took the early rounds from *Cowboy Jess,* as Willard was called, the latter came back to win a knockout in the 26th round. It has long been suspected that the outcome of the fight was fixed, and Johnson later maintained he had thrown the fight. But nothing was ever proven, and Willard went into boxing history as the successful *Great White Hope.*

WILLIAM, DUKE OF AUSTRIA (?–1406)

One of the most popular members of the court of Vienna, William, duke of Austria, was known for his elegance and brilliance. Because of those characteristics and his success in handling the affairs of state during the absence of the actual monarch—Duke Albert IV, who much preferred pilgrimages to the Holy Land and stays in monastaries to ruling— William was referred to by the people as *The Delightful.* (See also Albert IV, Duke of Austria.)

WILLIAM II, KAISER (1859–1941)

Kaiser Willam II of Germany was known to the American doughboys of World War I as *Kaiser Bill.* Although he was more accurately Frederick William (Friedrich Wilhelm Viktor Albert), ''Frederick'' did not become the operative name, probably because he did not wish to invite comparisons with Frederick the Great. This did not prevent the British press from lampooning him as *Frederick the Greatest.*

WILLIAM IV—See Silly Billy.

WILLIAM FREDERICK, DUKE OF GLOUCESTER—See Silly Billy.

WILLIAM OF ORANGE (1650–1702)

William of Orange, or William III of England, became known as *The Deliverer in England* after the Glorious Revolution of 1689. In league with disaffected English nobles he drove James II from the throne because of James' Catholicism. He reigned with Mary II and was called *Dutch Billy,* which in England was less of a drawback than being labeled a Catholic.

William the Bad: WILLIAM I OF SICILY (1120–1166)

Generally regarded as one of the worst of all monarchs, William I of Sicily was generally known as *William the Bad*. His reign was marked by intrigues, feuds and wars, and his subjects suffered many calamities. Ironically, and justly, his son and successor was called William the Good.

William the Conqueror—See PRYNNE, WILLIAM.

William the Good: WILLIAM II OF SICILY (1152–1189)

Unlike his dissolute father, William the Bad, William II of Sicily, who succeeded to the throne at the age of 14, was called *William the Good*. A youth of beguiling innocence and beauty, he was embraced by the nation, and the warring factions that thrived during his reign were reconciled in support of the young ruler. Until his death at the age of 37, his rule was a period of tranquility and justice.

William the Silent: WILLIAM I, PRINCE OF ORANGE (1533–1584)

William the Silent, prince of Orange and chief founder of the Dutch Republic, was also called *The High-Born Demosthenes,* after the great Greek orator-statesman. This did not contradict the previous sobriquet, which alluded to the fact that he knew when to hold his counsel.

William the Testy—See KIEFT, WILLIAM.

WILLIAMS, ALEXANDER S. "Clubber" (1839–1910)

One of the most corrupt and brutal police officers in American history, Inspector Alexander S. Williams gained his sobriquet *Clubber* while a patrolman. He used his nightstick viciously against the toughs, or anyone he presumed to be a tough,

on his beat. He was the originator of the famous observation, "There's more law in the end of a policeman's nightstick than in a decision of the Supreme Court." There is some speculation that Williams was the inspiration for Theodore Roosevelt's "Speak softly and carry a big stick." While Roosevelt, then chief of police, had a certain admiration for Williams' ability, he also wanted a force that was both tough and honest. He forced *Clubber* into retirement in 1895.

WILLIAMS, EDWARD BENNETT (1920–)

Because he defended so many criminal types at congressional hearings, attorney Edward Bennett Williams was nicknamed *The Burglar's Lobby in Washington.* He answered such criticism by noting, "The Sixth Amendment of the Constitution guarantees the right of legal counsel to *everyone.* It does not say to everyone *except* people like Frank Costello."

WILLIAMS, ESTHER (1921–)

Movie actress Esther Williams in her heyday was known in Hollywood as *The Wet Star* because her acting abilities were limited to her swimming prowess. Or as Fanny Brice put it: "Wet she's a star. Dry she ain't."

WILLIAMS, G. MENNEN "Soapy" (1911–)

Toiletries fortune heir G. Mennen Williams, who was Democratic governor of Michigan from 1949 to 1960, was inevitably nicknamed *Soapy*.

WILLIAMS, JAMES DOUGLAS (1808–1880)

As governor of Indiana in the 1870s James Douglas Williams was called *Blue Jeans Williams* and

The Blue Jeans Governor because he insisted on wearing clothes made of denim.

WILLIAMS, JOHN (1644–1729)

John Williams, a Massachusetts clergyman, was taken prisoner in a French and Indian attack in 1704 and held for two years before being set free. Returning to the members of his family who survived the massacre, he wrote a narrative entitled *The Redeemed Captive Returning to Zion* and was thereafter known as *The Redeemed Captive*.

WILLIAMS, JOHN STUART (1818–1898)

After the Mexican War John Stuart Williams ran for a seat in the Kentucky legislature on his service record. His opponent, Roger Hanson, was a member of Williams' company and disputed Williams' claim of heroism. The incident in dispute occurred at the Battle of Cerro Gordo, where Williams' claimed he had been the first to carry the American flag into the enemy's lines. Hanson insisted that in the dash for cover he had lost half a foot in height trying to keep up with Captain Williams, and in his speeches he derided his opponent as *Cerro Gordo Williams*. Williams won the election by six votes and retained the nickname as a mark of honor in furthering his later political and Confederate military careers.

WILLIAMS, RICHARD PERRY (1874–1966)

Many sports experts consider Richard Perry Williams to be the greatest athlete of all time, dubbing him *The All-Around Wonder*. English-born Williams came to the United States and obtained a coaching job at Tufts College in 1899. In the ensuing dozen years he set what appears to have been the records for their time in such events as the 100-yard dash (9 seconds); 100 meters (9.8 seconds); 400 meters, (46.6 seconds); mile (4 minutes 25 seconds); standing broad jump with weights (15 feet 4 inches); standing jump backwards with weights (13 feet 3 inches); running broad jump (26 feet ½ inches); running high kick (10 feet 3 inches); hitch and kick (9 feet 6 inches); shot put, 16 lb. (47 feet 9 inches); shot put, 12 lb. (57 feet 3 inches); discus throw (142 feet 9 inches); high jump on ice skates (4 feet 6 inches); baseball throw (415 feet 3 inches); circling baseball bases (12 seconds). He also beat the legendary Jim Thorpe in 19 track and field events, and the latter called him "the fastest sprinter who ever lived." However, *The All-Around Wonder* never had any of his marks accepted. The problem was Williams' coaching job, which, the Amateur Athletic Union said, made him a professional. Since the AAU was at the time the only widely recognized authority on sports records, Williams' accomplishments were simply ignored.

WILLIAMS, ROGER (c. 1603–1683)

As a minister in Salem, Roger Williams became embroiled in a dispute with the Massachusetts authorities on his advocacy of separation of church and state, especially his insistence that the civil magistrates should have no authority over the consciences of men. Dubbed *The Rebel of Salem,* he was banished from the colony and founded the Rhode Island Colony. There he put into practice his religious tenets and also carried out a far fairer policy toward the Indians, paying them for their lands, something that had not been done in Massachusetts. He became known to both white and red men as *The Indian's Friend*.

WILLIAMS, TENNESSEE (1911–1983)

Because he considered his son effeminate, Tennessee Williams' father called the future playwright *Miss Nancy*.

Williamson Clan—See Terrible Williamsons, The.

WILLIS, BROWNE (1682–1760)

Often described as an eccentric by members of his own class, English antiquary and landlord Browne Willis dressed in such ragged attire he was often mistaken for a beggar. He gained his nickname *Old Wrinkle-Boots* from wearing patched, 40-year-old boots. Much beloved by his tenants, Willis denied himself many pleasures of life so that he could use most of his money for charity to others.

WILLIS, NATHANIEL P. (1806–1867)

A British writer whose works were subjected to much criticism, Nathaniel P. Willis was nicknamed *Namby-Pamby Willis,* a play on his initials and the fact that his works were often careless regarding facts. He was also called *Penciller Willis* after one of his works, *Pencillings by the Way.* Unenthusiastic critics referred to him as *Leaden Penciller Willis.*

WILLKIE, WENDELL L. (1892–1944)

In the 1940 U.S. presidential race, Republican Wendell L. Willkie, a former Democrat, campaigned as more of a "common man" than President Franklin D. Roosevelt. Secretary of Commerce Harold L. Ickes, noted for his cutting wit, deflated the claim by referring to him as "a simple barefoot Wall Street lawyer." This was later refined to *The Barefoot Boy from Wall Street,* a political sobriquet Willkie was never able to escape.

WILLS, FRANK—See Watergate Guard, The.

WILLS, HARRY (1889–1958)

One of the finest boxers in the 1920s, Harry Wills was a black fighter never permitted to fight for

the heavyweight championship, a situation for which Jack Dempsey was much criticized. However, the opposition to Wills, who was called *The Dark Menace,* ran much deeper. As one authority put it, "The so-called better minds in government and boxing (A) didn't want a mixed title bout while postwar racial tensions were high and (B) didn't want a Negro champion."

WILLS, HELEN (1905–)

Female tennis star Helen Wills, several times U.S. and Wimbledon champion, was nicknamed *Little Miss Poker Face,* a court demeanor that has become much rarer in recent years.

WILMOT, JOHN (1647–1680)

Because he blushed so readily, John Wilmot, earl of Rochester, was nicknamed *Virgin Modesty.* It was said the term was first used by Charles II.

WILSON, CHARLES KEMMONS (1913–)

While on "the most miserable vacation trip of my life," spent in cramped but high-priced lodgings, Charles Kemmons Wilson got the idea for a "brand name" motel chain that would be subject to quality control, have reasonable rates and provide standardized room sizes and furnishings. The result was Holiday Inns and the sobriquet *The Father of the Modern Innkeeping Industry* for Wilson.

WILSON, EDITH BOLLING (1872–1961)

The wife of President Woodrow Wilson, Edith Bolling Wilson, was referred to as *The First Lady of the World* immediately after World War I. When her husband suffered a prolonged illness brought on by a blood clot on the brain, she became known as *The Presidentress of the U.S.*, especially to her husband's political foes. Senator Albert Fall stormed: "We have a petticoat government! Mrs. Wilson is President!" Mrs. Wilson took on much of her husband's work so that he could remain in office because Vice President Thomas Riley Marshall was considered more an entertainer than a statesman and hardly a viable alternative. Marshall's contribution to political thought was, "What this country needs is a good five-cent cigar." When informed once he might have to become president, he buried his hands in his face and could not speak. Not everyone attacked Mrs. Wilson in the performance of her duties. The London *Daily Mail* reported she was a quite capable "President." The 25th Amendment would today prevent any such "presidentress" from running the country.

WILSON, EDMUND (1895–1972)

One of the most influential literary and social critics of the 20th century, Edmund Wilson was hailed as *The Dean of American Letters*. Wilson was actually reticent, quiet and quite shy, and his intimates thus called him *Bunny*.

WILSON, HENRY (1812–1875)

Ulysses S. Grant's vice-president during his second term, Henry Wilson, was called *The Cobbler* and *The Natick Cobbler* since in earlier years he had worked as a shoemaker in that Massachusetts town.

WILSON, LEWIS "Hack" (1901–1948)

Because he was obtained by the Chicago Cubs baseball team for the payment of a mere $5,000 to the New York Giants, *Hack Wilson* (so called after a Chicago strongman of the era named Hackenschmidt whom Wilson resembled in stature) became celebrated as *The Million Dollar Slugger*

from the Five-and-Ten-Cent Store. Bought at that bargain price, Wilson went on to set the National League home run record of 56 in one season.

WILSON, SAMUEL—See Uncle Sam.

WILSON, THORNTON ARNOLD (1920–)

Boeing chairman of the board Thornton Arnold Wilson is referred to in the business press as *The Engineer of Success*. His efficiency is said to have engineered the company to great financial success. Among his colleagues he is known as *Old Shoe* because, even after appointed to his high post, he did not bother to move out of his noisy office to the more elegant surroundings to which he was entitled. Each morning he sheds his suit jacket and dons a navy blue sweater for the day. When it gets too cold in winter, he can be observed working in his overcoat and hat.

WILSON, WOODROW (1856–1924)

Woodrow Wilson, 28th president of the United States, never inspired any permanent flattering nicknames. He was actually ecstatic when during the campaign of 1912 a member of the audience at a rally shouted, "Hello, Woody," but his somber bearance would not permit the name to catch on. His enemies had no trouble coming up with derisive sobriquets for him. He was *The Schoolmaster in Politics* and thus unsuited, they said, for the harsh facts of political life. They also denounced him as *The Phrasemaker* and *Coiner of Weasel Words*, deriding his high-sounding slogans. Former president William Howard Taft called him *That Mountain of Egotism and Selfishness*.

WINCHELL, WALTER (1897–1972)

For many years a powerful and influential gossip columnist and radio commentator, Walter Winchell was called *The King of Broadway* and *America's One-man Newspaper*. In his waning years, however, he lost much of his clout, and celebrities who had feared him either ignored or denounced him. Gloria Swanson once exploded: '' . . . you are washed up, and everybody knows it except you.'' Perhaps the full measure of his decline was that in his last years Winchell, who had once ''owned'' the streets of Manhattan, confided to friends he would not venture out after dark without a gun.

Windmill, The—See BACALL, LAUREN.

WINGATE, ORDE CHARLES (1903–1944)

A British general who uncharacteristicly befriended the Jewish settlers in Palestine in the 1930s, Orde Wingate was regarded as the father of the Israeli army for the military training he gave young Jews in the settlements. He was nicknamed *Hayedid,* or *The Friend*. He used the same training tactics during World War II to whip a group of 2,000 Ethiopians and Sudanese into a fighting force that routed the Italians in Abyssinia. He later died in the Burma campaign, directing behind-the-lines operations against the Japanese.

Winsted Liar, The: LOUIS STONE (1875–1933)

In 1895 a young reporter in Winsted, Conn., named Louis Stone realized that newspaper readers and indeed many newspaper editors tended to believe anything they read. Thus many editors bought and published stories without checking the facts. Stone invented and sold hundreds of wild yarns, such as a tree that produced baked apples and a cow belonging to two spinsters that was so modest she would not permit a man to milk her. Eventually Stone became known nationally as *The Winsted Liar*.

WINSTON, JOHN A. (1812–1871)

Since he adamantly vetoed bills that would offer subsidies to railroads and other corporations, John A. Winston, governor of Alabama in the 1850s, was dubbed *The Veto Governor*.

Winter King, The—See FREDERICK V, ELECTOR PALATINE.

Wire-Master, The—See BUTE, LORD.

Wisdom—See EHRLICHMAN, JOHN.

WISE, ISAAC MAYER (1819–1900)

Because of his profound impact on and leadership of Jews in the United States in the 19th century as well as his advocacy of progressive Judaism, Rabbi Isaac Mayer Wise was called *The Moses of America*.

Wise, The—See ALBERT II, DUKE OF AUSTRIA.

Wise Man—See NEHRU, JAWAHARLAL ''Pandit.''

Wise Woman of Walkern, The—See WENHAM, JANE.

Wisecracker, The—See WALKER, JAMES J.

Wisest Fool in Europe (or Christendom)—See JAMES I.

Wisest Man of Greece, The—See
SOCRATES.

WISNER, EDWARD (1860–1915)

Having been wiped out in the Panic of 1893, Louisiana landowner Edward Wisner became convinced that the wetlands along the Mississippi River were unusually fertile because of the silt deposits. He bought more than a million acres of this supposedly worthless wasteland, which he drained and turned into very profitable farmland. It was his pioneer efforts that led to other reclamation projects around the country, both by private individuals and the state governments. He won the honorific *The Father of Reclamation*.

Witch of Wall Steet, The—See
GREEN, HENRIETTA "Hetty."

Witchfinder General—HOPKINS,
MATTHEW.

Withered Little Apple-john, A—See
MADISON, JAMES.

WITHER, GEORGE—See Worst
Poet, The.

Wizard, The—See JOHN III, KING
OF POLAND.

Wizard of Ooze, The—See DIRKSEN,
EVERETT MCKINLEY.

Wizard of Sussex, The—See
DAWSON, CHARLES.

Wizard of the Chorus Line, The—See
BERKELEY, BUSBY.

Wizard of the North, The—See
SCOTT, WALTER.

*Wizard of the Wacky Inventions,
The*—See GOLDBERG, RUBE.

Wolf, The—See VIDOCQ,
FRANCOIS EUGENE.

Wolf of Badenoch, The—See
STEWART, ALEXANDER.

WOLK, ABRAHAM L. (1891–1983)

A former political leader and judge in Pittsburgh, Pa., Abraham Wolk was called *The Father of Smoke Control*. After World War II he was instrumental in making the smoky steel city cleaner through the urban renewal program that became known as the Pittsburgh Renaissance.

WOLLSTONECRAFT, MARY (1759–1797)

The 18th century British feminist writer Mary Wollstonecraft made demands for social and sexual equality for women that caused many shocked foes to denounce her as *The Hyena in Petticoats*, a label first pinned on her by Horace Walpole.

WOLSEY, THOMAS (1471–1530)

The most powerful man of his time in England next to Henry VIII, Cardinal Thomas Wolsey was often disparaged by such nicknames as *The Mas-*

tiff Cur and *The Butcher's Dog* since he was the son of a butcher. During his youth he was called *The Boy-Baccalaure,* having taken his degree at a young age. Henry VIII called him *The Vicar of Hell,* especially when Wolsey was to be brought up on a number of charges, including infecting the monarch with a venereal disease by whispering in his ear.

Woman Who Always Prays, The—See **DUCHESNE, ROSE PHILLIPPINE.**

Wonder Child, The—See **CARDIAC, JEAN LOUIS.**

Wonder of the World—See **OTTO III OF THE HOLY ROMAN EMPIRE.**

Wonderful, The—See **GONGORA, LUIS Y AGROTE.**

Wonderful Doctor—See **BACON, ROGER.**

WOOD, JOHN B. (?–1884)

U.S. printer and journalist John B. Wood was the scourge of 19th century writers, who feared his blue pencil. He was credited with the ability to remove so much verbiage from a manuscript that he was called *The Great American Condenser.*

WOOD, MATTHEW (1768–1843)

Jocularly known as *The Absolute Wisdom,* in 1821 Sir Matthew Wood was an advisor to the ill-behaved and the even more ill-treated Queen Caroline of England. He was savaged by the political wits of the day after he allowed that his tactics perhaps had not been absolute wisdom and was thereafter referred to as *The Absolute Widsom.* However, he does seem to have acted wisely in extending considerable sums of money to the duke of Kent when the duke was being hounded by creditors. After the duke's death his daughter, Victoria, ascended the throne and made Wood a baronet.

Wooden Leg Stuyvesant—See **STUYVESANT, PETER "Wooden Leg."**

WOODFALL, WILLIAM (1745–1803)

William Woodfall, the brother of the publisher of the *Junius Letters,* was famed for his ability to attend a debate and without notes report the comments accurately the following day. He was nicknamed *Memory Woodfall.*

WOODHULL, VICTORIA (1838–1927)

Unconventional reformer Victoria Woodhull, whose interests included spiritualism, equal rights for women, free love and a single moral standard, became in 1872 the first woman candidate for the U.S. presidency on the Equal Rights ticket. Since most of her stands were unpopular, especially when advanced by a female advocate, she was dubbed *The Terrible Siren.*

WOOLDRIDGE, CLIFTON (1850–1915)

Possibly the most flamboyant police office in U.S. history, Clifton Wooldridge was known to the Chicago public as *The Incorruptible Sherlock Holmes of America* in an era when police standards were low and honesty rare. The underworld concurred in that opinion by referring to him as *That Damned Little Flycop.* In a 22-year career that began in 1888, Wooldridge made 19,500 arrests, closed down 100 panel houses, rescued at least 100 teenage girls from brothels and white slavery and turned down hundreds of bribes ranging from $500 to $5,000. He was shot 23 times and wounded 46 criminals in return, and at any given moment literally hundreds of residents of Joliet prison could thank Wooldridge for their presence there. Corrupt politicians did not look kindly on him, and Wooldridge was often shifted to some remote neighborhood only to be returned to the center of the city when the newspapers raised a storm of protest.

WOOLDRIDGE, WILLIAM O. (1922–)

As the Army's sergeant-major, William O. Wooldridge was celebrated in the 1960s as *The Army's Topmost Sarge*. Later in a burgeoning Army post exchange kickback scandal, he was dubbed by the press *The P.X. Millionaire*.

WOOLF, VIRGINIA (1882–1941)

An enigma both in her writing and in her personal life, English novelist Virginia Woolf (nee Stephen) was dubbed *The Goat* by her brother for her ability to butt in the relationships of others, often maliciously turning friend against friend. While there were those who thought her work brilliant, Edith Sitwell was not among them. Sitwell enjoyed talking to Woolf but "thought nothing" of her writing, labeling her *A Beautiful Little Knitter*.

WOOLLCOTT, ALEXANDER (1887–1943)

Author and journalist Alexander Woollcott, a man with an opinion on practically everything, was referred to as *The Town Crier*. He was also *The Man Who Came to Dinner* in real life, as in the play George S. Kaufman wrote satirizing him. An invitation to the 230-pound Woollcott could make him an almost permanent dinner guest, most assuredly good for a second, third and fourth helping at least.

WOOLMAN, JOHN (1720–1772)

In 1743 a young tailor "saw the light" and became a Quaker preacher. He traveled throughout the colonies preaching the evils of slavery and gaining the nickname *The Child of Light*.

Wooly-Head—See JULIAN, GEORGE WASHINGTON.

WORDSWORTH, WILLIAM (1770–1850)

A leader of the English Romantic movement, in his twenties poet William Wordsworth was a fervent supporter of the French Revolution, but he grew steadily more conservative. By 1843, when he was made poet laureate, he was a strong supporter of Tory landlordism. While some admiringly called him *The Poet of Nature* and *The Great God Pan,* others saw him in a less favorable light. Robert Browning dubbed him *The Lost Leader* and in that work said:

> Just for a handful of silver he left us,
> Just for a riband to stick in his coat.

The chief source of perjoratives for Wordsworth was Byron who offered: *The Blockhead, The Clownish Sycophant, The Converted Jacobin, Poet Wordy, This Poetical Charlatan* and *This Political Parasite*.

Worker in Souls, The—See MOODY, DWIGHT LYMAN.

World Citizen No. 1—See DAVIS, GARRY.

World's First Historian, The—See
CADMUS OF MILETUS.

World's Greatest Tenor, The—See
CARUSO, ENRICO.

*World's Greatest Trencherman,
The*—See **MILLER, EDWARD
ABRAHAM "Bozo."**

*World's Most Admired Woman,
The*—See **ROOSEVELT, ELEANOR.**

*World's Most Pulchritudinous
Evangelist*—See **MCPHERSON,
AIMEE SEMPLE.**

*World's No. 1 Industrial Architect,
The*—See **KAHN, ALBERT.**

*World's Second Richest Man,
The*—See **MELLON, ANDREW W.**

World's Wonder, The—See
ELIZABETH I.

Worst Actress of the Year, The—See
GRABLE, BETTY.

*Worst Poet, The: GEORGE WITHER
(1588–1667)*

A Parliamentary partisan during the English Civil
War, English poet George Wither was captured
by Royalist troops and sentenced to death. Another
poet, Sir John Denham, won a pardon for him from
Charles I on the ground that as long as Wither was
alive, he [Denham] ''should not be the worst poet
in England.'' Wither, thereafter known as *The
Worst Poet,* despised Denham for the rest of his
life.

Worst President's Friend, The—See
MITCHELL, JOHN N.

WORTH, ADAM (1844–1902)

U.S.-born master criminal Adam Worth was
called *The Napoleon of Crime* because his thefts
were spread over many countries and covered at
least three and possibly four continents.

Would-Be Cromwell of America—See
ADAMS, SAMUEL.

Wrecker, The—See **MORSE,
WAYNE.**

*WRIGLEY, WILLIAM, JR.
(1861–1932)*

William Wrigley, Jr., built a great chewing-gum
empire in the early 1900s and became known as
The Monarch of Mastication. It was a well-timed
nickname since it coincided with the mastication
craze that hit the nation. Health advocates recom-
mended people chew their food 30 to 70 times before swallowing, their slogan being ''Nature will
castigate those who don't masticate.'' The idea was
to make the food more digestible, but Americans
mistakenly transferred the practice to the mere
chewing of gum, much to the profit of *The
Monarch of Mastication.*

Writer of the Replusive, The—See
NABOKOV, VLADIMIR.

Writer of the Universe, The—See ASIMOV, ISAAC.

Wrong Way Riegels—See RIEGELS, ROY "Wrong Way."

Wrong-Way Corrigan—See CORRIGAN, DOUGLAS "Wrong-Way."

Wunderkind—See MOZART, WOLFGANG AMADEUS.

WYCLIFFE, JOHN *(1320?–1384)*

English religious reformer John Wycliffe, his way paved by Walter Lollard and John Huss in Bohemia, first raised the banner in England against what he considered popish tryanny. He was aptly nicknamed *The Morning Star of the Reformation,* a movement that he foreshadowed. He has also been dubbed *The Father of English Prose* since he began an English translation of the Bible, thereby becoming, as it has been put, "an industrious instructor of the people in their own rude but ripening dialect."

YAMANI, AHMED ZAKI *(1930–   )*

Saudi Arabian oil minister Sheikh Ahmed Zaki Yamani rose to international prominence with the emergence of OPEC as a cartel controlling the price and production of oil. Yamani was usually hailed as *The Good Guy of OPEC,* although generally his call for limitation in oil price increases was almost always followed by a rise in the price of Saudi oil. Thus some observers preferred referring to him as *The Shah of OPEC*.

YAMASHITA, TOMOYUKI *(1885–1946)*

Tomoyuki Yamashita, the Japanese general who scored that nation's greatest land victory in World War II, the lightning conquest of Malaya and Singapore, was hailed as *The Lion of Malaya* by the Japanese people. After the war he was executed as a war criminal for atrocities committed by his troops in the Philippines.

YANCEY, WILLIAM L. *(1814–1863)*

Perhaps the earliest consistent advocate of secession from the Union, William L. Yancey even carried his campaign into northern states, defending the right of the slave states to secede. In 1850 he launched a major campaign in his native Georgia to convince the state to secede, and at that early date he was already called *The Orator of Secession*.

YANG KUEI-FEI *(719–756)*

Yang Kuei-fei, the celebrated imperial concubine of the T'ang emperor Hsuan-tsung, has been labeled by historians *The Chinese Pompadour*. Initially the favorite of the emperor's 18th son, Kuei-fei attracted the attention of the emperor and became his consort for the next 20 years. To her physical charms she added a gaiety, wit and intelligence that were said to have distracted the ruler from the business of state. A civil war then ravaged China, and when the emperor was forced to evacuate the capital, his own troops mutinied. Their price for renewed support was that the emperor give up his corporeal delights and agree to the death of Kuei-fei. It was said that his chief eunuch strangled her.

Yankee Aristotle, The—See **WARD, LESTER FRANK.**

Yankee Doodle Dandy, The—See **COHAN, GEORGE M; HANCOCK, JOHN.**

Yankee Nigger, The—See **MOLINEAUX, TOM.**

Yassar Arafat's Best Friend in Congress—See **FINDLEY, PAUL.**

YEATS, WILLIAM BUTLER (1865–1939)

Poet and playwright William Butler Yeats led the Irish literary renaissance and, because he remained influenced by Irish mythology to some degree throughout his literary career, G. K. Chesterton dubbed him *The Man Who Knew the Fairies*.

Yellow Hair—See **CUSTER, GEORGE ARMSTRONG.**

Yellow Henry—See **STEWART, "Yellow" HENRY.**

Yiddish Mark Twain, The—See **ALEICHEM, SHALOM.**

Yorick—See **STERNE, LAURENCE.**

YORK, HENRY BENEDICT MARIA CLEMENT STUART (1725–1807)

Cardinal Henry Stuart York was called *The Last Stuart* since he was a male descendant of Great Britain's House of Stuart. Queen Anne, who reigned from 1702 to 1714, was the last of the dynasty.

YORKE, PHILIP (1690–1764)

Lord Chancellor of England Philip Yorke, first earl of Hardwicke, was frequently called *Judge Gripus*, an allusion to his well-known avarice.

YOUNG, BRIGHAM (1801–1877)

Mormon leader Brigham Young, who led the great trek to Utah, has been called *The Lion of the Lord*. Because he encouraged and practiced polygamy—reputedly having 27 wives and 47 children—he was called *Bigamy Young*.

YOUNG, GRAHAM (1947–   )

When he was 14, Graham Young was accused of poisoning his stepmother and attempting to poison his father, his sister and a school chum, and was found criminally insane. Released nine years later, he was hired as a tea boy by a photographic instruments firm that knew nothing of his past record. Young poisoned several of his coworkers, two of whom died. Actually some 70 employees had suffered strange illnesses. He kept a diary of the poisonings, listing his victims and intended victims. When it was found, Young, called by the press *The Obsessive Poisoner*, was sentenced to life imprisonment.

YOUNG, LORETTA (1913–   )

It is perhaps disillusioning to discover that Holly-wood actress Loretta Young, famed for angelic-type roles, was dubbed in the film colony as *The Steel Butterfly* and *Gretch the Wretch* (Gretchen being her real name).

Young, The—See Louis the Foolish.

Young English Giant, The—See TOLLER, JAMES.

Young Fellow—See SWANSON, GLORIA.

Young Hickory—See HILL, DAVID BENNETT; POLK, JAMES K.

Young Man with a Sneer, The—See WIDMARK, RICHARD.

Young Napoleon, The—See MCCLELLAN, GEORGE B.

Young Pretender, The—See STUART, CHARLES EDWARD.

Young Roscius, The—See BETTY, WILLIAM HENRY WEST.

Young Slasher, The—See STOCKMAN, DAVID A.

Young Steer, The—See ALEXANDER III OF RUSSIA.

Young Thunderbolt—See LEA, LUKE.

Younger Blitz from Kitz, The—See SAILER, TONI.

Youngest Millionaire, The—See COOGAN, JACKIE.

YOUNGMAN, HENRY "Henny" (1906–   )

Comedian Henny Youngman insists he adopted the nickname of *Henny* because everyone used to call him *Hen* when he went under his real name of Henry. He said, "I realized it was a bad name for anyone in show business. A hen can lay an egg, so I changed it to 'Henny.' With a name like that you could only lay a little egg."

Your Obedient Servant—See WELLES, ORSON.

YUGASIE (or YOGIA)—See Squaw Man.

YULCH, ADAM (1885–1950)

Although in 1936 Capt. Adam Yulch of the Nassau County Police Department was not the first policeman ever to identify and arrest a suspect through a laundry mark on a piece of clothing, he was the first to think of creating a complete file of such marks from each cleaner, tailor and laundry in the New York metropolitan area. Doing so, he aided various investigative agencies, some as far away as the West Coast, to solve cases. He constantly expanded his files and was nicknamed *The Laundry-mark Hawkshaw*.

Z

ZAHAROFF, BASIL (1850–1936)

Anglo-Greek munitions magnate and international financier-intriguer, Sir Basil Zaharoff was behind so many monumental plots that he was correctly labeled *The Mystery Man of Europe*. His early career clearly provided the inspiration for Eric Ambler's spy classic *A Coffin for Dimitrios*.

Zany of Debate, The—See CANNING, GEORGE.

Zany of His Age, The—See HENLEY, JOHN.

ZARATE, LUCIA (1863–1889)

Dubbed *The Mexican Midget*, Lucia Zarate hit her maximum height, 20 inches, at the age of 20. She weighed five pounds.

ZELL, HARRY VON (1906–1982)

U.S. radio announcer and actor Harry von Zell worked with so many top comedians and laughed so much at their jokes that within the profession he was called *Giggles*.

Zero—See MOSTEL, SAMUEL JOEL "Zero."

ZHUKOV, GEORGI (1896–1974)

Marshal Georgi Zhukov, the Red Army hero of World War II, was nicknamed by the Russian people *The General Who Never Lost a War*. His postwar popularity was perceived as a threat by Josef Stalin and later Nikita Khrushchev, and in 1957 he was relieved of his official duties and permitted to retire. He was rehabilitated in 1965.

ZIEGFELD, FLORENZ, JR. (1867–1932)

Florenz Ziegfeld, Jr., the great U.S. theatrical producer whose extravagant *Ziegfeld Follies* glorified the "American girl," was dubbed *The Lorenzo the Magnificent of the Stage*.

ZIEGLER, RONALD (1939–   )

Ron Ziegler, press secretary in the Nixon White House, was often referred to by some newsmen as *Ziggy Ron,* an allusion to their claims that his pronouncements often came out "backwards."

Ziggy Ron—See ZIEGLER, RONALD.

Zinjanthropus boisei—See Nutcracker Man.

ZIONCHECK, MARION A. (1900–1936)

One of the wildest and most reckless men ever to inhabit the halls of Congress, Rep. Marion A. Zioncheck of Washington was soon dubbed *The Congressional Playboy* by the press of the 1930s. Many of his playboy pranks and speeding violations in the District of Columbia landed him on the front pages. He committed suicide in 1936.

ZISKA, JOHN (1360–1424)

The gifted Bohemian general John Ziska came to the fore in the religious wars following the burning of John Huss at the stake in 1415. He confounded many of Europe's leading military strategists with his armored wagons and fanatical peasant followers armed only with flails. His favorite tactic was to draw the enemy into attacking apparently harmless wagons and then encircle them by wheeling his outer wagons in a lightning movement, whereupon his foot soldiers would flail the trapped enemy soldiers to death. Carlyle was to dub him *Rhinoceros Ziska,* an allusion to his impregnable wagons.

Zodiac Killer, The (fl. 1966–mid-1970s)

From 1966 until sometime in the early 1970s, a mysterious killer in California flooded newspapers with letters and cryptograms with zodiac symbols, which explained why he had killed a number of victims, mostly young girls, whom he said he was "collecting for my afterlife." The estimate of the number of murders attributed to the killer, some of them most gruesome, has ranged as high as 37 or 40. Since the mid-1970s nothing further has been heard from *The Zodiac Killer,* and it has been concluded that he is either dead or being held in some prison or mental institution, his identity not realized.

ZOILUS (fl. c. 4th century B.C.)

The Greek rhetorician Zoilus was called *The Scourge of Homer* because of his strong criticisms of his work.

Zubie Baby—See MEHTA, ZUBIN.

ZUCCA, RITA LOUISE—See Axis Sally.

ZUKOR, ADOLPH (1873–1976)

In his later years the movie pioneer and builder of the Paramount Pictures empire Adolph Zukor was referred to as *Pops.* This nickname was perhaps more in awe that he lived to such a ripe old age than to unbridled affection for a man who had exercised tremendous power in Hollywood. In fact, in Zukor's earlier days Nicholas Schenck and other top movie moguls called him *Creepy* or *Creeping Jesus.*

ZWEIBACK, MAX—See Kid Twist.

ZWILLMAN, ABNER "Longy" (1899–1959)

A crime syndicate chief of New Jersey, Abner Zwillman was nicknamed *Longy* by other crime leaders because he was always long on talk. He was found hanged to death in 1959 in his luxurious mansion in West Orange, N.J. The official verdict was suicide, but there was much speculation that to stay out of prison Zwillman was getting "long" on talk with the authorities about syndicate secrets.

ZWORYKIN, VLADIMIR KOSMA (1889–   )

While Vladimir Zworykin can hardly be given the entire credit as the inventor of television, he fully deserves the title *The Father of Television* for first demonstrating, in 1929, a practical all-electronic TV system in utililizing his two inventions, the iconoscope, or TV transmitter, and the kinescope, or TV receiver.

INDEX

Ancients—Greek

AESCHYLUS
ALEXANDER THE GREAT
APELLES
ARISTIDES
ARISTOPHANES
ARISTOTLE
CADMUS OF MILETUS
CALLIMACHUS
DEMOCRITUS
GALEN, CLAUDIUS
HERODOTUS
HIPPOCRATES
HIPPONAX
ISOCRATES
LONGINUS, DIONYSIUS CASSIUS
LUCIAN
MNESARETE
ORPHEUS
PARRHASIUS
PERICLES
PINDAR
PLATO
PYRICUS
SOCRATES
SOPHOCLES
THESPIS
ZOILUS

Ancients—Roman

ANTONINUS
APOLONIUS OF ALEXANDRIA
AURELIAN
BRUTUS, LUCIUS JUNIUS
CAESAR, JULIUS
CALIGULA
CICERO
COMMODUS, LUCIUS AELIUS
   AURELIUS
CRASSUS, MARCUS LICINIUS
ENNIUS, QUINTUS
HORACE

JULIAN
LUCILIUS, CAIUS
LUCRETIUS
MARIUS, CAIUS
OVID
PETRONIUS, CAIUS
SALLUST, CAIUS CRISPUS
TIBERIUS CAESAR
TITUS
VARRO, MARCUS TERENTIUS
VERRUCOSUS, QUINTUS FA-
   BIUS MAXIMUS

Ancients—Other

ABBAS
AMMONIUS
CLEOPATRA
DIDYMUS
HAMILCAR
IKHNATON

Arcthitects, Artists and Visual Arts Practitioners

ALBANI, FRANCESCO
ANDERSON, ALEXANDER
APPIANI, ANDREA
BEARDSLEY, AUBREY
BEHAM, HANS SEBALD
BOUCHER, FRANCOIS
BREECHES MAKER, THE
BROWN, LAUNCELOT
   "Capability"
BUNBURY, HENRY WILLIAM
CALDER, ALEXANDER
CAMBIO, ARNOLFA DEL
CANIFF, MILTON
CANO, ALONZO
CARAVAGGIO,
   MICHAELANGELO
   MERISI DA
CATLIN, GEORGE
CERQUOZZI, MICHAEL ANGELO

CEZANNE, PAUL
COELLO, ALONZO
COOPER, SAMUEL
COYSEVOX, ANTOINE
DAVID, JACQUES LOUIS
DAVIDSON, JO
DUERER, ALBRECHT
GILBERT, CASS
GILBERT, JOHN
GIORGIONE DE CASTELFRANCO
HIGGINS, EUGENE
HOGARTH, WILLIAM
HOPPER, EDWARD
HOUBRAKEN, JAKOB
JAMESON, GEORGE
JONES, INIGO
KAHN, ALBERT
KENT, ROCKWELL
KIKI
KRUGER, FRANZ
LA SUEUR, EUSTACE
LANMAN, CHARLES
LEBRUN, CHARLES
LEE, STAN
LEETEG, EDGAR
LEWIS, WYNDHAM
LOW, DAVID
MASACCIO, TOMMASO *"Bad
   Tom"*
MICHELANGELO
MIND, GOTTFRIED
NASMYTH, PATRICK
NAST, THOMAS
PENNI, GIOVANNI FRANCESCO
PISSARRO, CAMILLE
PUGET, PIERRE
PUGIN, AUGUSTUS WELBY
   NORTHMORE
RAPHAEL
REINHARDT, AD
REMINGTON, FREDERIC
REYNOLDS, JOSHUA
RIVERA, DIEGO
ROBUSTI, JACOPO
RUBENS, PETER PAUL

547

STROUD, ROBERT F.
STRUCK, LYDIA
SUTTON, WILLIE *"the Actor"*
TERRANOVA, CIRO
THAW, EVELYN NESBIT
THAW, HARRY W.
THRILL KILLERS, THE
TOMBS ANGEL, THE
TOUHY, ROGER *"Terrible"*
TRASH BAG MURDERER, THE
UNDERHILL, WILBUR
UNRUH, HOWARD
WANDERER, CARL
WEISS, HYMIE *"the Polack"*
WHITE, STANFORD
WHITMAN, CHARLES
WILCOXSON, BOBBY RANDELL
 "One Eye"
ZODIAC KILLER, THE
ZWILLMAN, ABNER *"Longy"*

Crime, Other—Criminals and Criminal Associates and Victims

BLUEBEARD
BODY SELLERS, THE
BRODIE, WILLIAM
DEEMING, FREDERICK BAILEY
DEVI, PHOOLAN
FLYING HIGHWAYMAN, THE
FOUNTAIN, THE
FRENCH RIPPER, THE
GALLOPING DICK
GETTY, JOHN PAUL, III
HAARMANN, FRITZ
HALF-HANGED SMITH
JACK THE RIPPER
JOHNSTONE, WILLIAM
KELLY, NED
LEE, JOHN
LIGHTFOOT, CAPTAIN
MACHINE GUN MOLLY
MIDDAY MURDERER THE
MOLL CUTPURSE
MONSTER OF DUSSELDORF
PETER
PETIOT, MARCEL
RAT, THE
REIS, ARTURO ALVES
RICORD, AUGUST
SCOTT, ADAM
SINGING STRANGLER, THE
SIXTEEN-STRING JACK
SMITH, GEORGE JOSEPH
SYMMONDS, JOHN
THREE-FINGERED JACK
TURPIN, DICK
WILD, JONATHAN

WORTH, ADAM
YOUNG, GRAHAM

Dancers (see Theatrical Personalities and Dancers)

Dentists (see Medicine and Dentistry)

Duelists

BAGENAL, BEAUCHAMP
CLAY, CASSIUS MARCELLUS
TROUSSE, MARQUIS DE LA

Eccentrics and Faddists (see also Freaks and Survivors)

BELL, WILLIAM
BRADY, DIAMOND JIM
BROADWAY ROSE
COUE, EMILE
CRUDEN, ALEXANDER
DEMARA, FERDINAND WALDO
DOUGLAS, WILLIAM
ELWES, JOHN
FAGAN, MICHAEL
FINK, MIKE
FLETCHER, HORACE
FOWLER, ORSON SQUIRE
GALIANI, FERDINAND
GRAHAM, SYLVESTER
GREEN, HENRIETTA *"Hetty"*
HATFIELD, BASIL MUSE
HENLEY, JOHN
HOW, JAMES EADS
JOHNNY APPLESEED
JONES, EDWARD
KELLY, ALVIN *"Shipwreck"*
LEARY, TIMOTHY
LOWSHER, JAMES
MCLEAN, EVALYN WALSH
MAN IN THE ZOO, THE
MAN ON THE LEDGE, THE
MAN WHO ATE DEMOCRATS,
 THE
MANGO, KING OF PICKLES
MERRY ANDREW
MOODY, JOSEPH *"Handkerchief"*
NORTON I, EMPEROR OF THE
 UNITED STATES
OTTO THE MAD
PRATT, DANIEL
RIPON, MARQUESS OF
ROBERT THE HERMIT

SMITH, JAMES HENRY *"Silent"*
SPOONER, WILLIAM
 ARCHIBALD
SYMMES, JOHN CLEVES
 "Hollow Earth"
VORONOFF, SERGE
WELBY, HENRY
WEST, JAMES MARION *"Silver
 Dollar,"* JR.
WILLIS, BROWNE

Economists

BURNS, ARTHUR F.
GEORGE, HENRY
KAUFMAN, HENRY
KEYNES, JOHN MAYNARD
MALTHUS, THOMAS ROBERT
MILL, JOHN STUART
RIVLIN, ALICE MITCHELL
SINCLAIR, JAMES E.

Educators and Historians (see also Ancients— Greek; Ancients—Roman; Ancients—Other)

ACTON, JOHN EMERICH
 EDWARD DALBERG, LORD
ADAMS, HENRY BROOKS
ALCUIN
ANGHIERA, PIETRO MARTIRE
BEDA, NOEL
BICKMORE, ALBERT SMITH
BLOW, SUSAN ELIZABETH
CAMDEN, WILLIAM
CHENEY, FRANCES NEEL
FROEBEL, FRIEDRICH
FROISSART, JEAN
GREGORY OF TOURS
HIGGINSON, STEPHEN
JONES, CHARLES COLCOCK
MCGUFFEY, WILLIAM HOLMES
NESTOR
PEABODY, ELIZABETH PALMER
PETTY, WILLIAM
STURLASON, SNORRI
VILLEHARDOUIN, GEOFFROI
 DE
WEBSTER, NOAH

Explorers and Travelers

CARR, JOHN
COLUMBUS, CHRISTOPHER
COOK, FREDERICK A.
DAVIS, JEFF

LEAHY, FRANK
NAMATH, JOSEPH *"Joe"*
RIEGELS, ROY *"Wrong Way"*
ROZELLE, PETE
STAGG, AMOS ALONZO
SUTHERLAND, JOCH BAIN
  "Jock"

Freaks and Survivors (see also Eccentrics and Faddists)

BARTLEY, JAMES
BIDDENDEN MAIDS, THE
CROWBAR MAN, THE
DEEP FREEZE WOMAN, THE
EDWARD THE FAT MAN
ELEPHANT MAN, THE
FRAUMARK BEAR-GIRL
HESSIAN WOLF-BOY
HUDSON, JEFFREY
KNOWLES, JOE
LUDWIG THE LEAPER
NASHNUSH, SULAIMAN
PARR, THOMAS
SELKIRK, ALEXANDER
SIAMESE TWINS, THE
SOBER SUE
TARZANCITO
TELLER, JAMES
TOM THUMB
WILD BOY OF AVEYRON, THE
ZARATE, LUCIA

Gamblers and Gambling Fixers and Con Artists

BERMAN, OTTO *"Abbadabba"*
BOLTON, *"Ice Box"* Bernie
BREADLINE CHARLIE
BRINKLEY, JOHN RICHARD
  "Goat Gland"
CARLETON, MARY
CHADWICK, CASSIE
GATES, JOHN W. *"Bet-a-Million"*
HARGRAVES, DICK
HARRIS, MAC
IVERS, ALICE
KELLY, HONEST JOHN
KORETZ, LEO
KREUGER, IVAR
LAW, JOHN
MAN WHO BROKE THE BANK
  AT MONTE CARLO, THE
MEANEST GAMBLER IN NEW
  YORK THE
MEANS, GASTON BULLOCK
MILLER, WILLIAM F. *"520%"*
POWELL, JOHN
ROMANOFF, *"Prince"* MICHAEL

SCARNE, JOHN
SMITH, JAMES MONROE *"Jingle
  Money"*
SOUTH'S MOST CROOKED
  GAMBLER, THE
TERRIBLE WILLIAMSONS, THE
TITANIC THOMPSON

Golfers (see Sports and Games)

Hockey Players (see Sports and Games)

Indians, Indian Agents, and Indian Fighters

CORNPLANTER
GERONIMO
HAWKINS, BENJAMIN
HOWARD, OLIVER OTIS
  "Bible-Quoting"
IRON SHIRT
ISHI
MCLAUGHLIN, JAMES
MAYHEW, THOMAS
PARKER, ELY SAMUEL
POWELL, DAVID FRANKLIN
SQUAW MAN
STRAIGHT TONGUE
VAN CORTLANDT, PHILIP
WILLIAMS, JOHN

Jockeys (see Sports and Games)

Journalists

BERNSTEIN, THEODORE
CANHAM, ERWIN D. *"Spike"*
CHAPIN, CHARLES
COBBETT, WILLIAM
COOKE, ALISTAIR
FRENEAU, PHILIP
GREELEY, HORACE
HABER, JOYCE
KILGALLEN, DOROTHY
KROCK, ARTHUR
LASKY, VICTOR
LEE, IVY L.
LIPPMANN, WALTER
MCCLENDON, SARAH
MARKEL, LESTER
PACKARD, VANCE

PEARSON, DREW
PEGLER, WESTBROOK
RIIS, JACOB AUGUST
RIPLEY, ROBERT
ROSENTHAL, A. M.
SALISBURY, HARRISON
STEFFENS, LINCOLN
STERLING, EDWARD
STODDART, JOHN
SULLIVAN, ED
SULLIVAN, MARK
THOMPSON, DOROTHY
WHITE, ISAAC DEFOREST *"Ike"*
WHITE, WILLIAM ALLEN
WINCHELL, WALTER

Judges (see Lawyers and Judges)

Labor Leaders and Labor Officials

BRENNAN, PETER J.
CHEVEZ, CESAR
DEMARIA, ALFRED T.
DORE, JOHN FRANCIS
DURKIN, MARTIN P.
FURUSETH, ANDREW
GOLDBERG, ARTHUR
HILL, JOE
HUTCHESON, MAURICE A.
KEARNEY, DENIS
KERRIGAN, JAMES
LEWIS, JOHN L.
MARKHAM, EDWIN
MBOYA, THOMAS JOSEPH
MEANY, GEORGE
PERKINS, FRANCES
PETRILLO, JAMES CAESAR
RANDOLPH, A. PHILIP
REUTHER, WALTER P.
WELESA, LECH

Law Enforcement Officials and Private Detectives

BAKER, ANDERSON YANCEY
BATMAN AND ROBIN
BECKER, CHARLES
BERTILLON, ALPHONSE
BURNS, WILLIAM J.
ELLIOTT, ROBERT G.
FAUROT, JOSEPH A.
GRAY, L. PATRICK
HEINRICH, EDWARD OSCAR
HOGAN, FRANK S.
HOOVER, J. EDGAR

JOHNSTON, JAMES A.
KETCH, JACK
LAFFEMAS, ISAAC DE
LAWES, KATHRYN
MILLER, DAISY ORR
MILLIGAN, MAURICE M.
MONSIEUR NEW YORK
NESS, ELIOT
OSBORNE, GEORGE O.
PARKER, ISAAC C.
PINKERTON, ALLAN
PURVIS, MELVIN
RIZZO, FRANK L.
SPILSBURY, BERNARD HENRY
SUTHERLAND, EDWIN H.
VALENTINE, LEWIS J. *"Night Stick"*
VIDOCQ, FRANCOIS EUGENE
WEDGWOOD, EDGAR A.
WILLIAMS, ALEXANDER S. *"Clubber"*
WOOLDRIDGE, CLIFTON
YULCH, ADAM

Lawyers and Judges

AVORY, HORACE EDMUND
BAILEY, F. LEE
BELLI, MELVIN
BLACKMUN, HARRY A.
BLACKSTONE, SIR WILLIAM
BRADSHAW, JOHN
BRANDEIS, LOUIS D.
BURROWES, PETER
CLARK, ABRAHAM
DARROW, CLARENCE SEWARD
DEIMAS, DELPHIN MICHAEL
FALLON, WILLIAM J.
FIELDING, JOHN
GOFF, JOHN W.
GROTIUS, HUGO
HAND, LEARNED
HOLMES, OLIVER WENDELL, JR.
HOUSTON, TEMPLE
HOWE, WILLIAM F.
HUGHES, CHARLES EVANS
INERIUS
KENT, JAMES
LEIBOWITZ, SAMUEL S.
LINDSEY, BEN B.
MARIS, HERBERT L.
MARSHALL, JOHN
MARSHALL, THURGOOD
MINTON, SHERMAN
MR. FANG
MITCHELSON, MARVIN
NORBURY, EARL OF
PARKER, ELLIS
RAGGED LAWYER, THE
REHNQUIST, WILLIAM

REMI, PHILIPPE DE
ROOT, GLADYS TOWLES
SABATH, JOSEPH
SENTIMENTAL TOMMY
SIRICA, JOHN J. *"Maximum John"*
TANEY, ROGER B.
WHITE, BYRON RAYMOND *"Whizzer"*
WILLIAMS, EDWARD BENNETT

Literary Figures—American

ALGER, HORATIO
ASIMOV, ISAAC
BEEBE, LUCIUS
BIERCE, AMBROSE
BRAND, MAX
BRYANT, WILLIAM CULLEN
CAIN, JAMES M.
CAPOTE, TRUMAN
CHANDLER, RAYMOND
CLARKE, McDONALD
CONVERSE, HARRIET
CRANE, STEPHEN
CUMMINGS, E. E.
DICKINSON, EMILY
DREISER, THEODORE
DUNBAR, PAUL LAURENCE
DUNLAP, WILLIAM
EASTMAN, CHARLES G.
EMERSON, RALPH WALDO
FROST, ROBERT
GINSBERG, ALLEN
GOULD, JOE
GUEST, EDGAR A.
HALE, SARAH JOSEPHA
HARRIS, JOEL CHANDLER
HAWTHORNE, NATHANIEL
HAYNE, PAUL HAMILTON
HEADLEY, JOEL TYLER
HEMINGWAY, ERNEST
HOWELLS, WILLIAM DEAN
IRVING, WASHINGTON
KIRCHHOFF, THEODORE
LEWIS, ESTELLE ANNA
    BLANCHE ROBINSON
LINDSAY, VACHEL
LONDON, JACK
LONG, WILLIAM J.
LONGFELLOW, HENRY
    WADSWORTH
MACDONALD, DWIGHT
MENCKEN, HENRY LOUIS
MILLER, JOAQUIN
MOORE, CLEMENT CLARKE
NEAL, JOHN
O'HARA, JOHN
PARKER, DOROTHY
PATTEN, GEORGE
    WASHINGTON

ROYALL, ANNE NEWPORT
RUNYON, DAMON
SHULMAN, MAX
SIMON, NEIL
SMITH, H. ALLEN
THOREAU, HENRY DAVID
UPDIKE, JOHN
WHEATLEY, PHILLIS
WHITMAN, WALT
WHITTIER, JOHN GREENLEAF
WILLIAMS, TENNESSEE
WILSON, EDMUND
WOOD, JOHN B.
WOOLLCOTT, ALEXANDER

Literary Figures—British

ADDISON, JOSEPH
ARNOLD, MATTHEW
BAILLIE, JOANNA
BALLANTYNE, JOHN
BLAKE, WILLIAM
BOSWELL, JAMES
BOWDLER, THOMAS
BRAITHWAITE, RICHARD
BROWNING, ROBERT
BURNS, ROBERT
BUTLER, SAMUEL
CAPERN, EDWARD
CARLYLE, THOMAS
CHATTERTON, THOMAS
CHAUCER, GEOFFREY
CHESTERTON, GILBERT KEITH
CIBBER, COLLEY
CLARE, JOHN
CLARKE, SAMUEL
COLERIDGE, SAMUEL TAYLOR
COLLINS, CHURTON
CONRAD, JOSEPH
COWLEY, ABRAHAM
CROWNE, JOHN
CUMBERLAND, RICHARD
DE QUINCEY, THOMAS
DEFOE, DANIEL
DENHAM, JOHN
DENNIS, JOHN
DODSLEY, ROBERT
DOYLE, ARTHUR CONAN
DRYDEN, JOHN
ELLIOTT, EBENEZER
FITZGERALD, WILLIAM
    THOMAS
FLETCHER, JOHN
FOOTE, SAMUEL
FORD, FORD MADOX
GAY, JOHN
GOLDSMITH, OLIVER
GOWER, JOHN
GRAY, THOMAS
HAMILTON, JANET

HARVEY, GABRIEL
HEBER, RICHARD
HERBERT, GEORGE
HILL, JOHN
HOLLAND, PHILEMON
HUMPHREY, DUKE OF
  GLOUCESTER
HUNT, LEIGH
IRELAND, WILLIAM HENRY
JENYNS, SOAME
JOHNSON, SAMUEL
JONSON, BEN
KEATS, JOHN
LEE, NATHANIEL
MACPHERSON, JAMES
MARLOWE, CHRISTOPHER
MASSINGER, PHILIP
MATHIAS, THOMAS JAMES
MILLER, WILLIAM
MILTON, JOHN
MONTAGU, MARY WORTLEY
NASH, THOMAS
OLDHAM, JOHN
ORWELL, GEORGE
OSBORNE, JOHN
OVERBURY, THOMAS
PHILIPS, AMBROSE
POPE, ALEXANDER
RAMSAY, ALLAN
RAWLINSON, THOMAS
RITSON, JOSEPH
ROGERS, SAMUEL
RUSKIN, JOHN
RYMER, THOMAS
SCOTT, WALTER
SHAKESPEARE, WILLIAM
SHELLEY, PERCY BYSSHE
SHIRLEY, JAMES
SIDNEY, SIR PHILIP
SMITH, EDMUND
SPENSER, EDMUND
STEELE, RICHARD
STEEVENS, GEORGE
STERNE, LAURENCE
STRACHEY, LYTTON
SUCKLING, JOHN
SWIFT, JONATHAN
SWINBURNE, ALGERNON
TENNYSON, ALFRED LORD
THACKERAY, WILLIAM
  MAKEPEACE
THEOBALD, LEWIS
THOM, WILLIAM
TROLLOPE, ANTHONY
WARBURTON, WILLIAM
WELLS, H. G.
WEST, REBECCA
WILDE, OSCAR
WILKIE, WILLIAM
WILLIS, NATHANIEL P.
WOOLF, VIRGINIA

WORDSWORTH, WILLIAM
WORST POET, THE

Literary Figures—French

ANGILBERT
BAYLE, PIERRE
BEAUMARCHAIS, PIERRE
  AUSUSTIN CARON DE
BOILEAU-DESPREAUX,
  NICHOLAS
BOURDEILLE, PIERRE DE
CHARTIER, ALAIN
CHENIER, ANDRE
CORNEILLE, PIERRE
CREBILLON, PROSPER JOLYOT
  DE
DEFORGE, EVARISTE DESIRE
DINEMANDY, JEAN
DU BARTAS, SALUSTIUS
DUMAS, ALEXANDER, PERE
FLAUBERT, GUSTAVE
FRERON, ELIE-CATHERINE
GARNIER, ROBERT
GROLIER, JEAN
HARDI, ALEXANDRE
HUGO, VICTOR
LA FONTAINE, JEAN DE
LABE, LOUISE
LAMARTINE, ALPHONSE
LEBRUN, PONCE-DENIS
  ECOUCHARD
MALHERBE, FRANCOIS DE
MAROT, CLEMENT
MAUPASSANT, GUY DE
MOLIERE
MONTIFAUD, MARC DE
MORELLET, ANDRE
RABELAIS, FRANCOIS
RACINE, JEAN
RESTIF, NICOLAS EDME
RIMBAUD, ARTHUR
RIVE, JEAN JOSEPH
RONSARD, PIERRE DE
SCUDERI, MADELINE DE
SERMENT, LOUISE ANASTASIE
  DE
THIBAUT IV
VERLAINE, PAUL
VERNE, JULES
VOLTAIRE

Literary Figures—Other
(see also Ancients—Greek;
Ancients—Roman)

ALEICHEM, SHALOM
ALVES, CASTRO
ANDERSEN, HANS CHRISTIAN

ANGENSOLA, BARTOLOMEO
  LEONARDO DE and LUPERCIO
  LEONARDO DE
ARETINO, PIETRO
ARIOSTO, LUDOVICO
ASCH, SHOLEM
BELINSKY, VISARION
  GRIGORYEVICH
BERKOWITZ, ITZHAK DOV
BOCCACCIO, GIOVANNI
CAMOENS, LUIS
CHARLETON, WILLIAM
CHIABRERA, GABRIELLO
CROKER, THOMAS CROFTON
DANTE ALIGHIERI
DOSTOEVSKI, FEODOR
ERASMUS, DESIDERIUS
FLEMING, PAUL
GHIBBES, JAMES ALBAN
GIOVANNI, DOMENICO DI
GOETHE, JOHANN WOLFGANG
  VON
GOLDONI, CARLO
GONGORA, LUIS Y ARGOTE
GRONOVIUS, JAMES
GROSSMANN, GUSTAVUS
GROTO, LUIGI
HACKLAENDER, FRIEDRICH
  WILHELM
HAFIZ, MOHAMMED
HARRIS, FRANK
HOFMANNSTHAL, HUGO VON
HOLBERG, LOUIS, BARON DE
KALIDASA
KARAMZIN, NICHOLAS
  MIKHAELOVITCH
KLOPSTOCK, FRIEDRICH
  GOTTLIEB
KRASICKI, IGNATIUS
LEOPARDI, GIACOMO
MALGLIABECCHI, ANTHONY
MERCK, JOHANN HEINRICH
MOLK, HEINRICH VON
MOORE, THOMAS
MORATIN, LEANDRO
  FERNANDEZ
NABOKOV, VLADIMIR
NASSER BEN HARETH
OMAR KHAYYAM
OPITZ, MARTIN
OSSIAN
PEREDA, JOSE MARIA DE
PETRARCH, FRANCESCO
PUSHKIN, ALEXANDER
QUERNO, CAMILLO
RAMLER, CHARLES WILLIAM
SACHS, HANS
SADI, MOSLEHEDIN
SAINTE-BEUVE, CHARLES
  AUGUSTIN
SCIOPPIUS, GASPAR

SERVICE, ROBERT WILLIAM
SHAW, GEORGE BERNARD
SOUMAROKOV, ALEXANDRE
 PETROVITCH
STRINDBERG, AUGUST
TOLSTOY, LEO
VALDES, JUAN MELENDEZ
VEGA, LOPE DE
WILLAMOW, JOHANN
 GOTTLIEB
YEATS, WILLIAM BUTLER

Medicine and Dentistry—Dentists, Disease Spreaders, Medical Entrepeneurs, Physicians, and Psychiatrists

ABERNATHY, JOHN
BARTON, CLARA
BERTHOLLET, CLAUDE LOUIS,
 COUNT
DAVIS, NATHAN SMITH
GALL, FRANZ JOSEPH
HERING, CONSTANTINE
JUNG, CARL GUSTAV
NIGHTINGALE, FLORENCE
NOGUCHI, THOMAS
PAINLESS PARKER
PALMER, DANIEL D. *"Fish"*
PARE, AMBROISE
PHYSICK, PHILIP SYNG
SPOCK, BENJAMIN M.
STRUGHOLD, HUBERTUS
SZOLD, HENRIETTA
TARNOWER, HERMAN
TYPHOID MARY

Military and Intelligence Notables (see also Ancients—Greek; Ancients—Roman; Ancients—Other; Civil War Notables, American; Revolutionary War Notables, American; World War I Notables; World War II Notables)

ANTOINE DE BOURGOGNE
ATTENDOLO, MUZIO
BADEN-POWELL, ROBERT
 STEPHENSON SMYTHE
BANIER, JOHAN
BARRY, JOHN
BART, JEAN
BAYARD, PIERRE DU TERRAIL,
 CHEVALIER DE

BEAUCHAMP, REICHARD DE
BLIGH, WILLIAM
BLUCHER, GEBHARD
 LEBERECHT VON
BULLER, REDVERS HENRY
BUTLER, SMEDLEY
 DARLINGTON
CALLEY, WILLIAM
CARNOT, LAZARE NICHOLAS
 MARGUERITE
CATINAT, NICHOLAS
CHARLES JOSEPH, PRINCE DE
 LIGNE
CHURCHILL, JOHN
CLIVE, ROBERT, LORD
CRABB, LIONEL
DE CLARE, RICHARD
DE RUYTER, MICHAEL
DERBY, CHARLOTTE,
 COUNTESS
DORIA, ANDREA
DOUGLAS, ARCHIBALD,
 FOURTH EARL OF
DRAKE, FRANCIS
DUNOIS, JEAN
EYTAN, RAFAEL
FITZGERALD, A. ERNEST
FOIX, GASTON DE
FORRESTAL, JAMES V.
GASSION, JEAN, COMTE DE
GENGHIS KHAN
GOETZ OF THE IRON HAND
GORDON, CHARLES GEORGE
 "Chinese"
HAWKWOOD, JOHN
HAYNAU, JULIUS JAKOB VON
HERSHEY, LEWIS B.
HILL, ROWLAND
HOWEL-Y-PEDOLAU, SIR
JUNOT, ANDOCHE
KHALID
LA MARCK, GUILLAUME DE
LA TOUR D'AUVERGNE,
 THEOPHILE MALO CORRET DE
LOISON, LOUIS HENRI, COMTE
MARQUEZ, LEONARDO
MASSENA, ANDRE
MILITARY HUMBOLDT, THE
MILORADOWITCH, MICHAEL
MOLTKE, HELLMUTH KARL
 BERNHARD VON
MONTBARS
MONTMORENCI, FRANCOIS
 HENRI
MURAT, JOACHIM
NELSON, HORATIO
NEY, MICHEL
PAGET, HENRY WILLIAM
 "One-Leg"
PERCIVAL, JOHN
PERCY, HENRY
PERO NINO, DON
PICHEGRU, CHARLES

ROSENBERG, JULIUS and
 ETHEL
RUPERT, PRINCE
SANTERRE, ANTOINE JOSEPH
SCHWERIN, COUNT KURT
 CHRISTOPH
SCOTT, WINFIELD
SINCLAIR, WILLIAM
SMITH, HARRY
SNELL, HANNAH
STEWART, CHARLES
STIEBER, WILLIAM
SWANSON, CLAUDE A.
TAMERLANE
THAYER, SYLVANUS
VERNON, EDWARD
WALKER, WILLIAM
WEDELL, H. C.
WEINBERGER, CASPAR
WELLINGTON, ARTHUR
 WELLESLEY, FIRST DUKE OF
WESTMORELAND, WILLIAM C.
WINGATE, ORDE CHARLES
WOOLDRIDGE, WILLIAM O.
ZISKA, JOHN

Mothers, Wives and Sweethearts (see also Presidents' Wives; Relatives of the Famous)

ARMSTRONG, LUCILLE
AYESHA
BARKLEY, ELIZABETH JANE
 RUCKER HADLEY
CHAMPDIVERS, ODETTE DE
CUNNINGHAM, MARY
FAIR PERDITA
FAIR ROSAMUND
FORD, CLARA
HIGHLAND MARY
JENNINGS, SARAH
LA VALLIERE, LOUISE DE
ROSE OF CIMARRON
SCHULENBURG, EHRENGARD
 MELUSINA VON DER
SHREWSBURY, COUNTESS OF
SOREL, AGNES

Music—Composers, Conductors, Musicians, Singers & Songwriters

ABU NASR MOHAMMED AL
 FARABI
ADDERLEY, JULIAN
 "Cannonball"
ANDERSON, MARIAN
ANTHEIL, GEORGE

JACOBI, FRIEDRICH HEINRICH
JUDAEUS, PHILO
KANT, IMMANUEL
LEIBNITZ, GOTTFRIED
    WILHELM VON
LESSING, GOTTHOLD EPHRAIM
MAIMONIDES
ROUSSEAU, JEAN JACQUES
RUSSELL, BERTRAND
SCHOPENHAUER, ARTHUR
SPENCER, HERBERT
TOUSSAIN, JACQUES

**Physicians (see Medicine
and Dentistry)**

**Politics—American (see
also Presidents; American;
Vice Presidents,
American)**

ABZUG, BELLA
ADAMS, EVA B.
ADAMS, SHERMAN
ALLEN, WILLIAM *"Fog Horn"*
ALTGELD, JOHN *"Pardon"*
ASHLEY, CHESTER
ATHERTON, CHARLES GOR-
    DON *"Gag"*
BAKER, HOWARD, JR.
BALLINGER, RICHARD
    ACHILLES
BANKHEAD, WILLIAM B.
BARTON, BRUCE
BARUCH, BERNARD M.
BEAME, ABE
BEARES, JAMES D.
BENTON, THOMAS HART
BIDDLE, NICHOLAS
BILBO, THEODORE GILMORE
BLAINE, JAMES G.
BLAIR, FRANCIS PRESTON, JR.
BLANKENBURG, RUDOLPH
BLANTON, THOMAS LINDSAY
BLOCK, JOHN R.
BOIES, HORACE
BORAH, WILLIAM E.
BRADY, JAMES
BREWSTER, RALPH OWEN
BROOKS, PRESTON S. *"Bully"*
BROWN, (EDMUND G., JR.)
    JERRY
BRYAN, WILLIAM JENNINGS
BUCKLEY, CHRISTOPHER A.
    "Blind Boss"
BURFORD, ANNE M. (GORSUCH)
BURR, AARON
BYRD, HARRY F.

CALHOUN, JOHN C.
CANNON, ISABELLA W.
CANNON, JOSEPH GURNEY
CARAWAY, HATTIE
CARR, WILBUR JOHN
CERMAK, ANTON J.
CHANDLER, WALTER
CHASE, SALMON P.
CLARKSON, JAMES SULLIVAN
    "Headsman"
CLAY, HENRY
COLSON, CHARLES W. *"Chuck"*
COUGHLIN, FATHER
    CHARLES E.
COUZENS, JAMES
COX, JACK
DAUGHERTY, HARRY M.
DAVIS, JEFF
DE SAPIO, CARMINE
DEAN, JOHN W.
DEWEY, THOMAS E.
DIES, MARTIN
DINGELL, JOHN D.
DIRKSEN, EVERETT MCKINLEY
DONE BROWN
DOUGHTON, ROBERT L.
    "Muley"
DOUGLAS, HELEN GAHAGAN
DOUGLAS, STEPHEN
DRINAN, ROBERT
EARLE, GEORGE H., III
EATON, MARGARET O'NEILL
EGAN, PATRICK
EHRLICHMAN, JOHN
ELLSWORTH, OLIVER
ERVIN, SAMUEL JAMES, JR.
FARLEY, JAMES A.
FARWELL, CHARLES B.
FENWICK, MILLICENT
FINDLEY, PAUL
FINN, DANIEL E.
FITZGERALD, JOHN F.
FOOTE, HENRY STUART
FORAKER, JOSEPH B.
FORBES, CHARLES R.
FULBRIGHT, J. WILLIAM
FUNSTON, EDWARD H.
    "Foghorn"
GLASS, CARTER *"Sound Money"*
GLEASON, PATRICK JEROME
GOEBEL, WILLIAM
GOLDWATER, BARRY M.
GORE, THOMAS PRYOR
GRASSO, ELLA
GRAY, FINLY HUTCHINSON
GROSVENOR, CHARLES HENRY
HAGUE, FRANK *"I Am The Law"*
HAIG, ALEXANDER M.
HALDEMAN, H. R.
HALL, ABRAHAM OAKLEY
HAMILTON, ALEXANDER
HAMMOND, JAMES H.

HARDIN, BENJAMIN
HAYAKAWA, SAMUEL I.
HEMPHILL, JOSEPH *"Single
    Speech"*
HILL, DAVID
HOLMAN, WILLIAM STEELE
HOLTZMAN, ELIZABETH
HOPKINS, HARRY L.
HOWE, LOUIS
HUNT, E. HOWARD
HUNTER, WHITESIDE GODFREY
HUSTON, TOM CHARLES
HYLAN, JOHN F. *"Honest John"*
JACKSON, HENRY M. *"Scoop"*
JOHNSON, J. MONROE
    "Rowboat"
JONES, JOHN P.
JULIAN, GEORGE WASHINGTON
KELLEY, WILLIAM DARRAGH
KELLY, *"Honest"* JOHN
KENNEDY, EDWARD M.
KENNEDY, JOHN PENDLETON
KENNEDY, JOSEPH P.
KENNEDY, ROBERT F.
KERR, ROBERT S.
KING, WILLIAM HENRY
KING, WILLIAM RUFUS
KISSINGER, HENRY
KNOX, PHILANDER CHASE
KNUTSON, HAROLD
KOLB, REUBEN FRANCIS
KROGH, EGIL
KYLE, JAMES HENDERSON
LA GUARDIA, FIORELLO H.
LANDON, ALFRED M.
LAWSON, JOHN DANIEL
LEA, LUKE
LEMKE, WILLIAM
LEWIS, JAMES H.
LODGE, HENRY CABOT
LONG, HUEY
LOWDEN, FRANK O.
LUDLOW, LOUIS LEON
MCCARTHY, EUGENE
MCCARTHY, JOSEPH R.
MCCLELLAN, JOHN
MCCLINTIC, JAMES V.
MCFARLANE, WILLIAM D.
MCGOVERN, GEORGE S.
MACON, NATHANIEL
MADDOX, LESTER G.
MAGRUDER, JEB STUART
MARCANTONIO, VITO
MARTIN, LUTHER
MASON, STEVENS THOMSON
MEESE, EDWIN, III
MESTA, PERLE
MITCHEL, JOHN PURROY
MITCHELL, JOHN N.
MITCHELL, MARTHA
MORGANTHAU, HENRY, JR.
MORSE, WAYNE,

MORTON, OLIVER
MORTON, WILLIAM THOMAS
   GREEN
MOTT, JAMES W.
MOUTON, ROBERT L.
MUNDT, KARL
MURPHY, CHARLES
NIMMO, ROBERT P.
O'NEILL, THOMAS P. *"Tip,"* JR.
PATMAN, WRIGHT
PEPPER, CLAUDE
PERKINS, GEORGE W.
PINGREE, HAZEN, S. *"Potato"*
PITTMAN, KEY
POTTER, JOHN FOX *"Bowie
   Knife"*
QUINN, JAMES ALOYSIUS
RAMSPECK, ROBERT
RANDOLPH (OF ROANOKE),
   JOHN
RANKIN, JEANETTE
RANKIN, JOHN E.
RAYBURN, SAM
REED, THOMAS B. *"Czar"*
RICHARDSON, ELLIOT L.
ROOSEVELT, JAMES
ROSENMAN, SAMUEL I.
   "Sammy the Rose"
RUSSELL, WILLIAM E.
SABATH, ADOLPH JOACHIM
SANDERS, CARL
SCHLAFLY, PHYLLIS
SCHMITT, HARRISON R.
SCOTT, WILLIAM LLOYD
SHANK, SAMUEL L.
SHERMAN, JOHN
SIMPSON, JERRY
SMALL, LEN
SMITH, ALFRED E.
SMITH, JESSE
SMITH, WILLIAM
SMITH, WILLIAM A. *"Watertight"*
SMYTHE, J. HENRY
STEVENS, THADDEUS
STEVENSON, ADLAI
STIMSON, HENRY L.
STOCKMAN, DAVID A.
STRAUSS, ROBERT S.
STURGEON, DANIEL
SULLIVAN, TIMOTHY *"Big
   Tim"*
TAFT, ROBERT A.
TALMADGE, EUGENE *"Gene"*
TAYLOR, ALFRED ALEXANDER
TAYLOR, ROBERT LOVE
THOMAS, J. PARNELL
THOMPSON, WILLIAM HALE
   "Big Bill"
TICHENOR, ISAAC
TILDEN, SAMUEL J.
TILLMAN, BENJAMIN RYAN
TUGWELL, REXFORD G.

VOORHIS, JERRY
WAITE, DAVIS HANSON
WALKER, JAMES J.
WATERGATE GUARD, THE
WEBSTER, DANIEL
WHEELER, BURTON K.
WILLIAMS, JAMES DOUGLAS
WILLIAMS, JOHN STUART
WILLIAMS, G. MENNEN
   "Soapy"
WILLKIE, WENDELL L.
WINSTON, JOHN A.
ZIEGLER, RONALD
ZIONCHECK, MARION A.

Politics—British

ARCHIBALD, MARQUIS OF
   ARGYLE
ASHTON, RALPH
ATTLEE, CLEMENT RICHARD
BACON, FRANCIS
BAILLIE, ROBERT
BARNARD, JOHN
BEVIN, ERNEST
BROUGHAM, HENRY PETER,
   LORD
BURKE, EDMUND
BUTE, LORD
CANNING, CHARLES JOHN
   "Clemency"
CANNING, GEORGE
CASTLEREAGH, ROBERT
   STEWART
CECIL, WILLIAM LORD
   BURLEIGH
CHAMBERLAIN, NEVILLE
CHESTERFIELD, PHILIP
   DORMER STANHOPE, LORD
CHURCHILL, WINSTON
CRIPPS, STAFFORD
CROMWELL, OLIVER
CROMWELL, RICHARD
CROMWELL, THOMAS
DANGERFIELD, THOMAS
DISRAELI, BENJAMIN
EDEN, ANTHONY
FITZ-WALTER, ROBERT
FOX, CHARLES JAMES
GAITSKELL, HUGH
GLADSTONE, WILLIAM
HAMILTON, WILLIAM
   "Single-Speech"
HARDIE, KEIR
HARLEY, ROBERT
HATTON, CHRISTOPHER
HEATH, EDWARD
HERVEY, JOHN
HOLLAND, HENRY FOX, LORD
HUME, JOSEPH
LAW, ANDREW BONAR

LLOYD GEORGE, DAVID
LORD PORN
MACDONALD, RAMSAY
MACKINTOSH, JAMES
MACMILLAN, HAROLD
MARVELL, ANDREW
NEVILLE, RICHARD
PEEL, ROBERT (the younger)
PITT, WILLIAM (the younger)
PYM, JOHN
RAT, CAT AND LOVEL OUR
   DOGGE
ROBINSON, FREDERICK
ROEBUCK, JOHN ARTHUR
SHELBURNE, LORD
SMITH, WILLIAM HENRY
STANLEY, LORD
STUCLEY, THOMAS
THATCHER, MARGARET
TIPTOFT, JOHN
URQUHART, DAVID
WALPOLE, ROBERT
WHITELOCKE, BULSTRODE
WILKES, JOHN
WOOD, MATTHEW
YORKE, PHILIP

Politics—French

ALBERT THE WORKINGMAN
ANACREON OF THE
   GUILLOTINE, THE
BABEUF, FRANCOIS NOEL
BLUM, LEON
BOULANGER, GEORGES ER-
   NEST JEAN MARIE
CADOUDAL, GEORGES
CLEMENCEAU, GEORGES
CORDAY, CHARLOTTE
DAMIENS, ROBERT FRANCOIS
DANTON, GEORGES JACQUES
DESMOULINS, CAMILLE
DREYFUS, ALFRED
HOPITAL, MICHEL DE L'
JOYEUSE, ANNE DE
LEDAIN, OLIVER
MAZARIN, JULES
MENDES-FRANCE, PIERRE
MIRABEAU, COMTE DE
POT, PHILIPPE
POTIER, AUGUSTIN
RICHELIEU, CARDINAL
ROBESPIERRE, MAXIMILIEN
   FRANCOIS MARIE ISIDORE
   DE
ROLAND, JEANNE MANON
   PHILIPON
SULLY, MAXIMILIEN DE
   BETHUNE, DUC DE
TALLEYRAND-PERIGORD,
   CHARLES MAURICE DE

Reformers and Protesters
(see also Patriots, Politics—American; Politics—British; Politics—French; Politics—Radical; Politics—Russian; Politics—Other; Revolutionaries)

ALINSKY, SAUL D.
ANTHONY, SUSAN B.
BEAL, ABRAHAM
BECCARIA, MARCHESE DE
BENTHAM, JEREMY
BERGH, HENRY
BISHOP, CORBETT
BLOOMER, AMELIA JENKS
BONAPARTE, CHARLES JOSEPH
BOOLE, ELLA A.
BRIGHT, JOHN
BURNS, ROBERT ELLIOTT
CANNON, JAMES, JR.
CHAMPION, EDME
CLARK, CHARLES DISMAS
CLARKSON, THOMAS
COBDEN, RICHARD
COMMONER, BARRY
COMSTOCK, ANTHONY
DAVIS, GARRY
DIX, DOROTHEA LYNDE
DOLCI, DANILO
DOW, NEAL
ELLSBERG, DANIEL
FOLSOM, ABIGAIL
FRIEDAN, BETTY
FRY, ELIZABETH
GARRISON, WILLIAM LLOYD
GOUGH, JOHN BARTHOLOMEW
GRANT, ROBERT
GUYER, ULYSSES SAMUEL
HOFFMAN, ABBOTT *"Abbie"*
HOPKINS, SAMUEL
HOWARD, JOHN
HOWE, SAMUEL GRINDLEY
JOHNSON, WILLIAM *"Pussyfoot"*
KAGAWA, TOYOHIKO
KELLEMS, VIVIEN
KING, MARTIN LUTHER, JR.
KUHN, MARGARET *"Maggie"*
LADD, WILLIAM
LUNDY, BENJAMIN
MARTIN, RICHARD
MORRELL, ED
MOTT, LUCRETIA
MURPHY, FRANCIS
NADER, RALPH
NATION, CARRY

NHAT CHI MAI
OASTLER, RICHARD
PERKINS, CHARLES NELSON
PRINCE OF CRANKS, THE
SCHURZ, CARL
SEWARD, WILLIAM H.
SHEPPARD, MORRIS
SIMS, PHILIP
STONE, LUCY
TRUTH, SOJOURNER
TUBMAN, HARRIET
TUTWILER, JULIA STRUDWICK
VOLSTEAD, ANDREW J.
WARREN, JOSIAH
WILD HORSE ANNIE
WILLARD, FRANCES E.
WOLLSTONECRAFT, MARY
WOODHULL, VICTORIA

Relatives of the Famous
(see also Presidents' Wives)

BRYON, AUGUSTA ADA
LINCOLN, ROBERT TODD
LINDBERGH, CHARLES A., JR.
LONGWORTH, ALICE LEE ROOSEVELT
MADEMOISELLE LA GRANDE
PEARY, MARIE AHNIGHITO
POOR LITTLE RICH GIRL
TALBOT, FRANCES JENNINGS
TRUMAN, JOHN ANDERSON
VAN BUREN, JOHN

Religion—Fakes, Inquisitors, Leaders, Martyrs, Reformers, Saints and Victims (see also Popes)

ABU BAKR *"The Upright"*
ALBERTUS MAGNUS
ALLEYN, SIMON
ANSGAR OF DENMARK
ANTHONY (or ANTONY), ST.
ATHANASIUS
AUGUSTINE, ST.
BACON, JOHN
BALL, JOHN
BARROW, ISAAC
BARTON, ELIZABETH
BECKET, THOMAS "à"
BECKX, PETER
BEECHER, LYMAN
BEGGING BISHOP, THE
BELSUNCE, HENRI FRANCOIS

BERNARD OF MENTHON, ST.
BIDDLE, JOHN
BISHOP OF HELL, THE
BONNIVARD, FRANCOIS DE
BOOTH, WILLIAM and CATHERINE
BRUNO, GIORDANO
BURRITT, ELIHU
CALVIN, JOHN
CELLIER, ELIZABETH
CHANNING, WILLIAM ELLERY
COMESTOR, PETER
CYRIL OF ALEXANDER, ST.
DUCHESNE, ROSE PHILIPPINE
DUNS SCOTUS, JOHN
DYER, MARY
ECK, JOHANN
EDWARDS, JONATHAN
ELIOT, JOHN
EZRA, ABRAHAM BEN MEIR IBN
FABER, JOHANN
FAREL, GUILLAUME
FIGHTING PRELATE, THE
FURMAN, RICHARD
GILPIN, BERNARD
GRAHAM, BILLY
GREGORY THE GREAT, ST.
HEBER, REGINALD
HOWE, JOHN
HUS, JOHN
INGE, WILLIAM RALPH
INGERSOLL, ROBERT G.
JOHN CHRYSOSTOM, ST.
JOHN FREDERICK, DUKE OF SAXONY
JOHNSON, HEWLETT
JONES, WILLIAM
JOSEPH OF COPERTINO, ST.
KENNEDY, CRAMMOND
KIMURA, HENRY SEIMATSU
KNOX, JOHN
LAS CASAS, BARTOLOME DE
LASSERAN-MASSENCOME, SEIGNEUR DE MONTLUC
LEE, ANN
LOLLARD, WALTER
LOYOLA, IGNATIUS OF, ST.
MCPHERSON, AIMEE SEMPLE
MAHARAJ JI
MARSHALL, STEPHEN
MARTIN, BISHOP OF TOURS, ST.
MASSILLON, JEAN BAPTISTE
MELANCHTHON, PHILIPP
MENOT, MICHAEL
MEZZOFANTI, GUISEPPE
MILBURN, WILLIAM HENRY
MOHAMMED
MOHAMMED AHMED
MONK, MARIA

MOODY, DWIGHT LYMAN
MORNAY, PHILIPPE DE
MUHAMMAD, ELIJAH
NAIGEON, JACQUES ANDRE
NUTCRACKER MAN
OATES, TITUS
ORIGEN
PAGE, KIRBY
PARKER, MATTHEW *"Nosey"*
PARKER, SAMUEL
PILLAR SAINT, THE
PRYNNE, WILLIAM
RAWSON, EDWARD
RUSSELL, JOHN
RYAN, JOHN A.
SAVONAROLA, GIROLAMO
SEWALL, JOSEPH
SOUTH, ROBERT
SPRUELL, JOHN
SUNDAY, BILLY
TAUSEN, HANS
TAYLOR, JEREMY
THAYER, JOHN
THOMAS AQUINAS
THOMAS THE APOSTLE
TORQUEMADA, TOMAS DE
UTLEY, ULDINE
WADDEL, JAMES
WALLER, JOHN
WHITE, JOHN
WILBERFORCE, SAMUEL *"Soapy Sam"*
WISE, ISAAC MAYER
WOLSEY, THOMAS
WOOLMAN, JOHN
WYCLIFFE, JOHN
YOUNG, BRIGHAM

Revolutionaries (see also Patriots; Politics—American; Politics—British; Politics—French; Politics—Radical; Politics—Russian; Politics—Other)

BUNKE, HAYDEE TAMARA
CADE, JOHN *"Jack"*
CAILLET, GUILLAUME
CAMERON, EVAN
CARLOS THE JACKAL
CLOOTZ (or CLOOTS), JEAN BAPTISTE
CONDORCANQUI, JOSE GABRIEL
DEFREEZE, DONALD D.
FIERRO, RODOLFO
IBARRURI, DELORES
PEZZA, MICHELE

REED, JOHN
SEVEN DAYS' KING, THE
SOLTYSIK, PATRICIA
VESEY, DENMARK
VILLA, PANCHO

Revolutionary War Notables, American

ADAMS, SAMUEL
ALLEN, ETHAN
ALLEN, THOMAS
ARNOLD, BENEDICT
ATTUCKS, CRISPUS
BIDDLE, CLEMENT
BURGOYNE, JOHN
BUTLER, THOMAS
CLEVELAND, BENJAMIN
DEWEY, JEDEDIAH
DICKINSON, JOHN
DOWNER, ELIPHALET
FISHER, HENDRICK
FORMAN, DAVID
FRANKLIN, BENJAMIN
GAGE, THOMAS
GATES, HORATIO
GIRTY, SIMON
GRAY, CHARLES
GREENE, NATHANAEL
HAMILTON, HENRY
HANCOCK, JOHN
HARNETT, CORNELIUS
HENRY, PATRICK
HOPKINSON, FRANCIS
JONES, JOHN PAUL
LAURENS, JOHN
LEE, CHARLES
LEE, RICHARD HENRY
LIVINGSTON, ROBERT R.
LIVINGSTON, WILLIAM
MARION, FRANCIS
MORRIS, ROBERT
PAGE, JOHN
PITCHER, MOLLY
SAMPSON, DEBORAH
SCHUYLER, PHILIP JOHN
SNYDER, CHRISTOPHER
SOWER, CHRISTOPHER
STARK, JOHN
THOMPSON, CHARLES
TRUMBULL, JONATHAN
WARREN, MERCY OTIS
WAYNE, *"Mad Anthony"*

Rulers and Nobility—British

ALBERT THE GOOD
ANDREW, PRINCE
ANNE, PRINCESS

ANNE, QUEEN
ANNE OF CLEVES
ARTHGAL, EARL OF WARWICK
BLACK DOUGLAS
BLACK PRINCE, THE
BLOODY MARY
BOLEYN, ANNE
CHARLES I
CHARLES II
CUMBERLAND, WILLIAM AUGUSTUS, DUKE OF
CURTHOSE
DEVEREUX, ROBERT
DOUGLAS, JAMES
EDGAR THE PEACEFUL
EDWARD III
EDWARD VI
EDWARD LONGSHANKS
EDWARD THE CONFESSOR
EDWARD THE MARTYR
EDWARD THE ROBBER
ELIZABETH I
ETHELRED THE UNREADY
FREDERICK AUGUSTUS, DUKE OF YORK
GEORGE I
GEORGE III
GEORGE IV
GRAY, JANE
HENRY, PRINCE
HENRI I
HENRY V
HENRY VI
HENRY VII
HENRY VIII
HENRY CURTMANTLE
JAMES I
JAMES I OF SCOTLAND
JAMES II
JAMES II OF SCOTLAND
"JAMES III"
JAMES V OF SCOTLAND
JOAN MAKEPEACE
JOAN OF KENT
JOHN LACKLAND
MACDONALD, JAMES
MAGNUS, EARL OF NORTHUMBERLAND
MARY OF MODENA
MONMOUTH, JAMES, DUKE OF
PHILIPS, MARK
PLANTAGENET
RICHARD THE LION HEARTED
RICHARD III
SEYMOUR, CHARLES, DUKE OF SOMERSET
SHEFFIELD, JOHN, DUKE OF BUCKINGHAMSHIRE
SILLY BILLY
SNOWDON, LORD
STEWART, ALEXANDER

GUIDARELLI, GUIDARELLO
HENRY, JOHN
HUDLUN, ANNA ELIZABETH
JORGENSEN, CHRISTINE
KOENIGSMARK, AURORA
MAN IN THE IRON MASK, THE
MEIER, SALLY
PFIESTER, DORIS
UNCLE SAM
UNSINKABLE MOLLY BROWN,
   THE
WINSTED LIAR, THE

Vice Presidents, American

AGNEW, SPIRO T.
BARKLEY, ALBEN W.
CURTIS, CHARLES
FAIRBANKS, CHARLES W.
GARDNER, JOHN NANCE
   "Cactus Jack"
HUMPHREY, HUBERT H.
MARSHALL, THOMAS RILEY
   "Five Cent Cigar"
ROCKEFELLER, NELSON
WALLACE, HENRY A.
WILSON, HENRY

Western Frontiersmen

ANDERSON, CHARLIE
AVERILL, JAMES
BASS, SAM
BEAN, ROY
BELL, TOM
BIG NOSE PARROTT
BILLY THE KID
BILLY THE KID (BILLY
   CLAIBORNE)
BLACK RIFLE
BRIDGER, JIM
BUFFALO BILL
BULETTE, JULIA C.
CALAMITY JANE
CASS, LEWIS
CASSIDY, BUTCH
CATTLE KATE
CHINA POLLY
CHIVINGTON, JOHN M.
CLUM, JOHN P.
CROCKETT, DAVY
CUSTER, GEORGE ARMSTRONG
DEADWOOD DICK
DEATH VALLEY SCOTTY
DYNAMITE DICK
EARP, WYATT
FORD, ROGER NEWTON
FREMONT, JOHN C.
GARRETT, PAT
GODFREY, HOLLEN

HANKS, O. C. *"Deaf Charley"*
HARE, WILLIAM HOBART
HICKOK, JAMES BUTLER *"Wild
   Bill"*
HOLLADAY, BENJAMIN
JENNINGS, AL
JOHNSTON, JOHN *"Liver-Eating"*
JONES, CHARLES JESSE
   "Buffalo"
KETCHUM, CATACORNERS
KONARSKY, MATT
LILLIE, GORDON W.
LOWE, JOSEPH *"Rowdy Joe"*
MACKENZIE, KENNETH
MAN BURNER, THE
MAN-EATER, THE
MASTERSON, WILLIAM BAR-
   CLAY *"Bat"*
MATHER, MYSTERIOUS DAVE
MATTHEWSON, WILLIAM
   "Buffalo Bill"
MEEK, *"Colonel"* JOSEPH L.
MILLER, CHARLES *"Bronco
   Charlie"*
MILLER, JAMES P. *"Deacon
   Jim"*
MINER, WILLIAM *"Old Bill"*
MORROW, *"Pegleg"* ANNIE
MORROW, *"Prairie Dog"* DAVE
MURIETA, JOAQUIN
MURPHY, JOHN *"Bear-Tracks"*
O'NEILL, WILLIAM O. *"Buckey"*
PLUMMER, HENRY
RATTLESNAKE DICK
RUSSELL, WILLIAM HEPBURN
SKULL, SALLY
SMITH, JEDEDIAH
SMITH, JEFFERSON RANDOLPH
   "Soapy"
SNOWSHOE THOMPSON
STARR, BELLE
STARR, HENRY
STRATTON, WINFIELD SCOTT
SUNDANCE KID, THE
TRACY, HARRY
UTTER, CHARLES H.
WALLACE, WILLIAM *"Big
   Foot"*

World War I Notables

BULLARD, EUGENE
HALL, WESTON B.
JELLICOE, JOHN RUSHWORTH
JOFFRE, JOSEPH JACQUES
   CESAIRE
LUCKNER, COUNT FELIX VON
LUKE, FRANK, JR.
PERSHING, JOHN JOSEPH
RICHTHOFEN, BARON MAN-
   FRED FREIHERR VON

ROOSEVELT, QUENTIN
THOMPSON, JOHN T.

World War II Notables

AXIS SALLY
BARBIE, KLAUS
BORMANN, MARTIN
BRADLEY, OMAR N.
BURKE, ARLEIGH *"31-Knot"*
CARLSON, EVANS F.
CARRE, MATHILDE
CIANO, COUNT GALEAZZO
CLARK, MARK WAYNE
COLLINS, JOSEPH LAWTON
   "Lightning Joe"
FREISLER, ROLAND
GOERING, HERMANN
GUDERIAN, HEINZ
HARRIS, ARTHUR *"Bomber"*
HESS, RUDOLPH
HEYDRICH, REINHARD
HITLER, ADOLF
JAMES, CLIFTON
KALTENBRUNNER, ERNST
KEITEL, WILHELM
KESSELRING, ALBERT
KOCH, ILSE
KRULAK, VICTOR H. *"Brute"*
KUHN, FRITZ
LAST OF THE SAMURAI, THE
LORD HAW HAW
LUCHAIRE, CORINNE
MACARTHUR, DOUGLAS
MARSHALL, GEORGE C.
MENGELE, JOSEF
MORSHEAD, LESLIE
MOUNTBATTEN, LORD LOUIS
MUELLER, HEINRICH
PATTON, GEORGE S., JR.
PELLEY, WILLIAM DUDLEY
PRELATE OF RESISTANCE
PULLER, LEWIS B. *"Chesty"*
QUISLING, VIDKUN
RIBBENTROP, JOACHIM VON
ROMMEL, ERWIN
SMITH, EDWARD H. *"Iceberg"*
SMITH, HOLLAND M. *"Howling
   Mad"*
STILWELL, JOSEPH *"Vinegar
   Joe"*
STREICHER, JULIUS
TOJO, HIDEKI
TOKYO ROSE
WAINRIGHT, JONATHAN
   MAYHEW
YAMASHITA, TOMOYUKI
ZHUKOV, GEORGI

Wrestlers (see Sports and Games)